Preface

In 1789 Thomas Paine, then in London, wrote to his friend, the first President of the United States: 'I am going over to France—A Share in two revolutions is living to some purpose.'[1] Paine lived an extraordinary life in an extraordinary era that still grips the attention of many readers. What were that era's meanings and lessons? Readers have often turned for authoritative answers to Paine's texts. But their evolving afterlives in later decades had the consequence that Paine became one of those canonical figures who have often been less studied than celebrated. More than many other authors in the current canon of the history of political thought, the 'usable Paine' obscured the 'historic Paine'. He was too often taken for granted; Paine became public property. This allowed assumptions about the meanings of his texts to be linked with inherited preconceptions about the societies in which he lived and wrote. When the causes of the American and French Revolutions or the threat of revolution in Britain were made to seem self-evident, myth-making was not far away. A reconsideration of the 'age of revolution' is overdue, and historians have begun to explore just such a revision.

In that polemical and rhetorical age, Paine was a highly effective polemical and rhetorical author. This book is, necessarily, a study of polemic and rhetoric rather than of the detached writing of an author in his library. Its subject is argument, both then and now, but argument that led to slaughter and destruction on both sides of the Atlantic in ways that Paine did not intend. Explaining these outcomes is not easy. The task of historians of political thought is not to pronounce that 'Paine was right' or 'Paine was wrong'; rather, to discover why he wrote as he did, what his meanings were, and how he was received. That is, to take him seriously as a contributor to extended arguments in a period populated by principled and mutually antagonistic political actors for whom the outcomes were often unhappy. It was once observed that all political careers end in failure. But this is a truism that applies equally to careers in such fields as political theory, philosophy, and economics; Utopia would otherwise have arrived. The historian of political thought makes no such judgement. This book does not argue that Paine was 'a failure'; he did not 'fail' to write *this*, or 'fail' to think *that*. Historians seek, instead, to understand what Paine did and did not write and think, and why: for them he succeeded, but in relation to his goals and those of his contemporaries.

Paine's authorial intentions are hard, and often impossible, to reconstruct in the absence of an extensive cache of his manuscripts; he can scarcely be assessed as if he were another Thomas Hobbes or John Locke, both Oxford or Cambridge dons by vocation though excluded from their universities for political reasons, both leaving extensive paper trails. Consequently what Paine thought could not easily be distinguished from what he wrote, either by his contemporaries or by later scholars.

---

[1] Paine to Washington, 6 Oct. 1789: Washington, *Papers*, iv. 196–7.

Instead, this book is chiefly about texts as public acts. It gives much attention to Paine's writings, but also to the texts of other activists, both pro- and anti-revolutionaries. It argues that contexts must be given due weight if these texts are to be understood. That, indeed, is why it could not be a short book: contexts are, necessarily, larger than texts.

By this method, the book arrives at a different view both of Paine's political and social thought and of the intellectual history of the 'age of revolution', an age in which religion is here reinstated as a leading political preoccupation. It gives central attention to such themes as radicalism, reform, republicanism, revolution, and rights: alliteration should not distract us from the momentous present-day significance of these issues, and to these must be added others including slavery, democracy, and poverty. This study derives from my reservations over many years about assumptions that the long eighteenth century was the 'birthplace' of 'the modern': these doubts have led me in turn to a fascination with the man himself. Paine is compelling because he poses a series of historical problems of the greatest present-day importance. Others must join me in a renewed attention to their solution if this foundational era and its consequences are to be better understood. Some readers of Paine still see themselves as Guardians of the Sacred Flame; I see the role of the historian as being to investigate, to question, and to challenge.

I hope that readers will share my willingness to test new explanations of this most remarkable of English revolutionaries. In my writing on another extraordinary figure of that age, Edmund Burke, I sought to avoid hagiography by removing successive layers of later varnish to reveal the eighteenth-century portrait beneath; not to judge Burke as a hero or a villain, nor to claim his obvious relevance to present-day politics, but to understand him as an historical character.[2] Here I pay the same compliment to Thomas Paine. In both cases, removing accretions of later misinterpretation allows a better understanding of their thought and an appreciation that neither's writings give privileged or shorthand access to the complex and still controversial 'age of revolution' in which they found themselves. Indeed it frees us to examine the age of revolution afresh at a time when the destabilization of states needs urgently to be better understood.

Readers should note two basic aims of this study. Previous writers on Paine were sometimes drawn to produce either denunciations or, later, eulogies. Paine was from an early date the subject of deliberately denigratory biographies.[3] Not until

---

[2] Burke, *Reflections*, ed. Clark, introduction.

[3] [George Chalmers], *The Life of Thomas Pain, The Author of Rights of Men. With a Defence of his Writings. By Francis Oldys, A.M. of the University of Pennsylvania* (London: Stockdale, 1791); James Cheetham, *The Life of Thomas Paine, author of Common Sense, The Crisis, Rights of Man, &c. &c. &c.* (New York: Southwick and Pelsue, 1809). Some alleged evidence presented in these hostile works may deserve consideration, but caution is necessary. For the increasing assessment in the late eighteenth century of many public figures (not just Paine) in respect of their private lives, see Corinna Wagner, 'Loyalist Propaganda and the Scandalous Life of Tom Paine: "Hypocritical Monster!"', *British Journal for Eighteenth-Century Studies* 28 (2005), 97–115.

THOMAS PAINE

Portrait bust of Thomas Paine by John Wesley Jarvis, 1809 (New York Historical Society)

Thomas Paine

*Britain, America, and France in the
Age of Enlightenment and Revolution*

J. C. D. CLARK

CLARENDON • OXFORD

OXFORD

UNIVERSITY PRESS

Great Clarendon Street, Oxford, OX2 6DP,
United Kingdom

Oxford University Press is a department of the University of Oxford.
It furthers the University's objective of excellence in research, scholarship,
and education by publishing worldwide. Oxford is a registered trade mark of
Oxford University Press in the UK and in certain other countries

First Edition published in 2018

Impression: 1

Published in the United States of America by Oxford University Press
198 Madison Avenue, New York, NY 10016, United States of America

British Library Cataloguing in Publication Data
Data available

Library of Congress Control Number: 2017954437

ISBN 978-0-19-881699-7

Printed in Great Britain by
Clays Ltd, St Ives plc

the late nineteenth century did academic opinion turn in his favour,[4] but since then his depiction has often been as normatively positive as it once was hostile. This study is a work neither of celebration nor of demonization. It seeks to explain him historically; it invites renewed attention to its remarkable subject in that non-partisan spirit. When this book expresses a professional historiographical scepticism towards the interpretation of themes like republicanism, rights, revolution, and religion, that scepticism is not a normative response to any individual.

Secondly, this account of Paine necessarily relates to my earlier work, and this relation calls for an explanation. My *English Society 1660–1832* might be misunderstood as arguing in general terms for the residual survival of an 'old' world into a 'new'. This study makes clear that my intention is to argue for a reinterpretation of that 'new' world itself. The radical and revolutionary tradition in America, France, and Britain is a subject of great and lasting intellectual importance; it must now be thought about in radical and even revolutionary ways. In the present age of religious wars, Paine has a renewed significance.

CALLALY CASTLE
NORTHUMBERLAND
DECEMBER 2017

---

[4] The first favourable biography was Thomas Clio Rickman, *The Life of Thomas Paine* (London: Rickman, 1819), but the key work of scholarship was Moncure Daniel Conway, *The Life of Thomas Paine* (2 vols., New York, 1892).

Acknowledgements

The extensive aims of this book, outlined in the Introduction, mean that it draws with gratitude on the work of several generations of scholars whose many achievements are set out in detail in the footnotes. Where others have anticipated the ideas presented here, my wish is to honour them by specific references. Historiography is often a collaborative enterprise; by acknowledging intellectual debts one can also appreciate how scholarship itself has developed over time, and this helps historians to see beyond their immediate commitments. If I have seen further, it is by standing on the shoulders of orthodoxies. Other historians have sought to contextualize Paine as a figure of the eighteenth century, which is my purpose also; it is older assumptions about the content of that context that I question here.

In a work that nevertheless differs from some historians in points of method and interpretation, it would have been distracting and discourteous to have listed every disagreement. I do so here only where it was necessary to situate my argument, usually with respect to lastingly influential interpretations (for example, of classics like those of R. R. Palmer and E. P. Thompson, historians for whom I have a high regard); I normally prefer to present primary evidence to support my own vision. Where I have written in general terms of 'conventional interpretations' of Paine, I ask only that these remarks be read as self-criticisms of misinterpretations that I myself once entertained.

For the convenience of readers, references to Paine's writings are here given to the most readily available collected version, Philip Foner's two-volume edition of 1945. Despite its merits, it had its shortcomings; I have noted 'text corrected' where I have conformed to the originals, and I argue for the de-attribution of texts and passages that Foner (and many others) accepted as Paine's. A new edition, undertaken to the latest standards, would be valuable; none was available at the time of writing. Similarly, a project to identify Paine's prose by computer modelling, and so to attribute to him material published anonymously, has not yet been completed. Both may contribute to knowledge.

'Every work of this kind is by its nature deficient, and I should feel little solicitude about the sentence, were it to be pronounced only by the skilful and the learned.'[5] Scholarship on the 'age of revolution' will continue to develop. To its future success this book is intended as a small contribution.

---

[5] 'Preface', in *The Plays of William Shakespeare ... To which are added Notes by Sam[uel] Johnson* (8 vols., London: J. and R. Tonson et al., 1765), i. lxxii.

Contents

PART III. DIVERGENCES AND LEGACIES

Illustrations

Abbreviations

Adams, *Diary and Autobiography*	*Diary and Autobiography of John Adams*, ed. L. H. Butterfield (4 vols., Cambridge, Mass., 1961)
Adams, *Works*	*The Works of John Adams, Second President of the United States: With a Life of the Author*, ed. Charles F. Adams (10 vols., Boston, 1850–6)
Aldridge, *Man of Reason*	Alfred Owen Aldridge, *Man of Reason: The Life of Thomas Paine* (London, 1960)
Aldridge, *American Ideology*	Alfred Owen Aldridge, *Thomas Paine's American Ideology* (Newark, Del., 1984)
BL Add MSS	British Library, Additional Manuscripts
Burke, *Reflections*, ed. Clark	Edmund Burke, *Reflections on the Revolution in France*, ed. J. C. D. Clark (1790; Stanford, Calif., 2001)
Cheetham, *Life*	James Cheetham, *The Life of Thomas Paine, author of Common Sense, The Crisis, Rights of Man, &c. &c. &c.* (New York: Southwick and Pelsue, 1809)
Claeys, *Paine*	Gregory Claeys, *Thomas Paine: Social and Political Thought* (London, 1989)
Clark, *English Society*	J. C. D. Clark, *English Society 1660–1832: Religion, Ideology and Politics during the Ancien Regime* (2nd edn, Cambridge, 2000)
Clark, *Language of Liberty*	J. C. D. Clark, *The Language of Liberty 1660–1832: Political Discourse and Social Dynamics in the Anglo-American World* (Cambridge, 1994)
Conway, *Life*	Moncure Daniel Conway, *The Life of Thomas Paine* (1892; ed. Hypatia Bradlaugh Bonner, London, 1909)
Conway (ed.), *Writings*	Moncure Daniel Conway (ed.), *The Writings of Thomas Paine* (4 vols., New York, 1894–6)
CW	Philip Foner (ed.), *The Complete Writings of Thomas Paine* (2 vols., New York, 1945)
EHR	*English Historical Review*
Franklin, *Papers*	*The Papers of Benjamin Franklin*, ed. Leonard W. Labaree et al. (New Haven, 1959–)
HJ	*Historical Journal*
Jefferson, *Papers*	*The Papers of Thomas Jefferson*, ed. Julian P. Boyd et al. (Princeton, 1950–)
Jefferson, *Writings*	Albert Ellery Bergh (ed.), *The Writings of Thomas Jefferson* (20 vols., Washington, 1907)

Keane, *Paine*   John Keane, *Tom Paine: A Political Life* (London, 1995)

Lounissi, *Paine*   Carine Lounissi, *La Pensée politique de Thomas Paine en contexte: Théorie et pratique* (Paris, 2012)

ODNB   *Oxford Dictionary of National Biography* (online)

P&P   *Past & Present*
PMHB   *Pennsylvania Magazine of History and Biography*

Rush, *Autobiography*   *The Autobiography of Benjamin Rush*, ed. George W. Corner (Princeton, 1948)
Rush, *Letters*   *Letters of Benjamin Rush*, ed. L. H. Butterfield (2 vols., Princeton, 1951)

Thale (ed.), *LCS Papers* Mary Thale (ed.), *Selections from the Papers of the London Corresponding Society 1792–1799* (Cambridge, 1983)

Washington, *Papers*   *The Papers of George Washington. Presidential Series*, ed. W. W. Abbot and Dorothy Twohig (Charlottesville, Va, 1987–)
WMQ   *William and Mary Quarterly*

Introduction
The Age of Paine?

Thomas Paine has plausibly been presented as England's greatest revolutionary, a pioneer of democracy, and the greatest champion of a natural rights discourse that triumphed in 1776 and 1789 with permanent implications thereafter. He had an astonishing career, even for his era. It was meteoric in personal terms, for he rose from humble origins to consort with some of the most famous of his contemporaries. By his own genius, he became a best-selling political author, reaching large numbers of readers with a striking message. That message had an undoubted impact, and Paine cannot be ignored. His writings bear on many of the values and practices that are internationally affirmed, and challenged, in the present day.

In his lifetime, he was once (although only once) even held to characterize his age: as John Adams wrote (although only in a private letter), 'I know not whether any Man in the World has had more influence on its inhabitants or affairs for the last thirty years than Tom Paine...Call it then the Age of Paine.'[1] Yet this retrospect from 1805 was not all it seems: what appears to be a ringing endorsement was an extrapolation of Adams's personal aversion for Paine, which dated back to 1776, and of Adams's detestation of the French Revolution, with which he now associated his *bête noire*: his hostility prompted an overstatement. Paine's role was considerable, but not necessarily all that his enemies claimed it to be. Are progressive ideologies framed, and favoured practical outcomes secured, chiefly by remarkable individuals? This heroic theory is one with which states conventionally labelled democracies now grapple as the old certainties seem to weaken.

This book explores a range of arguments that reinterpret the currently prevalent estimates of Paine, but do not deny his importance. It argues that Paine had his undoubted impact by being a figure of the eighteenth century, not by anticipating and explaining what is conventionally seen as modernity: he was so influential in his day precisely because he was not original, but because he brilliantly mobilized anglophone political languages already widely familiar.[2] This too was why he was so controversial, since he often appropriated shared languages of politics to which defenders of the existing order in Britain and North America also subscribed.

---

[1] John Adams to Benjamin Waterhouse, 29 Oct. 1805, in *Statesman and Friend: Correspondence of John Adams with Benjamin Waterhouse 1784–1822*, ed. Worthington Chauncey Ford (Boston, 1927), 31.

[2] In this he might be compared with another self-professedly unoriginal figure whose influence was enormous: John Wesley. By contrast, original thinkers like Thomas Spence received much less attention in their own lifetimes.

The book offers reinterpretations of prevalent eighteenth-century discourses. It adds that the most influential activists and reformers tended to have their impact by focusing attention on narrow bands of the available spectrum of discourse rather than by assembling rainbow alliances (an assumption that present-day accounts of 'the Enlightenment' have promoted): reform did not sweep all before it, even in America and France. And it proposes a model of the development of anglophone revolutionary and reforming discourse into the nineteenth century: it was less the achievement of a few innovative pioneers or heroic martyrs, more the unplanned consequence of the competing contributions of large numbers of men and women in fast-changing settings. An implication is that securing favoured outcomes in public life is a harder and more complex task than the old historiography of heroic individual action and the clear instantiation of lasting ideologies implied.

This is not a conventional narrative biography of Paine, and does not attempt to supersede any such works; consequently, it does not examine every episode in Paine's varied public career. In some sections, it is not primarily about Paine. It is a book about the 'age of revolution' in the North Atlantic world of the late eighteenth century, about the interpretation of political, social, and religious thought in that setting, and about the significance of that thought for explaining the development of the revolutionary tradition from Paine's lifetime forwards.

This is a study in the history of political thought, but Paine never sought to be an academic theorist. Rather, he spoke mostly to the practicalities of his day. Analysis of his writings therefore engages with the recent debate on whether there are 'perennial problems' in political theory, problems that persist in similar terms over long time periods. This book contends that attempts to depict Paine as a perennial teacher (on matters like natural rights) often rest on insufficient knowledge of the historical contexts within which he operated. Instead, it seeks to recover what the local and specific significance of his thought was in his own time. Anachronism, the imposition of the values or categories of one age upon another, forbids us to use what has been called the historic present tense: 'Paine says . . .' In the present, the achievement of good things in the political arena proves more difficult than it would be, were it a matter of the expression and application of general principles (like natural rights) to solve perennial problems.

Perspectives on many such political leaders have silently changed, in part because of scholarly logistics. Even a few decades ago, the primitive catalogues then available in most libraries made it laborious and difficult adequately to reconstruct the antecedent intellectual contexts of even major figures in the past. Instead, many schools of historiography were led implicitly to treat political activists as acting pragmatically in response to the needs and challenges of their own present. Such individuals could then be assumed to have been free agents, pioneers mapping out the course of politics and of theory in future decades, but themselves standing strangely out of time. More recently, the availability of computerized catalogues, and of databases like Early English Books Online and Eighteenth Century Collections Online, has wrought an unappreciated reversal. Today, these iconic figures can more easily be understood in relation to the events and ideas of their immediate pasts in all their richness and complexity. Metaphorically, they emerge as more the inheritors of old houses than the architects of new ones. Consequently, these figures' subsequent impacts are revealed as less determinative. They had, indeed, significant legacies, but seldom unchanging, foundational, or definitional ones, for the recovery of the detail of political and social debate reveals the complexities of scenes that evolved rapidly away from those into which the 'pioneers' had been born.

So it was with Paine. His writings had wide currency in his lifetime, but not as wide as the recent believers in his perennial significance suppose. Contextual studies of the world from which Paine emerged help explain his fame in his own day more than does the myth of any timeless, or proleptic, or transcultural influence. The answers presented here show Paine successfully deploying languages of politics that his English-speaking contemporaries had long employed, rather than his anticipating any modern, Utopian or cosmopolitan future, however conceived. Such new answers also help explain the only modest resonance of Paine's writings in France after 1789 and in present-day politics, where a greater impact would have been expected had 'perennial problems' been clearly evident at all times.[3] This was not a problem specific to any one author: if Paine's *Rights of Man* had little impact in France, Sieyès's *Qu'est-ce-que le tiers-état?* had little impact in Britain.

Partly because perennialism is still asserted, a reinterpretation of Paine's thought is especially necessary. That is a daunting task, for any adequate historical study of the subject demands attention to five vast areas: the American Revolution; the French Revolution; late eighteenth-century Britain, where Paine expected a revolution that did not occur; Ireland, where a revolution was indeed attempted in 1798; and the early United States, which did not witness the second American Revolution for which Paine called. Each of these scenes demands a lifetime's study; to address them all in a single volume is an act of scholarly temerity. Such a task is unavoidable, and this study necessarily extends far beyond Paine's writings to reconsider the great settings in which his writings had their chief engagement in his lifetime. It is therefore offered as a series of steps towards linked understandings of his ideas and the events in which he participated.

Because it is not a narrative biography but a study of Paine's thought in the 'age of revolution', this book accords different coverage to different areas: most to America during its Revolution, where Paine had a role in events that demands to be explicated against his writings; some to Britain, where his writings had a wide and lasting reception; some to France, where (although he did not prominently shape the course of events or of subsequent political thought) many of his most famous works appeared in the context of France's Revolution. Less space is given to the new American republic after 1802, in which Paine rightly found himself not at home, and less again to Ireland, which (despite its importance) supplied few explanatory contexts for Paine's thought.

That thought is now problematic. Paine has long been associated with the assumption that the values he is supposed to have championed were self-evident,

---

[3] Posthumous appeals to Paine are highly selective, as the omission in current debate of his preoccupation with the damaging level of national debt reveals. For this theme see especially Michael Sonenscher, *Before the Deluge: Public Debt, Inequality, and the Intellectual Origins of the French Revolution* (Princeton, 2007).

but this assumption needs reconsideration.[4] He chose the titles of his tracts brilliantly, but their contents did not always match their labels. *Common Sense* said nothing about why it was common sense that the Thirteen Colonies should pursue independence via world war and social revolution rather than via peaceful political negotiation and compromise, as Canada was to do. After American independence, Paine never wrote the systematic reflection he promised on the events of 1776–83. Similarly, *Rights of Man* had little to say about natural rights theory, although this was a long-standing tradition of European thought whose reactivation for religious reasons in the early 1770s had preceded revolution in America,[5] and Paine never wrote an extended analysis of the part played by natural rights language in the French Revolution. He often used the term 'rights', but he hardly expounded it: rights had long become truisms, and did not belatedly emerge as inspirational neologisms. *The Age of Reason*, in turn, invoked 'reason' but did not define it, or establish why reason validated Deism rather than any other religion (or, indeed, rather than atheism). Instead of explaining his age, Paine's works themselves demand historical explanations, and the answers often prove to be unexpected.

Many of Paine's surviving papers were evidently lost in a fire in the early nineteenth century, and the absence of any substantial single archive of hitherto-unused Paine manuscripts means that much about his intellectual development often remains inaccessible; contextual studies are therefore even more necessary. It is a central contention of this book that Paine cannot be understood by neglecting his contexts and engaging only in close readings of his texts: close readings alone, often adopted in the past, have necessarily proved problematic. Instead, both approaches are pursued here. This is a textual and a contextual study; it is an intellectual history that calls for a critical analysis of texts, and also a social history of ideas which asserts that texts did not talk to other texts. It is about attempting to discern the meanings of authors from the study of their writings, but also about discovering what the intellectual equipment of their societies permitted those authors to mean. Such enquiries lead to another goal: analysing not only what was in Paine's texts, but what was absent from them; considering at several points the significance of what Paine did *not say*, but contemporary discourse allowed him to say (for example, on slavery). Such analyses of absences are not normative judgements on Paine, but are integral to understanding his impact.

Where readers sometimes use classic texts as shorthand summaries of complex episodes, historians use the age to interpret the author, often by employing the forms of contextual interpretation and discourse analysis developed by historians of political thought since Peter Laslett; here and elsewhere I add to their approaches a greater attention to concepts as limiters and as enablers. During the era of twentieth-century modernism, its characteristic concepts were made to seem the self-evident building blocks of history; this assumption proves especially problematic when examined with respect to Paine's lifetime. A concept, even a famous one, does not validate itself: to label the events of 1776–83 'the American Revolution'

---

[4] John Locke, *An Essay Concerning Humane Understanding* (London: Thomas Basset, 1690), 299–306, had sought to assert the reality of certain 'Maxims' as self-evident 'Knowledge', but only to defend his position against the belief in innate ideas; he did not apply the argument to rights.

[5] Clark, *Language of Liberty*, 93–110 and *passim*.

does not establish that 'it' was a single thing, or solely American, or socially revolutionary. Similarly, understandings of French events depend on what phenomena are arbitrarily placed within that seemingly self-evident category, 'the French Revolution'. Attention to contexts and categories shows that Paine was highly intelligent and well informed, but was so with respect to his own time and to preceding decades, not to an unknowable future. Modernism was never his context.

In particular, I invoke sometimes unfamiliar components of political argument, including dynastic discourse (the rending arguments over political authority that persisted for decades after the armed expulsion of James II in 1688) and the discourse of England's 'Patriot' opposition of the 1730s (that uneasy alliance of opposites, Tory-Jacobites and extreme Whigs, against the corruption of Sir Robert Walpole's regime), with both of which I here establish the anti-Jacobite Paine's direct links. I emphasize the contextual significance for his politics of the limitations of his understanding of American and French events; instead, I indicate the lasting importance of his prior English preconceptions, including his Deism. Paine's politics emerge as less abstract than they appear in the pages of political scientists; even his antipathy to hereditary monarchy was drawn from specific English antecedents. Paine's Deism, in itself no secret to historians, is also shown here to have been a home-grown English plant rather than a set of Enlightenment generalizations learned in revolutionary America or France.

By placing Paine in his age, I seek to avoid prolepsis, the assumption that some later thing had already come into being. Like his contemporaries, he could not without prophetic foresight have adopted any of a series of political positions that were formulated only decades after his death; but his not adopting them was no personal shortcoming. It is no criticism of Paine that he did not anticipate Mill or Marx; it is, however, important. Contexts also help illuminate the counter-factuals, the things that might have happened; but an argument that Paine *could have* done something does not imply that he *should have* done it. If I dispense with some of the historiographical orthodoxies that have surrounded him, these revisions are not to be read as normative judgements on Paine himself.

Yet Paine was, and remains, enmeshed in value judgements. Some of his contemporaries argued that his role was more negative than positive, and focused on what they thought were his negations. In America, John Adams, although a hostile witness, wrote at an early date of the still-anonymous author of *Common Sense* that 'this writer has a better hand in pulling down than building... This writer seems to have very inadequate ideas of what is proper and necessary to be done in order to form constitutions for single colonies, as well as a great model of union for the whole.'[6] Later, in France, Marie-Jeanne Roland, though Paine's Girondin ally, similarly thought him 'better at throwing out sparks, so to speak, than at discussing the foundations or preparing the formation of a government'.[7] These reactions are theorized here as an argument that political thinkers must be understood in terms of their negations as well as in terms of their affirmations. The origins of such

---

[6] John Adams to Abigail Adams, Philadelphia, 19 March [1776]: *Familiar Letters of John Adams and his wife Abigail Adams, during the Revolution*, ed. Charles Francis Adams (1875; Freeport, NY, 1970), 146.

[7] *Mémoires de Madame Roland*, ed. Paul de Roux (Paris, 1966), 169–70.

negations are far from obvious: the answers do not necessarily emerge from a close reading of Paine's texts alone. Paine's prose is often exciting; it can seem to offer a possibility of beginning the world over again; but examined in context, it becomes itself the thing to be explained, and these new explanations are excitingly different.

Positive value judgements, by Paine's contemporaries and their successors, saw him put to a succession of uses, and I attempt to clarify how perspectives on his achievements changed into the early nineteenth century. Despite Paine's recruitment into later causes, and thanks to growing doubts and revisions by a number of historians, on which I gratefully draw here, scholarship on Paine may be at a turning point. His involvement in episodes that were later reified and put to powerful practical uses tended to trap him in a series of 'myths of origin', whether national (as with 'the American Founding'), sectional (as with 'the working-class movement'), stadial (as with 'the birth of modernity'), or credal (as with 'the rise of modern secularism').[8] These myths were powerful sources of anachronism, but they can now often be explained historically.

These larger anachronisms seriously hindered the understanding of Paine. The historic Paine was later obscured not least because of his dramatic part in two episodes, the American and French Revolutions, that were later unquestioningly held to have been 'modern' and to have articulated simply identifiable founding principles. Yet those two revolutions, complex and still disputed episodes as they were, produced a profusion of symbols and assertions of principle, often inconsistent, often retrospective, often the result of 'accident, mischance or miscalculation', often evolving in unexpected ways;[9] these revolutions cannot easily be summed up in conveniently simple formulae, extracted from the writings of Paine or any of his contemporaries. It is a conclusion of this study that one cannot say 'the American Revolution stood for *this*', 'the French Revolution had, at its heart, *that*', or 'the Enlightenment was united around *the following*'; and such renunciations compel major reconsiderations. A consequence is the untenability of the old assumption that the United States or the French Republic today have secular 'founding principles' or 'core ideals', any more than does Paine's home country.

In the twentieth century, when the opposite view was accepted, Paine was not merely explained but celebrated in various ways, notably as an architect of 'modernity', hailed as the prophet of a new age, his prophetic status seemingly confirmed by his unique role of acting in and expounding these two formative revolutions. In contrast, by taking modernity to be an intellectual *project* of the late nineteenth century rather than a social *process* of the late eighteenth, I argue that Paine's role was both more important and more difficult to grasp. Paine lacked not only the concept of 'modernity', a term that was absent from his published work, but even the now-ubiquitous idea of social 'process' itself.[10]

---

[8] The myth of origin of the United States has proved more resistant to revision than the myth of origin of the French republic, but even here dissenting voices have been raised, e.g. Francis Jennings, *The Creation of America: Through Revolution to Empire* (Cambridge, 2000).

[9] William Doyle, 'The Principles of the French Revolution', in Doyle, *Officers, Nobles and Revolutionaries: Essays on Eighteenth-Century France* (London, 1995), 163–72. This book advances a similar argument for the American Revolution also.

[10] In the eighteenth century a 'procession' was said to 'process' from one place to another. The reified present-day meaning of 'process' was absent from *Common Sense, Letter Addressed to the Abbe*

This argument is compatible with recent scholarship which has in general shown that less was new in the causes of either the American or French Revolutions than was once popularly assumed. Their agents necessarily drew on what they knew of the past as a guide to their own actions; indeed the more fraught the crises they experienced, the more desperate their recourse to past examples was.[11] The same is true of the present day, when the return of contingency in historical analysis has weakened the old faith in 'underlying' causes and re-emphasized the incomprehensible randomness of things, against which all historians contend. Genuinely new ideas not acting as causes of revolution in 1776 or 1789 (for example: anti-slavery, universal manhood suffrage, the redistribution of land, and equality for women) were indeed developed in the late eighteenth century, primarily in England, but the evidence presented here shows that Paine was not a leading framer of any of them. If the American and French Revolutions were thought to have created a new world, this book suggests that they did so more because of their then hardly understood consequences than because of any already-understood intellectual origins. That world, after 1783, often proved indifferent or hostile to the historic Paine. When it later wished to celebrate him, it reconstructed him.

The conceptual lexicon of the society from which Paine came therefore deserves careful attention. Like his contemporaries he lacked much of the intellectual equipment devised only in the century after his death (concepts denoting political positions, like radicalism, liberalism, and conservatism; models of social and economic change, like the Industrial Revolution; processes, like modernization and secularization; symbols of identity, like social class and nationalism; psychological states, like emotion or nostalgia).[12] Certainly, Paine could not offer 'a liberal theory

---

Raynal, Rights of Man, The Age of Reason, The Age of Reason. Part the Second, Dissertation on First-Principles of Government and *Agrarian Justice*. Even in the famous chapter V of *Rights of Man. Part the Second*, the word appeared in a far from Utopian context: 'As to mere theoretical reformation, I have never preached it up. The most effectual process [i.e. manner of proceeding] is that of improving the condition of man by means of his interest; and it is on this ground that I take my stand': *CW*, i. 400 (text corrected). Other instances of 'process' similarly referred to legal or constitutional procedure, not to a logic of events: *CW*, i. 350, 378, 447; 'To the Citizens of the United States', Letter II (1802): *CW*, ii. 915. This linguistic argument is not conclusive: did Paine nevertheless have the concept, without a label for it? His closest instance was his 'figure' of a budding twig as a harbinger of spring, a metaphor for the extension of revolution across Europe: *Rights of Man. Part the Second* (1792): *CW*, i. 453–4. But metaphor fell short of analysis, and he framed no account of revolution as process.

[11] For challenges to the claims of French revolutionaries that they were starting afresh, and explorations of their recourse to historical examples, including seventeenth-century English ones, see Rachel Hammersley, *French Revolutionaries and English Republicans: The Cordeliers Club, 1790–1794* (Woodbridge, 2005); Hammersley, *The English Republican Tradition and Eighteenth-Century France: Between the Ancients and the Moderns* (Manchester, 2010); Pierre Serna, 'In Search of the Atlantic Republic: 1660–1776–1799 in the Mirror', in Manuela Albertone and Antonino De Francesco (eds), *Rethinking the Atlantic World: Europe and America in the Age of Democratic Revolutions* (Basingstoke, 2009), 257–75.

[12] For an argument that 'emotion' was a category only invented in the early nineteenth century see Thomas Dixon, *From Passions to Emotions: The Creation of a Secular Psychological Category* (Cambridge, 2003). The term appears in Paine's publications only once: 'could I find a miser whose heart never felt the emotion of a spark of principle': *The American Crisis Extraordinary* (4 Oct. 1780): *CW*, i. 177. But the term there carried meanings different from its later ones. Rather, he wrote of 'the passions and feelings of mankind': [Paine], *Common Sense* (1776): *CW*, i. 22. Paine's rejection of monarchy and aristocracy was not an 'emotional' one.

of human rights', or move from 'liberalism' to 'radicalism', since neither liberalism nor radicalism had been conceptualized in his lifetime.

The older 'grand narratives' of an age of Enlightenment and revolution, long widely taken for granted, now call for careful reconsideration. This has been difficult partly because Paine's appropriation by later causes often detained his reputation within the historical assumptions of late modernism, the world view that achieved its greatest ascendancy from the 1960s to the mid-1980s. Where much else then moved on, these reforming scenarios were sometimes slow to change. I attempt to take further the explorations that other scholars have also engaged in: instead of refining any of the 'usable Paines' (the models of him constructed to be relevant to later debates) I seek to recover a 'historic Paine', a significantly different figure and one who finds his place within a revised understanding of his age and its dominant themes.[13] The historic Paine was not in any simple sense merely the opposite of any of the usable Paines; a more nuanced picture is necessary.

Three historiographical schools of recent decades, bearing on the age of revolution, may be briefly reviewed here. Not all are as influential as they were, but their cogency demands attention even in their decline. Other historians have since sought to understand Paine in his eighteenth-century setting; but the historiographies that they often assumed to be accurate accounts of Paine's intellectual and social contexts have become problematic since the mid-1980s, and a conscious readjustment is overdue.

First, the integration of Paine into a later world of socialism and capitalist industry. In Britain, where political discourse was overlaid by no domestic revolution comparable to the American or French, Paine was, decades later, caught up instead in the genealogy of a political project that derived from a teleological account of the formation of 'the working class'. This scenario has become problematic with changing interpretations of class formation and economic development: historians' sense of process is everywhere weakening.[14] In particular, some models of a usable Paine remained within the historiographical tradition, dating in England from the 1890s, that reached its apogee in a remarkable and influential work by E. P. Thompson.[15] It is a book that still deserves admiration. Much of it retains its value. It established assumptions for this period that were hegemonic until the mid-1980s and influential for longer still. Nevertheless, the subject is here taken in different directions, and some of the intellectual contexts that Thompson so eloquently offered are reconstructed. On this reconstruction depends, in turn, a

---

[13] Recent historiography is largely omitted in this study. But for the construction since the late nineteenth century of a succession of 'usable Paines' see J. C. D. Clark, 'Thomas Paine: The English Dimension', in *Selected Writings of Thomas Paine*, ed. Ian Shapiro and Jane E. Calvert (New Haven, 2014), 579–601. That essay offers evidence that Paine was often and influentially characterized, although not by every scholar of the subject, in ways that are questioned in the present book.

[14] For the present author's interpretations see Clark, *English Society*, 164–200 (class), 446–70 (Industrial Revolution).

[15] E. P. Thompson, *The Making of the English Working Class* (London, 1963). Since his book has been so important in the field, I think it appropriate respectfully to note some points of difference and of agreement.

reinterpretation of the later radical and revolutionary traditions that Thompson thought looked back to Paine as their framer.

In 1963 Thompson's key assumption was that the interpretation of what he saw as Britain's radical and revolutionary movement from the late eighteenth century to 1914 depended primarily on the interpretation of 'the Industrial Revolution'. Since that date, quantifying economic history, 'cliometrics', has recast understandings of late eighteenth-century economic change (in the broadest terms, it is now clear that there was no short, rapid 'Industrial Revolution' but a long, slow commercial evolution). As a consequence, I contend that the interpretation of Britain's subsequent radical experience today depends primarily on the interpretation of the relation between the American Revolution and the French. The reconstruction of Paine's role is therefore of far greater importance. Here I offer reconsiderations of both.

In Britain, Paine, although from a humble background, was not an investigator of popular culture or of the economic life of the poor. For his own reasons, he had a definitional confidence in an unspecific category, 'the people', writing: 'All property is safe under their protection. Even in countries where the lowest and most licentious of them have risen into outrage they have never departed from the path of *natural* honour.'[16] Holding this as a premise, Paine did not allow his experiences in America or France fundamentally to revise his prior commitments.

Thompson and I are at one, however, in our sense of our remits. He famously wrote: 'I am seeking to rescue the poor stockinger, the Luddite cropper, the "obsolete" hand-loom weaver, the "utopian" artisan, and even the deluded follower of Joanna Southcott, from the enormous condescension of posterity.'[17] Here I seek to rescue the American Patriot, the French Jacobin, the English reformer, and even the undeluded Thomas Paine himself, from the enormous approbation of posterity. Such ideal types are always oversimplifications. But since condescension and approbation equally distort the subject, these two tasks are symmetrical.

A second historiographical trend admirably sought to link events in North America and Western Europe. Paine's expression, an 'age of revolution', was taken up and generalized especially in the transatlantic vision of the historian R. R. Palmer and his followers. For Palmer it became a worked-out thesis that these episodes of governmental upheaval were manifestations of 'a common impulse', creating 'a single revolutionary movement'.[18] But what was their principle of unity? The idea of the international acceptance and self-evident meaning of 'democracy' in the

[16] [Paine], 'The Forester's Letters' (1776): *CW*, ii. 87.

[17] Thompson, *The Making of the English Working Class*, 12. Except in this justified case, and in quotation, I have avoided those dangerous terms, 'we' and 'our'.

[18] R. R. Palmer, *The Age of the Democratic Revolution: A Political History of Europe and America, 1760–1800* (2 vols., Princeton, 1959–64), i. 4, 7, 9. A second edition (Princeton, 2014), edited by David Armitage, is evidence of a present-day trend to revive Palmer's 'progressivist narrative' as global history, xx. Palmer appreciated that he was writing about 'certain predilections and biases which the author at the outset confesses to sharing' (i. 4), but could not analyse how those commitments shaped his account. 'The Enlightenment' was absent from this work, but eventually his 'democratic revolution' metamorphosed into 'the democratic Enlightenment', as in Simon P. Newman and Peter S. Onuf (eds), *Paine and Jefferson in the Age of Revolutions* (Charlottesville, Va, 2013), 4.

late eighteenth century now seems less persuasive than it did in the 1950s,[19] and Palmer's vision looks more like an international projection of egalitarian, populist assumptions dominant in his society in his own day, combined with post-1945 confidence in the United States as the beacon of democracy. There were indeed links between the American Revolution and the French; but historians now give more weight to the financial crisis triggered in France by its participation in the American war.[20] During the ascendancy of modernism, political scientists once sought to devise taxonomies of revolution and so to trace linkages between its examples;[21] but this enterprise is vulnerable to the counter-factual observation of historians that all revolutions could have been avoided, and most were.[22]

Paine's understanding of democracy is here revised by emphasizing the gulf between his idea of the 'representative system', which he consistently urged, and the new doctrine of universal suffrage, which he never quite embraced. Consequently, the theory of novel and integral relations between democracy, equality, and revolution in the 'age of the democratic revolution' becomes problematic. For Palmer the unifying theme was democracy; he repudiated nationalism. But others, later, did not, integrating nationalism with democracy in the idiom of 1848 and projecting both back to 1789 and 1776. This reconsideration of 'democracy' therefore relates to the reinterpretation of 'nationalism', which can now be identified as a new ideology coined only after Paine's death. His sense of national identity was far from new; it derived in familiar ways from England's long history. The American and French Revolutions were even recently assumed to have been obviously and similarly democratic protests against old orders whose contrary natures could be easily diagnosed, but this self-evidence is here questioned. Both revolutions now seem far less homogeneous, far less familiar, far less benign, far less normative, far less part of any single 'movement'.

Their differences outweigh their similarities. Both revolutions followed political conflicts in earlier decades that had often come to be expressed as conflicts between liberty and despotism, or liberty and tyranny; and these episodes defined political languages that found later expression in 1776 and 1789.[23] Both revolutions quickly rowed back from the sanguinary implications of mass democracy, the American in 1787, the French in 1794. Both revolutions replaced oligarchies speaking the language of status hierarchy with oligarchies speaking the language of liberty and equality, but these seemingly new languages obscured the older points at issue.

---

[19] For reappraisals of the long-tern trajectory of this phenomenon see John Dunn, *Democracy: A History* (London, 2005).

[20] 'It now seems clear that the direct impulse to the events of 1789 came not from an ideological struggle or a class struggle, but from a financial and fiscal crisis of the French monarchy, and that this crisis was above all the product of a geopolitical struggle in which that monarchy found itself engaged': Timothy Tackett, *The Coming of the Terror in the French Revolution* (Cambridge, Mass,, 2015), 39–40.

[21] e.g. Crane Brinton, *The Anatomy of Revolution* (New York, 1938; 3rd edn, 1965); Hannah Arendt, *On Revolution* (New York, 1963).

[22] The non-inevitability of these revolutions is taken as axiomatic in Wim Klooster, *Revolutions in the Atlantic World: A Comparative History* (New York, 2009), which also offers qualifications to Palmer's focus on democracy, 2, 62.

[23] For this argument applied to 1789 see Keith Michael Baker, *Inventing the French Revolution: Essays on French Political Culture in the Eighteenth Century* (Cambridge, 1990).

Both created societies whose egalitarianism was more cultural than securely political. But the two were very different. The American Revolution took place in a new, developing society totalling little more than two million inhabitants, its activists often seeking a return to past certainties; the French, in an old, developed society of some twenty-eight million, its activists often seeking a break with its past.

While seeking to avoid the sin of 'essentialism', this book presents an American Revolution whose leaders often and swiftly became bitterly anti-monarchical, contrasting with a French Revolution whose leaders, until the 'flight to Varennes', often looked to a re-pristinized constitutional monarchy and the repair of its finances. The book depicts an American Revolution in which the impassioned negations expressed by a dynamic Protestant Nonconformity and its claims to a right of resistance were often heard, against a French Revolution issuing in a sanguinary phase of de-Christianization that had no American parallel. It offers an American Revolution often led into extreme courses of action by minorities not authorized by their communities, against a French Revolution occurring in a nation much of which was initially swept by idealistic euphoria. In the Thirteen Colonies appeal was often made to 'the rights of Englishmen' to express the just relations of centre and periphery; in France, the principled resistance of the *parlements* to royal attempts at modernization were important precursors of revolution. In both cases this book depicts revolutions whose theoretical expressions drew on the particularist older discourses of their host societies more than on universalist ideological novelties.

Both revolutions were ideological and religious civil wars from the outset, but in America Loyalists were more often intimidated before 1775 or forced into exile thereafter; in France, Royalists and counter-revolutionaries more often stayed and challenged the Revolution from within, provoking reactions like the Terror.[24] Many French revolutionaries targeted ideas of privilege underlying a feudal system; few American revolutionaries used these concepts. The American Revolution began with a Declaration of Independence, the French with a Declaration of the Rights of Man and of Citizens. Both the American and French republics found great difficulty in inspiring their neighbours peacefully to follow their examples on theoretical grounds, and were quickly led into military action (Congress's invasion of Canada; France's war against Austria, Prussia, and Britain). In both cases, war upstaged potential social reforms. Even so, revolutionary France freed its slaves in 1794; revolutionary America embodied slavery in its constitution of 1787. France destroyed status hierarchy; the United States preserved it as racial and gender hierarchy. France saw significant early initiatives for the emancipation and participation of women;[25] America did not. In constitutional terms, American bicameralism, expressing an ideal of checks and balances to counteract democracy, contrasted with initial French unicameralism, expressing an ideal of equality and unified

---

[24] American *émigrés* have been estimated at 24 per thousand of the population, French *émigrés* at 5 per thousand; confiscations of property were, pro rata, comparable: Palmer, *The Age of the Democratic Revolution*, i. 188.

[25] Tackett, *The Coming of the Terror in the French Revolution*, 89–90, 252–4, 296–7.

popular sovereignty. In neither theatre of war did 'the Enlightenment' establish commonalities. The long-term legacy of both revolutions was less to promote democratic practice than to allow democracy's opponents to reify it, to demonize it, and so to delay its possible arrival for at least a century.

In both instances this book is led to attend to contingency and to the dynamic of revolutionary violence, against which it proposes that the texts of activists like Paine need to be read.[26] The book is not a narrative history of the American Revolution or the French, but it advances an interpretation of the leading thinker to have participated in both episodes that gives more weight to the unavoidable dissimilarities of the two revolutions than to their undeniable similarities. These last included, in both cases, principled violence, the negation of social hierarchy, lawlessness, mass casualties, the destruction of property, emigration, inflation, the persecution of Anglican or Catholic clergy, all amounting to a fundamental breach in the social fabric. Among those alleged similarities, not even democracy emerges here as a core value. Yet, as this book argues, there were no core values, no essential meanings: the unspoken paradox of the American and the French Revolutions is that they happened in America and France. On all conventional explanations, revolution should have broken out first in England.

No democratic doctrine was available to help Paine to foresee either great revolution in the form it took, but this is not a criticism of him: humanity can never foretell its future, except by chance. In Paine's case, historians must seek to discern what expectations he did entertain, and for what reasons. Such expectations, when revealed, help to re-establish Paine as a man of his time, indebted to a still-recent past, rather than as a prophet of any soon-to-be-realized future. Several observers in the mid- and late eighteenth century had predicted that, as Rousseau put it in 1762, it was 'impossible for the great monarchies of Europe to last much longer', so that 'we are approaching the state of crisis and the century of revolutions'.[27] As Voltaire wrote to d'Alembert in 1772, 'My dear philosopher, doesn't this appear to you to be the century of revolutions?'[28] Such statements may have been rhetorical wish-fulfilment; even so, Paine's provincial isolation may have delayed his echoing such ideas. When he finally did so, democracy and nationalism were not components of his rejection of monarchy and aristocracy. The argument that 'Paine sketched out the first revolutionary history to put the French Revolution squarely in an Atlantic perspective, based on the "diffusion" of America's example to France' depends on his authorship of the key narrative section in *Rights of Man*; but this narrative was not primarily by Paine.[29]

---

[26] For the nature and origins of revolutionary violence see Arno Mayer, *The Furies: Violence and Terror in the French and Russian Revolutions* (Princeton, 2000); Sophie Wahnich, *In Defence of Terror: Liberty or Death in the French Revolution*, trans. David Fernbach (2003; London, 2012); Tackett, *The Coming of the Terror in the French Revolution*, and work there reviewed. For increasing and numerous instances of popular violence in the decades before 1789, and attitudes towards it, 24–5, 33–8.

[27] Jean-Jacques Rousseau, *Emile, ou de l'éducation*, quoted in Sonenscher, *Before the Deluge*, 28; for anticipations of revolution, ch. 1.

[28] Quoted in Baker, *Inventing the French Revolution*, 203.

[29] Allan Potofsky, 'The One and the Many: The Two Revolutions Question and the "Consumer-Commercial" Atlantic, 1789 to the Present', in Manuela Albertone and Antonino De Francesco (eds),

A third historiographical school emphasized the ubiquity of natural rights, centrally carried forward in 'the Enlightenment', and sought to celebrate Paine's role in the triumph of that discourse.[30] Yet the future can take longer to arrive than was once assumed. It has been argued that rights discourse has achieved its present salience only since the 1970s, and that it may be on the verge of decline; far from universal, rights discourse is itself an evolving historical formation.[31] Indeed, 'The new historiography of human rights can be divided into these two tendencies: one that searches for stabilizing points for the present and finds them in the *longue durée* evolution of human rights (deep history) and one that seeks to demonstrate in revisionist fashion the instability of such universalist narratives and thereby the historicity, that is, the transcience, of our political and moral convictions (recent history).'[32] Both alternatives are explored in this book.

As for 'the Enlightenment', it has been aptly observed that

> Unlike many revolutions of late-modern history, the events in France [of 1789–93] were not based on a preexisting, well-defined ideology. They did not represent a simple appropriation of one strand or another of the philosophy of the Enlightenment. The writers and thinkers of the eighteenth century had produced an extraordinarily complex and often contradictory assemblage of ideas, on the basis of which one might have supported any number of programs for change or justifications for the status quo.[33]

The same argument holds for the American Revolution also. 'The Enlightenment', the principal supposed vehicle of human rights discourse in the age of revolution, can now be shown to be, in anglophone discourse, a term of historiographical art devised in the late nineteenth century and propagated only from the mid-twentieth, not a social and intellectual process in the eighteenth.[34]

Before that historical revision, 'the Enlightenment' was used to support the idea of the arrival in Paine's era of what has recently been termed 'universalism'.

Rethinking the Atlantic World: Europe and America in the Age of Democratic Revolutions (Basingstoke, 2009), 17–45, at 17–20, 24, 32. For the de-attribution of this narrative, see Appendix: Paine De-attributions.

[30] For an explicit rejection of the methods of the Cambridge School and the consequent transformation of Paine into a modern, secular, liberal natural rights theorist, see Robert Lamb, *Thomas Paine and the Idea of Human Rights* (Cambridge, 2015).

[31] 'Almost unanimously, contemporary historians have adopted a celebratory attitude toward the emergence and progress of human rights … they have rarely conceded that earlier history left open diverse paths into the future, rather than paving a single road toward current ways of thinking and acting … the heroes who are viewed as advancing human rights in the world—much like the church historian's apostles and saints—are generally treated with uncritical wonderment': Samuel Moyn, *The Last Utopia: Human Rights in History* (Cambridge, Mass., 2010), 6–7; Moyn, 'The End of Human Rights History', *P&P* 233 (2016), 307–22.

[32] Stefan-Ludwig Hoffmann, 'Human Rights and History', *P&P* 232 (2016), 279–310 at 280, 291, dating the triumph of human rights discourse to the 1990s but calling for a re-examination of 'social and economic rights' in the late eighteenth century as a consequence, 282, 307; Lynn Hunt, 'The Long and the Short of the History of Human Rights', *P&P* 233 (2016), 323–31.

[33] Tackett, *The Coming of the Terror in the French Revolution*, 343.

[34] J. C. D. Clark, 'The *Enlightenment*: catégories, traductions et objets sociaux', in Gérard Laudin and Didier Masseau (eds), *Lumières* 17–18 (2011), 19–39; the article anticipates the conclusions of a monograph. I place the term within inverted commas to signify a need for its re-evaluation.

Universalism is presented as the Enlightenment's central assumption that natural rights apply to, and therefore naturally occurred to, all men and women equally in 'modern' societies and so found appropriate expression in a single international movement. Paine's doctrines can be held up as key examples of universalism, that is, of democratic, secular, and egalitarian ideas, naturally proliferating in 'the West' in a post-Christian age. He seemingly provided evidence for this interpretation with ringing statements like 'The cause of America is in a great measure the cause of all mankind'[35] and 'my principle is universal. My attachment is to all the world, and not to any particular part.'[36] Even some present-day scholars can invoke the idea of 'the universality of the American experience'.[37] This assumption now calls for careful reconsideration.

Universalism is not wholly wrong. But the reality was more complex: centrally, it can be shown that rights discourse did not undergo a novel transformation in the late eighteenth century from what might be called particularism (here, its embeddedness within a particular culture) to universalism (embracing a newly liberating conception of human rights), since particularist and universalist ideas of rights had long coexisted.[38] Universalism is consequently problematic as an all-encompassing historical scenario.[39] Universalism must be traced alongside particularism, but any simple binary alternatives cannot do justice to an age in which universal claims were indeed made by individuals who can be shown not to have significantly or easily transcended their local identities during their lifetimes (their disembodied posthumous influence is another matter).

Paine was one such individual. His Deism was a central source of his universalist aspirations, but in this area Paine was to suffer his greatest reverses: neither the American republic nor the French became the Deist societies that he had hoped for, and particularist commitments came to dominate in both (in the American case, a huge wave of biblical fundamentalism). Paine advocated transfer payments from rich to poor, but cannot be shown to have held, or initiated, a rights-based universalist humanitarian sensibility. Moreover, attention to thinkers' negations as well as to their affirmations rebalances the older picture, since negations are more likely to be particularist where affirmations can more easily be phrased in universalist terms: Paine hated George III specifically, not all kings equally. Paine enjoyed a wide popularity in Britain, Ireland, and America, but only because of specific political forms and discourses that were still largely shared on both sides of the anglophone Atlantic and within which his writings could resonate. Behind what now appears to be universalist and secular discourse about rights stood resurgent English Deism and anti-Trinitarianism; behind Paine's advocacy of transfer

---

[35] [Paine], *Common Sense* (1776): *CW*, i. 3. If not rhetorical, Paine's locution disclosed a superhuman omniscience.

[36] [Paine], *The American Crisis*, VII (1778): *CW*, i. 146; in France, the National Assembly 'have established universal right of conscience, and universal right of citizenship': Paine, *Rights of Man* (1791): *CW*, i. 293. This was not quite the case.

[37] Introduction, in Newman and Onuf (eds), *Paine and Jefferson in the Age of Revolutions*, 7.

[38] See Ch. 5, section on Natural rights discourse.

[39] See especially the discussion of Paine's cosmopolitanism, Ch. 3, section on Cosmopolitanism.

payments in *Rights of Man. Part the Second*, often hailed as the origin of the idea of a welfare state, stood England's poor law, in which such payments had long been standard practice.

Like his contemporaries, Paine employed only a selection from the many political discourses available in his age. Rights were prominent among them, but not every right for everyone. Notably, universal suffrage was an available discourse in England from *c.*1780, and some interpretations have depicted Paine as being on a journey towards that end. Here I question whether he intended any such journey, and doubt whether he ever quite arrived at that destination. Such revisions illuminate larger problems of historical explanation that have hitherto made Paine difficult to interpret. Seemingly a key player in the 'age of revolution', Paine has been assumed to have stood on the threshold of a new age, even (mixing metaphors) to have been its leading midwife; but the steps in any such putative grand transition have never been adequately spelled out.

A revised understanding of Paine helps to explain in general terms how the political discourses of the eighteenth century related to those of the nineteenth, and my arguments on that large question can be better summarized in the Conclusion. Here it is sufficient to say that the old idea of a transformation in natural rights theory at the end of the eighteenth century, involving the liberating emergence of ideas of 'human rights', is now problematic. Indeed many of the problems confronted in the present day derive from the only late and fragmentary influence of such notions of human rights, where an older historiography depicted their secure instantiation in 1776 or 1789. Friends of the notion of human rights may well trace their neglect to new ideologies of the early nineteenth century like utilitarianism and socialism, in which human rights played little or no part.

Secularization theory, a key component of the present-day notion of 'the Enlightenment', can also be given a more balanced examination: it now emerges as a number of autonomous and self-referential changes within certain discourses rather than as a social process, a unified and overdetermined response to social change.[40] The 'age of revolution' was not driven by any proliferating secularism, and only a few individuals were then able to be openly atheist in a way hardly possible before. Within historical contexts now seen as being without any *process* of secularization, it becomes more important that Paine was a theist, not an atheist or a secularizer, since Paine's theism had a determinative impact on his social and political thought.

Paine's writings have hitherto posed a difficulty of interpretation for those not sharing (for example) Thompson's wider scenario of political change. In 1985 John Pocock rightly observed that Paine 'remains difficult to fit into any kind of category'; *Common Sense* 'does not consistently echo any established radical vocabulary'.[41]

---

[40] J. C. D. Clark, 'Secularization and Modernization: The Failure of a "Grand Narrative"', *HJ* 55 (2012), 161–94.

[41] J. G. A. Pocock, 'The Varieties of Whiggism from Exclusion to Reform: A History of Ideology and Discourse', in Pocock, *Virtue, Commerce, and History: Essays on Political Thought and History, Chiefly in the Eighteenth Century* (Cambridge, 1985), 276. Another author who greatly influenced the subsequent historiography of this period, Caroline Robbins, in her classic *The Eighteenth*

Historical scholarship since that date has set the scene for a re-examination, especially of 'radical' categories, yet even recently it was lamented that Paine and Jefferson 'defy easy categorization'; Paine has not been 'fully integrated into any of the major historiographical schools of the American founding'.[42] Here I propose different categories, vocabularies, discourses, and contexts to help integrate Paine into a different eighteenth century. Historians have seen in the age of revolution an 'entreprise de démystification sémantique', hugely promoted by Paine;[43] here I argue that new languages were often difficult to coin (as they still are) and that even revolutionaries were (and still are) indebted to older languages.

Contexts and discourses, then, are crucial, and concepts provide a vocabulary for both. One conclusion of this enquiry is the lasting importance in his world view of the contexts set by Paine's English preconceptions: he learned less than is often presumed from his experiences in America and France, just as his message secured a less direct bearing on the future intellectual and political dynamics of those two societies than his enthusiasts allow. That, indeed, is why the development of the United States, Britain, and France after Paine's lifetime cannot be understood as a simple extrapolation of universalist values.

Both experiences and pre-commitments need re-examination if a more nuanced and positive account of Paine is to emerge. Part I offers overviews of the languages of politics current in the anglophone world of the late eighteenth century, and of how far Paine shared or did not share them. Part II traces Paine's involvement in the American and French Revolutions, and relates his most famous texts, including *Common Sense*, *Rights of Man*, and *The Age of Reason*, to those contexts. Finally, Part III argues that events and discourses in the revolutionary and post-revolutionary world, on both sides of the Atlantic, evolved rapidly away from the British and American setting of 1776, and so made possible the successive afterlives of Paine's writings. For to have evolving afterlives is a characteristic of political classics.

Century Commonwealthman (Cambridge, Mass., 1959), significantly chose that Paine 'will be ignored here', 323.

[42] Introduction, in Newman and Onuf (eds), *Paine and Jefferson in the Age of Revolutions*, 1, 3.
[43] Lounissi, *Paine*, 190.

PART I

DISCOURSES AND CONTEXTS

1

Contexts and Biography

CHURCHES AND KINGS: EARLY ENGLISH CONTEXTS

The first word in the text of John Locke's *Two Treatises of Government* (1690) was 'Slavery': not chattel slavery, which he condoned, but the political condition to which 'an *Englishman*', or, worse still, 'a *Gentleman*' was reduced by living under a monarch who was a tyrant. 'Slavery' and 'Tyranny', 'Scripture' and 'Reason', 'absolute Power' and 'a Right to natural Freedom' were key terms in Locke's first three pages; in this usage he spoke an English opposition language in his day, and long afterwards. He was not a republican or a leveller: the aim of his book, as its Preface announced, was '*to establish the Throne of our Great Restorer, Our present King* William' and '*to make good his Title, in the Consent of the People*'. This title Locke had demonstrated, he claimed, by '*Scripture-proofs*'. His opponents spoke a congruent but contrary language of dynastic legitimacy: they condemned usurpation; they spoke of the hereditary right of top-down authority, and expounded the divine right of an authoritative Church established by revelation.

Nor was this discourse abstract theory. Paine was born in a society still divided over the political conflicts that stemmed from the restoration of the monarchy in 1660 and the attendant restoration of a hegemonic episcopal Church. This sudden reversal of the republican, sectarian experiments of 1649–60 was lastingly challenged, notably in the rending Exclusion Crisis of 1679–81 when a newly defined political group, the Whigs, had sought to bar Charles II's brother James, then Duke of York, from the succession to the throne on the grounds of his Catholicism and its alleged political implications. In this crisis the new doctrines of Whiggism and Toryism were worked out, with proliferating consequences. At issue was not just the hereditary right of one individual, but the claims of popular authority to override hereditary right as such and reshape the government at will: renewed civil war might not seem far away in a society long distinctive for its degree of popular political involvement.

The same doctrines were at issue in the Revolution of 1688–91, when James II was forced into exile, his attempts to dismantle a High Church Anglican hegemony frustrated, and Scotland and Ireland ravaged by armed conflict. The interpretation and implications of 'the Revolution' were contested for decades. The title of the invading William of Orange, seizing the throne as William III, was lastingly challenged during the European war into which he took his newly conquered kingdoms. These issues were not resolved by the Hanoverian accession in 1714, when another foreign dynasty, also seen by some as usurpers, was placed on the throne in a coup intended to prevent a Stuart restoration and to secure Whig, Low Church control over Church and state together. The resulting regime was precariously balanced and repeatedly challenged by rebellion and conspiracy. It was defended by a Whig minister, Sir Robert Walpole, at (said some) a high price: gross corruption, employed to repress widespread disaffection from George I and George II. Even so, neither a 'classical republicanism' nor a 'Lockeian liberalism' were among anglophone political discourses.

In this disputed dynastic context was fought a theoretically articulate contest for ascendancy between Anglicans, Catholics, and Protestant Dissenters; from the 1690s, spreading Deist and anti-Trinitarian theologies sought to upstage them all. 'Rights' were a shared currency of political debate, if chiefly employed in relation to the crown or to the Church rather than to the individual. The integrally related political and religious consequences of dynastic vicissitude were disputed in sustained theoretical conflicts whose framing languages hardly began to change before the 1750s: the defeat of the Jacobite rising of 1745–6 took time to modify political discourse, and religious controversy still periodically flared. Meanwhile, the instability of the political order, the (to some) self-serving and platitudinous nature of Whig apologias for the regime, the vulnerability of monarchs to revolutionary overthrow, the primacy of religious commitments, and the absence of a lasting religious settlement were inescapable determinants of political action and political theorizing. Neither in political practice nor in political theory had stability been attained, and after a brief and illusory mid-century hiatus the lid was blown off this seething pot once more in 1776.[1] The dynastic conflicts of *c.*1679–1750 were first expressed as a choice between rival dynasties, but finally, and for a few, led to the rejection of monarchy itself. Religious conflicts were similarly first expressed as a choice of which denomination was to form the hegemonic established Church; these conflicts too, for some individuals, turned into a freethinking rejection of revealed, Trinitarian Christianity itself. Both these small groups, which largely overlapped, were part of the tradition from which they came.

How much did Paine, in his early life, know of these theoretical conflicts? How did he react to them? How did his own political and theological ideas develop as the world about him changed? How did his politics and his religion relate to each other? These issues have proved difficult, since reconstructing Paine's early intellectual development faces a problem of the sheer lack of evidence. For the thirty-seven years from his birth to his arrival in Philadelphia in 1774 the outlines of his

---

[1] This dynastic and religious context is largely or wholly absent from many works on Paine's thought. Since they overlook the theoretical conflicts of *c.*1660–1760, except as found in Caroline Robbins's *The Eighteenth Century Commonwealthman* (Cambridge, Mass., 1959), they have difficulty in explaining where his ideas came from. Instead, they commonly adopt as their premises historiographical traditions drawn primarily from research on the decades after 1760. These works often treated the position of the social elite as previously unchallenged; hailed Paine as moved by novel indignation against the upper classes; credited him with the creation of a mass reading public; described him as the iconic figure of democracy, bringing the lower orders into political action for the first time; depicted him as a herald of modernity and an anti-slavery pioneer; and devised ideologies like 'popular radicalism' as the rationale for revolution. Such a context for Paine's youth is no longer historically tenable. Whether it is tenable for his later years is explored in this book.

life have been recovered, but much less is known about his developing thought. For the next thirty-five years from 1774 to his death in New York in 1809, more evidence survives; enough is known to establish that Paine was seldom forthcoming about his ideas at any time, least of all during the period before 1774.

This famine of evidence is obscured by the satisfaction of researchers who have recovered details of Paine's parents' biographies, or of their son's surroundings in Thetford, Lewes, or London; but these discoveries seldom establish with any certainty Paine's intellectual development. Which ideas influenced the young Paine most, which influences operated in what order, and how he reacted to them, are often unclear. With his emigration he also tried to wipe this slate clean. After 1774 he was able to present himself as emerging fully formed onto an international stage, honourably consistent in his support of rational ideas which he held, and had therefore always held, because they were self-evidently true; but such timeless pictures are seldom historically plausible. Paine's ideas changed over time, but it is not easy to trace their evolution. This chapter explores some of the problems in reconstructing Paine's early intellectual formation.

Thomas Paine was born in the Norfolk town of Thetford in 1737, and remained there until he ran away to sea in 1756. Thetford was the annual scene of the Lent Assizes and the execution of convicted criminals; it was a town dominated by the great estate and house of the dukes of Grafton. To some authors it seemed obvious to attribute Paine's later commitments against monarchy and aristocracy, or in favour of democracy and republicanism, to childhood experiences of the local exercise of state and private power; yet no evidence of Paine's youthful views survives to make such connections other than conjectural. Paine wrote nothing of the formation of his early political opinions, and he was therefore vulnerable to the projection onto him of later ideas about the self-evident unpopularity of early eighteenth-century social structures and practices.[2] Their unpopularity was not obviously the position of the early Paine: despite his later defence of the life of Louis XVI, Paine wrote nothing systematic against the death penalty,[3] while his eagerness to serve on board a privateer during the early stages of the Seven Years War suggests no fundamental alienation from the state or its warlike actions at that time. The later Paine was against costly wars if they could be attributed to aristocrats, but the early Paine was no pacifist.

Similarly, Paine was brought up in a household mixed in religious affiliation: his mother, Frances Cocke, was a member of the Church of England, while his father, Joseph Pain, was a Quaker. Yet there is no evidence from Thomas Paine's writings of any consequences in his own mind of a divided inheritance, and only a single

---

[2] This limitation may be partly overcome if it can be shown by computer modelling of prose styles that Paine contributed to the anonymously published *Letters* of 'Junius' (1768–72), overtly hostile to Grafton, but this attribution has not yet been established.

[3] In the Appendix to *Opinion de Thomas Paine sur l'affaire de Louis Capet, adressée au Président de la Convention Nationale. Imprimée par ordre de la Convention Nationale* (Paris, 1792), Paine was quoted as saying, 'je ne croirais jamais que nous avons reçus le pouvoir de prononcer la sentence de mort d'un homme': quoted in Bernard Vincent, *Thomas Paine ou la religion de la liberté* (Paris, 1987), 264. But Paine never wrote at greater length on this theme. The appendix is not printed in *CW*, ii. 555–8.

vignette of his childhood rejection of the Anglican doctrine of the atonement.[4] Whether this rejection was the result of Quaker influence is unknown; in any event, it was insufficient to persuade him formally to join that denomination. The adult Paine was not a campaigner for the rights of the denominations of Protestant Nonconformists, as many of his contemporary reformers were, and he quickly became hostile towards the Quakers in the Philadelphia of 1776 because of their pacifist unwillingness to join the rebellion. In later life Paine did little to effect a rapprochement with that sect, and by the 1790s did nothing to present them as pioneers or allies of the Deism that he then openly professed in *The Age of Reason*. Present-day opinion often treats Anglican discrimination against Dissenters in the eighteenth century as a self-evident major grievance, but Paine, here as elsewhere, did not act as later values predict. By the 1790s he articulated an Anglican Deist critique of revelation and priestcraft, not a Quaker or Dissenting critique of their civil disabilities.[5]

Nor, again, is much known about why Paine left home in 1756 to enlist on board the *Terrible* privateer, commanded by the unforgettably named Captain William Death, to fight in the war against France just then beginning. Whether he was moved by nascent patriotism, by anti-French sentiment, by an understanding of the strategic significance of the war, by a desire for profit as a privateer, by a quest for adult status, by a rejection of local aristocratic hegemony, by the boredom of small town life, or by several of these, is unknown. It was a choice that may have echoed the 'blue water' foreign policy preferences of the anti-Walpole 'Patriot' opposition, but no evidence survives to establish a link. Paine much later recorded that he was 'raw and adventurous, and heated with the false heroism of a master [at Thetford Grammar School] who had served in a man-of-war'; but this explanation was perfunctory, and distant in time from the events.

> From this adventure I was happily prevented by the affectionate and moral remonstrance of a good father, who, from his own habits of life, being of the Quaker profession, must have begun to look upon me as lost. But the impression, much as it effected at the time, began to wear away, and I entered afterwards in the *King of Prussia* privateer, Captain Mendez, and went in her to sea.[6]

From these fragmentary later recollections the Paine of the 1750s hardly emerges as any universalist critic of national assertion; nor does he sound like a rejecter of fatherly authority in explaining his decision a second time to go to sea in a warlike enterprise.

CAREER CHOICES AND THE AGRARIAN IDEAL

Paine's career choices once he arrived in the American colonies suggest that, whatever his intentions, he never attempted to set up business as a schoolmaster or a

---

[4] See Ch. 6, section on *The Age of Reason*.
[5] He was, however, well aware of the significance of the Test and Corporation Acts: see Ch. 5, section Paine, Jefferson, and Rousseau.
[6] Paine, *Rights of Man. Part the Second* (1792): *CW*, i. 405.

surveyor (both suggested in Benjamin Franklin's letter of reference), nor did he seek to re-establish himself as a shopkeeper or staymaker. His later choices suggest that he was a small-town craftsman whose ambition was an escape to the country-side and to life as an independent small freeholder:[7] it was a vision that looked back to 'Country party' ideals of early eighteenth-century England, not forward to the politicized artisan workshops of London in the 1790s or the class-based urban politics of the Victorian age. If Paine had any premonitions of the future, he dis-approved of some of its social forms. In 1805 he advised Jefferson on the settlers best able to counter the French Catholic presence in newly purchased Louisiana, warning against two groups: 'The Scotch turn their attention to traffic, and the English to manufactures. These people are more fitted to live in cities than to be the cultivators of lands.'[8] This remark had a specific application and a general one: it was the cultivation of land that Paine respected most.

By the 1770s the increasingly challenged ideal of the independent small farmer, derived immediately from England and distantly from ancient Rome, survived most powerfully in the American colonies; it could be appealed to even by colonists who had already moved into a larger economic role. John Dickinson, by the 1760s a wealthy large landowner, a trader in agricultural produce, and a successful lawyer who had not yet emancipated his slaves, used this older yeoman image to establish an innocent but fictitious persona at the opening of his best-selling pamphlet argu-ing against the Townshend duties:

> *My dear* Countrymen, I am a *Farmer*, settled, after a variety of fortunes, near the banks of the river *Delaware*, in the province of Pennsylvania. I received a liberal education, and have been engaged in the busy scenes of life; but am now convinced, that a man may be as happy without bustle, as with it. My farm is small; my servants are few, and good; I have a little money at interest; I wish for no more; my employment in my own affairs is easy; and with a contented grateful mind, undisturbed by worldly hopes or fears, relating to myself, I am compleating the number of days allotted to me by divine goodness.[9]

However inaccurate as an account of Dickinson's economic role, the ideal spoke to large numbers of people in humbler circumstances. Although Paine's life took him from small-town Thetford to London and on to Philadelphia and Paris, he expressed no perception that urbanization was transforming the social structures of the world in which he lived. Indeed, it is no longer clear in recent historiography that urbanization was then generally perceived as transformational: Paine did not respond to an obvious trend, for it was not obvious.

This bucolic ideal stood behind Paine's tract *Agrarian Justice* (1797). In it he devised a vision of rural society in which cultivators paid death duties to 'the com-munity' to compensate the 'half' of the inhabitants who had been 'dispossessed' of

---

[7] In 1821, Wiliam Hazlitt wrote similarly of the reformer William Cobbett that he was 'the perfect representation of what he always wished to be—an English gentleman-farmer': quoted in E. P. Thompson, *The Making of the English Working Class* (London, 1963), 754.

[8] Paine to Jefferson, 25 Jan. 1805: *CW*, ii. 1457.

[9] [John Dickinson], *Letters from a Farmer in Pennsylvania, to the Inhabitants of the British Colonies* (Philadelphia: David Hall and William Sellers, 1768), 3.

their 'natural inheritance' by the invention of landed property, yielding modest sums of money to be paid to the elderly and to 'the rising generation' at age 21 to buy 'a cow, and implements to cultivate a few acres of land',[10] not to apprentices or journeymen to allow them to set up as craftsmen (which Paine had been), nor to shopkeepers (which Paine had also been), nor to schoolteachers (which, again, Paine had been), and not to relieve workers from the consequences of manufacturing (which Paine had seen in the Sheffield iron industry). His was still a rural vision; Paine did not anticipate an urban society dominated by artisan workshops, let alone the concentration of manufactures in 'factories', and not the socialist common ownership of property. His pamphlet was aptly entitled *Agrarian Justice*, not *Workshop Justice*, let alone *Factory Justice*. Back in America from 1802, Paine tried to realize his agrarian ideal, for in 1784 the New York State Legislature had granted him the farm confiscated from a Loyalist in New Rochelle. But the reality of rural life was boredom and isolation. Paine was too old and ill to be a farmer, trying instead to live by selling firewood. His farm did not pay.[11] Needing care, Paine moved to Greenwich Village in New York in 1808, and died there in 1809.

Although Paine cooperated with ironmasters over his project for an iron bridge, he did not become the spokesman for any newly self-aware industrial social constituency. In 1787 he acknowledged that 'The manufacturers of Manchester, Birmingham and Sheffield have had of late a considerable spring', but 'this appears to be rather on speculation than certainty... in the best state which manufactures can be in, they are very unstable sources of national wealth'.[12] Paine was sometimes depicted in the twentieth century as the spokesman of the urban artisan, yet his economic views had little in common with such men; as he claimed in 1780: 'Lands are the real riches of the habitable world, and the natural funds of America.'[13] Nor was this an unusual position. Benjamin Franklin had argued in 1768 that 'Agriculture is truly *productive* of *new wealth*; Manufactures only change Forms.'[14] Even Adam Smith was close to that position. In Paris in 1766, Smith associated with physiocrats like François Quesnay and Anne-Robert-Jacques Turgot. In *Wealth of Nations*, Smith argued in 1776 that the physiocrats had gone too far in their argument that manufacturers and merchants did not add to real wealth, but even Smith attached great importance to agriculture.[15] Colonial America was still a deeply agrarian society; Paine was to learn few new lessons there, or in Paris, about economics.

[10] Paine, *Agrarian Justice* ([1797]): *CW*, i. 611–13, 618.

[11] 'Paine's correspondence about the practical problems of his farm shows that he had no knowledge of agriculture. He had a theoretical devotion to farming as the noblest of professions ... But he would never have undertaken a country life had his farm not been given to him by New York State. In New Rochelle, Paine depended entirely upon hired help or tenants and was able to keep things running only by selling off parcels of land': Aldridge, *Man of Reason*, 291.

[12] Paine, *Prospects on the Rubicon* (1787): *CW*, ii. 639.

[13] [Paine], *Public Good* (1780): *CW*, ii. 329.

[14] Benjamin Franklin to Cadwallader Evans, 20 Feb. 1768: Franklin, *Papers*, xv. 52; cf. Franklin, 'Remarks on Agriculture and Manufacturing' [late 1771]: Franklin, *Papers*, xviii. 273–4.

[15] Adam Smith, *An Inquiry into the Nature and Causes of the Wealth of Nations*, ed. R. H. Campbell and A. S. Skinner (1776; 2 vols., Oxford, 1976), 426–7, 674–7.

In political economy, as in other subjects, Paine saw in his English sources what he was predisposed to see. He condemned Edmund Burke for falling short of Adam Smith's talents in *Wealth of Nations*.[16] Yet from that work Paine took just one quotation, not about any new world of manufactures but about the old world, preoccupied as it was with the negative effect of government debt:

> 'The progress,' says Smith, 'of the enormous debts, which at present oppress, and will in the long run *most probably ruin*, all the great nations of Europe [he should have said *governments*] has been pretty uniform.' But this general manner of speaking, though it might make some impression, carried with it no conviction.[17]

The English, argued Paine, had ignored Smith's too-restrained warnings about national indebtedness, and would soon pay a heavy price.

Even when most preoccupied with the economic realm, Paine wrote of high finance, not of manufactures, urbanization, or class.

> It is worthy of observation that every case of failure of finances, since the system of paper began, has produced a revolution in governments, either total or partial. A failure in the finances of France produced the French Revolution. A failure in the finance of the assignats broke up the revolutionary government, and produced the present French Constitution. A failure in the finances of the Old Congress of America and the embarrassments it brought upon commerce, broke up the system of the old confederation, and produced the Federal Constitution. If, then, we admit of reasoning by comparison of causes and events, the failure of the English finances will produce some change in the government of that country.[18]

This was not written by a theorist of the transformative powers of capitalism. If Paine learned little from the Sheffield ironmasters, he may have learned more from an English banker, Sir Robert Smyth, an enthusiast for the French Revolution, whom Paine knew in Paris: finance had long been more politically literate than manufactures.

THE INTELLECTUAL WORLD OF EARLY NEWTONIANISM

A recurring argument of this study is that Paine's mental world looked back to early eighteenth-century English natural science, more than forward to early nineteenth-century political economy: to Newton, more than Ricardo or Marx. Newton's work had early become controversial, not least because of its theological implications. Even so, there was no rainbow alliance: Newton himself, together with his early followers like Richard Bentley, Samuel Clarke, Roger Cotes, and William Whiston,

---

[16] Paine, *Rights of Man* (1791): *CW*, i. 282.

[17] Adam Smith 'says, that in the year 1696, exchequer bills fell forty, fifty and sixty per cent; bank notes twenty per cent; and the bank stopped payment. That which happened in 1696 may happen again in 1796': Paine, *The Decline and Fall of the English System of Finance* (1796): *CW*, ii. 652, 654–6, 663–4.

[18] Paine, *The Decline and Fall of the English System of Finance* (1796): *CW*, ii. 664.

used natural science to defend an interventionist God and revelation against what they perceived as a widespread threat of atheism, including, from the 1690s, Deism.[19] Paine and his contemporaries were heirs to these earlier conflicts.

Paine used the profits of his privateering cruise on *The King of Prussia* to live in London in 1757–8. Perhaps in these years he attended subscription lectures by men who provided a popular introduction to what was already recognized as a Newtonian system or world view.[20] Much later, in *The Age of Reason*, Paine recorded: 'As soon as I was able I purchased a pair of globes [i.e. terrestrial and astronomical], and attended the philosophical lectures of [Benjamin] Martin [1705–82] and [James] Ferguson [1710–76], and became afterward acquainted with Dr. [John] Bevis [1695–1771], of the society called the Royal Society, then living in the Temple, and an excellent astronomer.'[21] Since Bevis did not take up residence in the Middle Temple until 1764 or secure election to the Royal Society until 21 November 1765,[22] this suggests that if Paine attended Martin's and Ferguson's lectures in 1757–8 he perhaps met Bevis during a later residence in London in 1766–8; if so, this is evidence of Paine's continuing commitment to natural science.[23] Martin's, Ferguson's, and Bevis's astronomical knowledge was elaborate, and far more complex than Paine's later account of the galaxy: Paine's education in scientific matters may have been superficial, but it may nevertheless have had consequences in other areas. What may these consequences have been?

In 1780 Paine made universalist claims for the significance of natural science:

> men who study any universal science, the principles of which are universally known, or admitted, and applied without distinction to the common benefit of all countries, obtain thereby a larger share of philanthropy than those who only study national arts and improvements. Natural philosophy, mathematics and astronomy, carry the mind from the country to the creation, and give it a fitness suited to the extent. It was not Newton's honour, neither could it be his pride, that he was an Englishman, but that he was a philosopher: the heavens had liberated him from the prejudices of an island, and science had expanded his soul as boundless as his studies.[24]

This was powerful rhetoric, but what precisely did it convey? One implication concerns national identity. Yet it is in question how far Paine escaped from an English frame of cultural reference, and how far he made real his rhetorical claim to be a citizen of the world. A second implication may be that Paine's Deism derived from his encounter with Newtonian science. Yet Paine's recollection of his childhood

[19] Richard H. Popkin, 'The Deist Challenge', in Ole Peter Grell, Jonathan I. Israel, and Nicholas Tyacke (eds), *From Persecution to Toleration: The Glorious Revolution and Religion in England* (Oxford, 1991), 195–215; John Redwood, *Reason, Ridicule and Religion: The Age of Enlightenment in England 1660–1750* (London, 1976; 2nd edn., 1996), 93–115.

[20] Alan Q. Morton (ed.), *Science Lecturing in the Eighteenth Century*, special issue of *British Journal for the History of Science* 28 (Mar. 1995).

[21] Paine, *The Age of Reason* (1794): *CW*, i. 496.

[22] Ruth Wallis, 'John Bevis, M.D., F.R.S. (1695–1771), Astronomer Loyal', *Notes and Records of the Royal Society* 36 (1981–2), 211–25, at 217.

[23] Paine was also in London from late 1772 to mid-April 1773; by then, Bevis was dead.

[24] Paine, *The American Crisis*, VIII (Mar. 1780): *CW*, i. 164.

reaction against a Trinitarian Christian doctrine of the atonement suggests that this event preceded his encounter with Martin and Ferguson in London.

Aside from these lectures, the young Paine had been surrounded by what was known, in the first half of the century, as physico-theology after William Derham's best-seller:[25] this was an English 'rhapsodic style of apologetic' that sought to confirm belief in a Creator from the regularities increasingly observable in 'Creation'. It had been anticipated before Newton but was soon greatly strengthened by his work; in an English context it had deployed the developing natural science of the 1660s and after to demonstrate the truth of Christianity. This was a characteristically Anglican school: 'Although most British deists were Newtonians, none before Paine had the character of rhapsodic physico-theology.'[26] Before the 1740s English Deists were 'not hostile to Newtonian philosophy, as is generally believed, but were critical of the conception of God which they believed served as its foundation'. They 'viewed the unpredictable God of the Newtonians as the God of the Tories and High Churchmen'; rather, the Deists 'separated Newton's laws of motion and conception of gravity from Newton's active God who guided them, and replaced that God with the God of their theology'.[27]

What, then, by the mid-eighteenth century, were understood to be the religious implications of Newton's work?[28] From the publication of the 'General Scholium' in the second edition of his *Principia* (1713), the Arian Newton's 'religious speculations created consternation amongst his supporters' and clearly associated him with anti-Trinitarianism.[29] Theological controversy had regularly explored the issue of the Trinity. Yet the three astronomers known to Paine in London did not evidently teach heterodox theology as an analogue of their natural science. There is no evidence in their writings of the heretical pantheism that has recently been ascribed to Newton as its founder, and recently projected forward to imply a republican and democratic critique of political authority.[30] The idea that Newtonianism pointed to republicanism calls for re-examination.

[25] W[illiam] Derham, *Physico-Theology: or, a Demonstration of the Being and Attributes of God, from his Works of Creation. Being the Substance of XVI Sermons Preached in St. Mary le Bow-Church, London, at the Honble Mr. Boyle's Lectures, in the Years 1711 and 1712* (London: W. Innys, 1713; 12th edn, 1754).

[26] In *The Age of Reason* 'Paine innovated on this tradition by adapting some of the arguments of this species of Christian apologetic into a defense of deism *against* Christianity': David C. Hoffman, '"The Creation We Behold": Thomas Paine's *The Age of Reason* and the Tradition of Physico-Theology', *Proceedings of the American Philosophical Society* 157 (2013), 281–303, at 283, 287.

[27] Jeffrey R. Wigelsworth, *Deism in Enlightenment England: Theology, Politics, and Newtonian Public Science* (Manchester, 2009), 71–108, 142–66, 204–8, at 72.

[28] The religion of the early Newtonians, apart from William Whiston, has not been at the centre of attention of recent studies, e.g. Patricia Fara, *Newton: The Making of Genius* (London, 2002); Roy Porter (ed.), *The Cambridge History of Science*, iv, *Eighteenth-Century Science* (Cambridge, 2003).

[29] Larry Stewart, 'Seeing through the Scholium: Religion and Reading Newton in the Eighteenth Century', *History of Science* 34 (1996), 123–65, at 127, 132; Larry Stewart, *The Rise of Public Science: Rhetoric, Technology and Natural Philosophy in Newtonian Britain, 1660–1750* (Cambridge, 1992).

[30] Margaret Jacob, *The Radical Enlightenment: Pantheists, Freemasons and Republicans* (London, 1981), 21, 31, 33, 87 and *passim*; Justin A. I. Champion, 'Deism', in Richard H. Popkin (ed.), *The Columbia History of Western Philosophy* (New York, 1999), 437–45.

Bevis seems to have published nothing on theology and to have had little interest in Newtonianism's possible theological implications.[31] Ferguson was given to including on the title pages of his publications biblical quotations like '*He made the* WORLDS' (Hebrews 1: 2); for him, astronomy made 'our Understandings clearly convinced, and affected with the Conviction, of the Existence, Wisdom, Goodness, Power, and Superintendancy of the SUPREME BEING: So that without an Hyperbole, *An undevout Astronomer is mad*…Minds capable of such deep Researches derive their Origin from Heaven, and are incited to aspire thither as to their proper and final Habitation.' The Universe was 'the Work of an infinite Power, prompted by infinite Goodness, having an infinite Space to exert itself in'.[32] Ferguson's cosmology did not posit a First Cause who then stood aside from Creation; his locution 'the supreme being' was evidently laudatory. On the contrary, for Ferguson 'wherever the Deity exerts his power, there he also manifests his wisdom and goodness'. Gravity 'seems to surpass the power of mechanism', and one explanation of it was 'the immediate agency of the Deity'. The motion of planets and comets was owing to 'the free choice and power of an intelligent Being'.[33] Ferguson published much, but nothing against revealed Trinitarian Christianity.

The same was true of Benjamin Martin. From the 1730s he had presented the claims of natural religion in terms that anticipated the Paine of the 1790s. For Martin, the 'noble Faculty of Reason' was 'the *Light of Nature*'; it allowed 'a Discovery of a *Prime* or *First Cause*, the *Great Author and Maker of all Things*, and which, by us, is called *GOD*'. Reason was exercised in a particular sphere: 'what is necessary to be known of God, (or indeed can be known of him by us) is manifest in the Works of Creation…Nor is there any Part of Nature within our view…which doth not loudly call upon us to receive and confess this great and divine Truth.' Natural religion was sufficient to discover 'the Being and Perfections of God, his Providence, and the Certainty of a future State after Death'. God, to natural religion, was a 'first Cause', a 'first Mover'. An atheist was merely 'a Fool', lacking 'natural Reason'.

So far, the Paine of *The Age of Reason* might have agreed. But Martin went further, arguing that '*Religion* is twofold, *viz. Natural* and *Reveal'd*'. The latter was found in a particular text: 'The sacred Writings of the *Old* and *New Testament* are

---

[31] The sale catalogue of Bevis's library joined it with that of another, so that one cannot be certain about the ownership of particular volumes: *A Catalogue of the Genuine Library and Philosophical Instruments of the late ingenious James Horsfall, Esq. Sub-Treasurer of the Middle Temple, and Fellow of the Royal Society, Deceased: Including the Library, Manuscripts, and Instruments of the late learned John Bevis, M.D. F.R.S. deceased … which … Will be Sold at Auction, By Mr. Paterson … On Saturday the 17th of December, 1785* (no place [?London], no printer, [?1785]). Nevertheless, since the books listed before the section of Bevis's manuscripts on p. 16 contained very few astronomical books, and the books after p. 16 were overwhelmingly astronomical, it is likely that Horsfall's library was listed on pp. 1–15, Bevis's on pp. 16–37. The latter contained no heterodox theology (unless one includes William Whiston's *Astronomical Principles of Religion, natural and reveal'd* (1717)), but instead included Henry Grove's *A System of Moral Philosophy* (1749) and James Beattie's *An Essay on the Nature and Immutability of Truth* (1774 edn), both orthodox texts.

[32] James Ferguson, *An Idea of the Material Universe, Deduced from a Survey of the Solar System* (London: for the Author, 1756), i, 4–5, 8, 27. For Ferguson, the planets were 'designed as commodious Habitations for Creatures endowed with Capacities of knowing, obeying and adoring their beneficent Creator … all Candidates for Heaven', 29–30.

[33] James Ferguson, *Astronomy Explained upon Sir Isaac Newton's Principles, and made easy to those who have not studied Mathematics* (London: for the Author, 1756), 30, 58–9.

the Oracle of God, or his revealed Will to Mankind.' Scripture afforded knowledge of many things, but especially 'the *Institution* of a more perfect, rational, and noble *Scheme* of *Religion* and *Devotion*, by JESUS CHRIST, the promised MESSIAH and SAVIOUR of the World, the SON and ANOINTED of God, who delegated and sent him with full Power and Commission so to do. And this is the *greatest* and most *momentous Point* of *Revelation*.' Martin then elaborated the 'Doctrine of the Scriptures concerning *Jesus Christ*', including the Incarnation, the Virgin Birth, miracles, and the Resurrection.[34]

It was just such an extension of natural religion that Paine condemned in *The Age of Reason*. Moreover, Martin continued this teaching into the 1750s.[35] When in a work of 1759 he announced that 'We propose to treat of Theology here, not in the usual Way as a Matter of *Faith*, but as a true and genuine *Science*, or Subject of real Knowledge', what he had to say of the solar system as a divine creation still found its place next to 'CHRISTIANITY; or Christian Revelation', in which Martin covered again, in more detail, his teaching on revealed religion in his text of 1737.[36] It is not known how far revelation featured in the subscription lectures by Martin and Ferguson that Paine attended, but the published writings of these astronomers provide no evidence that those lectures promoted religious scepticism. Nor is there evidence that their audiences were predisposed to religious scepticism or free-thought. If the 'first generation' of early Newtonians often tended to Arianism,[37] it is not clear that Paine imbibed any such lesson from the second or third generation of Newtonians whose lectures he attended. On the contrary, he left no evidence of any conversion from Arianism to the Deism that he later so militantly avowed.

Even in the 1750s, open Deists may have been few in number in London. It is 'highly probable' that Martin was a Baptist.[38] Ferguson had an orthodox upbringing in Scotland; he proudly used his astronomical science to calculate the year of the crucifixion, which does not suggest a commitment to Deism; he used a mechanical analogy to defend the doctrine of the Trinity; and he died a pious death, his will resigning his soul into the hands of God, 'hoping to be saved by the attonement of Christ my Redeemer'.[39] Such evidence suggests that early Newtonianism did not automatically, or generally, lead to Deism; this may have been Paine's later conclusion, not an inference widely drawn in the 1750s. If so, it may be that

[34] Benjamin Martin, *Bibliotheca Technologica: or a Philological Library of Literary Arts and Sciences* (London: S. Idle for John Noon, 1737), 1–5, 9, 29, 34, 37–9.

[35] Benjamin Martin, *A Plain and Familiar Introduction to the Newtonian Philosophy, In Six Sections* (London: W. Owen, 1751), hailed the galaxy as 'so noble a Work of Creation' that 'displays so much of the infinite Wisdom and Power of God', 91.

[36] Benjamin Martin, *A New and Comprehensive System of Philology; or, a Treatise of the Literary Arts and Sciences, According to their present State* (2 vols., London: W. Owen, 1759–64), i. i, 1–59, 218–410.

[37] Brian Young, 'Newtonianism and the Enthusiasm of Enlightenment', *Studies in the History and Philosophy of Science* 35 (2004), 645–63, at 649.

[38] John R. Millburn, *Benjamin Martin: author, instrument-maker, and 'country showman'* (Leiden, 1976), 9. Martin, *Bibliotheca Technologica*, 40, defined 'Christian Church' on the Nonconformist model of a gathered church, not in the Anglican terms of the Apostolic succession or the establishment.

[39] 'A Short Account of the Life of the Author' [by Ferguson] and Ferguson to the Revd Mr. Cooper, 10 Apr. 1776, in Ebenezer Henderson, *Life of James Ferguson, F.R.S.* (Edinburgh: A. Fullarton, 1867), 3, 5–6, 19, 145–8; 448, 452; John R. Millburn, *Wheelwright of the Heavens: The Life and Work of James Ferguson, FRS* (London, 1988), 75, 95–106, 250.

Paine's childhood rejection of a Christian doctrine of the atonement (and perhaps revealed religion more generally) came first, his adoption of Newtonianism second. But a secure conclusion awaits further evidence.

It has recently seemed obvious to link the rational and predictable cosmos out-lined by Newton with the rational Creation, imbued with general laws, posited by those thinkers now labelled Deists. Yet open and self-identified Deism was rare until a later date.[40] Not until the 1740s, in the person of Peter Annet (1693–1769),[41] did a variety of sceptical theologies within Protestantism resolve themselves into an open repudiation of revealed religion, and perhaps only then could this theological position potentially form an alliance with popularized Newtonian science; but no such alliance did Annet conclude.[42] His preferred strategies included a scathing rhetoric against revelation, the identification of inconsistencies in Scripture texts, a critique of the Pentateuch, the denial of miracles, and a repeated 'character attack' on the orthodox, but not a deployment of Newtonianism.

After seemingly not publishing in the 1750s, Annet again propagated his doc-trine of the supremacy of reason through his periodical, *The Free Inquirer*, pub-lished in nine issues in 1761; it led to his trial and conviction for blasphemous libel the next year.[43] These themes had similarities with those explored in Paine's *Age of Reason*, as did Annet's deliberate targeting of a wide audience; his writings were very different in tone from those of the early, and scholarly, Deists. The 1750s was evidently Paine's formative decade; yet evidence is lacking that he then encoun-tered Annet's theological writings. Even had he done so, Paine could have learned nothing from Annet on natural science. Newton himself had not been a Deist; nor were most of his followers among the natural philosophers. The generation of writers including Anthony Collins (1676–1729) and Matthew Tindal (1657–1733) were obliged publicly to identify themselves as Low Churchmen, not Deists. The writers of the early eighteenth century today labelled Deists were pre-occupied with textual biblical criticism and usually had little participation in experimental natural science as distinct from philosophical speculations on the soul, necessity, space, matter, or motion (William Whiston was no exception, for he was an Arian, not a Deist).[44] Similarly, the theologian who most famously sought to write the obituary of the subject wrote nothing about any link between Deism and natural science.[45]

---

[40] Charles Blount was unusual in accepting the term: 'An Account of the *Deist*'s Religion' in his *The Oracles of Reason* (London: no printer, 1693).

[41] James A. Herrick, *The Radical Rhetoric of the English Deists: The Discourse of Skepticism, 1680–1750* (Columbia, SC, 1997), 125–44, at 128.

[42] [Peter Annet], *Deism Fairly Stated, and Fully Vindicated from the Gross Imputations and Groundless Calumnies of Modern Believers ... By a Moral Philosopher* (London: W. Webb, 1746) assumed the exist-ence of a group, 'the Deists', 4.

[43] Wayne Hudson, *Enlightenment and Modernity: The English Deists and Reform* (London, 2009), 12, 22.

[44] '[T]he difference between deist and non-deist presentation of contemporary natural philosophy becomes almost indistinguishable near the middle of the eighteenth century': Wigelsworth, *Deism in Enlightenment England*, 101.

[45] John Leland, *An Account Of the Principal Deistical Writers that have Appeared in England in the last and present Century* (3 vols, London: B. Dod, 1754–6).

It is not clear that the young Paine drew any Deistical conclusion from his encounter with popularized Newtonianism, however much he later wished to present the two as mutually reinforcing. Evidence is lacking.[46] But it seems that Paine prioritized religion over natural science. As late as 1797, in an address to the Society of Theophilanthropists in Paris, he urged that 'all that which is called natural philosophy is properly a divine study'. Astronomy and the other natural sciences had been taught 'as accomplishments only; whereas they should be taught theologically, or with reference to the *Being* who is the Author of them: for all the principles of science are of divine origin'. Teaching the sciences instead as 'accomplishments' had the result 'of generating in the pupils a species of atheism'. Paine's only argument in favour of his theism was the familiar one: the existence of God as a First Cause was 'a belief deducible by the action of reason'. But Paine evidently added a personal motivation to this argument, since instruction along these lines, he argued, would 'render theology the most delightful and entertaining of all studies'.[47]

This was a late statement, and not necessarily evidence for Paine's early beliefs. But in the absence of evidence for Paine's religious beliefs changing, where the horrors of the American and French Revolutions might have prompted his theological development, it may be an indicator of an attitude dating from at least the 1750s. Like early eighteenth-century English natural philosophers Paine began with a fascination with physico-theology, a fascination evident in *The Age of Reason*, and seems to have interpreted Newtonianism as profoundly congruent with it.

METHODISM AND DEISM

If mid-eighteenth-century Newtonianism had no necessary heterodox theological implications, did it nevertheless carry anti-monarchical political implications? Little suggests that Newtonian natural philosophers of those decades adopted any particular political position.[48] Equally, little is known of the politics of the Deists of those years. Few positive reforming commitments can be identified among them; their preoccupations were negative, in condemning the sort of relation between religion and politics that they held to be embodied in the Jacobite threat (a preoccupation also of Paine). Paine left evidence of the wider political significance of

---

[46] Edward H. Davidson and William J. Scheick, *Paine, Scripture and Authority: The Age of Reason as Religious and Political Idea* (Bethlehem, Pa, 1994), 28, cite a letter to 'Paine' of 18 Dec. 1767 from the American clergyman Jacob Duché as evidence of Thomas Paine's early Deism; its text is derived from Désirée Hirst, *Hidden Riches: Traditional Symbolism from the Renaissance to Blake* (London, 1964), 10–12. But from internal evidence ('your Kempis, your discourses & excellent answer to Warburton') the recipient can only have been the author John Payne (fl. 1762–1800). Duché's observation that 'A wrathfull God whose anger could only be appeased by the blood of His own Son pour'd out in behalf of Sinners always appear'd to me next to blasphemous' was familiar ground in the 1760s.

[47] Paine, 'A Discourse at the Society of Theophilanthropists' (1797): *CW*, ii. 749–50, 754, 756.

[48] The best-selling text on the subject was J[oseph] Harris, *The Description and Use of the Globes, and the Orrery. To which is prefixed, By way of Introduction, a Brief Account of the Solar System* (London: Thomas Wright et al., 1731; 12th edn, 1783). Harris drew no political inferences.

his simplifying conceptions of science. By 1780 he presented Newtonianism as his pathway of escape from Englishness; it was a pathway that led him necessarily to the 'principles...universally known' that underlay the physical world.[49] This was in the middle of the American Revolution, when Paine needed just such a theoretical justification; yet he left no evidence of having possessed it when he arrived in Philadelphia in 1774.

The natural inference from Paine's remark of 1780 was a universal creator, regulating creation via general laws and committed to a general benevolence towards creation. By 1792, this had become: 'man, were he not corrupted by governments, is naturally the friend of man, and...human nature is not of itself vicious.'[50] It was a principle to which Paine held, whatever the scenes that unfolded around him. Even in *Agrarian Justice* (1797), Paine argued the inadequacy of charities to remedy poverty, and urged a systematic response: 'It is only by organizing civilization upon such principles as to act like a system of pulleys, that the whole weight of misery can be removed.'[51] It was a mechanical metaphor from the 1750s, and showed no deep understanding of the manifold dimensions of human suffering.

By a series of steps, the exact nature and chronology of which is now unclear, Paine's aversion to his native country became associated in his mind with principled humanitarianism and with Deism. Paine's benevolence was an abstract position, a consequence (as he finally saw it) of his Newtonianism; evidence does not establish that it was a reaction to suffering and squalor. Paine was a theorist, a friend of mankind in the abstract, more than of individual human beings in particular. By 1792, in *Rights of Man. Part the Second*, he drew a political inference from his Deism:

> We must shut our eyes against reason, we must basely degrade our understanding, not to see the folly of what is called monarchy. Nature is orderly in all her works; but this is a mode of government that counteracts nature. It turns the progress of the human faculties upside down. It subjects age to be governed by children, and wisdom by folly. On the contrary, the representative system is always parallel with the order and immutable laws of nature, and meets the reason of man in every part.

It followed that 'The Revolution of America presented in politics what was only theory in mechanics.'[52] This was metaphor, not argument, but it was consistent with Paine's position throughout that part of his life for which evidence survives.

By contrast, some later linkages were unavailable to Paine. His attendance at the London lectures of Benjamin Martin and James Ferguson cannot have led him towards 'political radicalism',[53] since this ideology was newly coined only in *c*.1820; in its absence, the formation of Paine's political views, especially his negation of monarchy, becomes a problem. The politics of Benjamin Martin and James Ferguson are unknown. A shared interest in Newtonianism does not seem to have led Paine to meet that other famous scientist of the age, Joseph Priestley, for whom natural

---

[49] [Paine], *The American Crisis*, VIII (Mar. 1780): *CW*, i. 164.
[50] Paine, *Rights of Man. Part the Second* (1792): *CW*, i. 397.
[51] Paine, *Agrarian Justice* ([1797]): *CW*, i. 618.
[52] Paine, *Rights of Man. Part the Second* (1792): *CW*, i. 353–4, 373–4.
[53] Keane, *Paine*, 43.

science formed part of a world view including Unitarianism in theology and republicanism in politics.[54] Paine never became a Unitarian; rather, his early religious explorations may have been in the opposite direction, towards Methodism.

'Methodism' in the early eighteenth century was not the formalized denomination that it later became, nor the rigid, stifling system conjured up (with exaggeration) by the historian E. P. Thompson (1924–93). On the contrary, the term was from the 1740s a loosely applied nickname, stretched to cover a variety of novel theologies and religious practices which sprang up independently in many parts of the kingdom more than they were imposed from above by George Whitefield or John Wesley. Methodism was initially religious experiment, not disciplined conformity, and drew people eager to explore the unfamiliar. Paine may have heard John Wesley preach in Thetford; in Dover in 1758 his then employer, the stay-maker Benjamin Grace, reportedly took him to the Methodist chapel where Paine presented himself as a believer,[55] and he may later have read printed sermons to that congregation when a preacher did not arrive (although this is unlikely to have happened often).[56] These traditions are not now supported by strong evidence, and must be treated with caution; but it is possible that the young Paine had brief contacts with Methodism while on a spiritual quest that ended in explicit Deism. It is also possible that his rhetorical rejection of established churches and their

[54] Robert E. Schofield, *The Enlightenment of Joseph Priestley: A Study of his Life and Work from 1733 to 1773* (University Park, Pa, 1997) records no contact with Paine. Priestley, after escaping from the riots in Birmingham, seems to have met Paine for the first time in London in 1791: Robert E. Schofield, *The Enlightened Joseph Priestley: A Study of his Life and Work from 1773 to 1803* (University Park, Pa, 2004), 294. They were not necessarily at one: while Priestley was teaching at New College, Hackney, in 1792, described by Burke as 'a hot bed of sedition', the students invited Paine to dinner as a gesture of defiance against their instructors. In 1794, Priestley was to attack Paine's *Age of Reason*, 305, 377–8.

[55] *The Journal of the Rev. John Wesley, A.M.*, ed. Nehemiah Curnock (London, 1916), viii. 31 n., citing an anonymous article, 'The White Cliffs of Dover: Methodism in a Great Fortress', *The Methodist Recorder and General Christian Chronicle* (19 Aug. 1906), 9. The author of the article presented no evidence.

[56] The Methodist Archives and History Center, Drew University, Madison, NJ, has a copy of the first volume of John Wesley's *Sermons on Several Occasions* (1746), with an inscription: 'Out of this volume Thomas Paine, author of the Age of Reason, used to read sermons to the Congregations at the Methodist Chapel in Dover when they were disappointed of a Preacher. At that time he belonged to the Methodist Society in that place': Keane, *Paine*, 544 n. 29. The reference to *The Age of Reason* places the inscription much later, and it may not be reliable evidence for 1758. Slightly differently, George Chalmers reported: 'There is a tradition, that in his lodging [at Sandwich] he collected a congregation, to whom he preached as an independent, or a methodist.' He added that Paine had sought ordination in the Church of England while in London in 1767, but without a recommendation to the bishop from the schoolmaster who employed him, Paine was unsuccessful; so 'he preached in Moorfields, and in various populous places in England, as he was urged by his necessities, or directed by his spirit': [George Chalmers], *The Life of Thomas Pain, The Author of Rights of Men. With a Defence of his Writings. By Francis Oldys, A.M. of the University of Pennsylvania* (London: Stockdale, 1791), 8, 21. Evidence does not survive to confirm Chalmers's claims, but he took care to consult original sources, and his arguments may have had some basis. An Anglican clergyman in the 1790s wrote that Paine was 'once an itinerant preacher', but this is unreliable evidence, since the same author also believed that Paine 'was a Dissenter': David Rivers, *Observations on the Political Conduct of the Protestant Dissenters* (London: T. Burton, [?1799]), 35–6. However, the fragmentary evidence for Paine's Methodism and possible attempt at Anglican ordination suggests, if true, an unfamiliar context for his early intellectual formation.

priests was related in some way to his not securing ordination. But the evidence is inadequate to establish such a possibility.[57]

It is therefore not clear what, if any, lasting influence Methodism had on Paine. If he had any contact with Wesleyan Methodism, its confident reliance on revelation may have only prompted Paine to define more clearly his Deist beliefs. Paine recorded no lingering respect for Methodism, as he did for Quakerism. After his return to the United States in 1802, he seemingly made no contact with the Methodism then burgeoning in that country. He did not follow Wesley's unmissable example of nationwide organization: Paine was usually a loner. No Paineite political movement developed in either Britain or America, led by Paine himself, with anything resembling Wesley's zealous structuring of local 'classes', district itinerants, and national organization: if there were Paine clubs, there is no evidence that he visited them or corresponded with them. Paine never became an orator, and never mobilized large open-air meetings with a fervent political message.

Nor did he evidently learn democratic lessons from the internal life of any religious denomination. He taught nothing about the self-improvement, empowerment, or resistance of ordinary men and women through local organizations. He did not address any expanding working class in the growing manufacturing districts of the north of England, which he evidently visited only when pursuing his plan for an iron bridge: Paine was always a figure from the rural small towns of the south-east, drawing on the intellectual life of London. Just as Paine's objection to hierarchy was an abstract objection to the hereditary principle rather than a litany of grievances against the specific local tyrannies of squires or noblemen, so his objections to the Church were abstract objections to its theology, proved by Paine from the Bible rather than from examples of the particular local misdeeds of parsons or bishops. John Wesley's published *Letters* contain no single item from Paine,[58] and Paine's writings contain no allusions to John or Charles Wesley, George Whitefield, or the Methodists collectively, except for one belated letter offering a critique of their orthodox theology: 'Their religion is all creed and no morals.'[59]

Evidence, then, does not establish a relation between Paine's alleged early brushes with Methodism and his subsequently avowed Deism. All that can be done is to establish possibilities. The most important of these possibilities is suggested by the persistence of Deism in early eighteenth-century England not just in centres of learning, but in the countryside. English Deism had enjoyed its greatest flourishing in the 1720s. It was as much in circulation in small town and rural locations as in the metropolis; indeed Paine had a parallel in the self-taught Salisbury glovemaker Thomas Chubb (1679–1747), a prolific author of Deist tracts who was initially inspired by William Whiston. But Chubb had two patrons in England, a local merchant and Sir Joseph Jekyll, MP; Paine had none. Chubb seems to have had easy access to books; Paine did not. Except for two years in London, the retiring Chubb lived his whole life in Salisbury; Paine moved continually. Chubb chose a

---

[57] Nathalie Caron, *Thomas Paine contre l'imposture des prêtres* (Paris, 1998), 54–9.
[58] *The Letters of the Rev. John Wesley, A.M.*, ed. John Telford (8 vols, London, 1931).
[59] Paine to Andrew Dean, 15 Aug. 1806: *CW*, ii. 1485.

life of privacy and writing, supported by Jekyll's pension; his work is scholarly and extensive. Paine's life was public, and financially precarious; his work was addressed beyond the elite. Chubb argued for natural law as the basis of political authority, but without passing through natural science; Paine's respect for Newtonianism was prominent, though difficult to assess.[60] But their religious views had much in common.

GOVERNMENT AND ITS CRITICS

Paine's early antipathy to the English monarchy and the English government have often been taken for granted, but their origin is difficult to trace; his career may offer a clue. From early 1768 Paine was again posted as an exciseman, this time to Lewes in Sussex, a town with an active Dissenting tradition. But there he secured appointment to the Society of Twelve, the self-selecting oligarchy that ran the town. He became a member of the Vestry of St Michael's parish; it administered, among other things, poor relief. This hardly suggests a youthful antipathy to government as such. In addition, he allegedly joined the Headstrong Club, a debating society meeting at the White Hart Inn.[61] Its records have been lost, if any were kept. Nothing is known of the subjects that caught its, and Paine's, attention. It has been suggested that Paine must have been informed about the developing American crisis,[62] but the absence in *Common Sense* of attention to the dispute makes this unlikely. Given the later importance of the American Revolution, it is significant how few people on either side of the Atlantic saw it coming; there is no evidence that Paine was one of those few. Since he later wrote *Common Sense*, it may be significant that Paine seemingly left no evidence that he was concerned about long-standing colonial American disputes before he left England in 1774.

One fragment of evidence on the relation between his religious and political views refers to his years in Lewes. The English reformer James Cheetham related an anecdote that he can only have heard, from Paine, after 1802:

> The following anecdote, which in conversation he related himself, first turned his thoughts, he remarked, to government. 'After playing at Bowls, at Lewes, retiring to drink some punch, Mr. Verril, one of the Bowlers, observed, alluding to the wars of Frederick, that the king of Prussia was the best fellow in the world for a king, he had so much of the devil in him. This, striking me [Paine] with great force, occasioned the reflection, that if it were necessary for a king to have so much of the devil in him, kings might very beneficially be dispensed with.'

The thought was not, however, in England, followed up by action. *There*, he was neither a ministerialist nor an anti-ministerialist. Whenever he turned his attention to

---

[60] T. L. Bushell, *The Sage of Salisbury: Thomas Chubb 1679–1747* (London, 1968), 8–9, 42, 50.
[61] Rickman, *Life of Paine*, 38. Rickman's informant was 'My friend Mr. Lee, of Lewes' in 1810, not a proximate source.
[62] Keane, *Paine*, 67–8.

government, it was only for a place, or for an increase of the salary of that which he held: he was thirty seven when he left England.[63]

Such, reportedly, was Paine's self-understanding after 1802. This was long after the event; but if true, the anecdote suggests that Paine's position in his Lewes years might better be described as anti-monarchical rather than pro-republican.

A clue to Paine's early political knowledge was the content of his local newspaper, *The Sussex Weekly Advertiser; or, Lewes Journal*, which he could have read while an exciseman in that town from 1768 to 1774.[64] It reprinted the letters of the anonymous 'Junius', then a sensation in the London press: they set the tone for much of the paper's political comment. Its issue of 10 December 1770 reprinted a speech by Sir William Meredith of 27 November calling for a reform of the criminal law, since the widespread use of the capital penalty 'is the way to render the people ferocious and sanguinary'. Its issue of 1 April 1771 carried a letter (not obviously in Paine's prose) signed 'COMMON SENSE' defending 'our Liberty of the Press' since 'It is better to cease to exist, than to cease to be free.' The issue of 15 April 1771 carried a mock petition to the king claiming 'the undeniable evidence of fact and experience, that the arbitrary and violent measures which have for several years past been invariably pursued by your Majesty's Ministers, are the sole, genuine, and adequate causes of the present general discontent in the minds of your faithful people'.

Readers on 29 April 1771 would have found a letter from 'TRIBUNUS' to the king beginning: 'Be not deceived, Sir, by the impunity with which your wicked Ministers have hitherto passed in their treasonable attempts to undermine the constitution, and destroy our liberties. Do not think Vengeance is dead, while it only sleepeth; or that the people feel not for freedom, and conceive an utter abhorrence of those who would betray it, because they have not *yet* attempted to do themselves ample justice': it was a veiled threat of resistance. 'TRIBUNUS' returned to his theme on 17 June 1771: whenever the laws are 'converted into the traitorous instruments of betraying the peoples liberties; this will tempt the subject to think for himself; and discharge him at once from all fealty and allegiance:—for what shall bind the subject to allegiance, when Governors cease to obey the laws?' In such a case,

> The people at once divest him [the king] of that illustrious figure in which he was once to appear, and reduce him to a mere definition of a man...When veneration is once lost, Sir, duty will not stay long behind...Believe me, Sir, the Prince that too hastily discovers fears of rebellion, is not without all intentions to provoke it.

Even in a quiet Sussex market town in the early 1770s, in a time of peace, people might read of 'tyranny', 'slavery', and a right of resistance. The language of 1776 in the American colonies was not specifically American. It was transatlantic.

---

[63] Cheetham, *Life*, 32–3.
[64] I have consulted the files of the paper in the Beinecke Library, Yale University.

Mild, by contrast, was a series of essays in the *Sussex Weekly Advertiser* (an initial series from 19 October 1772 to 14 December 1773) signed 'A Forester', the pen name that Paine was to use for his own letters in the *Pennsylvania Journal* from 3 April to 8 May 1776. The anonymous Sussex author (not Paine) engaged in a gentler form of apolitical moralizing, but one that sometimes had extensive implications. He claimed only to write against superstition in the name of 'plain truth' and 'a little common sense' (7 Sept. 1772); but on 14 September 1772 he declared that the 'divine spark' of 'understanding' seemed 'indiscriminately let fall upon poor and rich; at least, your fine folks have not monopolized it. Who finer than Lords or Ladies? And yet we hear, that "ONE OF THE NOBILITY," and "ONE OF NO ABILITY," are now become little less than synonymous terms.' It was a form of words later used in Paine's *Rights of Man*, and Paine has been suspected as the anonymous author of these letters. But by republishing the essays in book form in 1787, the author revealed himself as the Revd Richard Michell, a local Anglican clergyman.[65] It was a world in which politics and religion naturally joined, as evidenced by the *Sussex Weekly Advertiser*'s extensive printing of debates in Parliament on the application for the repeal of clerical subscription to the Thirty-Nine Articles (23 Dec. 1771–23 Mar. 1772).[66] The issue was of wide general interest.

There is no evidence that Paine wrote for the paper. The issue of 8 July 1771 contained a verse, 'An Arithmetical Paraphrase on the Lord's Prayer', sent in by 'a constant Reader: P___', but this cannot be shown to be Paine. It is not obviously satirical or dismissive, but evidence of the way in which the wording of so familiar a prayer could be used in daily discourse. 'A Forester' also echoed conventional ideas about the theological significance of nature:

Certain it is, nothing can tend more to elevate and enlarge the human mind, than the study and contemplation of nature, especially in her more magnificent productions. By tracing and exploring second causes, we are led to admire and adore the great first cause of all things. In our present state of existence the Deity discovers himself to us two ways, by his word and his works. The Creation therefore may be consider'd as a kind of natural bible, written in the most legible characters, and in an universal language; a language, which in one respect has the advantage even of the scriptures themselves, because it appeals to our bodily senses for the truth of what it maintains. From the astonishing variety, magnificence, beauty, and usefulness of the things *made*, we are taught by clear and undeniable deduction to infer the wisdom, power, and goodness of the *Maker*. And are we then so stupified and besotted by low-thoughted cares

---

[65] Richard Michell, *Fugitive Pieces on Various Subjects* (2 vols, Lewes: for the Author, by W. and A. Lee, 1787); George Spater, 'The Author of the "A Forester" Articles', *Bulletin of the Thomas Paine Society* 7 (1992), 53–5. Michell was generally unpolitical, but did condemn 'our taking such a mad step as that of going to logger-heads with our fellow-subjects on the other side of the Atlantic': Letter XXXVIII, n.d., *Fugitive Pieces*, ii. 42–51, at 43. After the peace in 1783, he printed verses that recorded: 'Thus Pride, and Folly, and Expence, | Have forc'd us into Common Sense': *Fugitive Pieces*, ii. 142–6, at 145.

[66] The issue of 29 June 1772 reprinted 'Lord Mansfield's speech on the Negro cause', his crucial judgement in *Somerset's Case* that established the illegality of slavery in England. To this landmark ruling Paine nowhere responded.

and pursuits, as to have no inclination to turn over and peruse a few leaves of this immense treatise, which is as instructive as it is beautiful and sublime?[67]

With much of this Paine agreed, differing on revelation through the divine 'word'. But this agreement only showed how far Paine was from originality in holding up Creation as evidence of a divine Creator: by the 1770s, it was a commonplace. And the political languages available in rural Lewes were equally old ones.

---

[67] Michell, Letter XLVI, n.d.: *Fugitive Pieces*, ii. 123–9, at 126–7. Michell's sceptical remarks about Hume, Bolingbroke, Deists, and 'infidels' (ii. 56, 159, 161-5) did not align him with Paine.

2

Pathways of Political Change
From (Anti-)Jacobite to Jacobin

ENGLISH DYNASTIC POLITICS AND
THE 'PATRIOT' OPPOSITION

Paine claimed in the 1790s that his objection to the French monarchy was abstract, directed against the institution in general. It was a claim easily understood within the conventional model of 'universalism'; but it obscured the highly specific nature of his objection to the British monarchy, aimed as it was at the historic reality of the Hanoverian dynasty. Despite his later reputation as a forward-looking man of 1776 or 1789, Paine's mind, like Burke's, had been formed in the world before 1760, a world preoccupied with dynastic politics and its ideological implications. Paine was not a Jacobite: his principles were the opposite. Indeed he extended his anti-Jacobite principles to a condemnation of all monarchy, the Orange and Hanoverian monarchies included. Nevertheless, his writings are full of examples of the anti-Hanoverian rhetoric that was so prevalent in Britain in the early eighteenth century; he drew on this inheritance to the point where other political traditions were almost wholly absent from his lexicon.[1] This rhetoric was shaped by the way the choice then open in English politics was not between a monarchy and a republic (in the sense of a state headed by an elected president), but between two rival dynasties. Only this long survival of Jacobite discourse explains the long survival, importance, and force of its opposite: anti-Jacobite discourse.

The terms of Paine's critique of monarchy were not recent, but of long standing. In *Rights of Man. Part the Second* (1792), he added a note on monarchs after 1688, unrestrained as Paine claimed they had been by the absence of a written English constitution. After the Revolution,

> another William, descended from the same stock, and claiming from the same origin [as the Stuarts], gained possession; and of the two evils, James and William, the nation preferred what it thought the least; since, from the circumstances, it must take one... As to what is called the convention parliament [of 1689, which recognized William and Mary as sovereigns], it was a thing that made itself, and then made the authority by which it acted.

[1] 'Although Jacobin and Tory are at opposed political poles, sparks of feeling and argument are continually exchanged between them': E. P. Thompson, *The Making of the English Working Class* (London, 1963), 344.

Politics became even worse thanks to 'the corruption introduced at the Hanover succession, by the agency of Walpole'.[2]

For Whigs like Burke, the Revolution was the bulwark of liberties; for Paine, it had opened Pandora's box.

I happened to be in England at the celebration of the centenary of the revolution of 1688. The characters of William and Mary have always appeared to me detestable; the one seeking to destroy his uncle, and the other her father, to get possession of power themselves: yet, as the nation was disposed to think something of that event, I felt hurt at seeing it ascribe the whole reputation of it to a man who had undertaken it as a jobb, and who, besides what he otherwise got, charged six hundred thousand pounds for the expence of the little fleet that brought him from Holland. George the First acted the same close-fisted part as William had done, and bought the Duchy of Bremin with the money he got from England, two hundred and fifty thousand pounds over and above his pay as king; and having thus purchased it at the expence of England, added it to his Hanoverian dominions for his own private profit. In fact, every nation that does not govern itself, is governed as a jobb [i.e. as a corrupt arrangement]. England has been the prey of jobbs ever since the revolution [of 1688].[3]

Paine condemned the summons of George I to the British throne:

Besides the endless German intrigues that must follow from a German elector being king of England, there is a natural impossibility of uniting in the same person the principles of freedom and the principles of despotism, or, as it is usually called in England, arbitrary power. A German elector is, in his electorate, a despot: how then could it be expected that he should be attached to principles of liberty in one country, while his interest in another was to be supported by despotism?[4]

Paine's condemnation of hereditary monarchy in general was partly that it produced civil wars of succession all over Europe; in Britain, the Wars of the Roses and the wars 'of 1715 and 1745, were of the same kind'.[5] He wrote of the Jacobite risings against the Hanoverians. The Hanoverian link had also dragged Britain into continental wars: 'The miseries of Hanover's last war [the Seven Years War] ought to warn us against connections.'[6] 'With the revolution of 1688, and more so since the Hanover succession [in 1714], came the destructive system of continental intrigues, and the rage for foreign wars and foreign dominion; systems of such secure mystery, that the expences admit of no accounts; a single line stands for millions.'[7]

For Paine poverty was caused by a variety of things, age, infirmity, and war among them. But—as a former exciseman—he focused on taxation as a cause, and taxation had been inflated by an illegal regime: 'So much has the weight and oppression of taxes increased since the Revolution, and especially since the year 1714.'[8] The tax

---

[2] Paine, *Rights of Man. Part the Second* (1792): *CW*, i. 383.
[3] Paine, *Rights of Man. Part the Second* (1792): *CW*, i. 419–20 (text corrected).
[4] Paine, *Rights of Man* (1791): *CW*, i. 327.
[5] Paine, *Rights of Man. Part the Second* (1792): *CW*, i. 366–7.
[6] [Paine], *Common Sense* (1776): *CW*, i. 19.
[7] Paine, *Rights of Man. Part the Second* (1792): *CW*, i. 417.
[8] Paine, *A Letter To Mr. Secretary Dundas* (1792): *CW*, ii. 453.

burden was also unequal: 'Before the coming of the Hanoverians, the taxes were divided in nearly equal proportions between the land and articles of consumption, with the land bearing rather the largest share; but since that era, nearly thirteen millions annually of new taxes have been thrown upon consumption.' In total, 'It has cost England almost seventy millions sterling, to maintain a family imported from abroad, of very inferior capacity to thousands in the nation; and scarcely a year has passed that has not produced some new mercenary application.'[9]

Paine condemned the Septennial Act of 1716, which arbitrarily lengthened the duration of Parliaments from three years to seven in order to frustrate a Stuart restoration.[10] The Act of 3 Geo. II sanctioning special juries 'served to throw into the hands of Walpole, who was then Minister, the management of juries in crown prosecutions' for the same reason.[11] Colonists who had not yet taken the oath of allegiance to Congress, Paine argued in 1780, were 'the non-jurors', and should be subject to a special tax; he well knew who the English Nonjurors had been.[12]

The Hanoverian regime responded to him, true to form: the legal indictment of *Rights of Man. Part the Second* in 1792 cited paragraphs that, judged Paine, 'relate chiefly to certain facts, such as the Revolution of 1688, and the coming of George the First, commonly called the House of Hanover, or the House of Brunswick, or some such house' and cited too the Bill of Rights of 1689, condemned by Paine for declaring that the Lords and Commons '*submit themselves, their heirs, and posterity for ever*' to William and Mary as king and queen. This was merely the contrivance of courtiers 'for the purpose of keeping up an expensive and enormous Civil List... Let such men cry up the House of Orange, or the House of Brunswick, if they please. They would cry up any other house if it suited their purpose, and give as good reasons for it.'[13] Although Paine, as an anti-monarchist, was no friend of the House of Stuart, his denunciations were mainly aimed at the House of Hanover. He urged the French not to execute Louis XVI by employing an English analogy: Charles I had been executed, yet Charles II was restored; in 1688 the later Stuarts had merely been exiled, and their family 'sank into obscurity, confounded itself with the multitude, and is at length extinct'.[14]

This anti-Hanoverianism was seldom an American phenomenon, but often an English one. New England colonists had rejected James II more unanimously in 1688 than had the English, and thereafter remained (or could present themselves as) more noisily loyal to the Houses of Orange and Hanover.[15] A critique of monarchs

---

[9] Paine, *Rights of Man. Part the Second* (1792): *CW*, i. 410, 421.

[10] Paine, 'Answer to Four Questions on the Legislative and Executive Powers' (1792): *CW*, ii. 526. In America, such a bill would have been blocked by the constitution: Paine, *Rights of Man. Part the Second* (1792): *CW*, i. 390.

[11] Paine, *Letter Addressed to the Addressers* (1792): *CW*, ii. 493.

[12] Paine to Joseph Reed, 4 June 1780: *CW*, ii. 1186–8.

[13] Paine, *Letter Addressed to the Addressers* (1792): *CW*, ii. 495–6.

[14] Paine, 'Reasons for Preserving the Life of Louis Capet' (15 Jan. 1793): *CW*, ii. 554.

[15] David S. Lovejoy, *The Glorious Revolution in America* (1972; 2nd edn, Middletown, Conn., 1987); Benjamin Lewis Price, *Nursing Fathers: American Colonists' Conception of English Protestant Kingship, 1688–1776* (Lanham, Md, 1999); Brendan McConville, *The King's Three Faces: The Rise and Fall of Royal America, 1688–1776* (Chapel Hill, NC, 2006); Eric Nelson, *The Royalist Revolution: Monarchy and the American Founding* (Cambridge, Mass., 2014).

(and, by extension, of monarchy) was more English than American. Nor was the title *Common Sense* original, or drawn from the American controversy. The term was widely used, and Paine's pamphlet was even preceded by a journal of the same name in 1737–43, 'funded initially by Jacobites', edited by Charles Molloy with the approval, from Rome, of James Francis Edward Stuart, King James III in the Stuart succession.[16] The term is conventionally associated with the leading work of the Scots philosopher and empiricist Thomas Reid,[17] but no party had a monopoly. Many authors employed it, without reification.[18] In the years preceding Paine's emigration to Philadelphia, it was most often used by defenders of revealed religion.[19]

Common Sense of 1737–43 continued the work of the famous journal *The Craftsman*. The political ideas of the latter 'are essentially a reworking of Bolingbroke's Patriot platform, though its outspokenness is signalled by its inclusion of the scurrilous print and allegorical satire on Walpole and George II, the *Vision of the Golden Rump*.'[20] No evidence establishes that Paine read this journal, but its existence suggests that the persona 'common sense' was common property as a rhetorical ploy, not exclusively confined in the 1770s to one political cause; it could mean 'quotidian wisdom of a preexisting community of everyday people' or 'a basic human faculty that allowed individuals to make elemental judgements about ordinary matters'.[21] There is no evidence that Paine discovered the idea of common sense in the writings of Lord Shaftesbury or of Thomas Reid:[22] the term was commonplace. Although Benjamin Rush may have sought to imply that

---

[16] James Sambrook, 'Charles Molloy', *ODNB*. See also Paul Kléber Monod, *Jacobitism and the English People 1688–1788* (Cambridge, 1989), 29; G. H. Jones, 'The Jacobites, Charles Molloy, and Common Sense', *Review of English Studies* new ser. 4, 13 (1953), 144–7; David Greenwood, *William King, Tory and Jacobite* (Oxford, 1969), 77–80. Two years of the periodical were reprinted in book form as *Common Sense: or, the Englishman's Journal* (2 vols, London: J. Purser and G. Hawkins, 1738–9).

[17] Thomas Reid, *An Inquiry into the Human Mind, On the Principles of Common Sense* (Edinburgh: A. Kincaid and J. Bell, and London: A. Millar, 1764).

[18] Lounissi, *Paine*, 235–6.

[19] e.g. [James Oswald], *An Appeal to Common Sense in Behalf of Religion* (2 vols, Edinburgh: Kincaid and Creech, and London: Cadell, 1768–72); [Herbert Lawrence], *The Life and Adventures of Common Sense. A Historical Allegory* (London: Montagu Lawrence, 1769); [John Wesley], *The Desideratum: or, Electricity Made Plain and Useful. By a Lover of Mankind, and of Common Sense* (Bristol: W. Pine, 1771); Thomas Morgan, *An Appeal to The Common Sense of plain and common Christians, in Behalf of the Old Christianity of the Gospel* (Leeds: J. Bowling, 1771); *Common Sense: In some Free Remarks on the Efficiency of the Moral Change... By a By-Stander* (New York: Samuel Inslee and Anthony Car, 1772); [Edward Evanson], *The Doctrines of a Trinity and the Incarnation of God examined upon the Principles of Reason and Common Sense* (London: S. Bladon, 1772); [John Fletcher], *An Appeal to Matter of Fact and common Sense. Or a Rational Demonstration of Man's corrupt and lost Estate* (Bristol: William Pine, 1772); Joseph Priestley, *An Examination of Dr. Reid's Inquiry into the Human Mind on the Principles of Common Sense, Dr. Beattie's Essay on the Nature and Immutability of Truth, and Dr. Oswald's Common Sense in Behalf of Religion* (London: J. Johnson, 1774); *Duelling and Suicide Repugnant to Revelation, Reason, and Common Sense* (London, no printer, 1774); [William Hopkins], *An Appeal to the Common Sense of all Christian People* (London: J. Johnson, 1775).

[20] Christine Gerrard, *The Patriot Opposition to Walpole: Politics, Poetry, and National Myth, 1725–1742* (Oxford, 1994), 39–40.

[21] For an argument that Paine's *Common Sense* reconciled both meanings, and that these dated from the late seventeenth century, see Sophia Rosenfeld, 'Tom Paine's *Common Sense* and Ours', *WMQ* 65 (2008), 633–68 and Sophia Rosenfeld, *Common Sense: A Political History* (Cambridge, Mass., 2011).

[22] [Lord Shaftesbury], *Chatacteristicks, &c. Volume I... Sensus Communis, or an Essay on the Freedom of Wit and Humour* (no place, no printer, 1711); Thomas Reid, *An Inquiry into the Human Mind, On*

Paine's title was owed to Rush himself, he made his claim long afterwards,[23] and its truth is doubtful; certainly, Paine seized on the title, and often used 'Common Sense' thereafter as his nom de plume. But other writers used it too: it was never Paine's monopoly, nor was it even specifically American. In 1775 American readers could peruse a reprint of Jonathan Mayhew's incendiary 30 January sermon, preached in 1750, in which he had represented himself as 'on the side of Liberty, the BIBLE and Common Sense, in opposition to Tyranny, PRIEST-CRAFT and Non-sense'.[24] But this was the freethinking idiom of the British authors John Trenchard and Thomas Gordon, at its height in London periodicals like *The Independent Whig* (1720–1 and collected editions), and of the extreme Latitudinarian bishop Benjamin Hoadly.[25]

Paine was well aware that the Hanoverian dynasty had in the past maintained itself by force. In 1781 he introduced the dynastic issue in a neutral tone that spoke volumes: 'We all know that the Stuart family and the House of Hanover opposed each other for the crown of England. The Stuart family stood first in the line of succession, but the other was the most successful.' How that success was brought about Paine illustrated with a long quotation from Tobias Smollett's *History of England* to show the Hanoverian Duke of Cumberland's savagery in devastating areas of Scotland after his victory at Culloden. The same would have happened in America, argued Paine, had Britain won the revolutionary conflict.[26] Paine's most evocative challenge was expressed in the same document. Why did George III obstinately persist in the American war? In case of defeat, 'Is he afraid they will send him to Hanover, or what does he fear?'[27] Paine returned to this point in 1797. European wars in the eighteenth century, he argued, had been caused by 'the mischievous compound of an elector of the Germanic body and a king of England...Let the elector retire to his electorate, and the world will have peace.'[28] As political analysis, this was by 1797 strangely outdated.

In *Rights of Man* (1791), Paine excused the 'few' casualties of the French Revolution: 'They all of them had their fate in the circumstances of the moment, and were not pursued with that long, cold-blooded, unabated revenge which

the Principles of Common Sense (Edinburgh: A. Kincaid and James Bell, 1764); Aldridge, *American Ideology*, 47.

[23] See Ch. 4, section on Republicanism.

[24] J[onathan] M[ayhew], *A Mysterious Doctrine Unriddled, or Unlimited Submission and Non-Resistance to the Higher Powers Considered* (Boston and Newry: Daniel Carpenter and J. Gordon, 1775), viii–ix.

[25] St Paul does not 'mention any thing of a *Passive Submission* in such cases; but plainly leaves Nations to the Dictates of common Sense': Benjamin Hoadly, *The Measures of Submission to the Civil Magistrate Consider'd. In a Defence of the Doctrine Deliver'd in A Sermon Preach'd before the Rt. Hon. The Lord Mayor, Aldermen, and Citizens of London, Sept. 29. 1705* (London: Tim[othy] Childe, 1706), 9.

[26] Paine cited T[obias] Smollett, *A Complete History of England, from the Descent of Julius Caesar, to the Treaty of Aix la Chapelle, 1748* (3rd edn, 11 vols, London: Richard Baldwin, 1760), xi. 239–40.

[27] [Paine], *The American Crisis*, X (5 Mar. 1781): *CW*, i. 191, 195–6. This number was in reality a compilation by the editor James Carey in 1797: Thomas Paine, *Collected Writings*, ed. Eric Foner (New York, 1955), 856–7.

[28] *Letter of Thomas Paine to the People of France, and the French Armies, on the Events of the 18th Fructidor, and its Consequences* (1797): *CW*, ii. 607–8.

pursued the unfortunate Scotch, in the affair of 1745.' In 1789 some individuals were killed and their heads carried around Paris on pikes.

> Let us therefore examine how men came by the idea of punishing in this manner. They learn it from the governments they live under; and retaliate the punishments they have been accustomed to behold. The heads stuck upon spikes, which remained for years upon Temple Bar, differed nothing in the horror of the scene from those carried about on spikes at Paris; yet this was done by the English Government.

It was a sequel to the executions of some of the Jacobite prisoners in 1746 that their heads were displayed in this fashion on a gate above one of London's main thoroughfares; Paine would have seen the last of them, for they remained impaled there for many years until brought down by decay.[29]

A partial political reconciliation had taken place under George III, but Paine did not condemn it. 'The present reign, by embracing the Scotch, has tranquillized and conciliated the spirit that disturbed the two former reigns. Accusations were not wanting at that time to reprobate the policy as tinctured with ingratitude toward those who were the immediate means of the Hanover succession', but wrongly.[30] Yet Paine was not reconciled. In the preface to the French edition of *Rights of Man*, Paine wrote of 'l'électeur de Hanovre, ou, comme on l'appelle quelquefois, le roi d'Angleterre'.[31] England was governed by 'a foreign house of kings...the House of Brunswick, one of the petty tribes of Germany'. Was wisdom 'at such a low ebb in England, that it was become necessary to import it from Holland [in 1688] and from Hanover [in 1714]?' Indeed, 'A German elector is, in his electorate, a despot'; how could he be attached to 'principles of liberty'? Things had deteriorated under George III: 'George I and II were sensible of a rival in the remains of the Stuarts; and as they could not but consider themselves as standing on their good behavior, they had prudence to keep their German principles of government to themselves; but as the Stuart family wore away, the prudence became less necessary'. 'German principles of government', a phrase Paine repeated, had a recognizable early eighteenth-century political reference.[32]

As late as 1793 Paine predicted that 'France, through the influence of principle and the divine right of men to freedom, will have a stronger party in England than she ever had through the Jacobite bugbear of the divine right of kings in the Stuart line.'[33] In 1797 he still referred to 'the Hanoverian Government of England'.[34] By 1800 he reported to Jefferson:

> the internal state of England, at this moment, is such, as makes it impolitic for France to press her on the subject of peace. There is, to my knowledge, a great change in the political principles of that country. Besides the aversion which many of them have to

---

[29] Paine, *Rights of Man* (1791): *CW*, i. 259, 265–6 (text corrected).
[30] Paine, *Prospects on the Rubicon* (1787): *CW*, ii. 627.
[31] Thomas Paine, *Les Droits de l'homme*, présenté par Claude Mouchard (Paris, 1987), 69.
[32] Paine, *Rights of Man* (1791): *CW*, i. 321–2, 325, 327–8.
[33] Paine to anon., 16 Mar. 1789: *CW*, ii. 1285–6.
[34] Paine, *Letter... to Camille Jordan* (1797): *CW*, ii. 761.

the Hanover family, there are much greater numbers who have an aversion to hereditary succession, and wish to establish government by representation.[35]

From the first, Paine had proceeded to the second; in describing both, he overstated his case.

His frame of reference was unchanged. In 1800, Paine, in France, continued to urge
a plan for the invasion of England. Together with the main force of gun-boats, aimed
to convey a large army to England's east coast, there should, he urged, be an expedition
from Brest or Rochelle to the north of Scotland. His perspective was still historical:

> The French revolution has many friends in that country, and the destination will not
> be suspected. This is the only part of the plan that is necessary to keep secret. The des-
> cent that was made there in 1745 had nearly proved fatal to the Anglo-Hanoverian
> government of England. That small force, with its partisans penetrated to the centre
> of England and then retreated.[36]

In 1806, anticipating Napoleon's successful conquest of England and a change of
government, Paine added: 'The dynasty of the Guelphs have continued ninety two
years which is somewhat longer than the dynasty of the Stuarts continued.'[37]

Paine understood the toppling of monarchy in a backward-looking perspective
rather than as offering a blueprint for a wholly different form of society. As late as
1807 his essay 'Of the Affairs of England' set out in the American press a very old
interpretation of English history:

> In 1714 the English nation, for the principles of government were not understood at
> that time, sent to Hanover for a man and his family, George the first, to come and
> govern them. The poor man knew nothing about England, he had never been there,
> knew nothing of its laws, and could not spake [*sic*] a word of English, but when he got
> in a passion, which he often did, he used to kick his hat about the room.
>
> His son, George the second, was the same sort of man as to dullness of capacity as
> his father was but not so peaceable, for the wars of George the first were carried on
> against his hat, but as George the second thought he knew something of military wars
> he was often engaged in continental wars in which England as a nation and an Island[38]
> ought to have had nothing to do; and the present incumbent George the third and *last*
> has hardly ever been at peace; but he is sly enough to stay at home and set other nations
> together by the ears, and the poor English have to pay the expense till they have hardly
> bread to eat themselves. This is the short history of the Guelphs or *Whelps* of Hanover.[39]

It was a history that, in Paine's mind, had changed little since the 1750s. This
was not an abstract critique of monarchy on natural rights grounds; its detail and
chronological extension suggests it is likely to have taken shape in Paine's mind

---

[35] Paine to Thomas Jefferson, 1 Oct. 1800: *CW*, ii. 1413.
[36] Paine to Thomas Jefferson, 1 Oct. 1800: *CW*, ii. 1416.
[37] Paine to Thomas Jefferson, 30 Jan. 1806: *CW*, ii. 1476.
[38] England shares an island with another kingdom and a principality: this slip reveals Paine's
Englishness and draws attention to his general neglect of Scotland, Wales, and Ireland.
[39] *Public Advertiser*, 1 June 1807, quoted in Aldridge, *Man of Reason*, 304–5.

well before 1774. Having taken shape, it persisted with little revision to the end of his life.

How did Paine absorb this political idiom? In 1779 he provided evidence for a personal link to this political language via the amateur mathematician George Lewis Scott (1708–80):

> As I always had a taste to science, I naturally had friends of that cast in England; and among the rest George Lewis Scott, Esq., through whose formal introduction my first acquaintance with Dr. Franklin commenced. I esteem Mr. Scott as one of the most amiable characters I know of, but his particular situation had been that in the minority of the present King he was his sub-preceptor, and from the occasional traditionary accounts yet remaining in the family of Mr. Scott, I obtained the true character of the present King from his childhood upwards, and, you may naturally suppose, of the present ministry.[40]

Scott was tutor to George, Prince of Wales, in 1750–1 and sub-preceptor in 1751–6: he was in a position to speak about the character of the boy who became king in 1760. He also had motives for doing so, and was by nature a raconteur: in 1769, the young Frances Burney spent an evening with Scott at a party, and recorded that 'he is very sociable & facetious too, & entertain'd me extremely with droll anecdotes & storys among the Great & Court'.[41]

Why was Scott important? Despite his ambitiously pro-Hanoverian parents, who had given him the Christian names of George I, Scott in 1752–3 became embroiled in accusations that unnamed people around the young Prince of Wales were, or had been, Jacobites. According to the paranoid Whig Horace Walpole, ineffectual but well-connected son of Sir Robert, Scott had been 'recommended by Lord Bolingbroke'; but Scott was also described by the level-headed Archbishop Thomas Herring as 'brought up in the school of Bolingbroke'.[42] Additionally, Henry Pelham, the Prime Minister, thought Scott had been 'recommended, as I understand, by Lord Bolingbroke, I suppose thro the channel of Lord Bathurst', a Tory and long-standing associate of Bolingbroke's.[43] In December 1752 Horace Walpole anonymously circulated a memorandum complaining of the covert or former Jacobite views of some of Prince George's courtiers, and so triggered a crisis that

---

[40] Paine to Henry Laurens, 14 Jan. 1779: *CW*, ii. 1162.

[41] *The Early Journals and Letters of Frances Burney*, ed. Lars E. Troide (5 vols, Kingston, Canada, 1988), i. 71. Burney's experience adds to the probability that Scott was a source for Paine. In May 1791, according to William Godwin, Paine borrowed £40 from a 'Scott' to help finance the publication of *Rights of Man*: Aldridge, *Man of Reason*, 135. Aldridge wrongly identified him as George Lewis Scott, who had died in 1780.

[42] Herring to Lord Hardwicke, 14 Sept. 1752: BL Add MSS 35,599 fo. 64, cited in *Letters from George III to Lord Bute 1756–1766*, ed. Romney Sedgwick (London, 1939), xxv.

[43] 'As to the Jacobitism of the nation, you know I have often said, I thought it increased, and grew more desperate; but I was laughed at for thinking so, even by the Royal Family themselves': Henry Pelham to the Duke of Newcastle, 16 Oct. 1750, BL Add MSS 32,723 fos 159–62; Barbara Brandon Schnorrenberg, 'Who Was George Lewis Scott?', *New Perspectives on the Eighteenth Century* 2 (2005), 39–53, at 41. Allen, 1st Earl Bathurst (1684–1775). Later Scott wrote a long letter to Bathurst vindicating his conduct after the accusations of 1752–3, including a denial that he had discussed with Bishop Hayter 'evidence for the being of a God': BL Add MSS 6,249 fos 302–8, cited by Schnorrenberg, 44.

the ministry silenced with some difficulty.[44] Of Andrew Stone, the sub-governor, James Cresset, the secretary to the Dowager Princess, and George Lewis Scott, the sub-preceptor, Lord Waldegrave later wrote in ironic dismissal of the charges: 'The Crimes objected against them were Jacobite Connections, instilling Tory Principles and Scott was moreover pronounced an Atheist on the presumptive Evidence of being a Philosopher and a Mathematician.'[45] This last allegation is explored below.

These charges were formerly disbelieved by historians,[46] but one of those suspected, William Murray MP (1705–93), Solicitor General in 1742–54, has now been shown to have written while an Oxford undergraduate in 1723–7 'offering my service' to the Stuart claimant and professing 'my duty and loyalty to the King [James III]'. As the Duke of Newcastle admitted to Andrew Stone in 1762, Murray had been gravely hampered in his political career by his family's Jacobitism; 'his own character not known in that respect; his first appearance in the world marked with the most intimate connection with the late Lord Bolingbroke and Mr. [Alexander] Pope' (a Catholic Nonjuror).[47] Not all smoke is without fire, and such evidence lends plausibility to Horace Walpole's observations that William Murray and Andrew Stone 'had been bred at Christ Church together, and had tasted of the politics of Oxford as well as of its erudition...they were converted by their own interest', and that Scott and Cresset were 'disciples of Lord Bolingbroke'.[48] By the 1750s, however, the meaning of that charge needs careful specification.

Personal self-interest was in play, as well as ideological inheritance. In 1756, when the Prince's household was changed, Horace Walpole claimed that the Prince 'himself condescended to desire Mr Stone to prevent Scott, his sub-preceptor, from being continued in any employment about him...the reason given for his exclusion was, his having talked with contempt of the Prince's understanding, and with freedom of the Princess's conduct'.[49] These opinions Scott may have communicated to Paine. This rearrangement was the occasion when John Stuart, 3rd Earl of Bute, joined the Prince's household as Groom of the Stole; Scott may have associated Bute with his own ejection, and may have judged George III's ministries negatively as a result, but evidence on this point is lacking. In his letter to Laurens,

[44] Horace Walpole, *Memoirs of King George II*, ed. John Brooke (3 vols, New Haven, 1985), i. 56, 193, 199n., 204–23.

[45] *The Memoirs and Speeches of James, 2nd Earl Waldegrave, 1742–1763*, ed. J. C. D. Clark (Cambridge, 1988), 143–4; for the crisis of 1752–3, introduction, 55–60.

[46] *Letters from George III to Lord Bute*, ed. Sedgwick, xxiv ('one of the hardiest legends in English history'), xxxvii, xlii. Sedgwick exposed the origins of a political stratagem and historical legend, but he thereby occluded the ideological issues that gave that stratagem some plausibility to contemporaries.

[47] [Romney Sedgwick], 'William Murray', in *The History of Parliament: The House of Commons 1715–1754*, ed. Sedgwick (2 vols, London, 1970), ii. 285–6.

[48] Walpole, *Memoirs of King George II*, i. 34; 'Sir Robert Walpole on quitting the ministry had cautioned Mr Pelham against Stone, having touched upon the scent of some of his intrigues, as he [Sir Robert] was hunting after Jacobite cabals', 193.

[49] Walpole, *Memoirs of King George II*, ii. 182 (this was the Dowager Princess of Wales). In 1804, George III judged Dr Thomas Hayter, Bishop of Norwich, guilty of a 'gross and wicked calumny on George Scott', who was 'a man of the purest mind, and most innocent conduct'. But in 1753 the Whig politician Richard Rigby had reported differently of Scott: 'he seems shrewd and cunning...I would not trust him with untold [i.e. uncounted] gold': *Memoirs and Speeches of James, 2nd Earl Waldegrave*, ed. Clark, 52, 60.

however, Paine associated Scott's view of Prince George's character with Scott's view of the new king's ministers, after George III's accession in 1760. Moreover, Paine's brief remark may have disclosed more than passing dealings with Scott, since Paine recorded that he owed information to Scott's family as well as to Scott himself.

Horace Walpole was not necessarily a reliable guide to Scott's politics, and some contextual explanation is required; but the context is complex, and conclusions must be cautious and provisional. Henry St John, 1st Viscount Bolingbroke (1678–1751), had explored the Stuart option in his early career, and had been attainted in 1715; but after the defeat of the rising of that year he professed to renounce any Jacobite commitment, negotiated a formal if ambiguous reconciliation with the regime, and returned to England in 1723. There, however, he became a prominent architect of the 'Patriot' opposition, seeking to combine Tories and opposition Whigs in an attempt to bring down Sir Robert Walpole. This did not end Bolingbroke's openness to a Jacobite restoration, which he discussed with Chavigny, the French ambassador, in 1732–3; he is not known to have gone so far at any later date.[50] From 1744, when he finally returned from France to pass his last years at Battersea, he had some association instead with the rival Hanoverian court of Frederick, Prince of Wales (1707–51). Although evidence is scant for Bolingbroke's conduct in 1744–51, it appears that what were at issue were persisting dispositions, not active Jacobite conspiracies.[51]

The opposition's case was most famously embodied in its journal *The Craftsman*, which arguably expressed a position implicitly but not actionably critical of the Hanoverian monarchy;[52] Bolingbroke's contributions ran from 1727 to 1735. The paper played on the themes of ministerial incompetence, the malign role of the monied interest, the centrality of trade and commerce to national prosperity, the negative impact of debt and taxes, the subversion of the constitution by crown influence, the menace of corruption and luxury, the erosion of popular liberties, the iniquity of the Septennial Act, the need for frequent elections, and the duty of independent freeholders to act to redress these ills. Only religious issues, which deeply divided Tories from opposition Whigs, remained off limits and hardly appeared in its pages. *The Craftsman* sought opposition unity in its implication that a majority of men were virtuous; the minority, the court and the ministers, were self-interested and corrupt. It was ministerial corruption that sustained one-party rule; sound gov-

[50] Eveline Cruickshanks, *Political Untouchables: The Tories and the '45* (London, 1979), 12.

[51] Clark, *English Society*, 114–19. Cresset, Murray, Scott, and Stone seem to have left no trace in the Jacobite negotiations and occasional conspiracies that followed Culloden: Doron Zimmerman, *The Jacobite Movement in Scotland and in Exile, 1746–1759* (Basingstoke, 2003).

[52] Lord Bolingbroke, *Contributions to The Craftsman*, ed. Simon Varey (Oxford, 1982); *Bolingbroke's Political Writings: The Conservative Enlightenment*, ed. Bernard Cottret (Basingstoke, 1997). 'Patriot Whiggery and Jacobitism deployed overlapping sets of images and metaphors, especially those of redemptive kingship. But Patriot Whigs were rarely Jacobites': Gerrard, *The Patriot Opposition to Walpole*, 232; 'both Patriot verse and Jacobite verse might in some sense be seen as parallel and overlapping forms, both predicating a national regeneration through the agency of a redemptive Patriot prince', 76; 'The history of the rival "Princes of Wales" [Frederick and Charles Edward] deserves further exploration, not least the mutually interchangeable set of political languages and princely images both deployed', 194.

ernment could only be restored by a patriotic reunion of virtuous men, transcending the parties of Whig and Tory. In this vision, the new 'Patriotism' succeeded the older 'Country party' ideal as the key denominator; opposition Whigs now came to outweigh but not to merge with their partners the Tories. 'Patriot' aggression became a leading theme of the War of the Austrian Succession of 1740–8 and the Seven Years War of 1756–63 (in the second of which Paine willingly fought).[53]

None of these themes was necessarily anti-Hanoverian; in practice, many could be made so by implication, since George II chose the ministers who sustained or condoned these national vices or failings.[54] As indefeasible divine right was diluted to a divine right to govern well, the monarch was set up for another form of devastating criticism from the discontented. Bolingbroke's *The Idea of a Patriot King* (1738) devised a eulogy of future princely virtue that could only imply a contrast with present kingly vice. In this current of ideas Bolingbroke's role was both formative and ambiguous, as he moved unreliably from Jacobite Toryism to the opposition Whiggism of Prince Frederick's court: his argument of 1738 might serve a future king from either dynasty,[55] though at the equally high price of a critique of actually existing monarchy. But his works sold. Some of his *Craftsman* essays were republished separately, and became best-sellers; he added more.[56] More problematically, Patriot Whiggery contained a prominent streak of heterodoxy and militant anticlericalism.[57] In Bolingbroke's religious writings, published posthumously in his collected *Works* of 1754 and edited by David Mallet, it became apparent that Bolingbroke's political position, especially his conception of public virtue, had been deeply involved with his Deism.

Little of this critique was altogether new; but Bolingbroke and his political and literary allies in the 1730s and 1740s drew these themes together, articulated this discourse brilliantly, and gave it contemporary application. No surviving evidence records whether Paine read Bolingbroke, or whether George Lewis Scott spoke to Paine about Bolingbroke. Nevertheless, a letter from Bolingbroke,

[53] The speech drafted by Lord Egmont for Frederick, Prince of Wales, to use after his accession, at the dissolution of the old Parliament, committed the new king to 'abolish those unhappy [party] distinctions, which have so long subsisted, and are productive of every mischief that can attend a divided state': A. N. Newman, 'Leicester House Politics, 1748–1751', *EHR* 76 (1961), 577–89, at 588. In 1760, George III was heir to this political ideal.

[54] Gerrard, *Patriot Opposition*, 12–13, rightly emphasizes that many Patriots, especially in wartime, were militantly pro-Hanoverian. By the 1750s Bolingbroke's drama of salvific monarchy could hardly avoid a Hanoverian in the leading role.

[55] Howard Erskine-Hill, 'Alexander Pope: The Political Poet in his Time', *Eighteenth Century Studies* 15 (1981–2), 123–48, at 139.

[56] Notably [Bolingbroke], *The Freeholder's Political Catechism* (London: J. Roberts, 1733); [Bolingbroke],, *A Dissertation upon Parties* (London: R. Francklin, 1734); [Bolingbroke], *Remarks on the History of England* (London: R. Francklin, 1743); [Bolingbroke], *Letters, on the Spirit of Patriotism: on the The Idea of a Patriot King: and On the State of Parties, At the Accession of King George the First* (London: A. Millar, 1749); [Bolingbroke], *Letters on the Study and Use of History* (2 vols., London: A. Millar, 1752). They were often reprinted. For Bolingbroke's *The Idea of a Patriot King*, first circulated in manuscript in 1738, see especially Gerrard, *Patriot Opposition*, 185–229.

[57] Gerrard, *Patriot Opposition*, 24–34, 39.

then living in Battersea, to his London publisher Richard Francklin in 1747
shows Bolingbroke using David Mallet and George Lewis Scott to negotiate in a
dispute with that bookseller.[58] Scott, then, was evidently someone Bolingbroke
knew well enough to entrust with a mission. Mallet, too, was already recognized
as a freethinker. That Bolingbroke chose to pair Scott with Mallet does not prove
that Scott shared Mallet's religious opinions, but it raises the possibility that the
aged statesman patronized younger men open to his religious views; and, if this
proves a valid hypothesis, it would explain something of Paine's later relationship
with Scott.

This was important since what was at issue by the 1750s were not plausible
Jacobite schemes to effect a restoration but the survival in changed circumstances,
and the continuing vitality, of a political lexicon hostile to the Hanoverians.[59] The
opposition of the 1730s created or reformulated a political language that spread
widely, including in the American colonies where *The Craftsman* was reprinted,
and could be used in different circumstances in the 1760s. It was so used when the
ascendancy of the Earl of Bute provided a new target and made it possible to claim
the existence of a new absolutism in the policies of George III and his ministers.
Paine's own politics were no exact copy of the opposition rhetoric of the 1730s and
1740s; but there were important similarities. Among them was the very prominent
role given to public virtue, and the negative stance towards the Hanoverian monarchy; Paine was unusual in carrying the second far further, but he did so not only
for abstract reasons but on historical grounds that were easily recognizable to his
contemporaries.

When did Paine know George Lewis Scott? Paine did not list him among the
scientists whose lectures he attended in London, probably in 1757–8 or 1766–8.
But Scott was an Excise Commissioner from February 1758 until his death, and
this suggests that Paine may have known him in the early 1770s during his, Paine's,
involvement in the Commissioners' scheme to raise the salaries of excisemen. If so,
this would distance their dealings even further from the events of 1752–3. What
was in question by the early 1770s was not conspiracy, but idealism; and of the
two, idealism would prove the more potent.

In 1776, Paine adorned the title page of his *Common Sense* with two lines of poetry:

> Man knows no Master save creating HEAVEN,
> Or those whom choice and common good ordain.

The passage is conventionally understood, if noticed at all, as an echo of a new age
of populist, egalitarian, and contractarian personal emancipation. In reality, their
author, James Thomson (1700–48), a college friend of the freethinker David Mallet,
with whom he lastingly collaborated, was a central literary figure in the 'Patriot'

---

[58] Bolingbroke to Richard Francklin, 7 Nov. 1747: *The Unpublished Letters of Henry St John, First
Viscount Bolingbroke*, ed. Adrian Lashmore-Davies (5 vols, London, 2013), v. 295–7, where Scott is
identified as a 'reputed Jacobite', n. 3. I owe this reference to Dr Lashmore-Davies.

[59] For which see especially Gabriel Glickman, 'Cultures and Coteries in Mid-Century Toryism:
Johnson in Oxford and London', in Jonathan Clark and Howard Erskine-Hill (eds), *The Politics of
Samuel Johnson* (Basingstoke, 2012), 57–89.

opposition to George II's ministries, was recruited into the circle of Frederick, Prince of Wales, and spoke the old political language of Paine's youth.[60] Thomson was a Scot. His poem of 1735–6 was an account of how not England but 'BRITAIN' had risen from '*Celtic* Night' to 'present Grandeur' by the exercise of Liberty. It did not in any very obvious sense anticipate the grievances that led to the American Revolution.[61] But nor, it is argued here, did Paine.

Paine (b. 1737) can hardly have known Thomson (d. 1748). But in 1777 James Boswell wrote to tell Samuel Johnson, then working on his *Lives of the Poets*, that George Lewis Scott and the poet John Armstrong were Thomson's 'only surviving companions, while he lived in and about London'.[62] Did Scott speak to Paine about Thomson? No evidence survives; but this contextual setting suggests that it is possible. It is, however, known that the colonial American rebels of the 1770s called themselves 'Patriots': the ideologies of the 1730s and 1740s were still current politics. The colonists' extraordinarily rhetorical public idealism had many sources; but one source was disclosed by the wife of John Adams, writing to her husband, then serving in Congress in Philadelphia, and quoting not a Commonwealthman, not John Locke, but thirty-nine lines of verse. They were by 'my favorite Thomson, from some spirited and patriotic speeches of his in the reign of George II', including:

> Oh! are ye not those patriots in whose power
> That best, that godlike luxury is placed
> Of blessing thousands, thousands yet unborn
> Thro' late posterity?[63]

The same vision had just been expressed in Paine's *Common Sense*.

---

[60] Thomson was a founder member of the Society for the Encouragement of Learning, as was George Lewis Scott. The society was established in 1736 'to institute a republick of letters, for the promoting of arts and sciences': quoted Gerrard, *Patriot Opposition*, 54–5.

[61] James Thomson, *Antient and Modern Italy Compared: Being the First Part of Liberty, a Poem* (London: A. Millar, 1735); *Greece: Being the Second Part of Liberty, a Poem* (London: A. Millar, 1735); *Rome: Being the Third Part of Liberty, a Poem* (London: A. Millar, 1735); quotations from *Britain: Being the Fourth Part of Liberty, a Poem* (London: A. Millar, 1736), 35. Paine's quotation came from the same page.

[62] James Boswell, *The Life of Samuel Johnson, LL.D.* (2 vols, London: Henry Baldwin for Charles Dilly, 1791), ii. 117. John Armstrong (1708/9–70), a college friend of James Thomson in Edinburgh and a practising physician, was a close friend of John Wilkes from *c.*1751, though they later quarrelled; he was also a cousin of Andrew Lumisden, until 1768 a secretary to the Stuart claimants James Francis Edward (1688–1766) and Charles Edward (1720–88), and called on Lumisden in Paris in 1770: James Sambrook, 'John Armstrong', *ODNB*. The Whig Armstrong, then, was at least aware of the possible grounds for anti-Hanoverian commitment on the part of others.

[63] Abigail to John Adams, 2 Apr. 1776: *Familiar Letters of John Adams and his Wife Abigail Adams, during the Revolution*, ed. Charles Francis Adams (1875; Freeport, 1970), 161–3. She quoted James Thomson, *The Seasons* (London: no printer, 1736), 187. Caroline Robbins, *The Eighteenth Century Commonwealthman* (Cambridge, Mass., 1959), 259, called Thomson 'the laureate of the Commonwealthmen'. It may on the contrary be suggested that Thomson calls in question the coherence into the early eighteenth century of a 'Commonwealth' tradition in the sense in which Robbins so influentially described it for the late seventeenth.

IDIOMS OF POLITICS: THE ALTERNATIVES

Paine's remarks on recent English history might be less striking if they had been diversified by remarks in other available political idioms.[64] He could have commended the 'Good Old Cause', the tradition of the revolutionaries of the 1640s and 1650s. He could have adopted the religious sectarianism militant in the 1640s and 1650s, which had periodically resurfaced after the Restoration of 1660. Paine could have endorsed the 'Commonwealthmen', those early eighteenth-century figures like Andrew Fletcher, Walter Moyle, John Trenchard, and Thomas Gordon, who drew inspiration from the mid-seventeenth century but re-expressed it in a newly commercial idiom.[65] He could have invoked Anglo-Saxon constitutionalism, as many reformers did. He could have endorsed the mainstream Whig image of a checked and balanced constitution. He could have adopted the language of 'Old Dissent', expressing the linked litany of pertinacious grudges against the establishment and its legal defences, like the Test and Corporation Acts, spoken by the denominations of Protestant Nonconformity (notably Presbyterians, Congregationalists, and Baptists) that took shape outside the Church after 1660. Paine could have echoed those Whigs who sought to place extensive interpretations on the Revolution of 1688 (especially from its anniversary in 1788), including the claim that it vindicated the sovereignty of the people. He could have praised John Locke.

All these well-defined political idioms Paine could have used; he used none of them, although these languages of politics were rehearsed by others in Britain at the time of the American and French Revolutions. These omissions were not shortcomings on Paine's part, but markers of a position different from those that much recent scholarship expects. Paine did in *Common Sense* quote one phrase from Milton, not from his political works but from *Paradise Lost*, on the impossibility of 'true reconcilement';[66] but this single instance only emphasized the absence of references elsewhere by Paine to Milton, his contemporaries, or their politics. Paine wrote intolerantly of the Protestant Dissenting denominations: 'give power to a bigot of any sectary [sect] and he will use it to the oppression of the rest', that is, of the other sects.[67] Paine was 'known not to be a Presbyterian; and therefore the cant cry of court sycophants, about church and meeting, kept up to amuse and bewilder the nation, cannot be raised against me'.[68] In *Common Sense* he even

---

[64] For which see especially J. G. A. Pocock, 'The Varieties of Whiggism from Exclusion to Reform: A History of Ideology and Discourse', in Pocock, *Virtue, Commerce, and History: Essays on Political Thought and History, Chiefly in the Eighteenth Century* (Cambridge, 1985), 215–310.

[65] Robbins, *The Eighteenth Century Commonwealthman*; Bernard Bailyn, *The Ideological Origins of the American Revolution* (Cambridge, Mass., 1967); Gordon Wood, *The Creation of the American Republic 1776–1787* (Chapel Hill, NC, 1969); J. G. A. Pocock, *The Machiavellian Moment: Florentine Political Thought and the Atlantic Republican Tradition* (Princeton, 1975). When the 'Commonwealth' paradigm was formulated in the 1950s, little was known in academe of the dynastic idiom discussed here.

[66] [Paine], *Common Sense* (1776): *CW*, i. 23. Ironically, Paine cited Satan's words warning his followers not to abandon their rebellion against God. For an argument that Paine was not indebted to Milton see Aldridge, *American Ideology*, 98.

[67] Paine to Jefferson, 25 Jan. 1805: *CW*, ii. 1460.

[68] Paine, *Rights of Man. Part the Second* (1792): *CW*, i. 442.

called the widely accepted idea of a mixed and balanced constitution 'farcical',[69] and his attitude to that emblematic figure of Whiggism, Locke, was dismissive. There are elements in Paine's historical vision of the idea of the 'Norman Yoke' (although without appeal to an antecedent libertarian Saxon constitution);[70] but the Norman Yoke was, by the 1770s, subsumed in something else. For Paine spoke in the language of anti-Hanoverian politics still sustained by the Jacobites in his youth, and absorbed by opposition Whigs, Paine among them, for whom a Stuart restoration would have been anathema. Paine borrowed this anti-Hanoverianism, but went further to condemn monarchy as such.

At local level, others were influenced by the dynastic idiom, however much political activists tended to be associated with any of the discourses just listed. Survivals of dynastic discourse were evident to the American Loyalist and merchant Samuel Curwen, sitting out the American Revolution in exile in Britain. After a religious service in that manufacturing centre, Manchester, in 1777, he witnessed 'the free unrestrained chat' of his companion's landlady,

> named Hudson a Quaker in religion and Jacobite in political principle, the numbers of which since the English born prince [George III] has mounted the throne is somewhat lessened here, as I am told by our Landlady, who is in the abdicated family's interest, which is here openly professed; all of that sect putting up large Oak boughs over their doors on the 29 May to express joy at the glorious Event of the restoration of the Stuart family to the English throne [in 1660]; many such I saw. The Ladies, who if they take a party are ever violent, scruple not, openly and without restraint to drink Prince Charles's health and their wishes for his restoration to his paternal Kingdom.

In that leading port, Bristol, on 29 May 1780, he added: 'This being Restoration Day, some houses are distinguished by oak branches in front. 'Tis a mark of attachment to Monarchy, and by many of regard to the excluded family at least in some places as Manchester, Exeter &c.'[71] If nonjuring religious practice was by that date almost extinct in England, a wider orientation against the Hanoverian monarchy was not.

Recent historiography has often minimized the significance and the incidence of this political allegiance: even if the Jacobite rising of 1715 is given some attention, the rising of 1745 is more often dismissed as an impractical, romantic gesture, a survival far beyond its time. Yet this judgement has distracted attention from three phenomena of considerable significance: first, the longer and wider survival of the language of Stuart allegiance in some quarters; second, the pathways of development by which its speakers evolved away from it; third, the importance, prominence,

---

[69] [Paine], *Common Sense* (1776): *CW*, i. 7.

[70] Christopher Hill, 'The Norman Yoke', in Hill, *Puritanism and Revolution: Studies in Interpretation of the English Revolution of the 17th Century* (London, 1958; Panther edn, 1969), 103–6, 119, discussed Paine but argued that, in *Common Sense* and *Rights of Man*, 'the appeal to the past' was abandoned in favour of 'the appeal to reason'; 'Paine brushes history aside to rest his claims on natural right.' Hill was unaware of the dynastic dimension of anti-monarchical argument and the weakness of its relation to natural rights theory.

[71] *The Journal of Samuel Curwen Loyalist*, ed. Andrew Oliver (2 vols, Cambridge, Mass., 1972), i. 366–7; ii. 616. These incidents do not appear in the index to this work, and have escaped attention.

and long persistence of *anti*-Jacobite ideology and rhetoric within a shared dynastic idiom. By 'Jacobitism' historians no longer mean, as they once did, an emotional, nostalgic and therefore intellectually empty attachment to one individual as their candidate for an office that had already been reduced to a constitutional monarchy. By 'Jacobitism' historians now mean many things, in complex and changing interaction: a dynastic option in European power-politics; a worked-out and sophisticated political ideology; an aspect of religious duty and observance; a cultural formation. In that last form it persisted longest.

FROM JACOBITE TO JACOBIN?

Paine's hostility to the hereditary principle seems so self-evidently valid in the present that the question is seldom asked: where in Paine's background did such an idea come from? The mental landscape in which Paine grew up, polarized between Stuart and Hanoverian, was one that he shared with others, born into one political world and forced to adapt to profoundly changing dynastic circumstances. The long shadow of seventeenth- and early eighteenth-century dynastic politics did not wholly disperse in 1760, nor was it confined to those who had been drawn to that political idiom. Jeremy Bentham, Major John Cartwright, Edward Gibbon, and James Mill illustrate other pathways of development that allow an understanding of Paine's own.

There was, however, one clearer but extreme case that highlights the pathway not taken by these four famous men. The phrase 'from Jacobite to Jacobin', sometimes heard in recent historiography, is too simple to capture their transitions; the chronological distance between the 1740s and 1790s would have meant that very few individuals could have completed that journey.[72] Contemporaries were nevertheless sometimes aware of a possible affinity, and at least one man did fall into that category: Joseph Ritson. In 1817 Robert Southey (1774–1843), looking back over the previous half century, argued that John Wilkes, important though he had been in sowing 'seeds of insurrection and insubordination', was not their sole cause: 'the ground was ready for the sower. Wilkes would have produced little effect if the public mind had not been apt at the time to receive such influences.' Wilkes played on a 'great body of latent discontent'. Southey offered an explanation:

Some influence must be attributed to the leaven which Jacobitism had left behind. The Jacobites, indeed, no longer existed as a faction, their hopes having no longer an object whereon to fix; but when disloyalty had ceased, disaffection would in very many instances remain; and men who had been trained up to regard the reigning family with dislike, and desire their overthrow, would be disposed to unite with any party in whom they could find the mere sympathy of opposition. If a generation of perfect tranquility had intervened, this feeling would have worn out; and all the adherents of the old family would gradually and imperceptibly have transferred their entire allegiance,

---

[72] For one other, see Dominic Green, 'From Jacobite to Jacobin: Robert Watson's Life in Opposition', in Allan I. Macinnes, Kieran German, and Lesley Graham (eds), *Living with Jacobitism, 1690–1788: The Three Kingdoms and Beyond* (London, 2014), 185–96.

as many unquestionably did. But there was no such interval; and it is a curious fact that the last man in England who was a professed Jacobite became a furious Jacobine.[73]

His footnote identified the man he meant: 'Ritson'.

The Co. Durham antiquary and vegetarian Joseph Ritson (1752–1803), from 1775 a lawyer in London, published in 1778 a broadside entitled *The Descent of the Crown of England*. Its preface made its intentions plain:

> we arrive at the Revolution, when (as the word imports) the Constitution appears to have suffered so violent and total a Change, that the very nature of things should seem to have been perverted along with it, and reduced to the original Chaos. The shock, like that of an earthquake, has appalled us so, we have not yet recovered the use of our reason; and possibly never may. In viewing this transaction, we dare not examine into its causes and effects as we do with regard to most other human events:—We are not even suffered to look upon it but through the deceitful glass of party prejudice.—The ever amiable and adorable Goddess Truth is abandoned by the historian as an infectious hag:—3,00 are 3,000000:—and our senses nothing but deception. In short, this affair must be considered as a monstrous birth, which, though we know it has existed, it does not so well become us to speak of, much less to argue upon.

Ritson however offered a more detailed account of the Revolution:

> William III. (prince of Orange) invaded England, under an invitation from some of the discontented nobility, with a pretence of redressing certain misunderstandings between King James and his subjects; and having obliged the King (whose eldest daughter he had married) to *abdicate* the Realm, and by his own writs convened an assembly consisting of some of the peers, the lord mayor, aldermen, and common council of London, and the whiggish members of the exclusion parliaments:—These men alone, without possessing the least shadow of authority from the law, government, or constitution, or from the people in general, in the name of the whole English nation, presented him and his princess with the royal diadem, on *Ash-Wednesday*, February 13[th], 1688!!!—A proceeding as replete with treachery, inhumanity, and injustice, as ever disgraced the annals of a civilized country; and, in order to be sincerely abhorred by every person of virtue or principle, only remains to be examined and known.—The antient heredit[a]ry government being thus rendered elective, two acts of parliament were soon afterwards made, whereby the crown was limited to William and Mary, and the survivor, for life; and after their death, to the issue of Mary; and failing that, to the princess Ann and her issue; and failing that, to Sophia electress of Hanover, youngest daughter of Elizabeth Queen of Bohemia, and her issue. Under the authority of which acts, the following princes have since ascended to the throne (the prince and princess of Orange dying childless).

Ritson then provided a list of monarchs after 1688.

His biographer perceptively commented: 'Ritson's Jacobitism was not so symptomatic of a devotion to royalty in its abstract principle as of a distaste for the present state of affairs.' By the 1790s Ritson was an enthusiast for the French Revolution,

---

[73] Robert Southey, 'On the Rise and Progress of Popular Disaffection' (1817), in Southey, *Essays, Moral and Political* (2 vols, London: John Murray, 1832), i. 72–3.

a friend of Thomas Holcroft, William Godwin, and John Thelwall. Visiting France for two months from August 1791, he wrote: 'I admire the French more than ever. They deserveed [*sic*] to be free, and they really are so. You have read their new constitution: can anything be more admirable? We, who pretend to be free, have no constitution at all... They are more than a match for all the slaves in Europe.' France had attained happiness 'owing to the dissemination and establishment of those sacred and fundamental principles of liberty and equality'.

In August 1793 Ritson thought a revolution in Britain 'at no great distance'. In early 1794, he addressed his nephew:

> I send you a beautiful edition and copy of Rousseaus *Inégalité des homes*. The [print of that] excellent author looks down upon me; on the other side of the fireplace hangs the sarcastic Voltaire; while the enlightened and enlightening Thomas [Paine] fronts the door: which is probably the reason, by the way, that scarce anybody has entered it since he made his appearance.

Ritson recommended a friend 'to enlighten your mind by an attentive perusal of the "Rights of man," and Godwin's "Enquiry concerning Political Justice"'. Like Paine, Ritson became disillusioned with the unfolding French Revolution. By March 1794 he was casting scorn on the idea, in the first edition of *Political Justice*, that, in Ritson's words, 'it is entirely in ones own power to be healthy and immortal'; by early 1796, he added: 'G[odwin], I suspect, is writing some sort of a history of the French revolution; with a view, perhaps, to wash the blood off his favorite Robespierre. I have no doubt of its proving a parcel of lies and sophisms.' Ritson went mad in 1803, and told his neighbour in Gray's Inn, Robert Smith, who disarmed him of a knife, that he was 'then writing a Pamphlet proving Jesus Christ an Impostor'; he died shortly afterwards.[74]

'From Jacobite to Jacobin', then, was a rare journey, even if one individual can be shown to have made it. More typical were men born in the early eighteenth century, like John Wesley (1703–91)[75] and Samuel Johnson (1709–84),[76] who, having one militantly Jacobite parent and being strongly influenced by that culture in their youth, later made some form of accommodation with the new dynasty: Wesley before 1745, Johnson after 1760. Thomas Paine had an Anglican mother, Frances Cocke (born 1696/7, married 1734, died 1790), daughter of Thomas Cocke, a local attorney and Town Clerk of Thetford from 1701; although nothing is known of her politics, or of the political culture discussed in Paine's parents'

---

[74] Bertrand H. Bronson, *Joseph Ritson: Scholar-at-Arms* (2 vols, Berkeley, 1938), i. 57–9, 145–7, 151, 164–5, 289–90; *The Letters of Joseph Ritson, Esq.* (2 vols, London: William Pickering, 1833), i. xiii–xiv, 203–4, 208–9; ii. 39–40, 42–3, 49, 117; Stephanie L. Barczewski, 'Joseph Ritson', *ODNB*.

[75] The extent of his political and social critique of his society is best evident in John Wesley, *A Concise History of England* (4 vols, London: R. Hawes, 1776); cf. J. C. D. Clark, 'The Eighteenth-Century Context', in William J. Abraham and James E. Kirby (eds), *The Oxford Handbook of Methodist Studies* (Oxford, 2009), 3–29.

[76] J. C. D. Clark, *Samuel Johnson: Literature, Religion and English Cultural Politics from the Restoration to Romanticism* (Cambridge, 1994); Jonathan Clark and Howard Erskine-Hill (eds), *Samuel Johnson in Historical Context* (Basingstoke, 2002); Clark and Erskine-Hill (eds), *The Politics of Samuel Johnson*; Clark and Erskine-Hill (eds), *The Interpretation of Samuel Johnson* (Basingstoke, 2012).

household, there is a possibility that the household tension between a Quaker father and an Anglican mother had a political as well as a religious component.[77] But evidence on this point has not been uncovered.

Other men, not divided in family background, offer clearer examples. Jeremy Bentham (1748–1832) was born to a High Church family in the City of London, and was well aware of the City's allegiances.[78] Of his paternal grandfather Jeremiah (1685–1741) Jeremy wrote: 'My grandfather on my father's side being a Jacobite, my father [also Jeremiah (1712–92)], *comme de raison*, was bred up in the same principles. My father subsequently, without much cost in conveyancing, transferred his adherence from the Stuarts to the Guelphs.' Converting from this mental nexus, the young Jeremy found an opposite ready to hand. One of his great uncles had been a bookseller, Thomas Woodward, who 'brought out Tindal's "Christianity as Old as the Creation"'; Woodward

> used to talk to Bentham of books and booksellers—of 'Honest Tom Payne,' whose shop was then contiguous to the Mewsgate,[79] and was a sort of gathering-place for the lettered aristocracy of the times. Woodward retired from business—was crippled and rich. Such part of his stock as was unsold and unsaleable, formed a large portion of the library at Browning Hill [an uncle's house near Reading, often visited by the young Jeremy], and served for young Bentham's intellectual pabulum.[80]

Appropriately, Jeremy Bentham's first publication, in 1774, was a translation of Voltaire's *Le Taureau blanc*, with a lengthy but anonymous Preface in which Bentham by implication assailed Scripture as an assembly of '*contradictions*, and *prolepsises*, and *allegories* and *interpolations*'.[81]

Matthew Tindal's *Christianity as Old as the Creation* had appeared in 1730, prudently without a publisher's name (no publisher has subsequently been ascribed to it); but Thomas Woodward's other titles (published alone or in partnership) are relevant. They included *An Historical Account of all the Tryals and Attainders of High-Treason: from the Beginning of the Reign of King Charles the First, chronologically digested* (1716), which evolved into *A Complete Collection of State-Trials and Proceedings for High Treason* (3rd edn, 6 vols, 1742) and the works of two Jacobites: the Chevalier Andrew Michael Ramsay's *The Travels of Cyrus* (2 vols, 1727; 4th edn, 1730) and Bishop

[77] A gap in the parish register means the absence of a written record of whether Thomas Paine was baptized in February 1737, but since the register records that his parents' second child, Elizabeth, was baptized in September 1738, it is likely that Thomas was also. He was confirmed by the Bishop of Norwich at about 12, a ceremony which required prior baptism, and twice married in the Church: Keane, *Paine*, 16–18.

[78] Clark, *English Society*, 93, 151–4.

[79] When Woodward ceased trading has not been established. For the bookshop at the Mewsgate, near Charing Cross, run by Thomas Payne (1719–99) from at least the 1750s (not to be confused with Thomas Paine the subject of this study), see the *ODNB* entries for Clayton Cracherode (1730–99) and Walter Wilson (1781–1847). Payne later published Bentham's *A Fragment of Government* (1776) and *An Introduction to the Principles of Norals and Legislation* (1789).

[80] 'Memoirs and Correspondence', in *The Works of Jeremy Bentham*, ed. Bowring (London, 1843), x. 2–4.

[81] *The White Bull, an Oriental History. From an Ancient Syrian Manuscript, communicated by Mr. Voltaire* [trans. Jeremy Bentham] (London: J. Bew, 1774), xxxiii.

Francis Atterbury's *Sermons and Discourses on Several Subjects and Occasions* (2nd edn, 1737; 6th edn, 1751). In a quite different key, Woodward also published John Trenchard and Thomas Gordon's *Cato's Letters* (4 vols, 1724; 5th edn, 1748), as well as Gordon's translations of two indictments of governmental corruption: *The Works of Tacitus* (2 vols, 1728–31; 2nd edn, 1737) and *The Works of Sallust* (1744), as well as a Commonwealth classic, *Memoirs of Edmund Ludlow* (3 vols, 1720–2). Such might have been the reading of a convert from one political camp to its opposite.

Bentham's associate John Bowring wrote:

> Bentham has assured me, not only that multitudes of the citizens of London were friendly to the Stuarts, but that even in the corporation there were aldermen waiting to bring about the restoration of the exiled family, whenever a fit occasion could be found. In the year 1745, the addresses of the Pretender had a wide circulation; and many papers, showing the zeal and interest which his forefathers felt in the success of the Stuarts, fell into Bentham's hands.[82]

One of those aldermen was Edward Gibbon II (1707–70), father of the historian Edward Gibbon III (1737–94).[83] Edward II was educated by the Nonjuror William Law (1686–1761), of whom Edward III later wrote that Law, as a Nonjuror,

> could disclaim all obedience to the new Usurpers of the Crown and Mitre, and might avow his loyalty to the indefeasible right, the banished heir of the house of Stuart. After the Revolution, oaths of allegiance had been multiplied and imposed by the foolish jealousy of the reigning party. Did they hope, by such cobwebs, to bind the conscience of Sunderland or Marlborough, of Bolingbroke or Atterbury? The majority of Jacobites were resolved to *ab*jure and *per*jure, as occasion might serve.[84]

Edward Gibbon II indeed took the oaths in order to be educated at Emmanuel College, Cambridge, and to sit in the Commons as Tory MP for Petersfield in 1734–41 and for Southampton in 1741–7. Nevertheless, determined on the downfall of Sir Robert Walpole, he was one of those who had talks in 1743 with James Butler, sent by Louis XV to assess support for a Jacobite rising with French military backing.[85] He may therefore have taken the oaths with mental reservations, as many did.

The father of Edward II of this family line was Edward Gibbon I (?1675–1736), a Jacobite who, despite his principles, prospered as an army contractor after 1689 but was a Director of that Tory project, the South Sea Company, when it crashed in 1720. In political revenge the Whigs deprived him of much of his fortune by an Act of Pains and Penalties: 'the avowal of Tory and the suspicion of Jacobite principles exposed him to the resentment of a Whig majority', and 'It must be lamented that the Whigs have too often sullied the principles of freedom by the practice of

---

[82] 'Memoirs and Correspondence', in *The Works of Jeremy Bentham*, ed. Bowring, x. 2.

[83] J. G. A. Pocock, *Barbarism and Religion*, i: *The Enlightenments of Edward Gibbon, 1737–1764* (Cambridge, 1999), 13–49.

[84] *The Autobiographies of Edward Gibbon*, ed. John Murray (London, 1896), 388 (Memoir A, composed 1788–9). Gibbon's drafts were written long after the events described, and display the limitations of hindsight.

[85] Cruickshanks, *Political Untouchables*, 40.

violence and tyranny.'[86] He later rebuilt his finances, but Edward Gibbon III long recalled this Act's 'pernicious violation of liberty and law'; in this political context 'the frequent imposition of oaths had enlarged and fortified the Jacobite conscience' of Edward I. 'His own wrongs had not reconciled him to the House of Hanover; his wishes might be expressed in some harmless toasts; but he was disqualified from all public trust; and in the daily devotions of the family the name of the King for whom they prayed was prudently omitted.'[87]

Edward Gibbon III, the historian, therefore inherited both enough wealth to give him freedom of action, and also knowledge of his family's political traditions as well as of the positions of his Deist neighbours in Putney, David and Lucy Mallet. At the age of 7, Edward began to be taught by a private tutor, the Revd John Kirkby; 'his principles were those of a Nonjuror, and it was on his omission of the prayer for the Royal family that loyalty or prudence obliged my father to dismiss him from his house'. In 1745, recorded the historian, 'Without daring, perhaps without desiring to aid the rebels, my father invariably adhered to the Tory opposition.' Of Kingston Grammar School the historian later recalled: 'nor have I forgot how often, in the year forty-six, I was reviled and buffeted for the sins of my Tory ancestors.' Matriculating as an undergraduate at Magdalen College, Oxford, in April 1752, Gibbon well understood the politics of the place, and his memorable rhetorical understatement about the fellows—'their constitutional toasts were not expressive of the most lively loyalty for the house of Hanover'—summed up a wealth of experience. In reaction against the disappointments of Oxford (of which university, before arriving, he would have held high expectations), the 16-year-old future historian's first public act was to convert (temporarily) to the Catholic Church. In London in 1758–60, Gibbon was short of intelligent company, being reduced 'to some old Tories of the Cocoa-tree [club]'; but this offered no future, and he was led instead into the company of freethinkers David and Lucy Mallet, whose mindset he increasingly explored.[88]

Less easy to trace are the more distant influences of the dynastic idiom. The Unitarian and supporter of universal manhood suffrage John Jebb (1736–86) was influenced by his uncle Samuel Jebb (1694–1772), a Nonjuror; 'Unable to take orders he became librarian to Jeremy Collier (1650–1726), the outspoken critic of political and moral corruption...While their religious and political views differed, Samuel Jebb set an example for his nephew as a scholar who adhered to principles to the detriment of his career prospects in the Church, turning to medicine as an alternative profession.'[89] Jebb's close friend John Cartwright (1740–1824), a supporter of the American Revolution, wrote in 1775:

> I am much amused when I hear people speak of abiding by and supporting their family principles: mine was a Tory family as I have been told, and Popery was once its religion;

[86] Gibbon, *Autobiographies*, 215 (Memoir C, composed c.1789); 378 (Memoir A, composed 1788–9).
[87] Gibbon, *Autobiographies*, 11, 13, 16–17 (Memoir F, composed 1792–3).
[88] Gibbon, *Autobiographies*, 31, 44, 76 (Memoir F, composed 1792–3); 113, 115, 126 (Memoir B); 215, 220–1, 226, 245 (Memoir C, composed c. 1789); 375 (Memoir A, composed 1788–9).
[89] Anthony Page, *John Jebb and the Enlightenment Origins of British Radicalism* (London, 2003), 12.

but as for myself I shall neither be Papist nor Tory, until I can believe in the infallibility of popes and kings. On every point which materially affects a man's moral conduct, either as an individual or as a member of society, he must judge and act for himself.

As his niece recorded, his was a family that had 'suffered by their exertions in the cause of Charles the First'.[90] The best known of Cartwright's publications were the anonymous *American Independence the Interest and Glory of Great Britain*, which denounced 'the wretched system of the base-minded Walpole' that every man has his price as being the root of national corruption,[91] and *Take Your Choice! Representation and Respect: Imposition and Contempt. Annual Parliaments and Liberty: Long Parliaments and Slavery* (London: J. Almon, 1776), a work that in some ways went further than Paine's *Rights of Man* to argue for universal manhood suffrage, annual Parliaments, the secret ballot, equal electoral districts, and the payment of MPs.

Another distantly influenced figure was the Scot James Mill (1773–1836), instinctively drawn to Bentham in 1807 or 1808 after his arrival in London in 1802. Mill had been born to a poor family but one also conscious of an alienation from the existing order that James absorbed and developed. In his ambition he was driven by his dominating mother, Isabel Fenton (1755–1801), whose father had been impoverished by participation on the Stuart side in the rising of 1745 and by Cumberland's 'ravages' after that episode. Isabel 'looked upon herself as one that had fallen from a better estate', consequently displayed a 'haughty superiority' to her neighbours, and set out 'to rear her son to some higher destiny'. She, according to her neighbours, 'was the source of her son's intellectual energy'.[92]

In some cases, like Bentham and Gibbon, the pathway of intellectual development was a rebound from one end of the spectrum to the other. Bowring recorded of Bentham:

> It was amusing to hear Bentham talk of the early impressions of his life respecting great people. For kings, and especially the kings of England, he had felt unbounded reverence. 'Loyalty and virtue,' I have heard him say, 'were then synonymous terms.' . . . In after life far different sentiments filled his mind. His opinion of George the Third was as low, as mean, as one human being could well have of another. He called him treacherous, selfish, deceitful, tyrannical, vehemently attached to all abuses—violently opposed to all reforms—a hypocrite and a liar.
>
> I do not believe he ever conversed with George the Third.[93]

---

[90] F. D. Cartwright, *The Life and Correspondence of Major Cartwright* (2 vols, London: Henry Colburn, 1826), i. 1, 57.

[91] [John Cartwright], *American Independence the Interest and Glory of Great Britain* (London: for the author by H. S. Woodfall, 1774), xii, Preface, iii. Cartwright did not make common cause with the luminaries of his day, denouncing 'the mad genius of Geneva' [Rousseau], 'the scribbling buffoon of Ferney' [Voltaire], and the 'see-saw sceptic from the remotest North' [Hume], x–xi. Woodfall was also the publisher of *The Public Advertiser*, in which the letters of 'Junius' appeared between 1768 and 1772.

[92] Alexander Bain, *James Mill: A Biography* (London, 1882), 4–5, reporting testimony gathered by himself in Mill's native parish, Logie Pert in Forfarshire.

[93] 'Memoirs and Correspondence', *The Works of Jeremy Bentham*, ed. Bowring, x. 42.

In Paine's case there is no evidence of such a reversal, as there is of his childhood rejection of the Church's teaching on the atonement. The evidence suggests that Paine absorbed and never modified the fundamental rejection of the Hanoverian monarchy and its supporting nobility that had been sustained into the 1750s by the Jacobite opposition.

Paine was not a Jacobite, indeed the opposite; but his stance was influenced by the dynastic antithesis, and he had no separate indebtedness to any other political position. One pathway of development has recently been identified as being from Jacobite to Conservative;[94] if Paine is a guide, another pathway may have been from anti-Jacobite to Jacobin. He could not wipe the slate clean; like his contemporaries, he could not easily escape from the intellectual preoccupations of the world in which he had been educated. The most he could do was to seek to transmute the indefeasible, hereditary rights of kings into '*the indefeasible, hereditary rights of man*', and his choice of words was not coincidental.[95] Equipped with this sweeping denigration of a malaise introduced into English society by false politics, Paine emigrated to America as a man largely already primed with a world view that awaited its moment to express itself.

AMERICAN COLONIAL DISCOURSE AND ENGLISH DYNASTICISM

The American colonies in which Paine arrived in 1774 were already complex societies, but ones in which typecast historical memories and resentments were deeply engrained; those memories and resentments were British ones, with local colonial variations, more than they were uniquely American. Ezra Stiles (1727–95), a Congregational minister and slaveowner in Newport, Rhode Island, wrote in his diary on 30 January 1770, the anniversary of Charles I's execution:

> This Day if observed at all, ought to be celebrated as an annivy Thanksgiving for or Memorial, that one Nation on Earth had so much fortitude & public Justice, as to make a Royal Tyrant bow to the Sovereignty of the People, institute a judicial Trial of a Monarch, & sentence him to the Punishm^t & Execution which he merited; by dissolving his Parl^t. 12 years, deforcing Loans on the subject by rigorous fines & arbitrary Imprisonments, by burying Dr Layton in a Dungeon for 12 years for boldly telling the truth, for those proclam^a & Edicts by which Pym, Bastwick & others suffered most barbarous Cruelties, & for exalting and sustaining that Scourge of Justice, Religion & Humanity, ABp. Laud, for arbitrarily vacating the New Engl^d Charter in 1635 within 7 or 8 years after he had granted it, & for establishing under ABp. Laud a Commission to rule the Colonies by subjecting to Episcopal & military government, with Authority

---

[94] James J. Sack, *From Jacobite to Conservative: Reaction and Orthodoxy in Britain c. 1760–1832* (Cambridge, 1993).

[95] Paine, *Rights of Man. Part the Second* (1792): *CW*, i. 356; Clark, *English Society*, 123. This locution was not original: [John Adams], *A Dissertation on the Canon and Feudal Law* (1765) had written of the people's 'right, an indisputable, unalienable, indefeasible, divine right to that most dreadful and envied kind of knowledge, I mean of the characters & conduct of their rulers': Adams, *Works*, iii. 456.

of remandg all offenders from hence to be tried in England at the pleasure of those who could with good will have bro[t] on an Extirpation of Puritanism from England and America by Fire & Sword—in a word, K. Charles I. had established Maxims of civil & religious Polity utterly subversive of all the principles of Runemede Liberty & the English Constitution.[96]

Such ancient antipathies, ready to hand and easily rehearsed again in the minds of many intelligent and well-informed colonists, were now about to be reactivated. Of this denominational and historical landscape in the colonies there is no evidence that Paine was aware; but he was well informed about the English historical land-scape. Indeed, it was not very different, as his impact in America was soon to show.

It was a colonial culture kept in repair by continual contemporary borrowings from England. As Stiles recorded on 4 April 1772: 'Reading Mrs. [Catharine] MacAulay's History', a famous English republican author (1731–91) with whom he later corres-ponded.[97] Stiles looked forward to English America becoming an independent state at some unspecified future date, and that 'in all future Ages the Puritans will make the bigger two Thirds of all English America'. This prospect he thought the 'Episcopalian and deistical Crown Officers' were then working to frustrate, seeking to break up the 'religious and political principles' of New England (18 February 1773).[98] Although well informed about current London politics, Stiles took care to quiz a visiting clergy-man, Mr Martin, who 'says he had an interview with the Pretender 1767—& I think three Times in all...I asked him whether the Pretender & his Adherents did not des-pair of his reachg the Crown. He said their only Hopes were in some interior Divisions & Convulsions, which they were watching for. I observed in that Case the Pretenders Religion would be an insuperable & common Objection against him. He said, Charles [Edward Stuart] was no Papist' (19 April 1775).[99]

That summer, Stiles (torn between scepticism and credulity) thought worthwhile transcribing at length a report that Lord North was conspiring with the Pretender to bring about a Stuart restoration by denuding Britain of the troops sent to America (19 July 1775).[100] When on 6 September 1775 'the Town of Manchester in Engld addressed the King against America', Stiles commented: 'N.B. Manchester proclaimed the Pretender King 1745—raised £2500M for the Chevalier & raised a Reg[t] & joined him. High Tory Jacobites! & now subscribe £600,000 to harass Americans' (28 November 1775).[101] By contrast with the prominence he gave to the historical dimension, Stiles wrote only that he 'read Common Sense', but did not comment further on Paine's pamphlet (24 February 1776).[102] These were not the views of a backwoodsman, for Ezra Stiles had an academic training and was soon to be president of his alma mater, Yale College, from 1778 to his death. Nor was Yale unique. The President of Harvard similarly warned the Congress of

---

[96] *The Literary Diary of Ezra Stiles, D.D., LL.D.*, ed. Franklin Bowditch Dexter (4 vols, New York, 1901), i. 34–5 (30 Jan. 1770).

[97] Stiles, *Diary*, i. 220, 230, 293, 321, 501.   [98] Stiles, *Diary*, i. 344–5.

[99] Stiles, *Diary*, i. 535. Charles Edward Stuart had indeed converted (at least nominally) to the Church of England on a clandestine visit to London in 1750.

[100] Stiles, *Diary*, i. 590.   [101] Stiles, *Diary*, i. 637.   [102] Stiles, *Diary*, i. 662.

Massachusetts in 1775: 'have we not great reason to suspect that all the late measures respecting the Colonies have originated from popish schemes of men who would gladly restore the race of Stewart and who look on popery as a religion most favourable to arbitrary power?'[103]

The situation had escalated since 1768 when the *Boston Gazette* had warned of a conspiracy between 'the French King, the Pretender, and Lord B[ute]': they had 'laid a plan to dethrone King George, enslave Great-Britain with her colonies and to introduce the Romish religion'. The significant change was that the royal assent to the Quebec Act in June 1774 made it possible, and politically advantageous, to direct such denigratory rhetoric against George III personally.[104] This rhetoric was effective, as Daniel Barber of Claremont, Connecticut, found when he enlisted in a militia company in 1775.

> We were all ready to swear, that this same [king] George, by granting the Quebec Bill, (that is, the privilege to Roman Catholics of worshipping God according to their own consciences,) had thereby become a traitor; had broke his coronation oath; was secretly a Papist; and whose design it was to oblige this country to submit itself to the unconstitutional powers of the English monarch, and, under him, and by his authority, be given up and destroyed, soul and body, by that frightful image with seven heads and ten horns. The real fears of Popery, in New England, had its influence; it stimulated many timorous pious people to send their sons to join the military ranks in the field and jeopardize their lives in the bloody contest. The common word then was, 'No King, no Popery.'[105]

The situation had evolved tactically, but changed less in its premises, since the New England theologian Samuel Willard (1640–1707) had warned his congregation in 1684 against a papal conspiracy: 'It is the Master Plot of the World.'[106] It was such antipathies more than any secular natural rights theory that awakened ancient fears of secret conspiracies against the liberties of Protestants; that turned transatlantic debates on tax jurisdiction into a struggle of cosmic significance; that gave the complexities of legal controversy a Manichean simplicity; and that justified the

---

[103] Samuel Langdon, *Government corrupted by Vice, and recovered by Righteousness. A Sermon Preached Before the Honourable Congress Of the Colony of the Massachusetts-Bay Assembled at Watertown, On Wednesday the 31st Day of May, 1775* (Watertown: Benjamin Edes, 1775), 29. Langdon was serious in his anti-popery. While still pastor of the First Church at Portsmouth, New Hampshire, he had preached *A Rational Explication of St. John's Vision of the two Beasts, In the XIIIth Chapter of the Revelation. Shewing That the Beginning, Power, and Duration of Popery are plainly predicted in that Vision, and that these Predictions have hitherto been punctually verified* (Portsmouth, NH: Daniel Fowle, 1774).

[104] 'Anti-pope', in *Boston Gazette*, 25 Apr. 1768, quoted in Francis D. Cogliano, *No King, No Popery: Anti-Catholicism in Revolutionary New England* (Westport, Conn., 1995), 51. The *Providence Gazette* of 3 Sept. 1774 reported: 'According to advices from Rome, the Chevalier Stuart (commonly called the Pretender) is preparing to set out on a voyage to New-England; and several assert he will go on board some Spanish vessels which are ready merely for that purpose': Cogliano, *No King*, 56–7.

[105] Daniel Barber, *The History of my Own Times* (3 vols, Washington: S. C. Ustick, 1827–32), i. 17.

[106] Samuel Willard, quoted in Thomas M. Brown, 'In the Image of the Beast: Anti-Papal Rhetoric in Colonial America', in Richard O. Curry and Thomas M. Brown (eds), *Conspiracy: The Fear of Subversion in American History* (New York, 1972), 1–20, at 12. For the antecedent history of colonial anti-Catholicism see Owen Stanwood, *The Empire Reformed: English America in the Age of the Glorious Revolution* (Philadelphia, 2011).

morality of bloodshed. This was congruent with the position in England, but went beyond it; Paine could therefore act as a catalyst.

Anti-Catholicism may have been at its most intense in New England and New York, but it had long been used for political advantage in the factional politics of the Philadelphia in which Paine landed in 1774. Indeed the tactical use of anti-popery was a game in which Paine's referee Benjamin Franklin had joined (by contrast Franklin, while demonizing 'popery', was a slaveowner).[107] In the Philadelphia press, as in New England, the Quebec Act was denounced: 'We may live to see our churches converted into mass houses and our lands plundered by tythes for the support of the Popish clergy... the Inquisition may erect her standard in Pennsylvania and the city may yet experience the carnage of St. Bartholomew's Day.'

Philadelphia papers printed reports[108] that an army of 30,000 Canadian Catholics had been formed and was about to be used to suppress colonial resistance.[109] Guy Fawkes' Day, 5 November 1774, was celebrated in the city with especial fervour, 'to show their abhorrence and detestation of the *Pope*, Pretender, etc., and such of their *Adherents* as would overthrow the GOOD OLD ENGLISH 'CONSTITUTION'.[110] From the spring of 1774, arguments of a British conspiracy against colonial liberty became 'commonplace' in Pennsylvania; 'After the imposition of the Coercive Acts virtually every piece of Whig rhetoric published in Philadelphia maintained, directly or indirectly, that there could no longer be any doubt of England's intentions towards America.' Correspondents in the Philadelphia press in 1774–5 pointed out the inconsistency of the practice of slavery with colonial claims for freedom: Paine was not to mention this line of argument. By late 1774, Philadelphia newspapers were carrying articles that blamed George III personally: this element in *Common Sense* was not new.[111]

Such evidence suggests that Paine's *Common Sense* may have owed much of its impact to an already widespread colonial belief in a British conspiracy. That belief, applied to questions of tax jurisdiction, was historically premised on religious hatred. Nor was such language confined to the mob. The American Philosophical Society temporarily discontinued its meetings in protest against 'the Bill for establi[shi]ng popery and arbitrary power in Quebec'.[112] The Continental Congress, also meeting in Philadelphia, framed an appeal *To the People of Great-Britain* that declared in the same idiom its 'astonishment, that a British Parliament should ever consent to

---

[107] 'Hostility to Catholicism remained strong in the colonies, and even reached a peak in the mid-eighteenth century, just as it was beginning to weaken in the mother-country': Joseph J. Casino, 'Anti-Popery in Colonial Pennsylvania', *PMHB* 105 (1981), 279–309, at 281; for Franklin, 298; Francis Jennings, *The Creation of America: Through Revolution to Empire* (Cambridge, 2000), 203; McConville, 112–19, 261–6.

[108] *Pennsylvania Packet*, 31 Oct. 1774: Casino, 'Anti-Popery', 307.

[109] *Pennsylvania Gazette*, 19 Oct. 1774; *Pennsylvania Journal*, 2 Nov. 1774: Casino, 'Anti-Popery', 307.

[110] *Pennsylvania Journal*, 9 Nov. 1774: Casino, 'Anti-Popery', 308.

[111] Stephen E. Lucas, *Portents of Rebellion: Rhetoric and Revolution in Philadelphia, 1765–76* (Philadelphia, 1976), 101, 103, 113. For the incidence of slavery in that colony, see Gary B. Nash and Jean R. Soderlund, *Freedom by Degrees: Emancipation in Pennsylvania and its Aftermath* (New York, 1991).

[112] *Early Proceedings of the American Philosophical Society for the Promotion of Useful Knowledge compiled by one of the Secretaries, from the Manuscript Minutes of its Meetings from 1744 to 1838* (Philadelphia, 1884), 87.

establish in that country [Canada] a religion that has deluged your island in blood, and dispersed impiety, bigotry, persecution, murder and rebellion through every part of the world'. The plan of the British ministry was, with 'the aid of our Roman Catholic neighbours' to 'reduce us to a state of perfect humiliation and slavery'.[113] These were not stylized rhetorical gestures, unimportant in practice, but applications of clearly defined dynastic and religious discourse. Appropriately, given this mindset, Congress's first offensive military action was to dispatch an army to conquer Catholic Canada.

It has been conventional to see the American Revolution in general, and the American colonial elite in particular, as forward-looking, appropriately galvanized by a forward-looking pamphlet, *Common Sense*, that articulated the new and abstract language of natural rights. An appreciation of the ways in which stereotypes and hatreds were mobilized in colonial politics for personal and sectional advantage suggests that this model calls for reconsideration. In neither America nor Britain did Paine sow the seeds of resistance: those seeds were already native in both soils, and regularly flowered on both sides of the Atlantic for reasons that Paine only partly appreciated. The events of 1775–6 were only their greatest flowering, not a wholly novel set of developments. Even so, as will be shown, Paine understood less of the American Revolution than has often been assumed. What languages of politics, then, did he speak?

---

[113] 'To the People of Great-Britain, from the Delegates…in General Congress, at Philadelphia, September 5th, 1774', in *Extracts From the Votes and Proceedings Of the American Continental Congress, Held at Philadelphia on the 5th of September 1774* (Philadelphia: William and Thomas Bradford, October 27th, 1774), contents separately paginated, 3, 12–13; *Journals of the Continental Congress, 1774–1789*, ed. Worthington Chauncey Ford (34 vols, Washington, 1904–37), i. 88.

3

Discourses and their Exponents

THE LANGUAGE OF POLITICS

The celebration of Paine as a reformer across a range of issues has as one premise an assumption about his political discourse. Paine allegedly has an 'uncanny familiarity'; he 'strikes our times like a trumpet blast from a distant world'; he is 'strikingly one of us'.[1] He is held to speak 'our' political language. What was that language, and what did it cover? Reformers are often presented as people who were offended by injustice or suffering wherever they saw it and who therefore supported a diversity of novel reforming crusades, understanding by their original insights the intellectual affinity of those issues. But this assumption is problematic, set against evidence that reformers shared most of the assumptions of their host societies and had their impact by placing new emphasis on narrowly focused elements of their societies' commonplaces. Even leading reformers tended to identify with specific agendas rather than with a broad range of causes that only in later decades were thought to have a necessary coherence. Particularist reforming languages were as common as universalist ones.[2]

One geopolitical influence is especially evident. Later readers seeking guides to the timeless promise and morality of Paine's first republic looked to him as 'a profound myth-maker' who 'wove together powerful emotive strands to create enduring myths about American size, uniqueness, open-mindedness, and goodness—America's fundamental difference from the rest of the world'.[3] Paine was used in the United States from the late nineteenth century in the re-formulations of discourse that reshaped its national myth in the age of modernism. But there were hardly any parallel uses of Paine in nineteenth- or twentieth-century France, and Paine's part in the creation of a national identity for the United States can now be traced in particularist terms.[4]

The historic Paine's discourse is difficult to relate to the discourses of these two new republics partly since he disparaged the culture of Greece and Rome, condemning it for lacking contemporary utility. This meant that, unlike many of his contemporaries, his understandings of republicanism and of democracy were not

---

[1] Keane, *Paine*, ix–x.   [2] See Ch. 5, section on Natural rights discourse.
[3] William H. Goetzmann, *Beyond the Revolution: A History of American Thought from Paine to Pragmatism* (New York, 2009), 4–5.
[4] See Ch. 7, section The framing of a national myth of origins.

indebted to the ancient world.[5] Yet the new American republic, in its ubiquitous classical architecture and its reflections on classical political precedent, became pre-occupied with Greece and Rome even more than did revolutionary and Napoleonic France.[6] Unable to appeal to this still normative past, Paine had to draw on other discourses.

His participation in daily politics offers a better guide to the discourses he commanded as an author. He had a role as a catalyst in 1776 because his discourses were inherited from pre-revolutionary Anglo-America. In France in 1789 (it will be argued) he did not even act as a catalyst. Paine's role there appears much larger in recent English-language celebrations of him than in detailed French histories of the French Revolution. That self-absorbed cataclysm rolled forward with a seemingly incomprehensible logic, irrespective of anything that its contemporary English-speaking commentators could say to discern in it an essence or causes. Consequently Paine's *The Age of Reason* was ineffective in its main goal, to prevent the French Revolution from turning towards atheism. But to expect more of Paine is to mistake his languages of politics.

The languages then available were significantly different from those current by the mid-nineteenth century. Even by Paine's death in 1809, the anglophone world still lacked much of the conceptual apparatus that was soon to be constructed. Paine and his contemporaries did not think in terms of 'modernity' or discern a 'process' of 'modernization'. They did not know the political ideologies coined in the 1820s as 'radicalism' and 'socialism', or cast them as antitheses to that English child of the 1830s, 'conservatism'. They might deplore, or pursue, 'luxury', but they knew no way to discuss the effects of 'industrialization'. They idealized 'reason' and treated it as the means to the mental state of 'enlightenment', but this was a commonplace and not evidence of the existence in their minds of a unified and universal movement now known as '*the* Enlightenment'. In this particularist world, a liberty was defined by James Scott in 1765 as 'some privilege that is held by charter or prescription'; only partially, in the 1760s, did English opinion reify this in the singular, as in the slogan 'Wilkes and Liberty'. Although American colonists who questioned the application of 'the liberties of Englishmen' were also drawn to reify a singular 'Liberty', Paine often continued to echo the old plural usage: in 1778 he wrote of 'The idea of freedom and rights'; in 1804, of 'rights, privileges, advantages, immunities'.[7]

---

[5] By contrast Robert Bisset, *Sketch of Democracy* (London: J. Smeeton, 1796), drew its examples wholly from Greek and Roman history. Few passages in Paine's writings show a positive estimation of the classics. Most of his references were disparaging: A. Owen Aldridge, 'Thomas Paine and the Classics', *Eighteenth-Century Studies* 1 (1968), 370–80.

[6] M. N. S. Sellers, *American Republicanism: Roman Ideology in the United States Constitution* (Basingstoke, 1994); Carl J. Richard, *The Founders and the Classics: Greece, Rome, and the American Enlightenment* (Cambridge, Mass., 1994).

[7] James Scott, *A General Dictionary of Arts and Sciences* (London: S. Crowder, 1765–6), ii (not paginated); Paine, 'A Serious Address to the People of Pennslyvania' (1778): *CW*, ii. 282; Paine, 'To the French Inhabitants of Louisiana' (1804): *CW*, ii. 966; quoted in Lounissi, *Paine*, 192.

Does this matter? A concept can, in principle, exist before the name for that concept;[8] but any such disembodied pre-existence is rare in historical actuality, and the episode of profoundly important conceptual formation witnessed in the English-speaking world mainly from the 1820s creates a challenge for historical interpretation if the preceding age is to be understood in other ways than as a collective failure of foresight. Until recently, eighteenth-century debates surrounding the American and French Revolutions were sometimes discussed as if those debates sprang as novelties from a hitherto intellectually vacuous English-speaking political culture, belatedly awakening to the implications of the Enlightenment; it is now understood that that culture had rung with controversy, often rooted in the seventeenth century, in ways that powerfully influenced the conflicts that followed.

Such indebtedness did not mean that Paine was a Lockeian. Confusion is generated by the twentieth-century convention of treating John Locke as almost an honorary Founding Father of the United States, a ubiquitous revolutionary who therefore needs to be linked to Paine.[9] Yet Paine was explicit in 1807 that Locke had been a supporter of William III and therefore of 'hereditary and *elective monarchy*', which Paine rejected: 'I never read Locke, nor ever had the work in my hand.' Locke had spoken to the situation in 1689, not 1776, Paine insisted. 'The people of America, in conducting their revolution, learned nothing from Locke; nor was his name, or his work, ever mentioned during the revolution, that I know of.'[10] Paine was aware of Locke, writing conventionally in 1792 of 'Locke, Hampden and Sydney' as Whig victims of persecution, but never appealed to Locke's texts where he might effectively

---

[8] Quentin Skinner, 'Language and Political Change', in Terence Ball, James Farr, and Russell L. Hanson (eds), *Political Innovation and Conceptual Change* (Cambridge, 1989), 6–23. But a functional specification of the 'criteria' that give meaning to a term may result in an under-appreciation of the autonomous shaping force of concepts; changing language is then likely to seem only a reflex of changing 'social beliefs...social perceptions...social values'. Thus 'social change' can appear as a 'process' (9, 20). I here offer an account of conceptual change that is determined neither by a 'social reality' nor by a discourse's putative logic.

[9] For the restricted circulation or impact of Locke's political writings in colonial America see John Dunn, 'The Politics of Locke in England and America in the Eighteenth Century', in John W. Yolton (ed.), *John Locke: Problems and Perspectives* (Cambridge, 1969), 45–80; J. G. A. Pocock, 'The Myth of John Locke and the Obsession with Liberalism', in J. G. A. Pocock and Richard Ashcraft (eds), *John Locke: Papers Read at a Clark Library Seminar 10 December 1977* (Los Angeles, 1980), 3–24; Donald S. Lutz, 'The Relative Influence of European Writers on Late Eighteenth-Century American Political Thought', *American Political Science Review* 78 (1984), 189–97; Oscar Handlin, 'Learned Books and Revolutionary Action, 1776', *Harvard Library Bulletin* 34 (1986), 362–79; J. G. A. Pocock, 'Between Gog and Magog: The Republican Thesis and the *Ideologia Americana*', *Journal of the History of Ideas* 48 (1987), 325–46; J. G. A. Pocock, 'Negative and Positive Aspects of Locke's Place in Eighteenth-Century Discourse', in Martyn P. Thompson (ed.), *John Locke und/and Immanuel Kant* (Berlin, 1991), 45–61; Clark, *Language of Liberty*. That Locke remains a prophet in the civil religion of the United States is evidenced in Steven M. Dworetz, *The Unvarnished Doctrine: Locke, Liberalism and the American Revolution* (Durham, NC, 1990) and Jerome Huyler, *Locke in America: The Moral Philosophy of the Founding Era* (Lawrence, Kan., 1995).

[10] Paine, letters in *The New York Public Advertiser*, 5 and 26 Sept. 1807, discussed in Clark, *English Society*, 139–40. For an analysis and disavowal of Paine's alleged indebtedness to Locke, see Aldridge, *American Ideology*, 107–36. In respect of the social contract, the explanatory device conventionally associated with Locke, Paine was ambiguous and inconsistent: Lounissi, *Paine*, 41–66, 144–8.

have done so.[11] Paine had never heard of 'Lockeian liberalism', another twentieth-century invention. Indeed Paine could not have heard of 'liberalism' of any kind, since liberalism was a new political doctrine, reified (and then weakly) only after his death.

The conceptual vocabulary (and the consequent political discourses) available to Paine was different, even when it provided apparent synonyms for later terms. In particular, he could not have been 'a radical'. A 'radical', as a substantive noun, was in the last decades of Paine's lifetime a shortened form of the phrase 'a radical reformer', meaning an advocate of parliamentary reform on the principle of universal suffrage. This usage was familiar in England by the 1780s: 'annual parliaments and universal suffrage' was a slogan devised to simplify and drive home the creed of that prominent champion of parliamentary reform Major John Cartwright, but Paine never adopted this shorthand formula.[12] 'Radicalism' went much further than the commitments of earlier 'radicals': when coined in England around 1820, it signified initially a cocktail of universal suffrage, militant atheism, and Ricardian economics.[13] Paine never quite arrived at the first, and held views at odds with the second and third. It once seemed plausible that 'Paine established a new framework within which Radicalism was confined for nearly 100 years, as clear and as well defined as the constitutionalism which it replaced',[14] but that view cannot now be sustained. Yet if his conceptual vocabulary was different, what of his style?

STYLE, RECEPTION, AND AUDIENCE

In 1776 and in the 1790s Paine secured the attention of English-speaking audiences to a degree matched in his time only by John Wesley (who shared with Paine a remarkable ability to mobilize and revitalize already-conventional discourses while saying little that was wholly new). Paine's discursive affinities in the English-speaking world were hardly replicated in France after 1789, but of his only modest reception there his anglophone admirers often knew little.[15] Recent explanations of his wide English influence addressed his prose: that it was

---

[11] Paine, *Letter Addressed to the Addressers* (1792), in *CW*, ii. 485; Aldridge, *American Ideology*, 107–22.

[12] F. D. Cartwright, *The Life and Correspondence of Major Cartwright* (2 vols, London: Henry Colburn, 1826), i. 82, 133; John Cannon, *Parliamentary Reform 1640–1832* (Cambridge, 1973), 80, 82, 88–9; Clark, *English Society*, 384, 396–406, 411–13. Paine did in 1776 once briefly commend the idea of annual parliaments, but without emphasis. He did not link it to the franchise, and did not return to the theme: [Paine], *Four Letters on Interesting Subjects* (1776), in Thomas Paine, *Common Sense and Other Writings*, ed. Gordon S. Wood (New York, 2003), 57–80, at 79.

[13] J. C. D. Clark, 'Religion and the Origin of Radicalism in Nineteenth-Century Britain', in Glenn Burgess and Matthew Festenstein (eds), *English Radicalism, 1550–1850* (Cambridge, 2007), 241–84.

[14] E. P. Thompson, *The Making of the English Working Class* (London, 1963), 94. Thompson treated 'radicalism' (sometimes with a leading capital) as a tradition of proletarian protest that *emerged* rather than, as it first had to be, a political theory that was *conceptualized* (e.g. 466, 469, 471, 674).

[15] Of what was once characterized as the Burke–Paine debate it has been observed: 'Il est manifeste que ce débat était considéré en France comme interne à la scène intellectuelle Anglaise': Lounissi, *Paine*, 565.

appropriate to a new world of democratic populism. Such explanations cited Thomas Jefferson in 1821:

> No writer has exceeded Paine in ease and familiarity of style, in perspicuity of expression, happiness of elucidation, and in simple and unassuming language. In this he may be compared with Dr. Franklin; and indeed his Common Sense was, for awhile, believed to have been written by Dr. Franklin, and published under the borrowed name of Paine, who had come over with him from England.[16]

Read closely, Jefferson had not invoked democratic populism, and his interpretation of Paine's prose as plain, artless, and therefore inherently populist laid the basis for a series of misunderstandings of the thematic unities that tied the historic Paine to his historic audience.

Paine's style is better identified as that of 'an eighteenth-century secular preacher in the long tradition of preaching', one of the 'preacher-prophets' whose sense of divine mission 'excluded doubt from his realm of vision'.[17] Appropriately, it has been observed that 'Paine's political ideas cannot be evaluated apart from his religious attitudes.'[18] His possible early brushes with Methodism soon found expression in proselytizing Deism. To promote Deistic ends, Paine's style was as carefully calculated and as ornamented as that of his late eighteenth-century opponents, and in some ways more traditional.[19] Yet Paine's very accessibility makes him a difficult author to understand because of the ease with which layers of interpretation could be subsequently superimposed on his work.

Some of Paine's title to count as a leader in the American Revolution derives from the assumption that, if not a theorist, he was at least an inspired journalist, giving expression in the public arena to the emergent voice of 'the people' through the new medium of the newspaper. Yet American newspapers during the Revolution retained the elite orientation of their colonial precursors: not until the 1790s in embryo, and the age of Jacksonian democracy in full realization, did newspapers emerge as partisan, populist voices in their own right.[20] That role was fully developed in the Paris of the 1790s, but with this francophone world Paine had contact mainly through just one French friend.

---

[16] Thomas Jefferson to Francis Eppes, 19 Jan. 1821: Jefferson, *Writings*, xv. 304–6. For Paine's supposedly democratic style see Olivia Smith, *The Politics of Language 1791–1819* (Oxford, 1984); Robert A. Ferguson, 'The Commonalities of Common Sense', *WMQ* 57 (2000), 465–504; Edward Larkin, *Thomas Paine and the Literature of Revolution* (Cambridge, 2005); for a recent corrective see Thomas Clark, 'A Note on Tom Paine's "Vulgar" Style', *Communications Quarterly* 26 (1978), 31–4.

[17] Paine's writing was 'profoundly religious in content and homiletic in style': Jack Fruchtman, Jr, *Thomas Paine and the Religion of Nature* (Baltimore, 1993), ix–x and *passim*.

[18] John W. Derry, *The Radical Tradition: Tom Paine to Lloyd George* (London, 1967), 41.

[19] Jane Hodson, *Language and Politics in Burke, Wollstonecraft, Paine, and Godwin* (Aldershot, 2007), 115–48.

[20] Arthur M. Schlesinger, *Prelude to Independence: The Newspaper War on Britain 1764–1776* (1957; Boston, 1980); Donald H. Stewart, *The Opposition Press of the Federalist Period* (Albany, NY, 1969); Culver H. Smith, *The Press, Politics and Patronage: The American Government's Use of Newspapers 1789–1875* (Athens, Ga, 1977); William David Sloan and Julie Hedgepeth Williams, *The Early American Press, 1690–1783* (Westport, Conn., 1994); Thomas C. Leonard, *News for All: America's Coming-of-Age with the Press* (New York, 1995); Carol Sue Humphrey, *The Press of the Young Republic, 1783–1833* (Westport, Conn., 1996); William E. Huntzicker, *The Popular Press, 1833–1865* (Westport, Conn., 1999).

Paine was not primarily a newspaperman, and his association with a particular journal in Philadelphia in 1775 was brief. Far from using a position as editor of *The Pennsylvania Magazine* to master the details of the transatlantic controversy in exchanges with Philadelphian leaders, the evidence does not securely establish that Paine was ever its editor, as opposed to its publisher's assistant. The most that Paine said at the time was that Robert Aitken, the magazine's owner, 'has applied to me for assistance' and that 'I assisted him'.[21] Even later, Paine only claimed that 'A person of this city [Aitken] desired me to give him some assistance in conducting a magazine, which I did without making any bargain': that is, without agreeing the terms and conditions of his employment.[22] This fell far short of claiming to have been the editor of the journal. Rather, Paine was that much older English phenomenon: a pamphleteer.

His forte was not the newspaper article or 'leader' but the pamphlet, a free-standing essay, more slowly written, in which the author had space to unpack his arguments for a literate audience. Paine lived in early 1778 at the house of William Henry in Lancaster; Henry's son John Joseph later recalled 'I knew Paine well' while Paine was writing *The American Crisis* no. V. This was

> a labour of three months in the enditing...Mr. D. Rittenhouse inhabited the front room, in the upper story...There he kept the office of the treasury of Pennsylvania...While that excellent man was employing his hours in the duties of his office, for the benefit of the people, Paine would be snoring away his precious time in his easy chair, regardless of those injunctions imposed upon him by congress, in relation to his political compositions. His remissness, indolence or vacuity of thought, caused great heart-burning among many primary characters, in those days...His Crisis, No. V, lay on his table, dusted: to-day three or four lines would be added, in the course of a week, a dozen more, and so on...I was so passionately engaged at heart, in the principles of our cause, that Paine's manner of living and acting, gave me a high disgust towards him.[23]

Paine was the last and most inspired of the old order of pamphleteers, just as William Cobbett, who brought his remains back to Britain, was the first master of the new world of newspaper journalism. As such, Paine's fictional persona was 'common sense', not 'the common man': Paine's aim was to destroy the old antithesis of patrician and plebeian, not to adopt a plebeian journalistic persona in order to champion plebeian interests. Paine, self-consciously a man of ability, sought the position in an extended elite to which he thought his talents entitled him, using what social standing he could win to benefit 'humanity', not 'the working class'. His discourse aimed at the good of 'the people', but he did not employ their discourses to achieve social or cultural change.

---

[21] Paine to Benjamin Franklin, 4 Mar. 1775: *CW*, ii. 1131.
[22] Paine to Henry Laurens, 14 Jan. 1779: *CW*, ii. 1161.
[23] John Joseph Henry's journal (1812), reprinted in *Pennsylvania Archives* 2nd series, ed. William H. Egle (Harrisburgh, 1890), xv. 61–191, at 144, 149.

SELF-IMAGE AND SOURCES

Paine created an image of himself as a reasoner from first principles. When he arrived in America, he claimed,

> I did not, at my first setting out in public life... turn my thoughts to subjects of government from motives of interest... I saw an opportunity, in which I thought I could do some good, and I followed exactly what my heart dictated. I neither read books, nor studied other people's opinions. I thought for myself.[24]

This personal myth of origins was related to the claims he made for the new republic: as he put it to the abbé Raynal in 1782,

> Our style and manner of thinking have undergone a revolution more extraordinary than the political revolution of the country. We see with other eyes; we hear with other ears; and think with other thoughts, than those we formerly used. We can look back on our own prejudices, as if they had been the prejudices of other people.[25]

But this image could only be a transposition to the political sphere of the early eighteenth-century English idea of the spiritual rebirth, propagated by rising Methodism and Evangelicalism; it was not an informed report on the situation on the ground in the colonies.

Paine presented himself after 1776 as having always been fully formed, holding the same opinions because they were rational, not developing over time, and almost without debts to other authors. To 'Cato' [William Smith], the critic of *Common Sense* in 1776, he replied: 'Cato may observe, that I scarcely ever quote; the reason is, I always think.'[26] But whatever his self-image, Paine did read books,[27] and was indebted to them; and to some degree he did change over time. However much Paine's image was that of a man invoking first principles and acting on them in a world made new by revolution, this was far from the case. Paine travelled to America and to France with heavy intellectual baggage which he never escaped; and although he did not read as widely as other famous figures of his age, he reflected on his reading. The English reformer and now newspaper editor James Cheetham, who knew Paine in America from 1802, wrote: 'He had read but little in the course of his life, much less than may have been supposed, but that little he had sorted, laid up in his intellectual store-house with care, and could deal it out with a facility and discrimination, which, however hated or despised, or on whatever account, was truly admirable.'[28] Paine consistently denied any intellectual indebtedness, but that did not mean that he

---

[24] Thomas Paine, *Rights of Man. Part the Second* (1792): *CW*, i. 406.

[25] Paine, *A Letter to the Abbe Raynal* (1782): *CW*, ii. 243.

[26] [Paine], 'The Forester's Letters' (1776): *CW*, ii. 78.

[27] Caroline Robbins, 'The Lifelong Education of Thomas Paine (1737–1809): Some Reflections upon his Acquaintance among Books', *Proceedings of the American Philosophical Society* 127 (June 1983), 135–42.

[28] Cheetham, *Life*, xxii. Paine terminated his friendship with Cheetham in 1807, and ceased to publish in his paper, *The American Citizen*: Cheetham was thereafter a hostile witness, but this comment is not on the surface hostile.

was not indebted. He was a teacher more than a learner: he made up his mind at an early age, and his views developed less in later years than has been thought.

Paine's sources were overwhelmingly English, or books available in English translation. This English frame of reference was unclear to his contemporaries as well as to later commentators since Paine's favourite author was evidently himself. On a brief trip to France in 1781 another American, Elkanah Watson, who 'officiated as interpreter', thought Paine 'coarse and uncouth in his manners, loathsome in his appearance, and a disgusting egotist, rejoicing most in talking of himself, and reading the effusions of his own mind'.[29] Paine's young friend Henry Redhead Yorke, visiting him in Paris in 1802, was astonished that Paine could quote verbatim from one of his pamphlets written twenty years before. Yorke commented:

> One of the most extraordinary properties belonging to Mr. Paine, is, his power of retaining every thing he has written in the course of his life. It is a fact, that he can repeat word for word, every sentence in his *Common Sense*, *Rights of Man*, &c., which I attribute first, to the unparalleled slowness with which he composes every passage he writes; secondly, to its having been profoundly meditated, and lastly, to his dislike of every sort of reading. The Bible is the only book he has studied, and there is not a verse in it, that is not familiar to him.[30]

This was only partly true: Paine read much in addition to Scripture, and some of his reading is reconstructed below. Yet Yorke's comment illuminates one central characteristic of Paine: because he was so self-referential, his ideas developed less over time than if he had followed current publications more closely. Without a greater adaptation to changing circumstances, Paine could be overtaken by events; by the mid-1790s his older intellectual inheritance engaged less and less with the new things happening in both America and France.

DEMOCRACY, RIGHTS, AND 'THE PEOPLE'

Paine's attitude to political representation can also be traced to a prior world. Since the 1980s it has become increasingly clear that eighteenth-century anglophone political theory was not secular; that democracy as universal suffrage was not a leading cause of the revolutions of 1776 and 1789, or an immediate outcome of either; and that if there was a single 'age of revolution', its unities and commonalities are now difficult to identify. Indeed the term 'democracy' was popularized in everyday English political discourse after 1790 less by Paine, its putative champion, than by its eloquent opponent, Burke.[31]

---

[29] *Men and Times of the Revolution; or, Memoirs of Elkanah Watson*, ed. Winslow C. Watson (New York, 1861), 127–8.

[30] Henry Redhead Yorke, *Letters from France, in 1802* (2 vols, London: H. D. Symonds, 1804), ii. 365.

[31] Mark Philp, 'Talking about Democracy: Britain in the 1790s', in Joanna Innes and Mark Philp (eds), *Re-imagining Democracy in the Age of Revolutions: America, France, Britain, Ireland 1750–1850* (Oxford, 2013), 101–13 at 104–5.

When rights language rose to prominence in the late twentieth century, democracy seemed the key right; it could be retrojected onto the age of revolution. It was once conventional to depict, in that era, a new world based on universalist natural rights as displacing an old particularist world of discourse that conceived of rights only as specific privileges. If the two are logically inconsistent, this would imply a sudden break that demanded a chronological location. Yet both senses had long coexisted (rights as legally defined entitlements, and rights as metaphysical ideals); over time the two alternated in prominence without either eliminating the other.[32] They coexisted for so long partly because 'rights' objectivized claims, and also because 'rights' could establish the morality of those claims within a Christian world view.

Paine's contemporaries could combine both usages in their political discourses, and two publications illustrate those discourses' composite nature. A reforming work on the English constitution, attributed to Obadiah Hulme and published before Paine left for America, urged the restoration of 'the constitution...established in England, by our Saxon forefathers' and the elimination of the constitution introduced to replace it at the Norman Conquest. In the Saxon system 'every man, who had so far distinguished himself, as to become a housekeeper, and as such, liable to pay his shot, and bear his lot [i.e. pay local taxation, more generally known as scot and lot], might give his consent to every law, that was made for his obedience'. A housekeeper franchise might seem arbitrary, or customary. But Saxon constitutionalism and natural rights were present together in this account:

> Whoever had the honour of being the first inventers of this mode of government, it is very evident, that the natural rights of mankind were their guide, and truth and justice their ends, in all their establishments. They considered every man alike, as he came from the hands of his maker, man as man, simply and detached from any foreign advantages, one might, accidentally, have over another...Every man, under that institution, was preserved in his natural, and equal rights, whether he were rich or poor.

The Saxon constitution was 'grounded upon the natural rights of mankind, in the constant annual exercise of their elective power, and the latter [the Norman] upon the despotick rule of one man'.

This binary and creationist formula, reminiscent of Paine's, might seem to anticipate universal manhood suffrage based on natural rights. But when the author came to spell out his preferred reforms, he fell back on advocating a familiar taxpayer franchise to apply

> throughout the kingdom. And this general rule should be the ancient rule, and the same that is now used in Westminster, and many other boroughs: where every resident inhabitant, that pays his shot, and bears his lot, should be entitled to his election, for a member of parliament, in that division to which he belongs.[33]

---

[32] See Ch. 5, section Natural rights discourse.

[33] [Obadiah Hulme, attrib.], *A Historical Essay on the English Constitution: or, An impartial Inquiry into the Elective Power of the People, from the first Establishment of the Saxons in this Kingdom* (London: Edward and Charles Dilly, 1771), iv, 4, 6, 8, 11, 154.

Evidence is lacking that Paine knew this text. But in 1774, James Burgh, in a text that was known to Paine, quoted Hulme's argument that 'Where annual election ends, slavery begins'; Burgh got no further in tying representation to natural rights alone, writing of 'the right or privilege of choosing representatives' and contending only that 'every person, who pays tax, ought to have a vote'.[34]

Paine too traced individual rights to a divine gift and initially favoured a tax-payer franchise rooted in customary privilege; in *Common Sense*, outlining his proposed election to a 'CONTINENTAL CONFERENCE' to frame a 'CONTINENTAL CHARTER', the equivalent of England's Magna Carta, he was casual about how electors to that conference were to be chosen.[35] His later views departed little from this arguably inconsistent combination. Even in the discussions of the Pennsylvania constitution of 1776, Paine merely 'argued that rights of citizenship in the new Pennsylvania republic should be extended to all men who served in the militia'.[36] Only after Paine's departure for America did the argument develop, and in England, not the colonies. John Cartwright in 1776 expanded the notion of 'what is vulgarly called property' that should qualify men for the franchise, quoting Locke's remark that 'every man has a property in his own person'. Yet even Cartwright did not abandon the argument from taxation: since all men paid some taxes, all were covered by the principle that '*no man* shall be *taxed* but with his own consent, given either by himself or *his representative in parliament*. Hence we find that, according to *the received doctrine of property*, no man can be without a right to vote for a representative in the legislature.' As to the poor, continued Cartwright, 'Their poverty is, surely, the worst of all reasons, for stripping them of their natural rights!' All men possessed freedom;

> doubtless it is the immediate gift of God to all the human species, by adding *free-will* to *rationality*, in order to render them beings which should be accountable for their actions. All are by nature free; all are by nature equal: freedom implies choice; equality excludes degrees in freedom. All the commons, therefore, have an equal right to vote in the elections of those who are to be the guardians of their lives and liberties; and none can be intitled to more than one vote.[37]

Paine would reach similar conclusions about a broad (though only male) electorate by 1795, but not on premises that led him to adopt Cartwright's formula 'annual parliaments and universal suffrage'.

---

[34] [James Burgh], *Political Disquisitions: or, An Enquiry into public Errors, Defects and Abuses* (3 vols, London: E. and C. Dilly, 1774-5), i. 38–9, 83.

[35] It would be composed of two members of Congress for each colony, plus 'Two members from each house of Assembly', plus 'five Representatives of the people at large, to be chosen in the capital city or town of each province, for, and in behalf of the whole province, by as many qualified voters as shall think proper to attend from all parts of the province for that purpose; or if more convenient, the Representatives may be chosen in two or three of the most populous parts thereof'. Such an assembly would be 'impowered by the people'. [Paine], *Common Sense* (1776): *CW*, i. 28–9 (text corrected). The qualification of voters was not specified.

[36] Francis D. Cogliano, '"The Whole Object of the Present Controversy": The Early Constitutionalism of Paine and Jefferson', in Simon P. Newman and Peter S. Onuf (eds), *Paine and Jefferson in the Age of Revolutions* (Charlottesville, Va, 2013), 26–48, at 34. In his proposals of 1776 for a Virginia constitution, Jefferson equally did not advocate universal male suffrage, 36.

[37] [John Cartwright], *Take your Choice!* (London: J. Almon, 1776), 19–22.

The widely shared argument from divine gift evolved over time; there was no sudden shift from particularist prescription to universalist natural rights.[38] Still less did reformers like Hulme, Burgh, and Cartwright invoke natural rights to demolish aristocracy and kingship. That was Paine's characteristic contribution, and it rested more on his particularist negations than on universalist affirmations drawn from natural rights theory. His originality in *Rights of Man* derived not from an affirmation of the principle of universal manhood suffrage but from his Deist negation of what his Deism identified as the hereditary principle, so that his generalized advocacy of a wider franchise was now set in a context of the abolition of monarchy and aristocracy. This was sensational. In this respect he went far beyond the reformers of the 1770s and 1780s: they had generally been Protestant Nonconformists who had said nothing against the Hanoverian monarchy and its supporting aristocracy, provided that the House of Commons could be reformed to become more responsive to the claims of their fellow Dissenters.

Paine often used the expression 'the people', but this locution alone did not make him a democratic theorist. Not until *Rights of Man* did he explicitly discuss 'democracy', and then to restrain it. His works occasionally mentioned but seldom closely examined the electoral machinery, the franchise, the age of majority, the structure and functions of the legislature, or the representation of women, all of which were to be major preoccupations of democratic reformers in the nineteenth and twentieth centuries. Paine stated at the outset of *Common Sense* his wish that elections be frequent, so that 'the *elected* might by that means return and mix again with the general body of the *electors* in a few months' and thereby 'establish a common interest with every part of the community',[39] but this remark needs interpretation. 'The prescription for "mixing" showed a new consideration for the common people, but it left old assumptions of rank mostly intact.'[40] In *Common Sense* the idea of 'the people' did appear, but even here was not heavily reified. It functioned rather as a default category to signify the totality of the population after the hereditary elements had been removed; it was an echo of scriptural uses to denote God's dealings with 'the people of Israel' and of the English political formula that described the king as the 'father of his people', rather than denoting a newly autonomous actor on the historical stage.[41]

Paine did not claim to speak for 'the people' conceived as 'the archetypal owners of all rights and liberties', a usage that later became widespread and heavily emphasized in the political discourse of the new American republic. This usage spread rapidly during the Revolution, as the colonial elite widely ceased to be self-identified as 'the better sort' and re-invented themselves as 'simple, ordinary citizens'. The same usage is still politically powerful in the present-day United States; but that does not authorize its projection back onto 1776.[42] Paine envisaged his favourite 'representative system' more negatively, as making impossible the tyranny of kings

---

[38] See Ch. 5, section Natural rights discourse.   [39] [Paine], *Common Sense* (1776): *CW*, i. 6.
[40] Michal Jan Rozbicki, *Culture and Liberty in the Age of the American Revolution* (Charlottesville, Va, 2011), 119–20.
[41] [Paine], *Common Sense* (1776): *CW*, i. 7–9, 11–12, 25.
[42] Rozbicki, *Culture and Liberty*, 120–1.

and aristocrats, than positively, as being the agent of social revolution. His political vision may be summed up as a negative critique of the English world of king, nobles, and bishops, linked to a positive Deistic vision of spontaneous, virtuous cooperation; but his negative critique was of little help in constructing and sustaining actual democracies. Paine's few passages that touched on democracy were not subtle and innovative, but often unspecific, chiefly because the positive advocacy of democracy was not central to his purposes. At the present, 'modernity' is often understood in terms of democracy, but Paine's relation to democracy requires careful qualification.

The new United States did not begin as, in any recent sense of the term, 'a democracy'. Nor was universal suffrage a lesson that Paine could learn in America. The franchise in the American colonies had been diverse; each colony had its own formula, tying the right to vote in different ways to the ownership of real estate or personal property; in some places but not others it explicitly excluded women, recent arrivals, freed slaves, servants, paupers, Jews, or Catholics. The proper extent of the electorate became an issue during the Revolution, with many arguing that the old criterion of personal independence, established by property owning, should be replaced by the criterion of personal participation, established by taxpaying and military service. But the outcome of these debates was highly varied; there was no wave of reforming opinion on the franchise that swept across the states. Only Vermont abolished both property and taxpaying qualifications.

Pennsylvania's new constitution of late 1776 ended property qualifications but instead enfranchised only adult male taxpaying freemen and their eldest sons; this meant that 'the increase in the size of the legal electorate was probably small'. Franchise reform was not a central cause of the Revolution, although it was in some places a consequence: 'Suffrage reform was advanced in a coherent fashion in only six states.'[43] The constitution of 1787 did not sweep away this diversity or affirm a principle of democracy derived from a natural right to vote in everyone: it only provided that the franchise in federal elections would be the same as that for 'the most numerous Branch of the State Legislature', and left this to be determined by each state for itself. In general, women, African Americans, and Native Americans were still denied the vote, as they had been before 1776.[44] Paine made no comment on this persisting discrimination. Nor did he protest when the new Pennsylvania constitution, professedly with a wide franchise, introduced test oaths

[43] Chilton Williamson, *American Suffrage from Property to Democracy 1760–1860* (Princeton, 1960), 92–7, at 92, 96. For the Pennsylvania constitution of 1776 see Theodore Thayer, *Pennsylvania Politics and the Growth of Democracy 1740–1776* (Harrisburg, Pa, 1953), 211–27.

[44] 'The American Revolution, in sum, produced modest, but only modest, gains, in the formal democratization of politics': Alexander Keyssar, *The Right to Vote: The Contested History of Democracy in the United States* (2nd edn, New York, 2009), 3–21, at 20; J. R. Pole, *Political Representation in England and the Origins of the American Republic* (London, 1966), 270–80. Appropriately, Paine figures little in these books, or in Richard R. Beeman, *The Varieties of Political Experience in Eighteenth-Century America* (Philadelphia, 2004), which emphasizes the differences in electoral practice across the colonies.

that effectively disenfranchised most potential voters and allowed power to be monopolized by the minority of Presbyterians.[45]

Whatever its earlier sources, universal manhood suffrage was an idea re-invented and placed in the political arena not in the colonies but in England; not by natural rights theorists per se but by a powerful group of intellectuals in the 1760s and 1770s, mostly Nonconformist Arians and Socinians, patronized by reforming aristocrats like Richmond and Shelburne. It was squarely on the agenda of English politics by the time of the election for the large popular constituency of Westminster in 1780.[46] Universal manhood suffrage implied a rejection of the ideal of a 'mixed and balanced' constitution, an ideal reaffirmed in the new American constitution of 1787; Paine too rejected that ideal, and this makes it even more notable that he did not find his way to the new ideology of representation.

As a Deist, Paine's attention was elsewhere. From the outset of his career he urged in general terms that the electorate be extensive, but wrote nothing about any individual right to vote deriving from personality; his starting point was the individual's unmediated access to God rather than the individual's common humanity. Paine's preferred company was that of freethinkers rather than of any self-conscious class constituency. In 1778, urging a wide electorate for Pennsylvania, he even argued that large groups be excluded from it: servants had forfeited their 'freedom', and servants he defined as not only 'servants in families' but those in 'offices or employments in or under the state, voluntarily accepted, and to which there are profits annexed'. Such people were 'detached by choice' from 'their original independent character of a man'.[47] 'Servants' here included white indentured labourers, who had by contract surrendered their freedom for a period of years in return for free passage to the colonies, and who made up a substantial part of the white workforce. Paine had paid for his own passage; he did not comment on the disenfranchisement of indentured labourers or black slaves. This was far from universal manhood suffrage. Only in the 1790s did a wide franchise begin to achieve prominence in his thought, but even then it did not engage with Paine's ideas about the modification of existing practices of state-funded poor relief.

Some historians have argued that Paine's position changed fundamentally over time, and that as a result of his experience in the American Revolution and in the transformational setting of the French he adopted an ideology of revolutionary democracy; but this cannot be squared with his writings. Even in *Rights of Man* (1791) the term 'democracy' appeared on only three pages, and there functioned

---

[45] 'By means of smoke and mirrors, this [constitution] has become Holy Writ in histories as "the most democratic" constitution of all the Revolutionary states': Francis Jennings, *The Creation of America: Through Revolution to Empire* (Cambridge, 2000), 174. For the actual working of this 'pretense', 180–92. The constitution was driven through by a provincial convention, self-appointed after the violent exclusion of moderates and Loyalists, in which voting was by county, not by head, so handing power to the less populated but Presbyterian western counties; it was never voted on by the people of Pennsylvania as a whole. The myth is, however, alive and well, e.g. in Terry Bouton, *Taming Democracy: 'The People', the Founders, and the Troubled Ending of the American Revolution* (New York, 2007).

[46] Clark, *English Society*, 411–12.

[47] Paine, 'A Serious Address to the People of Pennsylvania on the Present Situation of their Affairs' (Dec. 1778): *CW*, ii. 287–8.

as an abstract category, part of the familiar analytical trilogy of 'Monarchy, aristocracy, and democracy', which, for Paine, 'are but creatures of imagination'.[48] Nor
was there any transformation by the time of *Rights of Man. Part the Second* (1792),
and no systematic treatment of the idea. In that work 'democracy' again appeared
on only three pages, referring historically to 'the democracy of the Athenians' and
meaning the Athenians' 'simple democracy', which Paine summarily dismissed as
an 'inconvenience' in favour of his preferred form of government, 'the representative system'.[49] In this respect these two works were fully consistent, and not at odds
with *Common Sense*. Even the term 'equality' appeared only twice in *Rights of Man*,
in the context of 'The Mosaic account of the creation',[50] and nowhere in *Rights of
Man. Part the Second*: where readers today might expect Paine to have linked democracy with equality, he did not do so.

In *Rights of* Man (1791), Paine protested most prominently against the dis-
proportion of the representation, for in England two MPs were similarly
returned by counties and most boroughs irrespective of their populations; but
he framed no case for the franchise to be based on personality in numerically
equal constituencies. Indeed he praised the French draft constitution, which
embodied a taxpayer franchise; it said 'That every man who pays a tax of sixty
sous *per annum* (2s and 6d. English), is an elector.—What article will Mr. Burke
place against this?' He continued similarly: 'The French Constitution says, that
the National Assembly shall be elected every two years. What article will Mr.
Burke place against this?'[51] Paine did not echo Major Cartwright's slogan
'annual parliaments and universal suffrage', when he could relevantly have done
so. His premises were different.

His conception of a wide franchise was initially derived more from ideas of the
rights of taxpayers than from ideas of personal independence. Later in *Rights of
Man*, he declared that 'the election' of the House of Commons should be 'as universal as taxation', but did not base the franchise on a shared humanity.[52] His sense
of the size of the electorate that this entailed widened over time. As late as 1792,
he wrote: 'As every man in the nation, of the age of twenty-one years, pays taxes,
either out of the property he possesses, or out of the product of his labor, which is
property to him; and is amenable in his own person to every law of the land; so has
everyone the same equal right to vote, and no one part of the nation, nor any individual, has a right to dispute the right of another.'[53] He ignored women taxpayers,
whose rights were disputed by men. Only by July 1795 had this silently changed
to 'The true, and only true basis of representative government is equality of rights.

---

[48] Paine, *Rights of Man* (1791): *CW*, i. 289, 340 (71, 155–6 in the 1st edn).
[49] Paine, *Rights of Man. Part the Second* (1792): *CW*, i. 369, 371–2 (28, 33–4 in the 1st edn). For
a different interpretation, premised on R. R. Palmer's *The Age of the Democratic Revolution*, see Armin
Mattes, 'Paine, Jefferson, and the Modern Ideas of Democracy and the Nation', in Newman and Onuf
(eds), *Paine and Jefferson in the Age of Revolutions*, 95–117.
[50] Paine, *Rights of Man* (1791): *CW*, i. 274 (46–7 in the 1st edn).
[51] Paine, *Rights of Man* (1791): *CW*, i. 280–1 (text corrected).
[52] Paine, *Rights of Man* (1791): *CW*, i. 330.
[53] Paine, *Letter Addressed to the Addressers* (1792): *CW*, ii. 505.

Every man has a right to one vote, and no more, in the choice of representatives.'[54]
Even so, this was not quite the doctrine of universal manhood suffrage, let alone
universal suffrage including women, and the idea of a broad franchise performed
work no different in Paine's *Dissertation on First-Principles of Government* (1795)
than it had in *Common Sense* (1776): the tract of 1795 still framed the great alternative as being between a representative (not a democratic) and a hereditary system. The rationale for a wide electorate, in Paine's view, was that it would underpin
the representative system, not that it would affirm the value of the individual.

The passage from Paine's *Dissertation* just quoted was preceded by a short paragraph that demands close scrutiny:

> In contemplating government by election and representation, we amuse not ourselves
> by inquiring when, or how, or by what right it began. Its origin is ever in view. Man is
> himself the origin and the evidence of the right. It appertains to him in right of his
> existence, and his person is the title-deed.[55]

This seems from a present-day perspective to capture the case for universal suffrage
derived from individual personality. But for Paine, the phrase 'of the right' referred
back to 'government by election and representation', that is, his favourite and long-
standing ideal of the representative system, not to a universal franchise possessed
by every man (as others even at the time saw it) and leading to a direct democracy.[56]
The difference of principle was fundamental.[57] After this point, in his tract of
1795, Paine returned to the old language and the old assumptions: 'Personal rights,
of which the right of voting for representatives is one, are a species of property of
the most sacred kind.'[58] Property and personality were related; yet they were not
the same. As late as 1804, Paine did not treat democracy (in the sense of individual

---

[54] Paine, *Dissertation on First-Principles of Government* (1795): *CW*, ii. 577–8 (text corrected). A
few days later, on 7 July 1795, Paine protested in the National Assembly at the property qualification
for the franchise embodied in the constitution then proposed: 'The Constitution of 1795': *CW*, ii.
588–94. Even then, he framed only a negative critique of a tax qualification and not a positive affirmation of universal suffrage based on personality.

[55] Paine, *Dissertation on First-Principles of Government* (1795): *CW*, ii. 577, 583.

[56] Keyssar, *The Right to Vote*, 9, notes Paine's belief in the 1770s in the importance of voter independence, but argues that he had, while in France, accepted universal suffrage by 1795. Such a transition is questioned in the present work. Keyssar rightly criticizes the old scenario of a transition from
property to personality in the American franchise as a 'triumphalist presumption', a Whig interpretation in Herbert Butterfield's sense, inconsistent with the overriding interplay of 'war…Class, race,
gender, ethnicity, and religion'. Thanks to such an interplay, 'the United States was one of the last
countries in the developed world to attain universal suffrage' in the twentieth century: xxi, xxiv–xxvi.

[57] For an argument that Paine consistently held the principle of universal suffrage from *Common
Sense* to 1795, merely expressing it more clearly, see Bernard Vincent, 'Thomas Paine and the Issue of
Universal Suffrage', in Vincent, *The Transatlantic Republican: Thomas Paine and the Age of Revolutions*
(Amsterdam, 2005), 117–24.

[58] Paine immediately contradicted himself: 'In any view of the case it is dangerous and impolitic,
sometimes ridiculous, and always unjust to make property the criterion of the right of voting':
Dissertation on First-Principles of Government (1795): *CW*, ii. 578–9. He had done just that, and in
1797 did so again: 'The right of voting for persons charged with the execution of the laws that govern
society is inherent in the word liberty, and constitutes the equality of personal rights. But even if that
right (of voting) were inherent in property, which I deny, the right of suffrage would still belong to all
equally, because, as I have said, all individuals have legitimate birthrights in a certain species of property': *Agrarian Justice* ([1797]): *CW*, i. 607.

representation) as a major option, and still insisted that the choice was between 'the two systems of government, the *hereditary* and the *representative*',[59] not between a hereditary and a democratic option.

In his own self-image, Paine always advocated effective representative government, 'representation engrafted upon democracy', not direct democracy itself.[60] Yet the most successful example of representative government in any major state was the Westminster Parliament, in the homeland that Paine repudiated. Paine's anti-English rhetoric has obscured the degree to which he was, here as elsewhere, indebted to an older English model. In 1778, he wrote: 'I am as little fond of drawing observations from England as any man, because I know their modes of government are too wretched and ridiculous for imitation, but I would here remark, that the best representation comes from those places where the electors are most numerous and various, and their worst from the contrary places.'[61] The point was 'representation'; but England had to be repudiated. 'If ever we cast our eyes towards England, it ought to be rather to take *warning* by, than *example*.'[62]

It was as a series of negations that England featured, but in that role it dominated Paine's thought. Paine was anti-English more than he was pro-American or pro-French. The government of England he identified as being 'as great, if not the greatest, perfection of fraud and corruption that ever took place since governments began'.[63] But in this he largely reversed familiar English Whig self-praise rather than finding his way to a different analysis.

RELIGION

If Paine's political discourses were dependent on his religion, what can be learned of this more profound commitment? Paine wrote in 1776 of 'the English church, of which I profess myself a member'.[64] To what extent he agreed with its theology by that date is unclear. Yet Paine was evidently baptized in the Church of England, and was certainly twice married in that Church; his appointment in the excise service would have required a certificate of his having received the sacrament. His aversion to Anglican theology was the reaction of an insider, not of a Nonconformist. At Paine's trial *in absentia* in 1792 for *Rights of Man. Part the Second*, the first printer of that work, Thomas Chapman, recounted a quarrel with Paine that Chapman claimed justified him in withdrawing from an agreement to print a text that he feared would be legally actionable: 'Mr. Paine rose up in a great passion, declaring as I was a dissenter, he had a very bad opinion of dissenters in general, believing

---

[59] Paine, 'To the People of England on the Invasion of England' (6 Mar. 1804): *CW*, ii. 675.

[60] Paine, *Letter Addressed to the Addressers* (1792): *CW*, ii. 489–90.

[61] [Paine], 'A Serious Address to the People of Pennsylvania on the Present Situation of their Affairs' (Dec. 1778): *CW*, ii. 289.

[62] [Paine], 'A Serious Address' (Dec. 1778): *CW*, ii. 301.

[63] Paine to Sir Archibald Macdonald, Attorney General [11 Nov. 1792], to be read in court at his trial *in absentia* for *Rights of Man. Part the Second*: *CW*, ii. 512.

[64] [Paine], 'The Forester's Letters' (1776): *CW*, ii. 84.

them all to be a pack of hypocrites, and he should deal with them accordingly'.[65] Chapman's evidence should be treated with caution, since he was seeking to defend himself from legal penalty, but evidence is lacking that Paine anywhere praised Nonconformists.

It is important to investigate any influence on Paine from his father's Quakerism. Paine's inflation of 'reason' to be an historical actor, characterizing his times (as in his tract *The Age of Reason*) seems to parallel the famous text of the Quaker Robert Barclay of 1678, reprinted throughout the eighteenth century as that sect's classic defence. Barclay wrote always of men as 'rational Creatures endued with Reason', possessed of 'the natural reason of Man': 'Man, as he is a rational Creature, hath Reason as a natural Faculty of his Soul'. Barclay had appealed to 'men, that will be pleased to make use of that reason and understanding that God hath given them, and not be imposed upon, nor abused by the custom or tradition of others'. For Barclay, 'Revelations... neither do nor can ever contradict the outward Testimony of the Scriptures, or right and sound Reason'. But the two men importantly differed, chiefly over the Fall. Reason for Barclay was not a sufficient guide to salvation since it was 'the faln, corrupt, and defiled reason of man'.[66] Reason for Paine was 'the choicest gift of God to man', which man 'despises... and having endeavored to force upon himself the belief of a system against which reason revolts [revealed religion], he ungratefully calls it *human reason*, as if man could give reason to himself': 'It is only by the exercise of reason that man can discover God.'[67]

In 1737, the year of his birth, the English Quakers adopted a policy extending membership to the immediate family of members;[68] Paine could therefore have claimed membership of that society, whatever the level of his participation, despite being formally also a member of the Church of England. Yet in Philadelphia in 1776 Paine attacked the Quakers as if he were not one of them,[69] just as he never appealed to Presbyterians or Congregationalists as fellow-believers in a right of resistance, despite their prominence in the American Revolution. Quakers were already prominent, on both sides of the Atlantic, as anti-slavery campaigners; Paine did not make that question a central one in his politics, as he might have done had he shared a Quaker mindset. His views were closer to the seething pot of the established Church.

In 1809, in New York, the dying Paine was visited at his request by a Quaker, Willett Hicks, and told him, 'I am now in my seventy-third year, and do not expect to live long: I wish to be buried in your burying ground. I could be buried in the Episcopal church [which he had never formally left], but they are so arrogant; or

---

[65] Paine's trial (1793 edn), quoted in Cheetham, *Life*, 169–70. Cheetham added his opinion that Paine's words were 'exactly in character', 171.

[66] Robert Barclay, *An Apology For the True Christian Divinity, As the same is held forth, and preached by the People, Called, in Scorn, Quakers* (London: no printer, 1678), [xii, 'The Second Proposition'], 3, 39, 144, 319, 381.

[67] Paine, *The Age of Reason* (1794): *CW*, i. 482, 484.

[68] Vikki J. Vickers, '*My Pen and my Sword have ever gone together': Thomas Paine and the American Revolution* (London, 2006), 79–80. Vickers emphasizes the significance of the Quaker influence on Paine.

[69] In the appendix to the third edition of *Common Sense* (Philadelphia: W. and T. Bradford, 1776), 90–9: *CW*, ii. 55–60.

in the Presbyterian, but they are so hypocritical!'[70] Paine made his position clearer in his will: 'I know not if the Society of people called Quakers, admit a person to be buried in their burying ground, who does not belong to their Society, but if they do, or will admit me, I would prefer being buried there; my father belonged to that profession, and I was partly brought up in it.'[71] The Quakers refused him, and he was buried on his own farm. Formal denominational affiliation meant little to Paine, but in his intellectual formation he was a 'spoiled Anglican'.

In that role, he was often driven by negations more than by affirmations. Against his self-image as a man benevolent to all, led by abstract ideals, may be set the estimate of his character written by Dr James Manley, the physician who attended him on his deathbed:

> His anger was easily kindled, and I doubt not that his resentments were lasting. His vanity and self-love were so excessive, that to differ from him in opinion was, in his estimation, to be deficient in common understanding; and his opposition to the doctrine of Christianity was so rancorous, that in the early part of his [final] illness, he would treat its professors with rudeness.
>
> I have had no opportunity of judging of the humanity of his disposition, but I may remark, that he considered himself under no obligation to those who administered to him in his illness, and acted accordingly: he was penurious to an extreme...In the latter part of his life, he had his companions, though he seemed unfitted for sociability; and perhaps the reason why he affected company rather inferior to himself in point of understanding and acquirement, might be found in the peculiarities of his temper, which required acquiescence in his opinions to recommend to his attention...during the whole course of his illness, his petulance, vanity, and self-will were so excessive, that I have been constrained frequently to remark, that he of all others should, from motives of policy, have been induced to keep terms with Christians, as his temper was such as to preclude a possibility of his enjoying the sincerity of friendship, and none but they (and the best of them too) could possess charity sufficient to cover its manifold imperfections.[72]

Universalism had its limits.

POVERTY, PROPERTY, AND CLASS

In few themes is the temptation to assimilate Paine to later expectations stronger than in that of poverty. Yet Paine's later influence in this field was seldom

---

[70] Willett Hicks forgot Paine's last term; 'hypocritical' was Cheetham's inference, as a term that Paine 'used to apply to' the Presbyterians: Cheetham, *Life*, 294. Another work, *Memoirs of the Life and Gospel Labours of Stephen Grellet*, ed. Benjamin Seebohm (2 vols, Philadelphia, 1860), i. 163, retailed the anecdote that Paine, on his deathbed, expressed regret to his nurse for writing *The Age of Reason* as 'the devil's work'. This claim is not elsewhere attested, and is incompatible with Paine's general consistency of religious principle.

[71] 'The Will of Thomas Paine' (1809): *CW*, ii. 1500.

[72] James Manley to James Cheetham, 2 Oct. 1809: Cheetham, *Life*, 300–11, at 309–11.

prominent,[73] and careful distinctions are necessary. The poverty of healthy adults in Paine's lifetime had diverse causes, and how eighteenth-century debates on the problem are reconstructed may be influenced by preferences for present-day policy responses. In the simplest terms, eight main analyses of the causes of adult poverty were debated in Paine's lifetime and immediately after; they overlapped, and could be mutually reinforcing, yet were conceptually distinct. The first saw poverty as caused by the random impact of adversity on individuals' lives; since the late six-teenth century the English state's response had been social security payments. The second identified poverty as a consequence of taxes and debts imposed by a corrupt aristocratic and monarchical state to finance wars; the solution would be the pol-itical overthrow of that state form. The third treated poverty as a consequence of individual moral shortcomings; its solution was the personal moral reform urged by Christian Evangelicalism. The fourth traced poverty chiefly to humanity's col-lective lack of wealth; the implied remedy was production. The fifth ascribed pov-erty primarily to inequality; this analysis suggested that the main solution would be redistribution (and, later, public ownership). A sixth, associated above all with T. R. Malthus, ascribed poverty to over-population; its solution was delayed mar-riage. The seventh reacted subjectively to poverty perceived principally as squalor; its general solution extended the eighteenth-century idea of 'improvement' to work-ing conditions. Finally the eighth, in the early nineteenth century, identified pov-erty as a consequence of a class structure that locked out the working class from economic opportunity; the implied remedy would be the cultural or political lev-elling of such barriers. How did Paine relate to these approaches, evolving as they did over time?

Paine largely expressed the second analysis, and the others were markedly miss-ing in his work. For example, he was hardly sensitive to the seventh. In his own life, as for the lives of his neighbours, he seldom showed concern with his material sur-roundings. He attached little priority to securing better accommodation, house-hold goods, clothes, or food; he was not good at caring for himself, as his visitors often remarked, and after the end of his second marriage often lived in what might be described as bachelor squalor. Paine did not write in similar terms to Condorcet, who in his essay 'Public Instruction' (1791) looked forward to men 'attaining in their housing, their dress, their food, in all the habits of their daily life, a measure of health and cleanliness, and even of comfort and attractiveness'.[74] This uncon-cern Paine extended to others. Certainly, he supported the cause of the poor; but what most evoked his indignation was seldom the spectacle of material want, more often the spectacle of injustice.[75]

---

[73] For one rare retrospective appropriation of Paine's *Agrarian Justice* to support the introduction of death duties in the Budget of 1894, see Gareth Stedman Jones, *An End to Poverty? A Historical Debate* (London, 2004), 209. But Paine's legacy evidently did not make a significant contribution in 1908–11 to developing policy on non-contributory old age pensions and national insurance, 212–16.

[74] Quoted in Stedman Jones, *An End to Poverty?*, 43. For a contrasting image of a Paine committed to a programme for 'the elimination of poverty' see 21–6, 29, 41–2, 57, 63, 199, 224, 234–5, and *passim*.

[75] For an analysis of Paine's stance on poverty as deriving from his natural rights theories see Lounissi, *Paine*, 400–17.

Paine's critique of inequality was not identical to those familiar from later decades. He condemned inequality caused by the hereditary principle and primogeniture, the underpinnings of great landed estates, rather than the inequality of property as such. From his writings in the 1770s into the 1790s, evidence is lacking that Paine considered that any of his many political proposals would abolish the general inequality of property. His earliest printed work in 1772 (although first published for sale only in 1793) was a pamphlet, addressed to Parliament, seeking an increase in salaries for his fellow excise officers. This document contained no analysis of poverty or of social class, instead appealing continually (if tactically) to 'the wisdom of Government' to rectify a problem that had, by implication, no systemic cause other than too low a rate of pay and no wider systemic consequences if this grievance of one pressure group, the excisemen, were redressed. Paine's chief argument for higher salaries was less to reduce poverty as such than to reduce the temptation of poor excise officers to commit fraud: in the language of the Patriot opposition of the 1730s to 'out-root the present corruptions', not to correct some structural inequity in the economy.[76]

Appropriately, this pamphlet of 1772 led nowhere in Paine's subsequent writings: for the later Paine, the poor were poor not because they were underpaid state employees, or 'the working class', but because they were oppressed by hereditary kings and aristocrats; they were to be relieved not by combining to expropriate private property, or by taking control of the means of production, but by political revolution to destroy the hereditary principle. Although Paine organized backing from excisemen for an approach to Parliament in 1772, there is evidence that he did so as part of an officially sponsored move by the Commissioners of Excise to improve the lot of their employees, not as his own independent initiative or some class-based collective initiative.[77] Paine was not a champion of working men as such; he never sought to form a 'combination', as they were then known, nor did he write of the need for labourers to combine in the face of either landlords or manufacturers. This is more notable since others by the 1790s were beginning to do just that.

Paine was also a friend of production and exchange. As one historian rightly observed, 'There is absolutely no tension between virtue and commerce in *Common Sense*, for Paine assumes that they can and should exist compatibly together.'[78] In 1778, defending the new and professedly highly democratic constitution of Pennsylvania, he outlined a vision of the social order in which 'The harmony of the whole is composed of the harmony of its parts', rich and poor together. Indeed the rich needed the labour of the poor, he argued: without it, if the poor of one state migrated elsewhere, the rich would become poor themselves, 'for where there are none to labor, and but few to consume, land and property is not riches'.

---

[76] [Paine], *The Case of the Officers of Excise* ([1772]): *CW*, ii. 8, 15.

[77] This was a step to a higher civil list revenue for the crown, once losses caused by corruption had been decreased, and that this application would have been supported at higher level than the Excise Commissioners. George III had in his library a copy of Paine's *Case*: George Hindmarch, *Thomas Paine: The Case of the King of England and his Officers of Excise* (printed for the author, 1998), 91.

[78] Aldridge, *American Ideology*, 152.

I have heard it advanced, by those who have objected against the present constitution [of Pennsylvania] *that it was a good one for a poor man*. I reply, that for that very reason it is the best government for a *rich* one, by producing purchasers, tenants, and laborers, to the landed interest, and consumers to the merchants besides which, to live in a country where half the people are deprived of voting, is to live in a land of mutes from whom no honours can be received. As a rich man, I would vote for an open constitution, as the political means not only of continuing me so, but of encreasing my wealth; and as a poor man I would likewise vote for it, for the satisfaction I should enjoy from it, and the chance of rising under it. I am not pleading for the cause of one against the other in either case; for I am clearly convinced that the true interest of one is the real interest of both.

Such passages point to Paine's reliance at that date on production more than on redistribution. In Philadelphia from 1774 to 1787 he seems to have played no part in any socially revolutionary reform of poor relief.[79] His ideal was 'freedom' irrespective of social rank: 'Consider her [freedom] as the rich man's friend and the poor man's comforter, as that which enlivens the prosperity of the one and sweetens the hard fate of the other.' But he had no systemic analysis of that 'hard fate' that made poor men poor aside from the burden of the taxes imposed to support placemen, pensioners and the military, all parts of the hereditary system. His only counsel was, 'Let the rich man enjoy his riches, and the poor man comfort himself in his poverty.'[80] Although he used the word 'comfort', he did not specify how it was to be delivered apart from by ensuring 'freedom'. This was far from a collectivist notion of the state. Nor was his view confined to a Pennsylvania debate of 1778. In 1787, warning against war, Paine wrote similarly: 'I defend the cause of the poor, of the manufacturers, of the tradesmen, of the farmers, and of all those on whom the real burden of taxes falls—but above all, I defend the cause of humanity.'[81] It was not an anti-capitalist who linked the interest of the masses in the same sentence with that of the manufacturer and the farmer.

There are, however, passages in Paine's later writings that seem to be evidence of the author's indignation against inequality; they need careful scrutiny. In 1791 Paine argued in a vividly memorable image that 'A vast mass of mankind are degradedly thrown into the background of the human picture, to bring forward, with greater glare, the puppet-show of state and aristocracy'; but it was the clearly visualized second image that he negated, more than the vaguely conceptualized first that he affirmed.[82] In 1792 he added, again memorably, that 'a spectator who knew nothing of the world', and who saw it afresh, 'could not suppose that the hordes of miseable poor, with which old countries abound, could be any other than those

[79] Paine is absent from John K. Alexander, *Render Them Submissive: Responses to Poverty in Philadelphia, 1760–1800* (Amherst, Mass., 1980).

[80] [Paine], 'A Serious Address to the People of Pennsylvania on the Present Situation of their Affairs' (1778): *CW*, ii. 278, 282–3, 286.

[81] Paine, *Prospects on the Rubicon* (1787): *CW*, ii. 632.

[82] Paine, *Rights of Man* (1791): *CW*, i. 267.

who had not yet had time to provide for themselves. Little would he think they were the consequence of what in such countries is called government.'[83]

By implication, however, if 'government' were corrected, such people could 'provide for themselves' by the option noted above, production. Paine's position had not changed. Successive wars led him to emphasize the malign impact of the taxes that paid for them and supported a social structure: 'there are two distinct classes of men in the nation, those who pay taxes, and those who receive and live upon the taxes.'[84] For Paine in 1792 taxation, not capitalism or class, created both poverty and social rank. Even in *Agrarian Justice* (1797) he added: 'I care not how affluent some may be, provided that none be miserable in consequence of it.'[85]

Nor was Paine obviously a cultural class warrior. Although he was happy with the company of the poor, he also enjoyed the company of the rich: when in England he claimed to Kitty Few to be 'in pretty close intimacy with the heads of the opposition—the Duke of Portland, Mr. Fox and Mr. Burke'. He knew the Marquis of Lansdowne, to whom he wrote from Thetford as 'Your Lordship's Humble Servant', Lord Stanhope, Earl Fitzwilliam, and the Duke of Portland. Paine's writings give no evidence that he thought he was crossing class divides: he saw none. Present-day biographers quote his apparently populist remark to Kitty Few: 'I had rather see my horse Button in his own stable, or eating the grass of Bordentown or Morrisania, than see all the pomp and show of Europe'; [86] but Paine's life choices hardly bear out his claim. This absence was not inappropriate, if class theory was devised only in the decades after *c.*1815.[87]

Even in 1795, Paine made clear his distance from any conception of collectivist economic organization:

> That property will ever be unequal, is certain. Industry, superiority of talents, dexterity of management, extreme frugality, fortunate opportunities, or the opposite, or the mean of those things, will ever produce that effect, without having recourse to the harsh, ill-sounding names of avarice and oppression. Oppression is often the *consequence*, but seldom or never the *means* of riches... *All that is required with respect to property, is to*

---

[83] Paine, *Rights of Man. Part the Second* (1792): *CW*, i. 355. For a discussion of this text and its social security proposals see Ch. 5, section Social security.

[84] Paine, *Letter Addressed to the Addressers* (1792): *CW*, ii. 478. Such a position reveals the difficulties in recruiting the historic Paine to ratify present-day political campaigns. Yet for Paine's much more extreme statement in the same tract, 'When the rich plunder the poor of his rights, it becomes an example to the poor to plunder the rich of his property', see Ch. 5, section The London Corresponding Society. William Cobbett was similarly drawn to remark, 'We are daily advancing to the state in which there are but two classes of men, *masters*, and *abject dependents*': Thompson, *Making of the English Working Class*, 759. This was not a clear precursor of later three-class theory.

[85] Paine, *Agrarian Justice* ([1797]): *CW*, i. 617.

[86] Paine to Lansdowne, 21 Sept. 1787; Paine to Jefferson, 9 Sept. 1788; Paine to Kitty Nicholson Few, 6 Jan. 1789; Paine to anon. [?Thomas Christie], 16 Apr. 1790: *CW*, ii. 1265–6, 1268–72, 1274–8 at 1276, 1300–2 at 1300.

[87] Clark, *English Society*, 164–200 and *passim*. For a critique of the idea that 'Paine's writing reflects his own class origins and appeals primarily to other members of the same social class', identified as the artisans, see A. Owen Aldridge, 'The Problem of Thomas Paine', *Studies in Burke and his Time* 19 (1976), 127–43, at 128.

obtain it honestly, and not employ it criminally; but it is always criminally employed, when it is made a criterion for exclusive rights.[88]

In *Agrarian Justice* (1797), Paine still acknowledged the right of private property, arguing that, in 'acquired property...equality is impossible'; he included under this heading the 'additional value made by cultivation' of land which, he argued, in its natural state was not subject to private ownership. Paine contended only for 'Equality of natural property', and even here he did not name a high rate for his proposed death duties, redirected to the poor, that would compensate them for the loss of the birthright in uncultivated land that their ancestors had enjoyed while in 'the first state of man'.

Examined more closely, Paine's arguments of 1797 for redistribution were not unambiguous. Rather little money, in his proposal, was necessary to 'furnish the rising generation with means to prevent their becoming poor', enough only to provide every young couple at 21 years of age with £15 each when they 'begin the world'. Individual industriousness, implied Paine, would do the rest, an assumption all the more noteworthy given his own repeated lack of success in business. Although *Agrarian Justice* included 'personal property' as liable to death duties, since it was acquired by 'the aid of society', it too would pay a tax of only 10 per cent. Far more extensive proposals were already in the public arena, which Paine did not adopt. Although in 1797 he mentioned the conspiracy of François-Noel 'Gracchus' Babeuf (1760–97), then just frustrated, he did not explain it in ways that would have identified it as an early attempt at what was later called communism.[89] On the contrary, Paine explained it solely in political terms: 'The defect in principle of the Constitution was the origin of Babeuf's conspiracy.'[90] Although Paine elsewhere deplored manufactures as a basis of national wealth he never argued that growing manufactures were the exemplification of any new system later to be called 'capitalism'.[91]

More generally absent in Paine's writings was any sense of collective action or social solidarity to combat poverty. His anticipations of such positions were few, and perfunctory; when he wrote that 'The great mass of the poor in all countries are become an hereditary race', he did not follow up the remark and make it a theorized position (the conjunction of the terms 'hereditary' and 'race' shows how far he still was from nineteenth-century ideas). Paine did not urge the poor to act as a collective body; one analytical difficulty, standing in the way of such a mobilization, was

[88] Paine, *Dissertation on First-Principles of Government* (1795): *CW*, ii. 580 (text corrected); repeating words used in *Common Sense* (1776): *CW*, i. 9.

[89] As in R. B. Rose, *Gracchus Babeuf: The First Revolutionary Communist* (Stanford, Calif., 1978).

[90] Paine, *Agrarian Justice* ([1797]): *CW*, i. 607, 611–12, 618, 620–1. For a full discussion of this text see Ch. 6, section *The Age of Reason* as a Context for *Agrarian Justice*.

[91] For a similar absence of 'capitalism' even from the work of Thomas Spence, who argued for the common ownership of land, see Jack Fruchtman, Jr, 'Two Doubting Thomases: The British Progressive Enlightenment and the French Revolution', in Michael T. Davis (ed.), *Radicalism and Revolution in Britain, 1775–1848* (New York, 2000), 30–40, at 33.

his belief that 'It is, perhaps, impossible to proportion exactly the price of labour to the profits it produces.'[92]

He did not respond to the homogenizing pressures of social life in the American republic; he did not mention the French revolutionary ideal of *fraternité*; he did not call members of the London Corresponding Society 'comrade'. His collective categories of analysis were abstractions and mostly referred to those men of whom he disapproved, notably kings, aristocrats, and priests. In his daily life Paine was often a socially isolated figure. His morality generally involved individual action, not group action, and was one that he ascribed to Confucius: '*Acknowledge thy benefits by the return of benefits, but never revenge injuries.*'[93] This morality Paine acted out on many occasions, declining to seek retribution against those who had insulted or injured him (with an exception in the case of George Washington in the 1790s); that morality did not point forward to class action to correct group injustice.

Paine famously outlined in *Rights of Man. Part the Second* and *Agrarian Justice* what has been hailed as the beginning of a system of social security financed by transfer payments from rich to poor, the start of a modern welfare state premised chiefly on a novel idea of redistribution. Yet such ideas were not as novel as they now appear, if viewed out of the context of eighteenth-century English practice. The English poor relief system dated from the sixteenth century. It already provided for cash payments both regular and discretionary, administered at parish level, to the needy: these regular payments even gave rise to 'popular notions of entitlement'.[94] Paine himself, while an exciseman in Lewes, Sussex, in 1768–74, was a member of the Vestry of St Michael's parish, and his signature survives on documents recording the Vestry's payments to the poor.[95] Here as elsewhere, Paine reasoned on the basis of his English experience. He did not present his proposed reforms to poor relief as heralding any new world initiated by a greatly extended degree of redistribution. In *Rights of Man. Part the Second* he did not offer his outlined social security system as an agent of future revolutionary change, but rather as a means of righting very ancient wrongs.

---

[92] Paine, *Agrarian Justice* ([1797]), *CW*, i. 619–20. For an argument that it was Charles Hall in 1805 who first attempted 'to measure what proportion of the product of labor was received by the laborer', this being 'indisputably a crucial turning point in modern social theory', see Gregory Claeys, 'The Origins of the Rights of Labor: Republicanism, Commerce, and the Construction of Modern Social Theory in Britain, 1796–1805', *Journal of Modern History* 66 (1994), 249–90, at 285. 'Now, contractual and economic relations were increasingly central to the new radical analysis of poverty, though competing theories were by no means simply swept aside.' Hall's estimate of this proportion was sensationally low: one ninth. For Hall, see Ch. 7, section Manufacturing, capitalism, and poverty.

[93] Paine, 'Of the Old and New Testament' (31 Mar. 1804): *CW*, ii. 805–6.

[94] Steve Hindle, *On the Parish: The Micro-Politics of Poor Relief in Rural England c.1550–1750* (Oxford, 2004), esp. 398–405; J. R. Poynter, *Society and Pauperism: English Ideas on Poor Relief, 1795–1834* (London, 1969); Geoffrey W. Oxley, *Poor Relief in England and Wales 1601–1834* (Newton Abbot, 1974); Paul Slack, *The English Poor Law 1531–1782* (Basingstoke, 1990); Lynn Hollen Lees, *The Solidarities of Strangers: The English Poor Laws and the People, 1700–1948* (Cambridge, 1998).

[95] Audrey Williamson, *Thomas Paine: His Life, Work and Times* (London, 1973), 37–8; payments illustrated in plate 4.

Paine, as a Deist, wrote always of generalized categories of people, including 'kings', 'aristocrats', 'Americans'; but that did not make him a prophet who had abandoned particular commitments. Like his contemporaries, Paine used the term 'class', but with another meaning to that which became dominant in the nineteenth century. He could argue that the French Constitution 'has raised the income of the lower and middle classes, and taken from the higher';[96] but here 'class' had its old meaning, synonymous with 'rank' and 'degree'. For Paine, as for his contemporaries including John Wesley, 'class' still meant a group, not a social stratum or an identity created within the means of production and exchange. If these were his assumptions, it becomes more intelligble that Paine did not anticipate the theory of class that achieved prominence in the nineteenth century. When it was assumed that 'the working class' necessarily had to emerge, it seemed plausible to trace its emergence in Paine's lifetime.[97] Yet Paine was a considerable distance short of the English socialism of the 1830s, and cannot easily be located within what was once pictured as a tradition of 'working-class' activism that later found fulfilment in trade unions.[98]

Not until 1797 did Paine prioritize a term now familiar, writing of 'what was the condition of France under the *ancient regime*', but to him it was 'the ancient regime of Kings and Priests', not of material social structure.[99] Instead of class, Paine wrote of 'the rich' and 'the poor'. His enemies were kings, popes, aristocrats, and bishops, not anything he labelled 'the ruling class'; although he championed 'the people', he never visualized them as 'the working class', still less as a working class led or failed by that even later conceptualization, 'the bourgeoisie'. Class analysis was a language coined only after Paine's lifetime. Once it had been coined, Paine was retrospectively recruited as a pioneer; this was understandable, but a misconception. Paine did not even write the Pennsylvania constitution of 1776,[100] and his growing commitment to a wide franchise had a different origin from the later doctrine of class.

Nor did he anticipate the economics of David Ricardo (1772–1823), a tripartite division of society between land, labour, and capital that anticipated Marx but

---

[96] Paine, *Rights of Man* (1791): *CW*, i. 290.

[97] E. P. Thompson, *The Making of the English Working Class* (London, 1963). Paine's '*Rights of Man* is a foundation-text of the English working-class movement...he pointed towards a theory of the State and of class power, although in a confused, ambiguous manner', 90, 92. The ambiguity disappears by 181, 194 ('the outstanding fact of the period between 1790 and 1830 is the formation of "the working class"'). Given this assumption, it has escaped notice how little of the extensive evidence zealously assembled and eloquently presented by Thompson actually bears on the question of class formation (as does Cobbett's remark in 1830, quoted 228). On the contrary, his remarkable book gives evidence that major social and ideological conflict, and even a revolutionary underground, could then exist in the *absence* of the later ideology of class. Indeed Thompson was led to pronounce that in *Rights of Man* 'we are close to a theory of anarchism', 93.

[98] An influential exposition of this theory of Paine's relation to such a movement was Henry Collins's able introduction to Thomas Paine, *Rights of Man* (Harmondsworth, 1969), 9–47. The argument that Paine anticipated socialism is not now generally proposed, but the counter-argument deserves brief mention.

[99] Paine, *Letter...to Camille Jordan* (1797): *CW*, ii. 759, 763 (text corrected). Paine did not use the French; '*ancien*' is here better translated as 'former'.

[100] Foner's correction: *CW*, ii. 269. Paine soon disappears from the story told by Gary Nash, 'Philadelphia's Radical Caucus that Propelled Pennsylvania to Independence and Democracy', in Alfred F. Young, Gary B. Nash, and Ray Raphael (eds), *Revolutionary Founders: Rebels, Radicals, and Reformers in the Making of the Nation* (New York, 2011), 67–85.

attributed economic ills to the landlord rather than to the capitalist. Paine, as a small-town craftsman, teacher, exciseman, and shopkeeper, wanted nothing more than to become a small landowner,[101] and applauded the spread of landownership in the new American republic. In the world before radicalism and socialism, religion rather than class was often a key to political mobilization.[102] Of thirty-nine English political activists who emigrated to the United States in the 1790s, mostly in 1793–4, 90 per cent were anti-Trinitarian in their religious beliefs.[103] By contrast, not all of the *émigrés* identified with the egalitarianism they found in their new host society, and it was religion rather than political economy that still had most to say on poverty and inequality. Joseph Priestley wrote from America to the English Unitarian clergyman Theophilus Lindsey on 12 July 1795 complaining of the servant problem in the new world and observing of the United States: 'If there was more subordination it would be better for them all.'[104]

WOMEN'S EMANCIPATION

English Deists of the early eighteenth century had not been prominent campaigners for female emancipation. Paine has been praised as an early champion of that cause primarily on the strength of an anonymous essay 'An Occasional Letter on the Female Sex', published in *The Pennsylvania Magazine* of August 1775; but this was not written by Paine, and has long been shown to have been lifted from the introduction to an English translation (London, 1773) of Antoine Léonard Thomas's *Essai sur le caractère, les mœurs et l'esprit des femmes dans les différens siècles* (2 vols, Paris, 1772).[105] During the rest of his career the rights of women hardly featured in Paine's writings, although the question began to appear in high-profile revolutionary writings. When in 1790 Mary Wollstonecraft published *A Vindication of the Rights of Men* and followed it in 1792 with *A Vindication of the Rights of Woman*, later seen as a landmark in 'the movement' towards women's rights, Paine did not mention her or explicitly react to any of her ideas.

This absence is more notable since Wollstonecraft knew Paine in London in 1791 and 1792. She met him at a dinner party held on 13 November 1791 by the bookseller Joseph Johnson;[106] 'to Paine's house, during his 1791–2 stay in London,

---

[101] 'It is an historical irony that it was not the rural labourers but the urban workers who mounted the greatest coherent national agitation for the return of the land': Thompson, *The Making of the English Working Class*, 231. The irony is created only by recent historiographical expectations.

[102] Clark, *English Society*, ch. 4, 'Before Radicalism'.

[103] This correlation did not hold for 18 Scots activist *émigrés*, most of whom left in 1794–5 after the success of government repression in Scotland (22 per cent anti-Trinitarian) or for 115 Irish activists, most of whom left after the rising of 1798 (14 per cent anti-Trinitarian). Of the Irish, 38 per cent held positions in the United Irishmen. For English activists, the anti-Trinitarian proportion of 90 per cent was striking: Michael Durey, *Transatlantic Radicals and the Early American Republic* (Lawrence, Kan., 1997), 7, 10.

[104] Durey, *Transatlantic Radicals*, 180.   [105] See Appendix: 'Paine De-attributions'.

[106] It was William Godwin's first meeting with Mary Wollstonecraft. 'I had...little curiosity to see Mrs. Wollstonecraft, and a very great curiosity to see Thomas Paine. Paine, in his general habits, is no great talker; and, though he threw in occasionally some shrewd and striking remarks, the conversation

she had been a visitor'.[107] She was in France from December 1792 to April 1794, and was like Paine in contact with the Girondins. Moreover, she was no tourist, for she was writing a book soon published as *An Historical and Moral View of the Origin and Progress of the French Revolution; and the Effect it has Produced in Europe* (London: J. Johnson, 1794),[108] which in its unfinished state extended to the October Days in 1789. Paine met and dined with her before his imprisonment on 28 December 1793; a visitor, I. B. Johnson, wrote: 'Sometimes we met at Mr Paines or formed dining parties.'[109] Paine had every opportunity to appreciate her views.[110]

Yet Paine had never discussed the question of women's franchise and had assumed that government should remain in the hands of men. Praising in December 1778 the way in which Pennsylvania's constitution had been framed, he had boasted: 'No person was excluded from voting but those who chose to exclude themselves': he ignored the exclusion of women.[111] This continued, unreflectingly, to be his assumption, as it was the assumption of almost all small-town Englishmen; it was an assumption that makes problematic any attempt to reinterpret Paine's writings as a modern theory of rights-based liberalism, in which gender equality is now salient. It was not that Paine systematically excluded women from his mental universe of rights; rather, that like the predicament of African slaves he scarcely and seldom thought about it.

When he did address the position of women it was usually in the context of interpreting the moment when God created humankind. Paine used Creation to emphasize that God had instituted no social hierarchy among humans; but in order to prove his key point of equality between individuals Paine consistently urged, quoting Genesis, that the only distinction God had ordained was 'the distinction of sexes', which, by implication, was real. Even then, Paine never spelled out the extent and degree of difference that God had instituted between men and women; it is reasonable to infer that Paine saw no immediate need to do so. As late as

---

lay principally between me and Mary. I, of consequence, heard her very frequently when I wished to hear Paine': William Godwin, *Memoirs of Mary Wollstonecraft*, ed. W. Clark Durant (London, 1927), 62–3. See Godwin's memoirs of Wollstonecraft and Godwin's diary, <http://godwindiary.bodleian. ox.ac.uk/index2.html>. I am grateful to Mark Philp for this reference.

[107] Mary Wollstonecraft to William Roscoe, 14 Feb. 1792; Mary Wollstonecraft to Everina Wollstonecraft, 23 Feb. 1793, in *Collected Letters of Mary Wollstonecraft*, ed. Ralph M. Wardle (Ithaca, NY, 1979), 206–10; Godwin, *Memoirs of Mary Wollstonecraft*, 225.

[108] Although its title page announced 'Volume the First', no more were published. See *The Works of Mary Wollstonecraft*, ed. Janet Todd and Marilyn Butler (London, 1989), vi. 1–235. The work did not mention Paine. For a study of this text see Steven Blakemore, 'Wollstonecraft and the French Revolution', in *Crisis in Representation: Thomas Paine, Mary Wollstonecraft, Helen Maria Williams, and the Rewriting of the French Revolution* (London, 1997), 89–101.

[109] Janet Todd, *Mary Wollstonecraft: A Revolutionary Life* (London, 2000), 210; Mary Wollstonecraft visited her friend Gustav, Count von Schlabrendorf, 'often', as he recalled, in the Luxembourg prison: Lyndall Gordon, *Mary Wollstonecraft: A New Genus* (London, 2005), 224. It is not known whether she visited Paine before prisoners there were cut off from further communication with the outside in late February 1794.

[110] In Paris, 'She renewed her acquaintance with Paine': Godwin, *Memoirs of Mary Wollstonecraft*, 67; Thomas Clio Rickman, *The Life of Thomas Paine* (London: Rickman, 1819), 131–2.

[111] [Paine], 'A Serious Address to the People of Pennsylvania on the Present Situation of their Affairs' (1778): *CW*, ii. 280.

Agrarian Justice Paine wrote that God 'gave them [Adam and Eve] the earth for their inheritance', but added nothing about equal property rights between men and women deriving from this divine donation.[112] Women already had many rights in Paine's England; if they seldom possessed a vote, and if married women did not enjoy equal property rights with their husbands, there were few calls that they should acquire these rights. Paine could (here as elsewhere) have broken from the prevalent assumptions of his native society, but evidence is lacking that on these two points he did so. All he argued was that 'not a man or woman born in the Republic but shall inherit some means of beginning the world',[113] which was a minor concession indeed. The absence of evidence is not necessarily evidence of absence; but there are times when it can incline historians to that provisional and tentative conclusion.

ANTI-SLAVERY

Slavery permeated British society by the 1770s, whether hidden or revealed. All Souls College, Oxford, drew part of its wealth from Christopher Codrington's bequest derived from slave estates in the West Indies; Paine was unlikely to have known this secret. He was more likely, while an exciseman in Lewes, to have read stories in the *The Sussex Weekly Advertiser; or, Lewes Journal* of the cruelties of colonial slaveowners; more likely again to have read the widely-printed press reports of the landmark case of *Somerset v. Stewart* (1772); more likely still to have seen African slaves in England (whom Lord Mansfield, presiding in the *Somerset* case, then estimated to number '14,000 or 15,000').[114] Within such a mental world, Paine was against the institution of slavery. The question is why he made so little of it.

Anti-slavery was a publicly articulated position in England by the 1760s;[115] Benjamin Franklin even published an anonymous article in the London press in 1770 defending his fellow colonial slaveowners from an imagined Englishman's charges of the slaveowners' hypocrisy in denouncing 'every little imaginary Infringement of what you take to be your Liberties' by the London authorities while the colonists were themselves owning slaves.[116] The same cause was openly championed in Philadelphia before Paine arrived there in 1774. The Quaker Anthony Benezet had long been an outspoken opponent.[117] In 1773 Benjamin Rush, who

---

[112] [Paine], *Common Sense* (1776): *CW*, i. 9; Paine, *Rights of Man* (1791): *CW*, i. 274; Paine, *Agrarian Justice* ([1797]): *CW*, i. 609.

[113] Paine, *Agrarian Justice* ([1797]): *CW*, i. 622.

[114] William R. Cotter, 'The Somerset Case and the Abolition of Slavery in England', *History* 79 (1994), 31–56, at 36–8, 40.

[115] e.g. Granville Sharp, *A Representation of the Injustice and Dangerous Tendency of Tolerating Slavery; or of Admitting the Least Claim of Private Property in the Persons of Men, in England* (London: Benjamin White and Robert Horsfield, 1769). See, in general, David Brion Davis, *The Problem of Slavery in the Age of Revolution 1770–1823* (Ithaca, NY, 1975).

[116] The English critique was 'not quite fair', he complained. [Franklin], 'A Conversation of Slavery', *The Public Advertiser* (30 Jan. 1770): Franklin, *Papers*, xvii. 37–44.

[117] [Anthony Benezet], *Observations On the Inslaving, importing and purchasing of Negroes* (Germantown, Pa: Christopher Sower, 1759; 2nd edn, 1760); [Anthony Benezet], *A Caution and*

soon met Paine, had published a tract, although anonymously, against the practice.[118] There is sufficient, though fragmentary, evidence that Paine disapproved of
slavery, as many of his contemporaries already did in a weak sense.

Yet despite Rush's commitment and Franklin's sensitivity, Paine did not join the
abolitionist initiatives. The anonymous article of 1775, 'African Slavery in America',
often cited to prove Paine's early anti-slavery views, was misattributed to him.[119]
Paine was no friend of slavery, but it enjoyed no prominence in his writing or
thinking. In *Common Sense* Paine was instead indignant that Britain had 'stirred up
the Indians and the Negroes to destroy us'.[120] In his third 'Forester's Letter', dated
24 April 1776, slavery featured in one perfunctory footnote: 'Forget not the
hapless African.'[121] But he nowhere wrote about Lord Mansfield's judgement in
Somerset v. Stewart (1772), in which the Lord Chief Justice had sensationally ruled
that slavery did not exist in England unless specifically provided for in 'positive
law' (as it was not); this judgement effectively ended domestic slavery. Paine did
not extend his natural rights condemnations of kings and aristocrats to include
slaveowners. Nor is there evidence that Paine kept silence on the issue during the
revolution in order not to destabilize the American cause.

This is more notable since anti-slavery already had a formal existence in the
colonies. Just before the skirmishes at Lexington and Concord, Philadelphians
formed the Society for the Relief of Free Negroes Unlawfully Kept in Bondage (an
objective which fell far short of the abolition of slavery itself), but Paine's name did
not then appear in its records as a member, and its activities were suspended during
the war. It was re-launched in 1784 as the Pennsylvania Society for Promoting the
Abolition of Slavery, and the Relief of Free Negroes, Unlawfully Held in Bondage,
its membership consisting almost wholly of Quakers. On 23 April 1787 it elected
thirty-six eminent new members (which suggests a concerted effort by the society),
including Paine.[122] But Paine had, by that date, already left for New York, and
from there he sailed for France on 26 April.[123] There is no evidence that he had
agreed to be a member of the society, and it is possible that that newly launched
body was merely trying to raise its profile by conscripting a large number of famous names. Paine absorbed and occasionally echoed anti-slavery ideas, but in his
years in England and America they never became prominent in his works.

---

*Warning to Great Britain and her Colonies, in a Short Representation of the Calamitous State of the Enslaved
Negroes in the British Dominions* (Philadelphia: Henry Miller, 1766); [Anthony Benezet], *Some Historical
Account of Guinea... With an inquiry into the rise and progress of the slave trade* (Philadelphia: Joseph
Cruckshank, 1771).

[118] [Benjamin Rush], *An Address to the Inhabitants of the British Settlements in America, upon Slave-
Keeping* (Philadelphia: John Dunlap, 1773; 2nd edn, 1773).

[119] See Appendix: Paine De-attributions.

[120] [Paine], *Common Sense* (1776): *CW*, i. 30.

[121] [Paine], 'Forester's Letter', III (*Pennsylvania Journal*, 24 Apr. 1776): *CW*, ii. 82.

[122] For a lack of evidence on Paine's abolitionism, see also Gary Nash and Jean R. Soderlund, *Freedom
by Degrees: Emancipation in Pennsylvania and its Aftermath* (New York, 1991), 115, 124–5; James
V. Lynch, 'The Limits of Revolutionary Radicalism: Tom Paine and Slavery', *PMHB* 123 (1999),
177–99, at 181–2.

[123] Paine to Benjamin Franklin, 31 Mar., 22 June 1787: *CW*, ii. 1260–3. Franklin was elected
president of the refounded society, but evidence is lacking that Paine ever mentioned that election.

Equally they did not do so while he was in France, where opinion against slavery had also been forming.[124] The slave revolt in the French colony of Haiti in August 1791 did not lead Paine to hail its success as another realization of the promise of the American or French Revolutions.[125] Paine did not write even a single paragraph against slavery in *Rights of Man*, although it contained the perfect lead-in with his assertion that 'Man has no property in man' and (many pages later) a relevant political application: 'It is no relief, but an aggravation to a person in slavery, to reflect that he was sold by his parent.'[126]

In England, the Society for Effecting the Abolition of the Slave Trade was founded on 22 May 1787. Paine is not known to have been a member of that Society, which he might have joined before he finally left for France in September 1792.[127] Paine's name was not in the published *List of the Society, Instituted in 1787, For the Purpose of effecting the Abolition of the Slave Trade* (London: no printer, 1788), although Lafayette and Brissot de Warville were recorded as honorary members. Nine of its founding twelve members were Quakers, and Paine was not a Quaker. The Society was thrown into consternation when on 2 April 1792 the House of Commons passed a Bill for abolition but only after the addition of the word 'gradual' before the phrase 'abolition of the slave trade', so wrecking the proposal: Paine is not known to have protested.[128]

The French society for the abolition of slavery held its first meeting in Paris on 19 February 1788; despite Paine's long stay in the capital, there is no record of his having any association with that society. On 30 March 1799 a 'M. Pain' was proposed for membership;[129] even then, it is not clear that this was the Englishman Thomas Paine. 'Pain' is a French surname, and many sharing it are listed in the Paris telephone directory to this day. Thomas Paine, in Paris in March 1789, did write to Rush in America: 'I despair of seeing an abolition of the infernal traffic in Negroes. We must push that matter further on your side of the water.'[130] But there

---

[124] Edward Derbyshire Seeber, *Anti-Slavery Opinion in France during the Second Half of the Eighteenth Century* (Baltimore, 1937).

[125] Paine knew of the episode—'We have distressing accounts here from St. Domingo. It is the natural consequence of Slavery and must be expected every where'—but drew no more extensive conclusions: Paine to William Short, 2 Nov. 1791: *CW*, ii. 1320–1. Paine later hoped the United States, to its own advantage, would mediate between the rebels and the French government, which was then pursuing their military repression. He did not urge support for the Haitian revolution: Paine to Jefferson, 1 Jan. 1805: *CW*, ii. 1453–5.

[126] Paine, *Rights of Man* (1791): *CW*, i. 251, 324.

[127] Fair Minute Books of the Committee for the Abolition of the Slave Trade; 22 May, 1787–9 July, 1819 (3 vols, BL Add MSS 21,254–21,256). Paine's name is not among the many individuals with whom the committee did business, including Brissot de Warville, William Frend, the Marquis de Lafayette, 'Mons. Lanthenar' [Lanthenas], Capel Lofft, John Wesley, and Christopher Wyvill. Nor is there any record of Paine being elected to honorary membership, as others were. The Society was in touch with 'the Society of Amis des Noirs at Paris' (III, f. 63, 29 May 1792); again, Paine's name did not arise.

[128] Fair Minute Books, III, fo. 53ff.

[129] Marcel Dorigny and Bernard Gainot, *La Société des Amis des Noirs 1788–1799: Contribution à l'histoire de l'abolition de l'esclavage* (Paris, 1998), 363 and *passim*. Similarly, Paine does not feature in Jean-Daniel Piquet, *L'Émancipation des Noirs dans la Révolution française* (Paris, 2002).

[130] Paine to [Rush], 16 March 1789: *CW*, ii. 1285–6. The recipient is identified in David Freeman Hawke, *Paine* (New York, 1974), 434.

is no evidence that Paine's commitment to that cause was sufficient to lead him to seek membership of the French anti-slavery society for ten years thereafter, or, perhaps, ever. On neither side of the Atlantic did Paine lend his pen to the cause.

In 1797, the Quaker physician and revolutionary Dr John Walker asked Paine why he did not write more on the subject, and recorded his reply: 'An unfitter person for such a work could hardly be found. The cause would have suffered in my hands. I could not have treated it with any chance of success; for I could never think of their condition but with feelings of indignation.'[131] It was a strange response; indignation never hindered Paine from writing on the other subjects in politics and religion that moved him most. But the reply made clear that Paine himself appreciated that he had not generally been vocal in that cause. Towards the end of his life, he was on one occasion open about it: he published a protest, dated 22 September 1804, criticizing the French inhabitants of Louisiana for demanding admission to the Union as a state in which their existing rights, because sanctioned by 'the laws of nature', would be confirmed. Even then, his objection to slavery appeared only at the very end of his text, and his objection was couched in theological, not natural rights, terms: '*Dare you put up a petition to heaven for such a power, without fearing to be struck from the earth by its injustice?*'[132] Yet he quickly seemed to change his ground: four months later, over the settlement of Louisiana, he advised Jefferson that the issues surrounding slavery 'do not belong to the class of principles' that were 'proper subjects for the consideration of Government'; they were to be considered by government as practical matters only.[133]

If Paine's writings did not demonstrate any sustained theoretical commitment to the cause of anti-slavery, his lack of involvement was seemingly confirmed by a famous contemporary. Thomas Clarkson (1760–1846) launched a coherent anti-slave trade campaign in England after 1784 and became its leading extra-parliamentary pioneer: he was at the very centre of events. After Parliament passed an act for abolition in 1807, he wrote a two-volume work on the subject, part history, part autobiography: it was the well-informed account of an insider. Clarkson included detailed surveys of the leading authors and activists in Britain and America before the American Revolution, but in these accounts Paine did not feature.[134] Clarkson also spent six months in Paris in 1789–90, campaigning to secure French cooperation in the cause. There he negotiated with many Frenchmen who knew Paine, including Brissot, Condorcet, and Lafayette; Clarkson did not record that they ever mentioned Paine's name.[135]

---

[131] John Epps, *Life of John Walker, M.D.* (London: Whittaker, Treacher, 1831), 140–1. Walker hero-worshipped Paine (143), and seems not to have questioned this explanation. Paine could be casual in claiming denominational affiliation; on one occasion, seeing the pacifist Walker not join in a toast that the tricolour would fly over the Tower of London, Paine allegedly said: 'Walker is a Quaker with all its follies; I am a Quaker without them', 133.

[132] Paine, 'To the French Inhabitants of Louisiana' (1804): *CW*, ii. 963–8, at 968.

[133] Paine to Jefferson, 25 Jan. 1805: *CW*, ii. 1458.

[134] Thomas Clarkson, *The History of the Rise, Progress and Accomplishment of the Abolition of the African Slave-Trade by the British Parliament* (2 vols, London: Longman et al., 1808). For the British 'forerunners', i. 44–130; for the colonial American pioneers, i. 131–92.

[135] Clarkson, *History*, ii. 118–66.

As Clarkson implicitly showed, the campaign's intellectual rationale was not indebted to Paine. Clarkson quoted James Foster arguing in 1752 that slavery was an 'outrageous violation of *natural rights*'; it was falsely justified by misrepresenting the Gospel, making that text 'an enemy to the *natural* privileges and rights of man'. Clarkson quoted also Bishop William Warburton, arguing in 1766 that slavery 'shocks all the feelings of humanity, and the dictates of common sense'; appropriately, since '*Nature* created Man, free'.[136] These were familiar arguments in English discourse. Paine's *Rights of Man* did feature briefly in Clarkson's account, but only as an obstacle to the campaign, creating an alarm that meant that 'the current was turned against us' in the House of Commons.[137]

If slavery and empire went together, Paine cannot easily be bracketed as an antiimperialist campaigner. The concepts 'imperialism' and 'colonialism' were absent from his writings. *Common Sense* (1776) did nothing to define a 'British empire', to explain the rise of any such phenomenon, or to argue that it was evil. Paine's writings on France equally did not generalize from France's overseas possessions, or reflect on the long-standing Anglo-French rivalry for slave-cultivated sugar islands and trading posts. Paine's imagination was seemingly not captured, like Edmund Burke's, by the early phases of British rule in India. It is possible (but not established) that Paine may have denounced (as did Edmund Burke) the cruelty, corruption, and profiteering of the East India Company,[138] but even so Paine did not write against empire as such. Finally, Paine did nothing to analyse Anglo-Irish relations in terms of colonialism or imperialism. In key respects, his mindset was different from what later readers expected. He was a campaigner against hereditary injustice and against superstition, not against phenomena reified only after his death.

COSMOPOLITANISM

Paine's self-image extended beyond 'the people'. He presented himself as 'a man who regards the whole human race as his family',[139] 'a citizen of the world'.[140] He announced that he was 'a man who considers the world as his home...I have long banished the contracted ideas, I was, like other people, brought up in.'[141] These were ringing generalizations, but their exact meaning in the late eighteenth century was not transparent unless they indicated merely a default position, the residual social relations that would necessarily be left after the withering away of the state. Most histories of nations published in Paine's lifetime gave central attention to monarchs and royal families; to the Church and its challengers; and to the actions of

[136] Clarkson, *History*, i. 50–1, 61–3. James Foster, *Discourses on all the Principal Branches of Natural Religion and Social Virtue* (2 vols, London: for the author, 1749–52), ii. 156–8, cf. 172–3; William Warburton, *A Sermon Preached before the Incorporated Society for the Propagation of the Gospel in Foreign Parts; at their Anniversary Meeting in the Parish Church of St. Mary-le-Bow, On Friday February 21, 1766* (London: E. Owen and T. Harrison, 1766), 26.
[137] Clarkson, *History*, ii. 208–10, 212.   [138] See Appendix: Paine De-attributions.
[139] Paine, 'Answer to Four Questions on the Legislative and Executive Powers' (1792): *CW*, ii. 521.
[140] Paine, 'Reasons for Preserving the Life of Louis Capet' (15 Jan. 1793): *CW*, ii. 552.
[141] Paine to Lansdowne, 21 Sept. 1787: *CW*, ii. 1265.

the aristocracy in war and politics. But Paine negated all of these, and was left with few structural features to give definition and purpose to the histories of nations. Indeed, for Paine, 'A nation is composed of distinct, unconnected individuals, following various trades, employments and pursuits; continually meeting, crossing, uniting, opposing and separating from each other, as accident, interest and circumstance shall direct.'[142] Cosmopolitanism might easily seem to be merely the common features that remained. Paine clearly meant something more by the idea than that,[143] but meant it without prioritizing the abolition of African slavery or the emancipation of Native Americans.

In other minds, however, the term had had other meanings. It was far from being an eighteenth-century invention. Edward, first lord Herbert of Cherbury (1582?–1648), while at Oxford in 1599, as he wrote, 'did without any master or teacher attain the knowledge of the French, Italian and Spanish Languages', and music; 'My intention in learning Languages being to make my self a Citizen of the World as far as it were possible', an effort soon to be well rewarded in his diplomatic career.[144] Paine made no effort to master foreign languages, even though simple grammars, phrasebooks, and dictionaries were widely available in the England of his youth. Indeed there is no evidence that Paine had any such polyglot ambitions before he left his native country in 1774.

The late eighteenth century is often held to be the birthplace of a different meaning, created by novel circumstances: it is held that cosmopolitanism now meant not being able to move freely and competently between national cultures, but being able to rise above those cultures in the name of a transcendent and undifferentiated human identity. The degree to which Paine actually transcended his inherited identities is questioned in this book; but how clearly did he ever formulate such an ideal? It should suggest caution that Paine 'had little impact in the German-speaking world, and virtually no impact at all elsewhere in continental Europe'.[145] Paine's idea of diplomatic cooperation between European nations to secure perpetual peace was an idea of shared subscription to the rights of man; but it was at this point that it became most evident that Paine's conception of the rights of man was negative more than positive, a critique of monarchy, aristocracy, and Church more than an explanation of the strength of a humanity united by a shared understanding of its rights.

---

[142] Paine, *Dissertations on Government, the Affairs of the Bank, and Paper-Money* (1786): *CW*, ii. 371.

[143] Lounissi, *Paine*, 479–517.

[144] *The Life of Edward Lord Herbert of Cherbury* (London: J. Dodsley, 1770), 26–7 (this had been preceded by Horace Walpole's Strawberry Hill edition of 1764, but its circulation was probably limited). By the 1620s, Francis Bacon (d. 1626) would write: 'The Parts and Signes of Goodnesse are many. If a Man bee Gracious and Courteous to Strangers, it shewes, hee is a Citizen of the World; And that his Heart, is no Island, cut off from other Lands; but a Continent, that ioynes to them': *The Essays or Counsels, Civill and Morall, of Francis Lo. Verulam, Viscount St. Albans. Newly enlarged* (London: Iohn Haviland, 1629), 70. Thomas Blount defined 'Cosmopolite' as 'a Citizen of the world; or Cosmopolitan': *Glossographia: or a Dictionary, Interpreting all such Hard Words . . . as are now used in our refined English Tongue* (London: Tho. Newcomb, 1656). It is not clear that Paine's usage represented a significant development from these already familiar ones.

[145] Thomas Munck, 'The Troubled Reception of Thomas Paine in France, Germany, the Netherlands, and Scandinavia', in Newman and Onuf (eds), *Paine and Jefferson in the Age of Revolutions*, 161–82, at 161.

Nor is it clear that many Americans and French agreed with Paine's rhetorical aspiration to the brotherhood of man, or did so for very long. The inhabitants of the Thirteen Colonies generally sought after 1776 to create a new nation with a more powerful sense of identity, not to eliminate all national identities, while the overriding goal of the French in 1789 was generally to re-pristinize France, not to dissolve their nation. One test of the implementation of cosmopolitan ideals was nationality law, and here Paine's unhappy experiences in the legal systems of republican France and in the new United States, as he sought to establish a nationality of choice, are a guide to the ways in which universalism and particularism might ambiguously interact without leading to the triumph of the first over the second.[146]

Examined more closely, Paine like many of his English-born contemporaries had a specifically English frame of reference: almost all his printed sources were English, as was his intellectual equipment. Paine was first briefly in France in 1781, and was there without interruption from September 1792 to September 1802: that so able a man should not acquire fluency in spoken French during that time suggests a degree of cultural parochialism in the presence of what was still Europe's most prestigious and widely spoken language.[147] As to any specifically American popular culture, Paine's writings disclose no awareness of such a thing. As to the international communication of his values, Paine's internationalism was that of a man who did not notice that foreigners might not share it.[148]

IRELAND

Paine's geographical horizon was not as wide as his image as a 'citizen of the world' suggests. The term he almost always used to identify his home country was 'England' rather than 'Britain'. One political flashpoint was almost wholly absent from his writings: Ireland. Although there was much admiration in Ireland for Paine, and *Rights of Man* sold very widely there,[149] Paine initially showed little interest in that island in return. He did not anticipate an attempted revolution, long feared, that finally broke out in 1798, until Irish activists called on him in Paris in the 1790s and enlisted his support for their cause. In 1787, Paine had argued that 'The suspicion that England governs Ireland for the purpose of keeping her low, to prevent her becoming her rival in trade and manufactures, will always operate to hold Ireland in a state of sentimental hostility with England';[150] but he did not predict an unsentimental rising against this subjection. Paine's influence was different in

---

[146] See Ch. 5, section Paine's imprisonment: nationality and cosmopolitanism; Ch. 7, section Party politics, Deism, and the Trinitarian interpretation of the new republic.

[147] For Paine's confessions of his inability to address the Convention in French, at the trial of Louis XVI in January 1793, see Lounissi, *Paine*, 708–9.

[148] Jack Fruchtman, 'A Note on Paine's National Consciousness', in Fruchtman, *The Political Philosophy of Thomas Paine* (Baltimore, 2009), 157–65, claims Paine as an American.

[149] David Dickson, 'Paine and Ireland', in Dickson, Dáire Keogh and Kevin Whelan (eds), *The United Irishmen: Republicanism, Radicalism and Rebellion* (Dublin, 1993), 135–50.

[150] Paine, *Prospects on the Rubicon* (1787): *CW*, ii. 635.

each of the societies which his writings reached, but he had an impact not least in the sectarian politics of Ulster, dominated as it was by the Presbyterians: there George Knox of Dungannon wrote in 1793 that Paine had led 'every man to think himself a legislator and to throw off all respect for his superiors'.[151] But Ulster Presbyterianism had long supported such anti-hierarchical dispositions, and with these dispositions Paine's works now resonated. Paine seems to have been unaware of Ulster's potential, however much Ulstermen were aware of him, still less of Ireland's complexities.

Despite his only distant understanding of English rule in Ireland, Paine's per-spective was confined to the present. In the regency crisis of 1789, he commented: 'Ireland will certainly judge for itself and not permit the English Parliament or Doctor's[152] to judge for her.' Paine was evidently more interested in the possibility of erecting his iron bridge in Dublin: 'as the Duke of Leicester [sc. Leinster] and the other Deputies from Ireland are arrived, I intend making an opportunity of speaking to them on that business.'[153] The Irish Parliament did invite the Prince of Wales to assume the regency in Ireland, but the Lord Lieutenant, the Marquis of Buckingham, refused to present the petition to the Prince, and Ireland was gov-erned in this matter as in others by the Westminster Parliament.

In October 1792 Paine was contacted in Paris by the Irish revolutionary Lord Edward Fitzgerald, seeking French help for an Irish rising and taking France up on the resolution of the National Convention of 19 November offering support to all revolutionaries everywhere. Fitzgerald gave Paine a misleading account of the strength of Irish preparations for an uprising, and the weakness of British troops there. Paine forwarded this information to the French ministry, urging French financial aid, but he proved not to be a skilled organizer. The French Minister of Foreign Affairs, Pierre le Brun, sent his own agent to Ireland, the Irish-American Colonel Eleazer Oswald, but his pessimistic report ended immediate prospects of French action.[154] If Paine had only a superficial understanding of Ireland, his understanding of French politics was not deep: it seems that he was responsible for giving Irish activists the misleading impression that the French ministry was com-mitted to back an Irish rising with a substantial body of troops, a belief that was seriously to mislead such activists throughout the decade.[155]

Later, after his release from the Luxembourg prison, Paine was visited in Paris by Theobald Wolfe Tone, again eager to trigger revolution in Ireland. Paine was sym-pathetic, but it took the presence of Fitzgerald and Tone to provoke him to con-cern himself. Tone, alone and leading 'the life of a dog here in Paris', necessarily admired 'the famous Thomas Paine', but Tone had to apologize for him:

[151] George Knox to Lord Abercorn, 14 Feb. 1793, in I. R. McBride, *Scripture Politics: Ulster Presbyterians and Irish Radicalism in the Late Eighteenth Century* (Oxford, 1998), 178.
[152] i.e. the English doctors then treating George III, on whose diagnoses depended the political feasibility of a regency.
[153] Paine to Thomas Walker, 26 Feb. 1789: *CW*, ii. 1278–81.
[154] David V. Erdman, *Commerce des Lumières: John Oswald and the British in Paris, 1790–1793* (Columbia, SC, 1986), 183, 264.
[155] Marianne Elliott, *Partners in Revolution: The United Irishmen and France* (New Haven, 1982), 61, 73.

He is vain beyond all belief, but he has reason to be vain and for my part I forgive him. He has done wonders for the cause of liberty, both in America and Europe, and I believe him to be conscientiously an honest man... He read me some passages from a reply to the Bishop of Landaff, which he is preparing for the press, in which he belabours the prelate without mercy. He seems to plume himself more on his theology than his politics, in which I am not prepared to agree with him, whatever my private opinion of the Christian religion may be... He drinks like a fish, a misfortune which I have known to befall other justly celebrated Patriots.[156]

Paine became a heavy drinking companion of the Irish revolutionary leader James Napper Tandy, who was in Paris from 1797 until the rising the following year, but this helped neither of them. Wolfe Tone, a more effective organizer, did not find Paine to be the linchpin of a plan for the invasion of his homeland, and Paine hardly reflected on Ireland in his major works. Paine was an Englishman, preoccupied with English history, and for him Ireland was a distraction from the heart of the matter.

Paine was even unable, as late as 1806, to explain the Union of 1801, commenting: 'As England could not domineer Ireland more despotically than it did through the Irish parliament, people were generally at a loss (as well they might be) to discover any motive for that union, more especially as it was pushed with unceasing activity against all opposition.' Paine could only offer an apocryphal story of Lord Malmesbury, the English diplomat in Paris entrusted with negotiating peace in 1802, meeting a French demand that George III drop the phrase in his titles claiming to be King of Ireland, and Pitt's adopting the union as a solution to that problem.[157] These few asides were almost Paine's only comments on Ireland throughout his published works and private correspondence; his neglect was all the more notable since Ireland was the most clear-cut example in the British Isles of a community many of whose leaders claimed to be inspired by Jacobin ideals and to be seeking a revolution with France's armed backing.

AN 'AGE OF REVOLUTIONS'?

'It is an age of Revolutions, in which every thing may be looked for.'[158] This is one of Paine's most memorable aphorisms. Yet despite his later image as a leading agent of the redefinition of a universalist idea of 'revolution',[159] Paine like his contemporaries did not conceptualize and so could not anticipate the dramatic events in America or France; the revolution he finally did predict was one that he claimed in the 1790s would take place in England, but it never happened. What, then, of revolution as such? Far from contributing to resolve the political conflicts of late eighteenth-century Europe and anglophone America by the use of universalist

---

[156] Tone diary, 3 Mar. 1797, in *The Writings of Theobald Wolfe Tone 1763–98*, ed. T. W. Moody, R. B. McDowell, and C. J. Woods (3 vols, Oxford, 1998–2007), iii. 29–30.
[157] Paine to William Duane, 23 Apr. 1806: *CW*, ii. 1482–3.
[158] Paine, *Rights of Man* (1791): *CW*, i. 344.   [159] Lounissi, *Paine*, 233–79, at 257.

language, Paine (once more, like his contemporaries) necessarily had a limited understanding of that language and those conflicts, but that was in no way unusual. It is noteworthy that even the classic recent historical work framing such a universalist scenario offered only the most perfunctory analysis of 'revolution',[160] and whether such an ideal type was widely recognized during the 'age of revolution' is still in doubt.

Did Paine have an authoritative insight into the nature of revolution as such? This enquiry must begin first with America. There is no evidence of what he may have learned about politics from such local figures as the Deists Benjamin Franklin, James Cannon, and Thomas Young, or the Presbyterian millenarian Benjamin Rush, although it is notable that many of Paine's early friends in Philadelphia were religiously heterodox, with all that that entailed, rather than having their politics shaped by any economic status as artisans.[161] Indeed *Common Sense* said very little about the colonial American controversy, despite this controversy having resounded on both sides of the Atlantic since 1765. This lack of specific knowledge was one reason why Paine was not led to theorize the idea of 'revolution' in the 1770s.

Like his contemporaries, Paine began his political career without the universalist understanding of 'revolution' that was to be developed by twentieth-century social science. For his contemporaries, the heavily reified term 'the Revolution' meant the particularist events of 1688–9, in which James II had been deposed and William of Orange and Mary placed on the throne: in that sense it could be transferred by anglophone observers to the events in America and France. The un-reified term 'revolution' was already a familiar one in eighteenth-century discourse (generally meaning only a sudden and dramatic change) and from the American Revolution into the 1790s it was not at once clear that it was acquiring a heightened meaning. Any such new meaning was not quickly defined, even among the French Revolution's most ardent English-speaking supporters. The pro-French satirist Charles Pigott (d. 1794), rejecting Samuel Johnson's definition of 'revolution' as referring to 1688, which for Johnson had been only 'an exchange of Tyrants', proposed his own: '*Revolution*,—the sudden overturning of an arbitrary government by the People...A Revolution is a total alteration of the forms of governments, and a re-assumption by the People of their long lost rights; a restoration of that equality which ought always to subsist among men.'[162]

Pigott's definition addressed politics alone, in seventeenth-century terms; it looked backward to the recovery of ancient particularist rights, not forward to the novel arrival of universalist ones. Even Paine wrote similarly:

> The revolutions which formerly took place in the world, had nothing in them that interested the bulk of mankind. They extended only to a change of persons and measures but not of principles, and rose or fell among the common transactions of the moment.

[160] Palmer, *The Age of the Democratic Revolution*, i. 20–2.

[161] Eric Foner, 'Tom Paine's Republic: Radical Ideology and Social Change', in Alfred F. Young (ed.), *The American Revolution: Explorations in the History of American Radicalism* (DeKalb, Ill., 1976), 189–232, at 204–5.

[162] This was so despite Pigott's universalist definition on the same page: '*Rights*,—those claims which belong to us by nature and justice': Charles Pigott, *A Political Dictionary: Explaining the True Meaning of Words* (London: D. I. Eaton, 1795), 117–18; Lounissi, *Paine*, 258.

What we now behold, may not improperly be called a *'counter revolution.'* Conquest and tyranny, at some early period, dispossessed man of his rights, and he is now recovering them.

Since he did not reify the terms, Paine could write insouciantly of 'reforms, or revolutions, call them which you please'.[163] It was a model that he still applied in his most redistributionist tract, *Agrarian Justice*.

Why, then, were English-speaking reformers so slow in reifying 'revolution'? Arians, Socinians, and Deists often provided the leaders of radical and revolutionary groups. They might seem to have little in common, but one thing that they shared was a necessary theological difficulty in interpreting the cataclysmic events unfolding around them as evidence of the imminent Second Coming of Christ foreshadowed especially in the Books of Daniel and Revelation.[164] Instead, the late eighteenth century witnessed the spread among some people of an enthusiasm that has been described as 'a secularized kind of pseudo-millenarianism'.[165] But this proved inadequate to generate clear political meanings.

In 1787, as central a figure as the Arian Richard Price foresaw 'a kingdom of Christ still to come' via 'a progressive improvement in human affairs' that would bring about what Scripture predicted as 'some great revolution in the state of the Gentiles'. Yet Price was ambiguous between a 'revolution in favour of human happiness' effected by the improvement of knowledge and 'the brightness of our Lord's second coming', 'the universal kingdom of the Messiah'. Price's account of the importance of the American Revolution was that of a Dissenter, since the ongoing promise of the new American republic, to him, was that 'There a total separation of religion from civil policy has taken place.' This had not occurred, but Price lacked knowledge of the complex situation on the ground in America. Far from anticipating a transformation on American lines in England, Price offered a reassurance: 'I cannot help taking this opportunity to remove a very groundless suspicion with respect to myself, by adding, that so far am I from preferring a government purely republican, that I look upon our own constitution of government, as better adapted than any other to this country, and, in THEORY, excellent.' Of the Protestant Dissenters, 'I know not *one* individual among them who would not tremble at the thought of changing into a Democracy our mixed form of government, or who has any other with respect to it, than to restore it to purity and vigour, by removing the defects in our representation, and establishing that independence of the three states on one another, in which its essence consists.'[166] This was not a threat of armed resistance, and Price was not therefore led to reify 'revolution'.

---

[163] Paine, *Rights of Man. Part the Second* (1792): *CW*, i. 356, 451 (text corrected).

[164] Theologians have tended to divide into two schools of thought on this matter. Pre-millennialists held that Christ's Second Coming would precede the millennium, a thousand-year era of blessedness; post-millennialists held that the Second Coming would follow the millennium, which would prepare the way for Christ's return.

[165] John Dinwiddy, 'Conceptions of Revolution in the English Radicalism of the 1790s', in Dinwiddy, *Radicalism and Reform in Britain, 1780–1850* (London, 1992), 169–94, at 171.

[166] Richard Price, *The Evidence for a Future Period of Improvement in the State of Mankind, with the Means and Duty of Promoting it, represented in a Discourse, delivered on Wednesday the 25th of April,*

Similarly, the Socinian Joseph Priestley, preaching a sermon on 5 November 1789 that paralleled Price's more famous one the day before, advised reform or emigration rather than revolution: 'Our Saviour says, *If ye be persecuted in one city, flee ye to another.*' Yet English Dissenters had received 'rest' from 'persecution', 'in part by the repeal of the laws that were hostile to us, and in part by the increasing liberality of the times'. In return, Dissenters had 'always shewn themselves as well affected to the constitution as it was settled at the revolution' of 1688. As late as November 1789 Priestley issued no threats, only observing that 'the present times are favourable to liberality of every kind' and claiming 'all the natural and just rights of men and Englishmen'. Even his closing invocation fell far short of a millenarian call to revolution, only expressing the hope that 'we may see the nearer approach of those glorious and happy times, when *wars shall cease to the ends of the earth*, and when *the kingdoms of this world shall become the kingdoms of God and of his Christ*'. All he called for was that his country should 'aid a neighbouring nation', by implication France.[167]

In this context even Price's sermon on 4 November 1789 was, in its dramatic peroration, strangely unspecific:

> Be encouraged all you friends of freedom, and writers in its defence! The times are auspicious. Your labours have not been in vain. Behold kingdoms, admonished by you, starting from sleep, breaking their fetters, and claiming justice from their oppressors! Behold, the light you have struck out, after setting AMERICA free, reflected to FRANCE, and there kindled into a blaze that lays despotism in ashes, and warms and illuminated EUROPE![168]

Even here was no notion of 'revolution', although that is exactly how the passage was read much later. The implications of Price's sermon were (in present-day terms) sensational, but not because he reified 'revolution'.[169]

In 1791 Priestley seemed to talk up the phenomenon, congratulating Burke

> on the great revolution that has taken place in France, as well as on that which some time ago took place in America... These great events, in many respects unparalleled in all history, make a totally new, a most wonderful, and important, aera in the history of mankind... How glorious, then, is the prospect, the reverse of all the past, which is now opening upon us, and upon the world... The empire of reason will ever be the reign of peace.

1787, at the Meeting-House in the Old Jewry, London, to the Supporters of a New Academical Institution among Protestant Dissenters (London: H. Goldney for T. Cadell and J. Johnson, 1787), 3, 5, 10, 19, 22, 24, 31.

[167] Joseph Priestley, *The Conduct to be observed by Dissenters in order to procure the Repeal of the Corporation and Test Acts, recommended in a Sermon, preached before the Congregations of the Old and New Meetings at Birmingham, November 5, 1789* (Birmingham: J. Thompson, [1789]), 3–5, 11, 14, 16.

[168] Richard Price, *A Discourse on the Love of our Country, delivered on Nov. 4, 1789, at the Meeting-House in the Old Jewry, to the Society for Commemorating the Revolution in Great Britain* (London: George Stafford for T. Cadell, 1789), 49–50.

[169] Burke, *Reflections*, ed. Clark, 62–5.

Examined more closely, Priestley had still not reified 'revolution', offering only an ironic definition (evoking, perhaps, 1745): 'every successful revolt is termed a revolution, and every unsuccessful one a rebellion'. His whole interpretation attempted to diminish its practical impact: 'I wonder that the [French] revolution was brought about with so much ease, and so little bloodshed'.[170] Similarly, the self-described atheist William Godwin in 1793, reflecting on 'the mode of effecting revolutions', reassured himself:

> If no question can be more important, there is fortunately no question perhaps that admits of a more complete and satisfactory general answer. The revolutions of states, which a philanthropist would desire to witness, or in which he would willingly co-operate, consist primarily in a change of sentiments and dispositions in the members of those states. The true instruments for changing the opinions of men are argument and persuasion.[171]

As a Deist, Paine like Godwin could not anticipate the literal Second Coming of Christ. This meant that he never responded to the millenarianism that formed one strand in the discourse of American colonists and of their crisis, and meant also that he was slow in theorizing the heightened expectations that increasingly spread after 1789 and that he briefly summed up in the phrase 'an age of Revolutions'. Where Arians, Socinians, and Deists entertained varying hopes of a great transformation, but stopped short of literal predictions of a millennium, it may have been the enemies of the French Revolution rather than its British or American friends who did most to reify the idea of 'revolution' itself in anglophone discourse; and, foremost among them, Paine's nemesis Burke.[172]

There is evidence that a substantial part of English reformers above the social ranks of the plebeian London Corresponding Society did not seek a total overthrow of the constitution; it may be that Paine's and other theorists' difficulty in re-conceptualizing 'revolution' was a significant handicap to those who would have preferred a more fundamental transformation of society than had occurred in 1688–9. By contrast, it has been argued that French speakers did reify 'revolution' in the 1790s, and as a consequence many of their heirs continued to seek to re-enact such a revolution through the nineteenth century.[173] There was a similar contest in the new American republic over the interpretation and application of its Revolution, but that contest was far less impassioned than that of France: in the

---

[170] Joseph Priestley, *Letters to the Right Honourable Edmund Burke, occasioned by his Reflections on the Revolution in France, &c.* (Birmingham: Thomas Pearson, and London: J. Johnson, 1791), vii, 9, 140, 147.

[171] William Godwin, *An Enquiry Concerning Political Justice, and Its Influence on General Virtue and Happiness* (2 vols, London: G. G. J. and J. Robinson, 1793), i. 202.

[172] Burke, *Reflections*, ed. Clark, 66–7, 69–85, 89–90, 92–3. For the difficulty of interpreting the meaning of Godwin's self-description as 'an atheist', but the lasting influence on him of his early Nonconformity, see Mark Philp, *Godwin's Political Justice* (London, 1986), 34–7.

[173] François Furet, *Revolutionary France 1770–1880*, trans. Antonia Nevill (1988; Oxford, 1992). Significantly, Paine plays no role in Furet's volume. See also Keith Michael Baker, 'Revolutionizing Revolution', and Dan Edelstein, 'From Constitutional to Permanent Revolution: 1649 and 1793', both in Keith Michael Baker and Dan Edelstein (eds), *Scripting Revolution: A Historical Approach to the Comparative Study of Revolutions* (Stanford, Calif., 2015), 71–102, 118–30.

United States 'the Revolution' henceforth meant 1776 in particular more than revolution in general, just as, in Britain, it had meant 1688.

With this reassessment of Paine's conceptual vocabulary must go a reassessment of his practical role in daily politics. It would not be accurate to picture Paine as the archetypal fly on a series of chariot wheels, since his part in the American Revolution and in the Britain of the 1790s was significant; nevertheless, the old image of Paine's ubiquitous and transformative impact calls for reconsideration. In the 1790s, not even the most ardent English-speaking friends of the French Revolution succeeded in reifying 'revolution', and the reasons for this were both specific and general. As the record of Paine's responses to a series of issues like slavery, the position of women, and poverty shows, Paine was some way short of being an instinctive campaigner against all forms of what later became widely identified as oppression and injustice: his sense of the fundamental corruption of the society in which he lived had different roots, and it was instead his critique of society's hereditarian and Trinitarian premises that had a major impact. The practical implications of his religious beliefs will feature prominently in this book.

PART II
TEXTS AND CONTINGENCIES

4

The Unexpected Revolution
America, 1774–1787

PAINE AND THE ANTECEDENTS OF REVOLUTION

Contingency and biography

The long term was, and is, made up of a series of short terms. After the Peace of Paris in 1763, experienced Britons on both sides of the Atlantic often expected that the American colonies would evolve towards, and in the long term secure, independence. But few, even among the colonists, expected that the crisis over the Stamp Act (1765–6) would lead to the American Revolution when it did, or in the form it took. The events of the next decade were dominated by contingencies, like the unwise revenue-raising schemes of a Chancellor of the Exchequer, Charles Townshend; the tightening of customs enforcement to bear down on widespread smuggling, so hitting colonial merchants; the carefully exploited colonial fears of the introduction of an Anglican bishop, which aroused colonial 'no-popery' passions; the 'Boston Massacre' of 5 March 1770, provoked and exploited by extremists; the 'black winter' of 1771 in the north and west of the British Isles and the associated emigration to the colonies of waves of politicized Scots-Irish, who later played prominent roles; the credit crisis of 1772, which bore heavily on colonial debtors to metropolitan creditors; the contrived 'Boston Tea Party' of 16 December 1773 and the disproportionate reaction to it in London; the Quebec Act of 1774, which compromised colonial land speculators; George III's proclamation of 23 August 1775, declaring the colonies to be in a state of rebellion and provoking colonial moderates to think the tie of allegiance broken.

All, and more, such things could easily have happened differently. No logic drove events forward down a pre-determined path. Few British or American publications in 1766–74 asserted any such logic. Few publications of these years could be read as containing recent analyses, aside from denunciations of royal 'tyranny', that might seem to be confirmed by the armed clashes at Lexington and Concord in April 1775. Contingency meant that the arguments of Paine for independence and against the hereditary principle need not have appeared prophetic or determinative. For those who lived through the events of 1776 onwards, those events did not have a single meaning: they had many meanings, and these were contested. Among them were, for some, ideals of hope, liberty, community, equality, and meritocracy; for others, the coercion of dissent, sanguinary violence, the devastation of property, the exile of Loyalists, the genocide of Native Americans, and the continued practice of chattel slavery.[1]

Paine initially saw no logic in events. He carried to Pennsylvania an innocent letter of recommendation from Benjamin Franklin to his son-in-law Richard Bache. It read:

> The bearer, Mr. Thomas Paine, is very well recommended to me, as an ingenious, worthy young man. He goes to Pennsylvania with a view of settling there. I request you to give him your best advice and countenance, as he is quite a stranger there. If you can put him in a way of obtaining employment as a clerk, or assistant tutor in a school, or assistant surveyor, (of all which I think him very capable,) so that he may procure a subsistence at least, till he can make acquaintance and obtain a knowledge of the country, you will do well, and much oblige your affectionate father.[2]

It is perhaps the most famous reference letter ever written, yet it is not known when Paine was introduced to Franklin,[3] how well they knew each other, or why Franklin commended him. Franklin wrote many such letters to introduce English migrants to his colonial contacts: there was nothing special in his support of Paine.[4] More importantly, in 1773 Franklin introduced the talented but unstable English army officer, Charles Lee, who sided with the cause of colonial resistance and on his arrival toured the colonies, meeting many elite leaders, before holding high military office under (and eventually in conflict with) George Washington.[5] By contrast, Franklin may have known little about Paine. Paine's life, to 1774, hardly conformed to the ideals of frugal application to self-employment and self-improvement that were later celebrated in Franklin's *Autobiography*, practices which, Franklin thought, had raised himself to a position of eminence in the British empire.

Examined more closely, it is clear that Franklin was a cautious referee. He himself did not recommend Paine; he only wrote that Paine had been recommended to him. He did not claim to know Paine or record any exchanges between them. His assessment of Paine's talents put the emigrant on a low rung of the professions: not a master of any, but merely an assistant. Franklin admitted, in effect, that Paine knew nothing of the country to which he was going. Franklin showed no appreciation of Paine's talent, or of the revolutionary scene in which that genius would flower. But perhaps Paine's standing has been unduly built up in retrospect.

---

[1] Alan Taylor, *American Revolutions: A Continental History, 1750–1804* (New York, 2016), 1–9 and *passim*.

[2] Benjamin Franklin to Richard Bache, 30 Sept. 1774: Franklin, *Papers*, xxi. 325–6.

[3] Paine only recorded that he was formally introduced to Franklin by the mathematician George Lewis Scott: Paine to Henry Laurens, 14 Jan. 1779: *CW*, ii. 1162. Franklin may have written at Scott's urging; if so, this suggests a closer link between Scott and Paine (see Ch. 2, section English Dynastic Politics and the 'Patriot' Opposition).

[4] Philipp Ziesche, 'Thomas Paine and Benjamin Franklin's French Circle', in Simon P. Newman and Peter S. Onuf (eds), *Paine and Jefferson in the Age of Revolutions* (Charlottesville, Va, 2013), 121–36, at 122–3.

[5] Lee was in touch with the anti-slavery activist Anthony Benezet: John Richard Alden, *General Charles Lee: Traitor or Patriot?* (Baton Rouge, La, 1951), 50–1. There is no record that Paine met Benezet. Alden contends that Lee's 'religious views' were 'fundamentally similar to those of Franklin, Jefferson, Tom Paine, and Washington', 299.

James Wilmer, a visitor to the camp of the Pennsylvania militia in 1776, in which Paine served, recorded a different impression: 'though Mr. Paine certainly possessed a strong mind in many respects, yet in his appearance and usual conversation, he scarce was up to mediocrity'.[6] This was too harsh, but must be weighed against later praise.

Franklin's letter also showed no understanding that Paine was about to find himself in the right place at the right time. Nor did Paine: according (though much later) to Benjamin Rush, 'His vanity appeared in everything he said or did. He once said he was at a loss to know whether he was made for the times or the times made for him.'[7] His animus against his homeland was noticed by others; one, James Cheetham, who knew Paine in America after Paine's return there in 1802, projected what he then claimed was Paine's disposition backwards to 1774: 'Paine, like Milton's vanquished fiend, looking back malignantly on England as a Paradise lost to him; availing himself of this awful pause [after the battle of Lexington], and joyously turning to his account the high-handed measures of an infatuated [British] cabinet, wrote his Common Sense; probably in revenge for his expulsion from the excise.'[8] Little evidence survives from 1774–5 to confirm or refute this claim.

Cheetham was a hostile witness using extravagant language, but felt drawn to account in some way for Paine's negations. These are by no means easily explained. No evidence has emerged that Paine went to America carrying in his mind any specific list of grievances against his homeland: he had not denounced in print the politics of Thetford, or the workings of the criminal law, or the local power of the Duke of Grafton, or the corruption of London politics, or the oppression of Dissenters, or the privileges of the Church of England, or the social hierarchy, or Britain's repeated wars. Now, the American crisis into which he stumbled may have provided the clue, the missing piece in the jigsaw puzzle, the link that explained to Paine his life's misfortunes: like colonial Americans, he could understand himself as the victim of the British monarchy and its aristocratic allies.[9] If so, everything now fell into place.

If Franklin did not appreciate Paine, the lack of understanding was mutual: there is no evidence that Paine had any significant prior appreciation of the American colonies. Before landing in Philadelphia in 1774 he showed no anticipation of an impending catastrophe,[10] despite the articulate and heated transatlantic controversies that had raged since 1765, and (like his English contemporaries) showed no sense that the American colonies were already united by any newly minted American identity. Yet political issues and political argument often ran in parallel

---

[6] James J. Wilmer, *Men and Measures from 1774 to 1809* (Washington, 1809), 8–9; quoted in Aldridge, *Man of Reason*, 47.

[7] Rush, *Autobiography*, 323.

[8] Cheetham, *Life*, 45.

[9] It is open to enquiry whether in this respect Paine trod the same path as Jeremy Bentham, whose political experiences similarly led him to adopt a visceral hatred for a man, George III, whom Bentham had never met.

[10] This is important, since the British press in 1774 was preoccupied with 'the possibility of armed conflict' with the American colonies: Troy Bickham, *Making Headlines: The American Revolution as Seen through the British Press* (De Kalb, Ill., 2009), 65–70. It seems likely that Franklin had not spoken candidly to Paine about the American situation.

on both sides of the Atlantic, the American colonies often echoing the issues and rhetoric recently rehearsed in the home country. What taxes could central government impose on the population? The colonial outcry over the Stamp Act of 1765 (repealed in 1766) in many ways repeated the terms of the English outcry over Lord Bute's cider excise of 1763 (also repealed in 1766). How could urban disorder be contained? In the absence of police forces in Britain and North America, the use of troops as a first resort might easily lead to the loss of civilian life. The 'Boston Massacre' of 5 March 1770, a confused skirmish in the dark in which five civilians were killed by troops who spontaneously and without orders fired on a mob that had been taunting and stoning them,[11] was a re-run of the 'St. George's Fields Massacre' in London on 10 May 1768: there troops fired on rioters incited by John Wilkes, killing six or seven of them (both events were minor by comparison with the capital's Gordon Riots of 1780, when about 285 rioters were killed by troops). The 'Boston Massacre' was evidence not of any metropolitan plan to kill colonists, but of the shared problems that arose from soldiers' unpreparedness and unsuitability for the task of restraining urban disorder.

The use of the lurid term 'massacre' to describe the minor skirmish in St George's Fields was itself an English locution, not owed to colonial Americans. It was an attempt rhetorically to exploit, against the ministry, English memories of the alleged Irish Catholic massacre of Protestants in 1641 (how far the casualties were inflated by Protestant propaganda to justify the seizure of Catholic lands is now disputed) or the better-evidenced French Catholic massacre of Protestants on St Bartholomew's Day 1572.[12] Constitutional issues concerning the relative powers of the metropolis and local assemblies had long been explored in the relations between the Westminster and Dublin Parliaments, and were repeated by American colonial assemblies seeking to enhance their positions vis-à-vis London. Religious denominations kept in close touch with their co-religionists on the other side of the Atlantic, and eighteenth-century religious 'revivals' were a regular feature of a rising Evangelicalism. London publications could be quickly reprinted by colonial publishers, and vice versa. Careers as politicians, administrators, lawyers, clergy, artists, or merchants could take men back and forth across the ocean, as many found: Joseph Galloway, Benjamin Franklin, the artist Benjamin West, and Paine's first employer in Philadelphia, the Scots printer Robert Aitken, were not unusual. The American colonies were different from the home country, but as yet primarily in the different balance of their social components, especially the balance between religious denominations, and did not display characteristics (for example, of shared accent) that people of the time were drawn to describe as deep differences between

[11] John Adams, as a young lawyer in Boston, appreciated that 'Endeavours had been systematically pursued for many Months, by certain busy Characters, to excite Quarrells, Rencounters and Combats single or compound in the night between the Inhabitants of the lower Class and the Soldiers, and at all risques to inkindle an immortal hatred between them. I suspected that this was the Explosion, which had been intentionally wrought up by designing Men, who knew what they were aiming at better than the Instrument employed': Adams, *Diary and Autobiography*, iii. 292.

[12] John Gibney, *The Shadow of a Year: The 1641 Rebellion in Irish History and Memory* (Madison, 2013).

Britain and the colonies: in the writings of contemporaries, there was as yet little sense of any nascent American exceptionalism.

Taking sides: some older origins of partisanship

Nor were there yet two 'sides' to the conflict that soon unfolded. Readers of popular history can still find statements cast in simple binary terms that 'the Americans' thought *this*, 'the British' thought *that*. In reality, opinion in the American colonies on what to do about the constitutional points in dispute with the metropolis spanned the whole of the spectrum of possibilities, from representation at Westminster to armed resistance and independence; in the British Isles and in the Westminster Parliament opinion was similarly spread across the same spectrum. Some British writers like Josiah Tucker and John Cartwright urged a pre-emptive British declaration of American independence;[13] others urged military reconquest. Many people found themselves between these extremes, torn in different directions. Only after fighting began did opinion tend to polarize; but even then there remained many Loyalists in the colonies, many supporters of American independence in the British Isles. To experienced and rational observers on both sides of the Atlantic, the solution to the complex and growing crisis was by no means simple or obvious. People often therefore took sides, once taking sides was unavoidable, on the basis of prior commitments; they were led to align themselves not so much by the minutiae of the protracted legal and constitutional disputes over charters and statutes as by their wider and deeper antecedent beliefs, especially concerning religion and dynastic politics, that prompted negations of metropolitans or of colonists.

If such beliefs can be traced on both sides of the Atlantic, other commitments were still absent. Colonists had been aware of their collective identities for decades, and the English, Welsh, Irish, and Scots for centuries,[14] yet these forms of identity belonged to their age, and their premises changed over time. None were synonyms for 'nationalism', the proper name for an ideology invented in early nineteenth-century continental Europe to codify and exploit the forms of collective self-awareness that arose in response to the military impact of the French Revolution; even in the nineteenth century, it never quite applied in Britain, or in the new United States.[15]

---

[13] John Cartwright, *American Independence the Interest and Glory of Great-Britain* (London: [H. S. Woodfall], 1774; new edn, 1775) was a collected edition of ten letters to the press from 20 Mar. 1774 to 14 Apr. 1774. This was a pietistic Christian denunciation of corruption, and evoked no echoes in Paine's *Common Sense*.

[14] J. C. D. Clark, 'Protestantism, Nationalism and National Identity 1660–1832', *HJ* 43 (2000), 249–76.

[15] 'Nationalism' is still sometimes applied to ideas of collective identity found in earlier centuries, but as an anachronism the term conveys no meaning. It can only be employed historically as the proper name for the new doctrine that was coined in the early nineteenth century, as were radicalism and socialism. For the conventional collapsing of this new ideology into older forms of identity see Gerald Newman, *The Rise of English Nationalism: A Cultural History 1740–1830* (New York, 1987); David A. Bell, *The Cult of the Nation in France: Inventing Nationalism, 1680–1800* (Cambridge, Mass., 2001).

Colonists did become more aware of their commonalities before the Revolution, though in ways not indebted to later ideas of 'blood' and 'soil'. One pathway was promoted by the first widely famous and charismatic individual ever to set foot in the colonies: again an Englishman, the Methodist pioneer and itinerant the Revd George Whitefield (1714–70). Where Paine was no orator, often ill at ease in society, frequently suspicious of people, and given to losing friends, Whitefield had an instantly compelling personality and an extraordinary, unprecedented, eloquence which he exercised to win souls to his conception of Christianity on a series of tours the length of the Atlantic seaboard (1739–41, 1744–8, 1751–2, 1754–5, 1763–5, 1769–70); he profited from, but was also a chief promoter of, that evangelical revival known from the 1840s as 'the Great Awakening'.

In 1774–6 Paine rode no comparable wave. But there was one point of similarity, where opposites met. Whitefield had a sense of the profound and general corruption of the society of his age, and like others this sense derived originally from a Jacobite milieu that, again like others, he had formally left behind: he was at Oxford in 1732–6, a member of the Jacobite Samuel Johnson's Pembroke College; he was an early member of the Wesleys' 'Holy Club'; he developed the practice of open-air preaching when pulpits were closed against him because of his mounting attacks on Anglican clergy, including the Williamite and Hanoverian regimes' favourite bishops like John Tillotson and Edmund Gibson.

Although he preached loyalty to George II during the rising of 1745, as did the Wesleys, Whitefield found patrons in two individuals of very different politics. The first was drawn from the leading Welsh family of Phillips: Sir John Phillips, 6th Bt (1700–64), who was a key player in the dwindling but as yet unreconstructed Tory/Jacobite interest in the House of Commons into the 1750s.[16] Second, Whitefield's patrons included that evangelical entrepreneur the Countess of Huntingdon, whose chaplain he became; she and her husband were dangerously outspoken Jacobites.[17] By 1745 Whitefield was formally loyal to the Hanoverian regime, but his perception of deep social malaise and Hanoverian royal malice persisted. In 1764 he announced in New England: 'My heart bleeds for *America*... There is a deep laid plot against both your civil and religious liberties, and they will be lost... My information comes from the best authority in *Great Britain*.'[18] Whitefield therefore engaged in a systematic denunciation of British policy towards the colonies; since he 'dominated American evangelical networks' from the 1740s to his death in 1770[19] his views commanded a special status, one that applied across the boundaries of the colonies and across denominations.

---

[16] Eveline Cruickshanks, 'John Phillips', in Romney Sedgwick (ed.), *The History of Parliament: The House of Commons 1715–54* (2 vols, London, 1970), ii. 344–5.

[17] Boyd Stanley Schlenther, *Queen of the Methodists: The Countess of Huntingdon and the Eighteenth-Century Crisis of Faith and Society* (South Church, 1997), 27–31.

[18] William Gordon, *The History of the Rise, Progress, and Establishment, of the Independence of the United States of America* (4 vols, London: for the author, 1788), i. 143–4.

[19] Dee E. Andrews, *The Methodists and Revolutionary America, 1760–1800: The Shaping of an Evangelical Culture* (Princeton, 2000), 31.

Indeed Whitefield became an iconic figure in America before any of those later termed Founding Fathers. He was buried in Newburyport, Massachusetts; in September 1775 soldiers from the Continental Army opened his coffin, cut off pieces of his clothing, and carried with them in battle 'amulets taken from the body of one whose life and ministry had become a symbol of hope and salvation'.[20] Evangelical revivalism in general, but Whitefield in particular, and Whitefield especially among the elite, played a part in breaking down the eighteenth-century patrician convention that in the public speech of the elite, disinterestedness and civic virtue were established by self-restraint and by an undemonstrative style: for the elite as well as the masses, the Revolution was soon to be rhetorically as well as physically violent, appealing openly to a supposed divine sanction.[21]

Paine hardly needed to coin a new political idiom, since wide swathes of colonial opinion had already been mobilized against the home country. When in March 1770 George III had given a cold reception to the remonstrances of the City of London, its representatives protesting at the lack of attention accorded to their previous petition in favour of John Wilkes, the *Boston Gazette*'s comment evoked the high expectations that England's 'Patriot' opposition, notably Bolingbroke, had attached to Frederick, Prince of Wales (d. 1751): 'Is this the virtuous the religious k[ing], who was to bring back the Golden Age, and to banish vice and impiety from the realm[?] How long is England to be the sport of Libertines and Tyrants[?]'[22]

Disillusionment with the monarch preceded Lexington and Concord. In Philadelphia, one observer wrote that 'scarcely, if any, notice was taken' of the king's birthday on 4 June 1774; 'Not one of our bells suffered to ring...no, nor not one bonfire kindled.' Similar distancing from royal symbolism in 1774 has been noted for New England, New York, South Carolina, and Virginia, an anticipation of the 'iconoclasm' that saw the widespread destruction of royal portraits, coats of arms, and statues in 1776.[23] Where British strategists initially saw the rebellion as primarily a New England phenomenon,[24] some colonists had already begun to think, in response to metropolitan policy, in pan-colonial terms; and it was this already spreading assumption to which Paine's generalized invocation of 'Americans' in *Common Sense* spoke.

[20] Frank Lambert, *'Pedlar in Divinity': George Whitefield and the Transatlantic Revivals, 1737–1770* (Princeton, 1994), 198–225, at 215; Jerome Dean Mahaffey, *Preaching Politics: The Religious Rhetoric of George Whitefield and the Founding of a New Nation* (Waco, Tex., 2007); Jerome Dean Mahaffey, *The Accidental Revolutionary: George Whitefield and the Creation of America* (Waco, Tex., 2011).

[21] Michal Jan Rozbicki, *Culture and Liberty in the Age of the American Revolution* (Charlottesville, Va, 2011), 95.

[22] *Boston Gazette*, 30 Apr. 1770, quoted in Pauline Maier, 'John Wilkes and American Disillusionment with Britain', *WMQ* 3rd ser. 20 (1963), 373–95 at 392.

[23] *Extracts from the Diary of Christopher Marshall, 1774–1781*, ed. William Duane (New York, 1969), 6; 'in 1774, the character of protest began to change and express a fundamental distrust of king and empire': Brendan McConville, *The King's Three Faces: The Rise and Fall of Royal America, 1688–1776* (Williamsburg, Va, 2006), 302–11.

[24] Julie Flavell, 'British Perceptions of New England and the Decision for a Coercive Colonial Policy, 1774–1775', in Julie Flavell and Stephen Conway (eds), *Britain and America go to War: The Impact of War and Warfare in Anglo-America, 1754–1815* (Gainesville, Fla, 2004), 95–115.

Republicanism

Monarchy was easily negated, and republicanism was not a colonial invention. The
Philadelphia physician Benjamin Rush (1746–1813) was proud of his Cromwellian
ancestry. He later claimed he had, while a medical student at Edinburgh in 1766–8,
converted to republicanism and to a belief in 'the absurdity of hereditary power...
no form of government can be rational but that which is derived from the Suffrages
of the people who are the subjects of it'. Claiming in 1800 to have held such views
before the Revolution, he provided the fullest account of Paine's early arrival in
America, albeit one written much later to magnify the contribution of Rush himself.
His evidence therefore needs careful scrutiny, and at length:

> About the year 1774 a certain Thomas Paine arrived in Philadelphia from England
> with a letter of recommendation from Dr. Franklin to his family in Philadelphia. Mr.
> Paine said his object was to teach a School, or to give private lessons upon geography
> to young ladies and gentlemen. While he was waiting for employment, Robt. Aitken
> applied to him to conduct the United States Magazine.[25] He did this with great ability
> and success for several months. In one of my visits to Mr. Aitken's bookstore, I met
> with Mr. Paine, and was introduced to him by Mr. Aitken. His conversation became
> at once interesting. I asked him to visit me, which he did a few days afterwards. Our
> subjects of conversation were political. I perceived with pleasure that he had realized
> the independence of the American colonies upon Great Britain, and that he considered
> the measure as necessary to bring the war to a speedy and successful issue.

This correctly reported on Paine's recent modest employment in London. But
Rush was soon magnifying his own role:

> I had before this interview put some thoughts upon paper upon this subject, and was
> preparing an address to the inhabitants of the colonies upon it. But I had hesitated as to
> the time, and I shuddered at the prospect of the consequence of its not being well received.
> I mentioned the subject to Mr. Paine, and asked him what he thought of writing a
> pamphlet upon it. I suggested to him that he had nothing to fear from the popular odium
> to which such a publication might expose him, for he could live anywhere, but that my
> profession and connections, which tied me to Philadelphia, where a great majority of
> the citizens and some of my friends were hostile to a seperation of our country from
> Great Britain, forbad me to come forward as a pioneer in that important controversy.

Rush, then, presented himself as the main actor, merely being cautious for business
reasons. Paine

> readily assented to the proposal, and from time to time he called at my house, and read
> to me every chapter of the proposed pamphlet as he composed it. I recollect being
> charmed by a sentence in it which by accident, or perhaps by design, was not pub-
> lished. It was as follows: 'Nothing can be conceived of more absurd than three millions

---

[25] The journal, at first *The Pennsylvania Magazine: or, American Monthly Museum*, was later called
The Pennsylvania Magazine or United States Monthly Museum. Rush's much later recollection is the
only evidence that Paine was actually its editor.

of people flocking to the American shore every time a vessel arrives from England, to know what portion of liberty they shall enjoy.' When Mr. Paine had finished his pamphlet, I advised him to shew it to Dr. Franklin, Mr. Rittenhouse, and Saml. Adams, all of whom I knew were decided friends to American independence. I mention these facts to refute a report that Mr. Paine was assisted in composing his pamphlet by one or more of the above gentlemen. They never saw it till it was written, and then only by my advice. I gave it at his request the title of 'Common Sense.'[26]

Rush's wording in the last sentence was carefully chosen, yet ambiguous; he was evidently unable to claim all the credit.

Benjamin Rush began his autobiography only in 1800. As he appreciated, a number of men prominent on the public stage in 1775 had tried retrospectively to appropriate some of the credit for the success of Paine's pamphlet; Rush's claim to influence is not supported from other sources. But it is possible that the idea of a pamphlet on these themes was not Paine's own. What were Paine's were its contents: as Rush elsewhere admitted, 'I did not suggest a single idea contained in it, and I believe Dr. Franklin's head and hand were equally distant from the author while he wrote it.'[27] Evidence is lacking that Paine learned significant lessons about the American crisis while in Philadelphia and deployed such new knowledge in *Common Sense*; on the contrary, it will be suggested that that work set out some consequences of what he had previously thought while in England. But given the deep divisions in Philadelphia politics in 1775, it is likely that his title was intended to signify common sense understood as 'unprejudiced reason' rather than as 'consensus'. With that meaning, Paine was not the only writer to apply the term to the American crisis.[28]

John Adams began his own autobiography in 1802. He too felt it necessary to devote space to Paine's role in 1774–6, to justify his open hostility to Paine from an early date:

> In the Course of this Winter appeared a Phenomenon in Philadelphia *a Star of Disaster* (Disastrous Meteor),[29] I mean Thomas Paine. He came from England, and got into such company as would converse with him, and ran about picking up what Information he could, concerning our Affairs, and finding the great Question was concerning Independence, he gleaned from those he saw the common place Arguments concerning Independence: such as the Necessity of Independence, at some time or other, the peculiar fitness at this time: the Justice of it: the Provocation to it: the necessity of it: our Ability to maintain it &c. &c. Dr. Rush put him upon Writing on the Subject,

---

[26] Rush, *Autobiography*, 46, 89, 112–14, 197–200. Benjamin Rush to James Cheetham, 17 July 1809: Rush, *Letters*, 1007–9, is in some respects inconsistent with this account, which casts doubt on its claim that 'Mr. Paine proposed to call it "Plain Truth."' One historian observes: 'Such partisan indirection—a respectable gentleman recruiting a mouthpiece from the ranks of the less respectable— would be a perennial theme in subsequent American political history': Jeffrey L. Pasley, '*The Tyranny of Printers': Newspaper Politics in the Early American Republic* (Charlottesville, Va, 2001), 36.

[27] Rush to John Adams, 14 Aug. 1809: Rush, *Letters*, 1013–15, at 1014.

[28] Aldridge, *American Ideology*, 47; [Jonas Hanway], *Common Sense: in nine conferences, between a British Merchant and a Candid Merchant of America, in their private capacities as friends; tracing the several causes of the present contests between the mother country and her American subjects* (London: J. Dodsley, 1775).

[29] These were evidently alternative readings.

furnished him with the Arguments which had been urged in Congress an hundred times, and gave him his title of common Sense. In the latter part of Winter, or early in the Spring he came out, with his Pamphlet. The Arguments in favour of Independence I liked very well: but one third of the Book was filled with Arguments from the old Testiment, to prove the Unlawfulness of Monarchy, and another Third, in planning a form of Government, for the seperate States in One Assembly, and for the United States, in a Congress. His Arguments from the old Testiment, were ridiculous, but whether they proceeded from honest Ignorance, or foolish Supersti[ti]on on one hand, or from willful Sophistry and knavish Hypocrisy on the other I know not.

If *Common Sense* had been so malign in its influence, and if Paine had known so little of America, Adams had to shift the blame to Rush, and to claim credit for frustrating Paine's intentions. Adams continued:

The third part relative to a form of Government I considered as flowing from simple Ignorance, and a mere desire to please the democratic Party in Philadelphia, at whose head were Mr. Matlock, Mr. Cannon and Dr. Young. I regretted however, to see so foolish a plan recommended to the People of the United States, who were all waiting only for the Countenance of Congress, to institute their State Governments. I dreaded the Effect so popular a pamphlet might have, among the People, and determined to do all in my Power, to counter Act the Effect of it. My continued Occupations in Congress, allowed me no time to write any thing of any Length: but I found moments to write a small pamphlet which Mr. Richard Henry Lee, to whom I shewed it, liked so well that he insisted on my permitting him to publish it: He accordingly got Mr. Dunlap to print it, under the Tittle of Thoughts on Government in a Letter from a Gentleman to his Friend ...

This pamphlet, Adams claimed, had been influential as well as Paine's:

The Gentlemen of New York availed themselves of the Ideas in this Morsell in the formation of the Constitution of that State. And Mr. Lee sent it to the Convention of Virginia when they met to form their Government and it went to North Carolina, New Jersey and other States. Matlock, Cannon, Young and Paine had influence enough however, to get their plan adopted in substance in Georgia and Vermont as well as Pennsilvania. These three States have since found them, such Systems of Anarchy, if that Expression is not a contradiction in terms, that they have altered them and made them more conformable to my plan.

Even on the decision for independence, Adams denied that Paine had been original:

The third part of Common Sense which relates wholly to the Question of Independence, was clearly written and contained a tollerable Summary of the Arguments which I had been repeating again and again in Congress for nine months. But I am bold to say there is not a Fact nor a Reason stated in it, which had not been frequently urged in Congress. The Temper and Wishes of the People, supplied every thing at that time: and the Phrases, suitable for an Emigrant from New Gate [prison], or one who had chiefly associated with such Company, such as 'The Royal Brute of England,' 'The Blood upon his Soul,' and a few others of equal delicacy, had as much Weight with the People as his Arguments. It has been a general Opinion, that this Pamphlet was of great Importance in the Revolution. I doubted it at the time and have doubted it to this day. It probably converted some to the Doctrine of Independence, and gave others an Excuse for declaring in favour of it. But these would all have followed Congress, with Zeal: and on the other hand it excited many Writers against it, particularly plain Truth,[30] who contributed very largely to fortify and inflame the Party against Independence, and finally lost us the Allens, Penns, and many other Persons of Weight in the Community.

Adams was well aware that colonial American opinion had been divided in 1776, and blamed Paine for making the division worse.

Adams now had to retrieve his reputation for goodwill, but still subtly disparage his rival:

Notwithstanding these doubts I felt myself obliged to Paine for the Pains he had taken and for his good Intentions to serve Us which I then had no doubt of. I saw he had a capacity and a ready Pen, and understanding he was poor and destitute, I thought We might put him into some Employment, where he might be usefull and earn a Living. Congress appointed a Committee of foreign affairs not long after and they wanted a Clerk. I nominated Thomas Paine, supposing him a ready Writer and an industrious Man. Dr. Witherspoon the President of New Jersey Colledge and then a Delegate from that State rose and objected to it, with an Earnestness that surprised me. The Dr. said he would give his reasons; he knew the Man and his Communications: When he first came over, he was on the other Side and had written pieces against the American Cause:[31] that he had afterwards been employed by his [Witherspoon's] Friend Robert Aitkin, and finding the Tide of Popularity run (*pretty strong*)[32] rapidly, he had turned about: that he was very intemperate and could not write untill he had quickened his Thoughts with large draughts of Rum and Water: that he was in short a bad Character and not fit to be placed in such a Situation.—General Roberdeau spoke in his favour: no one confirmed Witherspoons Account, though the truth of it has since been sufficiently established. Congress appointed him: but he was soon obnoxious by his Manners, and dismissed.

Worse still, Adams questioned Paine's veracity.

There was one Circumstance, in his conversation with me about the pamphlets, which I could not Account for. He was extreamly earnest to convince me, that common Sense was his first born: declared again and again that he had never written a Line nor a Word that had been printed before Common Sense. I cared nothing for this but said nothing: but Dr. Witherspoons Account of his Writing against Us, brought doubts into my mind of his Veracity, which the subsequent histories of his Writings and publications in England when he was in the Custom house, did not remove.

At this day it would be ridiculous to ask any questions about Tom Paines Veracity, Integrity or any other Virtue.[33]

---

[30] See Ch. 4, section The Debate on *Common Sense*.
[31] Paine later recorded that one member had objected to his, Paine's, appointment as Secretary to Colonel Laurens, sent as envoy to the French court: the member 'doubted my principles, *for that I did not join in the Cause till it was late*': Paine to a Committee of the Continental Congress [October 1783]: *CW*, ii. 1234.
[32] These were evidently alternative readings.
[33] Adams, *Diary and Autobiography*, 330–5.

Adams evidently meant that Paine was by 1802 a national hero, beyond reproach. Whether this was true or not, no evidence has yet been uncovered of any journalism by Paine before he joined Aitken's magazine, and Witherspoon's reported claim stands alone. But it is evident that the American colonies, before 1776, lacked theorists of republicanism.

Paine in Pennsylvania

Paine's intentions in travelling to America were seemingly unrevolutionary. In 1766–7 he had been employed in the humble and ill-paid role of a teacher in two schools in London. Yet he intended to embark only on a similar career in the colonies: 'My particular design was to establish an academy on the plan they are conducted in and about London, which I was well acquainted with.'[34] Paine landed in Philadelphia on 30 November 1774, ill with the 'putrid fever' that cut down most of the passengers and crew of the *London Packet*, and only on 4 March 1775 did he declare himself 'perfectly recovered'. His earliest thoughts were not political but often scientific, for he was well enough to consider the relations of 'Dr. Priestley's late experiments on air' to the nature of the fever, and to write home to ask for a copy of Oliver Goldsmith's *An History of the Earth, and Animated Nature* (8 vols, London: J. Nourse, 1774).[35] For Paine, not God but science was English.

Paine came to express a militantly anti-elitist world view, and in *Common Sense* and later writings devised a series of negative images of kings and aristocrats. This rhetoric evoked latent American predispositions, but exactly how it did so needs interpretation. The conventional account has been that the American Revolution was a rejection of hierarchy in order to create a deliberately egalitarian and modern state; that the absence of nobility in the colonies made the emergence of this egalitarianism natural. But it has been argued that this image is owed to a later myth of origins; that the colonial elite sought to reject the authority of only the metropolitan elite, but not to destroy patrician values and ascendancy as such. The elite that so many colonists opposed was the English elite, the elite that had often rejected colonial pretensions to patrician status.[36] Paine's writings had some uses for colonial elites, but were importantly different: Paine was against all patricians as such, not merely English ones. Part at least of the colonial elite also professed loyalty to George III, and implicitly invited him to assume the role of an imperial monarch, ruling Britain and each colony directly and equally, rather than acting as one of the three elements (King, Lords, and Commons) fused in a sovereign Westminster Parliament.[37] Consequently the colonial elite was never fully to warm to Paine, any more than was the elite leadership of the early stages of the French Revolution or the Directory. Paine could be recognized by them as something challenging, a populist, even if he did not theorize 'the people'.

---

[34] Paine to Henry Laurens, 14 Jan. 1779: *CW*, ii. 1161.
[35] Paine to Benjamin Franklin, 4 Mar. 1775: *CW*, ii. 1130–2.
[36] Rozbicki, *Culture and Liberty in the Age of the American Revolution*, 98–100.
[37] Eric Nelson, *The Royalist Revolution: Monarchy and the American Founding* (Cambridge, Mass., 2014).

Paine's anti-ministerial and anti-monarchical commitments were chiefly derived from public debates in a home country in which both were well-rehearsed languages of politics; in the American colonies, open anti-monarchical rhetoric had been the exception among the elite, but common intellectual and denominational origins meant that colonists had not far to travel to reach that end. In the metropolis, those languages, classically reformulated in the 'Patriot' opposition to Sir Robert Walpole's ministries of the 1730s and early 1740s, had been revived in the political crises of 1754–7 and restated in the political conflicts of the 1760s: they were the political languages of which intelligent contemporary Englishmen would have known most, and they had currency in the colonies also.[38]

Other, more abstract, languages were less in evidence. By 1776 Paine had crossed the Atlantic only once; he was not a frequent traveller, and not a member of any Deist International as Jefferson and Franklin are sometimes depicted as having been. The three months he took to recover his health after his arrival reduced the time available for him to learn about the American colonies, yet evidence is lacking that he sought seriously to do so. Before the publication of *Common Sense* in January 1776 it is not clear that he had set foot outside Philadelphia. He was no Tocqueville, who later toured the new republic and assiduously collected evidence before writing *Democracy in America*. Indeed 'America' appears in *Common Sense* only as a homogeneous abstraction, not as a specific set of places and people.

Even Pennsylvania hardly featured as a place in Paine's writings. The Pennsylvania in which he landed in 1774 was a diverse society that already experienced internal conflict between its component groups, often ethno-religious conflict.[39] In 1766 a Stamp Act commissioner in that colony had written to London to complain that 'the presbyterians...are very numerous in America, and are...as averse to Kings, as they were in the days of Cromwell.'[40] He was a hostile witness, but a supporter of the colonists' 'godlike cause' wrote similarly in 1776: 'The Scotch, in the Province of Pennsylvania, act like and speak like their ancestors. They covenanted against the tyranny of a Stewart, their own countryman; and they are determined with us never to become the slaves of any Parliament or Potentate on earth.' The Scots Presbyterians 'are here the very warmest advocates for liberty.'[41] Much similar

---

[38] Colonial devotion to Wilkes 'in one instance could achieve the intensity of religious commitment': Maier, 'John Wilkes and American Disillusionment with Britain', 395. In the constitutional conflicts that led to an effective breakdown of royal government after the South Carolina Commons House voted money to support Wilkes, the colonist Arthur Lee argued in 1774 that the Commons was combating a doctrine that went 'back somewhat more than a Century, into the Days of omnipotent Prerogative': Jack P. Greene, 'Bridge to Revolution: The Wilkes Fund Controversy in South Carolina, 1769–1775', *Journal of Southern History* 29 (1963), 19–52, at 47.

[39] Owen S. Ireland, 'The Ethnic-Religious Dimension of Pennsylvania Politics, 1778–1779', *WMQ* 30 (1973), 423–48; Owen S. Ireland, 'The Crux of Politics: Religion and Party in Pennsylvania, 1778–1789', *WMQ* 42 (1985), 453–75. Appropriately, Paine does not feature in these studies.

[40] John Hughes to the Commissioners of Customs, 13 Jan. and 20 Feb. 1766, quoted in Eric Foner, *Tom Paine and Revolutionary America* (London, 1976), 112, 292 n. 7.

[41] Letter from a Gentleman of Philadelphia to W.L., merchant, in London, 18 May 1776, *Gazetteer and New Daily Advertiser*, 13 July 1776, in Margaret Wheeler Willard (ed.), *Letters on the American Revolution 1774–1776* (Boston, 1925), 312–18.

evidence illuminates the denominational dimension of colonial public life.[42] This religiously based conflict was only to grow, as the unfolding revolution forced the inhabitants to make choices, for a wide variety of reasons, between rebellion, neutrality, and loyalism;[43] of these sectarian complexities Paine wrote nothing. Nor was he a high-profile political activist. As in Paris after 1789, Philadelphia politics was increasingly dominated by 'the committee movement': between May 1774 and July 1776, 'over one hundred and eighty Philadelphians served on civilian committees. Probably another hundred sat on the city militia's committee of privates.' But Paine's name has not been traced among them.[44]

For his understanding of the early history of the British empire in North America, especially in relation to the land claims of the states, Paine cited in all his published works only one source, Oldmixon's *The British Empire in America*.[45] It was long out of date: much had changed in the colonies since its first publication in 1708. Even so, Paine showed no sign of having used Oldmixon before the appearance of his own tract *Public Good* on 30 December 1780; Oldmixon did not inform Paine's *Common Sense* (1776).[46] Paine's account of the impact of *Common Sense* is telling. 'It was in a great measure owing to my bringing a knowledge of England with me to America that I was enabled to enter deeper into politics, and with more success, than other people.' In 1780 Paine offered to return to England, 'keep himself concealed', and use his knowledge of America in England's 'free and open' press to convert English opinion to American independence.[47] This, he thought, was the area in which he could be of most use. He had good reason to think so.

So Paine stumbled by accident into the American Revolution, an episode that he therefore understood primarily in English terms. He operated more as a catalyst, triggering a reaction while remaining unchanged by it. As will be seen, Paine's ideas did in some ways develop over his lifetime, but the degree of his evolution has often been overstated; in other ways he retained the ideas he held in 1774. Nor is it clear that Paine's effect in America was fundamentally to change American opinion. In 1797, the English reformer William Godwin warned an Irish revolutionary of

> an error in your calculation, & that you take the effect of political publications at a higher estimate than perhaps my experience will authorize. It seems to me that the success of such writings very much depends upon the previous preparation of the public mind. Paine's pamphlet of Common Sense produced a great effect in America, but the bulk of the Americans were in a temper considerably congenial to the advices he gave.[48]

[42] Clark, *Language of Liberty*, 218–391.

[43] Gregory T. Knouff, *The Soldiers' Revolution: Pennsylvanians in Arms and the Forging of Early American Identity* (University Park, Pa, 2004).

[44] Richard Alan Ryerson, *The Revolution is Now Begun: The Radical Committees of Philadelphia, 1765–1776* (Philadelphia, 1978), 4, 275–81.

[45] [John Oldmixon], *The British Empire in America, Containing The History of the Discovery, Settlement, Progress and present State of all the British Colonies, on the Continent and Islands of America* (2 vols, London: John Nicholson et al., 1708; 2nd edn, 1741).

[46] [Paine], *Public Good* (1780): *CW*, ii. 307, 318.

[47] Paine to Nathanael Greene, 9 Sept. 1780: *CW*, ii. 1188–90.

[48] Godwin to [Hugh Skeys], 17 Oct. 1797: *The Letters of William Godwin, Volume I 1778–1797*, ed. Pamela Clemit (Oxford, 2011), 255.

An American historian has argued: 'Paine did not convert readers. Rather, he legit-imated inchoate notions about the abuse of power.'[49] Another urged: 'What made Paine's pamphlet [*Common Sense*] so compelling...was that, though in many senses original, in its fundamentals it simply expressed what people were already thinking.'[50]

Although independence was not yet widely discussed in the press, 'The entire direction of the [Pennsylvanian] resistance effort and all of its achievements up to December 1775 pointed toward a separation from Great Britain.' Nor was *Common Sense* the first publication to broach the issue: 'Salus Populi', writing in the *Pennsylvania Journal* of 27 December 1775, argued that one set of people seeking peace favoured independence, 'as the only state in which they can perceive any security for our liberty and privileges'.[51] Yet there were differences: especially, Paine was evidently a religious freethinker in a colonial world dominated by com-peting denominations of Trinitarian Christians or Quakers. Despite common ground on political matters such as English liberties and the contractual nature of govern-ment, Paine was therefore different in the key respect of religion from most of the American colonists among whom he found himself in 1775, just as he was differ-ent from the Parisians among whom he lived after 1787. He may never have appre-ciated how different from both of them he was.

Common Sense was, in its sections relating to the colonies, a generalized work, able mainly because of its religious premises to address many of the components of the colonies' diverse populations. It was a work in which the colonies appeared proleptically as an undifferentiated single actor: 'America is in a great measure the cause of all mankind.'[52] However inspiring as rhetoric, this gesture subsumed too many different cases into one category. Nor was this argument wholly original to Paine: the Congress had already asserted that 'The cause of America is now the object of universal attention',[53] a similar though not identical amalgamation.

However inspiring this rallying cry was to subsequent generations, its universal-ism, the wider applicability of the American example, was not often obvious in 1776. The jurisdictional location of Britain's North American colonies was largely peculiar to themselves; Protestant Nonconformity cut them off from the English mainstream, and their common law tradition from the European continent. War and independence did not solve the problems these polities confronted (as the second civil war of 1861–5 showed); after 1783 the new republic often turned in on itself until 1917. Not until the presidency of Woodrow Wilson, or even of Franklin Delano Roosevelt, did a world-historical international mission and the

---

[49] T. H. Breen, *American Insurgents, American Patriots: The Revolution of the People* (New York, 2010), 262. Significantly, Paine plays almost no part in Breen's story.

[50] Michael A. McDonnell, *The Politics of War: Race, Class, and Conflict in Revolutionary Virginia* (Chapel Hill, NC, 2007), 200.

[51] Ryerson, *Revolution is Now Begun*, 151–2.

[52] [Paine], *Common Sense* (1776): *CW*, i. 3.

[53] 'To the People of Great-Britain, from the Delegates...in General Congress, at Philadelphia, September 5th, 1774', in *Extracts From the Votes and Proceedings Of the American Continental Congress, Held at Philadelphia on the 5th of September 1774* (Philadelphia: William and Thomas Bradford, October 27th, 1774), contents separately paginated, 2. William and Thomas Bradford later published Paine's *Common Sense*; it is possible that Paine read this publication before finishing his pamphlet.

assumptions now labelled 'universalism' come to dominate the self-perceptions of many Americans. Paine's memorable sentence is evidence for the generalized nature of his understanding of politics rather than for any sense of imminent transatlantic transference. Moreover, fond of his best remarks, Paine used this one again in thanking the French in 1792 for citizenship and election to the National Convention, declaring that 'the cause of France is the cause of all mankind'.[54] At most, this locution was a secular translation of millennial aspirations, not a perceptive identification of how the particular circumstances of France related to the shared interests of 'all mankind'. In the terms used in this book, the relation between particularism and universalism was a problem not to be solved by rhetoric.

The meaning of Paine's remark is also not as clear as it first appears. If 'America' was already exceptional, in what ways could it be exemplary for a 'mankind' from which its exceptional nature established its difference? If 'America' was not exceptional, why was it alone to be a beacon of hope? There is, on the contrary, much evidence that the American colonies shared many or most elements of British political discourse. In the approach to war, the colonial press reprinted many essays and letters from British newspapers that assured colonists of support for their cause by British opinion, that complained in extravagant terms about the 'tyranny' of ministries at home, and urged that the British too were threatened with 'slavery'; this had long been the common coin of anglophone political discourse, reinvigorated in the 1730s and the early 1760s.[55] Some on both sides of the Atlantic were sceptical of this rhetorically heightened discourse, like Benjamin Franklin, in London in 1768: 'To be apprehensive of chimerical dangers, to be alarmed at trifles, to suspect plots and deep designs where none exist, to regard as mortal enemies those who are really our nearest and best friends, and to be very abusive'[56]—all these things, for Franklin, were mistakes that could be corrected by rational discussion among experienced, moderate men of affairs.

For large numbers of people in the colonies who lacked Franklin's connections at the top, reports of conspiracies against shared English liberties could only seem more plausible because others, across the Atlantic, were making similar claims. Of all the groups that gave most credence to stories of the revival under George III of 'popery and arbitrary power', the most credulous and angry were American Congregationalists and Presbyterians, numerous in the colonies but in English eyes still 'Dissenters', who wove new legislation like the Townshend duties and the Quebec Act into their old scenarios of persecution, martyrdom, and final, God-assured, triumph. Of all parts of the English-speaking world, the most intolerantly anti-Catholic were the New England colonies; so that, as one historian has

[54] Paine, *Address to the People of France* (25 Sept. 1792): *CW*, ii. 538; cf. Paine, *Rights of Man* (1791), Preface to the French edition: *CW*, i. 247: 'Every country in Europe considers the cause of the French people as identical with the cause of its own people, or rather, as embracing the interests of the entire world.'

[55] John Brewer, *Party Ideology and Popular Politics at the Accession of George III* (Cambridge, 1976), 139–216; Paul Langford, 'British Correspondence in the Colonial Press, 1763–1775: A Study in Anglo-American Misunderstanding before the American Revolution', in Bernard Bailyn and John B. Hench (eds), *The Press & the American Revolution* (Worcester, Mass., 1980), 273–313.

[56] Franklin, 'To the Printer of the Gazetteer', 13 Jan. [1768]: Franklin, *Papers*, xv. 18–19.

concluded, in colonial America 'no intellectual tradition was more prominent, or more omnipresent, than anti-Catholicism'.[57]

English controversies, colonial audiences

The backward-looking perspectives of all parties to the conflict made it even more important that English political discourse for many decades had been far more divided, trenchant, and anti-Hanoverian than anything seen in the American colonies. In recent decades, high points had been reached first by John Wilkes, notably in his periodical *The North Briton*, published in 218 issues from 5 June 1762 to 11 May 1771. Its most famous issue, for which Wilkes was prosecuted, was no. 45, of 23 April 1763, an attack on the terms of the peace of Paris and on the cider excise (an issue likely to have caught the attention of Thomas Paine, who had since the spring of 1761 been preparing for a career in the excise service and whose first appointment in Grantham, Lincolnshire, was in December 1762).

Wilkes professed to defer to the royal virtues of George III, but expended his ire on the king's chosen first minister, the 3rd Earl of Bute. The king's speech at the opening of parliament, for which the ministers were responsible, was 'the most abandoned instance of ministerial effrontery ever attempted to be imposed on mankind'. In the peace treaty Britain's former ally the King of Prussia had been 'basely deserted by the *Scottish* prime minister of *England*'. The ministers 'have sent the *spirit of discord* through the land' by the cider excise, 'and I will prophecy, that it will never be extinguished, but by the extinction of their power'. Through the cider-making counties 'the *spirit of liberty*' has gone forth, 'and a noble opposition has been given to the wicked instruments of oppression'. Lord Bute's surname was Stuart. Although a firm Whig, this did not save him from Wilkes's pen: 'The *Stuart* line has ever been intoxicated with the slavish doctrines of the *absolute, independent, unlimited* power of the crown.' But the English had fought back: 'The *king of England* is only the first magistrate of this country; but is invested by law with the whole executive power. He is, however, responsible to his people for the due execution of the royal functions, in the choice of ministers, &c. equally with the meanest of his subjects in his particular duty.' Wilkes insisted: 'The people too have

[57] Thomas M. Brown, 'In the Image of the Beast: Anti-Papal Rhetoric in Colonial America', in Richard O. Curry and Thomas M. Brown (eds), *Conspiracy: The Fear of Subversion in American History* (New York, 1972), 1–20, at 1. See also 'Catholics and the American Revolution', *The American Catholic Historical Researches* new ser. 2, no. 1 (Jan. 1906), 1–40; Sister Mary Augustina Ray, *American Opinion of Roman Catholicism in the Eighteenth Century* (New York, 1936); Charles H. Metzger, *Catholics and the American Revolution* (Chicago, 1962); Timothy W. Bosworth, 'Anti-Catholicism as a Political Tool in Mid-Eighteenth-Century Maryland', *Catholic Historical Review* 61 (1975), 539–63; Joseph J. Casino, 'Anti-Popery in Colonial Pennsylvania', *PMHB* 105 (1981), 279–309; Clark, *Language of Liberty, passim*; Francis D. Cogliano, *No King, No Popery: Anti-Catholicism in Revolutionary New England* (Westport, Conn., 1995); Thomas S. Kidd, '"Let Hell and Rome Do their Worst": World News, Anti-Catholicism and International Protestantism in Early-Eighteenth-Century Boston', *New England Quarterly* 76 (2003), 265–90. The fewness of these studies in the vast field of scholarship on the American Revolution is significant.

their *prerogative.*'[58] However ironic were his professions of regard for George III, Wilkes's implication was clear: the king could not be dissociated from the acts of his ministers; both king and ministers were absolutists.

The stream of anti-monarchical invective was reinforced in other periodicals, most famously in the series of 70 letters signed 'Junius', published in *The Public Advertiser* from 21 November 1768 to 21 January 1772. Their first target was the administration presided over by the Duke of Grafton as First Lord of the Treasury from 2 August 1766 until he was succeeded by Lord North on 10 February 1770; Paine would have been aware of the Grafton family, the local magnates in Paine's birthplace, Thetford ('The finances of a nation, sinking under its debts and expences, are committed to a young nobleman already ruined by play'). The first crusade of the Junius letters was over John Wilkes: the constitutional issues raised by Parliament's exclusion of Wilkes, returned in the general election of March 1768 for Middlesex and barred from taking his seat on the grounds of his outlawry. Junius inflated this to be 'the greatest constitutional question, that has arisen since the revolution' of 1688. From there, the points at issue broadened to include charges of governmental corruption, debt, and taxes. Success was not instantaneous (an early letter was delayed while the *Public Advertiser* printed a backlog of other correspondence, including a letter from 'Common Sense'—not by Paine), but 'Junius' soon became a cult figure.

Junius depicted Grafton's ministry as a threat to the constitution and laboured to bring it down, but according to his most recent editor 'the desperate plot to destroy the liberties of the subject existed only in his own mind...The world Junius depicts is too full of malevolent and dastardly villains to tell us much except that his own mind was inflamed and suspicious...he saw himself as defending the constitution from attack by the crown and its collaborators'. But among a public supplied with little inside information, conspiracy theories could gain currency. Junius's rhetoric therefore grew in intensity, although this disguised the limited nature of his constitutional aims: he was an admirer of the British Constitution, abusive of the king but not of the institution of monarchy, and no friend to parliamentary reform. As Junius explained in the 'Dedication to the English Nation' in the collected edition of his letters, 'let me exhort and conjure You never to suffer an invasion of Your political constitution, however minute the instance may appear, to pass by, without a determined, persevering resistance. One precedent creates another.'[59] In 1776, this pertinacious suspicion was to be Paine's attitude also.

Junius expressed an already familiar dynastic critique of George III:

Are You a prince of the House of Hanover, and do You exclude all the leading Whig families from your councils?—Do you profess to govern according to Law, and is it consistent with that profession, to impart your confidence and affection to those men only, who, though now perhaps detached from the desperate cause of the Pretender,

---

[58] John Wilkes, *The North Briton*, 45 (23 April 1763), facsimile in Adrian Hamilton, *The Infamous Essay on Woman* (London, 1972), 79–86.

[59] *The Letters of Junius*, ed. John Cannon (Oxford, 1978), xv, xx, xxii, xxiv–xxvi, 8, 27, 177.

are marked in this country by an hereditary attachment to high and arbitrary principles of government?

The origins of Paine's anti-hereditarian principles have been obscure, but sources may be found in the widespread and principled rejection of Stuart claims, and in the still vividly expressed fears that these claims influenced the ministerial and courtly politics of Britain in the 1760s.

Junius focused this critique on Grafton, descendant of an illegitimate child of Charles II:

> The character of the reputed ancestors of some men, has made it possible for their descendants to be vicious in the extreme, without being degenerate. Those of your Grace, for instance, left no distressing examples of virtue, even to their legitimate posterity, and you may look back with pleasure to an illustrious pedigree, in which heraldry has not left a single good quality upon record to insult or upbraid you. You have better proofs of your descent, my Lord, than the register of a marriage, or any troublesome inheritance of reputation. There are some hereditary strokes of character, by which a family may be as clearly distinguished as by the blackest features of the human face. Charles the First lived and died a hypocrite. Charles the Second was a hypocrite of another sort, and should have died upon the same scaffold. At the distance of a century, we see their different characters happily revived, and blended in your Grace. Sullen and severe without religion, profligate without gaiety, you live like Charles the Second, without being an amiable companion, and, for aught I know, may die as his father did, without the reputation of a martyr.[60]

By comparison with Junius's vilification of hereditary nobility, Paine's later remarks seem mild.

Junius's letter no. 35 (19 Dec. 1769) led to the prosecution of the publisher, Henry Sampson Woodfall, for seditious libel. Echoing Wilkes's deep sarcasm, Junius constructed an imaginary address from 'an honest man' to the king: 'We are far from thinking you capable of a direct, deliberate purpose to invade those original rights of your subjects, on which all their civil and political liberties depend.' But the admission of the Scots to office at the expense of 'the ablest servants of the crown', and the exclusion of Wilkes from the House of Commons, meant 'the constitution betrayed', and this reflected on the king himself: 'Are you not sensible how much the meanness of the cause'—the persecution of Wilkes—'gives an air of ridicule to the serious difficulties into which you have been betrayed?...The circumstances to which you are reduced, will not admit of a compromise with the English nation.'

Junius also invoked the American colonists. They had ceased to distinguish between the monarch and his ministers: 'They consider you as united with your servants against America...They left their native land in search of freedom, and found it in a desert. Divided as they are into a thousand forms of policy and religion, there is one point in which they all agree:—they equally detest the pageantry

---

[60] *Letters of Junius*, ed. Cannon, 23, 69. Junius initially professed to acknowledge the rectitude of George III's supra-party ideals, 26–7, but claimed that this royal idealism had miscarried.

of a King, and the supercilious hypocrisy of a bishop.' Yet America appeared only rarely in Junius's journalism; even an assiduous reader of every letter could have learned little of the substance of the transatlantic dispute. The letters were focused instead on England. If the friends of liberty, as they saw themselves, were now in opposition there, the fictitious interlocutor addressed George III: 'You are not however, destitute of every appearance of support: You have all the Jacobites, Non-jurors, Roman Catholics, and Tories of this country, and all Scotland, without exception.' The Scots, especially: 'one would think they had forgotten that you are their lawful King, and had mistaken you for a pretender to the crown.' But this illegality might turn against the monarch. 'The same pretended power, which robs an English subject of his birth-right, may rob an English King of his crown.'

The dynastic element was still inescapable, and therefore still raised the issue of the right of resistance necessarily disguised behind a fig-leaf of loyalty:

> The people of England are loyal to the house of Hanover; not from a vain preference of one family to another, but from a conviction that the establishment of that family was necessary to the support of their civil and religious liberties. This, Sir, is a principle of allegiance equally solid and rational;—fit for Englishmen to adopt, and well worthy of your Majesty's encouragement. We cannot long be deluded by nominal distinctions. The name of Stuart, of itself, is only contemptible;—armed with the Sovereign authority, their principles are formidable. The Prince, who imitates their conduct, should be warned by their example; and while he plumes himself upon the security of his title to the crown, should remember that, as it was acquired by one revolution, it may be lost by another.[61]

In his later letters, Junius built on these earlier assertions as if they were securely established: 'When the loyalty of Tories, Jacobites, and Scotchmen, has once taken possession of an unhappy Prince, it seldom leaves him without accomplishing his destruction.'[62] For over a decade before Paine's arrival in Philadelphia in 1774, the American colonies had imported such strident rhetoric. It was the belatedness of their responses that needs explanation.

Nor was Paine's *Common Sense*, published in January 1776, the first publication to call openly for independence. John Adams also claimed that this distinction was unexpectedly his own, when letters of 24 July 1775 that he wrote from Philadelphia, where Congress was sitting, to his wife and to General James Warren in Massachusetts fell into British hands en route and were published in the newspapers. 'The Ideas of Independence, to be sure were glaring enough, and they thought they should produce quarrels among the Members of Congress, and a division of the Colonies...Accordingly from this time at least if not earlier, and not from the publication of "Common Sense" did the People in all parts of the Continent turn their Attention to this Subject. It was, I know, considered in the same Light by others.'[63]

Paine's outspoken assaults on monarchy as such and on the person of the monarch were like almost nothing made explicit by the colonial elite since the Hanoverian accession. Anti-monarchical doctrine that professedly focused on more safely distant

---

[61] *Letters of Junius*, ed. Cannon, 159–73, at 159–60, 162, 164–5, 167–8, 170, 173.
[62] *Letters of Junius*, ed. Cannon, 187.   [63] Adams, *Diary and Autobiography*, iii. 319.

targets like Charles I could still occasionally be expressed by the theologically het-
erodox, most famously in the Arian Jonathan Mayhew's virulently anti-monarchical
*A Discourse Concerning Unlimited Submission and Non-Resistance to the Higher
Powers* (1750). Mayhew had claimed to be 'engaged on the side of Liberty, the BIBLE,
and Common Sense, in opposition to Tyranny, PRIEST-CRAFT, and Non-sense'.
If the end of 'the *making* and *executing of good laws*' were attained, 'it is enough.
But no form of government seems to be so unlikely to accomplish this *end*, as *absolute monarchy*—Nor is there any one that has so little pretence to a *divine original*,
unless it be in this sense, that God *first* introduced it into, and thereby overturned,
the common-wealth of *Israel*, as a *curse* upon that people for their *folly* and *wickedness*, particularly in *desiring* such a government. (See I Sam. viii chap.)' Nothing
could 'well be imagined more directly contrary to common sense, than to suppose
that *millions* of people should be subjected to the arbitrary, precarious pleasure of
one single man (who has *naturally* no superiority over them in point of authority)';
'It would be stupid tameness, and unaccountable folly, for whole nations to suffer
one unreasonable, ambitious, and cruel man, to wanton and riot in their misery.'
Mayhew ended his tract with profuse expressions of loyalty to George II, if the
implicit threat was hardly concealed.[64] There were as yet few such colonial publications, and surviving evidence does not establish that Paine knew Mayhew's
Discourse. Similar conclusions could, however, be drawn by any reader of the Book
of Samuel.

Recently, such negations were overtly paralleled only in English discourse. As
has been seen, Paine's critique nevertheless evoked a latent colonial discourse, hostile to monarchy and sustained in colonial religious denominations, but this implication had seldom been made public since the Revolution. There had been, however,
at least one exception to this general colonial reticence on kingship. An anonymous
essay entitled 'Political Observations', published on 14 November 1774 in the
Philadelphia press, combined a denunciation of monarchy and a defence of popular
sovereignty with a call for independence, and did so in arguments and language
that anticipated Paine's *Common Sense*.

> Has the impartial governor of the universe communicated his attributes of power,
> wisdom, justice, and mercy to kings only, and denied the least portion of them to
> every other class of mankind? Let history decide this question. The history of kings
> is nothing but the history of the folly and depravity of human nature...One man
> still continues to be the source of misery and depravity in all the kingdoms of the
> world.

Scripture, too, taught a clear lesson: 'God deals with all mankind as he did with the
Jews. He gives them kings only in his anger.' The American Congress, by contrast,
derived its authority from 'the people': 'A more august, and a more equitable legislative body never existed in any quarter of the globe.' Consequently,

---

[64] Jonathan Mayhew, *A Discourse Concerning Unlimited Submission and Non-Resistance to the
Higher Powers* (Boston: D. Fowle, 1750), Preface, 32n., 34–5, 40, 54–5. For Mayhew's use of Samuel,
12, 33. The work was reprinted in Boston in 1775.

The least deviation from the resolves of the Congress will be treason—such treason as few villains have ever had an opportunity of committing. It will be treason against the present inhabitants of the colonies—against the millions of unborn generations who are to exist hereafter in America; against the only liberty and happiness which remain to mankind; against the last hopes of the wretched in every corner of the world. In a word, it will be treason against God.

This trust had a momentous significance: 'We are now laying the foundation of an American constitution. Let us therefore hold up everything we do to the eye of posterity.' Independence was 'essential'. Indeed it originated elsewhere:

Wise and good men in Britain have lifted up the curtain of futurity in America. Let us not be afraid to look through it. Ye intuitive spirits who see through the connection of cause and effect: ye holy spirits who have been accustomed to trace the operations of Divine Providence: ye decisive spirits who resolve and execute at once—ye know what I mean.

That meaning was nothing short of independence. 'Let us neither think, write, nor act without keeping our eyes fixed upon the period which shall dissolve our connection with Great Britain.' No evidence survives to identify the author, but his sole named authority suggests his transatlantic frame of reference: 'To live (says Bishop Hoadly) by one man's will became the cause of all men's misery.' This was Benjamin Hoadly (1676–1761), the most famous Low Churchman of his age, storm centre of the Bangorian controversy, an iconic figure for the foes of the Church of England and an enemy of those holding 'high' views of monarchy.[65]

The ship *London Packet*, with Paine on board, docked in Philadelphia on 30 November 1774. Did Paine ever read the essay published in a local newspaper two weeks earlier? No evidence survives. But since newspapers were then printed on durable paper, and not yet the ephemera that they became in later centuries, it is possible. Was 'Political Observations' unique? Or was it the tip of an iceberg, an indication of popular opinion beyond the polite circle of elite politics?

Colonial newspapers often reprinted letters or articles first appearing in the British press, and their editors' choice of copy conveyed the seriously misleading impression that British opinion was substantially behind the colonists.[66] More dramatic texts also found a colonial market. With the passage of time, the most extreme British anti-ministerial rhetoric became much more virulent than the language of Wilkes and Junius. During the American war, Paine published a series of

---

[65] 'Political Observations, without Order: addressed to the People of America', *Pennsylvania Packet*, 14 Nov. 1774, in Merrill Jensen (ed.), *English Historical Documents: American Colonial Documents to 1776* (London, 1955), 816–18. The essay was reprinted in the *New York Gazetteer* and may have appeared in other newspapers.

[66] Benjamin W. Labaree, 'The Idea of American Independence: The British View, 1774–1776', *Proceedings of the Massachusetts Historical Society* 3rd ser. 82 (1970), 3–20. By contrast, copy on America in the British press gave the contrary and equally misleading impression that colonial opinion was unanimously in favour of resistance. 'British newspapers reflected the overall tenor of printed and private information coming from the colonies, which, thanks to American patriots' grassroots purges of loyalists from key positions and attacks on printers, was decidedly pro-American patriot in tone': Bickham, *Making Headlines*, 62–5, 73. From a British perspective, thus informed, a negotiated settlement may have seemed impossible.

sixteen pamphlets in 1776–83, each entitled *The American Crisis*. Just as *Common Sense* had echoed previous English titles, so Paine borrowed and adapted the title of an English paper, *The Crisis*, published weekly in London from 21 January 1775 to 12 October 1776 and extending to ninety-one issues.[67] The anonymous authors of *The Crisis* reached heights of invective as yet unknown in America, an invective now openly directed against the person of the king himself. It was unrepresentative of English reforming opinion,[68] but colonists were hardly to know this. Like many British publications, *The Crisis* was soon shipped across the Atlantic, was reprinted by colonial American publishers, and may have been 'the country's first bestseller' in the months following the battle of Lexington.[69] Among these publishers was Robert Aitken of Philadelphia, who had just employed Thomas Paine to assist him with Aitken's own periodical, *The Pennsylvania Magazine*. Paine could hardly have been unaware of the English paper *The Crisis*.

Since 1765 the colonies had seen a legal-constitutional critique of the tax jurisdiction claimed by the Westminster Parliament. It was formal and restrained. But it was only part of the debate, and echoed only part of the American commitments that turned a legalistic disagreement into a war. War and revolution had additional causes. The year before the Declaration of Independence and the publication of Paine's *Common Sense*, many colonial Americans were urged to opt for a repudiation of monarchical allegiance not just by colonial legal-constitutional reflections on taxing powers; not just by colonial Lockeian speculations on contract theory; not just by colonial natural rights language; but instead by outspoken denunciations of kingship in general and George III in particular that came straight out of English political culture, most recently reported to them in the London periodical *The Crisis*. It well exemplified the way in which dynastic rhetoric, in continual use from the Exclusion Crisis of 1679–81 to the Jacobite rising of 1745–6 and after, was redirected, after the Stuart threat was no more, against George III; and this redirection happened first and most emphatically in England, not America.

The first issue of *The Crisis* was addressed 'To the People of England and America', and sought to link the two cases by the claim that the American controversy proved the existence of a conspiracy at home. Indeed England, not America, was the paper's focus. Thanks to colonial resistance, '*America* will remain the Glory and Admiration of the World, and be held in the highest Veneration to the end of Time ... our *Danger* is the *same*, *their* Cause, is *our* Cause, with the constitutional Rights of *America*, must fall, the Liberties of *England*.'. The only alternatives to 'FIRMNESS and RESOLUTION', urged *The Crisis*, were 'MISERY and SLAVERY'. It offered: 'It is in your Defence I now stand forth to oppose, the most *sanguinary*, and *despotic*

---

[67] Its publisher was T. W. Shaw, who also published William Moore, *The Address for Blood and Devastation: and the addressers exposed; together with the idolatrous worship of kings and tyrants, and the Americans justified by several precedents from Scripture, in their Resistance to the Depredations and Lawless Violence of an English King, and his bribed servile Parliament. Which may serve as an answer to Tax[a]tion no tyranny, Wesley's Calm address, &c. &c* (London [1776]).

[68] Colin Bonwick, *English Radicals and the American Revolution* (Chapel Hill, NC, 1977), 83–4.

[69] Breen, *American Insurgents*, 262–74; Neil York, 'George III, Tyrant: *The Crisis* as Critic of Empire, 1775–1776', *History* 94 (2009), 434–60.

Court that ever disgraced a free Country.' Its virulence was indeed not confined to ministers, but aimed at the king himself: '*Bloodshed* and *Slaughter*, *Violence* and *Oppression*, *Popery* and *Lawless Power* characterize the present Reign'; George III was 'now tearing up the CONSTITUTION by the Roots, under the FORM of LAW'. The anonymous author offered a historical context: 'We can conceive no Reason, why the *Laws* and *Religion* of *England* should be sported with, and trampled under Foot, by a Prince of the House of *Brunswick*, rather than by one of the House of *Stuart*, surely upon every Principle of *Justice*, *Reason*, and *Common Sense*, whatever is *Tyranny* and *Murder* in one Man, is equally so in another.' Not content with that, the first issue of the paper contained a hint of a social critique: 'A Royal, Right Honourable, or a Right Reverend Robber, is the most dangerous Robber, and consequently the most to be *detested*.'[70]

This rhetoric was sustained over many issues. The king was 'firmly resolved on the People's RUIN' and 'drunk with Prerogative'; the recent unexpected dissolution of Parliament was 'a Piece of *Hanoverian* TREACHERY, BASENESS, and INGRATITUDE, which has far exceeded all the artful Villainy and low Cunning of the discarded *Stuarts*'.[71] The author rehearsed English incidents like that in St George's Fields; 'these and every other despotic and bloody Transaction of your Reign, will rise fresh in their [the people's] Minds; if they should be drove by your encouragement of Popery, your Persecutions, your Oppressions, your Violations of Justice, your Treachery, and your Weakness, into a fatal and unnatural CIVIL WAR in *America*'. The people might then 'pursue with implacable Revenge the Author of all their Miseries'. The colonies themselves would have many opportunities to 'throw off their Dependance on the Mother-Country'.[72] The call for American resistance was earliest and most loudly heard not in the colonies, but in London, and for metropolitan reasons. Paine's originality in *Common Sense* has seemed self-evident to those who did not read the English sources on which he drew; in reality, Paine was effective because he was a part of a shared Anglo-American culture, not because he related to any developing print culture in the American colonies that was not already present, to a greater extent, in England.

Examined closely, *The Crisis* was a journal resolutely committed to English causes, not to American independence. It did not anticipate the Declaration of Independence. When that document was promulgated, *The Crisis* printed it in its issue of 24 August 1776, but with an introduction primarily English: 'The following is the Declaration of INDEPENDENCE of the BRAVE, FREE, and VIRTUOUS *Americans*, against the most dastardly, slavish, and vicious TYRANT, that ever disgraced a Nation, whose savage cruelties are covered under a mask of Religion. Horrid Impiety! Execrable Hypocrisy!'[73] Even now, *The Crisis* did not issue a call for a literal revolution in England. Real war superseded the anti-monarchical rhetoric of 1775. Thereafter *The Crisis* only published seven more issues, five of them taken up with reprints from *The Principles of a Real Whig* by Robert, 1st Viscount Molesworth (1656–1725) and *The Freeholder's Political Catechism*, which it wrongly attributed to

[70] *The Crisis* I, 20 Jan. 1775.   [71] *The Crisis* II, 28 Jan. 1775.
[72] *The Crisis* III, 4 Feb. 1775.   [73] *The Crisis*, LXXXIV, 24 Aug. 1776.

the William Pulteney, Earl of Bath (1684–1764) rather than to Henry St John, 1st Viscount Bolingbroke (1678–1751). In any case, both texts had just been reprinted in London editions, and *The Crisis* was unlikely to make headlines by reprinting them yet again.

Far from the Declaration of Independence prompting the paper to a lasting examination of American issues, *The Crisis* lost momentum and ceased publication. Its linking of the English and American cases had always been only rhetorical; when it came to the point, the focus of *The Crisis* was shown to be on England. It neither expounded a principled republicanism, nor a systematic scheme for parliamentary reform. Instead, it took leave of its readers:

> We now lay down this PAPER, with grateful Thanks to the Public, and as LIBERTY and VIRTUE have taken their Flight to AMERICA, the only Asylum for Freemen, we are determined to follow, and not longer struggle in vain to animate our dastardly, degenerate Countrymen with the noble Spirit of their Forefathers, against the Ingratitude of a Tyrant, whose bare-faced System of Despotism and Blood, must soon end in the Ruin of England, and the Slavery of the present BASTARD Race of Englishmen.[74]

Evidently, too few Englishmen were republicans.

Positive arguments for republican government had been even more infrequent in North America than in Britain before 1776. Before 1763 many colonists had held, or found it politically advantageous to profess, a naive attachment to Britain's Protestant monarchy.[75] As the English reformer and American resident James Cheetham later but justifiably observed,

> Accident directed the thoughts of the Americans to a republick. When Common Sense was written, the friends of independence were not republicans. Paine's invectives against monarchy were intended against the monarchy of England, rather than against monarchy in general, and they were popular in the degree to which the measures and designs of the British cabinet were odious.[76]

It was not primarily in America (outside Puritan New England) but in Britain that anti-monarchical principle and sentiment had been openly expressed since *c.*1760.

Indeed British political culture was profoundly conflicted and self-critical, where that of the colonies was often far more consensual.[77] John Adams had boasted, not without cause, about the colonists' 'quiet temper for which they have

---

[74] *The Crisis*, XCI, 12 Oct. 1776. The idea of America as the 'last asylum of persecuted liberty' was familiar to English authors before Paine, e.g. *General [Charles] Lee's Letter to General Burgoyne, upon his Arrival in Boston* (New York: J. Anderson, 1775), 8; [Jonathan Shipley], *A Speech, Intended to have been Spoken on the Bill for Altering the Charters of the Colony of Massachusett's Bay* (London: T. Cadell, 1774), 40; Charles Lee to Sidney Lee, 1 Mar. 1766, in *The Lee Papers* (4 vols, New York, 1871-4), i. 42–4.

[75] Benjamin Lewis Price, *Nursing Fathers: American Colonists' Conception of English Protestant Kingship, 1688–1776* (Lanham, Md, 1999); McConville, *The King's Three Faces*.

[76] Cheetham, *Life*, 52.

[77] Bernard Bailyn, *The Ideological Origins of the American Revolution* (Cambridge, Mass., 1967), 18–19.

been remarkable, no country having been less disposed to discontent than this'.[78] England was quite different in that respect. Benjamin Franklin, returning to London in 1757, was astonished in 1758 on England's feeling 'itself so universally corrupt and rotten from Head to Foot, that it has little Confidence in any publick Men or publick Measures; and the Want of that Confidence turns, thro' Disunion, all their Strength into Weakness'.[79] Franklin was as yet an enthusiast for London, for England, and for the empire: he did not believe this flood of self-denigration. But many in the colonies, including American visitors to London, did.[80] A key feature of transatlantic culture was the way in which political news and political denigration from London were influential in a colonial culture less able to make adjustments for a distant British author's *parti pris*. There is evidence that colonists 'absorbed the news with a surprisingly uncritical eye'.[81]

As late as 1775 an English visitor recounted his experience of America:

> the leaders have...impressed on the minds of the people a belief that the Romish [religion] is going to be established in America by an act of Parliament...I have been frequently in the country, and had many opportunities of conversing with the country people; *'they say we had sooner die than be made slaves; it is a pity the King of England was turned Papist,'* and a great deal of such stuff. When I assured them to the contrary, they seemed surprized at my talking in that manner, and were quite enraged. *'What* (said they) *do you know better than the newspapers? are we not to believe what they tell us?'* It was with a great deal of difficulty I could get them appeased; they called me a Tory, a name as dangerous to the person so aspersed, as mad dog to the canine species in England.[82]

Even so, colonial echoes were nothing like the real thing, the rhetorically strident and passionate political debate in the home country. As England's leading itinerant, John Wesley, whose experience of what is today called public opinion was unequalled, wrote to the Secretary of State, the Earl of Dartmouth, in August 1775:

> I aver that the people in general all over the nation are so far from being well satisfied that they are far more deeply dissatisfied than they appear to have been even a year or two before the Great Rebellion, and far more dangerously dissatisfied. The bulk of the people in every city, town, and village where I have been do not so much aim at the Ministry, as they usually did in the last century, but at the King himself. He is the object of their anger, contempt and malice. They heartily despise His Majesty and hate him with a perfect hatred. They wish to imbue their hands in his blood; they are full of the spirit of murder and rebellion; and I am persuaded, should any occasion offer, thousands would be ready to act what they now speak.[83]

---

[78] [John Adams], *A Dissertation on the Canon and Feudal Law*, printed in the *Boston Gazette* (Aug. 1765), in *Papers of John Adams*, ed. Robert J. Taylor (Cambridge, Mass., 1977–), i. 103–28, at 123.

[79] Benjamin Franklin to Joseph Galloway, 17 Feb. 1758: Franklin, *Papers*, vii. 373–7, at 375.

[80] Gordon S. Wood, *The Americanization of Benjamin Franklin* (New York, 2004), 96.

[81] Breen, *American Insurgents*, 103.

[82] *Morning Chronicle and London Advertiser*, 30 Mar. 1775: Willard (ed.), *Letters on the American Revolution*, 67–8.

[83] John Wesley to the Earl of Dartmouth, Aug. 1775, in *The Letters of the Rev. John Wesley, AM*, ed. John Telford (8 vols, London, 1931), vi. 175.

It is easy to dismiss this passage as moralistic overstatement, but it echoed Wesley's own historical analysis of widespread antipathies to William III and to Hanoverian monarchs since 1714.[84] In London's Gordon Riots of 1780, many may have been moved by just such anti-monarchical feelings. This was not the general language of American colonists in the controversies of 1763–74. The seeming paradox of the American Revolution was that it happened in America. But history has no paradoxes, only unappreciated causes.

Guns and religion

All these English discourses Paine had many opportunities of knowing; but there were elements of the American scene of which he was lastingly unaware. What were later called the 'ostensible causes' of the American Revolution (that is, complex colonial grievances over legal rights in taxation and representation within the transatlantic polity) blanked out, for most later students, other important elements of the conflict. One such element was the significance of violence and the threat of violence, present through the 1760s and intensifying from 1774, passionate violence that quickly upstaged rational debate about principles and that made widespread armed resistance possible.[85] As General Thomas Gage, Governor of Massachusetts, complained by 1775, 'the name of God has been introduced in the pulpits to justify devastation and massacre'; the rebels 'make daily and indiscriminate invasions upon private property, and with a wantonness of cruelty ever incident to lawless tumult, carry depredation and distress wherever they turn their steps'.[86] It was left to the Loyalists to record 'a despotism cruelly carried into execution by mobs and riots', an 'enraged multitude'. But the Loyalist press was censored; even legislators were intimidated and silenced; other men were 'driven from their homes and families, and forced to fly to the army for protection', so that 'mutual confidence, affection and tranquillity' were 'succeeded by distrust, hatred and wild uproar'. The author of this account knew too much about politics in his native Massachusetts: 'these riots were not the accidental or spontaneous risings of the populace, but the result of the deliberations and mature councils of the whigs,

---

[84] Jonathan Clark, *From Restoration to Reform: The British Isles 1660–1832* (London, 2014), 178–9, 182, 205–6, 208, 210–11, 215.

[85] Breen, *American Insurgents*, 12–18, 76–98. For a study of how 'collective violence changed social relationships' in the 1740s and 1750s see Brendan McConville, *These Daring Disturbers of the Public Peace: The Struggle for Property and Power in Early New Jersey* (Ithaca, NY, 1999), 5 and *passim*. Holger Hoock, 'Mangled Bodies: Atrocity in the American Revolutionary War', *P&P* 230 (2016), 123–59, argues that the rebels engaged in 'systematic documentation' of British cruelties to create 'an atrocity narrative' but that the British forces were not similarly organized and 'never sustained a coherent counter-narrative', 124, 147–8.

[86] *By His Excellency The Hon. Thomas Gage, Esq.... A Proclamation* (broadsheet, no place [Boston], no printer, 12 June 1775); reprinted in the *Massachusetts Spy*, 21 June 1775. The context is significant: the *Massachusetts Spy* had been reprinting the periodical *The Crisis*, and its issue of 21 June led on the first page with the text of no. VI of that London paper. For the widespread coercion, torture, killing, or exile of Loyalists see Catherine S. Crary, *The Price of Loyalty: Tory Writings from the Revolutionary Era* (New York, 1973); Maya Jasanoff, *Liberty's Exiles: American Loyalists in the Revolutionary World* (New York, 2011).

and were sometimes headed and led to action by their principals'.[87] Of this process of collective coercion, Paine wrote nothing.

This 'wantonness of cruelty', in present-day language atrocities, was an element later removed from the sanitized accounts of the Revolution that were generated within the myth of origins of the new republic. It was, however, a theme prominent at the time: at local level rebels came together to intimidate, assault, torture, expel, or sometimes kill their Loyalist neighbours,[88] and in areas where the rebels did not achieve local superiority a savage guerrilla war gave combatants opportunities for violence away from the spotlight of publicity. In 1776 Paine argued:

> He that is wise will reflect, that the safest asylum, especially in times of general convulsion when no settled form of government prevails, is, *the love of the people*. All property is safe under their protection. Even in countries where the lowest and most licentious of them have risen into outrage they have never departed from the path of *natural* honor. Volunteers unto death in defence of the person or fortune of those who had served or defended them, division of property never entered the mind of the populace.[89]

But this was the opposite of the case, as Pennsylvania's persecution of the Quakers, incited by Paine himself, showed.[90] As early as June 1775, the Massachusetts Congress wrote to the Continental Congress asking for 'immediate advice':

> The situation of any Colony or People, perhaps, was never before such as made it more necessary for fully exercising the powers of civil government than the present state and situation of the Colony of the *Massachusetts-Bay*. The embarrassments, delays, disappointments, and obstructions, in executing every undertaking necessary for the preservation of our lives, and, much more, of our property, are so great and many, as that they cannot be represented or enumerated; and that is chiefly to be attributed to our want of a settled civil polity or government... There are, in many parts of the Colony, alarming symptoms of the abatement of the sense in the minds of some people of the sacredness of private property, which is plainly assignable to the want of civil government; and your Honours must be fully sensible that a community of goods and estate will soon be followed with the utter waste and destruction of the goods themselves.[91]

In the light of the local realities of the American Revolution, Paine's contrary claim itself calls for explanation.

So does any anodyne statement about the local realities of the revolution. In the 1790s, Lafayette reproached the French, whose revolution had taken a savage turn,

---

[87] [Daniel Leonard], *Massachusettensis* ([Boston: no printer, 1775]), 4–5, 12, 14, 16, 26, 36–7, 72, 77, 104, 108.

[88] David H. Villers, '"King Mob" and the Rule of Law: Revolutionary Justice and the Suppression of Loyalists in Connecticut 1774–1783', in Robert M. Calhoon et al. (eds), *Loyalism and Community in North America* (Westport, Conn., 1994), 17–30, at 22–3, 25.

[89] [Paine], 'The Forester's Letters', IV (8 May 1776): *CW*, ii. 87.

[90] See Ch. 4, section Fear and hatred.

[91] Massachusetts Congress to the Continental Congress, 11 June 1775, in Peter Force (ed.), *American Archives: Fourth Series. Containing a Documentary History of the English Colonies in North America, from the King's Message to Parliament, of March 7, 1774, to the Declaration of Independence of the United States* (Washington, 1833), ii. cols 959–60.

with an account of the American: 'So spirited was the perseverance of government, in maintaining good order, that not one drop of innocent blood, has been shed during that revolution. Hear this, oh France!—Not one drop of innocent blood has been shed during the whole of that glorious revolution!' But he also let slip a remark that told a different story: in the colonies, during the approach to revolution, 'party mobs met and fought daily in the streets'.[92]

Atrocities by all parties did not wait for the Declaration of Independence. In April 1775, to prevent the bombardment of Boston, a body of General Gage's troops marched out to destroy a magazine and cannon that Gage rightly believed was being collected at Concord. After a brush with local militia at Lexington, the troops left some of their wounded there and pressed on to Concord; 'on their return [to Lexington they] found two or three of their people Lying in the Agonies of Death, scalp'd & their Noses & ears cut off & Eyes bored out—Which exasperated the Soldiers exceedingly.' On the march back to Boston, the troops came under fire 'from behind Walls, & trees, & out of Windows of Houses, but this cost them [the rebels] dear for the Soldiers enterd those dwellings, & put all the Men to death'.[93] Such acts followed the torture and intimidation of Loyalists over several years; now, the mutilation of the wounded and the murder of civilian non-combatants was only the beginning of the mutual horrors of prolonged war. Colonial America was a rural society, with few substantial cities: most violence occurred in the countryside. It therefore normally passed unreported by foreign witnesses or journalists, and great crowds could seldom be gathered together: there were no direct American equivalents to events in revolutionary Paris like the September Massacres and the Terror. Yet the atrocities committed by Loyalists and Patriots alike were at the heart of the phenomenon of civil war.

Secondly, violence and the threat of violence were often orchestrated in America by self-appointed local committees, calling themselves committees of safety, that 'seized control of local government' in late 1774. What Loyalist victims perceived

---

[92] *The Marquis de la Fayette's Statement of his Own Conduct and Principles... Translated from the Original French, and most respectfully Inscribed to the Whig Club* (London: J. Deighton, 1793), 41, 53.

[93] Anne Hulton to Mrs Adam Lightbody, [Apr. 1775], in *Letters of a Loyalist Lady, being the letters of Anne Hulton, sister of Henry Hulton, Commissioner of Customs at Boston, 1767–1776* (Cambridge, Mass., 1927), 76–80. For mob coercion, violence and murder see 11–14, 18, 22–3, 25, 27, 29, 64–5, 70–2, 85. This episode has sometimes been dismissed as British propaganda and conflated with an attack by an American with an axe on a dying and helpless British solider on the bridge at Concord. But there is supporting evidence: Ensign Jeremy Lister wrote of four men 'scalp'd their Eyes goug'd their Noses and Ears cut of[f], such barbarity exercis'd upon the Corps could scarcely be paralelld by the most uncivilized Savages': Jeremy Lister, *Concord Fight: Being so much of the narrative of Ensign Jeremy Lister of the 10th Regiment of Foot as pertains to his services on the 19th of April, 1775, and to his experiences in Boston during the early months of the siege* (Cambridge, Mass., 1931), 27; Robert A. Gross, *The Minutemen and their World* (New York, 1976), 127. Both versions may be accurate, and the incident on the bridge at Concord may have been merged in the army's perception with other atrocities. As an officer recorded: 'The rebels fought like the savages of the country, and treated some, that had the misfortune to fall, like savages, for they scalped and cut off their ears with the most unmanly barbarity. This was irritated the troops to a very high degree; and if in future contests they [the rebels] should meet with some severities from them [the troops], they may thank themselves': letter from an officer at Boston, *Farley's Bristol Journal*, 17 June 1775, in *Letters*, ed. Willard, 76–7. Anne Hulton's evidence is reinforced in 'An Englishman Views the American Revolution: The Letters of Henry Hulton, 1769–1776', ed. Wallace Brown, *Huntington Library Quarterly* 36 (1972–3), 1–26, 138–51.

as an undisciplined, spontaneous mob could be a group of hitherto-respectable citizens taking prearranged action to coerce those of whom they disapproved in the name of 'the people'; but their actions were far from peaceful. One historian has adopted the term 'the American terror' to describe these 'campaigns of violent intimidation carried out by well-organized crowds'; campaigns that ended in 'sacrilege', that is, 'an attack on the monarchical fabric of provincial society'. Such violence began by being targeted against those personally involved in administering legislation like the Stamp Act, but 'A sudden change in the character and targets of these attacks began in 1773 and accelerated in 1774 as anyone assumed disloyal to the whig movement was a target for brutal reeducation.'[94]

The committees that stood behind collective action 'encouraged denunciations, often based on no more than personal animus and hearsay evidence. Moreover, these revolutionary bodies showed little patience for dissent. In communities throughout America the committees determined the progress of revolution'; they were 'fully prepared to intimidate, even terrorize those who dared to criticize the American cause' in 'local show trials'.[95] 'Intimidation by committee-sanctioned mobs became the chief means by which the revolutionaries negated the love of the king.' The same intimidation was practised in Philadelphia, and was reported in its press in 1775.[96] Paine had the opportunity to understand these things before publishing *Common Sense*, but it seems he did not take it. Had he reflected on the American experience of local committees in the war of 1776–83, he might have been sensitized in advance to the activities in Paris of the Cordeliers, the Jacobins, the Committee of General Security, and the Committee of Public Safety; but he evidently learned no such lessons.[97]

Together with violence went, thirdly, the mobilization of denominations. When in September 1774 local militias all over Massachusetts had spontaneously converged on Boston, mobilized by a false rumour that the British fleet had destroyed the city, many contingents were led by their ministers: as the Revd Ezra Stiles recorded their numbers, 'East Guilford 83 armed, with Mr Todd their pastor... Haddam—100 armed—animated by the Rev. Mr. May...Chatham—100 Marched with Rev. Mr. Boardman Pastor.'[98] The teaching of many more Congregationalist ministers who did not personally appear in arms reached a crescendo of incitement. Their denunciations of British policy, originating in the 1760s, scaled a peak in 1774–6. For patriots, this might seem a natural expression of principle. For Loyalists, it might appear differently. As a Masssachusetts lawyer expressed it,

> When the clergy engage in a political warfare, religion becomes a most powerful engine, either to support or overthrow the state. What effect must it have had upon the audience to hear the same sentiments and principles which they had before read in a newspaper, delivered on Sundays from the sacred desk, with a religious awe, and

[94] McConville, *The King's Three Faces*, 286–300, at 287–8, 291.
[95] Breen, *American Insurgents*, 160–240, at 162, 164.
[96] McConville, *The King's Three Faces*, 291, 293–8.
[97] For the role of violence see Simon Schama, *Citizens: A Chronicle of the French Revolution* (New York, 1989), 858–61 and *passim*.
[98] *The Literary Diary of Ezra Stiles, D.D., LL.D.*, ed. Franklin Bowditch Dexter (4 vols, New York, 1901), i. 484.

the most solemn appeals to heaven, from lips which they had been taught, from their cradles, to believe could utter nothing but eternal truths?[99]

Of this phenomenon too Paine did not write.

The confused skirmish in the dark at Lexington was initiated not by the regular troops, nor by the colonial militia, who were dispersing after an appeal by the British commanding officer, but by the flash of a pistol, fired (as Major John Pitcairn thought) from behind a wall: as with the Boston Massacre, someone evidently wished to provoke a violent confrontation. This person escaped detection, and his identity is unknown.[100] It is however known that one influential townsman had long been eagerly committed. In Lexington the ground had been prepared by its minister, who both left a self-exculpatory narrative of events and, on their anniversary, preached a sermon that assured his parishioners that 'all things are well-appointed for his chosen people—for them that fear Him', even in scenes of 'MURDER, BLOODSHED and WAR'. The British troops had been merely 'the enemies and oppressors of His people'; Americans were, after all, 'God's chosen people'; the British had 'violated their rights and liberties, religious and civil' out of a 'lust of domination'. The dead at Lexington had died 'in the cause of God'. In retaliation, '*Great Britain* shall be a desolation and *England* be a desolate wilderness'.[101] It is reasonable to assume that the minister, Jonas Clark, had preached in similar terms before the battle as well as afterwards.

The 'New Light' minister of Concord, William Emerson, who had been appointed on the recommendation of Jonas Clark, spent 1774–5 organizing resistance and finally sent his parishioners into battle with a sermon on 13 March 1775 from 2 Chronicles 13: 12, a ringing invocation of religious duty. The good soldier would be 'a happy Instrument, under God, of rescuing his invaded Rights from the iron Claws of Oppression'; 'we...are not willing, nay, dare not be guilty of such Edomitish Prophanity as to sell, or rather tamely resign our glorious Birthright into the bloody fangs of hungry Courtiers and greedy Placemen'. Therefore

> As a friend of Righteousness, as a Priest of the Lord who is under the Gospel Dispensation, I must say 'The Priests blow the Trumpets in Zion, stand fast, take the Helmet, Shield and Buckler and put on the Brigadine.'
>
> Arise my injured Countrymen, and plead even with the Sword, the Firelock and the Bayonet, plead with your Arms, the Birthright of Englishmen the dearly purchased Legacy left you by your never to be forgotten Ancestors, and if God does not help, it will be because your Sins testify against you, otherwise you may be assured... we shall expect you will be encircled in the Arms of God's protecting Providence, and that you will live to see Peace.

---

[99] [Leonard, Daniel], *Massachusettensis* ([Boston: no printer, 1775]), 16.

[100] Allen French, *The Day of Lexington and Concord: The Nineteenth of April, 1775* (Boston, 1925), 111–12, 120–8.

[101] Jonas Clark, *The Fate of Blood-Thirsty Oppressors, and GOD's Tender Care of His Distressed People. A Sermon, Preached at Lexington, April 19, 1776* (Boston: Powars and Willis, 1776), in Jonas Clark, *The Battle of Lexington: A Sermon & Eyewitness Narrative* (Ventura, Calif., 2007), 14–16, 39, 43, 45. The denominational dimension is missing even in the latest study, David Hackett Fischer, *Paul Revere's Ride* (New York, 1994), 193–4.

On 19 April, Emerson himself was in the middle of the skirmish at Concord, exhorting his militia. Yet he had no need to invoke 'America'; more rhetorically effective was to conjure up 'the Birthright of Englishmen'. Whatever his rhetoric, Emerson, the descendant and father of ministers, was himself a slaveowner who emancipated his slaves only on his deathbed.[102]

Clergy of the denominations of 'Old Dissent'—the denominations that had separated themselves from the Church of England after the restoration of the monarchy in 1660—were heirs to a political theology with roots in late sixteenth-century Separatism. It emphasized rights, confirmed to individuals by a covenant (the antecedent of the later language of compact or contract) with God. It gave the community of the 'gathered church' a large role in disciplining backsliders. Its forms of church government were democratic routes to communal coercion, providing for the election of clergy and sometimes even for their dismissal. In matters of state, that political theology had since the late sixteenth century asserted that rulers derived their authority from the consent of the governed, but made this platitude a potentially effective doctrine by imposing on the godly not just the right but the duty of resisting sinful monarchs, if necessary by armed force.

Later historians could reinterpret this mindset as secular assent, either explicit or instinctive, to the doctrines of John Locke (1634–1704), and treat this assent as an index to the self-assertion in the American Revolution of the 'common man'. But this conclusion bespeaks the imposition of present-day assumptions onto a Christian culture. Locke was certainly cited in the colonies during the Revolution, as he long had been and was into the 1770s much more widely cited in English culture as a (retrospectively adopted) patron saint of the Revolution of 1688. Between a few pamphleteers there was a brief transatlantic contest to claim the authority of Locke for the metropolitan or the colonial cause. But few even of the colonial elite had studied his political writings, and the mass of the colonists are unlikely to have heard of him. Given the deeply subversive implications of his *Two Treatises of Government*, the revealing evidence about Locke's role in the American Revolution is not that he was sometimes invoked by the rebels but that he was not more often and more widely invoked.

Locke was one among many seventeenth-century theorists to use the then vital notions of natural rights and political contract; in his day, as in the 1770s, these ideas were given practical force chiefly for those who already subscribed to the denominational idea of a divine covenant. Locke himself, from a Puritan family, did not invent the notion of contract but derived it from a seventeenth-century English debate, primarily a theological debate, which was the inheritance of many colonial Americans also. Given the other aims of their already old political theology, most colonists in the decades before the Revolution had done little or nothing to explore alternative republican or democratic frames of government, or even to anticipate independence. Locke's political writings were not republished in colonial

---

[102] *Diaries and Letters of William Emerson 1743–1776*, ed. Amelia Forbes Emerson (Concord, Mass.: privately printed, 1972), 42, 59–75, at 68, 74; Clark, *Language of Liberty*, 372; Fischer, *Paul Revere's Ride*, 205.

America until a single edition of the second of his *Two Treatises of Government* alone in Boston in 1773. Even then, its limited impact cautions against assuming that famous texts were in any simple sense a necessary and sufficient cause of the Revolution.[103]

The history of colonial publishing suggests that the tradition of natural law writing did not grow in the eighteenth century through sustained attention to its seventeenth-century authors (Grotius, Pufendorf, Selden, Locke) but was chiefly taken by eighteenth-century Britons on both sides of the Atlantic from the intellectual resources of their own time, notably religious resources. Colonists had not waited for the 1773 edition of Locke's *Second Treatise* to form their ideas. What mattered in 1774–6 was the triggering of notions of a right of resistance, providing not just a secular but a religious sanction for threatened violence or actual atrocity perpetrated by those who still wished to see themselves as God-fearing. In these years, several components came together in the American colonies to create a crisis, including older English Whig rhetoric denouncing tyranny, older English Puritan ideas stigmatizing unrighteousness, and the 'Patriot' language of the 1730s invoking idealistic self-sacrifice for the cause of one's posterity. Into this context intruded a recent English migrant who knew the language of the 1730s and 1740s, but was much less aware of colonial circumstances.

Appropriately, colonial clergy played key roles as catalysts of rebellion, especially in New England and the middle colonies.[104] Peter Oliver, Chief Justice of Massachusetts, called them with only some exaggeration 'Mr. *Otis's* black Regiment, the *dissenting Clergy*, who took so active a Part in the Rebellion'.[105] Joseph Galloway wrote in 1780 that the first Continental Congress in 1774 had at once divided into 'two parties...One intended candidly and clearly to define American rights' and 'to form a more solid and constitutional union between the two countries'; the other had, since the Stamp Act crisis, covertly intended the use of arms to establish 'American Independence'. The latter were 'congregational and presbyterian republicans, or men of bankrupt fortunes, overwhelmed in debt to the British merchants'.[106] Of their role Paine was apparently unaware. He was not an English Nonconformist: not a Presbyterian, Baptist, Congregationalist, or Quaker. He never showed an

---

[103] It was produced in 1773 by the Boston publishers Edes and Gill, who were closely associated with New England activists like John Adams and Samuel Adams (the second of whom was unusual in often citing Locke). Despite assiduous advertising in the *Boston Gazette*, the edition had not sold out by 1779; no other American publisher reprinted it. It 'might be advantageous...to treat the literature of revolution as an effect rather than a cause...In a certain sense, the Revolution helped canonize the *Second Treatise*...Locke was almost certainly more frequently read in the aftermath of the Revolution than in its prelude': Eric Slauter, 'Reading and Radicalization: Print, Politics, and the American Revolution', *Early American Studies* 8 (2010), 5–40, at 9, 18, 20–1, 25, 35, 37.

[104] New England clergy, with the gentry, were 'not only key transmitters of information, they were also gatekeepers who were broadly responsible for screening the passage of information and its diffusion to the public at large': Richard D. Brown, *Knowledge is Power: The Diffusion of Information in Early America, 1700–1865* (New York, 1989), 33, 65–81.

[105] *Peter Oliver's Origin & Progress of the American Rebellion*, ed. Douglass Adair and John A. Schutz (San Marino, Calif., 1961), 41, 53, 63–4, 106, 149.

[106] [Joseph Galloway], *Historical and Political Reflections on the Rise and Progress of the American Rebellion* (London: G. Wilkie, 1780), 66–7.

understanding of the connection between revolution, religion, committees of public safety, and mass violence.

The author's social location resisted contextual interpretation at the time, however, for Paine's pamphlet was anonymous. Its manuscript was conveyed through an intermediary to the Philadelphia printer Robert Bell, a Scottish migrant who had been ten years in the colonies; Bell published it on 9 or 10 January 1776. No evidence survives to establish why Paine wanted to preserve his anonymity, but he may thereby have sought to give weight to a publication by a man of no social standing. Ironically, Paine's first enemy was this Scot, who, in Paine's view, attempted to cheat him out of the author's rightful share of the profits. Paine turned to another publisher, W. and T. Bradford, and brought out an extended edition; Bell responded to the public protests of the still-anonymous author with a wave of personal abuse and denigration, pirated Paine's new material, and continued to sell his, Bell's, own further editions of the pamphlet. The subsequent controversy led each side to set out its case in the newspapers; this provoked what is probably Paine's statement in the *Pennsylvania Evening Post* of 30 January 1776 'That he first intended the above work to have been printed in a series of letters in the news-papers, but was dissuaded therefrom, on account of the impossibility of getting them generally inserted'.[107] If so, it seems that Paine became one of the greatest pamphleteers of the eighteenth century because he was no natural journalist.

PAINE'S ARGUMENT: *COMMON SENSE*

England's Patriot opposition and the absent alternatives

Common Sense argued that no negotiated compromise with Britain was possible, that the colonies should declare independence, and that they should adopt a republican system of government. It appealed in remarkably heightened language to the civic virtue and the self-sacrifice of the individual. This simple message, Paine's simple but inspiring prose, and the simple fact that independence was to be the outcome, have distracted attention from the considerable complexities of the pamphlet.

Where, first, did Paine's ideas come from? The ideological contexts explored above permit a better historical understanding of the contemporary meanings of *Common Sense*. Remarks made by George Lewis Scott in London may have formed in Paine's mind a negative image of George III, but more broadly Scott may have crystallized Paine's thinking drawn from the latter's indebtedness to the idioms of England's 'Patriot' opposition to the early eighteenth-century Hanoverian regime, with that opposition's reliance on civic virtue to conceptualize and combat the corruption of Sir Robert Walpole's ministry. Others may have drawn this idiom directly from ancient Rome; Paine's rejection of a classical education suggests that his

---

[107] Richard Gimbel, *Thomas Paine: A Bibliographical Check list of Common Sense with an Account of its Publication* (New Haven, 1956), 27. The controversy, and the competing editions, may also explain some of the pamphlet's initial sales.

sources were close at hand.[108] It is possible that neither this general orientation, nor Paine's images of George III, were immediately decisive when Paine landed in Philadelphia. He later claimed that the skirmishes at Lexington and Concord had been his catalyst, yet *Common Sense* appeared almost nine months afterwards: although he was not a fast writer, he may not have immediately appreciated the political implications of the bloodshed on 19 April 1775, implications that in the pamphlet he claimed were self-evident.

This slow reaction is evidence that Paine's advocacy of independence for the Thirteen Colonies may not have been primarily a swift, self-evident, natural-rights-driven, response to events but a gradual appreciation of some of the implications of prior English commitments against monarchy and the hereditary principle, and perhaps of prior Deist premises. Nor was his pamphlet any simple attempt to report or echo public opinion, as Paine acknowledged. He began his Introduction: 'Perhaps the Sentiments contained in the following pages, are not *yet* sufficiently fashionable to procure them a general Favor.'[109] Although Paine often thereafter used the nom de plume 'Common Sense', and described himself on the title pages of his subsequent publications as the author of that work, he did nothing to develop the persona or to reify the idea. This is comprehensible, if the chosen title was a last-minute afterthought. But these absences are also absences of evidence that Paine saw himself in 1776 or later in any coherent or developed way as the agent of a new cultural or political populism.[110] Moreover, it seems that no other colonial American publications used a reified notion of common sense in support of their armed resistance.

These antecedents for Paine's ideas make more understandable the absence of several large themes from *Common Sense*. It is too easy to project back assumptions drawn from later experience, and especially here. Whatever the uses to which *Common Sense* would be put in the 'civil religion' of the twentieth-century United States, it is important that the text contained no reified blueprint for revolution. Revolutionary changes unfolded in 1776–83 anyway, but in forms that Paine's contemporaries had never anticipated and did not fully understand. *Common Sense* did not include any call to enact 'the American Revolution', nor did it condemn 'the British Empire'.[111] Indeed the pamphlet did not reify or exploit a concept of 'revolution' at all.[112] The term 'revolution' did not yet embody a model of social revolution in any twentieth-century sense.[113]

---

[108] See Ch. 2, section English Dynastic Politics and the 'Patriot' Opposition.

[109] [Paine], *Common Sense* (1776): *CW*, i. 3.

[110] These continuing absences are more noteworthy since Paine's critics in 1776, like Charles Inglis, Henry Middleton, and William Smith, and his critics in the 1790s, did seek to appropriate the notion 'common sense' and use it against him, although (it might be argued) without significantly developing it: Lounissi, *Paine*, 238–46.

[111] The only empire in Paine's tract was the Russian: [Paine], *Common Sense* (1776): *CW*, i. 34.

[112] For an argument that in America 'the cause of constitutionalism superseded and subsumed the idea of revolution' see Jack Rakove, 'Constitutionalism: The Happiest Revolutionary Script', in Keith Michael Baker and Dan Edelstein (eds), *Scripting Revolution: A Historical Approach to the Comparative Study of Revolutions* (Stanford, Calif., 2015), 103–17, at 105.

[113] For the much later emergence of this idea, in a different theatre, see Keith Michael Baker, 'Inventing the French Revolution', in Baker, *Inventing the French Revolution: Essays on French Political Culture in the Eighteenth Century* (Cambridge, 1990), 203–23.

Instead, Paine, like many English observers,[114] soon pictured events in America as a civil war, a conflict of just two sides in which one side must be wholly in the right, the other wholly in the wrong. He was pre-committed to a simple binary interpretation, that 'The laying a country desolate with fire and sword, declaring war against the natural rights of all mankind, and extirpating the defenders thereof from the face of the earth' was solely the responsibility of 'the royal brute of Great Britain'. This conduct was, therefore, unforgivable: 'hath your house been burnt? Hath your property been destroyed before your face? Are your wife and children destitute of a bed to lie on, or bread to live on? Have you lost a parent or a child by their hands, and yourself the ruined and wretched survivor?' Only a coward could 'shake hands with the murderers', that is, the enemy. After news of the battle of Lexington, Paine claimed, 'I rejected the hardened, sullen-tempered Pharoah of England for ever; and disdain the wretch, that with the pretended title of FATHER OF HIS PEOPLE can unfeelingly hear of their slaughter, and composedly sleep with their blood upon his soul.'[115] It was an English idiom, found also in that English newspaper, *The Crisis*. Nothing specifically American informed Paine's alignment against monarchy.

What did Paine bring to the writing of *Common Sense*? In 1794, he wrote an autobiographical note which implied the chronological priority of his 'moral and philosophic principles':

> I had no disposition for what is called politics. It presented to my mind no other idea than as contained in the word Jockeyship. When, therefore, I turned my thoughts toward matter of government I had to form a system for myself that accorded with the moral and philosophic principles in which I have been educated. I saw, or at least I thought I saw, a vast scene opening itself to the world in the affairs of America, and it appeared to me that unless the Americans changed the plan they were pursuing with respect to the government of England, and declared themselves independent, they would not only involve themselves in a multiplicity of new difficulties, but shut out the prospect that was then offering itself to mankind through their means. It was from these motives that I published the work known by the name of 'Common Sense,' which was the first work I ever did publish; and so far as I can judge of myself, I believe I should never have been known in the world as an author on any subject whatever had it not been for the affairs of America.[116]

---

[114] e.g. [John Roebuck], *An Enquiry, whether the Guilt of the Present Civil War in America, Ought to be Imputed to Great Britain or America* (London: John Donaldson, 1776); David Hartley, *Substance of a Speech in Parliament. Upon the State of the Nation and the Present Civil War with America* (London: J. Almon, 1776); *An Unconnected Whig's Address to the Public; upon the Present Civil War, the State of Public Affairs, and the Real Cause of all the National Calamities* (London: G. Kearsley, 1777); [John Hall], *The History of the Civil War in America. Vol. I. Comprehending the Campaigns of 1775, 1776, and 1777. By an Officer of the Army* (London: T. Payne and J. Sewell, 1780) [all published]; Anthony Stokes, *A View of the Constitution of the British Colonies, in North-America and the West Indies, at the Time the Civil War broke out in the Continent of America* (London: for the author, 1783).

[115] [Paine], *Common Sense* (1776): *CW*, i. 3, 22, 25, 29.

[116] Paine, *The Age of Reason* (1794): *CW*, i. 496–7. Paine's pamphlet on the pay of excise officers had been printed for private circulation; his essays in the Philadephia press may not have counted, in his mind, as separate publications.

A key phrase was 'or at least I thought I saw', for it was this perception to which Paine's antecedent beliefs led him, not any independent reality. Religion and natural philosophy came first, then, but this was not obvious from the text: it is likely that in 1776 Paine did not put his Deist cards on the table.

Much else was absent from the pamphlet. In *Common Sense* and elsewhere, Paine wrote nothing about the sophisticated and detailed controversy on the legal and constitutional position of the colonies that had raged since the Stamp Act crisis in 1765.[117] He did not cite the hitherto-leading colonial contribution to the debate, John Dickinson's *Letters from a Farmer in Pennsylvania* (Philadelphia: David Hall and William Sellers, 1768). Paine detailed no grievances against colonial governors, clergy, or tax officials (a notable omission, given his own career as an excise officer). He wrote nothing on the history of the colonies, and framed no argument (as others did)[118] about how the early Puritan settlers had imbued the colonies with a love of liberty and detestation of 'arbitrary power'. Thomas Jefferson, in one of the most famous pamphlets of 1774, reprinted the same year in Philadelphia, combined natural rights language with an account of liberty-loving Saxon 'ancestors' whose private-enterprise invasion of Britain, he argued, did not materially differ from that of the 'individual adventurers', the Britons who conquered and settled America, unindebted to 'the British public'.[119] Paine omitted both the Puritans and the Saxons; he looked back not on some early founding of liberties but on 'dark and slavish times';[120] he offered no outline of colonial American history to prove his points about its future directions, or the independence of society from the state.

Similarly, where Jefferson in his *Summary View* set out an overview of the imperial legislation regulating trade that, he argued, disadvantaged colonial American producers and merchants,[121] Paine wrote nothing about these economic dimensions of the conflict. He also wrote nothing about the governmental role that the Second Continental Congress, sitting in Philadelphia from 10 May 1775, was creating for itself as it dealt with more and more practical business, or about the efforts of moderates among the delegates to find a negotiated settlement.[122] Paine did not discuss 'democracy', a term that only became widely popularized in American

---

[117] Appropriately, Paine does not feature in a recent survey: Jack P. Greene, *The Constitutional Origins of the American Revolution* (Cambridge, 2011).

[118] [John Adams], *A Dissertation on the Canon and Feudal Law* (1765) had framed such an historical argument, and excused the Puritans' 'enthusiasm' as 'founded in revelation and in reason too': Adams, *Works*, iii. 451–2. The Deist Paine did not repeat this excuse for Trinitarian Christian zeal.

[119] [Thomas Jefferson], *A Summary View of the Rights of British America. Set forth in some Resolutions Intended for the Inspection Of the present Delegates Of the People of Virginia, Now in Convention* (Williamsburg, Va: Clementina Rind, 1774), 6, 8, 20. The pamphlet was reprinted by John Dunlap in Philadelphia in 1774; Paine might have had easier access to this edition.

[120] [Paine], *Common Sense* (1776): *CW*, i. 6–7.

[121] [Jefferson], *Summary View*, 9–13, 23.

[122] Jack N. Rakove, *The Beginnings of National Politics: An Interpretive History of the Continental Congress* (New York, 1979), 64–91; Pauline Maier, *American Scripture: Making the Declaration of Independence* (New York, 1997), 9–28.

political discourse in *c.*1792–4.[123] He wrote nothing about what has been called 'the American Revolution within America': the social changes that produced, and were produced by, armed rebellion.[124]

Chapters 1 and 2 have offered evidence for the incidence of extreme anti-Hanoverian and sometimes (by extension) anti-monarchical commitment in England. American Loyalists were soon to argue that 'republican' (i.e. anti-monarchical) designs had been pursued by some colonists for many years before Lexington and Concord; they were not necessarily wrong. The widespread existence of such commitments, grounded in the political theology of many American denominations but as yet generally unexpressed, created social constituencies for Thomas Paine.[125]

The structure of *Common Sense*

If such themes were absent, what did his pamphlet contain? How was it structured? As the title page made clear (see Plate 1), the work was divided into four parts. It is seldom remarked that the first two parts were different from the last two, and that the two halves of the work did not fit well together. Indeed Parts I and II did not mention America at all. Parts III and IV were a total contrast, but invoked 'America' only in general terms to bolster the single main argument that Americans should not merely seek 'the repeal of the acts', but independence: 'the period of debate is closed. Arms as the last resource decide the contest.' The 'acts' were the 'Intolerable Acts' and the Townshend Acts, not mentioned in Parts I and II. Part III also began with its own introductory remarks, as if unrelated to what had gone before: 'In the following pages I offer nothing more than . . . and have no other preliminaries to settle with the reader, than . . .'[126]

How did Paine come to assemble his effective but awkwardly structured tract? In 1777, he wrote of its composition, and linked it with his ambition to write a history of the American Revolution:

> In October 1775, Dr. Franklin proposed giving me such materials as were in his hands, towards completing a history of the present transactions, and seemed desirous of having the first volume out the next Spring. I had then formed the outlines of *Common Sense*, and finished nearly the first part; and as I supposed the doctor's design in setting out a history, was to open the new year with a new system, I expected to surprise him with a production on that subject, much earlier than he thought of; and

---

[123] Seth Cotlar, 'Languages of Democracy in America from the Revolution to the Election of 1800', in Joanna Innes and Mark Philp (eds), *Re-imagining Democracy in the Age of Revolutions: America, France, Britain, Ireland 1750–1850* (Oxford, 2013), 14–27.

[124] Merrill Jensen, *The American Revolution within America* (New York, 1974).

[125] Clark, *Language of Liberty*, 141–381. William D. Liddle, '"A Patriot King, or None": Lord Bolingbroke and the American Renunciation of George III', *Journal of American History* 65 (1979), 951–70, argues that 'except for a very few, relatively timid colonial criticisms of the king, every instance of anti-monarchical rhetoric to be found in colonial publications of whatever kind during the years 1767–73 originated in England', 963. The conversion of many colonists to anti-monarchical doctrines in 1774–6 has, in this interpretation, to be ascribed wholly to the disillusionment of their loyal expectations. It is suggested here that there were additional, long-present, antecedents.

[126] [Paine], *Common Sense* (1776): *CW*, i. 17, 24.

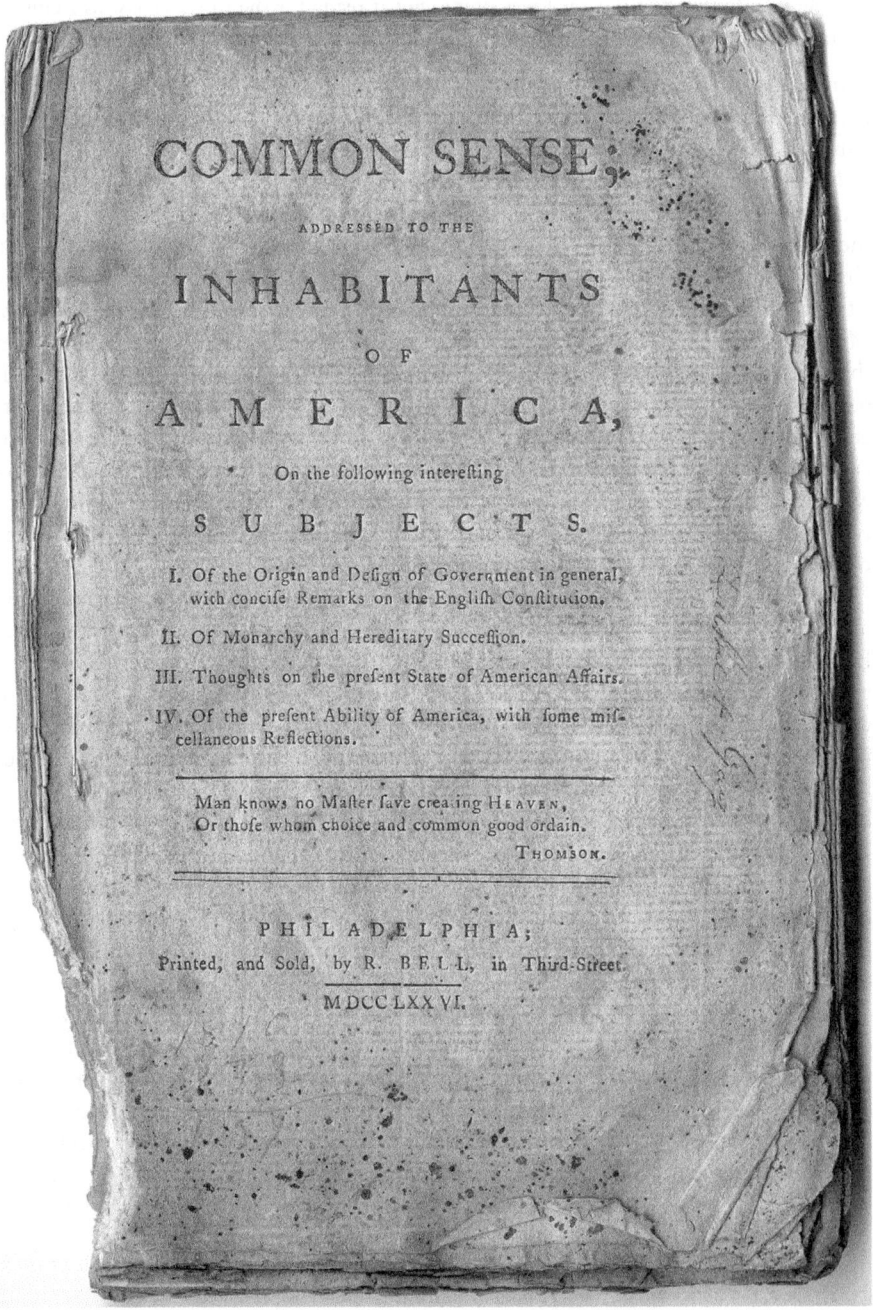

Plate 1. Title page of the first edition of *Common Sense* (American Philosophical Society).

without informing him what I was doing, got it ready for the press, as fast as I conveniently could, and sent him the first pamphlet that was printed off.[127]

Paine did not record that Franklin actually gave him materials for a history of 'the present transactions', only that Franklin proposed doing so, and *Common Sense* contained no history of transatlantic controversies.

More telling is Paine's phrase 'finished nearly the first part'. Given the circumstances of the work's composition, it is possible that the first half (Parts I and II of the four) was not written in the colonies, but was finished or drawn from material already drafted by Paine in England, and brought with him when he crossed the Atlantic. There is evidence that Paine brought over, and reprinted in the *Pennsylvania Magazine*, one piece (his poem on the death of General Wolfe, written soon after that event of 1759);[128] Paine may have brought other manuscript material also. If so, the absence from the two opening sections of *Common Sense* of specific references to the American controversy becomes comprehensible. So does the rhetoricized hatred of English political institutions, for Paine had not come into conflict with their colonial representatives in his few months in Philadelphia. Again, if the two opening sections were drafted in England, this would be evidence that Paine's negation of monarchy preceded his affirmation of republicanism.

It may lend support to this case that Paine's analysis in *Common Sense* often lacked specificity. His discussion was either of concepts (society, government) or of British institutions in general (the monarchy). Even in abstract matters of government, his conceptual vocabulary lacked many later key terms: 'democracy' and 'democratic' were absent from his text, and Paine did not discuss the franchise, only perfunctorily mentioning an ideal: 'The representation [should be] more equal.' But how much more equal, and between what, or whom, he did not explain. The very brevity of this remark on so important a matter is evidence that it was not central in Paine's thinking. The twentieth-century invention of a position anachronistically known as 'Lockeian liberalism' was premised on the existence of an acquisitive individualism that, to its recent champions, must naturally have issued in a campaign for franchise extension; yet Paine and his contemporaries were unaware of the existence of any such position.[129]

Nor in *Common Sense* did he use the term 'republicanism', or appeal to the example of England's republic of the 1650s, or draw on the works of the 'Commonwealthmen', those English thinkers who are thought to have reinterpreted the significance of that episode in the decades that followed 1660. In *Common Sense* Paine discussed no historically realized republic except ancient Israel before its adoption of monarchy. Indeed his conception of a 'republic' differed importantly from later usage. It was 'somewhat difficult to find a proper name for the government of England', he

---

[127] [Paine], *The American Crisis*, III (19 Apr. 1777): *CW*, i. 73–101, at 88–9.

[128] Thomas Clio Rickman, *The Life of Thomas Paine* (London: Rickman, 1819), 256–7.

[129] For a review of the recent historiographical controversy between 'Lockeian liberalism' and 'classical republicanism' or 'civic humanism' see Lee Ward, *The Politics of Liberty in England and Revolutionary America* (Cambridge, 2004), 1–7. But for the very limited attention in the American colonies to both Locke and the civic humanists see Clark, *Language of Liberty*, 20–9 and *passim*. The present book offers a third alternative.

argued. 'Sir William Meredith calls it a Republic', he acknowledged, citing the English opposition MP and ex-Jacobite Sir William Meredith (1724–90)[130] but (problematically for interpretations of Paine as an early campaigner for American freedoms) not mentioning Meredith's opposition in Parliament to the Stamp Act, the American tea duty and the Declaratory Act. Paine was even willing to treat England as having been a republic, although one now out of order: 'Why is the Constitution of England sickly, but because monarchy hath poisoned the Republic; the crown has engrossed the Commons.' Even so, the constitution had a 'republican part', the House of Commons, with which Paine identified himself.[131] Yet *Common Sense* did not explicitly champion anything called 'republicanism'; it did not discuss the nature of republicanism, or advocate it, except to say that 'The Republics of Europe are all (and we may say always) in peace',[132] a conclusion that was evidently deductive rather than inductive.

Instead of positively expounding republicanism the pamphlet negated monarchy, and argued on the basis of what Locke had called '*Scripture-proofs*' that God had condemned monarchy when the ancient Israelites requested a king. *Common Sense* achieved its republican significance primarily by negation. To many colonists (at least beyond the ranks of religious zealots) republicanism was a default position: to moderates, it was the reality of independence, produced by George III's identification of them as rebels in his proclamation of 23 August 1775 and his speech to Parliament of 26 October 1775,[133] that suddenly created thirteen separate republics unprepared for their new status by prior theorizing, not any abstract conversion to republican theory as a result of reading *Common Sense*. It contained no such theory. Indeed Paine himself wrote in 1779 of the British ministry's prior intention 'to conquer America' and claimed that 'The reception which the last petition of Congress met with put it past a doubt that such was their design, on which I determined with myself to write the pamphlet *[Common] Sense*.'[134] This suggests that even Paine's position, like that of other colonists, was a reaction to British acts rather than a programmatic application of a prior republican doctrine.

If England counted, at least in part, as a republic, Paine's use of the term was not unusual. From the 1660s into the 1770s, defenders of the established order in England and America were loud in their identification of 'republics', 'republicans', 'republicanism', and 'republican principles' with regicide and 'democratical government'.

---

[130] Patrick Woodland, 'Sir William Meredith', *ODNB*. For this author's libertarian interpretation of the constitution see especially [Sir William Meredith], *Letter to Dr. Blackstone, By the Author of the Question Stated* (London: G. Woodfall, 1770). Meredith, commending the relaxation of subscription, wrote of 'our present constitution' as 'a republic, under the administration of a king, whose title is sacred whilst he preserves our laws, but forfeited if he attempt to breach them': Meredith to G.K., a Dissenting minister, n.d., *Gentleman's Magazine* 43 (1773), 216.

[131] Later Paine added: 'All that part of the government of England which begins with the office of constable, and proceeds through the departments of magistrate, quarter-session, and general assize, including the trial by jury, is republican government': *Rights of Man* (1791): *CW*, i. 326.

[132] [Paine], *Common Sense* (1776): *CW*, i. 16, 27.

[133] *By the King. A Proclamation for suppressing Rebellion and Sedition* [23 Aug. 1775] (London: Charles Eyre and William Strahan, 1775); *His Majesty's most Gracious Speech to both Houses of Parliament, on Thursday the 26th of October, 1775* (no place, no printer [1775]).

[134] Paine to Henry Laurens, 14 Jan. 1779: *CW*, ii. 1162.

English reformers seeking to escape association with Charles I's judicial murder in 1649, with the sanguinary record of the republics of ancient Greece and Rome, or with the heavy-handed oligarchies of contemporary republics like the United Provinces and Venice, often affirmed their loyalty (whether sincerely or tactically) to limited monarchy, merely calling for the system of checks and balances to be restored to (what they claimed was) working order. James Burgh, John Cartwright, and Joseph Priestley all wrote in such terms.[135] After the Restoration in 1660 'a range of writers on politics whom we see as republican saw no difficulty in characterizing some states with monarchs as republics... they contrasted republics with despotisms or tyrannies, not with monarchies'.[136] In 1762 Rousseau had written: 'I therefore call every State ruled by laws a Republic, whatever the form of administration may be, for then alone the public interest governs and the commonwealth really exists.' If monarchy was the 'minister' of 'the general will, which is the law', then 'monarchy itself is a republic'.[137]

Was Paine's position on republicanism in *Common Sense* merely tactical? Did he subsequently adopt an open and undisguised doctrine which theorized rule by elected presidents? The evidence suggests that he did not. In 1786, he argued: 'the word *republic* means the *public good*, or the good of the whole, in contradistinction to the despotic form, which makes the good of the sovereign, or of one man, the only object of the government.'[138] But how was the good of the whole to be judged? Paine did not define this in any substantive and new way. Instead, in *Rights of Man* (1791) he made his continuing attachment to an older procedural position evident: 'The two modes of government which prevail in the world, are, *First*, government by election and representation: *Secondly*, government by hereditary succession. The former is generally known by the name of republic; the latter by that of monarchy and aristocracy.'[139]

Consistently, when in July 1791 Paine and his friends in Paris launched a journal, after their assertion that Louis XVI had constructively abdicated by his flight to Varennes, it was titled *Le Républicain; ou le défenseur du gouvernement Représentatif.*[140] Consistently again, Paine also wrote in *Rights of Man. Part the Second* (1792):

> What is called a *republic*, is not any *particular form* of government. It is wholly characteristical of the purport, matter, or object for which government ought to be instituted, and on which it is to be employed, *res-publica*, the public affairs, or the public good; or, literally translated, the *public thing*... It is not necessarily connected with

---

[135] W. Paul Adams, 'Republicanism in Political Rhetoric before 1776', *Political Science Quarterly* 85 (1970), 397–421, at 403–11.

[136] Mark Philp, 'English Republicanism in the 1790s', *Journal of Political Philosophy* 6 (1998), 235–62, at 240–1.

[137] Jean-Jacques Rousseau, *On the Social Contract, or Principles of Political Right* (1762), in *The Collected Writings of Rousseau*, ed. Roger D. Masters and Christopher Kelly (Hanover, 1994), iv. 153.

[138] Paine, *Dissertations on Government, the Affairs of the Bank, and Paper-Money* (1786): *CW*, ii. 372–3.

[139] Paine, *Rights of Man* (1791): *CW*, i. 338.

[140] Conway, *Life*, 127. Only four issues were published. Paine to Condorcet, Bonneville, and Lanthenas, June 1791: *CW*, ii. 1316 repeated this conception; 'I venture to think that the preceding opinions will show you that I am a sound Republican.'

any particular form, but it most naturally associates with the representative form, as being best calculated to secure the end for which a nation is at the expense of supporting it.[141]

Paine was not a theorist of republicanism; he was a critic of monarchy. The larger picture is important: it was not affirmations of a theory of 'republicanism' that posed such a threat to monarchy and aristocracy in the late eighteenth century,[142] but the negations of the existing social order derived from religious heterodoxy, especially from open and militant Deism.

Present-day commentators are often struck by Paine's language denouncing monarchy in *Common Sense*, seeing this language as marking the beginning of a new world, republican and egalitarian in the present-day meaning of these terms.[143] Especially, this language can seem an attack on patriarchy. Yet Paine nowhere framed such a critique of gender relations in his day, and did not systematically address the question of the position of women. If he attacked monarchy, he nevertheless in *Common Sense* almost wholly passed over aristocracy. His exception was a rhetorical flourish, 'The remains of Aristocratical tyranny in the persons of the Peers'; but this was a historical allusion, powerful in its context, not an analysis calling for social revolution in the future.[144]

Initial contemporary reactions to the pamphlet did not read it as emancipatory in the sense of marking a watershed between political discourses. The author's Deism was concealed, and his use of scriptural texts to denounce monarchy was, on the surface, traditional. Denunciations of monarchy were already old in England. On monarchy, Paine taught the English little that they did not already know, except in the key respect of ignoring Whig orthodoxy that the monarchy, after the Revolution of 1688 and the Hanoverian accession in 1714, was already limited and constitutional: the hereditary right of George III, according to Whigs, was strictly limited by statute and so (some would claim) no hereditary right at all. What was different in Paine from the adherents of the House of Stuart was that he drew these anti-Hanoverian conclusions from religious heterodoxy, and that after 1789 he took the

---

[141] Paine, *Rights of Man. Part the Second* (1792): *CW*, i. 369–70. 'By republicanism . . . I understand simply a government by representation—a government founded upon the principles of the Declaration of Rights.' For a contrasting argument that Paine learned a new doctrine of republicanism from his French contacts after 1787, see Richard Whatmore, '"A gigantic manliness": Paine's Republicanism in the 1790s', in Stefan Collini, Richard Whatmore, and Brian Young (eds), *Economy, Polity and Society: British Intellectual History 1750–1950* (Cambridge, 2000), 135–57.

[142] Until the 1790s 'republicanism' had been a term of disparagement, hardly defined, and seldom advocated: Blair Worden, 'Liberty for Export: "Republicanism" in England, 1500–1800', in Gaby Mahlberg and Dirk Wiemann (eds), *European Contexts for English Republicanism* (Farnham, 2013), 13–32, at 13–14, 30.

[143] Alternatively, Paine's anti-monarchical passion is sometimes traced to the Commonwealthman Algernon Sidney (1622–83), e.g. Ward, *The Politics of Liberty*, 388; but there is no evidence that Paine ever read that republican author. Sidney argued for a right of tyrannicide; Paine did not, and defended the life of Louis XVI.

[144] [Paine], *Common Sense* (1776): *CW*, i. 7. For a contrasting argument that *Common Sense* was 'an appeal for global change' and the *American Crisis* papers were considerations of how to 'export revolution', see Jack Fruchtman, Jr, 'Thomas Paine's Early Radicalism, 1768–1783', in Newman and Onuf (eds), *Paine and Jefferson in the Age of Revolutions*, 49–70, at 52, 60.

argument to greater lengths: not the replacement of one dynasty by another, but the abolition of dynasticism itself in favour of a vision of rule by those that Paine depicted as innocent, ordinary individuals. Republics could embody any form of government; but, Paine now added inconsistently, not monarchy.

Practicalities and sources

Common Sense was, then, a negation of 'the so much boasted Constitution of England' more than an affirmation of American grievances, of revolution as such, of the practical realities of the American colonies or of the nature of government in an independent American republic. Paine's critique of monarchy was (at least, overtly) based on a selective interpretation of Scripture texts, especially Samuel ('These portions of scripture are direct and positive. They admit of no equivocal construction') and the invocation of English anti-Catholicism ('monarchy in every instance is the popery of government'; the phrase 'mother country' had been 'jesuitically adopted by the king and his parasites'; George III was guilty of 'a low papistical design'). Scripture too, Paine claimed, gave no sanction to the hereditary principle, except by analogy with the doctrine of original sin ('original sin and hereditary succession are parallels'); he did not defend his implied dismissal of original sin, perhaps one of few places where his Deism was visible.[145] All these components played also to colonial American audiences; if they did not originate there, they could sometimes find in North America their fullest expression. Especially was this true of the anti-Catholicism on which Paine drew.[146]

Paine's practical examples (aside from ancient Israel) were all taken from English history: monarchs from William the Conqueror to Henry VII; a Prime Minister, Henry Pelham; Magna Carta; a lord of the Treasury, Charles Wolfran Cornwall; and the Marquis of Rockingham (neither the rebels of the 1640s nor those of 1688 featured). By contrast, *Common Sense* mentioned by name no single colonial American leader, and no single colonial American publication on the controversy. It is reasonable to infer that Paine knew little of either.[147]

Instead, in *Common Sense* Paine cited five recent texts as his sources. What can be learned from them? John Locke was not mentioned. Only one author (James Burgh) has been located among the civic humanists, and Paine's citation of him was perfunctory. The first text was by the Italian theorist Dragonetti, but this did not establish Paine's cosmopolitanism: Dragonetti's work had recently been republished

---

[145] [Paine], *Common Sense* (1776): *CW*, i. 12, 14, 19.

[146] Francis D. Cogliano, *No King, No Popery: Anti-Catholicism in Revolutionary New England* (Westport, Conn., 1995), 49–55 and *passim*; Jason K. Duncan, *Citizens or Papists? The Politics of Anti-Catholicism in New York, 1685–1821* (New York, 2005).

[147] By contrast, a leading Loyalist contribution engaged openly with such leading tracts as [John Dickinson], *Letters from a Farmer in Pennsylvania* (Philadelphia: David Hall and William Sellers, 1768), James Otis, *The Rights of the British Colonies Asserted and Proved* (Boston: Edes and Gill, 1774) and [William Knox], *The Interest of the Merchants and Manufacturers of Great-Britain, in the Present Context with the Colonies, stated and considered* (London: T. Cadell, 1774), as well as rehearsing the controversy since the Stamp Act: [Daniel Leonard], *Massachusettensis* ([Boston: no printer, 1775]), 55–7, 64, 83, 90, 92, 94, 99–102, 104.

in an English translation.[148] Paine cited Dragonetti again in 1792,[149] but there
and in *Common Sense* Paine combined the same two separated passages in
Dragonetti's *Treatise*: 'The science of the politician consists in fixing the true point
of happiness and freedom' and 'Next to the virtue of sovereigns, his might deserve
our attention, who should discover a mode of government that contained the
greatest sum of individual happiness, with the fewest wants of contribution.' Paine
probably repeated himself rather than retaining an influential copy of Dragonetti
from 1775 to 1792.

It has been argued that Dragonetti contains 'in embryo... the radical program
of the second part of Paine's *Rights of Man* and *Agrarian Justice*, and the foundation
of that program in an explicit utilitarianism'.[150] This goes too far: the two sentences quoted by Paine were almost the only ones in Dragonetti's book that echoed
Paine's own position, and its anonymous translator had been prompted to apologize for the 'compliments to kings, which the author [Dragonetti] has scattered up
and down his work, and which may appear suspicious or fulsome to a republican
reader'. The state of nature did not witness free-standing and peaceful society,
wrote Dragonetti, but 'savage sufferings'. As for utilitarianism as a route to a correct policy, 'Evil is so much interwoven with human nature, that virtue can never
be too much encouraged.'[151] Paine made no use of Dragonetti's argument that 'an
implicit faith in noble virtue distributes often considerable favours to birth only':
Paine's critique of the hereditary principle was differently premised. Dragonetti condemned 'that inequality which blasts our present state'; Paine did not. The Italian
urged that 'Without touching the immense estates of the rich, the poor might be
provided for by a distribution of the commons adjoining to most villages' and condemned 'the Agrarian laws, those sources of civil horrors';[152] again, Paine hardly
addressed such themes until *Agrarian Justice* (1797). The early Paine was not a
thinker who drew novel and extensive conclusions from the already commonplace
principle of utilitarianism, as Jeremy Bentham did. Paine's knowledge of Dragonetti's
work may suggest only that he had frequented the London bookshop of its publisher, his near namesake Tom Payne.

The second text cited by Paine was John Entick's *Naval History*, invoked to show
a specific point, the cost of building warships.[153] The third was Burgh's *Political
Disquisitions*, but it was cited by Paine to establish the beneficial 'consequence' of
'a large and equal representation' at Westminster rather than to show anything specific

---

[148] Giacinto, marchese Dragonetti, *A Treatise on Virtues and Rewards* (London: Johnson and Payne, and J. Almon, 1769).

[149] Paine, *Letter Addressed to the Addressers* (1792): *CW*, ii. 490.

[150] David Wootton, 'The Republican Tradition: from Commonwealth to Common Sense', in Wootton (ed.), *Republicanism, Liberty and Commercial Society, 1649–1776* (Stanford, Calif., 1994), 1–41 at 36–9.

[151] Dragonetti, *Treatise*, 17, 27, 153–5, 159.

[152] Dragonetti, *Treatise*, 41, 53, 75, 107, 125.

[153] John Entick, *A New Naval History: or, Compleat View of the British Marine* (London: R. Manby et al., 1757), lvi.

about the colonies.[154] The first American edition of this work had been published
in Philadelphia in 1775 by Robert Bell, who also printed the first edition of *Common
Sense*, and Paine may have encountered it in Philadelphia; yet whether he read it in
England or Philadelphia, he never entered into Burgh's detailed investigations of
rotten boroughs, or echoed Burgh's imagery, or considered (as Burgh did: i. 29) the
implications of parliamentary electoral malpractices for colonial governance.[155]

Paine's fourth source was a pamphlet by Sir John Dalrymple, held up by Paine
in English terms as 'a whining Jesuitical piece', 'toryism with a witness!'[156] Fifthly,
in the enlarged second edition of *Common Sense*, attacking the Pennsylvania Quakers
for their pacifism, Paine used a historical retrospect, invoking 'the honest soul of
[Robert] Barclay' (1648–90) and his protest against the restored monarchy's
oppression of the Quakers of that day. If the Quakers of Pennsylvania had the same
spirit, argued Paine, they would 'preach repentance' to George III.[157] This was not
praise of the colonial Quakers, but part of Paine's denunciation of them by comparison with their English co-religionists. These, then, were all books available in
London; his use of them makes more notable the absence of American colonial
books or pamphlets.[158]

Natural rights, the Fall, and society

Despite the title of Paine's later *Rights of Man*, his *Common Sense* too was hardly a
work of systematic natural rights theory. Nor did Paine seek to call his pamphlet
Rights of the Americans. Indeed, the role of natural rights even in Paine's *Rights of
Man* will be qualified below. The phrase 'natural right' was sometimes used in *Common*

---

[154] [James Burgh], *Political Disquisitions: or, An Enquiry into public Errors, Defects, and Abuses* (3
vols, London: E. and C. Dilly, 1774–5), i. bk II, chs 2–7.

[155] Burgh (*Political Disquisitions*, i. 72–5) quoted Locke. If Paine was correct in later claiming
never to have read Locke, this too may suggest that Paine's knowledge of Burgh was superficial.

[156] [Sir John Dalrymple], *The Address of the People of Great-Britain to the Inhabitants of America*
(London: T. Cadell, 1775).

[157] Paine, 'To the Representatives of the Religious Society of the People called Quakers', appendix
to the third edition of *Common Sense* (Philadelphia: W. and T. Bradford, 1776), 93–4: *CW*, ii. 57.
Paine referred to the introductory letter 'Unto Charles II' prefacing the Quaker Robert Barclay's classic
*An Apology For the True Christian Divinity, As the same is held forth, and preached by the People, Called,
in Scorn, Quakers* (London: no printer, 1678), sig. Br–v. It was also quoted in Voltaire's *Letters
Concerning the English Nation* (London: C. Davis and A. Lyon, 1733), 22–3. Barclay's *An Apology*
continued to be reprinted, and Paine's Quaker background suggests that he may have used the original
rather than borrowing Voltaire's quotation.

[158] [Paine], *Common Sense* (1776): *CW*, i. 3, 6, 10–12, 14–17, 28–9, 32–3, 38, 40–1. In a more
international vein, Paine mentioned, 29, 'Massanello', i.e. the fisherman Tommaso Aniello (1622–
47), the leader of a revolt against Spanish Habsburg rule in Naples; but this example was known to
English readers from Thomas D'Urfey's *The Famous History of the Rise and Fall of Massaniello* (London,
1700), recently reinforced by [Francis Midon], *Remarkable History of the Rise and Fall of Masaniello,
the Fisherman of Naples* (London: H. Fenwick, [?1770]). Wootton, 'The Republican Tradition', 30–1,
argues that Paine 'almost certainly' read J[ohn] H[all], *The Grounds and Reasons of Monarchy Considered
and exemplified out of the Scottish History* (Edinburgh: Evan Tyler, 1651), in the version rewritten by
John Toland and printed in Toland's eighteenth-century editions of James Harrington's *Oceana*, Hall
being 'the only widely available author who rejected hereditary monarchy in all its forms'. This argument fails since it is not established that Paine ever read Harrington's *Oceana*. Cf. Aldridge, *American
Ideology*, 98–101.

Sense, as in much contemporary discourse by reformers and their opponents alike, and similarly coupled with utilitarian arguments. It was as yet commonplace for both to be employed together in a weak sense, a sense in which appeal could be made to two different arguments without raising obvious problems about their logical consistency. In the 1770s, and for long afterwards, there were not two distinct camps of theorists, the adherents of natural law and the champions of utilitarianism; rather, almost all people subscribed to both, on the unifying premise that God had intended mankind to be happy by the practice of virtue.[159]

So natural law and its application, natural right, appeared in *Common Sense*, but as rhetorical emphasizers: 'A government of our own is our natural right.' Britain was 'declaring war against the natural rights of all mankind'. 'In this first parliament every man by natural right will have a seat.' Yet this was a figure of speech, not an extended argument. According to Paine, men had originally established government from the utilitarian operation of 'necessity, like a gravitating power', not from calculations about their rights: man 'finds it necessary to surrender up a part of his property to furnish means for the protection of the rest'. Paine did not explain the nature of 'natural right', or continue his argument about the first franchise. On the contrary, he proceeded at once to argue that future changes in representation violating this principle of direct representation as a natural right would be adopted because 'it will be found best' and 'prudence will point out the propriety'.[160]

Equally, Paine mounted no extended consideration of utilitarianism: among theists, brief appeals to utility were as common in the 1770s as appeals to natural right. Even into the 1790s, almost all reformers were theists. Not until the arrival of an atheist, Jeremy Bentham, publishing from the 1770s, was utility emphasized to the point of incompatibility with natural right. But for Bentham, there was no God who could have imbued Creation with natural law; the atheist Bentham would logically dismiss natural rights theory as 'nonsense upon stilts'.[161] This was not Paine's position; but the incompatibility of natural rights theory and utilitarianism was fully apparent only after his lifetime.

More important in *Common Sense* than any systematic and positive arguments about natural right were Paine's negative arguments against what he termed 'hereditary right', which, in his vision, was no right at all. His aim in 1776 was not primarily to expound an abstract idea of rights but to negate 'hereditary succession', specifically kingship rather than aristocracy, and his basic reasons for denouncing it were theological: for the Deist Paine, God had granted men rights, but not the rights that Trinitarians often asserted.

Perhaps his most famous aphorism was 'We have it in our power to begin the world over again.'[162] This is sometimes presented as a proof of his universalism, or

[159] For an argument tracing utilitarianism in rights theory to Samuel Pufendorf (1632–94) see Richard Tuck, *Natural Rights Theories: Their Origin and Development* (Cambridge, 1979), 1.

[160] [Paine], *Common Sense* (1776): *CW*, i. 3, 5–6, 29.

[161] Jeremy Bentham, *An Examination of the Declaration of the Rights of Man and the Citizen Decreed by the Constituent Assembly in France*, in *The Works of Jeremy Bentham*, ed. John Bowring (11 vols, London, 1843), ii. 501.

[162] [Paine], *Common Sense* (1776): *CW*, i. 45.

as a secularized echo of millenarianism. There was indeed a millenarian strand in American revolutionary discourse;[163] yet there is no evidence that Paine knew of it. For a Deist, Christ's literal Second Coming would have been impossible; this suggests that Paine's image may have been instead an echo of the 'new birth' often found in early eighteenth-century English religious revivalism. In practical terms, this memorable idea was appealing exactly because it was, in a secular sense, impossible. Even in the American colonies, successive groups of new immigrants used the opportunities created by their new lands not to jettison their cultural baggage but—in hundreds of unconscious ways—to become more like themselves, more attached to their values and practices.[164] Paine's phrase made sense only as an echo of a scriptural promise ('Behold, I make all things new': Revelation 21: 4), and was appropriately followed by the sentence 'A situation, similar to the present, hath not happened since the days of Noah until now.'[165] Such an argument could only be theological.

If this renovation of the entire human condition were to be made a reality, the central antecedent obstacle had to be eliminated. Hereditary right 'hath no parallel in or out of scripture but the doctrine of original sin'. If original sin were implicitly omitted as a fiction, Paine could open his pamphlet by arguing for the existence of 'society' as a prior, benign, and natural formation, uncorrupted by the Fall, distinct from that later construct, 'government' (he differed here from many of the 'classical republicans').[166] This was the point of his opening brief rehearsal of conventional social contract theory to explain the origin of government, but his new tactic was seen, and contested. An early critic, George Chalmers, attacked Paine's distinction between the state and society as 'a political discovery, which had escaped the sagacity of Sydney, and eluded the understanding of Locke... Government and society being... parts of one whole, and being thus directed to the same end, have the same origin, and cannot without each other exist.' Chalmers quoted George Washington's comment that 'Individuals, entering into society, must give up a share of liberty to preserve the rest' and observed: 'These must be allowed to be excellent observations, though they be not altogether new. All these and more are taught to every Englishman in his nursery, except, indeed, those Englishmen, who are educated at [those centres of Calvinism] Geneva and Lausanne, at [the Dissenting academies of] Warrington

---

[163] Ruth H. Bloch, *Visionary Republic: Millennial Themes in American Thought, 1756–1800* (Cambridge, 1985), 75–6, 80.

[164] David Hackett Fischer, *Albion's Seed: Four British Folkways in America* (New York, 1989).

[165] [Paine], *Common Sense* (1776): *CW*, i. 45. Paine's 'allusion implicitly posits a revolutionary Jehovah cleansing the corrupt world by creating it anew. Beginning by envisioning the regeneration of America and the world as a collective national endeavor, Paine's messianic vision culminated with himself as the exclusive creator of the new revolutionary world': Steven Blakemore, 'In the Beginning: Thomas Paine's Two Revolutionary Careers', in Blakemore, *Crisis in Representation: Thomas Paine, Mary Wollstonecraft, Helen Maria Williams, and the Rewriting of the French Revolution* (London, 1997), 25–44, at 41.

[166] Paine was arguably inconsistent, in *Common Sense* picturing the state of nature as a benign 'state of natural liberty', but in his *Letter to the Abbe Raynal* as a 'state of barbarism': Carine Lounissi, 'Thomas Paine's Reflections on the Social Contract: A Consistent Theory?', in Scott Cleary and Ivy Stabell (eds), *New Directions in Thomas Paine Studies* (New York, 2016), 175–93.

and Hackney'.[167] Paine was neither a Calvinist nor a Dissenter: his antecedents looked back to the Deism of the reign of George II.

In secular terms, Paine's argument at this point was arguably flawed, since, according to him, society and government had been formed in the same way, for utilitarian advantage; only his theological commitments established a normative difference between a world of equal individuals (society) and a world of kings and bishops (government). Consequently, Paine's instincts pulled him in two directions. It was in the same paragraph that he attributed government to 'the inability of moral virtue to govern the world' and then immediately followed this contention with the claim: 'however our eyes may be dazzled with show, or our ears deceived with sound; however prejudice may warp our wills, or interest darken our understanding, the simple voice of nature and reason will say, 'tis right.'[168] Paine did not explain why the simple voice of nature and reason, shared among mankind, had not already changed the minds of his political opponents.

Hitherto the term 'society' in anglophone political thought had been synonymous with 'civil society' or 'Body Politick', as it had been in Locke's *Two Treatises of Government*,[169] and meant what is today called the state. Paine's novel idea of 'society' seemed to correspond to what had earlier been termed the 'state of nature', a condition of innocent cooperation of which mankind had, by some means, been deprived. The most obvious cause of this deprivation (and an idea which Locke had never been able to integrate into his account of the origins of government) was the Fall. Paine the expounder of Scripture seemed to accept the Fall in the opening pages of *Common Sense* in order to condemn the sinfulness of government, but his tactic at once created a problem for Paine the Deist: the Fall denigrated postlapsarian human nature.

Consequently, Paine the Deist silently distanced himself from the Fall, arguing for 'society' as the spontaneous creation of uncorrupt individuals. Without this theological dimension, Paine's argument can only appear today as a tactic, a claim that colonial Americans already possessed ordered relations that would survive the removal of British rule, the dissolution of government.[170] This seeming acceptance of the Fall was also at odds with Paine's argument a few months later in the 'Forester's Letters' that 'no nation of people, in their true senses, when seriously reflecting on the rank which God hath given them, would ever, of their own consent, give any *one man* a negative power over the whole', since 'No man since the fall hath ever been equal to the trust.'[171] He did not explain why this argument did not apply equally to the president of a republic, equipped with a veto over legislation; and this omission suggests that the Fall was a doctrine that Paine was using for tactical advantage only.

---

[167] [Chalmers], *Life of Thomas Pain*, 41–2, 50.
[168] [Paine], *Common Sense* (1776): *CW*, i. 6.
[169] [John Locke], *Two Treatises of Government*, ed. Peter Laslett (Cambridge, 1988), 277, 282–3, 315, 323–6, 329, 337, 358, 406, 427 (although cf. 318–19).
[170] e.g. Ward, *The Politics of Liberty*, 380.
[171] [Paine], 'Forester's Letters', III, 24 Apr. 1776: *CW*, ii. 79.

Elsewhere, Paine could coin a conception of 'society' close to its present-day meaning; this conception had much to do with peaceful exchange, that is, commerce, and did not examine the realities of conflict between commercial individuals.[172] The point of Paine's discussion of commerce was to prove his moral claim about the spontaneous association of innocent people, rather than to respond to the material facts of growing trade in the early 1770s. Even in 1792, he wrote: 'In all my publications, where the matter would admit, I have been an advocate for commerce, because I am a friend to its effects. It is a pacific system, operating to unite mankind by rendering nations, as well as individuals, useful to each other'[173] (by contrast, he did not prioritize the role of commerce in alleviating poverty). Paine nowhere theorized the artisan or discussed the rapid economic changes that were occurring in the American colonies.

For this notion of 'society' Paine received plaudits from some later commentators. So sure were they of his status as a 'modern' that they did not remark that Paine, having coined this sense for a collaborative 'society', did little with the idea in his subsequent writings. Paine's state was to be one characterized by freedom of contract, cheap government, individual effort, and competition, not collectivist social cooperation or a return to primitive agriculture (as Thomas Spence, for example, envisaged). Whether the fallen nature of man made such a social Utopia impossible was a question on which the Paine of 1776 was ambiguous.

By 1792 he hailed manifestations of a widespread desire for 'a friendly alliance' between Britain and France in ways that suggested a more profound barrier:

> It shows, that man, were he not corrupted by governments, is naturally the friend of man, and that human nature is not of itself vicious. That spirit of jealousy and ferocity, which the governments of the two countries inspired, and which they rendered subservient to the purpose of taxation, is now yielding to the dictates of reason, interest and humanity.[174]

But if the Fall had not occurred, why was that spirit of 'ferocity' so powerful? By 1804 he wrote openly against the doctrine of the Fall as an idea not present in the Gospels of Matthew, Mark, Luke, or John, or in the teachings of Jesus.[175] In *Common Sense*, he had moved in the direction of an implicit repudiation of it. Indeed this abstract demotion of the Fall ran parallel with, and contradicted, Paine's much more traditional English argument from 'Scripture chronology', citing Old Testament sources for the original absence of kingship. 'Government by kings' was 'the invention of the devil.... for the promotion of idolatry'. At the outset of *Common Sense*, kingship was ruled out not primarily by natural rights; rather, 'the will of the Almighty as declared by Gideon, and the prophet Samuel, expressly disapproves of government by kings'. Only withholding Scripture from the people hid this fact;

---

[172] For the role of commerce in Paine's thought, and the limits of his endorsement of it, see especially Claeys, *Paine*, 46–8, 55–6, 96–101.

[173] Paine, *Rights of Man. Part the Second* (1792): *CW*, i. 400.

[174] Paine, *Rights of Man. Part the Second* (1792): *CW*, i. 397.

[175] Paine, 'Of the Religion of Deism Compared with the Christian Religion, and the Superiority of the Former over the Latter', *The Prospect* (30 June–7 July 1804): *CW*, ii. 799; cf. 808.

hence 'monarchy in every instance is the popery of government'. In specifically English terms, the title of William the Conqueror (and therefore of his successors) 'hath no divinity in it'.[176] By contrast, Paine did not yet cite Scripture against the institution of aristocracy.

This scriptural teaching was Paine's central strategy in *Common Sense*, and it engaged explosively with a colonial population for whom seventeenth-century politico-theological conflicts were still very much alive. Indeed God appeared twenty-three times in Paine's text, as 'the Almighty' (7 times), 'God' (7), 'Heaven' (6), 'King of Heaven' (1), 'Lord of Hosts' (1), 'the King of America' (1), together with other biblical references to Pharaoh, Lucifer, Noah, creation, the Reformation, Jesuits, the Papacy, hell, redemption, and more: *Common Sense* was saturated with Christian reference.[177]

It was therefore noteworthy that the texts Paine cited were almost all from the Old Testament (Judges 8:. 23; 1 Samuel 8: 5–20, 9, 12: 17–19; 2 Samuel). Paine markedly avoided the New Testament and its many texts, from Jesus and the Apostles, which had long been used to support monarchy or that had been used to develop doctrines of Atonement. There was one exception, but in that instance Paine was able to argue against a passage's familiar meaning: '"*Render unto Caesar the things which are Caesar's*," is the scripture doctrine of Courts, yet it is no support of monarchical government, for the Jews at that time were without a King, and in a state of vassalage to the Romans.'[178]

It was immediately after his use of Samuel that Paine implied its application to the British present: 'To the evil of monarchy we have added that of hereditary succession.' By this crucial linking, a negation of the doctrine of original sin, the hereditary principle now came to occupy a growing place in Paine's vision. Because of human equality in sinlessness and in virtue by creation, 'no one by birth could have a right to set up his own family in perpetual preference to all others forever'. Even had people once chosen a monarch, 'they could not without manifest injustice to their children say [to the king] "that your children and your children's children shall reign over ours forever"'. He did not observe that the discontinuities of English government, from James II to William III to Anne to George I, had declared the opposite practice; instead, Paine relied on his earlier assertion: 'tho' we have been wise enough to shut and lock a door against absolute Monarchy, we at the same time have been foolish enough to put the Crown in possession of the key.'[179]

This was not Paine's point, however, for a new reason. In 1792 he was to argue that the pre-existence of a peaceful and cooperative state called 'society' was proved by a historic fact:

For upward of two years from the commencement of the American War, and to a longer period in several of the American states, there were no established forms of government. The old governments had been abolished, and the country was too much occupied in

---

176 [Paine], *Common Sense* (1776): *CW*, i. 4–5, 9–10, 12, 14, 45.
177 Nathalie Caron, *Thomas Paine contre l'imposture des prêtres* (Paris, 1998), 124.
178 [Paine], *Common Sense* (1776): *CW*, i. 10 (text corrected), citing Matthew 22: 21.
179 [Paine], *Common Sense* (1776): *CW*, i. 8, 13 (text corrected).

defence, to employ its attention in establishing new governments; yet during this interval, order and harmony were preserved as inviolate as in any country in Europe.[180]

But that was in 1792. In 1776, in the appendix to the third edition of *Common Sense*, he disclosed what he actually knew of the situation on the ground:

> The present state of America is truly alarming to every man who is capable of reflection. Without law, without government, without any other mode of power than what is founded on, and granted by, courtesy... The property of no man is secure in the present unbraced system of things. The mind of the multitude is left at random, and seeing no fixed object before them, they pursue such as fancy or opinion presents. Nothing is criminal; there is no such thing as treason; wherefore, every one thinks himself at liberty to act as he pleases.[181]

Paine's comment in 1792 is evidence that his views were deductive, deduced from a set of preconceptions, rather than inductive, drawn from observation of the realities of civil war.

Evidence supports Paine's comment of 1776. Even in Philadelphia, the American Patriot General John Lacey found in December 1776 that the people 'appeared all hostile to each other, Whig & Tory in a state little better [than] open Enemies'.[182] The colonies had long been torn by violence. Resistance theory was the reverse of which local ideas of legitimacy were the obverse: both were given concrete form in regional insurrections, most recently the march of the Paxton Boys against Philadelphia (1764); the Regulator phenomenon in the Carolinas (1768–71); the Pennamite v. Yankee clashes in Pennsylvania (1770–1) and the Green Mountain Boys in Vermont (early 1770s). Such phenomena continued after independence with the rebellion in North Carolina in 1784, Shays's rebellion in Massachusetts (1786–7), farmers' resistance to foreclosures in Pennsylvania in the same decade, the Whiskey Rebellion (1794) and Fries's Rebellion (1799), both in the same state. Such rebellions generally had denominational as well as economic dimensions.[183] In towns, the activity of mobs was ubiquitous, to coerce political opponents and enforce plebeian norms: mob action contributed powerfully to make the American Revolution socially revolutionary.[184]

---

[180] Paine, *Rights of Man. Part the Second* (1792): *CW*, i. 358.

[181] [Paine], *Common Sense* (1776): *CW*, i. 43.

[182] Quoted in J. Paul Selsam, *The Pennsylvania Constitution of 1776: A Study in Revolutionary Democracy* (Philadelphia, 1936), 239.

[183] Clark, *Language of Liberty*, 240–82. Of Shays's rebels, William Knox reported: 'Their creed is "that the property of the United States has been protected from the confiscations of Britain by the joint exertions of all, and therefore ought to be the common property of all ..." In a word, they are determined to annihilate all debts public and private and have agrarian laws which are easily effected by means of unfunded paper money': Knox to George Washington, 23 Oct. 1786, in Jensen, *American Revolution within America*, 82.

[184] Gordon S. Wood, 'A Note on Mobs in the American Revolution', *WMQ* 3rd ser. 23 (1966), 635–42; Gordon S. Wood, *The Creation of the American Republic 1776–1787* (Chapel Hill, NC, 1969), esp. 319–28. See also Pauline Maier, 'Popular Uprisings and Civil Authority in Eighteenth-Century America', *WMQ* 3rd ser. 27 (1970), 3–35; Pauline Maier, *From Resistance to Revolution: Colonial Radicals and the Development of American Opposition to Britain, 1765–1776* (London, 1973); Paul A. Gilje, *Rioting in America* (Bloomington, Ind., 1996); Terry Bouton, 'A Road Closed: Rural Insurgency

According to its victims, mass intimidation was not always spontaneous: as General Gage had reported to London of the Stamp Act disturbances in New York, 'The Plan of the People of Property has been to raise the lower Class to prevent the Execution of the Law.' In Boston, Thomas Hutchinson observed the same chain of command.[185] The coercive activity of mobs steadily increased after successfully rendering the Stamp Act unenforceable, and it fed on, and in turn contributed to, rising anger. Anger was a key theme of *Common Sense*, yet Paine neither led the mob, nor directly addressed it; he nowhere discussed the activities of crowds or the issues that their violence raised. Paine seems to have featured in the attention of American revolutionary mobs only once, and that in his absence, when a mob in New York intervened to destroy the print run of a pamphlet replying to *Common Sense*.[186]

Paine argued from Scripture history rather than from current events. How sincere was he in his use of that source? John Adams much later claimed to Benjamin Rush that he, Adams, had in early 1776 replied to Paine's criticism of Adams's *Thoughts on Government*:

> In return, I only laughed heartily at him and rallied him upon his grave arguments from the Old Testament to prove that monarchy was unlawful in the sight of God. 'Do you seriously believe, Paine,' said I, 'in that pious doctrine of yours?' This put him in good humor and he laughed out. 'The Old Testament!' said he, 'I do not believe in the Old Testament. I have had thoughts of publishing my sentiments of it, but upon deliberation I have concluded to put that off till the latter part of life.'[187]

In his *Autobiography* Adams offered a similar account:

> I told him further, that his Reasoning from the Old Testament was ridiculous, and I could hardly think him sincere. At this he laughed, and said he had taken his Ideas in part from Milton: and then expressed a Contempt of the Old Testament and indeed of the Bible at large, which surprised me. He saw that I did not relish this, and soon check'd himself, with these Words 'However I have some thoughts of publishing my Thoughts on Religion, but I believe it will be best to postpone it, to the latter part of Life.'[188]

This was written after Paine's return to the United States in 1802, and after his public notoriety produced by *The Age of Reason*; Adams was a hostile witness, and

---

in Post-Independence Pennsylvania', *Journal of American History* 87 (2000), 855–87; Kenneth Owen, 'Violence and the Limits of the Political Community in Revolutionary Pennsylvania', in Patrick Griffin, Robert G. Ingram, Peter Onuf, and Brian Schoen (ed.), *Between Sovereignty and Anarchy: The Politics of Violence in the American Revolutionary Era* (Charlottesville, Va, 2015). Since the work of George Rudé in the 1960s, scholarship has often analysed mob action as purposeful, focused, and strictly circumscribed in its use of force. Consequently, the significance of violence as violence has been obscured.

[185] Arthur M. Schlesinger, 'Political Mobs and the American Revolution, 1765–1776', *Proceedings of the American Philosophical Society* 99 (1955), 244–50, at 244.

[186] Paul A. Gilje, *The Road to Mobocracy: Popular Disorder in New York City, 1763–1834* (Chapel Hill, NC, 1987), 64.

[187] John Adams to Benjamin Rush, 12 Apr. 1809: *The Spur of Fame: Dialogues of John Adams and Benjamin Rush, 1805–1813*, ed. John A. Schutz and Douglass Adair (San Marino, Calif., 1966), 144.

[188] Adams, *Diary and Autobiography*, iii. 333.

this account must be treated with caution. Evidence from 1776 of Paine's insincerity is scant, but in the appendix to the third edition of *Common Sense* it may have slipped out in his denial of divine agency: 'Kings are not taken away by miracles, neither are changes in governments brought about by any other means than such as are common and human; and such as we are now using.'[189] Additionally, on 17 October 1780, Paine wrote to Major General Nathanael Greene in mockery of Providence and prayer.[190] By contrast, evidence has not emerged to substantiate Paine's orthodox piety in these years.

Adams's record was long after the event: he now had reasons for antedating Paine's disbelief in order to disparage him. On the other hand, Paine left no evidence of any fundamental reconsideration of his religious opinions during the course of his adult life. It seems likely, therefore, that his use of Scripture history in *Common Sense* was tactical. If so, this tactic was well judged, for it spoke to a colonial society still dominated by biblical fundamentalists, well aware of the passages on which Paine relied. This makes it notable that in his published American writings from 1779 onwards, Paine abandoned his hitherto-frequent references to religion.[191] Christianity was a theme that Paine could easily drop.

Paine's remark about Milton, if correctly reported, was possibly a reference to Milton's tract *Pro Populo Anglicano Defensio* (1651), which, like *Common Sense*, had cited Old Testament texts, especially 1 Samuel, to prove God's ban on monarchy as a blasphemous institution and the people's right to depose a king. But this reliance on Milton was unlikely, given the rarity of English translations of Milton's tract.[192] What was different in Paine, not present in Milton, was Paine's denunciation of kingship for its hereditary nature, and his attitude to the Fall; for despite Paine's opening remarks in *Common Sense* about human corruption, thereafter his doctrine was the opposite. Milton, moreover, was a concealed Arian; Paine was a Deist. Paine, then, may have named Milton to Adams in order to invoke an authority, but this does not establish that Paine had any significant intellectual debt to Milton or to any of the sectarians of the 1640s.[193]

In *Common Sense*, it was only after his lengthy interpretations of Judges and 1 Samuel that Paine turned to an inconsistent image of his own: it proved to be memorable for later readers, but is seldom explained. Exalting the idea of a constitution in the new American republic and repudiating earthly kingship, he urged: 'that we may not appear to be defective even in earthly honours, let a day be solemnly set apart for proclaiming the charter; let it be brought forth placed on the divine law, the Word of God; let a crown be placed thereon, by which the world may know, that so far as we approve of monarchy, that in America the law is king.'[194]

---

[189] Paine, 'Epistle to Quakers' (1776): *CW*, ii. 59.

[190] Printed in Aldridge, *American Ideology*, 104.

[191] Caron, *Thomas Paine contre l'imposture des prêtres*, 119, 'une totale dispartition du thème religieux'.

[192] Paine had no Latin, and Milton's tract had no English editions, before 1776, after *A Defence of the People of England. In Answer to Salmasius's Defence of the King* (no place, no printer, 1695); for Samuel, 24–30, 35–6, 42–3.

[193] For a similar argument see Aldridge, *American Ideology*, 98.

[194] [Paine], *Common Sense* (1776): *CW*, i. 29.

This was not the language of John Locke, or of the civic humanists. It was an image that echoed nothing that had happened in America or Britain up to that time. But it was a prescient anticipation of Robespierre's Deistic 'cult of the Supreme Being' and its invented civic festivals in revolutionary France.

In the address to the Quakers that formed part of the appendix to the third edition of *Common Sense* (appearing on 14 Feb. 1776), Paine (still publishing anonymously) claimed: 'The writer of this is one of those few who never dishonors religion either by ridiculing or caviling at any denomination whatsoever.'[195] But that was far from the case. Paine's text contained an overt attack on 'popery', and was an implicit attack on the Church of England for its willingness to support a corrupt state.[196] In 1803 he added a comment that did not correct anything he had previously written: 'Every sectary, except the Quakers, has been a persecutor. Those who fled from persecution persecuted in their turn, and it is this confusion of creeds that has filled the world with persecution and deluged it with blood... The key of heaven is not in the keeping of any sect, nor ought the road to it be obstructed by any.'[197] Whether the charges of superstition and persecution counted as ridiculing and cavilling was a point on which Paine differed from many of his contemporaries.

Fear and hatred

Religion was a particular instance (perhaps the key instance) of Paine's negations. *Common Sense* 'breathes an extraordinary hatred of English governing institutions':[198] hatred of George III; hatred of Catholics; hatred of Loyalists; hatred of all who did not commit themselves to the armed struggle. *Common Sense* 'fuels itself with images of blood, ashes, suffering, cruelty, corruption, monstrosity, hellishness, and villainy'; in this text, 'anger is the legitimate precursor of virtuous civic action', intensifying as the text continues.[199] Appropriately, Paine's one quotation from Milton invoked this theme to explain the impossibility of reconciliation: 'never can true reconcilement grow where wounds of deadly hate have pierced so deep'. In his appendix, responding to the king's speech of 26 October 1775, Paine announced that George III had 'procured for himself an universal hatred' (universalism, one might add, was not always benign). Anyone who 'can calmly hear and digest' Tory doctrine 'hath forfeited his claim to rationality—an apostate from the order of manhood—and ought to be considered as one who hath not only given up the proper dignity of man, but sunk himself beneath the rank of animals, and contemptibly crawls through the world like a worm'. Only a securely established independent government, he threatened, could protect the Tories from 'popular rage'.

---

[195] [Paine], 'To the Representatives of the Religious Society of the People called Quakers': *CW*, ii. 56.

[196] [Paine], *Common Sense* (1776): *CW*, i. 12, 14, 16, 21, 29, 37.

[197] Paine to Samuel Adams, 1 Jan. 1803: *CW*, ii. 1435, 1438.

[198] J. G. A. Pocock, 'The Varieties of Whiggism from Exclusion to Reform: A History of Ideology and Discourse', in Pocock, *Virtue, Commerce, and History: Essays on Political Thought and History, Chiefly in the Eighteenth Century* (Cambridge, 1985), 276.

[199] Robert A. Ferguson, 'The Commonalities of Common Sense', *WMQ* 57 (2000), 465–504, at 493, 495–7.

The lives of American Tories who had 'dared to assemble offensively' were 'forfeited to the laws of the state'; they were 'traitors'; such a traitor 'loses his head'.[200] 'Paine uses anger to urge the people as mob to express the general will of a republican citizenry... The unleashing and manipulation of group hatreds do not make for a pretty sight, and the success of *Common Sense* depends on them.'[201] Consequently, it is difficult to interpret Paine's negations as primarily the positive affirmations of a republicanism premised on communitarian notions of civic virtue. Instead, if everyday politics is normally an expression of distrust and dislike, it is clear that in revolutions and civil wars these controllable dispositions are greatly inflated into fear and hatred. These dispositions were prominent in the conflicts of 1776–83, as they were after 1789.[202]

So Paine provided a rationale for the 'popular rage' that was now directed against Loyalists, or, in Pennsylvania, against the pacifist Quakers. In the third edition of *Common Sense*, he published as an appendix an attack on the Quakers for not joining in the Revolution (it is a text that makes problematic any confidence in Paine's 'universalism', attributed to his partly Quaker upbringing). Denunciation of Quakers and Loyalists fuelled a campaign of violent persecution against them on the basis of forged evidence, a campaign that Paine actively encouraged and that led to widespread confiscation of property, the destruction of livelihoods, the arbitrary imprisonment without trial of many, the deaths in custody of two, and the executions of two more.[203]

All this took place under the umbrella of the new Pennsylvania constitution, laws being passed which disenfranchised those deemed disloyal and which abolished habeas corpus. This constitution's provisions about due process were ignored in widespread harassment, summary detentions, large scale expropriations of property, spoliation, and profiteering by informers and looters. Pennsylvania even for a time established a Council of Safety with the power of imposing capital punishment 'in a summary mode' on those 'who from their general conduct or conversation may be deemed inimical to the common cause of Liberty, and the United States of North America', arguably an anticipation of the Terror in the French Revolution.[204]

---

[200] [Paine], *Common Sense* (1776): *CW*, i. 23, 41, 43–4, 46.

[201] Ferguson, 'Commonalities of Common Sense', 498–9.

[202] '[F]ear was one of the central elements in the origins of Revolutionary violence'; 'In historical situations the arousal of hate is commonly associated with sentiments of betrayal, with the rejection of values and beliefs one holds most dear, and with real or imagined threats. In both individuals and groups, hate is often tightly interwoven with fear and to the stories one contrives to tell others and to tell to oneself to justify and envelop one's fears': Timothy Tackett, *The Coming of the Terror in the French Revolution* (Cambridge, Mass., 2015), 7, 140.

[203] Jane E. Calvert, 'Thomas Paine, Quakerism and the Limits of Religious Liberty during the American Revolution', in *Selected Writings of Thomas Paine*, ed. Ian Shapiro and Jane E. Calvert (New Haven, 2014), 602–29.

[204] 'The constitution was carefully contrived as an instrument of power for which its proclaimed rights were only eyewash': Francis Jennings, *The Creation of America: Through Revolution to Empire* (Cambridge, 2000), 180–92, at 183. Henry J. Young, 'Treason and its Punishment in Revolutionary Pennsylvania', *PMHB* 90 (1966), 287–313 estimated 'hundreds' of prosecutions for treason and 'perhaps a score' of executions, plus forty-eight more executions, perhaps of Loyalists, after convictions more easily secured for other felonies, as well as acts of attainder against 457 individuals (the last Loyalists being hanged in 1788). 'The legislative record for the state of Pennsylvania during the

Again, Paine offered no critical comment, even in his long essay 'A Serious Address to the People of Pennsylvania on the Present Situation of Their Affairs',[205] and his conduct needs to be set against his carefully shaped self-image as a supporter of a natural right to religious toleration. Similarly, in his writings at the time of the American Revolution, as later at the time of the French, the phenomena of forced mass emigration and financial ruin did not feature; but the proportion of *émigrés* per thousand of the population was even higher in the American case than in the French.

Hatred hardly appears in studies of the history of political thought; it is marginalized as a discreditable mode that fuelled ideas (by implication, low-level ideas) rather than as an idea itself. Yet if hatred can be analysed as a mode of action, like sociability, justice, or politeness, there is a case for subjecting it to enquiry. In the political theory of hatred, Paine played a role comparable with few of his contemporaries. In particular, Paine's personal hatred of George III, which occluded the monarch's modest actual part in governance, passed directly into the Declaration of Independence. No other named colonial propagandist had written in such terms against the sovereign as an individual, and it seems that Paine's influence in changing the terms of the debate in this respect was significant. Yet he did not invent this mode of action. Rather, *Common Sense* was effective because it resonated with what already existed. 'For ten years [from 1765] the propagandists unremittingly and with increasing bitterness aspersed the characters and defamed the names of the English ruling classes at home and abroad. By 1775 they had become objects of hatred and disgust.'[206]

Thanks primarily to *Common Sense* and its interpretation in the twentieth century, Paine has often been credited with a doctrine of American exceptionalism in a text held to give privileged access to an American reality;[207] this image needs reconsideration. True, Paine hailed an undivided and undifferentiated 'America', but this category derived primarily from his ignorance of the diverse patterns on the ground; at no point did he anticipate one recent historian in identifying four contrasting regional wars of independence, each differently motivated and supported.[208]

American Revolution presents a picture of harsh people unyielding in their determination to stamp out all opposition': Anne M. Ousterhout, 'Controlling the Opposition in Pennsylvania during the American Revolution', *PMHB* 105 (1981), 3–34, at 3. The author lists 1,256 persons 'accused of disloyal acts after July 4, 1776', 18.

[205] Francis D. Cogliano, "'The Whole Object of the Present Controversy": The Early Constitutionalism of Paine and Jefferson', in Newman and Onuf (eds), *Paine and Jefferson in the Age of Revolutions*, 26–48, at 32–3.

[206] Philip Davidson, *Propaganda and the American Revolution 1763–1783* (Chapel Hill, NC, 1941), ch. VIII, 'Hate', 139–52, at 139. For Paine in this context, 131–3, 144–5, 15; 'The personal abuse of the King began mildly at first . . . but did not become common until after the appearance of *Common Sense*', 150.

[207] Ferguson, 'Commonalities of Common Sense', 465–7. Ferguson's assessments of the pamphlet's cultural centrality, like other scholars', rest on the inflated circulation figures now rendered implausible by the work of Trish Loughran. Yet Ferguson also identifies the contradictions and ambiguities of *Common Sense*: 'Paine blithely punctuates his claims of reasonableness and disinterestedness with other, disconcerting demands for revenge', 467–8.

[208] Fischer, *Albion's Seed*, 827–8.

Any American exceptionalism was almost wholly an abstraction in Paine's mind, a projection not of detailed knowledge of American realities but, instead, of an English desire for a religiously inspired emancipation from English realities. In this sense, Paine's American exceptionalism was an extrapolation onto a blank canvas of his English pre-commitments. What had been different about 'America', he wrote in retrospect, in January 1789, was 'The innocence of her character that won the hearts of all nations in her favor . . . her inimitable virtue.'[209] It was an important claim, made for later purposes, although it correctly reflected the prominent part played by virtue in Paine's thought. Yet if human nature is everywhere mixed, this comment reveals more about Paine than about colonial and revolutionary America.

THE DIFFUSION AND RECEPTION OF *COMMON SENSE*

If *Common Sense* was not the first publication to call for independence, it was the most open demand for it, and the most denigratory of the London authorities. But what exactly was its impact? This is strangely difficult to assess, since the pamphlet was eventually assimilated into the new republic's myth of origins and was ascribed a legendary role, ubiquitous, transformative, and unifying. At the time, Paine assiduously magnified its circulation, claiming in his 'Forester's Letter' of 8 April 1776 a sale of 120,000; but this was implausible within three winter months of its first publication, rested on no extensive knowledge by Paine of the work's printing history, and was a claim made for rhetorical effect in controversy with the Loyalist 'Cato'.[210] In 1779 Paine raised his boast to 150,000 copies, again without substantiation.[211] By 1945 the historian Philip Foner asserted, again without evidence, that 'shortly after its publication almost half a million copies were sold'.[212]

Yet investigation of the limited and patchy diffusion of the pamphlet among its colonial audience shows that 'it was neither as widely produced nor as widely consumed as rumor has it. Indeed, this particular narrative of origin has always been a populist fantasy, for the Revolution was powered by a far more limited consensus than this myth can ever acknowledge.' That is: the American Revolution was driven forward by small groups. *Common Sense* was reprinted in only seven of the thirteen colonies at a time when the transport of significant numbers of books between colonies, especially in midwinter, was nearly impossible. Its markets were highly localized, especially the members of the Continental Congress, meeting in Philadelphia; Philadelphian political activists; their contacts in their home colonies, especially in New England, which were linked to Philadelphia by post roads; and individuals already politically mobilized by the controversies that had raged since 1765. Its diffusion was '[l]ess a spontaneous than an engineered phenomenon' as activists of

---

[209] Paine to Kitty Nicholson Few, 6 Jan. 1789: *CW*, ii. 1276. 'One of the real paradoxes of *Common Sense* is that in it Paine treats America as a privileged land, chosen by providence for special favors, while at the same time he assumes that the political principles which he applies to it have equal validity in the rest of the world': A. Owen Aldridge, 'The Problem of Thomas Paine', *Studies in Burke and his Time* 19 (1978), 127–43, at 127.

[210] [Paine], 'The Forester's Letters' (8 Apr. 1776): *CW*, ii. 67.

[211] Paine to Henry Laurens, 14 Jan. 1779: *CW*, ii. 1163.   [212] Foner, in *CW*, i. xiv.

some social standing in Philadelphia hid behind an obscure English newcomer in order to test the reception of an extreme political option while shielding themselves.[213] Its reach was extended by quotations in newspapers. Yet even in Philadelphia, *Common Sense* did not at once transform the views of those hitherto unpersuaded. When elections were held on 1 May to fill seventeen newly created seats in the Pennsylvania Assembly, three of the four seats assigned to Philadelphia went to moderates (though by small majorities). Only between May and July 1776 were the moderates 'defeated by the machinations of a group of men determined to bring Pennsylvania immediately into the independence column regardless of the expressed wishes of the electorate'. It was a coup that Paine implicitly promoted in his first and fourth 'Forester Letters', published on 3 April and 8 May.[214]

The impact within America of *Common Sense* was chiefly in 1776, and was not sustained thereafter: in one quantifying study of America's 'Most Cited Thinkers, 1760–1805' Paine does not feature in the top 36.[215] Even in 1776, evidence for its reception beyond Pennsylvania does not establish that *Common Sense* created the unanimity of opinion that was once presumed necessary to create a nation. Only later, in 1802, did Benjamin Rush assert its legendary status:

> Its effects were sudden and extensive upon the American mind. It was read by public men, repeated in clubs, spouted in Schools, and in one instance, delivered from the pulpit instead of a sermon by a clergyman in Connecticut. Several pamphlets were written against it, but they fell dead from the press. The controversy about independence was carried into the news papers, in which I bore a busy part. It was carried on at the same time in all the principal cities in our country.[216]

Yet this was a retrospective simplification, and presumed a ubiquity of circulation that did not exist in 1776. Initial reactions of members of the colonial American elite of the southern and middle colonies to *Common Sense* could be adverse. Some were outright Loyalists. Others condemned the anonymous tract for insisting on an armed bid for independence at a time when delicate negotiations with Britain might still be possible, or for its ignorance of what John Adams called 'the Science of Government', especially what moderates saw as the superiority of a constitution of checks and balances over Paine's favoured unicameral legislature embodying popular sovereignty.[217]

[213] Trish Loughran, 'Disseminating Common Sense: Thomas Paine and the Problem of the Early National Bestseller', *American Literature* 78 (2006), 1–28, at 3, 5–6, 13–15, 17; Trish Loughran, *The Republic in Print: Print Culture in the Age of U.S. Nation Building, 1770–1870* (New York, 2007), 33–103. Loughran suggests a maximum colonial print run of 75,000. A few early editions in Philadelphia may have numbered 3,000, but even if the 25 American editions had an average print run of as much as 1,000, which is unlikely, the total would have been substantially less. This would still have been an exceptional circulation, but far short of the legend.

[214] Stephen E. Lucas, *Portents of Rebellion: Rhetoric and Revolution in Philadelphia, 1765–76* (Philadelphia, 1976), 224–5. For the political manoeuvres that captured the colony, ch. 8.

[215] Donald S. Lutz, 'The Relative Influence of European Writers on Late Eighteenth-Century American Political Thought', *American Political Science Review* 78 (1984), 189–97, at 194. Assigned among categories of publications, citations of the Bible were almost always predominant, 192.

[216] Rush, *Autobiography*, 114–15.

[217] See the negative reactions of John Adams, Carter Braxton, Landon Carter, Daniel Dulany, William Franklin, Christopher Gadsden, Patrick Henry, Henry Laurens, Richard Henry Lee, and

In Philadelphia, leaders could be cautious; the reactions of delegates to Congress provide one sample of Paine's reception among the elite. In January, Samuel Adams sent a copy of *Common Sense* to his wife for James Warren: 'Don't be displeased with me if you find the Spirit of it totally repugnant with your Ideas of Government. Read it without Prejudice and give me your impartial Sentiments of it when you may be at Leisure.' John Hancock forwarded a copy to Thomas Cushing: 'I Send it for your and Friend's amusement', but did not comment further. When John Dickinson drafted an 'Address to the Inhabitants of America', at the end of January, it showed no influence by Paine. The rank and file might be less cautious: Josiah Bartlett noted that the pamphlet had been 'greedily bought up and read by all ranks of people' in the city. But when in February 1776 Thomas Nelson, in Philadelphia, sent Thomas Jefferson 'a present of 2/ worth of Common Sense', probably some twenty copies, there is no indication that Jefferson did anything with them. Joseph Hewes sent a copy to a correspondent: 'The only pamphlet that has been published here for a long time I now send you, it is a Curiosity, we have not put up [packed] any to go by the Wagon, not knowing how you might relish independency.' In February, John Adams wrote of Paine as the author of 'a certain Heretical Pamphlet'. Later he gave a mixed appreciation: 'all agree there is a great deal of good sense, delivered in a clear, simple, concise and nervous Style. His Sentiments of the Abilities of America, and of the Difficulty of a Reconciliation with G.B. are generally approved. But his Notions, and Plans of Continental Government are not much applauded. Indeed this Writer has a better Hand at pulling down than building.' The next month, Adams added: 'In Point of argument there is nothing new. I believe every one that is in it, had been hackneyed in every Conversation public and private, before that Pamphlet was written.'

Paine's greatest impact was in the political hub, Philadelphia; there Samuel Ward reported on 19 February, 'I am told by good Judges that two thirds of this City & Colony are now full in his Sentiments.' Yet not all contemporaries credited the pamphlet with a decisive influence, by comparison with colonial reactions against escalating British acts. As John Adams wrote to his wife in February: 'I sent you from New York a Pamphlet intituled Common Sense, written in Vindication of Doctrines which there is Reason to expect that the further Encroachments of Tyranny and Depredations of Oppression, will soon make the common Faith.' In March Oliver Wolcott, in Philadelphia, reported that 'It has had a Surprizing run, which is an Evidence it falls in with the general Sentiments of the People.' As Francis Lightfoot Lee wrote from the same city in March, 'Our late King & his Parliament having declared us Rebels & Enemies, confiscated our property, as far as they were likely to lay hands on it; have effectually decided the question for us, whether or no we shou'd be independent.'[218]

John Rutledge, in Bailyn, *Ideological Origins*, 288–92; Foner, *Tom Paine and Revolutionary America*, 120–3; Keane, *Paine*, 124–8.

[218] Samuel Adams to James Warren, 13 Jan. [1776]; Josiah Bartlett to John Langdon, 13 Jan. 1776; John Hancock to Thomas Cushing, 17 Jan. 1776; John Dickinson, Draft Address to the Inhabitants of America, [?24 Jan. 1776]; Thomas Nelson to Thomas Jefferson, 4 Feb. 1776; Joseph Hewes to Samuel

One newspaper writer in March 1776 contended that the effect of *Common Sense* was 'trifling compared with the effects of the folly, insanity and villainy of the King and his Ministers'.[219] In April Samuel Adams, a zealot for independence, agreed: 'Mankind are governed more by their feelings than by reason. Events which excite those feelings will produce wonderful Effects. The Boston Port bill suddenly wrought a Union of the Colonies which could not be bro[ugh]t about by the Industry of years in reasoning on the necessity of it for the Common Safety.' For Adams, 'one Battle would do more towards a Declaration of Independency than a long chain of conclusive Arguments in a provincial Convention or the Continental Congress'.[220] Indeed, *Common Sense* gained much from being luckily published at the same time that George III's speech to Parliament on 26 October 1775 arrived in Pennsylvania, declaring, 'The rebellious war now levied is become more general [than just Massachusetts], and is manifestly carried on for the purpose of establishing an independent empire.'[221]

Once people began to see a logic in events, Paine's pamphlet could become iconic, even in the south. In April, John Adams wrote of a report from John Penn, a Delegate from North Carolina who had returned home from Philadelphia 'to attend the Convention of that Colony, in which he informs, that he heard nothing praised in the Course of his Journey, but Common Sense and Independence'.[222] But the Declaration of Independence on 4 July was a political act, not a projection onto a larger screen of Paine's teaching. In April Carter Braxton, a delegate to the Continental Congress from Virginia, warned of the divisions and differences between the colonies: 'Upon reviewing the secret movements of men and things I am convinced the assertion of independence is far off. If it was to be now asserted the continent would be torn in pieces by intestine wars and convulsions.'[223] Arguably, that is what then happened.

Historians have appreciated such limitations. Among the delegates to the Congress, '*Common Sense* probably had little direct impact on their thinking about independence'; this depended on 'more prosaic considerations'.[224] State and local resolutions on independence suggest 'that Paine's influence was more modest than he claimed and than his more enthusiastic admirers assume. *Common Sense* helped provoke public debate on independence, as did the news from England that arrived

---

Johnston, 13 Feb. 1776; John Adams to Abigail Adams, 18 Feb. 1776; John Adams to Charles Lee, 19 Feb. 1776; Samuel Ward to Henry Ward, 19 Feb. 1776; Oliver Wolcott to Samuel Lyman, 16 Mar. 1776; John Adams to Abigail Adams, 19 Mar. 1776; Francis Lightfoot Lee to Landon Carter, 19 Mar. 1776; John Adams to William Tudor, 12 Apr. 1776 in *Letters of Delegates to Congress 1774–1789*, ed. Paul H. Smith (Washington, 1976–), iii. 87–8, 104, 139–44, 194, 247, 271, 277, 285, 389–90, 398–9, 407, 513.

[219] *Pennsylvania Evening Post*, 7 Mar. 1776, quoted in John C. Miller, *Origins of the American Revolution* (Stanford, Calif., 1959), 476.

[220] Samuel Adams to Samuel Cooper, 30 Apr. 1776: *The Writings of Samuel Adams*, ed. Harry Alonzo Cushing (4 vols, New York, 1904–8), iii. 281–3. The same argument informs Jack Rakove, 'The Decision for American Independence: A Reconstruction', *Perspectives in American History* 10 (1976), 217–75.

[221] *His Majesty's most Gracious Speech to both Houses of Parliament, on Thursday the 26th of October, 1775* (no place, no printer), broadsheet. Apart from the formal identification of rebellion, the language of the speech was moderate: 'I shall be ready to receive the misled with tenderness and mercy.'

[222] John Adams to James Warren, 20 Apr. 1776: *Letters of Delegates*, ed. Smith, 558.

[223] Carter Braxton to Landon Carter, 14 Apr. 1776: Jensen (ed.), *American Colonial Documents*, 866.

[224] Rakove, *Beginnings of National Politics*, 89, 95.

at the time of its publication. But thereafter the argument for separation from Britain among Americans turned, as it always had, on what the mother country did, who was responsible for its actions, and what implications those considerations carried for the American future.'[225]

Americans themselves often sought, in retrospect and for their current purposes, to scale down the significance of Paine's intervention. As Samuel Williams, a Federalist, a minister, and a historian of Vermont, put it in 1794, in reaction against the unfolding French Revolution, the realities of colonial life (rather than revolutionary innovation) had disposed the colonists against 'the distinctions which society had set up against nature', namely titles of honour:

> Nothing was left for them but to pursue the line and course of nature, which was that of utility and safety. And this could produce nothing but similarity of situation, rights, privileges, and freedom ….notwithstanding the perpetual interference of royal authority, every thing cooperated to produce that natural, easy, independent situation, and spirit, in which the body of the people were found, when the American war came on.—In such circumstances, the common farmer in America had a more comprehensive view of his rights and privileges, than the speculative philosopher of Europe, could ever have of the subject…Learning their principles from the state of society in America, *Paine*, and other writers upon American politics, met with amazing success: Not because they taught the people principles, which they did not before understand; but because they placed the principles which they [the writers] had learned of them [the people], in a very clear and striking light, on a most critical and important occasion.[226]

This was a sanitized version of the Revolution, written from the perspective of 1794 in an attempt to defuse the threat of French principles by depicting the revolutionaries of 1776 as moderates. But it nevertheless contained one important understanding of Paine's role. Colonial Americans at the moment of Paine's arrival in 1774 had already understood their business very well.

Williams's account also ignored what had turned negotiable colonial grievances into revolution. Another American, the New Jersey Presbyterian Ashbel Green (1762–1848), later a Presbyterian minister but in 1776 a teenager, looked back of these events from the vantage point of 1840. He could briefly characterize a general cause: 'On the whole, I think it is unquestionable, that the spirit which produced the American revolution had its origin and its fostering principally among those who were denominated *dissenters*.' Paine was not a Dissenter, and Green deplored the irreligion, as he now saw it, of *The Age of Reason*. But Green's analysis explained why Paine had been a catalyst, not an original ideologue.

> I lately looked into a copy of this pamphlet [*Common Sense*], and was ready to wonder at its popularity and the effect it produced, when originally published. But the truth is, it struck a string which required but a touch to make it vibrate. The country was

---

[225] Maier, *American Scripture*, 91.
[226] Samuel Williams, *The Natural and Civil History of Vermont* (Walpole, NH: Isaiah Thomas and David Carlisle, 1794), 372–3.

ripe for independence, and only needed somebody to tell the people so, with decision, boldness and plausibility. Paine did this recklessly, having nothing to lose... Paine's talent, and he certainly possessed it eminently, was to make a takeing and striking appeal to popular feelings, when he saw it tending toward a point to which he wished to push it, whether for good or evil.[227]

Whatever the impact of this pamphlet, Green's account of the American war then found no need to mention Paine's other writings.

If *Common Sense* had some, but not a decisive, influence as a catalyst in the decision of part of the elite to declare independence, it was less influential in converting the elite to any faith in popular rule. John Adams published the most famous if implicit reply to Paine, not mentioning *Common Sense* by name but instead offering a minimalist account of the revolution to counter Paine's extensive one: 'by an act of Parliament we are put out of the royal protection, and consequently discharged from our allegiance.' It followed, urged Adams, in contrast to Paine's doctrine, that 'The first necessary step' in forming a constitution 'is, to depute power from the many, to a few of the most wise and good'. Their influence should be secured, argued Adams, by a bicameral legislature, an executive power with a veto, and an independent judiciary.[228] The wide reception of Adams's remarks suggests that Paine did not set the terms of the debate for all colonists, even supporters of the Revolution. But a more penetrating critique of *Common Sense* came from colonists opposed to independence.

Although the Loyalist response to *Common Sense* did not widely discredit it, one Loyalist, Charles Inglis, unaware of Paine's authorship, did diagnose with some accuracy the mood of Paine's pamphlet: the author

seems to be every where transported with rage—a rage that knows no limits, and hurries him along, like an impetuous torrent... Yet I cannot persuade myself, that such fire and fury are genuine marks of patriotism. On the contrary, they rather indicate that some mortifying disappointment is rankling at heart; or that some tempting object of ambition is in view; or probably both.[229]

The anonymous author of *Common Sense* had ignored the cost of his political prescriptions; 'it is more than probable he has nothing to lose; and like others in the same predicament, is willing to trust to the chapter of accidents and chances for something in the scramble. He cannot lose; but may possibly gain.'[230] This was sometimes the case: as the subsequently eminent Charles Biddle later admitted, after the battle of Lexington, 'Being young, and considering my country unjustly persecuted, I was as willing to go to war as any man in America. Perhaps my having little to lose was another reason for my having no objection to it.'[231] It was too true of

---

[227] *The Life of Ashbel Green, V.D.M.*, ed. Joseph H. Jones (New York, 1849), 29, 46–7.

[228] [John Adams], *Thoughts on Government: Applicable to the Present State of the American Colonies. In a Letter from a Gentleman To his Friend* (Philadelphia: John Dunlap, 1776), 9, 11, 14, 16–17, 21.

[229] *The True interest of America Impartially Stated, in certain Strictures On a Pamphlet Intitled Common Sense. By an American* [Charles Inglis] (Philadelphia: James Humphreys, jun., 1776), 34.

[230] [Inglis], *The True interest*, 54, 61, 64–5, 67.

[231] *Autobiography of Charles Biddle, Vice-President of the Supreme Executive Council of Pennsylvania 1745–1821* (Philadelphia, 1883), 72.

Paine: he had no house, no lands, no ships, no business in America; but he had also experienced no reverse there. The sense of 'mortifying disappointment' was something that Paine had presumably brought with him from England. *Common Sense* has seemed such a collection of self-evident truths to generations of Americans that key questions are seldom asked. Why did Paine write it at all? Why did he side so fully with the cause (in 1774 a minority aspiration in the Thirteen Colonies) of colonial independence?

The answers to those questions can only be primarily English ones. But those answers must recognize that the debate in England on the American crisis did not come to turn on Paine. In London, *Common Sense* did not have a defining effect on public controversy, even among sympathizers with the American colonists. Debate did not focus on it, as much debate in the 1790s did focus on *Rights of Man*. Although there were more editions of *Common Sense* in the British Isles than in the colonies, it did not create any consensus in Britain in favour of American independence; on the contrary, British opinion seems to have hardened against the rebels over time.[232]

North's ministry reacted to seditious publications in the 1770s very differently from Pitt's ministry in the 1790s: North did little to suppress them. But beneath this toleration the text that flourished most was Richard Price's *Observations*: 'it was as a jeremiad on Britain's decline that it had its main impact. Price blended the style of an Old Testament prophet' in warning against Britain's moral corruption 'with the authority of a modern economist' warning of the economic impact of war. By contrast, even reformers were often 'dismayed' by the outbreak of fighting, which signified an implicit abandonment of the transatlantic common cause of reforming English abuses.[233] In 1776 Price wrote: 'I have reason, indeed, to believe, that independency is, even at this moment, generally dreaded among them as a calamity to which they are in danger of being driven, in order to avoid a greater.'[234] He was already out of date. For different reasons, both Price and Paine had been led to overlook the dynamic causes of revolution purely internal to the colonies.

In England, *Common Sense* was therefore 'not well received by the main body of the colonists' English friends...It is difficult to find in the opposition press as a

---

[232] Paine does not feature in the widespread and detailed newspaper debates on America studied in Troy Bickham, *Making Headlines: The American Revolution as Seen through the British Press* (De Kalb, Ill., 2009) or in Fred Junkin Hinkhouse, *The Preliminaries of the American Revolution as seen in the English Press, 1763–1775* (New York, 1926). Paine's brief mention in Solomon Lutnick, *The American Revolution and the British Press 1775–1783* (Columbia, SC, 1967), 46–7 evidently derived from Lutnick's acceptance of Paine's overstated figures for the sales of his pamphlet.

[233] John Sainsbury, *Disaffected Patriots: London Supporters of Revolutionary America 1769–1782* (Kingston, Canada, 1987), 126. A recent scholar has argued that Price's *Observations* 'had a sale of over sixty thousand in six months': Jon Erik Larson (ed.), *Richard Price and the Ethical Foundations of the American Revolution* (Durham, NC, 1979), 9. If so, this may be compared with Paine's *Common Sense*, which may have had a smaller initial circulation in the colonies. Yet Price's pamphlet had a far larger potential audience in London and England, and the figures are not directly comparable to Paine's disadvantage.

[234] Richard Price, *Observations on the Nature of Civil Liberty, the Principles of Government, and the Justice and Policy of the War with America* (2nd edn, London: T. Cadell, 1776); same pagination as 1st edn; 60.

whole any laudatory comment about the pamphlet.' When John Almon reprinted it, he published it with another tract, as he explained in the advertisement: 'The public have been amused by many extracts from the Pamphlet entitled *Common Sense*, which have been held up as Proof positive that the Americans desire to become independent; we are happy in this opportunity of publishing [James Chalmers'] *Plain Truth*; which we take to be as good a Proof that the Americans do not desire to become independent.' The anti-slavery reformer Granville Sharp recorded in his diary his meeting with Lord Dartmouth on 14 March 1777, Sharp urging: 'I ventured to pledge my life upon the success of an attempt to bring back the American Empire to the allegiance of the crown of Great Britain provided a proof of *Sincerity* in Treating with them was given and the proof which I proposed was the *Reformation of Parliament* at Home.'[235] He was lucky not to have been taken at his word.

English reformers generally had as little understanding as Paine of the nature of what was occurring in the American colonies; like Paine, they tended to see English colonies in English terms.[236] But after the Declaration of Independence, there could be no doubt of colonists' intentions. The reformers in England who had been eager to identify themselves as friends of America often fell silent, or redirected their rhetoric into a simple denunciation of North's ministry. The pioneer in the mobilization of an image of the American Revolution for English purposes was not Paine but, once more, Richard Price, and not until 1784.

Price's *Observations on the Importance of the American Revolution, and The Means of making it a Benefit to the World* (1784) hailed 'a revolution which opens a new prospect in human affairs, and begins a new aera in the history of mankind;—a revolution by which *Britons* themselves will be the greatest gainers, if wise enough to improve properly the check that has been given to the despotism of their ministers, and to catch the flame of virtuous liberty which has saved their American brethren'. By 'exciting a spirit of resistance to tyranny', the 'late war' had 'emancipated one *European* country, and is likely to emancipate others'. But of this 'virtuous liberty' Price showed no more knowledge in 1784 than in 1776. Instead, he rehearsed the English Nonconformist litany, hailing 'the excellent HOADLY', Joseph Butler, Samuel Clarke, David Hume, and James Burgh. He did not mention Paine, or any American, and offered little specific knowledge of the new American republic except that it had abolished religious establishments (which in 1784 was not entirely the case) and that it enjoyed economic equality—'the rich and the poor, the haughty grandee and the creeping sycophant, equally unknown' (which was far from true). Price's preoccupation, which took up most of his pamphlet, was still an English one: 'The injury which civil establishments do to Christianity'. Price's construction of a 'usable' American Revolution (usable, that is, in English Nonconformist

---

[235] Sainsbury, *Disaffected Patriots*, 127–8. Thereafter, Paine does not feature in Sainsbury's careful study.

[236] For a contrasting argument that America was formative for English reformers' thought from the 1770s, see Arthur Sheps, 'The American Revolution and the Transformation of English Republicanism', *Historical Reflections* 2 (1975), 3–28.

conflicts with the Church) was in wholly English terms.[237] With Price, as with Paine, universalist discourse could be made plausible by ignorance.

For most English reformers in the late 1780s Price, not Paine, was the leading intellectual. It was to be Price's restatement of his position of 1776 in *A Discourse on the Love of our Country* (1789), not any new intervention by Paine, that provoked Edmund Burke's *Reflections on the Revolution in France*. Price provided the catalyst; but Burke's seeming prescience about (what was much later called) the new age of totalitarian democracy then dawning was not primarily based on his observation of the very earliest stages of the French Revolution. For Burke had been, until 1776, a 'friend of America' who like others fell silent after the Declaration of Independence gave a disastrously unexpected turn to events. He was tactically unable to make public what he learned of the sanguinary situation on the ground in America, and instead transposed his haunting insights onto France.[238] In political theory, too, Burke's objections were first to Price's writings of 1776. Before 1791, Paine did not dominate the debate.

COMMON SENSE: THE DISCURSIVE CONTEXT

Paine, Priestley, and Price

Paine's late eighteenth-century world did not witness a 'universalism' that naturally united reformers everywhere. This argument can be tested in a number of ways. One is to analyse the differences as well as the similarities between Paine and one of the leading contemporary champions of a variety of reforming causes, the Dissenting intellectual and Unitarian Dr Joseph Priestley. This exercise is particularly necessary since Paine has been presented as a reader, 'we can be fairly confident', of Priestley's works. 'Here we find, not only Paine's distinctions between society and government, between political and civil liberty, but also the claims that all governments were originally equal republics and that men cannot renounce the rights of their descendants'.[239]

But there were major differences between the Socinian Priestley and the Deist Paine. Priestley wrote that 'The great instrument in the hand of divine providence, of this progress of the species towards perfection, is *society*, and consequently *government*'; in society 'men are connected with and subservient to one another',

---

[237] Richard Price, *Observations on the Importance of the American Revolution, and The Means of making it a Benefit to the World* (London: no printer, 1784; the dedication dated 6 July 1784), 2–3, 6–7, 14–15, 20, 35, 37, 42, 61, 65–6, 68–9. Benjamin Hoadly (1676–1761), from 1734 Bishop of Winchester, the most polemical Low Churchman of his age. Samuel Clarke (1675–1729), Anglican priest but an Arian. Joseph Butler (1692–1752), from 1750 Bishop of Durham.

[238] J. C. D. Clark, 'Edmund Burke's *Reflections on the Revolution in America* (1777); or, How Did the American Revolution Relate to the French?', in Ian Crowe (ed.), *An Imaginative Whig: Reassessing the Life and Thought of Edmund Burke* (Columbia, SC, 2005), 73–92.

[239] Wootton, 'The Republican Tradition', 34–5, relying on Felix Gilbert, 'The English Background of American Isolationism in the Eighteenth Century', *WMQ* 3rd ser. 1 (1944), 138–60, at 157: 'Their fundamental political ideals were identical...Paine's passages are nothing but a paraphrase of Priestley's words.'

so making possible 'general improvements'. 'Government' was 'the great instrument of this progress of the human species towards this glorious state', an end point 'glorious and paradisiacal, beyond what our imaginations can now conceive'.[240] In 1776 at least, Paine depicted society as the result of 'prudence', pragmatic utilitarian cooperation prompted by 'lost innocence', and regarded government as the evil agency that frustrated the promise of spontaneous society. Government, for Paine, had eventually given rise to the malign principles of kingship and hereditary right: he did not picture it as the instrument of progress in its present-day sense.[241]

Priestley, like 'almost all political writers... before us', depicted men leaving the state of nature to 'voluntarily resign some part of their natural liberty, and submit their conduct to the direction of the community'. In any large community, government must be by deputy; 'In England, the king, the hereditary lords, and the electors of the house of commons, are these *standing* deputies; and the members of the house of commons are, again, the *temporary* deputies.'[242] Paine accepted the passage from the state of nature to government, but rejected this conventional tripartite division.[243]

Priestley defined '*Political liberty*' as 'the power, which the members of the state reserve to themselves, of arriving at the public offices, or at least of having votes in the nomination of those who fill them'.[244] Paine largely ignored meritocratic access to office and the franchise question, and did not argue by deduction from a definition of 'liberty' (no such definition was offered in *Common Sense*, where the term 'liberty' was used infrequently and not reified). Priestley, moving towards the doctrine of universal suffrage, claimed that man had an indefeasible 'natural right... of relieving himself from all oppression, that is, from every thing that has been imposed upon him without his own consent', so that 'this can be the only true and proper foundation of all the governments subsisting in the world'.[245] Paine, as a Deist, made equality by creation the starting point of his analysis.[246]

Priestley's notion of utilitarianism was dependent on his conception of God: 'the good and happiness of the members, that is the majority of the members of any state, is the great standard by which every thing relating to that state must finally be determined'.[247] Priestley made the theological premises of his utilitarianism clear: 'the happiness of his creatures' was the wish of 'the divine being', as all could see who were 'not warped by theological and metaphysical subtilties'.[248] Paine's Deism led him to a primarily negative critique: the power of a king, if it needed checking, could not be 'from God'; the division of humanity into kings and subjects was one for which there was 'no truly natural or religious reason'; for a Deist, God did not intervene to prescribe particular courses of action. For Paine, 'human

---

[240] Joseph Priestley, *An Essay on the First Principles of Government; and on the Nature of Political, Civil, and Religious Liberty* (London: J. Dodsley, T. Cadell and J. Johnson, 1768), 5–6, 8.

[241] [Paine], *Common Sense* (1776): *CW*, i. 4–5, 13.   [242] Priestley, *An Essay*, 9–11.

[243] [Paine], *Common Sense* (1776): *CW*, i. 5–7.   [244] Priestley, *An Essay*, 12–13.

[245] Priestley, *An Essay*, 16.   [246] [Paine], *Common Sense* (1776): *CW*, i. 9.

[247] Priestley, *An Essay*, 17.   [248] Priestley, *An Essay*, 18.

wisdom' could do that; the last part of *Common Sense* was an analysis of England's and America's 'interest'.[249]

Priestley argued that although 'a body of people may be bound by a voluntary resignation of all their interests (which they have been so infatuated as to make) to a single person, or to a few, it can never be supposed that the resignation is obligatory to their posterity'. For Priestley, this was established by the utilitarian argument 'because it is *manifestly contrary to the good of the whole that it should be so*'. According to Priestley, 'systems of uniformity' in 'political and religious institutions', especially 'religious establishments', enforced by law, could not be imposed upon posterity: this would imply our 'infallibility'. Here there was a simple absence of natural right. 'What natural right have we to judge for them, any more than our ancestors had to judge for us?' But his main ground for this position was utilitarian: its opposite would make 'improvements' impossible.[250] For Paine, the absence of authority in ancestors over their descendants was because the hereditary principle was akin to the argument from original sin.[251]

Priestley envisaged large, advanced polities, since 'a state of perfect equality, in communities of individuals, can never be preserved'. He therefore approved of 'such states as England, France and Spain' as alternatives to 'very extensive, and consequently absolute monarchies'. He accepted that 'In general...none but persons of considerable fortune should be capable of arriving at the highest offices in the government', and 'the highest offices of all, equivalent to that of king, ought to be in some measure hereditary'. Although Priestley urged 'Let the livings of the clergy be made more equal', in setting their rewards 'Let nothing be considered but the work [i.e. the clergyman's duties], and the necessary expences of a liberal education': for him, clergy would still be educated gentlemen.[252] Paine hankered after an ideal of rural simplicity, condemned the monarchy of England, offered no sanction to the rule of the rich, made the hereditary principle his main target, and had no regard for educated gentlemen. For Priestley, 'the divine being' had 'raised up William the third of glorious memory' to effect 'our deliverance' at the Revolution of 1688, thanks to whom 'the government of this country is now fixed upon' a 'good and firm...basis'; as to the English Constitution, 'I can heartily join with the greatest admirers...I really think it to be the best actual scheme of civil policy', though open to improvement.[253] Paine condemned William III and the Revolution of 1688, and argued that England had no constitution.

Priestley announced 'a maxim, than which nothing is more true, that *every government, whatever be the form of it, is originally, and antecedent to its present form, an equal republic*; and, consequently, that every man, when he comes to be sensible of his natural rights, and to feel his own importance, will consider himself as fully equal to any other person whatever'.[254] By contrast Paine began with the equality of man at the creation, and in one explanation professed at least to believe in the

---

[249] [Paine], *Common Sense* (1776): *CW*, i. 8–9, 23, 26.   [250] Priestley, *An Essay*, 182–4.
[251] Priestley, *An Essay*, 17; [Paine], *Common Sense* (1776): *CW*, i. 14.
[252] Priestley, *An Essay*, 19–22.   [253] Priestley, *An Essay*, 35, 128.
[254] Priestley, *An Essay*, 41.

origin of government with 'the quiet and rural lives of the first Patriarchs'. But more generally Paine depicted governments as malign impositions: for him, governments did not originate as equal republics.[255]

Whatever the form of government, Priestley distinguished 'political liberty' from 'civil liberty'; 'whether a people enjoy more or fewer of their natural rights, under any form of government, is a matter of the last [i.e. utmost] importance; and upon this depends, what, I should chuse to call, the *civil liberty* of the state, as distinct from its political liberty'. It followed that 'even a republic' or 'a democracy' might be 'tyrannical, and oppressive' as well as a monarchy or an aristocracy. European governments differed greatly in form, but 'the present happiness of the subjects of them can by no means be estimated by a regard to the form'.[256] For Paine, republics and representative systems had inbuilt guarantees against oppression.

Finally, Priestley used by far the larger part of his *Essay* to argue for just two public policy goals: first, that the state should not provide a system of public education; second ('the most important question concerning the extent of civil government') 'whether the civil magistrate ought to extend his authority to matters of *religion*'. Here, despite Priestley's use of the idea of natural rights, he was also explicit in founding his conclusion on utility: 'as all arguments *a priori* in matters of policy are apt to be fallacious, fact and experience seem to be our only safe guide' to whether the civil magistrate's interference 'be for the public good'. His conclusion was: 'Let the system of *toleration* be completely carried into execution'; that attained, 'I do not pretend to define what degree of establishment is necessary for religion.' Even popery was no danger, since 'All the address and assiduity of man cannot, certainly, recommend so absurd a system of faith and practice to any but the lowest and most illiterate of our common people, who can never have any degree of influence in the state.' For Priestley, the 'progress of knowledge is chiefly among the thinking few'. Only eight years before the publication of *Common Sense*, Priestley had much to say about England in the 1640s and 1688, but ignored the American controversy.[257] By contrast, Paine largely ignored education, later condemned religious toleration as implying a right in the state to choose to tolerate, never spoke contemptuously of 'the common people', and used the second half of *Common Sense* to argue for the political independence of the American colonies.

Priestley thought it was the 'kind intentions of the deity' to provide for 'a state of constant, though slow improvement in every thing'; 'This seems to be the time, when the minds of men are opening to large and generous views of things.' In contrast to Priestley's gradualism, Paine from 1776 thought he saw the beginning of a new age not of slow improvement but of revolutionary transformation: 'The birthday of a new world is at hand'.[258]

Priestley held that 'ecclesiastical and civil jurisdiction, being things of a totally different nature, ought, if possible, to be wholly disengaged from one another'.

---

[255] [Paine], *Common Sense* (1776): *CW*, i. 10.   [256] Priestley, *An Essay*, 50–1, 53.

[257] Priestley, *An Essay*, 62–191, at 104–5, 116, 119–20, 138, 147. Priestley, 148, commended a famous book, [Francis Blackburne], *The Confessional* (London: S. Bladon, 1766), the key attack on subscription and establishment. Paine never mentioned *The Confessional*.

[258] Priestley, *An Essay*, 142, 188; [Paine], *Common Sense* (1776), in *CW*, i. 45.

It was his central goal. In his peroration, he announced: 'Let all the friends of liberty and human nature join to free the minds of men from the shackles of narrow and impolitic laws.' To secure that end, 'gentle measures' should be preferred unless 'the friends of arbitrary power' used coercion, in which case 'the disorders of the state' might 'absolutely force us into violent measures'.[259] Without anticipating 1776, Priestley in 1768 conveyed a polite threat of revolution. Paine left no evidence of such a commitment before the skirmish at Lexington.

The root cause of their difference was theological. Priestley was a Socinian; Paine, it seems, was already a Deist. Priestley advocated tolerance of Deism, but not the adoption of that cause. Indeed, for him Deism was a regrettably erroneous system only encouraged by persecution: 'it is, perhaps, principally owing to the laws in favour of Christianity, that there are so many deists in this country.'[260] There was much, then, that Paine and Priestley had in common, but much in which they differed; and there is no sufficient evidence to establish that Paine's views in *Common Sense* derived from a reading of Priestley.

By contrast, Paine in his *Crisis* papers later cited Richard Price. In *Common Sense* Paine cannot have drawn on Price's *Observations*, the latter published in London in February 1776; but how much did they share? The difference is clear: Price's tract, although it began with general reflections on liberty (pp. 2–18), was largely taken up with a detailed and well informed examination of the American controversy (pp. 19–109). Although Price professed 'to try this question by the general principles of Civil Liberty; and not by the practice of former times; or by the *Charters* granted the colonies', he included much recent detail. Paine's knowledge of the American debate was small: the last half of *Common Sense* was a projection into the future, not a review of past arguments.[261]

In general preconceptions, Price and Paine shared more. Price cited with approval Burgh's *Political Disquisitions*, 'a work full of important and useful instruction', and (in the same footnote as 'Mr. Locke on Government') Priestley's *Essay*, its author being one of those 'excellent writers' who had 'refuted' the notion that 'government is not the creature of the people' and had showed how 'a free government' had a 'tendency to exalt the nature of man'.[262]

Price offered the familiar Whig binary alternative 'between *Liberty* and *Slavery*', but with an emphasis on '*Human Authority*' in religion requiring conformity to particular modes of faith and worship, and superseding *private judgment*'. This led to a heightened rhetoric: 'without *Religious* and *Civil Liberty* he [man] is a poor and abject animal without rights, without property, and without a conscience, bending his neck to the yoke, and crouching to the will of every silly creature who has the insolence to pretend to authority over him.'[263] Paine shared this rhetorical overstatement, but without reifying 'liberty'. To Paine, the goal of the future 'Charter of the United

---

[259] Priestley, *An Essay*, 189–91.   [260] Priestley, *An Essay*, 174.

[261] Richard Price, *Observations on the Nature of Civil Liberty, the Principles of Government, and the Justice and Policy of the War with America* (2nd edn, London: T. Cadell, 1776), 32; same pagination as 1st edn.

[262] Price, *Observations*, 10, 16–17.   [263] Price, *Observations*, 4–6.

Colonies' was 'Securing freedom and property to all men, and above all things, the free exercise of religion, according to the dictates of conscience': for the heterodox, the world presented a series of threatening conspiracies against religious liberty. It was at this point in his argument that Paine cited Dragonetti; but for Paine, the Italian's shallow utilitarianism was dominated by Paine's goal of liberty of conscience. Paine wrote of natural rights, but these had meaning for him in a Deist cosmology: 'The Almighty hath implanted in us these unextinguishable feelings for good and wise purposes.'[264]

Price insisted that

> all civil government, as far as it can be denominated *free*, is the creature of the people. It originates with them. It is conducted under their direction; and has in view nothing but their happiness...In every free state every man is his own Legislator...All *laws* are particular provisions or regulations established by COMMON CONSENT...all *Magistrates* are Trustees or Deputies for carrying these regulations into execution.

But this was a lofty standard: if laws were not made by all, all were in a state of 'Slavery'. Price appreciated that this meant that '*Civil Liberty*, in its most perfect degree, can be enjoyed only in small states, where every member is capable of giving his suffrage in person, and of being chosen into public offices'. Paine did not tie liberty to the suffrage, and placed his confidence in the representative system. As with Paine, Price's remedy was also that individuals should give their consent via '*Substitutes* or *Representatives*' so that 'whatever can be done by such delegates, within the limits of their trust, may be considered as done by the united voice and counsel of the Community' and the state 'will still be *free* or *self-governed*'. This was long-familiar English doctrine. What elevated it above the status of a cliché for the heterodox was their renewed perception that their subjection to an Anglican establishment made them slaves, and it was their secularized chiliasm that created the expectation that 'any number of states might be subjected to a scheme of government, that would exclude the desolations of war, and produce universal peace and order'.[265] Paine argued on similar lines that before kings existed 'there were no wars' and forecast that in his ideal republic, civil war would henceforth not happen;[266] he would in turn see the French Revolution as the harbinger of universal peace.

What was chiefly different was Price's insistence, missing in Paine, that a state would be free 'in proportion as it is more or less fairly and adequately represented'.[267] Paine supported 'a large and equal representation',[268] but, indifferent to the franchise question, he never defined it. For Price, Burgh's statistics on English constituencies and voting meant that 'it will be an abuse of language to say that the [English] state possesses Liberty'. Given Price's earlier rhetoric about liberty and slavery, it now mattered little that he should briefly concede that 'Liberty may be enjoyed in every possible degree; from that which is complete and perfect, to that which is merely nominal'. Within a few lines, Price slipped back into his rhetoric of '*slavery*'.

---

[264] [Paine], *Common Sense* (1776): *CW*, i. 29–30, 37.   [265] Price, *Observations*, 6–9.
[266] [Paine], *Common Sense* (1776): *CW*, i. 9, 15, 27.   [267] Price, *Observations*, 9–10.
[268] [Paine], *Common Sense* (1776): *CW*, i. 38 (citing Burgh).

But once this rhetoric had been vindicated, Price recorded that he was quite happy with the idea of 'an *Hereditary Council*, consisting of men of the first rank in the state... This will form useful checks in a legislature.' The two extremes, he argued, were rule by 'a lawless body of *Grandees*' and 'a *lawless mob*'.[269] Like many reformers, Price shared most of the assumptions of his society, differing from it only on defined issues. Paine, rejecting the hereditary principle, went far further; he rejected 'rank', and he rejected the possibility of a government of checks and balances.

Price's critique of British policy was, at its root, theological:

> In this hour of tremendous danger, it would become us to turn our thoughts to Heaven. This is what our Brethren in the Colonies are doing. From one end of *North-America* to the other, they are FASTING and PRAYING. But what are we doing?—Shocking thought! We are ridiculing them as *Fanatics*, and scoffing at religion.—We are running wild after pleasure, and forgetting every thing serious and decent at *Masquerades*.—We are gambling in gaming houses; trafficking for Boroughs; perjuring ourselves at Elections; and selling ourselves for places.—Which side then is Providence likely to favour?

The American states were 'animated by piety'.[270] The conflict, according to Price, was between pious friends of liberty and corrupt, ungodly tyrants. Without understanding the theological dimension of colonial politics, he projected onto the colonists these illusions. Paine, who understood even less about social dynamics in the colonies, did something similar to a higher degree. Addressing the colonists, he announced that the object of independence was 'to preserve your native country uncontaminated by European corruption'.[271]

Whatever its claim to piety, Price's position contained a scarcely disguised threat of armed resistance, 'should any events ever arise that should render the same opposition necessary that took place in the times of King *Charles* the First, and *James* the Second'; 'An important revolution in the affairs of this kingdom seems to be approaching.' Paine was not the only revolutionary in the English-speaking world of the 1760s and 1770s. As to the American controversy, Price's position was deduced from his premises: 'the slavery of a people to internal despots may be qualified and limited; but I don't see what can limit the authority of one state over another. The exercise of power in this case can have no other measure than discretion; and, therefore, must be indefinite and absolute.'[272]

The hereditary principle and its colonial opponents

One distinguishing element in Paine's thought was his anti-hereditary commitments. Where did these originate? In Paine's view, the practical antidote to the hereditary principle was not republicanism, or democracy, or equality, but the representative principle: 'The system of government purely representative, unmixed with anything of hereditary nonsense, began in America.'[273] And the same year:

---

[269] Price, *Observations*, 10–13.   [270] Price, *Observations*, 98.
[271] [Paine], *Common Sense* (1776): *CW*, i. 41.   [272] Price, *Observations*, 18, 20, 109.
[273] Paine, *A Letter To Mr. Secretary Dundas* (1792): *CW*, ii. 449.

Two revolutions have taken place, those of America and France; and both of them have rejected the unnatural compounded system of the English Government. America has declared against all hereditary government, and established the representative system of government only. France has entirely rejected the aristocratical part, and is now discovering the absurdity of the monarchical, and is approaching fast to the representative system.

What the representative system legitimately represented was not the electorate, or popular sovereignty: for Paine, 'There ought to be, in the constitution of every country, a mode of referring back, on any extraordinary occasion, to the sovereign and original constituent power, which is the nation itself.'[274] It was not 'we the people' or a reified 'America' that had achieved this, but, for Paine, the representative system. But if this was the practical means, what had been the colonists' intellectual case against the hereditary principle?

An antipathy to titles of honour was already common ground among the heterodox. In Boston, Massachusetts, the Deist Benjamin Franklin had found in the 1720s that 'my indiscrete Disputations about Religion began to make me pointed at with Horror by good People, as an Infidel or Atheist'. He published an essay 'On Titles of Honour' in *The New-England Courant* of 18 February 1722–3 that used a reinterpretation of Scripture to enforce a lesson of social equality:

> In old Time it was no disrespect for Men and Women to be call'd by their own Names: *Adam*, was never called *Master* Adam; we never read to Noah *Esquire*, Lot *Knight* and *Baronet*, nor of the *Right Honourable* Abraham, *Viscount* Mesopotamia, *Baron* of Carran [Canan]; no, no, they were plain Men, honest Country Grasiers, that took Care of their Families and their Flocks. *Moses* was a great Prophet, and *Aaron* a Priest of the Lord; but we never read of the *Reverend* Moses, nor the *Right Reverend Father in God*, by Divine Providence, *Lord Arch-Bishop of* Israel... It was no Incivility then to mention their naked Names as they were expressed.

For Franklin as for Paine, an objection to nobility was a sub-set of a theological critique of hierarchical ecclesiastical offices.

Only later, in Philadelphia, did Benjamin Franklin's best-selling almanac *Poor Richard Improved* for 1751 carry a mathematical proof of the impossibility of pure noble descent, a table which 'shews the Impossibility of preserving Blood free from such Mixtures, and that the Pretension of such Purity of Blood in ancient Families is a mere Joke', long intermarriage 'rendring all the People related by Blood, and, as it were, of one Family'. When he came to begin his autobiography in 1771, Franklin smugly congratulated himself on 'Having emerg'd from the Poverty & Obscurity in which I was born & bred, to a State of Affluence & some Degree of Reputation in the World', a pride not unlike Paine's; Franklin's rejection of aristocracy, like Paine's, was rather theoretical than based on personal experiences of injustice at the hands of the nobility.[275] This colonial scene was only a pale echo of the conflicts over status that had marked the home country. Early eighteenth-century colonists

---

[274] Paine, *Letter Addressed to the Addressers* (1792): *CW*, ii. 482–3, 503–4.
[275] *Benjamin Franklin: Writings*, ed. J. A. Leo Lemay (New York, 1987), 49–50, 1269–70, 1307, 1325.

like Franklin were however trapped in a contradiction, rejecting the hereditary system for theological reasons but forced to be enthusiastic about the monarchy of George I and George II for political ones: for them, the Stuart threat still spelled popery and tyranny. After 1760, this could change for Franklin as it did for Paine. Paine, by 1792, trusted that 'every species of hereditary government might fall, as pope and monks had fallen before'.[276] It was to be a new Reformation.

Common Sense made use of scriptural language that engaged with the prevalent Trinitarian Christianity of American colonists, and this had long generated among them a nexus of political expectations. As a colonial American in Boston explained in 1774,

> The united language of almost every man is, that he has a right to be happy; that he is determined to be free; and that he chooses both under the auspices of the illustrious house of Brunswick, and in connection with our parent state.—These rights they claim not only under a charter from a temporary king, but from one under the broad seal of heaven— from the king of Kings, and Lord of all the earth. They say, these rights were created in them by the decrees of providence; that they were born with them—exist with them—are founded upon the immutable and eternal maxims of right, reason, and the never failing principles of strict justice; and therefore ought not to be surrendered but with the heart's blood—or to be torn from them by any power of human institution.[277]

It was a mindset still consumed by an atavistic hatred of Catholicism: as the future President of Yale College, Ezra Stiles, wrote in his diary on 23 August 1774:

> The King has signed the Quebec Act, extendg that Province to the Ohio & Mississippi and comprehending nearly Two Thirds of the Territory of English America, and established the Romish Church & IDOLATRY over all that space; in this Act all the Bishops concurred. Astonishing that King, Lds and Commons, a whole protestant Parliament should expressly establish Popery over three Quarters of their Empire.[278]

An English visitor noted:

> In their churches the Gospel is laid aside for politics, and nothing is more common than their offering up prayers for the destruction of the navy and army. I have talked with their patriots; they will not allow Great Britain to have any right whatever over the Colonies, and seem determined to shake off all connection with her. I was told by one of their principal leaders, that they waited for nothing but the Canadians to join them in the grand rebellion, (as he called it) to declare themselves independent.[279]

Such a mindset was ready to go to scriptural lengths of violence. A correspondent from Virginia promised 8,000 volunteers 'as ready to face death in defence of their

---

[276] Paine, *Letter Addressed to the Addressers* (1792): *CW*, ii. 496.

[277] Letter from an American, Boston, 15 Nov. 1774, in *Bristol Gazette* (12 Jan. 1775): Willard (ed.), *Letters on the American Revolution*, 7–10.

[278] *The Literary Diary of Ezra Stiles, D.D., LL.D.*, ed. Franklin Bowditch Dexter (4 vols, New York, 1901), i. 455 (23 Aug. 1774).

[279] Letter from on board the fleet at Boston, 20 Feb. 1775, in *Morning Chronicle and London Advertiser* (30 Mar. 1775): Willard (ed.), *Letters on the American Revolution*, 67–70.

civil and religious liberty as any men under heaven', that is, in armed action.[280] As another colonist in Philadelphia expressed it:

> Nothing but a total repeal of the acts of parliament of which we complain can prevent a civil war in America. Our opposition has now risen to desperation. It would be as easy to allay a storm in the ocean, by a single word, as to subdue the free spirit of the Americans without a total redress of their grievances. May a spirit of wisdom descend at last upon our Ministry and rescue the British empire from destruction! We tremble at the thoughts of a separation from Great Britain. All our glory and happiness have been derived from you. But we are in danger of being shipwrecked upon your rocks. To avoid these, we are willing to be tossed, without a compass or a guide, for a while upon an ocean of blood.

To its native speakers, this biblical language did not seem extreme. As the same writer added two days later, 'There cannot be a greater error than to suppose that the present commotions in America are owing to the arts of demagogues. Every man thinks and acts for himself in a country where there is an equal distribution of property and knowledge.'[281] Colonists could be, on the surface, rational and hospitable. A sergeant who deserted from the British army added: 'Before I knew these people, I was shocked at the thought of being sent out to *cut their throats*, and resolved not to turn human butcher, to destroy my *friends* and *countrymen*. Now I know them, I find them the best hearted, generous people in the world, ready to give everything to strangers.'[282] But in every colony a religious undertone redescribed secular objectives. The colonists' goal, as a correspondent in Philadelphia explained, was 'the preservation of their liberties, and salvation of North America'.[283] Another, from Charlestown, South Carolina, claimed: 'We do not fear all the force that can be sent against us, for we have a just cause in hand, and no doubt but we shall meet protection in a merciful God.'[284]

Consequently, widespread bloodshed followed Lexington and Concord as low-level warfare became endemic; by the summer of 1775 it was clear that 'Every hopes of reconciliation between the mother country and the colonies is now vanished.'[285] By the autumn of that year, a rebel correspondent in Philadelphia rejoiced that

> our troops have had such success in every enterprise, that the hand of Heaven seems visibly on our side...I cannot but conclude, in the words of an old fashioned book, seldom consulted by kings or their ministers: 'The kings of the earth stand up, and their rulers take council together; but He, by whom kings reign, shall laugh them to

---

[280] Letter from Virginia, 16 Apr. 1775, in *London Chronicle*, 1–3 June 1775: Willard (ed.), *Letters on the American Revolution*, 75.

[281] Letters from an American to a Member of Parliament, Philadelphia, 24 and 26 Dec. 1774, in *London Chronicle* (25–7 Apr. 1775): Willard (ed.), *Letters on the American Revolution*, 40–1.

[282] Letter to a tradesman at York from his son at Charles Town, 3 Feb. 1775, *London Evening Post* (11–13 Apr. 1775): Willard (ed.), *Letters on the American Revolution*, 60–2.

[283] Letter from Philadelphia, 7 May 1775, in *London Chronicle* (24–7 June 1775): Willard (ed.), *Letters on the American Revolution*, 102–3.

[284] Letter from Charles Town, South Carolina, 10 May 1775, *Gazetteer and New Daily Advertiser* (5 July 1775): Willard (ed.), *Letters on the American Revolution*, 104–6.

[285] Letter from Rhode Island, n.d., in *Morning Post and Daily Advertiser* (21 July 1775): Willard (ed.), *Letters on the American Revolution*, 131.

scorn, even the Holy one shall have them in derision.' Sooner or later he will vindicate his own divine prerogative by the overthrow of tyrants and of tyranny.[286]

The inescapable and horrifying phenomenon of widespread killing, drawn out over the spring, summer, and autumn of 1775, crystallized colonial opinion in favour of independence: it is possible that *Common Sense* achieved its success the following year in part by crystallizing for colonists what they had already been brought by violence to believe (if so, this was more a credit to Paine's journalistic talent than to his strategic originality).[287] Paine, who (like the quoted deserter) similarly enjoyed colonial support and (like other correspondents) had confidence in divine providence, differed from this rhetoric chiefly in his open condemnation of the House of Brunswick; for him, therefore, independence was a positive goal, not a default position, and to obtain it he was similarly willing to venture on an 'ocean of blood'.

To an English visitor to Boston, the analysis was similar but the valuation was different:

> The inhabitants of New England are the descendants of Cromwell's *elect*, and they not only inherit their sentiments in civil and religious matters, but they have copied after them during the context they have had with the Mother Country. They shew the same encroaching Jesuitical and hypocritical disposition; every concession on your part has only produced fresh demands on theirs. Nothing will satisfy them or conciliate them to your government, and nothing but force can extort submission and obedience from them. The Church of England are the only balance against them...Such...is the influence of the faction which presides at the head of affairs, that nine tenths of the people will greedily swallow the most glaring fictions which they shall think proper to propagate, and nothing can get the better of their infatuation, but a spirited exertion of power, which all good men are waiting to see take place.[288]

Or as a British army officer reported a few days later,

> The inhabitants of this province retain the religious and civil principles brought over by their forefathers, in the reign of K. Charles I. and are at least a hundred years behind hand with the people of England in every refinement. With the most austere shew of devotion, they are destitute of every principle of religion or common honesty, and are reckoned the most arrant cheats and hypocrites on the whole continent of America.[289]

In 1775, another added: 'It is impossible to give you a better description of the bulk of the people on this Continent (and particularly in the province of Massachusetts

---

[286] Letter from Philadelphia, 5 Oct. 1775, in *London Evening Post* (23–5 Nov. 1775): Willard (ed.), *Letters on the American Revolution*, 213–14.

[287] The much greater scale of casualties in the French Revolutionary and Napoleonic wars, and the eighteenth-century 'aristocratic culture', have occluded the significance of violence in decades following the end of Europe's 'wars of religion': David A. Bell, *The First Total War: Napoleon's Europe and the Birth of Warfare as We Know It* (Boston, 2007), 37–42, 44–51. Bell nevertheless excepts civil wars from this alleged growing moderation of savagery, 49.

[288] Letter from Boston, 20 Nov. 1774, in *Gazetteer and New Daily Advertiser* (19 Jan. 1775): Willard (ed.), *Letters on the American Revolution*, 10–14.

[289] Letter from Boston, 22 Nov. 1774, in *Bristol Gazette* (12 Jan. 1775): Willard (ed.), *Letters on the American Revolution*, 14–16.

Bay) than every English history gives of the principles of the Independents in Oliver's time. There their pictures are justly drawn.'[290]

Ensign Daniel Gwynne wrote to his brother in 1781 that to understand the colonists he should read Samuel Butler's satire on the Puritans, *Hudibras* (1663), and 'add to that as much Knavery, Roguery low Cunning and all kinds [of] Villany under the Mask of religion…as you can well put together'.[291] An Englishman in Boston in 1776 added:

> The Americans, like their brethren with you [in England] have been deluded by Patriots, Fishers in troubled waters, and hot-headed Republican Preachers… The real sentiments of true Englishmen are liberal, open, and generous. They detest Slavery, and only contend for a just and equal partition of Taxes, that every part of the Empire may contribute their proper share to the support of the whole. This is the light in which I see the present contest; but I know that the pious Saints of this Continent have accepted, with great chearfulness for a century past, above one hundred millions of English pounds, either in specie or in protection; and yet, when Britain required a small assistance, they thought their liberties in danger, and absolutely refused.[292]

A visitor to New York recorded his own experience:

> I came to this place highly prepossessed in their [the colonists'] favour, but find their behavior so mad, so inconsistent with that gratitude they owe Great Britain, that I have entirely changed my opinion of them, tho' at the same time I do not entirely side with Government in all their measures…should the liberty side get the better, it will end in the destruction of the colonies…Most sensible people here, people of property, whom I should suppose interested as much as any in the matter, are of this opinion, and say that one master is better than a thousand, and that they would rather be oppressed by a King than by a rascally mob…In the east and southern provinces they are in actual rebellion, raising troops, and seizing ammunition in the most daring manner; the common people are mad, they only hear one side of the question, and believe they are oppressed because they are told so, which is all they know of the matter.[293]

A Boston correspondent confirmed this: 'Many shocking violences have been perpetrated in the country. There is no sort of violence that they do not commit…All their leaders are poor miscreants, who could not live in affluence but in times of commotion; having nothing to lose by the disturbances, they exert themselves to keep up and increase them.'[294]

---

[290] Letter from Boston, 1 Mar. 1775, in *Farley's Bristol Journal* (29 Apr. 1775): Willard (ed.), *Letters on the American Revolution*, 70–1; for similar analyses, 120, 353.

[291] Daniel Gwynne to William Gwynne, 12 Oct. 1781, Gwynne Letters, Pembrokeshire RO, quoted in Stephen Conway, *The American War of Independence 1775–1783* (London, 1995), 39.

[292] Letter from Boston, n.d., in *Lloyds Evening Post and British Chronicle* (12–14 June 1776): Willard (ed.), *Letters on the American Revolution*, 266–8.

[293] Letter from New York, 28 Dec. 1774, in *Morning Chronicle and Daily Advertiser* (2 Feb. 1775): Willard (ed.), *Letters on the American Revolution*, 45–6.

[294] Letter from Boston, 16 Jan. 1775, in *Gazetteer and New Daily Advertiser* (1 Mar. 1775): Willard (ed.), *Letters on the American Revolution*, 53–6.

Nor was fraternity a lasting ideal, according to one British correspondent: 'Desertion no longer prevails among the troops, nor do they meet with that encouragement to desert as they did soon after their arrival; the common people are tired of treating them according to their first plan, as brothers; they now consider them as enemies, indeed they ever held them in that light, but under a mask which they have now laid aside.'[295] Paine, similarly, had no inhibitions about the use of armed force, and issued no warnings about the loss of property in war. He rejected the Church of England, but in the American colonies this placed him with the great majority. All colonists were not of one mind: the inhabitants of Paine's Pennsylvania were more divided in their views than those of New England, but by 1774 Boston Congregationalists and Philadelphia Presbyterians shared much in their political rhetoric.[296] Such brief fragments as these letters do not display the complexities of divided opinion on either side of the Atlantic, but they are evidence that before Paine's arrival in the colonies mutually hostile positions had been taken up that were not owed to him.

A minority of the heterodox among the colonists were close to Paine's own views on religion. Another Deist, Thomas Jefferson, in his pamphlet of 1774, expressed the same Deistic sense of the simplicity of human affairs, governed as he thought them to be by a Supreme Being's similarly general laws. He sought to vindicate 'those rights which God and the laws have given equally and independently to all'; the king was only 'the chief officer of the people, appointed by the laws, and circumscribed with definite powers, to assist in working the great machine of government...The great principles of right and wrong are legible to every reader; to pursue them requires not the aid of many counsellors. The whole art of government consists in the art of being honest...The God who gave us life gave us liberty at the same time.'

From such premises it was obvious to Jefferson that the colonies ranked equally with the home country, united in a polity only by allegiance to the same king:

> Not only the principles of common sense, but the feelings of human nature, must be surrendered up before his majesty's subjects here can be persuaded to believe that they hold their political existence at the will of a British parliament...Can any one reason be assigned why 160,000 electors in the island of Great Britain should give the law to four million in the states of America, every individual of whom is equal to every individual of them, in virtue, in understanding, and in bodily strength?

He continued: 'From the nature of things, every society must at all times possess within itself the sovereign powers of legislation', so that when the king overstepped the laws by 'dissolving one house of representatives' in the colonies and refusing to call another, 'the power reverts to the people, who may exercise it to unlimited extent'.[297] Jefferson had not met Paine when he wrote these words, but their simi-

---

[295] Letter from on board the fleet at Boston, 20 Feb. 1775, in *Morning Chronicle and London Advertiser* (30 Mar. 1775): Willard (ed.), *Letters on the American Revolution*, 67–70.

[296] Clark, *Language of Liberty*, 27, 329, 337, 369–71.

[297] [Thomas Jefferson], *A Summary View of the Rights of British America* (Williamsburg, Va: Clementina Rind, 1774), 5, 12, 19, 22–3.

larity to Paine's is easily explained: they derived from a shared body of ideas. 'Common sense' was an expression widely used; but to a Deist it had especial resonance.

The Debate on *Common Sense*

Not every colonist shared Jefferson's Deist attitudes. To Trinitarians, politics, like revealed religion, was complex, not simple. Paine's claim that armed rebellion was the prescription of 'common sense' was no sooner made than opponents targeted and denied that very claim.[298]

His earliest critic seized on the theological component of *Common Sense*. If its objection against the effects of the British government were valid, argued 'Rationalis', the argument would apply equally against 'the Jewish theocracy', which had been a direct gift of 'the Great Jehovah himself' but had (as in Deuteronomy, 9: 7, 24) led only to rebellion against God. Rationalis then turned the tables on *Common Sense* by citing John Trenchard, Francis Hutcheson, and John, 1st Baron Somers: all these Whig authorities had argued (Somers quoting Prov. 8: 16; 1 Sam. 8: 4, 7; 10: 25; 11: 1, 5, 6, 7, 14, 15; 12: 13) that men, not God, had established governments, so that men could legitimately choose whatever form of government they liked: it followed that 'monarchy is not inconsistent with the Holy Scriptures' and could be 'as pleasing to the Almighty, if agreeable to the people, as any other form of government, even the author's beloved republic'. Nor, insisted Rationalis, had *Common Sense* weighed the 'constant scenes of blood and devastation' that subsisted in 'ancient and modern republics' against the consequences of monarchy. Holland and Poland were examples of the collapse of a republic into aristocracy, and the weakness of elective kingship; consequently, 'hereditary is preferable to elective monarchy'. Only if an 'advantageous accommodation' with Britain proved impossible would independence be 'the dernier resort of America'.[299]

Another early commentator to take a different line wrote a series of letters in *The Pennsylvania Gazette* between March and June 1776 under the pen name 'Cato'. He was the Scottish born and educated Anglican clergyman William Smith, first Provost of the College of Pennsylvania since 1755, later the University of Pennsylvania, and pro-American in his sympathies.[300] His letters finally provoked the anonymous author of *Common Sense* to reply, under the pen name of 'The Forester'. For Smith, Paine was one of a 'few' who had had 'the astonishing boldness to aim at a total destruction of our charter constitution, and seizing into their own hands our whole domestic police, with legislative as well as executive authority'. Smith was open in his determination 'in executing the Resolves of Congress, and maintaining *American*

---

[298] Sophia Rosenfeld, 'Tom Paine's *Common Sense* and Ours', *WMQ* 65 (2008), 633–68, at 663–5.

[299] 'Rationalis', in *The Pennsylvania Gazette* (28 Feb. 1776), citing John Trenchard's *Cato's Letters*, no. 60 (6 Jan. 1721), Francis Hutcheson's *A Short Introduction to Moral Philosophy* (Glasgow: Robert Foulis, 1747), 285, and John, 1st Baron Somers's *The Judgment of Whole Kingdoms and Nations concerning the Rights, Power, and Prerogative of Kings* (London: T. Harrison, 1710). For the debate in general, see especially Aldridge, *American Ideology*, 158–253.

[300] For his sympathy with colonial resistance in 1775–6, see Albert Frank Gegenheimer, *William Smith Educator and Churchman 1727–1803* (Philadelphia, 1943), 162–77.

Liberty. But Congress had been given the remit of 'promoting reconciliation upon constitutional principles between Great-Britain and her Colonies' and other such ends, not to go beyond them. In Pennsylvania only the Assembly was 'vested with the authority of the people', not any ad hoc body like the Conventions that had met elsewhere.[301]

According to Smith, 'our presses' had 'lately groaned' with 'many publications in favour of *independency*', but 'little notice has yet been taken' of them; 'I am confident that nine-tenths of the people of Pennsylvania yet abhor the doctrine'. Such an idea had 'Possibly' been held by 'some men' from 'the beginning of this controversy', but it would have been thought 'slanderous, inimical to America' to express it. Even now, wrote Smith, the idea of independence had only recently been broached; it was not clear what 'men of consequence' supported it; 'Certainly it has no countenance from the Congress.' It followed that 'independence is not the cause in which America is *now* engaged, and is only the idol of those who wish to subvert all order among us, and rise on the ruins of their country!'[302]

Rightly, continued Smith, the Pennsylvania Assembly had given instructions to their Delegates to Congress that were an 'insurmountable barrier' against 'any change of our constitution, or...the least transfer of our allegiance'. The problem arose from 'strangers intermeddling in our affairs, and avowedly pressing their republican schemes upon us'. But if the Congress were led on to act without authority, 'we may be...plunged deeper into all the growing horrors of war and bloodshed, without ever being consulted!' 'To see America reduced to such a situation may be the choice of adventurers who have nothing to lose, or of men exalted by the present confusions into *lucrative* offices, which they can hold no longer than the continuance of the public calamities.' Set beside these inferences, the claims of *Common Sense* about American military and naval strength, the eagerness of other countries to trade with America, the disapproval of God for kingly government, England's constitution as 'a bungling piece of machinery', the idea that 'the nation itself is but one mass of corruption'—all these were only assertions.[303] Indeed the doctrines of *Common Sense* were 'out of the common way—bold, marvelous and flattering'. Its teaching would be accepted only by those who had 'a predilection for the doctrine...without wishing to hear the arguments on the other side'.[304]

The charges that the author of *Common Sense* was an outsider, a man of no consequence, someone ignorant of American affairs, a person who had nothing to lose and who sought to profit personally by promoting catastrophe, were evidently sufficient to sting Paine to reply (the only time he replied to a critic of *Common Sense*).[305] Even then, he did not sign his name to letters to the *Pennsylvania Packet* and *Pennsylvania Journal* in April and May 1776, which appeared over the pen name

---

[301] [William Smith], 'To the People of Pennslylvania. Letter I', *Pennsylvania Gazette* (13 Mar.1776), in Thomas Paine, *Common Sense*, ed. Edward Larkin (Peterborough, Ontario, 2004), 171–5.

[302] [Smith], Letter II, 20 Mar. 1776, in Paine, *Common Sense*, ed. Larkin, 175–80.

[303] [Smith], Letter III, 27 Mar. 1776, in Paine, *Common Sense*, ed. Larkin, 180–6.

[304] [Smith], Letter IV, 27 Mar. 1776, in Paine, *Common Sense*, ed. Larkin, 186–93. In this letter, Smith for the first time hinted that the author of Common Sense was one 'Pain', otherwise 'Payne'.

[305] Aldridge, *American Ideology*, 168.

of 'The Forester' (an echo of a pen name used by another correspondent in the *Sussex Weekly Advertiser* in 1771–4, while Paine was employed in Lewes). Perhaps Paine did not think he had a monopoly on the character 'Common Sense', since he did not use it here. He was obviously angry, addressing the still-anonymous Cato: 'Thou hast tauntingly called on me by name.' Paine insisted that it was the content of *Common Sense* that mattered, not 'the *rank* or condition of the man' who wrote it. He was furious that Cato had, by implication, identified him as one of the '*strangers intermeddling in our affairs*', and replied: 'He that *is* here and he that was *born* here are alike concerned.' Cato's letters were 'gorged with absurdity, confusion, contradiction and the most notorious and willful falsehoods', rhetoric that Paine frequently repeated in similar phrases.

Again Paine appealed to 'the plain doctrine of reason', avoiding Cato's pragmatic arguments with the assertions that no reconciliation was possible; that 'the people' had the right to change the constitution of Pennsylvania at any time, authorizing any men rather than the Assembly to act for them; that the colonists were not contending against the ministry in London but against 'an arbitrary king'; that European powers merely wanted 'a free and uninterrupted trade with the whole continent of America'; that all former statements of Congress against independence 'are out of date' since 'the people of America' had now found George III to be 'a royal savage'; that but for the British connection, 'nations...would otherwise seek our friendship'.[306] Paine's responses, then, were less detailed engagements with the substantive argument, than rhetorical counters; their effectiveness depended on their powerful expression. His most heartfelt passages in the 'Forester's Letters' were those in which he expressed negations of monarchical government. Unusually, Paine cited Rousseau's 'plan for establishing a perpetual European peace... This would be forming a kind of European Republic', but he did not work out the implications of the idea for republicanism as such or extrapolate the principles of the American Revolution to Europe, merely reflecting negatively on 'the proud and plundering spirit of kings'.[307]

One anonymous colonist, probably the delegate to the Continental Congress and wealthy South Carolina planter Henry Middleton, was easily able to identify and question Paine's premises, especially the difference between society and government: all individuals who cooperated together did so under some form of government, replied Middleton, and government was far better than Paine's 'necessary Evil'. Paine's picture of settlers in 'some sequestred Part of the Earth' forming a government *ex nihilo* was misleading: must they not 'be considered in a State of Society and Government, prior to any Formation of it, in the Method asserted by this Author?' The proposition of *Common Sense* that

'*Mankind are originally Equals in the Order of Creation,*' is a very levelling Principle. There are some natural Distinctions which cannot fail having very great Effects...however Nature may put a Ridicule upon hereditary Succession, 'by giving an Ass for a

---

[306] [Paine], 'The Forester's Letters' (1776): *CW*, ii. 61, 63–6, 68–70, 82.
[307] [Paine], 'The Forester's Letters' (1776): *CW*, ii. 78–80.

Lion,' it must be owned that some seem by Nature formed to rule, and others to obey... 'Male and Female are Distinctions of Nature;' but I suppose the Author would not give up the Government of the Male to the Female Part of the Creation.

In reply, Middleton asked 'Whether it never happens in Republicks that the Choice falls upon Asses as well as upon Lions?' Middleton, however worldly, nevertheless quoted Genesis and I Timothy to show the origin of government in God's institution, and in human dependence even before the Fall: 'Government and Society are nearly coeval, and... the very first Mode of Government must have resembled Monarchy more than any other.' Genesis too was called on to show that 'there was Murder before there were Kings', and the Book of Judges to show the 'Wickedness and Confusion' during their rule. But this did not entail 'that Monarchy is the only Government of Divine Institution', nor was Adam 'absolute Sovereign'; consequently, Middleton agreed with Paine, "*Whatever Form of Government appears most likely to ensure us Security, with the least Expense, and greatest Benefit, is preferable to all others*," and all I plead for is, that in some Instances Monarchy has done this, and may do this as much as any Form.'

According to Middleton, *Common Sense*'s insistence on simplicity worked against its case: 'the most perfect Government is where the most perfect Being rules, and all his good Creatures implicitly and perfectly obey.' As Middleton saw, his anonymous opponent began with a plea for simplicity in government, but then 'proposes a Plan of Government far more complex, and consequently far more unnatural, than those he pretends to abolish'. Denigration of monarchy was not necessarily appropriate: 'The present Emperor [Joseph II], and King of *Prussia* [Frederick II, "the Great"], are probably more minutely acquainted with the State of their Dominions than any one of their Subjects; I should think an *English* King also might be at Liberty to read *Common Sense*, or a News-Paper.' Middleton's was a pragmatic and well-informed vision from a man of affairs, but he too was steeped in biblical precedent: as he recognized, 'every Argument that has an Appearance of Scripture to support it, with many Persons, is decisive'.[308]

Paine's appeal to 'common sense' was not self-evidently valid for all readers. In a pamphlet first published in New York, its Preface dated 16 February 1776, the Anglican priest Charles Inglis (1734–1816) challenged the implication of his still-anonymous opponent's title, 'a figure in rhetoric, which is called a Catachresis, that is, in plain English, an abuse of words. Under this title, he counteracts the clearest dictates of reason, truth, and common sense... I find no *Common Sense* in this pamphlet, but much *uncommon* phrenzy.' Its author 'unites the violence and rage of a republican with all the enthusiasm and folly of a fanatic'. (Inglis rightly understood that religion and politics joined in Paine's account.) After its initial rhetorical

---

[308] *The True Merits of a Late Treatise, printed in America, Intitled, Common Sense, Clearly pointed out. Addressed to the Inhabitants of America. By a late Member of the Continental Congress, a Native of a Republican State* [?Henry Middleton] (London: W. Nicoll, 1776), 3–13, 16. Middleton also questioned Paine's assertion that only independence could safeguard America from civil war. The opposite might prove correct; 'Should this ever prove the Case, the Man will have much to answer for, whose Rancour and Rashness has hurried on so great a Calamity', 29–30.

indignation, Inglis's reply turned to practical debate. He urged that Paine's 'remedy is infinitely worse than the disease', would bring down upon the colonies 'dreadful evils', and was driven not by a rational appraisal of colonial grievances but by 'malice and antipathy to monarchical government'.

Instead, urged Inglis, the colonists should pursue 'a reconciliation with Great-Britain, on solid, constitutional principles, excluding all parliamentary taxation'. Rather than that, 'To realize his beloved scheme of Independent Republicanism, he [Paine] would persuade the colonists to renounce their allegiance to our true and lawful liege sovereign King George III—plunge themselves into a tedious, bloody, and most expensive war with Great Britain—and risque their lives, liberties and property on the dubious event of that war.'[309] Paine had not, indeed, offered a defence of the term 'common sense' or its application. He had said nothing of the balance of advantages and of why the balance lay with the option of war. If the impact in the colonies of *Common Sense* is to be explained, it must be in terms other than the self-evidence of its substantive arguments: that war was obviously preferable to negotiation.

Inglis made an attempt to explain his opponent, not knowing his identity, by calling into question Paine's distinction between the state and society and asserting instead that men were 'by an act of Providence in our birth, made members of society... Providence hath formed us for society, and placed us in it from the time of our first existence'. Inglis appealed to Richard Hooker (*c*.1554–1600). Men did not create society or 'government' by a conscious collective act in the beginning of the world. Rather, continued Inglis, 'nature has made us members of society, without any choice or will of ours... As we cannot doubt but the benevolent author of our being, wills our happiness in the state where he hath placed us, he surely wills also the means which lead us to that end—those means are order and government.' Consequently 'The first British emigrants to America, were in a state of Society before their emigration', and obtained before their departure 'grants, charters and instructions, which vested them with a legal title to those lands, and marked the outlines of those governments that were to be formed here'. The 'ends' of government 'cannot be obtained, but by subordination, order and the regulation of laws'.[310] These were long familiar positions in the eighteenth century, and neither Paine nor Inglis invented them.

If they were to be more loudly asserted in the debate over the French Revolution, these ideas were already common knowledge before the debate on the American. By the 1770s, a Whig monarchist like Inglis could express the modification of that doctrine which the eclipse of the Stuart dynastic alternative had produced: 'Thus far I hold, with the best republican writers on the subject, the divine right of government, whose end is the good of mankind; yet without appropriating that right to any particular form, exclusively of others.'[311] Anti-Jacobitism required him, as it later required Burke, to say that God had not specifically sanctioned the monarchy

---

[309] *The True Interest of America Impartially Stated, in certain Strictures On a Pamphlet intitled Common Sense. By an American* [Charles Inglis] (Philadelphia: James Humphreys, 1776), vi–vii (italics and Roman reversed), 10. Aldridge, *American Ideology*, 193–8.

[310] [Inglis], *The True Interest*, 10–14.   [311] [Inglis], *The True Interest*, 11–12.

of George III, but Inglis sought to claim a divine-right underpinning for that monarchy in a wider sense. Inglis was, overtly, a Whig, announcing that

> The constitution of England, as it now stands, was fixed at the revolution, in 1688—
> an aera ever memorable in the fair annals of Liberty...The lamp of science never
> shone brighter in any country than in Britain, nor did patriots of greater fame ever
> adorn the cause of freedom, than those who stood forth to assert her liberties, at that
> distinguished period...I am none of your *passive obedience and non-resistance men.*
> The principles on which the glorious Revolution in 1688 was brought about, consti-
> tute the articles of my political creed.

Thanks to those principles, 'the constitution of England approaches the nearest to perfection—that it is productive of the greatest happiness and benefit to the subject, of any constitution on earth'. Inglis briefly surveyed what King, Lords, and Commons could actually do, compared with what he claimed was Paine's parodic picture of them.[312] Burke in 1790 could say no more. And if *Common Sense* had cited some apparently anti-monarchical passages from Scripture, urged Inglis, it had ignored all the monarchical passages: these Inglis now rehearsed.[313] For a colonist, then, as for English Whigs, the idea of a checked and balanced constitution of three components went together with a claim to its divine authority.

Yet his closing arguments were pragmatic, not theoretical. Reconciliation would regain 'the protection of the greatest naval power in the world'; 'Agriculture, commerce and industry' would no longer 'languish and droop'. America would have access to British manufactures, which 'confessedly surpass any in the world'; but in the event of a war, 'All our property throughout the continent would be unhinged; the greatest confusion, the most violent convulsions would take place'; the colonists would be divided; 'Devastation and ruin must mark the progress of this war along the sea coast of America...Ruthless war, with all its aggravated horrors, will ravage our once happy land—our sea-coasts and ports will be ruined, and our ships taken. Torrents of blood will be spilt, and thousands reduced to beggary and wretchedness.' Nor would the political outcome even of independence be happy for America, since 'Limited monarchy is the form of government which is most favourable to liberty—which is best adapted to the genius and temper of Britons' as a middle path between democracy and absolute monarchy.

> The author of *Common Sense* is a violent stickler for Democracy or Republicanism
> only—every other species of government is reprobated by him as tyrannical: *I* plead for
> the constitution which has been formed by the wisdom of ages—is the admiration of
> mankind—is best adapted to the genius of Britons, and is most friendly to liberty.[314]

Nor would republicanism work in 'America', which was 'too extensive for it'. Independence would bring a massive annual tax burden on America; 'And all this, after being exhausted by a tedious war, and perhaps our shipping and sea-ports destroyed!'[315]

---

[312] [Inglis], *The True Interest*, 15–16, 19, 31.   [313] [Inglis], *The True Interest*, 16, 25, 31–3.

[314] [Inglis], *The True Interest*, 48–51, 53.

[315] [Inglis], *The True Interest*, 53, 58–61. For the maritime impact of the war that followed, see Richard Buel, *In Irons: Britain's Naval Supremacy and the American Revolutionary Economy* (New Haven, 1998).

Finally, Inglis challenged the great antithesis framed in 1679–81, the claim that the only alternatives were liberty and slavery; on the contrary, 'both may be equally avoided' by negotiation. But a Declaration of Independence would 'preclude treaty intirely', and would deprive America of the help of 'our friends in England': 'It would stop their mouths; for were they to say any thing in our favour, they would be deemed rebels, and treated accordingly.' Nor could America expect assistance from France, which would not embark on war from a '*disinterested* motive of aiding and protecting these colonies'. More probably, it would produce an alliance against America of European governments fearful of losing their colonies.

These were cogent points; only Inglis's prediction of the absence of foreign intervention was to prove obviously mistaken. Yet Inglis was candid that he had 'omitted every subject, the discussion of which might tend to raise jealousy among the colonists; such as religion'.[316] Indeed this subject was seldom overtly touched on by colonists in the published colonial controversies of 1775–6. Paine was not yet identified as a Deist, and the spiralling practical conflicts of these years quickly upstaged the theological disputes that had been such important precursors of the conflict.[317]

The first publisher of *Common Sense*, Robert Bell, found it prudent to preface a pamphlet that took the other side with eulogies to the freedom of the press by Junius and De Lolme. This was an anonymous work, *Plain Truth*, published in Philadelphia on 13 March 1776 and explicitly answering *Common Sense*.[318] It was written by James Chalmers (?1727–1806), a large landowner in Maryland since arriving there in 1760. *Plain Truth* has been judged to have been 'influential', and went through two editions and four printings in Philadelphia within two months; a considerable body of Loyalist opinion remained in America's most populous city.[319] The author dedicated his pamphlet to John Dickinson in recognition of his 'Endeavors to stop the Effusion of Blood, of Torrents of Blood'; to avert the 'horror, misery and desolation, awaiting the people at large in the siren form of American independence'. Chalmers confessed himself 'indignant'; he had written with 'ardor', faced with the prospect of 'Ruin, Horror, and Desolation'. This was indeed a characteristic response of Paine's opponents, who found no weighing of high ideals against human suffering in *Common Sense*. Chalmers too diagnosed 'malevolence' in *Common Sense*, and set it against 'the English constitution; which with all its imperfections, is, and ever will be the pride and envy of mankind'.

[316] [Inglis], *The True Interest*, 69.

[317] James B. Bell, *The Imperial Origins of the King's Church in Early America, 1607–1783* (Basingstoke, 2004); James B. Bell, *A War of Religion: Dissenters, Anglicans, and the American Revolution* (Basingstoke, 2008), esp. ch. 11, 'Critics of the Continental Congress and Common Sense: Jonathan Boucher and Charles Inglis'.

[318] *Plain Truth; addressed to the Inhabitants of America, Containing, Remarks on a late Pamphlet, entitled Common Sense. Wherein are shewn, that the Scheme of Independence is Ruinous, Delusive, and Impracticable: That were the Author's Asserations, Respecting the Power of America, as Real as Nugatory; Reconciliation on liberal Principles with Great Britain, would be exalted Policy: And that circumstanced as we are, Permanent Liberty, and True Happiness, can only be obtained by Reconciliation with that Kingdom. Written by Candidus* [James Chalmers] (Philadelphia: R. Bell, 1776); Aldridge, *American Ideology*, 178–90.

[319] Stephen E. Lucas, *Portents of Rebellion: Rhetoric and Revolution in Philadelphia, 1765–76* (Philadelphia, 1976), 159, 179–80.

Common Sense had argued that 'the antiquity of the English Monarchy will not bear looking into'; Chalmers in reply cited Hume to show that all property was originally 'founded on fraud and injustice', but that necessity forbade a continual reversion to origins. Similarly in Scripture, Old Testament example 'gives way to the Gospel Dispensation' in the New.[320]

Chalmers pointed to the wave of denigration directed even against a good monarch: 'The many unmerited insults offered to our gracious Sovereign; by the unprincipled Wilkes, and others down to this late Author; will forever disgrace humanity.' *Common Sense*, he reminded readers, had claimed that monarchy itself had 'laid not this or that kingdom only, but the World in blood and ashes'. The reality was the opposite, contended Chalmers: 'If we examine the republics of Greece and Rome, we ever find them in a state of war domestic or foreign. Our author therefore makes no mention of these ancient States.' Chalmers quoted 'the excellent Montesquieu': a democracy required a small state, with 'simplicity of manners', and 'a great degree of equality' among its people. Moreover, 'no government is so subject to CIVIL WARS, and INTESTINE COMMOTIONS, as that of the democratical or popular form'. *Common Sense* claimed that the colonies 'would have flourished as much, and probably much more, had no European power taken any notice of her'. Perhaps, countered Chalmers; but without British aid 'these delectable Provinces would now appertain to France; and the people of New England, horrid to think, would now be counting their beads' [i.e. worshipping as Catholics].[321]

Chalmers's pamphlet was mainly taken up with practical objections to *Common Sense*: its author was merely 'ignorant of the true state of Great Britain and her colonies'; those circumstances pointed to the colonies' weakness against 'such POTENT ANTAGONISTS' as the British 'fleets and armies', as demonstrated by their victories in the Seven Years War. By comparison, colonial troops had in the present crisis shown 'but few marks of Spartan or Roman enthusiasm'. Chalmers expected that 'zeal for liberty' would not animate the colonists to such 'glorious efforts of heroism' as 'religious enthusiasm' had done in human history; by implication, Chalmers admitted none in the colonies, while in Europe 'religious rancour, which formerly animated princes to arms, is succeeded by a spirit of philosophy extremely friendly to peace'. There was 'not the most distant gleam of aid from foreign powers'; would the kings of France or Spain supply aid 'which inspiring their subjects with a relish for liberty, might eventually shake their arbitrary thrones'? Added to that, Britain 'is said to contain more industry, consequently more wealth, than all the rest of Europe'; Britain could afford a conflict, and 'Britain joins to the commerce of Tyre, Carthage and Venice...the fire of old Rome'. *Common Sense* had grossly underestimated the British navy, the cost to America of seeking to rival it, and the feasibility of an American force of armed merchantmen. The ministry in London would 'exert every nerve of the British power' to preserve its colonies, for their 'political existence depends on our constitutional obedience'.[322]

---

[320] [Chalmers], *Plain Truth*, Dedication and Introduction, n.p.; 2–6, 66.
[321] [Chalmers], *Plain Truth*, 7–9, 12–13.
[322] [Chalmers], *Plain Truth*, 17–21, 24–5, 28, 42–3, 47.

In the same practical vein, Chalmers urged that reconciliation with Britain would not be 'the ruin of the Continent', as *Common Sense* predicted, but would 'conduct us to our former happy state'. Against these facts, Chalmers quoted an authority: 'All plans of government (says HUME) which suppose great reformation in the manners of mankind, are merely imaginary.'[323] If Paine had not grasped the Loyalist viewpoint, Chalmers did not grasp the rebel one: Chalmers did not enter into the *mentalité* that drove the revolution, but argued primarily as a trader, convinced that the colonies' trade could only be to the mother country, and that the colonies could not rival the home country in armies or fleets. So, indeed, it generally proved to be in the early years of fighting: only the entry of other European powers tipped the military and naval balance.

But Chalmers's pragmatic arguments did not explain why the revolution happened, why it took root, or why a decision to attempt independence spread like wildfire after the publication of *Common Sense*. Only at the end of his pamphlet did Chalmers begin to sound a different note. If independence came about, 'the New England men...will assume a superiority' in the new republic.

> Notwithstanding our Author's fine words about toleration: Ye sons of peace and true Christianity; believe me, it were folly supreme, madness, to expect angelic toleration from New-England, where she has constantly been detested, persecuted and execrated. Even in vain would our Author; or our CROMWELL cherish toleration; for the people of New-England, not yet arrived in the seventeenth or eighteenth century, would reprobate her.[324]

Colonists would not have welcomed being told that they had not yet made it into the eighteenth century. But the practically minded Chalmers, like the Anglican priest Inglis, did not explore more deeply the religious origins of rebellion. Both lived in societies in which Anglican discourse had very limited impact compared with anti-Anglican discourse. The reception of *Common Sense* was subsequently mythologized; although it did have a significant role, its impact was not always weighed against those works written to refute it. Explanations are consequently lacking why cogent practical responses like those of Inglis and Chalmers seem to have had such little effect on colonial opinion. This very formulation suggests an answer: Inglis and Chalmers wrote in an elite idiom of prudent, propertied affirmation; Paine partly echoed a populist idiom of hate-filled, religiously inspired negation.

Consequently, Inglis's pamphlet did not fall still-born from the press in New York: it provoked, and was suppressed by, mob violence. As he reported to the Society for the Propagation of the Gospel in London, he had placed himself 'at the Risque not only of my Liberty, but of my Life, I drew up an Answer [to *Common Sense*], and had it printed here [New York], but the Answer was no sooner advertised, than the whole Impression was seized by the Sons of Liberty and burnt. I then sent a Copy to Philadelphia, where it was printed, and soon went into a second edition...I was in the utmost Danger.' Inglis was clear that

---

[323] [Chalmers], *Plain Truth*, 44, 62.   [324] [Chalmers], *Plain Truth*, 64.

colonial motivations survived to the moment of the Declaration of Independence and its associated violence: although 'civil liberty was the ostensible object [of the Revolution], the Bait that was flung out to catch the Populace at large, and engage them in the Rebellion; yet it is now past all Doubt, that an Abolition of the Church of England was one of the principal springs of the Dissenting Leaders' Conduct; and hence the Unanimity of Dissenters in this Business, their universal Defection from Government—emancipating themselves from the Jurisdiction of Great Britain, and becoming Independent, was a necessary Step towards this grand Object'.[325] This opinion Inglis confided to a private letter: to have published it in New York in 1776 would have made his personal situation even more perilous, together with that of his Church.

To pragmatic arguments like these, Paine replied only in his 'Forester's Letters', and there perfunctorily: *Plain Truth* received the briefest dismissal as having 'withered away like a sickly unnoticed weed'.[326] That was all that Paine said in reply to Chalmers's case. Paine was not a controversialist in the sense of relishing the cut and thrust of printed exchanges, and (as in the 1790s, after *Rights of Man*) made little attempt to engage in the debate that *Common Sense* triggered. On occasion, he commented in press articles like the 'American Crisis' and 'Forester's Letters', but wrote no *Common Sense. Part the Second.* Yet whatever the specific and detailed case outlined by authors like Smith, Chalmers, and Inglis, it did not compare in its impact with that of Paine's generalized rhetoric. It seems that Paine's pamphlet was, for many, a catalyst, at least in the short term. Why?

One answer must be that many of its key premises were already widely accepted in the American colonies. In the 1760s, members of the American Philosophical Society in Philadelphia were heavily influenced by a form of rationalism that emphasized God as a first cause, the significance of the religion of nature and its accessibility to science, the immortality of the soul, and the need for virtue; yet Deism 'did not crystallize as a religion in the beliefs of most educated Philadelphians. Rather it tended to highlight certain emphases in the Christianity of those who came under its influence.'[327] In this dilute form, such attitudes could be widespread.

Intellectual developments accessible in small-town England were accessible in small-town America also. So were the books that embodied them. In 1755 John Adams's first job after graduating from Harvard was as a schoolteacher in Worcester,

---

[325] Charles Inglis to Richard Hind, 31 Oct. 1776, Society for the Propagation of the Gospel MSS, quoted in Bell, *A War of Religion*, 152–3. A dedication copy to William Eden, now in the John Carter Brown Library, has a MS leaf inserted: 'This pamphlet was first printed at New York, in March 1776; & when advertised for Sale, the whole impression seized & burned by the Sons of Liberty. The Author, with much Trouble & no less Hazard, conveyed a Copy to Philadelphia, after expunging some Passages that gave the greatest offence, softening others, inserting a few adapted to the Spirit of the Times, & altering the Title Page', had it printed: Thomas R. Adams, *American Independence: The Growth of an Idea* (Providence, RI, 1965), 157. The New York edition had been entitled *The Deceiver Unmasked; or, Loyalty and Interest United: In Answer to a Pamphlet Entitled Common Sense* (New York: Samuel Loudon, 1776).

[326] [Paine], 'The Forester's Letters', II (8 April 1776): *CW*, ii. 69.

[327] Harold E. Taussig, 'Deism in Philadelphia during the Age of Franklin', *Pennsylvania History* 37 (July 1970), 217–36, at 236.

Massachusetts: 'Here I found Morgan's Moral Philosopher,[328] which I was informed had circulated, with some freedom, in that Town and that the Principles of Deism had made a considerable progress among several Persons, in that and other Towns in the County', persons like Ephraim Doolittle and Nathan Baldwin, 'great readers of Deistical Books... They were great Sticklers for Equality as well as Deism: and all the Nonsense of these last twenty Years', Adams wrote in 1802, 'were as familiar to them as they were to Condorcet or Brissot'. Another was Joseph Dyer: 'An Arian by profession... He carried his Doctrine of Equality, to a greater Extremity, or at least as great as any of the wild Men of the French Revolution. A perfect Equality of Suffrage was essential to Liberty.'[329] It is possible that Paine learned his Deism in Philadelphia in 1775; but there is no evidence that he did so, and evidence that he was in touch with American Deists only after his return in 1802 suggests that Paine's religious outlook was already formed by 1774.

Colonial outlooks could be similarly formed before that date. Adams was drawn into politics by resisting the implementation of the Stamp Act; this led him to write *A Dissertation on the Canon and Feudal Law* (1765). There, although he used the phrase 'our privileges', he also wrote of the colonists' 'love of *universal Liberty*': even before Paine, the 'liberties' or specific entitlements of the English common law could be reified into a singular and abstract 'liberty', and both usages coexisted, despite their logical difference. Adams wrote without difficulty of colonists' (specific) 'RIGHTS', and of 'the inherent rights of mankind'. Even an Arian like Adams[330] could declare, whether sincerely or not: 'Be it remembered... that liberty must at all hazards be supported. We have a right to it, derived from our Maker'; liberty depended on '*Rights* derived from the great legislator of the universe'.

This discursive universalism Adams combined with a particularist historical case. The Puritans had 'established sacerdotal ordination, on the foundation of the Bible and common sense... They knew that government was a plain, simple, intelligible thing founded in nature and reason and quite comprehensible by common sense.' Common sense showed that 'Rulers are no more than attorneys, agents and trustees for the people; and if the cause, the interest and trust is insidiously betray'd, or wantonly trifled away, the people have a right to revoke the authority, that they themselves have deputed, and to constitute abler, and better agents, attorneys and trustees.' Some of this was shared ground with Paine; they differed in Adams's idea of the proper forum for such discussion. Already, in 1765, Adams wrote:

> Let the pulpit resound with the doctrines and sentiments of religious liberty. Let us hear the danger of thralldom to our consciences, from ignorance, extream poverty and dependance, in short from civil and political slavery. Let us see delineated before us, the true map of man. Let us hear the dignity of his nature, and the noble rank he holds among the works of God! That consenting to slavery is a sacriligious breach of trust, as offensive in the sight of God, as it is derogatory from our own honor or interest or

---

[328] [Thomas Morgan, d. 1743], *The Moral Philosopher. In a Dialogue between Philalethes a Christian Deist, and Theophanes a Christian Jew* (3 vols, London: for the Author, 1737–40).

[329] Adams, *Diary and Autobiography*, iii. 263, 265.

[330] Clark, *Language of Liberty*, 27, 38, 329, 337, 369–71.

happiness; and that God almighty has promulgated from heaven, liberty, peace, and good-will to man![331]

For Paine, the pamphlet rather than the pulpit was his instinctive home; but using the pamphlet, he spoke similarly to colonists' paranoia that they were about to be subjected to royal and Anglican 'slavery'.

Common Sense undoubtedly played a role in the decision to attempt armed resistance; yet the nature of its impact is not obvious. In interpreting its meaning, two considerations especially demand explanation. One is its large sale in the Thirteen Colonies in 1776, yet this sale can initially seem difficult to explain. The work hardly discussed the Anglo-American dispute. It denounced kings; yet no king had visited the American colonies. It hardly engaged with specific American grievances (however well it evoked latent American fears and hatreds), and sold widely not because most or even many of its American readers were Deists. Second, the nature of the colonial argument. It is not clear that *Common Sense* led to a widespread and major debate in America, with protagonists *pro* as well as *con*. The number of colonial replies was modest, and not out of line with other colonial pamphlet exchanges since 1764.[332]

After its publishing success in 1776, American editions of *Common Sense* were few until American publishers' interest in the work began to revive in the late nineteenth century. From the early twentieth century it became an 'American classic', calling for reprints edited by American historians, American political scientists, and at least one American literary scholar, all implicitly or explicitly using the text to celebrate a version of their state's myth of origins and omitting to compare it with other writings of the time. But after 1776, the interest of Americans in the text soon flagged. It might be suggested that *Common Sense* was important in America in the few years after publication because of its negations, more than over several decades because of its affirmations, its generalized promise of a new and wholly different future.

The impact of *Common Sense* was different in different societies. Quickly reprinted in Britain, it went into at least a fourth London edition in 1776, but was not as inspirational there as *Rights of Man* later was. The extensive British debate did not revolve around *Common Sense*: British critics tended to reply to the pro-American writings of Richard Price, or to challenge the actions and pronouncements of Congress. Price's famous tract *Observations on the Nature of Civil Liberty, the Principles of Government, and the Justice and Policy of the War with America* went through fourteen London editions in 1776, with others in Dublin

---

[331] John Adams, *A Dissertation on the Canon and Feudal Law* (1765), in *Papers of John Adams*, ed. Robert J. Taylor et al. (Cambridge, Mass., 1977–), i. 103–28, at 112, 114, 116–17, 120–1, 123, 126.

[332] Adams, *American Independence*, 183–7 provides a short-title list in chronological order of nineteen pamphlet exchanges in colonial America from 1764 to *Common Sense*. In the latter exchange, Adams lists only [James Chalmers], *Plain Truth*; *Remarks on a Late Pamphlet Entitled Plain Truth*; [Charles Inglis], *The Deceiver Unmasked*; [John Adams], *Thoughts on Government*; [Carter Braxton], *An Address to the Convention of the Colony and Ancient Dominion of Virginia*; and *Civil Prudence, Recommended to the Thirteen Colonies*.

and Edinburgh.[333] *Observations* received extensive publicity in the London press.[334] It was Price's work, not Paine's, that Thomas Hardy (later the founder of the London Corresponding Society) recorded had been the work that first aroused his interest in politics.[335]

This makes it more notable that after the immediate circumstances of 1776, *Common Sense* continued to be reprinted far from the colonies: in Copenhagen, Edinburgh, Greenock, Lemgo, Lima, London, Manchester, Newcastle-upon-Tyne, Paris, Rotterdam, Stirling.[336] Long after its original application in the Thirteen Colonies had passed into history, the work had a series of separate British afterlives: in the 1790s; in and after 1819; in 1831 and in the twentieth century, now serving the myths of origin of a series of British (and European) causes not present in America in 1776. In these locations and by these dates the American rebellion was dead and buried, but the Deist and later the freethinking and Jacobin assault on kings, lords, and bishops was very much alive.

THE AMERICANIZATION OF THOMAS PAINE? HIS WARTIME TRACTS AND AFTER

The 'Forester' and *Four Letters*

Paine's wartime journalism in the colonies has understandably captured the attention of American historians of the Revolution, and it has therefore been reconstructed as an American phenomenon without reference to what was being written at that time in the British press. Yet Paine's journalism, like his *Common Sense*, equally contained little, or perhaps nothing, that was specifically American. If colonial political debate before 1775 among the elite was marked by its reticence and formal politeness compared with its polarized British counterpart, the same forthright anti-ministerial rhetoric was even more evident in Britain after 1775.

The British press, not censored like American newspapers by mob action, teemed with denunciation: the ministry 'drove America into resistance by a series of such tyrannical acts as would have disgraced Algiers'; 'this unnatural war with America is a plan of raising butchers to attempt the murder of the injured innocent'; Britain's welfare was to be 'the Sport of Imbecility, Avarice, Obstinacy, Presumption, or Treason' on the part of Lord North's ministry. North himself was saluted: 'You have now begun the bloody business. You now find all America united, and that they have Spirit equal to Englishmen, because they are Englishmen.' 'A civil war is now the consequence of preferring falsehood to truth—tyranny to moderation—slavery to liberty: for it is certain where a disposition to rebellion appears among the people,

---

[333] Thomas R. Adams, *The American Controversy: A Bibliographical Study of the British Pamphlets about the American Disputes, 1764–1783* (2 vols, Providence, RI, 1980), i. 361–474.

[334] It was immediately serialized in the *London Chronicle* for 13, 15, and 17 Feb. 1776.

[335] *Memoir of Thomas Hardy, Founder of, and Secretary to, the London Corresponding Society... written by himself* (London: James Ridgway, 1832), 8, 102.

[336] Richard Gimbel, *Thomas Paine: A Bibliographical Check List of Common Sense with an Account of its Publication* (New Haven, 1956), 78–102.

the chief cause is tyranny in the rulers.'[337] This was a widely shared vocabulary in Britain, quickly applied in America; to it, Paine could add little beyond (what could not easily be said in Britain) a rejection of monarchy itself.

Paine remained in America from 1774 to 1787; how much did he learn about his new country? In the 'Forester's Letters', four replies to the critics of *Common Sense* published in the Philadelphia press in April and May 1776, Paine added few insights into America and, instead, chose to elaborate his denunciation of the British constitution, arguing inconsistently that George III could not himself repeal any oppressive Acts of Parliament and also that he was 'an arbitrary king'.[338] But the idea that Paine was the author of the Declaration of Independence, or that he cooperated with Jefferson in writing it, has been argued to be mythical.[339]

In the anonymous *Four Letters on Interesting Subjects* (1776),[340] first attributed to Paine by A. O. Aldridge, the author applied to colonial administrators an English critique of the 'servile character' of 'almost every man who held an office under George the Third'; such men were making a 'transition from Toryism to treason'. Once more, the whole responsibility was laid on the home country, and, specifically, its king:

> the British court wished from the beginning of this dispute to come to an open rupture with the [American] Continent, that she might have a colourable pretence to possess herself of the whole. The long and scandalous list of placemen and pensioners, and the general profligacy and prodigality of the present reign, exceed the annual supplies. England is drained by taxes, and Ireland impoverished to almost the last farthing, yet the farce of state must be kept up, every thing must give way to the wants and vices of a court.

The object of the court, claimed Paine, was to provoke armed rebellion, since 'persons conquered under that character forfeit their all, be it where it will, or what it will, to the crown'. The 'British court' never wished to have Lord North's conciliatory plan of 20 February 1775 'adopted by the colonies', and so provoked hostilities at Lexington and Concord before they could do so. Britain's victory would subject the American colonies to 'a repetition of all those savage and hellish oppressions and cruelties which she so unrelentingly inflicted on the wretched inhabitants of the East-Indies'. Such was the argument of Paine's first letter. It revealed the same preoccupations as *Common Sense* with Britain's conduct alone.

---

[337] Alfred Grant, *Our American Brethren: A History of Letters in the British Press During the American Revolution, 1775–1781* (Jefferson, NC, 1995), 61, 65, 72, and *passim*.

[338] [Paine], 'The Forester's Letters' (1776): *CW*, ii. 64–5.

[339] Keane, *Paine*, 135, 560 n. 70; Garry Wills, *Inventing America: Jefferson's Declaration of Independence* (Garden City, NY, 1978); Pauline Maier, *American Scripture: Making the Declaration of Independence* (New York, 1997), 90–1; David Armitage, *The Declaration of Independence: A Global History* (Cambridge, Mass., 2007). Fresh light on Paine's alleged involvement in the Declaration of Independence may be shed by computer analysis of his and that document's prose styles.

[340] The first and second letters were evidently written before the Declaration of Independence, but the whole pamphlet was not advertised as published until 17 July 1776: Adams, *American Independence*, 155–6.

The second letter urged unity on the Thirteen Colonies. The third letter questioned the authority of Charles II's royal charter for Pennsylvania, dated 1681: it had claimed to grant 'lands which were at that time in the possession of the natives', and had claimed to give William Penn's heirs the right to be 'perpetual and absolute governors of Pennsylvania'. William Penn's charters for his colony, and the corporations established under them, were constitutionally null. Corporations were only 'so many badges of kingly tyranny... The most flourishing towns in England, as, Birmingham, Sheffield, Manchester, have no Corporations.' Finally, in the fourth *Letter*, Paine insisted on a distinction between governments and constitutions: a country could have the first without the second. 'The form of government in England is by a king, lords and commons; but if you ask an Englishman what he means when he speaks of the English Constitution, he is unable to give you any answer. The truth is, the English have no fixed Constitution.' The crown could act in certain areas by prerogative; king, lords, and commons together could pass any Act they chose. England was consequently governed by 'an absolute legislative power'; there was 'no Constitution in that country which says to the legislative powers, "Thus far shalt thou go, and no farther."' Paine urged a constitution to restrain this legislative absolutism; but his discussion of the question was largely abstract.[341]

When Paine turned to recommend a unicameral legislature, he referred again to English examples, not American experience. 'The lords and commons in England formerly made but one house.' Two houses might as easily frustrate each other as produce wiser legislation:

> The two best bills in the last sessions in England were entirely lost by having two houses; the bill for encreasing liberty of conscience, by taking off the necessity of subscription to the thirty-nine articles, Athanasian creed, &c. after passing the lower house by a very great majority, was thrown out by the upper one;[342] and at the time that the nation was starving with the high price of corn, the bill for regulating the importation and exportation of grain, after passing the lower house, was lost by a *difference* between the two, and when returned from the upper one was thrown on the floor by the commons, and indignantly trampled underfoot.

Indeed, apart from his brief digression into the history of Pennsylvania, which was indeed mostly about Charles II and William Penn, Paine's *Four Letters* did little to extend the scant discussion of America already contained in *Common Sense*.[343]

---

[341] This was not Paine's first demand for a constitution as a blueprint antecedent to government, an idea which had appeared in *Common Sense* (1776): *CW*, i. 37.

[342] Paine confused several episodes: the motion on 6 Feb. 1772 to relieve Anglican clergy from the need to subscribe the Thirty-Nine Articles, which was lost in the Commons; a second motion on 5 May 1774 which met the same fate there; and a Bill for the relief of Dissenters, passed in the Commons on 3 April 1772 but defeated in the Lords on 19 May, the same happening to a second Bill in February and March 1773: Clark, *English Society*, 406–7; Richard Burgess Barlow, *Citizenship and Conscience: A Study in the Theory and Practice of Religious Toleration in England during the Eighteenth Century* (Philadelphia, 1962), 150–6, 158–9, 175–9, 185–9.

[343] [Paine], *Four Letters on Interesting Subjects* (1776), in *Common Sense and Other Writings*, ed. Wood, 57–80, at 60–4, 67, 69, 74–5. Paine quoted, 70–1, from documents on the history of

The American Crisis

While *Four Letters* were being written and published, political events were sweeping forward in Pennsylvania. They resulted in a new and formally democratic constitution for that state, adopted at a constitutional convention in mid-July 1776; it provided votes for all men who had paid taxes in the colony in the past year: a wide electorate, but not one including all males. Paine's hand has often been traced in this document. But Paine himself later made clear that he had been with the army when the Convention met; 'I held no correspondence with either party, for, or against, the present constitution. I had no hand in forming any part of it, nor knew any thing of its contents till I saw it published...I have kept clear of all argument for or against the constitution.'[344] Paine's preoccupation was with the geopolitics of the conflict with Britain and with persuading colonists to embrace independence, not with the implementation of any doctrine of universal manhood suffrage, much as he approved of an extensive electorate. Independence meant the overthrow of the old Pennsylvania Assembly, which was still unresolved on that break; and it was probably Paine who denounced in the press its members who held back. They had 'deserted the public trust in a time of the greatest danger and difficulty. Like James the Second they have abdicated the government, and by their own act of desertion and cowardice have laid the Provincial Conference under the necessity of taking instant charge of affairs.'[345] Overthrown it was, and on 2 July 1776 three of the five representatives of Pennsylvania voted in Congress for independence.

As Paine's sixteen *American Crisis* pamphlets were published over a period of years in 1776–83, they naturally reflected his growing knowledge of American events; but his underlying commitments and frame of reference hardly changed. In the *Crisis* papers he continually repeated the rhetorically heightened English Whig discourse, dating from the Exclusion Crisis of 1679–81, asserting that the only alternative to 'liberty', achieved via armed resistance, was 'slavery' imposed by 'tyranny'. He insisted on an unbridgeable divide between two unchanging identities, which he still called, in terms now outdated in England, 'Whigs' and 'Tories'. He reminded his audience of historic English defeats, like those inflicted by Joan of Arc. He briefly compared George Washington with William III. He warned the British joint commander Richard, Viscount Howe, that George III might desert him as Henry VIII had deserted Cardinal Wolsey, and later warned Sir Henry Clinton, British commander-in chief in 1778, 'Remember the times of Charles the First! For Laud and St[r]afford fell by trusting to a hope like yours.' Paine cited resistance to the Jacobite rebellion of 1745–6 as an example (to be expected by America) of ultimate victory despite initial defeats.[346]

In reality Washington was no William III, as Paine was aware, and no military genius; Washington had, indeed, been promoted early in life beyond his level of

Pennsylvania. His (presumably published) source has not yet been identified, although it was not [John Oldmixon], *The British Empire in America* (1708).

[344] [Paine], 'To the People' (18 Mar. 1777): *CW*, ii. 270, 272.
[345] 'To the People', *Pennsylvania Gazette* (26 June 1776): attributed to Paine in Keane, *Paine*, 137.
[346] [Paine], *The American Crisis*, I–VII (23 Dec. 1776–21 Nov. 1778): *CW*, i. 50–1, 53, 58–9, 70–1, 76, 84, 90, 94–5, 131, 133–4, 157.

professional competence. In the early months of the conflict Washington personally suffered a series of military defeats that almost destroyed his cause. He scored one minor victory in the battle of Trenton on 26 December 1776 and gained the advantage in an unimportant skirmish at Princeton on 3 January 1777; but not until the American generals Benedict Arnold and Horatio Gates won a significant victory at Saratoga on 17 October 1777, in Washington's absence, did independence begin to seem militarily attainable. Even then, Washington's decision to keep his army in the winter of 1777–8 at Valley Forge, 20 miles from Philadelphia, almost destroyed it.

There is evidence that Washington appreciated his limitations. Benjamin Rush recorded a story from early 1775:

> About this time I saw Patrick Henry at his lodgings, who told me that General Washington had been with him, and informed him that he was unequal to the station in which his country had placed him, and then added with tears in his eyes 'Remember, Mr. Henry, what I now tell you: From the day I enter upon the command of the American armies, I date my fall, and the ruin of my reputation.'[347]

Perhaps this was fiction; or perhaps a militarily skilled Washington made a profession of inadequacy to pre-empt criticism. At the time, Paine had written in the *American Crisis* papers in defence of Washington, and against moves to replace him as commander in chief. But when in the 1793–4 the American government did not secure Paine's release from the Luxembourg prison, Paine interpreted Washington's policy as deliberate inaction, and was moved either to take revenge, or to reveal what he saw as the truth. In a sensational pamphlet published in 1796,[348] Paine denounced Washington:

> had it not been for the aid received from France, in men, money and ships...your cold and unmilitary conduct...would in all probability have lost America; at least she would not have been the independent nation she now is. You slept away your time in the field, till the finances of the country were completely exhausted, and you have but little share in the glory of the final event. It is time, Sir, to speak the undisguised language of historical truth...when we speak of military character, something more is to be understood than constancy; and something more *ought* to be understood than the Fabian system of *doing nothing*. The *nothing* part can be done by anybody...By the advantage of a good exterior he attracts respect, which his habitual silence tends to preserve; but he has not the talent of inspiring ardor in an army.[349]

Or as Paine wrote in the press: 'I well knew that the black times of '76 were the natural consequence of his [Washington's] want of military judgment in the choice of positions into which the army was put about New York and New Jersey.'[350] It was less confidence in the military strength of the American cause or any detailed

---

[347] Rush, *Autobiography*, 113.

[348] For a different interpretation see Steven Blakemore, 'Revisionist Parricide: Thomas Paine's Letter to George Washington', in Blakemore, *Crisis in Representation: Thomas Paine, Mary Wollstonecraft, Helen Maria Williams, and the Rewriting of the French Revolution* (Madison, 1997), 57–73.

[349] Paine, *Letter to George Washington* (1796): *CW*, ii. 695, 718–21.

[350] Paine, 'To the Citizens of the United States', Letter III (29 Nov. 1802): *CW*, ii. 922.

knowledge of the transatlantic controversy that drove Paine during the American Revolution than his enmity to his home country.

Paine's own war service was at one remove. As an American officer wrote, 'Paine may be a good philosopher, but he is not a soldier—he always kept out of danger.'[351] Yet he wrote. The effect of Paine's *American Crisis* essays has passed into national myth, with the enduring vision of Washington reading an issue to his men on Christmas day, 1776, to inspire them to victory at the battle of Trenton. Yet little other evidence survives for the impact of the essays. The motivations of combatants on the rebel side were complex, and not wholly idealistic. One officer in the Pennsylvania Line, Alexander Graydon, a hostile witness against Paine and a man in reaction against the French Revolution, later claimed that the year 1776 was not

> a season of almost universal patriotic enthusiasm. It was far from prevalent in my opinion, among the lower ranks of the people, at least in Pennsylvania. At all times, indeed, licentious, levelling principles are much to the general taste, and were of course popular with us; but the true merits of the contest, were little understood or regarded. The opposition to the claims of Britain originated with the better sort: it was truly aristocratic in its commencement; and as the oppression to be apprehended, had not been felt, no grounds existed for general enthusiasm. The cause of liberty, it is true, was fashionable, and there were great preparations to fight for it; but a zeal proportioned to the magnitude of the question, was only to be looked for in the minds of those sagacious politicians, who inferred effects from causes, and who, as Mr. Burke expresses it, 'snuffed the approach of tyranny in every tainted breeze.'

Graydon documented the slow and difficult recruitment of troops. Among the soldiers, 'it appeared, that the sordid spirit of gain was the vital principle of this greater part of the army'; he was repeatedly struck by the 'very few gentlemen and men of the world, that at this time appeared in arms from this country [Pennsylvania], which might be considered as the cradle of the revolution'. If so, Paine's journalism had not reversed this reticence.

When, continued Graydon, the statue of George III in New York was demolished after the Declaration of Independence, 'so little was the spirit of seventy-six like the spirit of subsequent eras, that the act was received with extreme coldness and indifference…We were, indeed, beginning to grow angry with him; and were not displeased with Paine for calling him a *royal brute*, but we had not yet acquired the true taste for cutting throats.' Graydon noted Paine's presence as an observer at an early action, and that he 'gave us a handsome puff in one of the Philadelphia papers of the day', but this only prompted Graydon to the reflection that *Common Sense* had produced the author's

> good reception at Head Quarters, and acquaintance with the Commander-in-chief [Washington], whom he seems to have considered from that time, as embarked with him in the general cause of reforming, republicanizing, and democratizing the world; than which nothing was more foreign to the views of the General, or those of the others, who took a lead in the early stage of the contest. One of the most untoward

[351] Biddle, *Autobiography*, 87.

consequences of a successful resistance of government, is the unavoidable association in the undertaking, of the worst men with the best, of fools, fanatics, system-mongers, reformers and *philosophers*, with men of sense, moderation and virtue, who, wishing to stop when the true object of the controversy is attained, are seldom suffered to do it, or, if fortunate enough to prevail, they are, thenceforth viewed with suspicion and charged with apostasy.[352]

It was not a warm commendation of Paine's *The American Crisis*. But it might be inappropriate to expect a theoretical consideration of the work among American troops. The American general William Irvine observed of the western Pennsylvania militiamen that 'a great majority have no other views than to acquire lands'.[353]

Historians remain divided over the degree of idealism of the common soldiers in this conflict, but in Paine's own Pennsylvania it does not seem that *The American Crisis* settled the question: indeed Pennsylvanians were initially markedly reluctant to enlist. In this respect the American experience was to be different from the French, for large numbers of young Frenchmen enlisted in 1792–3 in a wave of patriotic idealism in order to defend the Revolution from the invading armies of Prussia and Austria.

The progress of the war

Nor was the war a preordained progression towards American victory: the military dimension of the conflict was complex, neither army was particularly skilled in land warfare, and the balance of advantage swung from one side to another. Each side scored victories; many military outcomes turned on small causes. Even after the British defeat at the battle of Yorktown in 1781, Britain's naval position recovered; France and Spain might still have been driven out of the war by their financial weakness. Several strategic outcomes were possible; there were plausible alternatives to the loss of half of Britain's twenty-six American colonies that was negotiated in 1783, and Britain's retention of Gibraltar and most of her possessions in the West Indies, and a strengthening hold on India, meant that her worldwide strategic position was not annihilated. Military historians have emphasized that only the uncertainty of Britain's command of the sea permitted outside intervention in the Thirteen Colonies, and it was fears for the loss of naval supremacy that finally induced the House of Commons in London to give up the war on land. But in these naval events George Washington played no part.[354] Paine's biographers can sometimes discuss the war as if an American victory was assured primarily by republican morale, and as if that morale was supported primarily by Paine; but this assumption ignores the complex military and geopolitical realities to which Paine's

[352] *Alexander Graydon's Memoirs of his Own Time*, ed. John Stockton Littell (Philadelphia, 1846), 134–5, 148, 157, 161, 188. It is open to debate whether Graydon's reaction to the French Revolution distorted his memory of the American, or allowed him to be candid about the earlier event.

[353] For the debate over the soldiers' motivation, see Knouff, *The Soldiers' Revolution*, 36, 39, 65 and *passim*.

[354] Piers Mackesy, *The War for America 1775–1783* (London, 1964), esp. 510–16; Jeremy Black, *War for America: The Fight for Independence 1775–1783* (Stroud, 1991).

simple journalism supplied a retrospective commentary. Military historians of the American war, by contrast, generally found it unnecessary to discuss Paine, and their silence is significant.

The argument from morale also ignores the diversity of opinion within the Thirteen Colonies. The coercion of Loyalists by 'systematic violence and intimidation' before 1776, and the failures of the British army consistently to sustain Loyalists once fighting had begun, make it impossible to arrive at any simple map of the distribution of colonial opinion between Loyalists and Patriots, a balance that also shifted as time went on; yet one historian has argued that 'there was always a vast middle ground of uncommitted men who more than anything wanted order and security'.[355] Little evidence reveals how Paine's writings influenced that mass of moderate opinion. What mattered more, it might be suggested, was the physical reality of war.

What Paine produced was propaganda, and to be effective it had to disguise war's realities. Long before the French Revolution, he addressed Lord Howe:

> I, who know England and the disposition of the people well, am confident, that it is easier for us to effect a revolution there, than you a conquest here; a few thousand men landed in England with the declared design of deposing the present king, bringing his ministers to trial, and setting up the Duke of Gloucester in his stead, would assuredly carry their point, while you are groveling here, ignorant of the matter.

Although this vision belonged to the era of dynastic instability before 1745 rather than to the era of deep-seated Hanoverian security after 1760, this was a claim that Paine later repeated in *Crisis* no. VI. He argued that a declaration of independence had been forced on the colonies; otherwise, 'There was reason to believe that Britain would endeavor to make a European matter of it, and, rather than lose the whole [of North America], would dismember it, like Poland.' Why, asked Paine, was America to be dragged into European wars? He echoed early eighteenth-century British Tory 'blue-water' strategists: 'Britain, for centuries past, has been nearly fifty years out of every hundred at war with some power or other'; the right policy for an independent America (as for Britain) was isolation, and naval strength. 'The most able English statesmen and politicians have always held it as a principle, that foreign connections served only to embarrass and exhaust England.'[356] Imperial expansion was an injustice: Britain's 'late reduction of India, under Clive and his successors, was not so properly a conquest as an extermination of mankind'. For Paine geopolitics, rather than internal American circumstances, pointed to American success.

Paine's argument, in *Crisis* nos VII and VIII, implied that military failure to suppress the rising was the fault of Britain more than the achievement of America. Indeed the Revolution, in Paine's account, was caused solely by 'a secret and fixed determination in the British Cabinet to annex America to the crown of England as

---

[355] Piers Mackesy, *Could the British have Won the War of Independence?* (Worcester, Mass., 1976), 5–6, 12. Mackesy recognized that the main alternative to his argument was that 'the guerre révolutionnaire which preceded the first shots at Lexington was irreversible'; but this local conflict was one that Paine had not seen, and in which he played no part.

[356] Paine, *Prospects on the Rubicon* (1787): *CW*, ii. 631.

a conquered country',[357] not by anything that happened in the colonies them-selves. For Britain's malaise, specifically the ruinous level of British taxation, he turned to a British work, Richard Price's *Observations on the Nature of Civil Liberty, the Principles of Government, and the Justice and Policy of the War with America.*[358] Warning the people of Rhode Island to consent to join the other states in a federal import duty to pay the interest on loans taken out in the money market in Holland to support the war, Paine reminded his readers of the heavier taxes paid on many commodities in England, citing as his authority Richard Burn's *Justice of the Peace and Parish Officer.*[359] Despite Paine's later reputation in the United States, in *The American Crisis* letters, as in *Common Sense*, there was little of principle that was specifically American. A century-old political discourse, shared on both sides of the Atlantic, had already provided all that was needed to promote or oppose resistance.

Paine, indeed, intended to set out his scenario in a history of the American Revolution; it would have focused wholly on Britain's provocative role. On 24 January 1775 an essay in the *Pennsylvania Magazine* looked back to the old world: 'The British magazines, at their commencement, were repositories of ingenuity. They are now the retailers of tale and nonsense. From elegance they sunk to sim-plicity, from simplicity to folly, and from folly to voluptuousness. The Gentleman's, the London, and the Universal, Magazines, bear yet some marks of their original-ity; but the Town and Country, the Covent-Garden, and the Westminster, are no better than incentives to profligacy and dissipation.'[360]

Yet Paine did not turn aside from these familiar sources. Rather, he planned to use them in an important work. In 1777, Paine promised Franklin: 'I intend next winter to begin on the first volume of the Revolution of America', asking Franklin for sources: 'the Gentlemans and Universal Magazines for '74, '75 and '76, the two Reviews and Parliamentary debates for the same year, and such as are come out since and the last Court Register.'[361] Next year he added: 'I live in hopes of seeing and advising with you respecting the History of the American Revolution, as soon as a turn of affairs makes it safe to take a passage for Europe.'[362] This was always postponed.

As I wish to render the History of this Revolution as complete as possible I am unwill-ing to begin it too soon, and should be glad to consult you first, because the *real motives* of the British King in commencing the War will form a considerable political part. I am sufficiently persuaded myself that they wished for a quarrel and intended to annex America to the Crown of England as a conquered country. They had no doubt

---

[357] [Paine], *The American Crisis*, V (21 Mar. 1776): *CW*, i. 118–19, 144, 157.

[358] [Paine], *The Crisis Extraordinary* (4 Oct. 1780): *CW*, i. 173 cited 96–8 of Price's work as the source for a table of tax revenues 'being the medium of three years before the year 1776'. The pagin-ation tallies with an American reprint of Price's *Observations* (Charleston: David Bruce, 1776), but not with the London editions of that year.

[359] [Paine], 'Six Letters to Rhode Island' (1782–3): *CW*, ii. 360–1.

[360] [Paine], 'The Magazine in America', *Pennsylvania Magazine* (24 Jan. 1775): *CW*, ii. 1110.

[361] Paine to Benjamin Franklin, 20 June 1777: *CW*, ii. 1132–3.

[362] Paine to Benjamin Franklin, 16 May 1778: *CW*, ii. 1143–51, at 1151.

of victory and hoped for what they might call a Rebellion, but we have not, on this side of the water, sufficient proof of this at present.[363]

By 1779, he wrote:

> I intend prosecuting a history of the Revolution by means of a subscription—but this undertaking will be attended with such an amazing expense, and will take such a length of time, that unless the States individually give some assistance therein, scarcely any man could afford to go through it. Some kind of an history might be easily executed made up of daily events and trifling matters which would lose their importance in a few years. But a proper history cannot even be begun unless the secrets of the other side of the water can be obtained, for the first part is so interwoven with the politics of England that that which will be the last to get at must be the first to begin with—and this single instance is sufficient to show that no history can take place for some time. My design, if I undertake it, is to comprise it in three quarto volumes and to publish one each year from the time of beginning, and to make an abridgement afterwards in an easy agreeable language for a school book.[364]

Without these English sources, which he considered essential, Paine never undertook his *History*. He had no appreciation that important explanations of the American Revolution lay all around him in America for he continued to understand that revolution chiefly in terms of his English preconceptions, blaming 'the *real motives* of the British King' for provoking the fighting. Britons serving in the American theatre of war saw much more. By the time he began again to spend time in England, from the late 1780s, his priorities had changed: no longer to blame the English ministry of 1776, but to vindicate his sense of the possibility of rational solutions to practical problems with a plan for a prefabricated iron bridge. Yet this pursuit of rational solutions in the field of engineering did not mean that Paine ever attempted a history of the American Revolution.

Paine, Raynal, and Crèvecoeur

Paine's undefended image of the history of the American Revolution now met a challenge from a French ally, the abbé Raynal. Raynal's book was written in a tone of breathless admiration of the Americans. It also provided a lengthy paraphrase of 'this celebrated performance', *Common Sense*. Even such language was not enough for Paine, for Raynal was drawn to point out that the American Revolution contained a paradox:

> None of those energetic causes, which have produced so many revolutions upon the globe, existed in North America. Neither religion nor laws had there been outraged. The blood of martyrs or patriots had not there streamed from scaffolds. Morals had not been there insulted. Manners, customs, habits, no object dear to nations had there been the sport of ridicule. Arbitrary power had not there torn any inhabitant from the

---

[363] Paine to Benjamin Franklin, 24 Oct. 1778: *CW*, ii. 1153–4.
[364] Paine to Henry Laurens, 14 Sept. 1779: *CW*, ii. 1179.

arms of his family and his friends, to drag him to a dreary dungeon. Public order had not been there inverted. The principles of administration had not been changed there; and the maxims of government had there always remained the same. The whole question was reduced to the knowing whether the mother country had, or had not, the right to lay, directly, or indirectly, a slight tax upon the colonies: for the accumulated grievances in the manifesto [the Declaration of Independence] were valid only in consequence of this leading grievance. This, almost metaphysical, question was scarcely of sufficient importance to cause the multitude to rise, or at least to interest them strongly in a quarrel for which they saw their land deprived of the hands destined to its cultivation, their harvests laid waste, their fields covered with the dead bodies of their kindred, or stained with their own blood.[365]

In 1782 Paine replied indignantly, his pamphlet containing two elements: an account of what the American Revolution had been, and a prediction of its wider significance.

Paine asserted that 'all' of Raynal's 'energetic causes', these gross abuses, had indeed come into being in the American colonies between 1765 and 1776. Paine wrote nothing about events internal to the colonies as causes of the Revolution, instead repeating the usual litany of oppressive British actions from the Stamp Act through the Declaratory Act to the Boston massacre. The Revolution was wholly Britain's fault: 'it was the fixed determination of the British Cabinet to quarrel with America at all events... They hoped for a rebellion, and they made one.' The inadequacy of Paine's account of the causes of the outbreak of the Revolution was only disguised by the circumstantial detail of the subsequent fighting, to which he now turned, and of which he naturally knew more than did Raynal. Yet behind this account of conflict on the ground in America lay Paine's view of the transoceanic dimension in earlier years: there, Britain's 'former overbearing rudeness, and insufferable injustice on the seas, have made every commercial nation her foe'. The exchange with Raynal was evidence, once more, that Paine's love of America was abstract, and general; his hatred of Britain was specific, and visceral.[366] Appropriately, Paine was secretly paid for this pamphlet and others by the French minister to the United States, Luzerne.[367]

To some historians, Paine's *Letter to Raynal* is most striking for its eulogy of the uniqueness and promise of the American Revolution; as Paine put it, 'Here the value and quality of liberty, the nature of government, and the dignity of man, were known and understood, and the attachment of the Americans to these principles produced the Revolution, as a natural and almost unavoidable consequence.' Americans now 'think with other thoughts'. These 'other thoughts' were international: 'As the mind closed itself towards England, it opened itself towards the

---

[365] Guillaume-Thomas, Abbé Raynal, *Révolution de l'Amérique* (London: L. Davis and La Haye: P. F. Gosse, 1781); English translation as *The Revolution of America* (London: Lockyer Davis, 1781), 79–90, 126–7 (reprinted by Robert Bell, Philadelphia, 1781). Historians still struggle with the 'ostensible causes' of the American Revolution, the inadequacy of the usual list notably acknowledged in Gordon S. Wood, *The Making of the American Republic 1776–1787* (Chapel Hill, NC, 1969), 3.

[366] Paine, *Letter to the Abbé Raynal* (1782): *CW*, ii. 216–19, 221, 262.

[367] Aldridge, *Man of Reason*, 97.

world.' Examined more closely, Paine still used the conditional: 'Should the present [American] revolution be distinguished by opening a new system of extended civilization, it will receive from heaven the highest evidence of approbation.'[368] This conditional is normally overlooked, as is the role in the argument of 'heaven', but they point to the limitations of Paine's understanding of what had happened within the Thirteen Colonies. Nor did Paine write in 1782 of the reception of the American Revolution in Europe, a subject of which he could yet know little.

Was this vision Paine's original insight? It has been argued that Paine's text echoed closely the rhetoric of the Frenchman Michel-Guillaume-Jean de Crèvecoeur's *Letters from an American Farmer*.[369] He had arrived in Canada, aged twenty, in 1755; as an Anglophile, he worked in the British colonies after 1759 as J. Hector St John, was naturalized in 1765, married, and lived as a prosperous farmer in Orange County, New York. There, before 1776, he wrote idealistically about colonial life; but he did so as a Loyalist, soon persecuted, who escaped to England in 1781. His book was first published in London in 1782; it is not established that copies reached Philadelphia before 21 August 1782, when Paine's *Letter to Raynal* was dated, in time for Paine to absorb its rhetoric.

Parts of Crèvecoeur's text do seem reminiscent of Paine's, notably Crèvecoeur's famous question 'What, then, is the American, this new man?' The American, he answered, had

> arrived on a new continent; a modern society offers itself to his contemplation, different from what he had hithero seen. It is not composed, as in Europe, of great lords who possess everything and of a herd of people who have nothing. Here are no aristocratical families, no courts, no kings, no bishops, no ecclesiastical dominion, no invisible power giving to a few a very visible one, no great manufactures employing thousands, no great refinements of luxury…We have no princes for whom we toil, starve and bleed; we are the most perfect society now existing in the world.

This superseded old world allegiances: 'What attachment can a poor European emigrant have for a country where he had nothing?' So wrote Crèvecoeur before the Revolution, with no sense of impending disaster. All this was common to Paine's rhetoric in 1776; and it was the vision also of many Loyalists of the early 1770s.

More promisingly for an argument of the two men's similarity, Crèvecoeur continued: 'The American is a new man, who acts upon new principles; he must therefore entertain new ideas and form new opinions.' Echoing this ideal, he outlined a claim of growing American homogeneity out of nationally diverse immigrants: 'From this promiscuous breed, that race now called Americans have arisen.' Such, at least, was the universalist rhetoric; but as Crèvecoeur's text went on, he developed a very different and particularist analysis of the different rates of worldly success of the new arrivals, Germans, Scots, and Irish, based on their national characters. Paine made no such point. Crèvecoeur was not as insensitive as was Paine to the diversities of American colonists: on the contrary, Crèvecoeur

---

[368] Paine, *Letter to the Abbé Raynal* (1782): *CW*, ii. 219, 243, 256.
[369] Jack Fruchtman, Jr, *The Political Philosophy of Thomas Paine* (Baltimore, 2009), 74.

attempted an analysis of changes of manners and morals from the polite society of the older tidewater settlements to 'the most vicious of our people' on the frontier, 'a mongrel breed, half civilized, half savage'. 'There, remote from the power of example and check of shame, many families exhibit the most hideous parts of our society.' Crèvecoeur depicted no Deist republic and no benign Paineite 'society' manifesting spontaneous peaceful cooperation; rather, he described carefully how 'the various Christian sects introduced [by immigrants] wear out and... religious indifference becomes prevalent'. Nor did Crèvecoeur celebrate the effect of any American Revolution; for him, writing before 1776, the European emigrant to America merely became 'an English subject'. In his pages it was economic opportunity that wrought a transformation in the emigrant's character, not participation in revolution or throwing off any English yoke. For Crèvecoeur, the American colonies before 1776 declared no Painite approbation of heaven.[370]

Had Paine and Crèvecoeur expressed the same vision, their coincidence might be evidence that they were in a broad sense reporting on American realities. But their accounts were significantly different. Their writings themselves demand historical explanation; they are not keys that provide such insights. Paine's republican Utopianism was never an empirically based position.

History, slavery, and the constitution

It has often been argued that the *Letter to the Abbe Raynal* constitutes a part of Paine's intended history of the American Revolution. Certainly, that *Letter* contains a brief summary of Paine's position, but it was not a fragment of a larger work. Even a year later, Paine continued to explore with Congress the possibility of being appointed 'Historiographer to the Continent'. Paine was torn between his belief that his services to America had been insufficiently acknowledged and rewarded, and his desire to pose as an independent, unpaid, and uncorrupted observer: 'for Congress to reserve to themselves the least appearance of influence over an historian, by annexing thereto a yearly salary subject to their own control, will endanger the reputation of both the historian and the history.'[371] Paine, then, sought to use this issue of principle to extract from Congress a grant or capital sum, but this they would not give. Nor are Paine's professions of unbought independence convincing, since in 1782–3 he was secretly in receipt of payments from Washington's government; payments were given to Paine in order to support him while he joined in the project of creating a strong federal government with its own powers of taxation.[372] The real reason for Paine's inability to write his planned *History of the American Revolution* was an intellectual one: he had convinced himself that the evidence from which it could be written was evidence of English high politics alone, and to such evidence he did not have access.

---

[370] J. Hector St. John de Crèvecoeur, *Letters from an American Farmer and Sketches of Eighteenth-Century America*, ed. Albert E. Stone (Harmondsworth, 1986), 67–70, 72–3, 77, 79, 83, 85–8.
[371] Paine, 'To a Committee of the Continental Congress' [Oct. 1783]: *CW*, ii. 1226, 1240.
[372] Keane, *Paine*, 216–26, 235–40.

Perhaps for that reason, Paine wrote nothing of the other American Revolution:[373] not the constitutional revolution that won independence for the Thirteen Colonies and established them as a single republic, but the social revolution that was triggered by war and rebellion, the social revolution that profoundly altered relationships in society between patrician and plebeian, master and servant, rich and poor, men and women, parents and children—even, in some cases, between white and black (although seldom, it seems, between white settler and Native American).[374] These social changes are often today identified through present-day categories like 'egalitarianism', 'meritocracy', 'feminism', and 'racial equality', the appropriateness of which for the 1780s may be questioned. Something like them did exist at that time, yet the present-day categories may subtly misstate the eighteenth-century phenomena. Paine, indeed, believed in equality; yet his sense of equality derived from a militant belief that a Creator God had literally created each individual with equal rights, a belief that is rarely found in the present day. Paine's critique of aristocrats did not, therefore, easily or directly translate into a celebration of an egalitarian social ethic (as between races, classes, or genders) in the present-day sense.

Paine's first wife had died, and he was separated from his second: he wrote no extended discussion of the position of women, and was insensitive to the changes in gender relations taking place around him in America. Paine had no offspring, and had no personal experience against which to judge changes in relations between parents and children; his only argument here was the theoretical one that each 'generation' was fully competent to decide in all matters. Paine, subsidized by Washington's government, wrote in favour of a fundamentally strengthened federal government succeeding the British crown in having the rights to all western lands, but in his most considered examination of the question of the westward territorial expansion of the new republic Paine ignored the land rights of Native Americans entirely. His silence was more notable, since he condemned 'all rights by mere conquest, power or violence'; nevertheless, the 'Indians', for him, were merely people who threatened 'incursions'. Paine even condemned the British proclamation of 1763, setting limits to the westward expansion of white settlers: 'It is easy for us to understand, that the frequent and plausible mention of the Indians was only a pretext to create an idea of the humanity of [the British] government.'[375] Indeed the rights of America's native inhabitants never occupied a prominent place in Paine's thinking. For a range of necessarily powerful reasons, Paine did not appreciate that he had lived through a social revolution in America.

Paine's hatred of George III did not extend to France's monarch: Paine's English preoccupations overrode any possible alignment against a French 'other'. In July

---

[373] For which see especially Gordon Wood, *The Radicalism of the American Revolution* (New York, 1992).

[374] Susan Juster, *Disorderly Women: Sexual Politics and Evangelicalism in Revolutionary New England* (Ithaca, NY, 1996); Michael A. McDonnell, *The Politics of War: Race, Class, and Conflict in Revolutionary Virginia* (Chapel Hill, NC, 2007).

[375] Paine, *Public Good* (1780): *CW*, ii. 306, 322, 330. For the massacre and spoliation of Native Americans by Patriots see Wim Klooster, *Revolutions in the Atlantic World: A Comparative History* (New York, 2009), 28–30.

1782 Luzerne, the French minister to Washington's court, gave 'a most splendid entertainment' to celebrate the birthday of the Dauphin. Paine was present, as were John Dickinson, Robert Morris, John Rutledge, George Washington, and others. Rush commented:

> It was impossible to partake of the joy of the evening without being struck with the occasion of it. It was to celebrate the birth of the Dauphin of France. How great the revolution in the mind of an American! To rejoice in the birth of a prince who must one day be the support of monarchy and slavery! Human nature in this instance seems to be turned inside outwards. The picture is still agreeable, inasmuch as it shows us in the clearest point of view that there are no prejudices so strong, no opinions so sacred, and no contradictions so palpable, that will not yield to the love of liberty... The celebrated author of *Common Sense* retired frequently from company to analyze his thoughts and to enjoy the repast of his own original ideas.[376]

But Paine did not write of the event, not even when the Dauphin, Louis-Joseph, born in 1781, died in 1789.

In retrospect, Paine's residence in the new American republic before 1787 was notable for his lack of interest in two subjects that would soon rise to dominate attention in that state: slavery, and the constitution.

Paine was not alone in his lack of attention to slavery: English Deists had not marked themselves out as anti-slavery campaigners. This absence has been obscured by the misattribution to him of an anonymous article on that theme in 1775, and of the preamble to an Act of the Pennsylvania Assembly for the emancipation of slaves, passed by that body on 1 March 1780.[377] By 1805, when anti-slavery was in full swing, Paine easily identified with it, but notably in biblical terms, not in terms of universalist natural rights language. The port of Liverpool, Paine knew, was the centre of the English slave trade. 'Had I the command of the elements I would blast Liverpool with fire and brimstone. It is the Sodom and Gomorrah of brutality.'[378] It was not an early and sustained commitment. This seeming insensitivity to a practice that Paine, when challenged, condemned was something that he shared with many of the revolutionaries who left the British Isles for the United States in the 1790s. As one survey of activists has shown, 'Of the thirty-two *émigrés* whose views in America have been discovered, only thirteen were adamantly opposed to slavery, no fewer than eleven owned slaves, and the views of the remaining eight were ambiguous or altered over time.'[379]

Second, the Federal constitution. Paine's aversion to his native land did not emancipate him from every English maxim of government. Soon after the new republic established its independence, Paine dropped his hostility to central power and reverted to an argument close to William Blackstone's *Commentaries on the*

---

[376] Rush to ?Elizabeth Graeme Ferguson, 16 July 1782: Rush, *Letters*, 280.

[377] Preamble to the Act Passed by the Pennsylvania Assembly, March 1, 1780: *CW*, ii. 21–2. See Appendix: Paine De-attributions.

[378] Paine to Thomas Jefferson, 25 Jan. 1805: *CW*, ii. 1462.

[379] Michael Durey, *Transatlantic Radicals and the Early American Republic* (Lawrence, Kan., 1997), 283. Paine should be deleted from the thirteen there recorded as 'adamantly opposed'.

Laws of England (1765–9). Defending the newly established Bank of North America in 1786, Paine began a pamphlet with a dictum: 'Every government, let its form be what it may, contains within itself a principle common to all, which is that of a sovereign power, or a power over which there is no control, and which controls all others; and as it is impossible to construct a form of government in which this power does not exist, so there must of necessity be a place, if it may be so called, for it to exist in.'[380]

In general, however, British examples served only as warnings. The federal constitution, urged Paine in 1786, should have a provision that laws would automatically lapse after thirty years; 'The British, from the want of some general regulation of this kind, have a great number of obsolete laws; which, though out of use and forgotten, are not out of force, and are occasionally brought up for particular purposes, and innocent, unwary persons trepanned thereby.'[381] When Paine condemned paper currency as being of no fixed value and therefore corrupting of all economic relations, he cited as an analogy not paper currency, but the issuing of coin made of other metals than gold and silver: 'It was the issuing base coin, and establishing it as a [legal] tender, that was one of the principal means of finally overthrowing the power of the Stuart family in Ireland.' Paine cited as his source Thomas Leland's *The History of Ireland from the Invasion of Henry II*.[382]

Nevertheless, Paine could hardly be said to have taken a close interest in what is now known as state formation.[383] By leaving for France in April 1787, he was abroad while the Convention met in Philadelphia from May to consider a new constitution for the United States, and afterwards showed no great knowledge of its proceedings. For their part, the delegates to that conference sat in almost daily weekday session from 25 May to 17 September without apparently discussing Paine's ideas or even mentioning him.[384] Paine's main use of the American example was in *Rights of Man. Part the Second* (1792). Yet even his enthusiastic editor, Philip Foner, admitted that 'Paine tends to romanticize early American History'. What Paine knew most about was the formation of the Pennsylvania constitution (although he did not admit its flagrantly undemocratic operation); he knew something about the Articles of Confederation at the Federal government level; but of the content of the new and very different constitution of 1787, as opposed to the procedure for its ratification, he understood less.[385]

---

[380] Paine, *Dissertations on Government; the Affairs of the Bank; and Paper Money* (1786): *CW*, ii. 368–9.

[381] Paine, *Dissertations on Government; the Affairs of the Bank; and Paper Money* (1786): *CW*, ii. 395–6.

[382] Paine, *Dissertations on Government; the Affairs of the Bank; and Paper Money* (1786): *CW*, ii. 407–8. Paine cited Thomas Leland's *The History of Ireland from the Invasion of Henry II* (3 vols, London: J. Nourse et al., 1773), iv. 265.

[383] For the de-attribution of 'Candid and Critical Remarks on a Letter signed Ludlow', see Appendix: Paine De-attributions.

[384] Max Farrand (ed.), *Records of the Federal Convention of 1787* (rev. edn, 4 vols, New Haven, 1966); the General Index is in the fourth volume, separately titled *Supplement to Max Farrand's The Records of the Federal Convention of 1787*, ed. James H. Hutson (New Haven, 1987). These records are not a verbatim transcript of every word spoken, so that the seeming absence of references to Paine cannot be conclusive.

[385] Paine, *Rights of Man. Part the Second* (1792): *CW*, i. 354, 376–81.

Paine: refugee

The world had already moved on. After 1783, the experience of some of the men later termed Founding Fathers was of neglect and official ingratitude. Politics had its new concerns; memories in a continually changing Congress were short. Thanks to American parochialism, this applied especially to those whose reputations were international. It even applied to the most internationally famous American of his age, Benjamin Franklin. Cheering crowds welcomed him when he returned to Philadelphia in September 1785, but this did not translate into national recognition or reward. Congress would not settle Franklin's accounts from his French mission; it would not give his grandson a post; it would not make him a land grant in the western territories as a reward for his services to the Revolution. Like Paine, Franklin drew up a memorandum for Congress setting out his many and important services to the new republic, but Congress did not act. 'Even the much hated British had not treated him as shabbily as the Congress had.'[386]

Paine was in a similar position. Congress, burdened with wartime debt, initially did nothing for him; some states did something; none, in Paine's eyes, did enough. It was the French minister, the Chevalier de la Luzerne, who in 1783 provided a reward of 2,400 livres for Paine's publications of the past year, so allowing him to buy at Bordentown a small house, land, and a horse. Only in the spring of 1784 did Paine learn that the New York Senate had awarded him the 300-acre estate confiscated from a Loyalist at New Rochelle. In October 1785 Congress, after much internal dissent, awarded him the sum of $3,000, 'enough to enable him to avoid want in the next twenty years of his life'.[387]

Paine, then, was not alone in being neglected by the new but impecunious American republic, and his neglect is not evidence against his significant role in the Revolution. Even so, no excuse was sufficient and no reward came in time to satisfy Paine, and his disillusionment may have had causes additional to Franklin's. 'The country that ought to have been to me a home, has scarcely been an Asylum. I sometimes ask myself, what am I better off than a refugee.'[388] He repeated the phrase in another letter. 'Trade I do not understand. Land I have none, or what is equal to none. I have exiled myself from one Country without making a home of another.' He deeply resented 'the continued neglect of the Country [the United States] towards me'; it 'did not afford me a home'; 'it does not afford to me a home'.[389] Paine's reiteration of the word 'home' was eloquent of his sense of loss.

It was as a refugee, claiming therefore to be 'a man who considers the world as his home',[390] that Paine returned to Europe. On a brief visit to l'Orient in March

---

[386] Wood, *The Americanization of Benjamin Franklin*, 213, 221–6.

[387] Foner, *Tom Paine and Revolutionary America*, 192; Keane, *Paine*, 250–4.

[388] Paine to anon. [?James Duane], 19 May 1783, in Hazel Burgess, *Thomas Paine: A Collection of Unknown Writings* (Basingstoke, 2010), 37–43, at 38.

[389] Paine, 'To a Committee of the Continental Congress' [Oct. 1783]: *CW*, ii. 1227–8.

[390] Paine to Lansdowne, 21 Sept. 1787: *CW*, ii. 1265–6.

1781 as a companion of the man sent to negotiate the French loan that was intended to make possible the continuation of the Thirteen Colonies in the war, he had written: 'I find myself no stranger in France; people know me almost as generally here as in America.'[391] This was an overstatement: the reality was to prove rather different after Paine arrived back in France on 26 May 1787.

---

[391] Paine to James Hutchinson, 11 Mar. 1781: *CW*, ii. 1195; Paine to the Senate of the United States, 21 Jan. 1808: *CW*, ii. 1490.

5

The Unexpected Revolution
France, 1787–1802

THE AMERICAN REVOLUTION AND FRANCE, 1787–1789

Contingency and foresight

The larger the episode, the greater the role of contingency. The greater the role of contingency, the more important were individual experiences as against the over-arching interpretations of ideologues.[1] Several writers in the late eighteenth century looked forward in highly general terms to the end of the Europe of monarchs and aristocrats, but none predicted the French Revolution in the form it took, or its timing. Given Louis XVI's caution and irresolution, and the diverse aims of elite and non-elite political activists, there were many points at which events could have taken a quite different course: official responses to the disastrous harvests of 1787 and 1788, leading to rural conflict and economic crisis in 1789; the bitter winter of 1788–9; the initial lack of royal definition of the procedure of the Estates-General; the king's dismissal of his reforming ministers on 11 July 1789 and their replacement by men hostile to the Revolution; the symbolic storming of the Bastille on 14 July; the forcible removal of the royal family from Versailles to Paris on 6 October; the king's 'flight to Varennes' on 20 June 1791 and its failure, promoting conspiracy theories, paranoia, Jacobinism, and republicanism; his imprisonment on 10 August 1792, and the suspension of monarchy, after an armed insurrection of *sans-culottes*; the Terror of 1793–4: all these episodes and more could have happened otherwise, and, in that case, the arguments of Sieyès for unified national sovereignty and against aristocracy need not have seemed prophetic or determinative.

Contingency meant that for those who lived through the events of 1789 onwards those events did not have a single meaning: they had many meanings, and these were contested.[2] In the simplest terms, the French Revolution, like the American, had two faces. For some of those who experienced it the Revolution was a moment

---

[1] See Peter McPhee, *Living the French Revolution, 1789–99* (Basingstoke, 2006), and his evocation of the kindred view of the historian Richard Cobb that 'the Revolution was irrelevant to the masses of French people when it was not being made against them', 3. McPhee depicts a Revolution that was primarily the work of urban elites, imposed, partly by force, on an often unwilling countryside.

[2] 'Indeed, it seems likely that in the Revolutionary dynamic no single array of factors was operative at all times. The Revolution evolved, rather, in an irregular fashion through a series of "phase changes," each initiated by unanticipated crises or events, each entailing a distinct configuration of cause and consequence': Timothy Tackett, *The Coming of the Terror in the French Revolution* (Cambridge, Mass., 2015), 4. The same is argued of the American Revolution in Chapter 4.

of euphoria, idealism, fraternity, liberation, the opening up of endless possibility, the vindication of principles. They might perceive events as a series of universalist affirmations. But others experienced a dark world of particularist negations, like the elderly Victoire de Froulay de Tessé, Marquise de Créquy, evidently writing in 1799:

> In the towns you see only insolent or evil people. You are spoken to only in a tone which is brusque, demanding or defiant. Every face has a sinister look; even children have a hostile, depraved demeanour. One would say that there is hatred in every heart. Envy has not been satisfied, and misery is everywhere. That is the punishment for making a revolution.[3]

Both perceptions were part of the intellectual context in which famous texts were composed and read. How did Paine integrate them? What was his vision of contingency or inevitability?

In 1802, finally back in America, he explained in a newspaper article: 'When I sailed for Europe, in the spring of 1787, it was my intention to return to America the next year, and enjoy in retirement the esteem of my friends, and the repose I was entitled to. I had stood out the storm of one revolution, and had no wish to embark in another.'[4] Other evidence supports the interpretation that these words record Paine's lack of anticipation in 1787 of an impending revolution in France. While there in 1787, and just about to cross the channel, Paine warned the British in a carefully written pamphlet not to engage in war with France over the revolution then proceeding in the United Provinces.[5] He described France as in many ways financially stronger than England; he showed no understanding that French finances were on the point of collapse, and that this would precipitate the country into revolution. On the contrary, what he thought he saw was that

> a very extraordinary change is working itself in the minds of the people of that nation. A spirit that will render France exceedingly formidable whenever its government shall embrace the fortunate opportunity of doubling its strength by allying, if it may be so expressed (for it is difficult to express a new idea by old terms), the majesty of the sovereign with the majesty of the nation... what has at this moment the appearance of disorder in France, is no more than one of the links in that great chain of circumstances by which nations acquire the summit of their greatness.

This 'appearance of disorder' would only solidify the French government and monarchy by restoring the freedom of the French people. The Franks 'were once the freest people in Europe; and as nations appear to have their periodical revolutions, it is very probable they will be so again'.[6] But 'revolution' here implied a return to

---

[3] Comte de Courchamps, *Souvenirs de la Marquise de Créquy de 1710 à 1803* (10 vols, Paris, 1903), ix. 144, translated in Peter McPhee, *Liberty or Death: The French Revolution* (New Haven, 2016), xi.

[4] Paine, 'To the Citizens of the United States' (15 Nov. 1802): *CW*, ii. 909.

[5] Before 1789 the prospects for revolution seemed less, or not at all, in the great and stable monarchies like France or Britain than in Geneva, the United Provices, and the Austrian Netherlands: Janet Polasky, 'Revolutionaries between Nations, 1776–1789', *P&P* 232 (2016), 165–201. But of these places Paine and other English reformers knew little.

[6] Paine, *Prospects on the Rubicon* (1787): *CW*, ii. 634, 641, 643–5.

origins, not a cataclysmic departure from them: 1776 had not transformed Paine's usage. In 1787 he did not yet write of himself as living through an age of revolution. On the contrary, he expressed admiration for 'the majesty of the sovereign', Louis XVI. This reinforces the conclusion that Paine had entertained no worked-out republican position when he sailed for Philadelphia in 1774. Republicanism was not Paine's leading idea.

In 1787, in Paine's view, England rather than France was now the nation at risk. Again, his evidential base for this claim was English, not French. Arguing in 1787 for the successive doubling of the cost of each of England's wars, and the division of the nation between those who profited from the national debt and those who shouldered its burden, he cited only William Playfair's *The Commercial and Political Atlas* but no French or American sources.[7] Paine was slow to perceive the larger significance of events in France. As he wrote to Washington in July 1791: 'After the establishment of the American Revolution, it did not appear to me that any object could arise great enough to engage me a second time. I began to feel myself happy in being quiet; but I now experience that principle is not confined to time or place, and that the ardor of Seventy-six is capable of renewing itself.'[8] But this was two years after the fall of the Bastille. In 1792 he confirmed his first reaction: 'When the American Revolution was established, I felt a disposition to sit serenely down and enjoy the calm. It did not appear to me that any object could afterwards arise great enough to make me quit tranquillity, and feel as I had felt before.'[9]

If Paine had not anticipated the American Revolution, he returned to France in 1787, and crossed to England, again without any sense that the American Revolution would be followed by kindred revolutions across Europe. But this was not at all unusual. The idea of a domino effect of revolutions, 1776 being the first in a series, later occurred to others, but it would be wrong to retroject it or to overstate its early acceptance or plausibility. In 1789 it was the doctrine of Richard Price, whose knowledge of America and France was limited, but was only subsequently adopted by Paine. On 28 November 1792 the Convention, in Paris, received a delegation from the London-based Society for Constitutional Information, predicting that further revolutions would follow; even then, nothing was said of Paine.[10]

Raynal, Paine, and the significance of America

There is however some evidence which initially seems to point in the opposite direction to establish Paine's foreknowledge, and it must be carefully examined. Guillaume Raynal in his *The Revolution of America* (1781) had expressed scepticism

---

[7] Paine, *Prospects on the Rubicon* (1787): *CW*, ii. 642, citing William Playfair, *The Commercial and Political Atlas: representing, by means of stained copper-plate charts, the exports, imports, and general trade of England: the national debt, and other public accounts, with observations and remarks* (London: J. Debrett et al., 1786).

[8] Paine to George Washington, 21 July 1791: *CW*, ii. 1319.

[9] Paine, *Rights of Man. Part the Second* (1792): *CW*, i. 347–8.

[10] *Réimpression de l'Ancien Moniteur*, 14, p. 593, quoted in Lounissi, *Paine*, 706.

about Americans having defended a universalist notion, 'the happiness of mankind', in their rebellion. Paine replied in 1782 by defending that idea:

> Who can say that the happiness of mankind made *no part of the* motives which produced the alliance [with France, in 1778]? To be able to declare this, a man must be possessed of the mind of all the parties concerned, and know that their motives were something else.
>
> In proportion as the independence of America became contemplated and understood, the local advantages of it to the immediate actors, and the numerous benefits it promised mankind, appeared to be every day increasing; and we saw not a temporary good for the present race only, but a continued good to all posterity; these motives, therefore, added to those which preceded them, became the motives on the part of America.

But Paine did not, indeed could not, claim to know 'the mind of all the parties concerned' himself. Attributing founding principles to the new republic was from the earliest date problematic, more so in proportion to those principles' generalization.

Paine added, in a piece of rhetoric already quoted, that 'Our style and manner of thinking have undergone a revolution more extraordinary than the political revolution of the country. We see with other eyes; we hear with other ears; and we think with other thoughts, than those we formerly used.' But following this memorable image he did not explain in what way that was the case with the former colonists or in what way the American Revolution was linked with 'the happiness of mankind' except to claim that 'the Revolution of America and the alliance with France' combined to 'expel prejudice'. Rather than explain that expulsion, his text then turned to other things.

Examined closely, and not in the hindsight of seven years later, his pamphlet of 1782 had attended only to the wartime alliance between the United States and France, not to any revolutionary effect the American Revolution was expected to have, in future, within France. Paine argued that 'A total reformation is wanted in England', but made no such point about France; still less did he predict such an episode in England's neighbour. Where Paine might reasonably have reflected on the universal significance of republicanism, he did no such thing. He wrote about 'the principles of universal society', but this was a rhetorical flourish that he did not develop other than to express his preference for peace over war. Clearly, Paine was as yet without the ideological equipment to visualize himself as an international revolutionary.[11]

Paine, then, implicitly admitted in his *Letter to the Abbe Raynal* that Americans' motives had been complex, had not at the outset of the Revolution included 'the happiness of mankind', and had developed over time. He also fell into the trap of baldly asserting the opposite of Raynal. Paine's remark was generalized and without specific application; it was a claim that he did not follow up or develop until his *Rights of Man. Part the Second* (1792). Indeed Paine in 1782 effectively disclaimed the idea of a domino effect of revolutions in disavowing any views on the 'Forms of government' of those two allies, the French monarchy and the

---

[11] Paine, *Letter to the Abbe Raynal* (1782): *CW*, ii. 238, 242–3, 255–6.

American republic: 'we have no more right or business to know how the one or the other conducts its domestic affairs, than we have to inquire into the private concerns of a family.'[12] It was not Paine but Richard Price in 1789 who famously wrote of a Revolution 'after setting AMERICA free, reflected to FRANCE, and there kindled into a blaze that lays despotism in ashes, and warms and illuminates EUROPE!'[13]

Paine adopted this analysis only in about 1792, probably influenced to do so by Lafayette's self-serving public relations exercise.[14] Paine's delayed response was understandable, since the American Revolution hardly performed the initiating role in any linked series of 'modern' revolutions; that role was to be invented for it only by twentieth-century political science. France, a far larger and more complex polity than the United States, was driven by its own self-absorbed conflicts more than by any influence of a distant and foreign population. In Britain the effects of the American Revolution might have been expected to have been more direct, but were initially limited. Not until after *c.*1815 was the example of the new American republic a significant element in the calls for parliamentary reform in Britain, and even then this role was not sustained.[15] As will become clear, the role of America in Paine's *Rights of Man. Part the Second* (1792) needs careful qualification.

Bankruptcy, principle, and the crowd

In recent scholarship the connection between the American Revolution and the French has steadily emerged as financial more than ideological. France's victory in the American revolutionary war was ruinously expensive. It triggered a slow-motion crisis that led to national bankruptcy in 1788 and the summoning of the Estates-General in May 1789; but Paine was pre-committed to the thesis that France's finances were strong, Britain's weak. The image of the American Revolution as an ideological trigger of revolutions elsewhere was still not fully formed in Paine's mind in May 1790 when he wrote from London to George Washington and enclosed the key to the Bastille, a present from Lafayette. Paine described the key as 'the first ripe fruits of American principles transplanted into Europe', but the idea was evidently that of Lafayette rather than of Paine. 'When he [Lafayette] mentioned to me the present he intended you, my heart leaped with joy. It is something so truly in character, that no remarks can illustrate it, and is more happily expressive of his remembrance of his American friends, than any letters can convey.'[16] Perhaps significantly, the Genevan reformer Étienne Dumont later wrote of 1789: 'They who anticipated a civil war, looked upon Lafayette as ambitious of becoming

---

[12] Paine, *Letter to the Abbe Raynal* (1782): *CW*, ii. 244.
[13] Richard Price, *A Discourse on the Love of our Country, delivered on Nov. 4, 1789, at the Meeting-House in the Old Jewry, to the Society for Commemorating the Revolution in Great Britain* (London: George Stafford for T. Cadell, 1789), 50.
[14] See Appendix: Paine De-attributions.
[15] David Paul Crook, *American Democracy in English Politics 1815–1850* (Oxford, 1965).
[16] Paine to George Washington, 1 May 1790: *CW*, ii. 1303.

the Washington of France.'[17] Dumont, who knew Paine, did not ascribe to him any such ambition with respect to that country.

In *Rights of Man. Part the Second* (written in London and published on 16 February 1792), dedicated to Lafayette and imbued with Lafayette's self-serving story of the French troops having brought back to France the libertarian lessons they had learned during the American war,[18] Paine wrote: 'One of the great advantages of the American Revolution has been, that it led to a discovery of the principles, and laid open the imposition, of governments.'[19] Even then, he did not specify what those principles had been (other than the principles in which he claimed he had himself always believed), and wrote almost nothing in detail in either part of *Rights of Man* about the supposed ideological communication of revolution from America to France. He merely stated that it had occurred: 'From a small spark, kindled in America, a flame has arisen, not to be extinguished.'[20] This is evidence that Paine may have echoed the language of Richard Price, although without adding local American understandings to Price's phrasing.[21] In September 1792 Paine added no analysis when he again claimed of the American Revolution: 'The principles on which that Revolution began, have extended themselves to Europe.'[22] But that was not at all what he had thought when he sailed to France in 1787.[23] Indeed, before Louis XVI's flight to Varennes in June 1791, republicanism was a minor strand in French politics.[24] The idea of a powerful ideology, 'republicanism', first triumphing in the American Revolution and then similarly providing the essential principle of the French, cannot now be historically substantiated.

Paine's understanding was hindered by two obstacles. First, he was pre-committed to the opinion that

> In viewing this subject, the case and circumstances of America present themselves as in the beginning of the world... We are brought at once to the point of seeing government begin, as if we had lived in the beginning of time. The real volume, not of

---

[17] Étienne Dumont, *Recollections of Mirabeau, and of the Two First Legislative Assemblies of France* (London: Edward Bull, 1832), 30.

[18] French opinion during the American war often eulogized colonial society, but had pictured it in French terms. The duplicitous Benjamin Franklin was fêted in Paris, but as exemplifying the simple and natural virtues recently celebrated by Jean-Jacques Rousseau: Durand Echeverria, *Mirage in the West: A History of the French Image of American Society to 1815* (Princeton, 1957).

[19] Paine, *Rights of Man. Part the Second* (1792): *CW*, i. 360.

[20] Paine, *Rights of Man. Part the Second* (1792): *CW*, i. 398.

[21] For an argument that Paine may have copied the English translation of the *Déclaration des droits de l'homme et du citoyen* from Price's *Discourse on the Love of our Country*, see Ch. 5, section The French *Déclaration*. If so, Paine may here have echoed Price's image of the communication of a revolutionary flame.

[22] Paine, *Address to the People of France* (25 Sept. 1792): *CW*, ii. 539. Political scientists conventionally omit the end of Paine's sentence: 'and an overruling Providence is regenerating the old world by the principles of the new'. It might be argued that Paine, as a Deist, had more difficulty in making sense of this second claim than of the first.

[23] For an argument that gives more weight to Paine's autonomous use of the American example see Mark Philp, 'The Role of America in the "Debate on France" 1791–5: Thomas Paine's Insertion', *Utilitas* 5 (1993), 221–37.

[24] Lounissi, *Paine*, 683.

history, but of facts, is directly before us, unmutilated by contrivance, or the errors of tradition.[25]

Such a pre-commitment excused his relative prior ignorance both of America and soon of France: their histories were, by definition, now irrelevant. He argued that the new government of America was 'representation ingrafted upon democracy',[26] but he focused on the first term rather than the second, and was initially unwilling to consider how the French Revolution was taking a different and more populist course from the American.

Second, his limited sense of the differences between the two revolutions prevented a better understanding of the French. As late as 1792, he wrote:

> Within the space of a few years we have seen two Revolutions, those of America and France. In the former, the contest was long and the conflict severe; in the latter, the nation acted with such a consolidated impulse, that having no foreign enemy to contend with, the revolution was complete in power the moment it appeared.[27]

Here as elsewhere, Paine echoed contemporary usage: one meaning of 'revolution' denoted a sudden event, quickly over. But of other differences between the two cases, Paine hardly wrote. As a response to long-contested events across France, the notion of an event already over was inadequate, as the revolt of 1793 in the Vendée, to name only one local war, was to emphasize (Paine saw Paris, but little else of the kingdom). In 1797, he added: 'Why has the Revolution of France been stained with crimes which the Revolution of the United States of America was not? Men are physically the same in all countries: it is education that makes them different. Accustom a People to believe that Priests, or any other class of men, can forgive sins, and you will have sins in abundance.'[28] This remark, too, disclosed only a populist English anti-popery combined with real ignorance of the situation on the ground in the American war, not a deep understanding of two revolutions. There were real differences between the American and French cases, in their political, ideological, religious, and social antecedents. But since Paine did not confront the divisions in colonial American attitudes over the best responses to the transatlantic problems of 1765–75, he could see no further into contrasts and commonalities.

While in England, and even when writing to Jefferson in France, the impending re-assembly of the Estates-General triggered no anticipations in Paine's mind of convulsion.[29] By February 1789, he wrote: 'I am very much rejoiced at the account you give me of the state of affairs in France. I feel exceedingly interested in the happiness of that nation. They are now got, or getting, in the right way, and the present reign will be more immortalized in France than any that ever preceded it.'[30] His comment disclosed no understanding of the political problems of the monarchy, even though, in March 1789, a new term appeared in Paine's writing:

---

[25] Paine, *Rights of Man. Part the Second* (1792): *CW*, i. 376.
[26] Paine, *Rights of Man. Part the Second* (1792): *CW*, i. 371.
[27] Paine, *Rights of Man. Part the Second* (1792): *CW*, i. 446.
[28] *Letter, from Thomas Paine to Camille Jordan* (1797): *CW*, ii. 759 (text corrected).
[29] Paine to Jefferson, 9 Sept. 1788: *CW*, ii. 1270.
[30] Paine to Jefferson, 26 Feb. 1789: *CW*, ii. 1281.

'With respect to the French revolution, be assured that every thing is going on right. Little inconveniences, the necessary consequences of pulling down and building up, may arise; but even these are much less than ought to have been expected.'[31] Confusing and diverse events in France had become 'the French revolution'. Like his contemporaries, Paine still used 'revolution' in the prevalent late eighteenth-century sense to mean an astonishing but completed change, not a cataclysmic social restructuring, still less a process that unfolded over a period of time, the results of which might be predicted from an understanding of its internal logic. This was not a lack of vision on Paine's part, but a mark of his necessary cultural embeddedness.

Raised in a small country town, Paine similarly did not appreciate what came from the late nineteenth century to be analysed as the psychology of crowds.[32] He was out of England during the episode that graphically illuminated for many late eighteenth-century English observers the potential for mass violence in urban settings, the Gordon Riots of June 1780. Paine mentioned this convulsion only in passing, and then only to blame it on the government;[33] but in the scale of the disturbances, the loss of property, and the numbers killed, the episode invites comparison with the early stages of the French Revolution in Paris. Edmund Burke looked back on the Gordon Riots as 'one of the most critical periods in our annals'.

Had the portentous comet of the rights of man...crossed upon us in that internal state of England, nothing human could have prevented our being irresistibly hurried, out of the highway of heaven, into all the vices, crimes, horrours and miseries of the French revolution...There was, indeed, much intestine heat; there was a dreadful fermentation. Wild and savage insurrection quitted the woods, and prowled about our streets in the name of reform. Such was the distemper of the publick mind, that there was no madman, in his maddest ideas, and maddest projects, who might not count upon numbers to support his principles and execute his designs.

Many of the changes, by a great misnomer called parliamentary reforms, went, not in the intention of all the professors and supporters of them, undoubtedly, but went in their certain, and, in my opinion, not very remote effect, home to the utter destruction of the Constitution of this kingdom. Had they taken place, not France, but England, would have had the honour of leading up the death-dance of Democratick Revolution.[34]

---

[31] Paine to [Benjamin Rush], 16 Mar. 1789: *CW*, ii. 1285–6 (addressee not given by Foner; the letter is in the Library of Congress).

[32] Its pioneer was Gustave Le Bon (1841–1931); see especially *La Psychologie des foules* (Paris, 1895; English translation as *The Crowd*, 1896) and *La Révolution française et la psychologie des révolutions* (Paris, 1912; English translation, 1913). Similar insights were pioneered by the historian Hyppolyte Taine (1828–93) in his *Origines de la France contemporaine* (6 vols, Paris, 1876–94); for a translation of volumes ii–iv see Taine, *The French Revolution*, trans. John Durand, ed. Mona Ozouf (3 vols, Indianapolis, 2002). Few American historians of the American Revolution learned from this line of investigation.

[33] Paine, *Rights of Man* (1791): *CW*, i. 266–7; *Rights of Man. Part the Second* (1792): *CW*, i. 359–60.

[34] *A Letter from the Right Honourable Edmund Burke to a Noble Lord* (London: J. Owen, 1796), 12–13.

Perhaps Burke here merely projected his fears of 1796 back onto the events of 1780; perhaps he identified a real political dynamic. If the second, to this dimension of politics Paine, a Deist and rationalist, was and remained oblivious.

His idealistic pre-commitments were unrevised if (as one report claimed) he was himself almost lynched by the Paris mob: on 21 June 1791, the day following the royal family's night-time escape from the Tuileries Palace (the flight to Varennes), Paine and his friend Thomas Christie were present to hear the reading of the National Assembly's declaration that government would continue. According to a near-contemporary,

> An officer proclaimed the will of the National Assembly, that all should be *silent*, and *covered*. In a moment, all tongues were still; all hats were on. Not so our author: He had lost his cockade; and to have a hat, without a cockade, was treason. A cry arose, *Aristocrat! Aristocrat! A' la lanterne! A' la lanterne!* He was desired by those who stood near him, to put on his hat. Whether he preserved his *usual coolness*, during this uncommon danger, we are unable to tell. A Frenchman, who could speak English, desired him to put on his hat: But, the hat having no cockade, he was involved in a sad dilemma, and the sentimental mob was at length in some measure satisfied by prudent explanation.[35]

The explanation was not Paine's: without command of spoken French, Paine was unable to placate the mob until Thomas Christie, a French speaker, established his identity. Paine did not write of the episode, although (if correctly reported) he had been only moments away from death. Again, if correctly reported, the cause of Paine's danger was merely his often-remarked negligence in dress; but the important conclusion is that he (and some other English observers in Paris) did not subsequently reflect on the significance of this and similar cases of crowd action, of which they can hardly have been unaware.

Paine, Jefferson, and Rousseau

Certain novel elements in Paine's political theory in *Rights of Man* have been traced in their genesis to Paine's meetings in Paris with Jefferson and Jefferson's kindred spirits among the French reformers between 1787 and 1789: a 'fully worked out account of natural rights'; the chronological priority of constitutions, governments coming later and being built on the blueprints that constitutions provided; and the autonomy of each generation to decide for itself in all matters.[36] This development has been traced in part to the influence of the French translation of a tract by the American John Stevens (1739–1838): *Observations on*

---

[35] [George Chalmers], *The Life of Thomas Pain, The Author of Rights of Men. With a Defence of his Writings. By Francis Oldys, A.M. of the University of Pennsylvania* (London: Stockdale, 1791), 127–8; evidently quoting Thomas Christie's letter from Paris of 22 June 1791, published in the *Morning Chronicle* of 29 June 1791.

[36] Mark Philp, 'Revolutionaries in Paris: Paine, Jefferson and Democracy', in Simon P. Newman and Peter S. Onuf (eds), *Paine and Jefferson in the Age of Revolutions* (Charlottesville, Va, 2013), 137–60.

Government (New York, 1787), and the 200 pages of notes that the French translation added to the American first edition.[37]

Is this inference justified? Although Paine's *Rights of Man* often used the term
'rights', a cliché by the 1790s, it is argued here that the book did not contain any
worked-out theory of natural rights, only a series of assertions which took natural
rights for granted as premises. Paine's inability to speak French, and his still poor
command of written French, would have limited his exchanges with Jefferson's
French friends.[38] For the same reason it is doubtful if he would have been able to
read Stevens's pamphlet in its French translation, with its important new appendix
in French. There is evidence that Paine read French newspapers by the time of his
arrest in 1793,[39] but not that he could write in French. But borrowings from
French sources in Paine's writings during his long stay in France from 1792 to
1802 are hard to find, and his not learning from French publications in that decade, when he was in France continuously and had more opportunity to master the
written language, casts doubt on any significant indebtedness during his short
visits in earlier years.

Paine's brief discussions of rights and of constitutions as blueprints in *Rights of
Man* were abstract ones. They did not rest on significant historical understandings
of the American or French Revolutions, or echo in a clear way any borrowings
from Stevens's pamphlet. They were not really different from the positions laid out
in *Common Sense*, for example in that text's arguments that society preceded government, which was then entered into by an explicit agreement (one might term it
a constitution); that participation in government was 'by natural right'; and that
there had been an early practice 'of having elections often', evidently to revise
arrangements previously made. The claim of the autonomy of each generation was
also implicit in the argument of *Common Sense* that 'We have it in our power to
begin the world over again',[40] but this perception had its much older origin in
English theology, not in reflection in the late 1780s on recent events in America.

In these respects Paine in 1787–9 is unlikely to have learned major lessons from
events, since in both America and France the history was the reverse of Paine's

---

[37] [John Stevens], *Examen du gouvernement d'Angleterre, comparé aux constitutions des États-Unis… Par
un cultivateur de New-Jersey. Ouvrage traduit de l'anglois, & accompagné de notes* [trans. J. L. Faure?]
(Londres [i.e. Paris?]: et se trouve à Paris, chez Froullé, 1789). The Bodleian attributes the notes to P. S.
Dupont de Nemours, Condorcet, and J. A. Gauvain Gallors. 'We do not know if Paine read it': Philp,
'Revolutionaries in Paris', 141n.

[38] Franklin, writing to a French friend in Paris, explained: 'This letter goes by Mr. Paine… He does
not speak French, or I would recommend him to your civilities': Franklin to Le Veillard, 15 Apr. 1787,
in *Benjamin Franklin's Autobiographical Writings*, ed. Carl Van Doren (London, 1946), 678. From
1797 Paine stayed for five years at the house of the printer of *Rights of Man. Part the Second* and *The
Age of Reason*, Nicolas Bonneville. He and his wife Marguerite later recalled Paine at this period: 'He
rose late. He then used to read the newspapers, from which, though he understood but little of the
French language when spoken, he did not fail to collect all the material information relating to
politics, in which subject he took most delight… It was seldom he went into the society of French
people… He could not speak French; he could understand it tolerably well when spoken to him, and
he understood it when on paper perfectly well': Conway, *Life*, 333, 339. By that stage, Paine had been
in France for a decade.

[39] Lounissi, *Paine*, 23.   [40] [Paine], *Common Sense* (1776): *CW*, i. 5–6, 45.

theory: in both the Revolution came first; constitutions, successively modified in agonizing amendments, came afterwards. Despite Paine's residence in Paris for part of the years 1787–9, he spent longer periods before the publication of *Rights of Man* in London, where he was in contact with the theorists of the Society for Constitutional Information: the new elements in *Rights of Man* on the need for national conventions to establish constitutions are as likely to have derived from these English influences as from anything Paine imbibed from Jefferson or his French circle.

Paine's argument on the autonomy of each 'generation' was appealing to individuals who sought a licence for their preferred actions, but it was problematic as an argument, since Paine did not define what counted as a generation or explain why it had an integrity.[41] In the absence of such a chronological unit, equal authority would inhere in every individual at every moment. In that case, no polity could commit itself to currencies, contracts, bureaucratic structures, laws, treaties, or alliances, since such decisions would always be liable to be overturned. That such an objection did not then occur to Paine suggests that his attention was elsewhere, on emancipating his present from the dead hand of its past, more than on providing a viable blueprint for its future.

English issues still loomed large for Paine. When he met the Whig leader Charles James Fox in London on 16 April 1790 Paine was distressed that Fox had not received Paine's letter, sent from Paris, which had 'laid down all the principal points with respect to the French Revolution, the Test Act, etc., which I intended for subjects for conversation when we met'.[42] Despite the scale of events in France, Paine mentioned in the same sentence the English legislation of 1673 and 1678 (conventionally referred to as one Act) that made communion in the Church of England a qualification for public office (for example, as an excise officer). Controversy over the Test Act still loomed large in many English minds, especially those of Dissenters, who made unsuccessful attempts in Parliament to secure its repeal on 28 March 1787 and 8 May 1789.[43] Paine's antipathies towards England continued to rise. 'This Court is now what the French Court used to be. It is conducted with Mystery and intrigue. It is maneuvering every where and every how.'[44] In 1792 Paine continued to write of 'The long subsisting fear of a revolution in England'.[45]

Paine did not initially see the French Revolution as a more momentous episode partly because he lacked the apprehensions, anticipations, or conspiracy theories that other people often later derived from their negative reactions to Rousseau and Freemasonry. Jean-Jacques Rousseau had earlier come to seem, for Burke, a prophet of revolution, but not for Paine. Paine's extensive writings gave Rousseau only passing

---

[41] He evidently appreciated the problem, since he attempted a definition later: Paine, *Dissertation on First-Principles of Government* (1795): *CW*, ii. 575–6, arguing that a generation would be terminated when the number of young men reaching the age of 21 exceeded the number of adults 'at the time that we count from'. But this criterion would create a plethora of minute generations, and so undermine the ideas of a substantial generation's giving its consent and of a generation's having rights against a preceding one.

[42] Paine to [?Thomas Christie], 16 Apr. 1790: *CW*, ii. 1300.

[43] Clark, *English Society*, 413–17.   [44] Paine to William Short, 1 June 1790: *CW*, ii. 1306–7.

[45] Paine, 'On the Propriety of Bringing Louis XVI to Trial' (20 Nov. 1792): *CW*, ii. 549.

mentions,[46] with one seeming exception. In 1791 an important passage in *Rights of Man* praised Rousseau as a key figure in the relay race of *philosophes*; but this was, it is argued below, an interpolation of material primarily written by Lafayette.[47] Elsewhere in *Rights of Man*, Paine's single use of the term 'the general will' was too unspecific to have revealed a clear debt to Rousseau.[48] In *Rights of Man. Part the Second* (1792) Rousseau was not named, and the two uses of 'the general will' were similarly unspecific.[49] In a text of the same year, attributed to Paine, there was an extended quotation only when Rousseau's text anticipated Paine's preoccupation with the vicious nature of kingly government:

> We have the following description of them in the *Contrat Social* of J. J. Rousseau: 'The men who take the foremost place in monarchies are often simply base marplots, ordinary rogues, mean intriguers. The trivial intellectual qualities that have raised these people to high positions in courts but serve to make more apparent to the public their real insignificance.' In a word, the story of all monarchies supplies the proof that, while monarchs do nothing, their ministers do nothing but evil.[50]

This fell short of Paine's attributing to Rousseau a leading role in bringing on the Revolution.

There was a second notable absence from Paine's world view. European counter-revolutionaries sometimes ascribed the French Revolution to a conspiracy in which Freemasons took a leading part; but Paine did not mention the leading conspiracy theorist, the Abbé Augustin Barruel (1741–1820).[51] For his knowledge of Freemasonry, Paine used three English sources, Samuel Pritchard's *Masonry Detected* (1730), Captain George Smith's *The Use and Abuse of Freemasonry* (1783), and William Dodd's *Oration* (1776), before checking them against Jérôme Lalande's entry in the *Encyclopédie*, in the last of which Paine was 'much disappointed'.[52] Paine's view of the French Revolution had other sources.

In general, Paine's information on the French Revolution was not extensive. He was resident in France for only a part of the time covered by *Rights of Man* and later tracts: from 26 May to 30 August 1787; from mid-December 1787 to not later

---

[46] e.g. [Paine], 'The Forester's Letters' (1776): *CW*, ii. 79; Aldridge, *American Ideology*, 137–46; Lounissi, *Paine*, 176–85.

[47] See Appendix: Paine De-attributions.   [48] Paine, *Rights of Man* (1791): *CW*, i. 299, 321.

[49] Paine, *Rights of Man. Part the Second* (1792): *CW*, i. 446, 453.

[50] [Paine], 'An Essay for the Use of New Republicans in their Opposition to Monarchy' (11 Oct. 1792): *CW*, ii. 543, quoting Jean-Jacques Rousseau, *Du Contrat social* (1762), livre III, ch. VI, 'De la monarchie'. This translation of a newspaper article is Foner's. Paine is unlikely to have read Rousseau in French, and this suggests that the passage he cited may have been drawn to his attention, and translated, by a French friend.

[51] Notably Augustin Barruel, *Mémoires pour servir à l'histoire du Jacobinisme* (4 vols, London: de l'Imprimerie Françoise, 1797–8).

[52] [Paine], 'Origin of Freemasonry' [1805]: *CW*, ii. 840, citing Samuel Prichard, *Masonry Detected: being a universal and genuine description of all its branches from the original to the present time* (London: J. Wilford, 1730; frequently reprinted, reaching a 21st edn, ?1790); Captain George Smith, *The Use and Abuse of Free-Masonry: a work of the greatest utility to the brethren of the society, to mankind in general, and to the ladies in particular* (London: G. Kearsley, 1783; 2nd edn, 1785); William Dodd, *An Oration: delivered at the Dedication of Free-Masons' Hall, Great Queen-Street, Lincoln's-Inn-Fields, on Thursday, May 23, 1776* (London: G. Robinson et al., 1776).

than mid-February 1788; from after 26 February 1789 to mid-March 1789; from November 1789 to 17 March 1790; from July to September 1790; from February to March 1791; from April to 13 July 1791; and finally for a decade, from 13 September 1792 to 1802. Although his tracts convey the impression that his accounts carried the authority of an eyewitness, he was often in England when crucial episodes took place, including the first meeting of the Estates-General (5 May 1789), the fall of the Bastille (14 July 1789), the murders of Foulon and Berthier de Sauvigny (22 July 1789), the National Assembly's adoption of the *Déclaration des droits de l'homme et du citoyen* (26 August 1789), the October Days (5–6 October 1789), and the September Massacres (2–6 September 1792).

In late 1792, Paine lamented 'my inability to express myself in French'.[53] Even in October 1794, petitioning the Convention for release from the Luxembourg prison, Paine was obliged to have his letter translated.[54] Paine was therefore out of his depth when elected to the French National Convention in 1792. Despite his decade in France, and his incarceration there, there is little evidence that he learned more than elementary spoken French or sought to use his limited knowledge of the spoken language to gain a deeper understanding of France and its revolution. *Rights of Man* (1791) and *Rights of Man. Part the Second* (1792) nevertheless became best-sellers in English, and Paine's already high profile lent credence to the impression, carefully nurtured in their pages, that these works gave readers a privileged access to events in France. In one way *Rights of Man* was a wholly different work from *Common Sense*: it did nothing to trigger the French Revolution, which had begun already regardless of any English catalyst. But both works shared one feature: they did not rest on deep knowledge of the episodes to which they were much later thought to be keys.

RIGHTS OF MAN: ANTECEDENTS

Political argument in Britain had developed since Paine left in 1774: how much did he learn of these changes after his return in 1787? He knew something; among other sources, from Edmund Burke, whose friend Paine now became. Both were Whigs, both were reformers, both (in different degrees) ill disposed towards George III, both in their own eyes friends to what they saw as Whig liberties for all peoples. When Burke's *Reflections on the Revolution in France* was advertised as forthcoming in February 1790, Paine heard of it in Paris; in London in March, he learned of its slow progress as Burke repeatedly revised his manuscript. In October, Paine, back in Paris, heard again of the book's imminent publication, and returned to London in time to witness its appearance on 1 November 1790. It seems that Paine had already been writing on the French Revolution in response to the promptings of Lafayette; now, he turned these materials into a reply to Burke. Paine took lodgings at the Angel Inn, Islington, and began to write; he finished his text there on

[53] Paine, 'On the Propriety of Bringing Louis XVI to Trial' (20 Nov. 1792): *CW*, ii. 548.
[54] Paine to James Monroe, 4 Oct. 1794: *CW*, ii. 1355.

29 January 1791, his fifty-fourth birthday.[55] *Rights of Man*, then, was written in England, indeed in London, and (like Burke's book) it was, implicitly or explicitly, primarily about England more than France (but also not about Scotland or Ireland).

When the publisher, Joseph Johnson, pulled out of the project on the scheduled day of publication, afraid of government action, Paine found a replacement. His book finally appeared on 16 March 1791, priced at three shillings as against the five shillings of Burke's *Reflections*. Paine then departed for Paris, leaving his printer to face any legal consequences. Yet the government did nothing. Although the numbers of copies printed cannot be known, and were exaggerated at the time and later, it circulated widely.[56] Even George III spent 'half an hour' in 'reading with marked attention' a copy which had just arrived in Charles Knight's Windsor book-shop, where the king's morning walk often took him, but he seems not to have bought it.[57]

Rights of Man has traditionally been explained as a text in debate with Burke's *Reflections on the Revolution in France*. This is not wrong, but it gives a partly mis-leading impression. In particular, the assumption that Paine was naturally and under-standably engaged in a dialogue with only one other author and only one other text has occluded the many other texts to which he might have responded; and it has distracted attention from the things that are missing from *Rights of Man*, things that readers might reasonably have expected to find there. For just as *Common Sense* had said nothing about the many sophisticated contributions to the transatlantic political debate of 1765–76, so *Rights of Man* said nothing explicitly about the many other strands in British political thought in the immediately preceding decades.

Historians must deal with the scant acknowledgement in Paine's writings of other political writers, even the most famous. He did not mention the significance of the works of the lawyer Sir William Blackstone,[58] although these had raised concerns among Dissenters and the heterodox on both sides of the Atlantic. Paine passed over David Hume, although Hume had popularized his political views in a collection of *Essays* that reached many editions.[59] Paine did not respond to nascent utilitarianism, although Jeremy Bentham had published his first key works in 1776

---

[55] Keane, *Paine*, 304.

[56] For corrections to older claims of huge circulation figures see William St Clair, *The Reading Nation in the Romantic Period* (Cambridge, 2004), 256–7, 623–4 and Peter De Bolla, *The Architecture of Concepts: The Historical Formation of Human Rights* (New York, 2013), 206–13, 218–37; 'Paine invested a great deal in giving the impression that his book was read by (or to) the entire (or at least a very substantial part) of the reading (or read-to) population. He was boasting', 233.

[57] George III was not offended with the bookseller for stocking *Rights of Man*. Knight's son recalled favourable memories of the king: 'an impression of the homely kindness of his nature … There was a magnanimity about the man': Charles Knight, *Passages of a Working Life during Half a Century*, ed. James Thorne (3 vols, 2nd edn, London, 1873), i. 37. There is today no copy of the first edition of *Rights of Man* in the royal library: ex inf. Emma Stuart, Curator of Books and Manuscripts, Windsor Castle.

[58] William Blackstone, *Commentaries on the Laws of England* (4 vols, Oxford: Clarendon Press, 1765–9).

[59] David Hume's *Essays, Moral and Political* was first published in 1741, and augmented in succes-sive editions; as *Essays and Treatises on Several Subjects* (1753–4) it saw editions in 1758, 1760, 1764, 1767, 1768, 1770, 1772, 1777, 1779, 1784, and 1788 before the publication of *Rights of Man*.

and 1789 in a secular reaction against Blackstone's theistic natural law arguments,[60] or to the work of Archdeacon William Paley who in 1785 had applied a theistic utilitarianism to defend the Anglican structure of the state.[61]

Nor did Paine cite the writings on government of the heterodox Dissenting intelligentsia, notably Richard Price[62] and Joseph Priestley.[63] He passed over the Swiss J. L. DeLolme's survey of the English Constitution,[64] already a best-seller in England. Paine did not mention Burke's earlier critique of the English monarchy, although this was continually reprinted.[65] Paine said nothing on the prolific writings of Dissenters in the late 1780s demanding a repeal of the Test and Corporation Acts,[66] commemorating the Revolution of 1688,[67] or celebrating the French Revolution. Paine's seclusion in the Angel Inn, Islington, while writing *Rights of Man*, suggests that his contacts with English reformers were not decisive in that period; indeed the Society for Constitutional Information, founded in 1780, was moribund by 1790 and only revived at a meeting on 7 March 1791, during the publishing delay that threatened to block the appearance of Paine's book.[68] Absence of evidence is not conclusive evidence of absence, but it is also the case that most of the themes for which these other authors were best known were also largely or wholly absent from Paine's writings. This should suggest that Paine's attention was elsewhere: he had a different intellectual formation and different overriding purposes.

Instead of responding in controversy to Blackstone, Bentham, or the others, Paine re-emphasized natural rights language. This, with the idea of a convention, was clearly prominent in Paine's thought in the 1790s. Yet before the publication of *Rights of Man*, many other activists had replied to Burke's *Reflections*: they too typically made prominent use of rights language.[69] Natural rights did not for

[60] Jeremy Bentham, *A Fragment on Government: Being an Examination of what is delivered, On the Subject of Government in General, In the Introduction to Sir William Blackstone's Commentaries; with a Preface in which is given a Critique of the Work at Large* (London: T. Payne, P. Elmsly and E. Brooke, 1776); Jeremy Bentham, *An Introduction to the Principles of Morals and Legislation* (London: T. Payne, 1789).

[61] William Paley, *The Principles of Moral and Political Philosophy* (London: R. Faulder, 1785) had reached an eighth London edition by 1791.

[62] Richard Price, *Observations on the Nature of Civil Liberty, the Principles of Government, and the Justice and Policy of the War with America* (London: T. Cadell, 1776).

[63] e.g. Joseph Priestley, *An Essay on the First Principles of Government; and on the Nature of Political, Civil, and Religious Liberty* (London: J. Dodsley, T. Cadell and J. Johnson, 1768).

[64] J. L. DeLolme, *The Constitution of England, or An Account of the English Government; In which it is compared with the Republican Form of Government, and occasionally with the other Monarchies in Europe* (London: T. Spilsbury for G. Kearsley, 1775) saw London editions in 1777, 1778, 1781, 1784, 1788, and 1790 before the publication of *Rights of Man*.

[65] [Edmund Burke], *Thoughts on the Cause of the Present Discontents* (London: J. Dodsley, 1770) reached a sixth and last London edition in 1784.

[66] e.g. [Samuel Heywood], *The Right of Protestant Dissenters to a Compleat Toleration Asserted* (London: J. Johnson, 1789). There were many such publications.

[67] e.g. Andrew Kippis, *A Sermon preached at the Old Jewry On the Fourth of November, 1788, before the Society for Commemorating the Glorious Revolution* (London: G. G. J. and J. Robinson, 1788); Joseph Towers, *An Oration delivered at the London Tavern, on the Fourth of November, 1788, on Occasion of the Commemoration of the Revolution, And the Completion of a Century from that great Event* (London: Charles Dilly, 1788).

[68] Jenny Graham, *The Nation, the Law and the King, Reform Politics in England, 1789–1799* (2 vols, Lanham, Md, 2000), 215.

[69] Claeys, *Paine*, 66–71, 90–6.

most writers override, but coexisted in a diverse political language with, the specific privileges (also called rights) that were guaranteed (with varying efficacy) by the laws. What Paine did was to place a highly effective rhetorical emphasis on a narrow aspect of a discourse that was already a truism, to express the idea in memorable prose, and to use natural rights in a series of new and sensational negations of monarchy and aristocracy. In his intellectual resources Paine was far from original. In his deployment of those resources he was remarkable.

After 1688 and 1714, deeper enquiries into the basis in natural rights of social and political institutions were politically inconvenient in Britain. As one reformer replied to Burke: 'I will neither follow you nor Dr. Price through a long inquiry into the nature of the rights which we acquired at the Revolution. The Princes of the Brunswick line have made the laws their rule.'[70] This had never been quite the case, and universalist rights had always featured to some degree in discussion alongside the 'rights of Englishmen', the particularist rights delivered by English law; but in the 1790s generalized rights, the 'rights of man', featured much more prominently before heading into their long obscurity.[71] Paine and his opponents all contributed to this trend. As one anonymous writer put it, Burke's *Reflections*, 'so far from answering the purpose for which it was intended, has had an entirely contrary effect, by producing a general recognition of those unalienable rights, the existence of which it imprudently and weakly questions'.[72] Everyone believed in rights; their schism was over what that familiar term meant.

Because of the ubiquity and lack of definition of 'rights', the implications of the 'rights of man' could steadily expand. In the 1790s Paine made increasing use of the idea of a convention, an anti-parliament that would have direct authority from the people to draw up a constitution and would supplant the Westminster body. This, too, was shared more widely. Since his departure from England in 1774 the undercurrent of alienation from the Hanoverian monarchy had taken clearer form, and had sometimes led to ideas for new structures of government. Especially, the idea of a national extra-parliamentary association in the late eighteenth century had emerged in Paine's absence, though slowly. It had been implicit in a work he was aware of: James Burgh's *Political Disquisitions*. Burgh termed the body he advocated 'a GRAND NATIONAL ASSOCIATION FOR RESTORING THE CONSTITUTION', and explained its authority in terms that anticipated Paine's: 'For whatever the majority desire, it is certainly lawful for them to have, unless they desire what is contrary to the laws of God.' But Burgh envisaged this association only as bringing pressure to bear on Parliament to induce it to reform; it would be an association 'for restoring the independency of parliament',[73] not for replacing Parliament.

In a pamphlet published only after Paine's departure for America, John Cartwright invoked Burgh's association, but with 'a wider basis', now in the context

---

[70] [John Scott], *A Letter to the Right Hon. Edmund Burke, In Reply to his 'Reflections on the Revolution in France, &c.' By a Member of the Revolution Society* (Dublin: J. Sheppard et al., 1791), 15.

[71] 'A major result of Burke's arguments was to give greater prominence to natural rights ideals than they had enjoyed in radical debates hitherto': Claeys, *Paine*, 71.

[72] *A Letter to a Member of the National Assembly* (no place [?London], no printer, [?1791]), 30.

[73] [James Burgh], *Political Disquisitions* (3 vols, London: E. and C. Dilly, 1774), iii. 428–34, 438, 455.

of Cartwright's much more extensive formula: annual parliaments and universal suffrage. Cartwright added: 'an associated nation may do more than petition, or remonstrate either. There is nothing it cannot do but what is naturally impossible. It can level a throne with the earth, and trample authority in the dust. And it can do these things of *right*.'[74] A London reformer, John Jebb, also cited Burgh but again went further to envisage a network of county associations combining together to coerce the House of Commons (in Yorkshire, the moderate Christopher Wyvill was then assembling just such a group; Jebb sought to place an extensive interpretation on its authority). Thus united and forming 'the community at large', the counties' 'command would proceed from the Principal to the Delegate, from the Master to the Servant'. Jebb urged that 'if such combined assemblies should in solemn council declare, that the present House of Commons was dissolved, such declaration would be truly constitutional, and that the requisite power would not be wanting to give validity to the decree'.[75]

Paine was now to take this idea further. *Common Sense* had been a call for American independence, not for an American Congress to act as a convention that would compel the Westminster Parliament or the colonial assemblies to reform themselves, and not a call for a convention that would draft a new British or American Constitution (the constitutional convention of 1787 was to be created by the American Congress, not 'the people' directly); the theme of a convention grew in Paine's thought only subsequently. In the 1790s Paine aligned himself clearly enough with the reforming wing of British politics; but there were many long-standing strands in British reforming discourse that he did not touch, even though he seems to have moved in increasingly extremist circles.

Some of the growing and potentially revolutionary influence of *Rights of Man* evidently arose from the distribution of very large numbers of free copies, as was also the case with some anti-revolutionary writings. Samuel Kenrick reported on 18 May 1791 that 'the London Constitutional Society have purchased the copyright (of the *Rights of Man*) & that it is their intent to circulate them gratis in every parish in England. Thirty thousand copies are already subscribed for & another subscription for fifty thousand more is nearly filled.' Paine is likely to have been involved; there is evidence that he offered the SCI £300 in May 1791, perhaps to forward this project. In Ireland, a Whig Club subscribed for 20,000 more copies for free circulation.[76] Circulation figures do not always measure the numbers of publications purchased; they are evidence for supply as well as for demand, and therefore not a reliable guide to the pattern of public opinion. But public opinion is likely to have been very well primed over many decades for an appeal to rights, even if it was poorly prepared for the idea of a convention.

---

[74] [John Cartwright], *Take Your Choice!* (London: John Almon, 1776), 89, 91, 93, 95–6.

[75] [John Jebb], *An Address to the Freeholders of Middlesex, assembled at Free Masons Tavern, in Great Queen Street, Upon Monday the 20th of December 1779, Being the Day appointed for a Meeting of the Freeholders, for the Purpose of Establishing Meetings to Maintain and Support the Freedom of Election* (London: J. Dixwell, T. Cadell and J. Bew, [1779]), 11–13, 15.

[76] Graham, *The Nation, the Law and the King*, 216–19.

PAINE'S ARGUMENT: *RIGHTS OF MAN*

The Revolution of 1688 and its lessons

What, then, did Paine's text contain? *Rights of Man* had something to say about the French Revolution, evidently repeating Lafayette's spin on that episode,[77] but the work was (as Paine emphasized at the beginning of its Preface and later) chiefly fuelled by anger at the decision of his friend and fellow reformer Edmund Burke to sound a dramatic warning in *Reflections on the Revolution in France* about the potential impact of French events on England. *Rights of Man*, first appearing as a book of 162 pages, was written or completed at speed, in indignation at Burke's intervention.

Paine's argument was specific as well as general. His reply began not with the French Revolution of 1789 and its claimed universal principles but with a particularist debate with Burke over the interpretation of England's revolution of 1688 and with a defence of Richard Price, whom Burke had criticized.[78] Burke had made the Parliament of 1689 'infallible', claimed Paine, and attributed to it a 'divine right' to rule over the yet unborn; this 'has shortened his journey to Rome'. Parliament thereby repeated 'the offence for which James II. was expelled'. This was backward-looking language, but it is evidence for Paine's lasting mindset. His negation of monarchical divine right may also have obscured a problem, for the body calling itself a parliament, that met at Westminster in 1689, claimed for itself the authority of just the sort of convention that Paine was soon to advocate; Paine's problem was not that this body had deposed James II, but that it had then affirmed the nation's permanent allegiance to William III.

Paine quoted from Burke a key text: '"The Lords Spiritual and Temporal, and Commons, do, in the name of the people aforesaid,"' (meaning the people of England then living) "most humbly and faithfully *submit* themselves, their *heirs* and *posterities*, for EVER."' Burke's claim was vulnerable, for it was at odds with the common law doctrine that no parliament could bind its successor; but Paine instead presented his own rebuttal of Burke in the language of natural rights. Appealing to Price, Paine described changing a government as 'a right resident in the nation', that is, 'the consent of the living'. To support natural rights, Paine introduced his hero the marquis de Lafayette at this point in the text, eulogizing his proposal of 'a declaration of rights' to the French National Assembly on 11 July 1789 and his service in the American war.[79]

Lafayette's words actually revealed that he held a different view of rights from Paine's: Lafayette 'applies to the living world, and emphatically says:—"Call to mind the sentiments which Nature has engraved in the heart of every citizen, and which take a new force when they are solemnly recognized by all"'. Rights, for Lafayette, were devised by a secular 'Nature' rather than by God; but Paine did not sense a

---

[77] See Appendix: Paine De-attributions.

[78] Burke had responded to Price, *A Discourse on the Love of Our Country* (1789): Burke, *Reflections*, ed. Clark, 62–5.

[79] Paine, *Rights of Man* (1791): *CW*, i. 244–5, 249–55 (text corrected).

contradiction. Rather, their universalist affirmations obscured their particularist differences. Paine now saw his own role as analogous to Lafayette's: just as Lafayette had exported the American Revolution to France, Paine would export the French Revolution to England.

What, however, was that revolution? Something momentous was clearly happening in France, but Paine's contemporaries found similar difficulty in diagnosing it. William Godwin, who then idolized Paine, wrote of *Rights of Man*:

> The seeds of revolution it contains are so vigorous in their stamina, that nothing can overpower them. All that remained for the illustrious author, after having enlightened the whole western world by the publication of Common Sense, was to do a similar service to Europe, by a production as energetic as that was, & adapted with equal skill to rouse & interest the mind. The effects, it may be, of this work will not be so rapid; but, if properly disseminated (& persecution cannot injure it), will be as sure.[80]

But 'seeds' and 'stamina' were metaphors, and did not capture the novelty or significance of French events. It may be asked whether Paine's tract, or the writings of any of his contemporaries, did better in the face of an astonishing crisis. Paine should not be censured for not doing what none of his contemporaries managed to do.

Rights of Man ended with the seemingly limitless invocation: 'a general revolution in the principle and construction of Governments is necessary.'[81] But Paine's usage in most of this text was not universalist. He was familiar with the terms 'the American Revolution' and 'the French Revolution', or 'the Revolutions of America and France', but for Paine 'the Revolution' meant, as it had in *Common Sense*, England's revolution of 1688. It was still a particularist understanding. Paine did occasionally write of 'a complete and universal revolution', but did not reify the term or work out the nature of any such universal revolution. For him, what was occurring in France was 'so transcendently unequalled by any thing in the European world' that 'the name of a Revolution is diminutive of its character', an announcement that would discourage attempts at definition.

Had Paine conceived of revolution in novel terms as a process or a pattern of events flowing in one direction, its converse would have been equally understandable. He wrote, on the contrary, that the idea of a counter-revolution was literally unthinkable: 'Those who talk of a counter revolution in France, shew how little they understand of man. There does not exist in the compass of language, an arrangement of words to express so much as the means of affecting a counter revolution.'[82] In 1776 and 1789, Paine invoked resistance theory; but this was at least as old as the Calvinism of the 1550s,[83] and had not thereafter issued in a reified sense of 'revolution'. Hence, for Paine as for his contemporaries, the interpretation of 1688 was crucial.

[80] William Godwin to [?Thomas Brand Hollis], [3–16 Mar. 1791]: *The Letters of William Godwin, Volume I 1778–1797*, ed. Pamela Clemit (Oxford, 2011), 52.
[81] Paine, *Rights of Man* (1791): *CW*, i. 341.
[82] Paine, *Rights of Man* (1791): *CW*, i. 244, 256, 284, 317, 320, 340.
[83] Quentin Skinner, *The Foundations of Modern Political Thought* (2 vols, Cambridge, 1978), ii. 239.

The Bastille, the October Days, and rights

Recent scholarship has argued that in 1789 (although there had been anticipations) 'the notion of revolution as a fact gave way to a conceptualization of revolution as ongoing act', a 'domain of lived experience with its own dynamic and its own chronology...a collective political act ushering in the birth of a new world...a dynamic, violent process with no clear end in sight'.[84] Alternatively, a slightly later time frame has been proposed: during the French Revolution, 'and more specifically in the years from 1792 to 1794, a new, far more radical model of revolution emerged. Its primary goal was no longer constitutional stability but rather the refashioning of the state and of society', a transformation effected as the Jacobins ceased to appeal to constitutional authority and appealed instead to the authority of 'the Revolution itself'.[85] Yet Paine left no evidence, in his writings of the 1790s or after, of having clearly sensed such a change. It may be that he observed French events from the outside, and was unaware of a widespread shift in linguistic usage around him; it may, alternatively, be that such linguistic shifts were as yet both confined to minorities and short-lived, so that the more generally understood changes waited until 1917.[86]

Natural rights discourse and the discourse of revolution were closely related. When Paine in *Rights of Man* turned away from the debate on the Revolution of 1688 to address what he wished to identify as 'the springs and principles of the French Revolution', he presented these in familiar terms as natural rights, not as novel aspects of revolution as such. 'The revolutions that have taken place in other European countries, have been excited by personal hatred.' By contrast 'the instance of France', he claimed, was not a revolt against 'the personal despotism of the men', as England had rebelled against Charles I and James II as individuals, but against 'the despotic principles of the government... the hereditary despotism of the monarchy': Paine was still more concerned to offer an older negation than a novel affirmation. For him, an appeal to rights was primarily a way of validating the negations of a long-standing Whig political discourse. As Paine argued, Burke was only siding with old English enemies, transposed to France: 'arbitrary power, the power of the Pope, and the Bastille'.[87]

---

[84] Keith Michael Baker, 'Revolutionizing Revolution', in Keith Michael Baker and Dan Edelstein eds, *Scripting Revolution: A Historical Approach to the Comparative Study of Revolutions* (Stanford, Calif., 2015), 71–102, at 71, 84, 95–6, 102. For the increasing prominence of the locution '*contre révolution*' in the *Archives parlementaires* between 1789 and 1793 (a locution that Paine predicted was impossible), 97–102.

[85] Dan Edelstein, 'From Constitutional to Permanent Revolution: 1649 and 1793', in Baker and Edelstein (eds), *Scripting Revolution* 118–30, at 119.

[86] After the overthrow of Robespierre in July 1794, 'For a while it looked as though the Jacobin script [of revolution justifying revolution] was destined for oblivion: in the wave of revolutions that swept across much of Europe and Spanish America, between 1808 and 1830, all followed the [older] constitutional script'. The 'Jacobin script' was not 'back...to stay' until 1917: Edelstein, 'From Constitutional to Permanent Revolution', 130. For a symmetrical argument that a fundamentally new sense of natural rights language, conventionally located in the 1790s, was clearly adopted only after 1948 see Ch. 5, section Natural rights discourse.

[87] Paine, *Rights of Man* (1791): *CW*, i. 256, 258, 260 (text corrected).

Only then did *Rights of Man* turn to specific happenings in France, vividly narrating the events leading to the fall of the Bastille in circumstantial detail. Paine did not reveal that he had been in England at the time. He mentioned only one source for these events: again, his friend Lafayette. Once more, Paine struck the old English Whig antithesis: 'The event was [i.e. the alternative outcomes were] freedom or slavery.' The Bastille was symbolic, like 'Bunyan's Doubting Castle and Giant Despair'. The taking of the Bastille, argued Paine, was the culmination of resistance to the comte d'Artois's royalist 'plot', defeated after Lafayette had been elected vice-president of the National Assembly. It was on 11 July 1789, wrote Paine, that 'a declaration of rights was brought forward by M. de Lafayette', a text that formed the basis for the *Declaration of the Rights of Man and of Citizens*, adopted on 26 August. It was Lafayette's account ('M. de Lafayette has since informed me ,....'), adopted by his English client.[88]

Rights of Man then jumped forward in time to a second brief but detailed narrative, this one covering the 'October Days' of 5–6 October 1789 when a Paris mob marched to Versailles and compelled the royal family to return to Paris; other observers saw it as the moment of the monarchy's effective deposition. Again, Paine had been in England, and inadvertently revealed that he had no sufficient explanation of this episode: 'After all the investigations that have been made into this intricate affair...it still remains enveloped in all that kind of mystery which ever accompanies events produced more from a concurrence of awkward circumstances, than from fixed design.' So Paine missed the way in which the expedition to Versailles was organized, not spontaneous. Again, the hero of Paine's account was Lafayette, who had 'hitherto been fortunate in calming disquietudes' and who took 20,000 of the Paris militia to Versailles to preserve order: 'M. de Lafayette became the mediator between the enraged parties.'[89]

From these two brief historical narratives *Rights of Man* then turned to a more extended account of 'the natural rights of man', expanding Paine's earlier asides. Again, however, Paine's account proved to be different from those then prevalent in Paris, including Lafayette's. Like many contemporary English theists, Paine defined rights as a divine gift, 'when man came from the hand of his Maker'; this was 'the divine origin of the rights of man at the creation'. Paine cited 'The Mosaic account of the creation' as his authority for the 'illuminating and divine principle of the equal rights of man', the *'unity or equality of man'*. It was a deeply English conception of human equality, appealing to no recent American or French document, statement, or founding principle; indeed Paine claimed that his doctrine 'shews that the equality of man, so far from being a modern doctrine, is the oldest upon record', found, that is, in the Book of Genesis.[90]

This doctrine, powerful also in the fundamentalist United States, still had much leverage in Britain but was more problematic in French society. By referring

---

[88] Paine, *Rights of Man* (1791): *CW*, i. 254–5, 260–5, 273.
[89] Paine, *Rights of Man* (1791): *CW*, i. 267–72. Paine gave his source (272, text corrected) for events from 3 to 10 October: Louis Marie Prudhomme's weekly journal *Révolutions de Paris*, no. 13, misprinted by Paine '*Revolution de Paris*'. He would have had difficulty in reading the French text.
[90] Paine, *Rights of Man* (1791): *CW*, i. 273–6 (text corrected).

everything to the immediate act of the Creator, it also had the effect of shutting down argument about the nature of rights claims and replacing that argument with bald authorial assertion. It may not be a coincidence that Paine's famous tribute to natural rights was followed in future decades not by the ascendancy of natural rights theory but by the rise of Jeremy Bentham's utilitarianism, in which natural rights discourse was repudiated. It is difficult to accept Paine's tract as a fully developed secular theory of natural rights; but such a secular theory was unnecessary in Paine's England, where rights (understood as divine rights) were ubiquitous truisms.[91]

Turning to civil rights, Paine now explained them in similarly established English terms as arising when men entered into civil society via the social contract to defend their natural rights: his account would have been familiar in the late seventeenth century. What distinguished it from other natural rights theories, notably Burke's, was Paine's argument about the degree to which men retained their natural rights after joining civil society: 'Man did not enter into society to become *worse* than he was before, nor to have fewer rights than he had before, but to have those rights better secured. His natural rights are the foundation of all his civil rights.' Man therefore directly retained some natural rights in civil society, prominently 'religion'; the others, where 'the power to execute them is defective', he indirectly retained because 'he throws [them] into the common stock as a member of society'. 'Society *grants* him nothing.' Consequently, 'every civil right grows out of a natural right; or, in other words, is a natural right exchanged'. Only, the rights surrendered 'cannot be applied to invade the natural rights which are retained in the individual'.[92] Paine, then, wished to talk up natural rights over civil rights, but he still acknowledged that some sort of surrender and exchange had taken place. It might be debated whether the ongoing authority of this partial exchange of natural for civil rights was consistent with the argument that no 'generation' had a right to bind subsequent generations, but Paine saw no such difficulty.

This familiar and older concession of a surrender and exchange had already been overtaken by the positions of British reformers like Thomas Christie, Capel Lofft, and Joseph Priestley who had written unambiguously about man's retention in civil society of *all* his natural rights. This was not clear at the time because the next step in the argument of *Rights of Man* was a dramatic set of negations of existing civil institutions claiming to exist by right, and it was these negations that captured attention: they were negations, Paine wrote, of Burke's 'catalogue of barriers...between man and his Maker' (not between man and Nature). Paine here advanced a brief stadial theory of the evolution of governments over time: 'The first was a government of priestcraft, the second of conquerors, and the third of reason.' But Paine's critique of the Church was not perfunctory. Divine right monarchy, invented 'in imitation of the Pope, who affects to be spiritual and temporal, and in contradiction to the Founder of the Christian religion, twisted itself afterwards into an idol of

---

[91] For a different view see Claeys, *Paine*, 71–5. *Rights of Man* 'does not look much like a classic text of modern political thought': Mark Philp, *Paine* (Oxford, 1989), 64. Philp argues that the pamphlet's 'disorganized appearance' added to its rhetorical impact.

[92] Paine, *Rights of Man* (1791): *CW*, i. 275–6.

another shape, called *Church and State*.[93] So Dissenters had long claimed it was in England, where Henry VIII created a new state form by claiming headship of the Church; in France the Catholic Church was not headed by the monarchy and was faced by few Protestants, but Paine's teaching was aimed primarily at England. There the phrase 'Church and State' was commonplace, and identified a large part of what was ordinarily understood by 'the constitution'; for the Deist Paine, committed to the view that the Church had no authority, there was no constitution.

Following a chain of deductive argument, Paine contended that if no institution in civil society possessed independent authority, government must be the result of an agreement among 'the people'; consequently, the constitution was that agreement, 'a thing *antecedent* to government'. He did not remark that in the recent case of the United States, the government had come first, and only later organized its constitution following the Convention of 1787 (its members had, indeed, exceeded the instructions given by the states; but Paine was probably unaware of this). If the Church and its teaching had no prescriptive authority, for Paine it was a constitution that, by default, 'contains the principles on which the government shall be established'. His point was to contend negatively that in England 'no such thing as a constitution exists, or ever did exist, and consequently that the people have yet a constitution to form'. The right to do so resided only in 'a general convention elected for the purpose'; Parliament had no right to reform itself. So it was, argued Paine, in France at that moment, where the National Constituent Assembly was such a general convention, drafting a constitution. Paine's proof was once again English and anti-Hanoverian: 'The act by which the English Parliament empowered itself to sit seven years, shews there is no constitution in England.' He referred to the Septennial Act of 1716 by which, at a time of anxiety over the Jacobite threat, Parliament had unilaterally and arguably illegally prolonged its term from three years to seven.[94] The idea of a convention, then, was clearly set out in *Rights of Man*, although not prominently or stridently; the degree of revolutionary change that a convention would entail was not described in detail.

Paine extended his discussion of civil rights to an advocacy of economic rights against 'monopolies', so that 'all trades shall be free'; his authority was not the work of any French political economist, but Adam Smith's *Wealth of Nations* (1776). Paine is famous for his aphorism at this point in *Rights of Man*: 'They order these things better in France.' Examined more closely, almost all of his arguments were English, and his comparisons of the English and French polities were more negations of England's than informed affirmations of France's. Paine's strongest argument against hereditary monarchy was a critique of William the Conqueror's title to the throne of England; he did not discuss Louis XVI's title to the throne of France.[95] By contrast, Paine followed his discussion of natural rights by framing no assertions of individuals' rights to universal suffrage, of women's rights to equality with men, or of slaves' rights to emancipation.

[93] Paine, *Rights of Man* (1791): *CW*, i. 275, 277.
[94] Paine, *Rights of Man* (1791): *CW*, i. 278–80 (text corrected).
[95] Paine, *Rights of Man* (1791): *CW*, i. 281–6.

Instead, in *Rights of Man* he next gave space to a negative critique of aristocracy, of aristocratic titles, and of an aristocratic chamber in the legislature.[96] *Common Sense* had been primarily aimed at effecting an American constitutional revolution, not at inciting social revolution, yet it still briefly denounced 'aristocratical tyranny' in the House of Lords;[97] it was a locution that could by implication have entailed a revolution in England also. The Thirteen Colonies in 1776 had no aristocracy; France in 1789 had a large and powerful one. Paine's theological commitment of 1776 against the hereditary principle now found an application appropriate in the new circumstances. The French Revolution gave occasion for Paine's anti-aristo-cratic utterances; it did not cause them. The new National Assembly had abolished the status of nobility in France while Paine was composing *Rights of Man*: he could hardly have resisted applying the lesson to England. But he correctly responded also to an extended significance given to a term in France. As Paine wrote to Burke, 'The Term Aristocrat is used here, similar to the word Tory in America;—It in general means an Enemy to the Revolution, and is used without that particular meaning formerly fixed to Aristocracy.'[98]

Paine then turned to the position of the clergy.[99] He knew that 'In France, the cry of "*the church! the church!*" was repeated as often as in Mr. Burke's book, and as loudly as when the dissenters' bill was before the English parliament.' Paine was no friend of what was 'called *The Church established by Law*'. Yet he referred here not to France but to the series of struggles in Parliament over attempts to repeal the Test and Corporation Acts, on 28 March 1787, 8 May 1789, and 2 March 1790. Paine was in England for the second of these; but it was an English preoccupation. The Catholic Church in France was denounced by French revolutionaries for other reasons, not for being 'established by Law' in the English sense. It was of England that Paine told a story: England, not France, was religiously intolerant; 'Soon after the rejecting the Bill for repealing the test-law, one of the richest manufacturers in England said in my hearing, "England, Sir, is not a country for a dissenter to live in—we must go to France."'[100]

The key narrative

Paine had earlier in *Rights of Man* offered short narratives of the events of 14 July and 5–6 October 1789, but his argument had then moved on. Now he back-tracked, inserting at this point in the text a longer connected narrative of events in France, looking back to Louis XIV but picking up the story in more detail from the American war to the taking of the Bastille.[101] The oddity of this duplication in

    [96] Paine, *Rights of Man* (1791): *CW*, i. 285–9, 296–7.
    [97] [Paine], *Common Sense* (1776): *CW*, i. 7.
    [98] Paine to Burke, 17 Jan. 1790, quoted in Philipp Ziesche, 'Thomas Paine and Benjamin Franklin's French Circle', in Simon P. Newman and Peter S. Onuf (eds), *Paine and Jefferson in the Age of Revolutions* (Charlottesville, Va, 2013), 121–36, at 131.
    [99] Paine, *Rights of Man* (1791): *CW*, i. 290–3.
    [100] Paine, *Rights of Man* (1791): *CW*, i. 290, 292, 294 (text corrected).
    [101] What I suggest is the interpolated passage of some 6,000 words is in *Rights of Man* (1791): *CW*, i. 298 ('The despotism of Louis XIV …') to i. 313 ('to act in unison with its object'). In the Penguin

the text has hitherto escaped attention; but several considerations suggest that Paine here drew on an account provided by someone else. Two considerations are noteworthy. At this point in the text, the prose style of *Rights of Man* subtly changes: it was English prose originally written by a native French speaker, with only a few interpolations that are recognizable as Paine's. In respect of substance, the author displayed a familiarity with French authors and French court politics to a degree that Paine never elsewhere matched.

Readers might naturally have expected a historical overview of the antecedents of the French Revolution in such a book, and *Rights of Man* seemed to provide this better than most other English pro-reform texts of the 1790s. This expectation has distracted attention from four further problems of this narrative section. First, it was wholly unlike what preceded and followed it in Paine's book. Second, it was a detailed, complex, insider's view of high politics, rather than an account of general political, intellectual, or social change. Third, the author boasted of knowing 'a sort of secret history'[102] of calculations behind the conduct of the nobles in the Estates-General. Fourth, this section cannot have been based to any significant degree on Paine's own involvement in French affairs of state. He did not move in circles sufficiently exalted to report personally on the higher reaches of politics or the people he here discussed (the Queen; the comte de Vergennes; M. Necker; M. Calonne; the comte d'Artois; Loménie de Brienne, Archbishop of Toulouse; the ducs de la Rochefoucauld, de Luxembourg, and de Broglie; the vicomte de Noailles, wrongly ranked by Paine as a duke; M. Lamoignon). Paine's knowledge of spoken French was insufficient to allow him to understand the conversations and complex political events set out in his narrative; and, most tellingly, he was in France for only a few months of the period (1778–89) covered by it. But all these practical limitations may have meant that Paine was aware of a shortcoming in his own writing: an account of the nature and origins of the French Revolution.

If so, Paine had a reason for accepting help from others.[103] His leading informant was probably Lafayette, who featured repeatedly and always favourably in this narrative section, whom Paine had acknowledged as a source in the briefer narratives of the taking of the Bastille and the October Days, and to whom Paine then dedicated *Rights of Man. Part the Second.* A further clue is provided by the text's central thesis that 'When the [American] war closed, a vast reinforcement to the cause of liberty spread itself over France, by the return of the French officers and soldiers.' Lafayette emerged as the hero of this narrative, and it embodied his perspective on events, as taught to Paine; but however enthusiastic opinion in France

---

edition, the passage is 115–31. The fall of the Bastille had occupied some 2,250 words, *CW:* i. 261–5; the October days, *CW*, i. 268–72, slightly less. Both these shorter passages seem to be in Paine's prose, although he evidently owed their detailed information to another. See Appendix: Paine de-attributions, and Jonathan Clark, 'Monuments to Liberty', *Times Literary Supplement*, 18 Sept. 2015, 14–15.

[102] Paine, *Rights of Man* (1791): *CW*, i. 309.

[103] Paine also probably drew on Jefferson's letters to him, although sometimes mis-remembering what Jefferson had said: Lounissi, *Paine*, 635–8. This suggests that Paine did not carefully transcribe Jefferson's information, and that another account (perhaps written) was Paine's chief source, to which he added passages.

had been about America in 1778–83, this dominant role for returning French troops has never been validated by historical research as a leading cause of the events of the French Revolution from 1789.[104]

By attributing so large a role to the American Revolution, the argument can only have been congenial to Paine. It is open to question whether this section is an insertion, borrowing from a text supplied to Paine by his closest French associate, or whether Paine drew on a published source available to him in London while he was composing his tract.[105] Since no such published source has yet been identified, and since a printed French text would have been beyond Paine's capacity to read unaided in the Angel Inn, the first alternative is probable. It might be argued that Paine made these ideas his own by incorporating them; but since evidence is lacking to show that Paine understood this claim of the domino effect of the American Revolution to have been historically accurate, such an argument would be inadequate.

Lafayette's own evidence also points to his authorship, for on 12 January 1790 he wrote to George Washington: 'Common Sense [Paine] is writing a Book for you—there you will See a part of My Adventures—I Hope they will turn to the Advantage of My Country and Mankind in General.'[106] If Lafayette's account is accurate, it suggests that Paine's *Rights of Man* was not solely a reaction to Burke's *Reflections on the Revolution in France*, published in London on 1 November 1790; and his words 'for you' may suggest Paine's desire to be the Washington of a British Revolution. Lafayette's role in the early months of the French Revolution was that of an ambitious, sophisticated politician with his own version of recent events and his own agenda; as Jefferson saw, Lafayette's '*foible*' was '*a canine appetite for popularity and fame*'.[107] Paine evidently did not see through the interpretation that he was being given by his worldly French friend. In particular, it is not clear that Paine saw the hand of Lafayette in the legislation of the National Assembly that confined the franchise to those who paid direct taxes of at least a silver mark each year, a considerable sum. Paine always saw Lafayette in highly generalized terms as an international champion of liberty, not as a quotidian politician.

---

[104] Of the French officers who served in America, 'there is no available evidence that any of the pro-American majority returned home as revolutionists. None were Brissots or Robespierres.' Of the role of the private soldiers in 'peasant revolts' the evidence is 'as yet inconclusive': Echeverria, *Mirage in the West*, 43–4, 98, 114–15. Others also used this argument from the influence of returning French troops: Lounissi, *Paine*, 594–5. There were a few such ex-servicemen in politics, notably Louis Marc Antoine, vicomte de Noailles (1756–1804), who received the British surrender at Yorktown in 1781. He took a leading part in the National Constituent Assembly in its abolition of privileges on 4 Aug. 1789 and its abolition of titles in June 1790; he became an *émigré* in 1791. Noailles was, however, the brother in law of Lafayette. Jean-Baptiste Donatien de Vimeur, comte de Rochambeau (1725–1807) commanded the French expeditionary force in America but played only a small part in the French Revolution.

[105] Paine, *Rights of Man* (1791): *CW*, i. 300–1. There was one apparent first-hand account, when Paine reported the Paris crowd's reception of the comte d'Artois at the Palais de Justice on 17 August 1787: i. 305. Paine was in Paris at the time, but no evidence establishes that the 'I' in the text referred to Paine rather than to Lafayette. Another interpolation was probably Paine's, the jibe that 'nobility' was a synonym for 'no-ability', which he may have remembered from the *Sussex Weekly Advertiser*: i. 310.

[106] Washington, *Papers*, iv. 567.

[107] Jefferson, from Paris, to James Madison, 30 Jan. 1787: Jefferson, *Papers*, xi. 95.

The French *Déclaration*

When the guidance of Paine's suggested source ceased, and when the seemingly interpolated section ended, Paine's discussion of France in *Rights of Man* reverted to an external view. Neither Burke nor Paine clearly analysed the differences between, and the similarities of, the American and French Revolutions. The American Revolution's first symbolic document was a declaration of *independence*, but Paine now held up for attention the French Revolution's declaration of *rights*: an English translation of the French *Declaration of the Rights of Man and of Citizens*,[108] adopted by the National Assembly on 26 August 1789. Paine followed it with his own 'Observations'. His comments on the French document were notable for their brevity. He focused on just one substantive issue, religious toleration, and once more did not notice the significant difference between his own leading conception of natural rights as a series of divine gifts to each individual at the moment of that person's 'creation' and the original *Declaration*'s conception of rights as almost wholly secular possessions, 'natural' in the sense of universal, their universality expressed by the operation of 'the law'.

It has not been remarked that the English text of the *Déclaration des droits de l'homme et du citoyen*, as printed in *Rights of Man*, gave that document a more theistic cast than its French original. The prologue to the *Déclaration* had concluded: 'En conséquence, l'Assemblée Nationale reconnaît et déclare, en présence et sous les auspices de l'Etre suprême, les droits suivants de l'Homme et du Citoyen.' But the version in *Rights of Man* read: 'For these reasons, the NATIONAL ASSEMBLY doth recognize and declare, in the presence of the Supreme Being, and with the hope of his blessing and favour, the following *sacred* rights of men and of citizens.'[109] The Almighty was perfunctorily acknowledged in the French original, but the English version implied an active God where the French text had said no such thing. Paine's English text was, however, not his own translation: it was almost identical to the English translation that had been printed by the Nonconformist minister Richard Price as an appendix to his famous sermon (whether Price's French was adequate to translate the French document is unclear).[110] Paine did not work from the French original. Because the Deist Paine borrowed unthinkingly from the Arian Price's pamphlet, Paine was probably lastingly unaware that attitudes to rights prevalent among French revolutionaries were increasingly different from attitudes to rights widespread among English theists.

Generations of readers have taken the inclusion of the French *Declaration of the Rights of Man and of Citizens* to be self-evidently appropriate; the *Declaration* seemingly validated Paine's text, and vice versa. Examined more closely, the *Declaration* relates to the rest of Paine's pamphlet not as an integrated argument, but as another interpolation. In his own text Paine provided, for the most part, an

---

[108] *Declaration of the Rights of Man and of Citizens*: *CW*, i. 313–15.

[109] Paine, *Rights of Man* (1791): *CW*, i. 314 (text corrected; italics original).

[110] Price, *A Discourse on the Love of our Country*, appendix, 6. Paine's text here repeated the capitals and italics in Price's text. Elsewhere, Paine's text differed only in punctuation and capitals from Price's, with two exceptions. Price's gave the title as *Declaration of the Rights of Men and of Citizens*, and I. as 'Men were born and always continue free'; Paine's printed the title as *Declaration of the Rights of Man and of Citizens*, and I. as 'Men are born, and always continue, free.'

array of particularist negations, negations of 'divine right' in the historic forms it had taken.[111] These he held up as contradicted by natural rights. The sections in which he did this preceded and followed a translated French document that contained a series of universalist affirmations. But on how the affirmations and negations related to each other, Paine had little to say other than the link he inherited from *Common Sense*: that the (false) doctrine of original sin undermined the hereditary principle.

In Paine's 'Observations on the Declaration of Rights' he complained of what he argued was the inadequacy of the guarantee of religious toleration in Article X. But he was distracted from this unease by the need to treat the French document as being of world-historical significance:

> In the declaratory exordium which prefaces the Declaration of Rights, we see the solemn and majestic spectacle of a Nation opening its commission, under the auspices of its Creator, to establish a Government; a scene so new, and so transcendently unequalled by any thing in the European world, that the name of a Revolution is diminutive of its character, and it rises into a Regeneration of man.

Revolutions, in Paine's usage hitherto, were not transcendent episodes. A 'Regeneration of man' echoed English Methodism's idea of the 'new birth' rather than any specific understanding by Paine of complex French events. Paine saw what he wanted to see in France, and saw it mainly through the eyes of one Frenchman. He provided no introduction to the *Declaration*, and in the 'Observations' that followed Paine closed not with analysis but with a highly rhetorical quotation.[112] 'I will close the subject with the energetic apostrophe of M. de Lafayette—*May this great monument, raised to Liberty, serve as a lesson to the oppressor, and an example to the oppressed!*'[113] Thanks in part to his admiration for Lafayette, Paine did not grasp the difference between English and French understandings of the issues.

Paine's crucial 'single idea', the thought that would prevent all error 'on the subject of religion', relegated to a footnote, was that

> before any human institutions of government were known in the world, there existed, if I may so express it, a compact between God and man, from the beginning of time; and that as the relation and condition which man in his *individual person* stands in toward his Maker cannot be changed, or any ways altered by any human laws or human authority, that religious devotion, which is a part of this compact, cannot so much as be made a subject of human laws; and that all laws must conform themselves to this prior existing compact, and not assume to make the compact conform to the laws, which, besides being human, are subsequent thereto.[114]

The French *Declaration* had not said that. Indeed, the French document was the ambiguous result of political contingency, for it was 'hammered out in committee after numerous revisions and compromises...the entire process became increasingly

---

[111] Paine, *Rights of Man* (1791): *CW*, i. 252, 277.
[112] Paine, *Rights of Man* (1791): *CW*, i. 317.
[113] Paine, *Rights of Man* (1791): *CW*, i. 313–17.
[114] Paine, *Rights of Man* (1791): *CW*, i. 316n.

bogged down in disputes over words and "metaphysical" battles'. God appeared as 'the Supreme Being', a locution that commanded wide agreement in the Assembly but that might have signalled a lowest common denominator. Finally a 'compromise version' was 'cobbled together'.[115] Of the second drafting committee's twenty-four proposed rights, the Assembly, after much disagreement and debate over six days, had time to agree on only seventeen; it then postponed discussion of the others, and never resumed the question.[116]

Far from solving all problems, the *Declaration* only highlighted them: did these rights apply to all men, or only to male citizens? To all 'passive citizens', or only to 'active citizens'? To all people, including slaves and women, or only to white males, or only to French male Catholic property owners?[117] Even the warmest advocates of 'the rights of man' had seldom intended their greatest extension. In the absence of agreement on these questions, could there be agreement on what the principles of the French Revolution were? Rights expressed in universal or general terms settled nothing, however much they triggered debate or were appealed to in later centuries. The *Declaration*, intended as the preamble to a new constitution that rested on its principles, did not securely and unambiguously instantiate rights in law; it merely sought to replace one legal fiction with another. The legal fiction that the monarch had authority to confer privileges and rank was superseded by the legal fiction that the privileges of individuals equal in rank rested on the authority of abstract, generalized rights. What this all meant was as disputable in the second case as it had been in the first.

Paine was evidently unaware of the significance of the tactical dimension of the *Declaration*'s framing. He may even have moved in an opposite direction to the Assembly. From his leading idea of rights as individual gifts from God to each individual at the moment of that individual's creation, Paine had even fallen back on an older idea of hereditary right, rights as a legacy descending from parents to children by unalterable divine appointment (this was far from what is today generally meant by 'democracy'). But Paine saw no contradiction.

It was here that Paine committed himself to his second conception of natural rights, inconsistent with the first of divine gift at the moment of each individual's creation. In order to argue that a previous generation could not interfere with the rights of the present one, he wrote: 'The rights of men in society are neither devisable, nor transferable, nor annihilable, but are descendible only; and it is not in the power of any generation to intercept finally, and cut off the descent.' It was a locution which looked forward to *Rights of Man. Part the Second* and its salute to '*the*

---

[115] Jonathan Israel, *Democratic Enlightenment: Philosophy, Revolution, and Human Rights 1750–1790* (Oxford, 2011), 905–8; cf. Dan Edelstein, 'A Reply to Jonathan Israel', in Kate E. Tunstall (ed.), *Self-Evident Truths? Human Rights and the Enlightenment* (London, 2012), 127–35. I am grateful to Dan Edelstein for discussions of this episode, although the interpretation here is my own.

[116] Lynn Hunt, *Inventing Human Rights: A History* (New York, 2007), 16, 130–1; Stéphane Rials, *La Déclaration des droits de l'homme et du citoyen* (Paris, 1988).

[117] The 'contentious debates provoked by the tension between universal claims and particular laws could only be temporarily resolved by legislative decisions': Lynn Hunt, 'The Declaration of the Rights of Man and of the Citizen, August 1789: A Revolutionary Document', in Rachel Hammersley (ed.), *Revolutionary Moments: Reading Revolutionary Texts* (London, 2015), 77–84, at 80–3.

indefeasible, hereditary rights of man. Paine's practical goal was to break up the indefeasible, hereditary right of kings and to distribute a share of that prize to everyman, not to devise a new version of natural rights theory as such. A new version would have seemed unnecessary: by the 1790s, natural rights theory was (before Bentham) seldom challenged. To that end, Paine wrote in 1792 of old and new governments: 'the one now called the old is *hereditary*, either in whole or in part; and the new is entirely *representative*'. He did not claim that the new governments, unlike the old, were distinguished by being based on natural rights or on reified revolutions.[118]

English and American rights

Paine concluded *Rights of Man* with a long 'Miscellaneous Chapter': it had little to say about France except to compare its finances favourably with England's. Instead, its opening was a reiteration of his English-centred case against 'hereditary rights', specifically as derived from William the Conqueror and extending to Burke's errors in interpreting 1688. It was this case that identified the entire English government as 'usurpation', again an echo of an early eighteenth-century dynastic critique. Burke, he argued, had already shown himself as a supporter of 'hereditary rights, and hereditary succession' by the role he had taken with the Foxite Whigs in 1788, when they attempted to pass a Regency Bill to vest full kingly authority in their patron, the Prince of Wales, following the illness of George III. 'This ought to be a caution to every country, how it imports foreign families to be kings.' France had not done so; Britain had.

To the contrary Paine cited not a French example but a speech of the Earl of Shelburne in the House of Lords in 1783, reporting Shelburne as arguing

> That the form of a government was a matter wholly at the will of the nation at all times: that if it chose a monarchical form, it had a right to have it so; and if it afterwards chose to be a republic, it had a right to be a republic, and to say to a king, 'We have no longer any occasion for you.'[119]

In contrast to Shelburne's generalized position Paine advanced a particularist anti-Hanoverian one, citing 'what one of the Brunswick soldiers told me, who was taken prisoner by the Americans in the late war': that America was 'a free country', but 'in my country, if the prince says, Eat straw, we eat straw'. Paine added: 'God

---

[118] Paine, *Rights of Man* (1791): *CW*, i. 313–17, 325; *Rights of Man. Part the Second* (1792): *CW*, i. 356, 364.

[119] Paine, *Rights of Man* (1791): *CW*, i. 317–28, at 318–19, 321–2. This went beyond Shelburne's words as recorded in *The Parliamentary Register; or History of the Proceedings and Debates of the House of Lords... During the Third Session of the Fifteenth Parliament of Great Britain* (London: J. Almon, 1783), xi. 25: 'He could easily conceive, he said, a case in which the people of this country might speak to the Crown in such language as this: "Sire, we called in the aid of your illustrious family to save us from Popery and arbitrary power. We have for three ages reaped the benefits of their attention to our interests and welfare, but not thinking that monarchy is any longer essential to our security, freedom, and happiness, we are determined to do all the business of the Crown ourselves: and therefore, with many thanks for your care and kindness, we make you our bow, and intreat you to relinquish the trust."'

help that country, thought I, be it England or elsewhere, whose liberties are to be protected by German principles of government, and Princes of Brunswick!'[120]

Rather than then returning to events in France, Paine closed his 'Miscellaneous Chapter' with 'a concise view of the state of parties and politics in England' from 1783 to 1791. Unlike the 6,000 word narrative of French events, here reattributed to Lafayette, this passage was informed by Paine's own knowledge. Finally, his Conclusion offered again his basic choice between 'government by election and representation' and 'government by hereditary succession'. A 'mixed government becomes a continual enigma', enabled to act only by 'corruption', especially the corruption that promoted wars to maximize governments' revenues. These arguments, echoing the Patriot opposition of the 1730s, were less remembered than his closing flourish: 'It is an age of Revolutions, in which every thing may be looked for.'[121] But why this was so, and what these revolutions were, Paine did not there set out. English arguments offered insufficient clues to the French Revolution. If so, it would help explain why *Rights of Man* was to have little impact in France itself, like *The Age of Reason* that followed it.

Revolutionaries differed. If *Rights of Man* terminated Paine's friendship with Burke, it almost did the same with Washington, to whom it was dedicated. On 21 July 1791 Paine sent the American President no less than fifty copies, boasting: 'The work has had a run beyond anything that has been published in this country on the subject of government.'[122] But an American edition had already appeared on 3 May with a note by Thomas Jefferson as an unauthorized Preface, saluting *Rights of Man* as countering the 'political heresies which have sprung up among us'. This was easily interpreted as a criticism of the Vice-President, John Adams, and of the President himself. Far from the consensual, benign, Deist polity that Paine had envisaged, the new United States was falling into bitter division between two political parties—a division more polarized and more embittered than in Britain itself.

The pro-French Republicans now drew up battle lines against the anti-French Federalists, the Republicans depicting the Federalists as friends of monarchy and aristocracy, the Federalists seeing the Republicans as friends of revolution and bloodshed. Paine's gift to the President was therefore politically embarrassing. Washington did not reply until 6 May 1792, and then coldly. Paine's dedication expressed the hope that 'the *Rights of Man* may become as universal as your benevolence can wish, and that you may enjoy the happiness of seeing the New World regenerate the Old'. If this was a serious invitation to join in an ongoing transatlantic revolution Washington did not respond, and he evidently blocked Republican demands that Paine be appointed to the newly vacant office of Postmaster General. Of the fifty copies of *Rights of Man* that Paine sent him, Washington kept forty-seven, undistributed.[123]

In the United States as in England, the French Revolution had potent domestic implications that partly reflected events in France and partly reflected the political

---

[120] Paine, *Rights of Man* (1791): *CW*, i. 322 (text corrected).
[121] Paine, *Rights of Man* (1791): *CW*, i. 328–38, at 328, 338, 343–4.
[122] Paine to Washington, 21 July 1791: *CW*, ii. 1318.
[123] Washington to Paine, 6 May 1792: Washington, *Papers*, x. 357–8.

preoccupations of the very different societies in which French events had their impact. The United States was no neutral yardstick against which revolution in general could be judged; but reformers in England, Paine included, were increasingly drawn to reflect on the significance of the American case. It would be a leading theme in Paine's *Rights of Man. Part the Second.*

THE DEBATE ON THE FRENCH
REVOLUTION, 1789–1792

Paine, Burke, and their circles

The English-speaking debate on the French Revolution was even more extensive than the agonized controversy that followed the American.[124] As in the earlier episode there is no evidence that Paine followed that debate of the 1790s with any closeness. He was not an instinctive controversialist, enjoying detailed argumentative exchanges with a range of named opponents;[125] in any case, that is not how the pamphlet war of the 1790s developed. One estimate suggests that of approximately 'four thousand pamphlets dealing with questions of reform and revolution [that] appeared in England between the fall of the Bastille and the Peace of Amiens' in 1802, only 340 clearly addressed Price, Burke, and Paine.[126] To understand this exchange as 'the Burke–Paine debate' is a misconception. There was no party of Burke confronting a party of Paine.[127] Paine did not debate within or between any such groups; he saw himself as a moral teacher, announcing his self-evident principles to a listening world. This identity both aided his declamatory force and isolated him to some degree from the developing discussion.

---

[124] Gayle Trusdel Pendleton, 'The English Pamphlet Literature of the Age of the French Revolution Anatomized', *Eighteenth-Century Life* 5 (1978), 29–37; Gayle Trusdel Pendleton, 'Towards a Bibliography of the *Reflections* and *Rights of Man* Controversy', *Bulletin of Research in the Humanities* 85 (1982), 65–103; Amanda Goodrich, 'Surveying the Ebb and Flow of Pamphlet Warfare: 500 Rival Tracts from Radicals and Loyalists in Britain, 1790–1796', *British Journal for Eighteenth-Century Studies* 30 (2007), 1–12. For the substance of the debate see especially Claeys, *Paine*, 110–76; Marilyn Morris, *The British Monarchy and the French Revolution* (New Haven, 1998), 56–78; Lounissi, *Paine*, 525–77.

[125] It is not known how many of the replies to *Rights of Man* Paine knew of. The following year he wrote that 'Not less, I believe, than eight or ten pamphlets intended as answers to the former part of the "Rights of Man" have been published by different persons': Paine, *Rights of Man. Part the Second* (1792): *CW*, i. 350 (text corrected). It is not clear whether this was Paine's attempt to disparage the replies. Later in 1792 he wrote: 'Not less than forty pamphlets, intended as answers thereto, have appeared, and as suddenly disappeared': Paine, *Two Letters to Onslow* (1792; second letter, dated 21 June): *CW*, ii. 461; Lounissi, *Paine*, 545. Paine correctly appreciated his own lasting currency, but it is unknown whether this led him to disregard other publications.

[126] Of the 340, Pendleton identified 104 works as 'reformist', 213 as 'conservative': Pendleton, 'Towards a Bibliography', 65, 74.

[127] 'It may also be noted that the famous "pamphlet war" which followed the publication of the two books was by no means a controversy between the followers of Burke on the one hand and those of Paine on the other. It was more like a collection of answers to Burke by people who did not agree with Paine, and of answers to Paine by people who did not agree with Burke': R. R. Fennessy, *Burke, Paine and the Rights of Man: A Difference of Political Opinion* (The Hague, 1963), 213–50, at 220.

Burke, a parliamentarian for whom controversy was his vocation, quickly replied. Paine's *Rights of Man* appeared on 13 March 1791; on 3 August Burke published a systematic response to his critics, none of whom he named but one of whom he quoted at length. It would have taken little work to identify Paine as the author of the passages that Burke transcribed and repudiated. His chosen extracts focused aptly on Paine's central claims. According to these quotations Britain had no constitution, this being a thing 'antecedent to government'. Aristocracy was 'a *monster*' and incapable of legislation; primogeniture was against 'every law of nature'. The House of Commons, Burke countered, did not 'arise out of the inherent rights of the people'. His unattributed quotations continued: charters and corporations were 'charters of oppression'. Man was so 'wretched' under 'the monarchical and hereditary systems of government' that 'a general revolution in the principle and construction of government is necessary'. Government 'is not, and from its nature cannot be, the property of any particular man or family, but of the whole community', which could at any time 'abolish any form of government it finds inconvenient'. In France, 'Monarchical sovereignty, the enemy of mankind, and source of misery, is abolished.' A crown was merely a 'metaphor'. In France, the right of war and peace now resided in 'the nation'. In England, the Convention Parliament of 1689 had claimed by usurpation an authority as tyrannical as that of James II; but the Revolution of 1688 was already 'eclipsed by the enlarging orb of reason, and the luminous revolutions of America and France'. The House of Hanover, in its native country, was a 'despotism', and in England its members were a 'Foreign House'; England had no need to have 'sent for' them. 'What are those men kept for?'[128]

Burke's tactic was mainly to hold up passages from Paine's original as if their obvious extremism needed no counter argument. Equally, however, Paine did not engage directly with Burke. Indeed Paine maintained a distance even from fellow reformers. William Godwin, who had encountered him briefly at 'a numerous meeting', the London Revolution Society's annual dinner on 4 November 1791, followed up with a letter to Paine in the most flattering terms:

> I regard you, sir, as having been the unalterable champion of liberty in America, in England & in France, from the purest views to the happiness and virtue of mankind. I have devoted my life to these glorious purposes, & am at this moment employed upon a composition, embracing the whole doctrine of politics, & in which I shall endeavour to convince my countrymen of the mischiefs of monarchical government, & of certain other abuses not less injurious to society. I believe that a cordial & unreserved intercourse between men employed in the same great purposes, is of the utmost service to their own minds & to their cause.[129]

---

[128] [Edmund Burke], *An Appeal from the New to the Old Whigs, in consequence of some late Discussions in Parliament, relative to the Reflections on the French Revolution* (London: J. Dodsley, 1791), 86–95.

[129] Godwin to Paine, [7 Nov. 1791]: Godwin, *Letters*, ed. Clemit, i. 64–6. Godwin invited Paine to join a dinner party on 12 March 1792, evidently prompted by reading *Rights of Man. Part the Second*, but 'Paine did not attend': Godwin to Paine, [16 Feb. –11 Mar. 1792]: Godwin, *Letters*, i. 67–8. Godwin's closing line, 'I am contented to wait with patience, confident that the time will come when you will acknowledge the kindred I claim', suggests no close acquaintance already achieved. After 12 March 1792 'Godwin never met Paine again'; 'It was Thomas Holcroft who undoubtedly had

Godwin, aged 35, was hardly a star-struck teenager. He asked Paine for a private meeting; but apart from their dining on 13 November at a dinner party given by Joseph Johnson, their shared publisher, there is no evidence that they had a serious discussion then or later. Paine made only the briefest of appearances in Godwin's *Enquiry Concerning Political Justice*, and Godwin made no appearances in Paine's writings. This non-meeting of minds is more notable since Godwin's book was 'fathered by the debate' on the French Revolution.[130]

Nor did Paine initially command a defined social constituency in England. Disssent did not obviously provide one. A leading Nonconformist, Samuel Heywood, struggling to defend his co-religionists from charges of disloyalty and extremism, even shied away from mentioning Paine by name. 'Dr. Price and the Dissenters', urged Heywood, did not hold the doctrine attributed to them by Burke in his *Appeal from the New to the Old Whigs*, namely 'that the people may lawfully depose kings, not only for misconduct, but *without any misconduct at all*'. The societies Burke referred to 'are *not dissenting* societies', and these doctrines 'have not been *"disseminated from a single dissenting pulpit!"*'

> And the only authority cited [by Burke] to prove these are the principles of *the Dissenters*, is a pamphlet written by a professed republican [Paine], and the subject of a foreign state! It has been sufficiently hard on the Dissenters to have had imputed to them, as a body, the sentiments of single individuals from among themselves, but it is doubly so to make them answerable for the opinions of a foreigner, with whom they have no connection.[131]

Heywood correctly appreciated that Paine would be toxic to the Nonconformist cause.

This was so since Paine was not seen in England as a foreigner; like other English reformers, Paine was already committed to see the French Revolution of 1789–90 as an exemplification of his own English principles. As with *Common Sense*, Paine therefore talked up the significance and the impact of *Rights of Man* where the real insight into American and French events of Paine's two texts was limited. In 1802, back in America, he wrote, evidently of *Rights of Man* and its sequel: 'It had the greatest run of any work ever published in the English language. The number of copies circulated in England, Scotland and Ireland, besides translations into foreign languages, was between four and five hundred thousand.'[132] A book enjoyed a wider sale if perceived as engaged in conflict with a rival volume, and that was so here: *Rights of Man* was inevitably read as Paine's response to Burke's *Reflections on the Revolution in France*. Even so, as with *Common Sense*, Paine's figures for its

---

the greatest influence on Godwin during the composition of *Political Justice*': Peter H. Marshall, *William Godwin* (New Haven, 1984), 85, 87.

[130] Mark Philp, *Godwin's Political Justice* (London, 1986), 74. Philp rejects the theory that Godwin was involved in the publication of Paine's *Rights of Man*, 75.

[131] [Samuel Heywood], *High Church Politics: being a Seasonable Appeal to the Friends of the British Constitution, against the Practices and Principles of High Churchmen; as exemplified in the late opposition to the repeal of the Test Laws, and in the riots at Birmingham* (London: J. Johnson, 1792), 190; [Burke], *An Appeal from the New to the Old Whigs*, 56.

[132] Paine, 'To the Citizens of the United States' (15 Nov. 1802): *CW*, ii. 910.

circulation rested on scant knowledge of the practicalities of printing and publishing. The true number must await future research, but was probably significantly less. Undoubtedly, *Rights of Man* enjoyed widespread acclaim and circulation; but, as with *Common Sense*, the assumption of its ubiquity and its transforming impact has the character of legend. If the real but lesser impact of *Rights of Man* is to be gauged, the legend must be investigated.[133]

The need for a careful assessment of the impact of *Rights of Man* was evident at the time, even to the Foxite MP Samuel Romilly. On 20 May 1791 he wrote:

> We have had violent debates in our House of Commons on the French Revolution; and they have produced a total, and, as it should seem, an irreparable breach between Fox and Burke. Fox has gained much with the public by his conduct, and Burke has lost as much. It is astonishing how Burke's book has fallen; though the tenth edition is now publishing, its warmest admirers at its first appearance begin to be ashamed of their admiration. Paine's book, on the other hand, has made converts of a great many persons; which, I confess, appears to me as wonderful as the success of Burke's; for I do not understand how men can be convinced without arguments; and I find none in Paine, though I admit he has great merit. It is a book calculated, I should have thought, to strengthen preconceived opinion, but not to convert any one. However, the event shows that I was wrong.[134]

Yet perhaps he had not been wrong; perhaps, as in 1776, so in 1791, Paine brilliantly captured and focused bodies of opinion hitherto widely diffused (a success he did not repeat in France with *The Age of Reason* or *Agrarian Justice*).

A reassessment of Paine involves also his former friend and fellow reformer. Burke had adopted a highly negative public response to the French Revolution from his speech in the Commons of 9 February 1790; his *Reflections on the Revolution in France* was published on 1 November that year. Partly his stance was his recognition, in the French case, of phenomena that he had come to appreciate in the American Revolution but had at that time been unable, for tactical Whig party reasons, to articulate. Partly it was a response to the crisis of November 1788 to February 1789, when George III's illness threatened a regency in the person of the Prince of Wales and, in consequence, a new ministry led by Fox and his allies. Although the king had recovered, no one knew if his illness might return, or when he would die: in either event, some form of fundamental change in Britain, directed from above by the French Revolution's most ardent British elite admirers, was a real possibility. Burke now knew that his position would be invidious in a new reign; as the Prince of Wales had said to Lord Thomond, after the appearance

---

[133] This reconsideration of Paine's impact began with Günther Lottes, *Politische Aufklärung und plebejisches Publikum: Zur Theorie und Praxis des englischen Radikalismus im späten 18. Jahrhundert* (Munich, 1979), 267–9 and 'Radicalism, Revolution and Political Culture: An Anglo-French Comparison', in Mark Philp (ed.), *The French Revolution and British Popular Politics* (Cambridge, 1991), 78–98, at 84.

[134] Romilly to Madame G—, 20 May 1791: *Memoirs of the Life of Sir Samuel Romilly, Written by Himself, with a Selection from his Correspondence, edited by his Sons* (3 vols, London, 1840), i. 426–7. Most of Romilly's letter gave an account of the recent Commons debate on the abolition of the slave trade, a cause with which he did not link Paine.

of Burke's *Reflections*, 'How the Devil could your friend Burke publish such a Farrago of Nonsense?'[135]

On 21 May 1791 Captain William Bentinck met Burke at a dinner party and had a long conversation with him afterwards. Burke had argued 'That he explained to Fox the situation of this country very quiet and safe, the King loved, the Ministry strong.' Bentinck's record of Burke's views continued:

> But suppose an accession to the throne and change of Ministers, what might be the consequences with a King [George IV] unpopular by his expenses and habits of life, with a great demand on the public, with the dissenters (who hate Fox though they use him) asking more than any Ministry can give and amounting to 700,000, having various meetings in different parts of England—obliged to make a new batch of peers—to lay on new taxes, and unpopular in the country, with the minds of men the views of the dissenters in England since the year 1789, of the democrats in France, conceiving those views to be highly dangerous to the quiet of the country...In all probability a Revolution here would be the consequence. Therefore, added Burke, as I found Fox was not to be checked by any friendly advice or by any reason, I thought it best to separate from the party as it was impossible for me to join on such terms.[136]

A spontaneous and self-sufficient revolution 'from below' in Britain was highly unlikely in November 1790, but a Fox ministry, and its unfolding consequences, was not: dramatic events might then have been led by a section of the elite, as they initially were in France and the American colonies, and might similarly have escaped from elite control. In the event, George III was not permanently incapacitated until 1810 and died only in 1820, but in 1790 such a prolonged active life may have seemed improbable. The possibility of transformative change was therefore in the public mind before the publication of *Rights of Man*.

If Burke was hostile, the opening months of the French Revolution could be welcomed even by many of Fox's opponents. Only a minority of elite authors initially agreed with Burke about events in France. Before *Rights of Man*, others had already replied to Burke's *Reflections*, and done so in terms very different from Paine's. They often urged that the French Revolution was a much more moderate, constructive, and hopeful event than Burke had depicted it; they recommended reforms in the British Constitution to return it to its ancient excellence, not its revolutionary abolition.[137] Even the Society for Constitutional Information sought

---

[135] *The Farington Diary*, ed. James Greig (8 vols, London, 1922–8), iv. 22, Joseph Farington reporting the recollection of Lord Thomond in 1806.

[136] Captain William Bentinck's diary, in Aubrey Le Blond, *Charlotte Sophie Countess Bentinck: Her Life and Times, 1715–1800* (2 vols, London, 1912), i. 162–4.

[137] Joseph Towers, *Thoughts on the Commencement of a New Parliament* (1790), who looked to a day when 'the people' might 'demand, as their undoubted, their unquestionable right, a more just and equal representation in Parliament', and the 'necessary renovation of the constitution', 22; Capel Lofft, *Remarks on the Letter of the Rt. Hon. Edmund Burke, Concerning the Revolution in France* (1790); [George Rous], *Thoughts on Government: occasioned by Mr Burke's Reflections, &c. In a Letter to a Friend* (London: J. Debrett, 1790); Robert Woolsey, *Reflections upon Reflections, including some Observations on the Constitution and Laws of England; particularly On Pressing, on the Excise, on Libels, &c. In Two Letters, to the Right Hon. Edmund Burke, In answer to his Pamphlet* (London: for the author, and sold by W. Stewart, 1790). Works taking such a position published soon after *Rights of Man* included James

in 1788–9 at least to appear to remain within this mindset, sensational though it would have been in the 1770s; as the toasts at their dinner on 21 May 1788 affirmed, 'The Majesty of the People...Annual Parliaments and the People's Rights restored...Repeal of the Septennial Act, Liberty of the Press; Abolition of the Slave Trade...May no one suffer in Civil Capacity for Religious Opinion.' This was an English agenda, owing little to America or to Paine.

These goals the SCI continued to profess, hopeful that the French Revolution would create a setting in which parliamentary reform would be more, not less, attainable in Britain.[138] As late as 1792 the Dissenter William Belsham quoted a statement that the SCI had published in the press:

> It was never in our contemplation to extend a reform beyond the manifest corruptions of that part of it which the people at large have an undoubted right to create; and reflect with perfect satisfaction, on no other mode of redress than what the established forms of the Constitution may sanction.

Belsham added a note on *Rights of Man*. True, Paine was a republican; but he was now 'the subject of a Republican State'.

> And it by no means follows, that those who admire and recommend his book as an excellent and decisive reply to Mr. Burke, must adopt his opinions relative to Monarchy; opinions totally extraneous, or rather opposite to the main design of the work, as a vindication of the French Revolution, the French Nation having very wisely retained the monarchical form of Government.[139]

Such an argument could only be compromised by the execution of Louis XVI on 21 January 1793.

Yet the position of even moderate English reformers had already shifted by that date. The London-based Revolution Society had affirmed at its centenary celebration on 4 November 1788 three principles (partly derived from recent English religious controversy) which it claimed had been embodied in the Revolution of 1688:

I. That all civil and political authority is derived from the people.
II. That the abuse of power justifies resistance.
III. That the right of private judgment, liberty of conscience, trial by jury, the freedom of the press, and the freedom of election, ought ever to be held sacred and inviolable.[140]

Mackintosh, *Vindiciae Gallicae* (1791) and [Sir Brooke Boothby], *A Letter to the Right Honourable Edmund Burke* (London: J. Debrett, 1791).

[138] Minute Book of the SCI, National Archives, TS 11/1133, fo. 180, quoted in Fennessy, *Burke, Paine*, 221–2. Paine was evidently not present on 21 May 1788, and may not have been immediately confronted with the anti-slavery commitments of members of the SCI.

[139] W[illiam] Belsham, *Examination of an Appeal from the New to the Old Whigs; to which is prefixed, An Introduction, containing Remarks on Mr Burke's Letter to a Member of the National Assembly* (London: C. Dilly, 1792), 34–5.

[140] *An Abstract of the History and Proceedings of the Revolution Society, in London. To which is annexed a copy of the Bill of Rights* ('Printed by Order of the Committee', 1789), 14–15.

Those subscribing to such views naturally saw the French Revolution as an echo of the English; but the euphoria of such early reactions against Burke's *Reflections* implicated these English sympathizers as French events unfolded. Such principles, innocent in the context of a commemoration of 1688, might be seen as a basis for a revolution in Britain in the evolving context of the French Revolution.

The publication of *Rights of Man* on 13 March 1791 revitalized a SCI that seemed to have become moribund in the previous few months.[141] Its meeting on 23 March 'inaugurated a new policy of the society; this policy was, quite simply, to support Paine, and gain publicity for his book'.[142] Why did the SCI, dedicated to the repair of the British Constitution, now endorse an activist who denied that Britain had a constitution? Why did the Society, committed to parliamentary reform, endorse a man who demanded Parliament's abolition?[143] Some of the members of the SCI may have been more extreme in their commitments than they revealed; others may have acted on the perilous principle that 'my enemy's enemy is my friend'.

How extreme, then, was Paine's book? *Rights of Man* went further than most reformist pamphlets of 1789–90; it accepted Burke's challenge, and outlined what seemed at first reading a polar opposite to Burke's position. Yet this appearance was partly misleading. The two men still agreed in much, now placing different valuations on what they similarly analysed. Paine, like Burke, saw in the French Revolution an episode holding out the promise of world revolution. Both thought they saw the doctrine of the rights of man as its activating principle. Both saw monarchy, aristocracy, and religion as providing the hegemonic structures of British society. Both saw the conflicts unleashed in 1789 as a war of ideas.

Each understood the other well. As Burke correctly claimed, Paine did not argue for the meliorist reform of the British Constitution; Paine argued that Britain had no constitution, and needed to be provided with one. Paine, as Burke feared, was moved by an antipathy to British institutions that has been captured with the word 'hate', and this was already clear to contemporaries. William Hazlitt later defined a Jacobin:

> To be a true Jacobin, a man must be a good hater ... The love of liberty consists in the hatred of tyrants. The true Jacobin hates the enemies of liberty as they hate liberty, with all his strength and with all his might, and with all his heart and with all his soul ... His hatred of wrong only ceases with the wrong.[144]

It was this mode of action that Paine most prominently represented: the negation of what he identified as England's central institutions. *Rights of Man* is today often analysed in isolation from Paine's other works, yet these supplied a context in which *Rights of Man* was then read. Even *Common Sense* continued to appear in England: there were five editions between 1791 and 1793, including London editions by

---

[141] Albert Goodwin, *The Friends of Liberty: The English Democratic Movement in the Age of the French Revolution* (London, 1979), 176–7.

[142] Fennessy, *Burke, Paine*, 223–4.

[143] Fennessy, *Burke, Paine*, 226.

[144] William Hazlitt, 'The Times Newspaper' (1817), in *The Complete Works of William Hazlitt*, ed. P. P. Howe (21 vols, London, 1930–4), vii. 151–2.

J. S. Jordan in 1791 and by H. D. Symonds in 1792. British readers of *Rights of Man* could have been well aware of the context that Paine had already created by his earlier writings, revolutionary, anti-monarchical, and egalitarian because appealing not to 1688–9 but to men's natural rights at the Creation and in the state of nature. The primitive community of goods, which was not what Paine overtly advocated for the present, could nevertheless seem not far off.

The peaceful euphoria of 1789 evolved during 1790 and 1791 as the implications of conflicts preceding 1789 were exposed by events. The growing element of hatred was eventually to compromise the often peaceful and moderate early goals of some leaders of the British reform societies, and potentially made revolution a mass phenomenon. This element was more clearly present in France, directed first against the aristocracy, the Church, the queen;[145] and finally, after the flight to Varennes, against the king. In *Rights of Man*, Paine denied its existence in the French case alone:

> The revolutions that have taken place in other European countries, have been excited by personal hatred. The rage was against the man, and he became the victim. But, in the instance of France, we see a revolution generated in the rational contemplation of the rights of man, and distinguishing from the beginning between persons and principles.[146]

But this was an interpretation that Paine deduced from his prior commitments, not one that he inferred from observation of events on the streets of Paris: it is doubtful if he ever knew a single *sans-culotte*,[147] and he discussed the details of no other European revolutions to support his comparison. As to the revolution he predicted in Britain, he could hardly deny the salience of his own 'personal hatred' of George III.

Even to the French vilification of aristocracy, Paine could add little to what his source, probably Lafayette, told him:

> The more aristocracy appeared, the more it was despised; there was a visible imbecillity and want of intellects in the majority, a sort of *je ne sais quoi*, that while it affected to be more than citizen, was less than man. It lost ground from contempt more than from hatred; and was rather jeered at as an ass, than dreaded as a lion. This is the general character of aristocracy, or what are called Nobles or Nobility, or rather No-ability, in all countries.[148]

Only the last phrase is likely to have been Paine's, but this English commitment now seemed to find expression in France. For English domestic reasons of the 1760s, Paine's *Rights of Man* contributed in the 1790s to a debate on the institution of

---

[145] Chantal Thomas, *The Wicked Queen: The Origins of the Myth of Marie-Antoinette*, trans. Julie Rose (New York, 1999).

[146] Paine, *Rights of Man* (1791): *CW*, i. 258.

[147] Except in the pre-revolutionary sense of the term, 'a writer without a patron': Michael Sonenscher, *Sans-Culottes: An Eighteenth-Century Emblem in the French Revolution* (Princeton, 2008), 58.

[148] Paine, *Rights of Man* (1791): *CW*, i. 310 (text corrected). The French phrase is unlikely to have been chosen by Paine.

aristocracy that the Lewes exciseman could hardly have anticipated.[149] But until the proposals for economic redistribution in *Rights of Man. Part the Second*, the terms in which Paine cast his critique had hardly changed.

Neither Lafayette nor Paine seem to have appreciated the extent of the hatred that lay beneath French universalist discourse. Paine let this slip only in an English context:

> The origin of the government of England, so far as relates to what is called its line of monarchy, being one of the latest, is perhaps the best recorded. The hatred which the Norman invasion and tyranny begat, must have been deeply rooted in the nation, to have outlived the contrivance to obliterate it. Though not a courtier will talk of the curfeu-bell, not a village in England has forgotten it.

But if it was 'impossible that such governments as have hitherto existed in the world, could have commenced by any other means than a total violation of every principle, sacred and moral',[150] the same hatred (despite Paine's denial) would have been directed against the French monarchy also. By 1793, this was shown to have been the case, and the English debate on the French Revolution developed in response; but Paine did not follow this line of inference.

The starting point of the clash between Burke and Paine was not the tone of public opinion: it began in part as a conflict over history, first over 1688, then over the historical understanding of French events. This conflict centred on their narratives of certain key episodes, especially the fall of the Bastille and the October Days. Paine chose to emphasize the fall of the Bastille, an episode that Burke had passed over since he considered the October Days, as the fall of the monarchy, to matter more. On this later episode Paine had to reply to Burke on Burke's own ground, if Paine—at this stage still envisaging a transformed constitutional monarchy in France rather than a republic—was to vindicate the feasibility of a moderate and idealistic outcome to the Revolution. Here both Burke and Paine omitted and carefully rearranged evidence to support their two interpretations of the events of 5–6 October 1789. At many points, Paine 'evades rather than contests' Burke's account; Paine 'consistently omits or forgets any suggestion of intimidation or coercion'.[151]

Yet not for nothing had Paine written in January 1789, 'I am in some intimacy with Mr. Burke.'[152] Burke summed up the events of 6 October 1789 as 'the most important of all revolutions, which may be dated from that day, I mean a revolution in sentiments, manners, and moral opinions'.[153] Paine echoed him in writing that the Revolution as a whole 'has apparently burst forth like a creation from a chaos, but it is no more than the consequence of a mental revolution priorily exist-

---

[149] Amanda Goodrich, *Debating England's Aristocracy in the 1790s: Pamphlets, Polemics and Political Ideas* (Woodbridge, 2005).

[150] Paine, *Rights of Man. Part the Second* (1792): *CW*, i. 361.

[151] Steven Blakemore, 'Paine's Revolutionary Comedy: The Bastille and October Days in the Rights of Man', in Blakemore, *Crisis in Representation: Thomas Paine, Mary Wollstonecraft, Helen Maria Williams, and the Rewriting of the French Revolution* (London, 1997), 45–56.

[152] Paine to Jefferson, 15 Jan. 1789: Jefferson, *Papers*, xiv. 454.

[153] Burke, *Reflections*, ed. Clark, 243.

ing in France'.[154] It was not an interpretation unique to them. With some insight, John Adams in 1815 was to apply it retrospectively to the American Revolution: for him, the revolutionary war was only the 'Effect and Consequence' of the real revolution; 'The Revolution was in the Minds of the People, and this was effected, from 1760 to 1775, in the course of fifteen Years before a drop of blood was drawn at Lexington'.[155] If Paine and Burke were slow to see this in 1775–6, they were forewarned to appreciate it in 1789–90.

Paine and Burke were agreed in their subscription to watered-down natural law premises, in their consequent attachment to rights, in their suspicion of kingly power, and in their championing of religious toleration. Both condemned the abuses of French society before the Revolution. Neither had ever had much to say on chattel slavery, the expropriation and massacre of Native Americans, the position of women, or economic change. It was precisely because Burke and Paine were, in 1788, not far apart in their political views that their conflict in 1790 expressed an agonizing schism within intelligent Whig opinion. In theoretical terms, this schism might be made to appear as a conflict between universalism and particularism; in reality, each author drew on both.

Before the publication of *Rights of Man*, Paine continued to correspond with Burke. In 1798, Burke's early biographer Robert Bisset wrote that Paine called on Burke 'frequently' in 1788, and tried to persuade Burke of his, Paine's, view of France:

> People in general, he [Paine] asserted, did not know the change speedily about to take place in that country. The French, he averred, were determined to surpass every nation in liberty, and to establish a pure democracy. Mr. Burke saw that this was not an opinion resulting from Paine's penetration into principles and their probable effects, but from his knowledge of actually declared intentions. He was therefore the more certain that attempts would be made to carry these designs into effect. Paine prophesied that the same species of liberty would be extended to other countries; and, led away by his wishes, fancied all Europe would unite in overturning monarchy. Whether of himself, or from the suggestion of his French friends, Paine expressed his wishes that the British Opposition should coincide in the republican views, and *use parliamentary reform as the pretext*.

Bisset claimed, in retrospect, that Burke had repudiated this position from the outset:

> Burke answered to him, 'Do you mean to propose that I, who have all my life fought for the constitution, should devote the wretched remains of my days to conspire its destruction? Do not you know that I have always opposed the things called reform; to be sure, because I did not think them reform?' Paine, seeing Burke totally averse to his projects, forbore repetition... Paine went to France early in 1789, and wrote several letters from Paris to Burke, explaining to him the schemes of the popular leaders.

---

[154] Paine, *Rights of Man* (1791): *CW*, i. 298 (text corrected).

[155] John Adams to Thomas Jefferson, 24 Aug. 1815: *The Adams–Jefferson Letters*, ed. Lester J. Cappon (Chapel Hill, NC, 1959), 454–6, at 455. Adams added: 'The Records of thirteen Legislatures, the Pamp[h]lets, Newspapers in all the Colonies ought [to] be consulted, during that Period, to ascertain the Steps by which the public Opinion was enlightened and informed concerning the Authority of Parliament over the Colonies.' Paine might have done this.

In one of these, dated July 11th, he copied a note just received from a distinguished American gentleman [Jefferson], at whose house the republican chiefs held their most confidential meetings. 'The leaders (said the note) of the assembly surpass in patriotism; they are resolved to set fire to the four corners of France, rather than not reduce their principles to practice, to the last iota. Do not fear the army, we have gained them.'[156] Here we see Mr. Burke learned from Paine, not only that they were determined to overthrow the existing orders, but that they had provided the most effectual means by debauching the army from their duty. From Paine, indeed, he learned enough to render him inimical to the French revolution, even if his knowledge of it had been confined to the result of that person's communications.[157]

One reason for Paine's confidence was that he shared the old assumption that a revolution was a sudden event, not the unleashing of a developing process that might go on to have malign consequences as yet undisclosed. As he wrote to Burke on 17 January 1790: 'If we distinguish the Revolution from the Constitution, we may say, that the first is compleat, and the second is in a fair prospect of being so.' Consequently, for Paine, it was innocuous that 'The Revolution in France is certainly a Forerunner to other Revolutions in Europe.'[158] Burke took a different view; this led to his speech of 9 February 1790 on the Army Estimates, in which he first raised apocalyptic fears about events in France, and on to the *Reflections*, in which he felt towards a new understanding of revolution itself.[159]

Natural rights discourse

If not a celebration of Rousseau, or a denial of a conspiracy by Freemasons and *philosophes*, Paine's *Rights of Man* does seem self-evidently to centre on the phrase he adopted as its title. It did help rights language gain a wider currency in the 1790s. Yet this was not a novel idea before Paine gave it such emphasis. Natural rights language was familiar by the late seventeenth century, and was taken for granted in that virulent anti-ministerial and anti-monarchical London paper *The Crisis* of 1775–6.[160] The Church's doctrine of monogenesis (that mankind was descended from a single couple, Adam and Eve) had long predisposed the English to think of all individuals having rights. The occasional locution 'the rights of mankind' could there-

---

[156] Bisset quoted, inaccurately, Jefferson to Paine, 11 July 1789: Jefferson, *Papers*, xv. 266–9. It is not clear whether Paine sent Burke a copy of Jefferson's letter or paraphrased it.

[157] Bisset added: 'These are facts which I did not know when I wrote the first edition', published in 1798; Bisset now quoted 'a very eminent literary gentleman' who had visited Burke and reported at length on his views: Robert Bisset, *The Life of Edmund Burke* (2nd edn, 2 vols, London: George Cawthorn, 1800), ii. 284–7, 424, 432.

[158] Paine to Burke, 17 Jan. 1790: *The Correspondence of Edmund Burke*, ed. Thomas W. Copeland et al. (10 vols, Cambridge, 1958–78), vi. 67–75. Paine insinuated that the duc d'Orléans had instigated the march to Versailles, Paine adding: 'I am in this respect confident of the Authority I speak from', presumably Lafayette. For part of what may be Burke's reply, vi. 78–81.

[159] Burke, *Reflections*, ed. Clark, 69–72.

[160] *The Crisis*, XII, 8 Apr. 1775; LXXXIII, 17 Aug. 1776. The phrase 'the native rights of man' appears in a text that Paine knew: Giacinto, Marchese Dragonetti, *A Treatise on Virtues and Rewards* (London: Johnson and Payne, and J. Almon, 1769), 13.

fore be found,[161] coexisting with the politically more particularist idea of 'the rights of Englishmen'. The former could then be shortened to 'the rights of man' in the work of even so unrevolutionary an author as Sir William Blackstone.[162]

Nevertheless, natural rights are conventionally taken to be the essential principles of the 'age of revolution'; some accounts of 1776 still claim that universal rights were novel and transformative, driving individual emancipation in that revolution and its successors as particularist, legal rights gave way to universal human rights.[163] Others suggest that the developing French usage of *les droits de l'homme* was determinative of anglophone usage. These scenarios are questioned here, a questioning stemming from the reinterpretation of colonial discourses in the American Revolution offered above. Certainly, the French Revolution then created a new context for English debates on natural rights going beyond the impact in England of the American. Examined more closely, however, neither context immediately resulted in a novel, clearly defined, or irreversible development of natural rights doctrine by any anglophone participant.

The term 'rights' was already familiar in anglophone political discourse from 1688 and before. Such instances were undeveloped before the 1790s, implying no great sense of novelty. Such novelty is implied only by the present-day convention of contrasting a seventeenth-century discourse of rights as specific legal entitlements (for example, entitlements of Englishmen) with a late eighteenth-century discourse of rights as universal metaphysical human attributes. If the two ideas were indeed so distinct, the difference ought to have entailed a clean break from one political discourse to the other; yet the evidence reveals no clear-cut transition. In the early 1770s English churchmen and Nonconformists demanding greater doctrinal latitude could invoke 'the rights of humanity', even while that debate was also conducted in particularist terms.[164] It seems that in England the earliest heavy emphasis on 'the rights of man' came in the anti-slavery debate, in which the slaves'

[161] e.g. [William Knox], *The Controversy between Great Britain and her Colonies Reviewed* (London: J. Almon, 1769), 16, quoting the resolution of the Assembly of Massachustts Bay, 29 Oct. 1765.

[162] For Blackstone, the term could be 'summed up' as 'the natural liberty of mankind', and was 'a right inherent in us by birth, and one of the gifts of God to man at his creation': William Blackstone, *Commentaries on the Laws of England* (4 vols, Oxford, 1765–9), i. 121; 'the rights and liberties of mankind': Ant[hony] Benezet, *A Caution and Warning to Great Britain and Her Colonies, in A Short Representation of the Calamitous State of the Enslaved Negroes in the British Dominions* (Philadelphia: Henry Miller, 1766), 28; [Allan Ramsay], *Thoughts on the Origin and Nature of Government. Occasioned by The late Disputes between Great Britain and her American Colonies. Written in the Year 1766* (London: T. Becket and P. A. De Hondt, 1769), 19.

[163] Lounissi, *Paine*, 191–232.

[164] Joshua Toulmin, *Two Letters on the late Applications to Parliament by the Protestant Dissenting Ministers* (London: J. Johnson, 1774), 30, 35, 40. See also [Benjamin Dawson], *A Free and Candid Disquisition on Religious Establishments in General, and the Church of England in Particular* (London: B. White, 1771), 20, 22–3, 25, 67; [Richard Watson], *A Letter to the Members of the Honourable House of Commons; respecting the Petition for Relief in the Matter of Subscription. By a Christian Whig* (London: W. Bowyer and J. Nichols, 1772), 11; [Francis Blackburne], *Reflections on the Fate of a Petition For Relief in the Matter of Subscription, Offered to the Honourable House of Commons, February 6th, 1772* (London: no printer, 1772), 79, 84–6, 88; Philip Furneaux, *An Essay on Toleration* (London: T. Cadell, 1773), 13, 20–3, 34, 43, 60–1, 71–2; [John Disney], *A Short View of the Controversies occasioned by the Confessional, and the Petition to Parliament for Relief in the Matter of Subscription to the Liturgy and Articles of the Church of England* (London: J. Johnson, 1773), iii; [Edmund Law], *Considerations on the*

common humanity was emphasized by campaigners on both sides of the Atlantic,[165] and was applied to politics by a parliamentary reformer who was also an anti-slavery pioneer.[166] But this usage did not at once pass into daily speech as something new. That transference was owed not least to Paine himself, despite his evident non-involvement in anti-slavery campaigns.

However logically inconsistent, particularist and universalist accounts of rights had coexisted and were conventionally invoked together even by reformers or activists. When in 1773 the Boston publishers Edes and Gill produced the sole colonial edition of the second of Locke's *Two Treatises of Government* (1690), they advertised it at length in the *Boston Gazette*, commending it as a work that 'will give to every intelligent Reader a better View of the Rights of Men and of Englishmen'; even so, appealing to both sources, the edition was not a best-seller.[167] The precocious Alexander Hamilton published a pamphlet in 1775 that appealed to the conventional learned tradition—'Apply yourself, without delay, to the study of the law of nature. I would recommend to your perusal, Grotius, Puffendorf, Locke, Montesquieu, and Burlemaqui'—but based its main argument on the colonial charters, which, he claimed, did not recognize an authority in the Westminster Parliament to tax the colonies. Universalist rights, according to Hamilton, were only one component of this rationale, recognized by Congress:

> The deputies, chosen in the several provinces met at Philadelphia, according to appointment; and framed a set of resolves declarative of the rights of America, all which, I have by general arguments proved, are consonant to reason and nature; to the spirit of the British constitution and to the intention of our charters.[168]

If revitalized rights discourse had a major impact in the English-speaking world after *c.*1774, it did so exactly because it was already widely and diffusely accepted, impelled by deeper commitments, and embedded in conventional formulae, not because it was a novel invention of one thinker (or any small group of thinkers).[169]

Propriety of Requiring a Subscription to Articles of Faith (Cambridge: J. Archdeacon for T. & J. Merrill et al., 1774), 27.

[165] E.g. Thomas Cooper, *Letters on the Slave Trade, first published in Wheeler's Manchester Chronicle* (Manchester: C. Wheeler, 1787), 23, quoting G[eorge] Gregory, *Essays Historical and Moral* (London: J. Johnson, 1785), 310; Peter Peckard, *Justice and Mercy recommended, particularly with reference to the Slave Trade. A Sermon preached before the University of Cambridge* (Cambridge: J. Archdeacon et al., 1788), v; [Peter Peckard], *Am I Not a Man? And a Brother? With all Humility addressed to the British Legislature* (Cambridge: J. Archdeacon, 1788), iii, 19, 43–4, 86–7, 89, 94; 'Africanus', *Remarks on the Slave Trade, and the Slavery of Negroes* (London: J. Phillips and T. Payne, and Norwich: Chase, 1788), 1, 29; T[homas] Clarkson, *An Essay on the Comparative Efficiency of Regulation or Abolition, as applied to the Slave Trade* (London: James Phillips, 1789), 76.

[166] Granville Sharp, *A Declaration of the People's Natural Right to a Share in the Legislature; Which is the Fundamental Principle of the British Constitution of State* (London: B. White, 1774), xxv.

[167] Eric Slauter, 'Reading and Radicalization: Print, Politics, and the American Revolution', *Early American Studies* 8 (2010), 5–40, at 25.

[168] [Alexander Hamilton], *The Farmer Refuted: or, A more impartial and comprehensive View of the Dispute between Great-Britain and the Colonies, intended as a Further Vindication of the Congress* (New York: James Rivington, 1775), 5, 53.

[169] The contributors to Barry Alan Shain (ed), *The Nature of Rights at the American Founding and Beyond* (Charlottesville, Va, 2007) often conclude that colonial American rights claims were

When Englishmen on both sides of the Atlantic invoked universalist rights, they necessarily did so in a theistic context. Hamilton had to admit that New York, his colony, had no charter. He was therefore forced to appeal to a much wider rationale: 'The sacred rights of mankind are not to be rummaged for, among old parchments, or musty records. They are written, as with a sun beam, in the whole *volume* of human nature, by the hand of divinity itself; and can never be erased or obscured by mortal power.'[170] His key words were 'sacred' and 'divinity'. Since he was only 18, his sentiments are likely to have reflected the surrounding culture; for that reason he anticipated Paine's choice of terms. Thomas Jefferson's first draft of the Declaration of Independence in June 1776 began: 'We hold these truths to be sacred & undeniable; that all men are created equal & independant, that from that equal creation they derive rights inherent & inalienable, among which are the preservation of life, & liberty, & the pursuit of happiness.'[171] Such generalized aspirations were so platitudinous (Jefferson's key words were 'sacred' and 'created') that they could easily be abbreviated to 'self-evident' in the final text.

In either case such rights would be guaranteed (in the opinion of theists) by humanity's Creator. God could as easily be understood to will the particularist rights of Englishmen as the universalist rights of mankind; the first might be a special case of the second, or a mark of exclusive favour. For Jefferson and most of his contemporaries it was God who made rights self-evident, not a humanity made universalist by its secularity. Although Locke was sometimes cited in 1775–6, he was invoked far less often than the one being to whom even Locke had deferred, the Almighty. Consequently it waited for one of the first clearly identifiable English-speaking atheists, Jeremy Bentham, openly to dismiss natural rights doctrine as 'nonsense upon stilts'. For theists, why were rights self-evident? In 1792 Paine gave a similar answer to Jefferson's in 1776, praising the French Constitution for having as its foundation 'the rights of man': 'the principle is too obvious to admit of argument. The man who should venture to gainsay it would thereby establish his kinship to the fool who said in his heart there is no God'.[172]

'not primarily individualistic' but 'corporate', as in ascribing rights to 'the people', and that not until 1775–6 was this discourse, for many colonists, 'free from any historical moorings in British constitutionalism': 2–3. The Declaration of Independence was 'a listing of grievances, rather than ... an original philosophical treatise laying out a novel theory of individual rights': Shain, 'Rights Natural and Civil in the Declaration of Independence', 116–62 at 144.

[170] [Hamilton], *The Farmer Refuted*, 38. T. H. Breen, 'An Appeal to Heaven: The Language of Rights on the Eve of American Independence', in Robert Fatton Jr and R. K. Ramazani (eds), *The Future of Liberal Democracy: Thomas Jefferson and the Contemporary World* (Basingstoke, 2004), 65–83, at 74.

[171] Quoted in Lynn Hunt, *Inventing Human Rights: A History* (New York, 2007), 15. Hunt contends this self-evidence indicates that the late eighteenth century saw a 'sudden crystallization' of a new idea of 'human rights'; that this reflected a widespread prior shift in sensibility towards empathy with the individual, embodied in the new literary genre of the novel; and that 'sometime between 1689 and 1776 rights that had been viewed most often as the rights of a particular people—freeborn English men, for example—were transformed into human rights, universal natural rights', 21–2. See also Dan Edelstein, 'Enlightenment Rights Talk', *Journal of Modern History* 86 (2014), 530–65, esp. s. III, 'From Reason to Sentiment'. The present work explores a different argument. Evidence is lacking that Paine ever read a novel.

[172] Paine, 'Answer to Four Questions on the Legislative and Executive Powers' (June–July 1792): *CW*, ii. 522.

Ascribing rights to divine fiat had discouraged further enquiry into their nature and content, but this lacuna presented no difficulties if familiar truths were being rehearsed on both sides of the anglophone Atlantic.[173] Even Mary Wollstonecraft's famous and impassioned reply to Burke did not explain the nature of rights other than to say (as would Paine) that 'the rights of men' were 'Sacred rights!' which 'we received, at our birth, as men...from God'.[174] No different explanation of rights was forthcoming from the Foxite political writer James Mackintosh, who also wrote of 'the sacred rights of Nature' (only later did this seem a contradiction). In his reply to Burke's *Reflections*, second only to Paine's, Mackintosh disclaimed 'any elaborate research into the metaphysical principles of politics and ethics'. 'We are besides absolved from the necessity of it in a controversy with Mr. Burke, who himself recognizes, in the most ample form, the existence of those natural rights.' Mackintosh was only incensed by Burke's claims that men had given up all their natural rights on entering into civil society. Only some rights were so surrendered, Mackintosh replied.[175]

For Thomas Christie, a Scots enthusiast for the French Revolution, rights were 'our most sacred rights'; the 'laws of nature' were 'his [God's] laws'; and for Christie 'The subsequent conventions of civilized society cannot take away the rights of nature, because such conventions were formed for the very purpose of maintaining these rights.' If violated, 'The right of resistance ought to be exercised.' Rights were known in that kingdom from the beginning, so that 'the present constitution of France is not an audacious novelty, but a glorious recovery of original rights; a restoration of the ancient system.'[176] The English Dissenter Joseph Priestley wrote similarly. For him, rights were merely those that had been 'usually termed *natural*'; he offered no deeper analysis. Instead, he negated the idea that 'mankind, when once they have entered into a state of society, necessarily abandon all their proper *natural rights*, and thenceforth have only such as they derive from society'. Consequently, if the magistrates violated those rights without 'an equivalent' the people were 'certainly at liberty to consider the original compact as broken'.[177]

Capel Lofft, a Peterhouse Latitudinarian, now a Unitarian and founder member of the Society for Constitutional Information, wrote similarly: he too argued contentiously that 'a surrender of primary independent rights, to preserve secondary adventitious rights, the whole of natural liberty for a precarious portion of civil, is

---

[173] For the 'vagueness' of much Anglo-American rights discourse in the eighteenth century see John Philip Reid, *Constitutional History of the American Revolution: The Authority of Rights* (Madison, 1986), 10–11, 93.

[174] [Mary Wollstonecraft], *A Vindication of the Rights of Men, in a Letter to the Right Honourable Edmund Burke; occasioned by his Reflections on the Revolution in France* (London: J. Johnson, 1790), 21, 73.

[175] James Mackintosh, *Vindiciae Gallicae. Defence of the French Revolution and its English Admirers against the Accusations of the Right Hon. Edmund Burke; including some Strictures on the late Production of Mons. De Calonne* (London: G. G. J. and J. Robinson, 1791), 204–13, 219–20, 304.

[176] Thomas Christie, *Letters on the Revolution in France, and on the New Constitution established by the National Assembly: occasioned by the Publications of the Right Hon. Edmund Burke, M.P. and Alexander de Calonne, late Minister of State* (Part I, London: J. Johnson, 1791), 16, 21, 25, 70–1.

[177] Joseph Priestley, *Letters to the Right Honourable Edmund Burke, occasioned by his Reflections on the Revolution in France, &c.* (Birmingham: Thomas Pearson, and London: J. Johnson, 1791), 24–5.

an imaginary compact'. But the nature of those natural rights he described in equally conventional terms: whatever men's civil rights, 'the rights of men, the honour of intellectual and moral agents, the illustrious rank of men determined to be free, is of date far higher, and of origin transcendently more venerable'. Lofft's catalogue of rights was therefore merely that which 'conscience, humanity, and the public interest requires us to recognize'. Natural rights were 'clearly ascertainable': Lofft saw no problem in specifying them. If they were violated, 'redress' could only be by 'the extraordinary and collective interposition of the Community as such'.[178] For the Arian Presbyterian minister and reforming pamphleteer Joseph Towers, rights were simply 'the common rights of mankind'.[179] But such generalized language was evidence that rights had become truisms in a diverse and ill-defined anglophone theistic rights discourse.

Without clear definitions of sources, all shades of opinion in England had long appealed to 'rights' both particularist and universalist.[180] Although universalist terms were available, the most practically effective and most common locution had been 'the rights of Englishmen' or some variant of it.[181] Specific and legally defined rights, privileges, or liberties were acquired by being born an Englishman, that is (in law), being born a subject of the king. Such legal privileges were therefore often described as being (like allegiance to the person of the king, what would now be called nationality) birthrights: inherent, hereditary, unalienable, or indefeasible, just as allegiance could not be renounced. Natural rights were also familiar to a learned audience since their seventeenth-century heyday in the works of authors like Hugo Grotius, John Selden, Samuel Pufendorf, and John Locke. Long before the meanings read into 'human rights' after 1948, older rights discourse could also be taken in an egalitarian direction. Thus a Latitudinarian clergyman in 1718 argued against a divine right in rulers: 'all Men are *equal* in Nature, and have *equal* Natural Rights; and so one Man cannot *naturally* have any more Power over another, than another over him.' Civil laws must therefore express 'the common Rights of Mankind'.[182]

---

[178] Capel Lofft, *Remarks on the Letter of the Rt. Hon. Edmund Burke, Concerning the Revolution in France, and on the Proceedings in Certain Societies in London, Relative to that Event* (London: J. Johnson, 1790), 32, 36, 38–40.

[179] Joseph Towers, *Thoughts on the Commencement of a New Parliament. With an Appendix, containing Remarks on the Letter of the Right Hon. Edmund Burke, on the Revolution in France* (London: Charles Dilly, 1790), 53.

[180] Hunt, *Inventing Human Rights*, 122.

[181] e.g. [Thomas Wagstaffe], *The Rights and Liberties of Englishmen* (London: A. Baldwin, 1701); *The Judgment of Whole Kingdoms and Nations... Shewing... An Account of the British Government, and the Rights and Priviledges of the People in the time of the Saxons, and since the Conquest* (London: T. Harrison, 1710); *A Guide to the Knowledge of the Rights and Privileges of Englishmen* (London: J. Scott, 1757); *The Rights and Liberties of the People of England Vindicated* (London: W. Nicoll, [?1770]); [Allan Ramsay], *A Plan of Reconciliation between Great Britain and her Colonies... By which the Rights of Englishmen, in Matters of Taxation, are preserved to the Inhabitants of America, and the Islands beyond Atlantic* (London: J. Johnson, 1776); [John Cartwright], *A Declaration of the Rights of Englishmen* (no place, no printer, [?1784]).

[182] John Jackson, *The Grounds of Civil and Ecclesiastical Government Briefly Consider'd, To which is added, A Defence of the Bishop of Bangor, Against the Objections of Mr Law* (2nd edn, London: James Knapton, 1718), 8, 11, 98, quoted in De Bolla, *The Architecture of Concepts*, 108; for indefeasible

Before the 1790s this appeal to 'mankind' did not prevalently reconceive claims as 'the rights of man', despite occasional anticipations in respect of religious rights.[183] But English friends of the American Revolution echoed or appropriated colonial universalist usages, and these usages grew in England into the 1790s. New usages were however new in placing emphasis on certain aspects of an old and diverse pattern of discourse. It is open to debate whether 'the rights of Englishmen' was a phrase only extended rhetorically into 'the rights of mankind', a locution also found throughout the century, and whether this phrase was in turn merely shortened to 'the rights of man' in the 1790s without these verbal changes marking a transformation in the content of the concept from rights as legal privileges and as divine gifts to rights as secular human attributes.[184] Indeed, if a wholly new and transformative understanding of 'rights' was born in 1776 or 1789 it becomes difficult to explain how such rights so soon receded in English, French, and American political discourse, not resuming a salient role until after (perhaps several decades after) the United Nations' Universal Declaration of Human Rights of 1948.

The use of universalist terms nevertheless grew. It was promoted in the English anti-slavery campaigns of the 1760s and 1770s, modest in size though these still were. It was taken further by heterodox Nonconformists in their campaigns against the Test and Corporation Acts in 1772–4. In colonial America from 1775 armed rebellion, which could not easily be justified on the basis of black-letter law, compelled recourse in some quarters to a far more rhetoricized and unspecific idea of natural rights.

Some Whig opponents of rebellion could therefore react with indignation at colonists' appropriation of a part of the Whig tradition; other Whigs endorsed it. On 20 January 1775, the 1st Earl of Chatham chose a debate in the House of Lords on a motion that the British troops be withdrawn from Boston for a major speech, siding with the colonists. Josiah Quincy, a New England activist who was present, reported the debate. Lord Camden '(undoubtedly the first common lawyer in England)' agreed with Chatham's defence of the colonists, Camden declaring: 'The natural rights of man and the immutable laws of nature are all with that people.' Another Whig politician, the widely experienced 1st Earl Gower, disagreed: 'a very remarkable saying of Lord Gower's I cannot omit. His Lordship said, "I am for enforcing these measures (and with great sneer and contempt); let the Americans sit talking about their natural and divine rights, their rights as men and citizens; their rights from God and nature."'[185] Quincy was evidently shocked; but Gower (if

---

right, 151, 155. De Bolla cautions against assuming 'that a "transformation" in conceptual architecture occurred between, say, 1730 and 1790', 112.

[183] [Matthew Tindal], *An Essay Concerning the Power of the Magistrate, and the Rights of Mankind, in Matters of Religion* (London: Andrew Bell, 1697).

[184] I have argued elsewhere that the phrase 'a radical reformer' (meaning a supporter of parliamentary reform on the principle of universal suffrage) was shortened to 'a radical' in the 1790s without anticipating that new coinage of the 1820s, 'radicalism'.

[185] 'Journal of Josiah Quincy, Jun., during his Voyage and Residence in England from September 28th, 1774, to March 3d, 1775', *Proceedings of the Massachusetts Historical Society* 3rd ser. 50 (1916–17), 433–96, at 462–3; Richard C. Simmons and P. D. G. Thomas (eds), *Proceedings and Debates of the British Parliaments Respecting North America 1754–1783* (6 vols, Millwood, NY, 1982–6), v. 267–87, at 273–4, 284. Quincy is the only source for Gower's remark.

correctly reported) had begun the demonization of an old truism, universalist rights, a demonization that was to have a major impact in Britain in the 1790s.

This universalist usage had been much less in evidence in the early 1760s. It was conventional in the Stamp Act crisis of 1765 for colonists to claim, as did Patrick Henry, 'all the Liberties and Privileges, Franchises and Immunities, that have at any Time been held, enjoyed, and possessed by the people of *Great Britain*'.[186] Benjamin Franklin wrote in 1771 of 'the Stand so generally made throughout the Colonies in Defence of their Privileges'.[187] Privileges, unlike rights, could easily seem unequal. A claim of 'equality' in colonial discourse still generally meant a legal fiction of colonial Englishmen's equality with metropolitan Englishmen (however different their perceptions), not the equality of all human beings with each other.

Into the 1770s, Englishmen in England and America could still appeal simultaneously to many different grounds for their claims without a sense of contradiction. In September 1774 the First Continental Congress resolved, in the words of John Adams, 'to found our rights upon the laws of Nature, the principles of the English Constitution, and charters and compacts'. But the Congress, after weeks of debate, did not specify the rights that had been violated, given the great differences between each colony's legal status; Congress therefore fell back on a claim (making much less use of rights) that each colony had the procedural authority to legislate for itself in internal matters. If they were no longer claiming the rights of Englishmen, however, colonists were soon led to appeal, as did Congress in October 1774, to 'the Natural Rights of Mankind'. Even then, Silas Deane still linked this phrase with 'The Rights of British Subjects, in general'.[188] Far from being a war of colonial liberation, fuelled by novel ideas rapidly and consensually adopted in a new world, the conflict of 1776–83 took the form of a civil war between long-familiar groups, established opinion on both sides of the Atlantic being divided in similar ways over the implications of a shared, long-standing, and diverse rights discourse.[189]

Although there were anticipations, only in 1775–6 did many colonists self-consciously seek to escape their allegiance by asserting that they had been placed outside of the state's protection by George III's declaration that they were in a state of rebellion. If so, the rebels no longer saw themselves as Englishmen; they had by default to claim an exalted, ennobling identity as men. Their understandings of rights could only be influenced by their violent act of self-isolation, with rights becoming of necessity 'comfortably vague'. Even then, ideas of equal human rights

---

[186] De Bolla, *The Architecture of Concepts*, 150n.; cf. James Otis in 1764: Hunt, *Inventing Human Rights*, 120.

[187] Benjamin Franklin, *Autobiography*, in Franklin, *Writings*, ed. J. A. Leo Lemay (New York, 1987), 1372.

[188] De Bolla, *The Architecture of Concepts*, 187, 193, 197.

[189] Clark, *Language of Liberty, passim*. Although colonists after 1775 began increasingly to use the phrase 'appeal to heaven' as an excuse for bloodshed, this usage was not novel, not especially American, and not necessarily indebted to Locke: his was one voice among many, and the major contest over the ownership of his legacy took place in England. An appeal to heaven was at that time an appeal to *heaven*, not to secular human rights. The phrase had been commonplace in seventeenth-century English religious discourse. Although less often found in the mid-eighteenth century, it survived in more backward parts of the empire, notably New England, and so could be given heavy emphasis.

'were in little demand' in the politics of the new American republic.[190] The phrase 'rights of man' was 'not much in use in the America of the 1770s'; there was, rather, much negative use made of the idea of the natural rights of individuals, that is, of American individuals, against the British state.[191] Equality now evolved into a legal fiction asserting that all 'men' (that is, property-owning white Trinitarian Protestant adult males siding with independence) possessed equal rights (however different their perceptions), not that such men were equal with Loyalists. In this form, universalist rights discourse was more a later consequence than a preceding cause of the American Revolution, and cannot be analysed as its essence.

The phrase *droits de l'homme* existed in French elite discourse from the 1760s in the writings of such authors as Voltaire and Rousseau, but with 'at first little explicit definition'.[192] This suggests that the locution was not widely perceived as a transformational novelty, calling for explanation. Only in and after 1789 were many Frenchmen led by events to see themselves less and less (and finally not at all) as subjects of a king but, instead, as men: like American colonists, their new need for an exalted conception of their rights-possessing humanity was suddenly urgent. Paine captured this need: in France, by the abolition of titles, 'the *peer* is exalted into MAN'.[193] In both cases there was an unexpected consequence as the legal fiction of the equality of 'man' gradually strengthened the legal fiction of the collectivity, the republic, or the nation. If all people were the same, they formed an undifferentiated mass: individualism paradoxically led on to totalitarian democracy. In both American and French geographical settings such practicalities came first, theory lagged confusedly behind.

No major shift of meaning was yet echoed by the Englishman Paine in *Common Sense*: there Paine was concerned to negate 'hereditary right', not to affirm or develop a new idea of natural rights as such. He continued to use an older language. His Introduction spoke of 'the natural rights of all mankind', but also announced that people had 'an undoubted Privilege' (not right) to enquire into abuses of power. His text continued to employ this positive sense of 'privilege'. By the Fall, man was subjected to 'Satan' and, by obedience, to 'Sovereignty': 'both disable us from

[190] De Bolla, *The Architecture of Concepts*, 131–205, at 138, 140, 148, 196. There was then 'an American turn away from universalism in the 1780s'; a 'long gap' intervened until 1948 in which 'talk of universally applicable natural rights subsided': Hunt, *Inventing Human Rights*, pp. 126, 176. This long gap signals a major difficulty in the interpretation of the American and French Revolutions. In recording the absence over many decades of a later-celebrated neologism, the recent historiography of universal human rights is symmetrical with the recent historiography of the concept of revolution.

[191] Michael Zuckert, 'Natural Rights in the American Revolution: The American Amalgam', in Jeffrey N. Wasserstrom, Greg Grandin, Lynn Hunt, and Marilyn B. Young (eds), *Human Rights and Revolutions* (2nd edn, Lanham, Md, 2007), 65–82, at 65–6. Zuckert outlines three interpretations of the role of rights language in the American Revolution, which he terms the Succession Thesis, the Irrelevancy Thesis, and the Amalgam Thesis. The interpretation advanced here, consistent with the idea of 'amalgam', might be identified as the Default Thesis. Much that followed 1776 and 1789 in political discourse was an unintended consequence, not a foundational novelty.

[192] 'Most of those using the phrase in the 1770s and 1780s in France, such as the controversial Enlightenment figures d'Holbach and Mirabeau, referred to the rights of man as if they were obvious and needed no justification or definition; they were in other words self-evident': Hunt, *Inventing Human Rights*, 23–6, at 25.

[193] Paine, *Rights of Man* (1791): *CW*, i. 286.

reassuming some former state and privilege.' In wholly conventional terms Paine explained the purpose of a written constitution, a 'Continental Charter', as being 'to support the right of every separate part, whether of religion, personal freedom, or property', not universal human rights.[194] In the revolutionary war, he continued to boast of a people resisting because of 'an attachment to rights and privileges',[195] not because they had devised a new understanding of universal natural rights.

In his publications of the 1790s Paine discussed none of the other replies to Burke. Consequently he gave the impression (as so often in his writings) of arguing from a novel access to first principles, where he was in reality restating the often-stated truisms of his contemporaries in more vivid language. Only in *Rights of Man* did 'privilege' begin to take on a newly pejorative meaning: in the Estates-General 'The majority of the aristocracy claimed what they called the privilege of voting as a separate body, and of giving their consent or their negative in that manner; and many of the bishops and the high-beneficed clergy claimed the same privilege on the part of their Order.'[196] But this sentence occurred in the passage here re-attributed to Lafayette. If Paine was not the primary author, he responded to French denunciations of *les privilégiés*, the privileged people, a more reified locution; he was not its pioneer.

Only by 1797 had Paine himself absorbed this different meaning and accepted an antithesis, writing to a French opponent: 'You claim a privilege incompatible with the Constitution and with Rights.'[197] Even then, he did not theorize any such change.[198] The pamphleteer who had caught the significance of the notion of privilege in the approach to the Revolution was not Paine but Emmanuel Joseph Sieyès, whose pamphlets, including *Essai sur les privilèges* (November 1788) and *Qu'est-ce que le tiers-état?* (January 1789), had great influence in shaping French thought.[199] Indeed Sieyès gave privilege a central place in his analysis, as Paine did not: 'The prejudice which supports privilege is the most pernicious that ever affected the earth, it is more intimately connected with the social organization than any other, it corrupts more deeply, and it interests a far greater number in its defence.' By contrast to 'privilege', the concept 'feudal', often found in the *cahiers des doléances*, made only two perfunctory appearances in Sieyès's text.[200] On the famous

---

[194] [Paine], *Common Sense* (1776): *CW*, i. 3, 14, 37 (text corrected).

[195] Paine, *The American Crisis*, V (21 Mar, 1778): *CW*, i. 124.

[196] Paine, *Rights of Man* (1791): *CW*, i. 308.

[197] *Letter from Thomas Paine, to Camille Jordan, of the Council of Five Hundred. Occasioned by his Report on the Priests, Public Worship, and the Bells* (1797): *CW*, ii. 759.

[198] For an argument that Paine's *Rights of Man* revealed the emergence of a concept of rights as residing not in the individual but in 'the collective category man' see De Bolla, *The Architecture of Concepts*, 244. But 'the rights of the people', an unambiguously collective category, had been a familiar locution throughout the eighteenth century. As De Bolla notes, 'Although there can be little doubt that the publication of *Rights of Man* increased the circulation of the phrase *the rights of man*, it is not so clear that Paine's text prompted, encouraged or effected widespread use of the noetic concept "rights of man"', 269, 272–3.

[199] Emmanuel Joseph Sieyès, *Political Writings Including the Debate between Sieyès and Tom Paine in 1791*, ed. Michael Sonenscher (Indianapolis, 2003). Only the first of these two titles was available in English translation in Paine's lifetime.

[200] *An Essay on Privileges, and particularly on Hereditary Nobility. Written by the Abbé Sieyes, a Member of the National Assembly; and Translated into English, with Notes, by a Foreign Nobleman, now*

night of 4 August 1789 (and again in a decree of 11 August) the National Assembly responded to a new usage, abolishing 'the feudal regime' by abolishing privileges (not by abolishing any tie between land tenure and military service).

It becomes more understandable that Paine was not fully aware of the significance of such changes in discourse if they were generally adopted later than was implied by the old historiographical practice of seeing the period from 1760 to 1800 as a unified 'age of the democratic revolution'. It is now evident that it was in and after 1789, not in and after 1776, that the phrases 'rights of man' and 'rights of men' grew exponentially in English usage: the senses in which the American Revolution created a new world of discourse need to be carefully qualified. That 'rights of man' and 'rights of men' grew so greatly in usage in England after 1789, and in such a short time frame, suggests a response to events in France and to the French idea of *les droits de l'homme* seems to have taken priority. Had the most likely dominant cause been the domestic British or American coinage of a new ideology, 1776 would probably already have had that effect.

If this numerical increase in anglophone usage was a reaction to the French Revolution, it suggests in turn that no new English meanings need have been central. As late as 1789, 'rights of man' was used only as frequently as 'rights and privileges'.[201] The location or ownership of rights may have changed more than the perceived nature of rights themselves. Where 'rights' had been most associated with the word 'church' in 1700–20, in the years 1780–1800 'rights' grew to be associated with 'people'. But even the locution 'human rights' was occasionally used in English-language publications throughout the century,[202] and if examples of its use grew in *c.*1780–1800 it was growth from a very low base: it is not clear that a few more such uses transformed familiar meanings.

Whether a secular idea of 'universal human rights' was *ever* formulated in a way to make it coherent or effective is beyond the scope of this study.[203] If it was not, however, one cannot employ an historical teleology leading in a straight line from rights as legal privileges in the seventeenth century to rights as universal, secular human attributes in the late twentieth. Discourse was always more plural, and more indebted to the past, than even contemporaries appreciated. Once more, in the late eighteenth century negations (the uses to which 'rights' were put to identify and denounce enemies) may have been as important as affirmations (the use of 'rights' to visualize or define a better future populated by friends). A new basis for a right

---

in England (London: J. Ridgway, 1791), 74–5; for 'feudal times' and 'the unenlightened remains of the feudal system', 32, 53. Its anonymous English translator, a critic of Burke, asserted that to the publications of Sieyès '*are attributed in a great measure, the important changes which have been so happily effected in France, and particularly the* abolition of Titles and Nobility', 2. The translator also drew explicit parallels with England, 3, 16–17, 27, 29, 37.

[201] Dan Edelstein, 'Intellectual History and Digital Humanities', *Modern Intellectual History* 31 (2016), 237–46.

[202] De Bolla, *The Architecture of Concepts*, 48–50, 83, 88, 102–3, 106, 113. De Bolla argues that in the 1790s 'this increase in use of the phrase *the rights of man* does not provide evidence for a generally accepted or understood concept of universal or "human rights" in any significant sense', 213, 273.

[203] For a rejection of this idea see G. R. Elton, 'Human Rights and the Liberties of Englishmen', *University of Illinois Law Review* (1990), 329–46.

to vote, individual personality, was indeed worked out in England from the 1760s; but it was an idea only slowly adopted, and was not openly and explicitly embraced even by Paine. New ideas were often less powerful than familiar ones that could bear a sudden rhetorical emphasis.

Before 1791 the most famous expression in England of a new emphasis on rights had been the sermon by Richard Price that triggered Edmund Burke's *Reflections on the Revolution in France*. Price had sought to re-express patriotism as a (universalist) 'principle of universal benevolence', the only alternative to which was, he claimed, a (particularist) 'principle holding together a band of robbers in their attempts to crush all liberty but their own'. By Price's standard, 'most' actually-existing governments were

> usurpations on the rights of men, and little better than contrivances for enabling the *few* to oppress the *many*. Convince them that the Deity is a righteous and benevolent as well as omnipotent being, who regards with equal eye all his creatures, and connects his favour with nothing but an honest desire to know and do his will; and that zeal for mystical doctrines which has led men to hate and harass one another will be exterminated.

It was this realization which 'helps to prepare the minds of men for the recovery of their rights, and hastens the overthrow of priestcraft and tyranny'. The usage was familiar, for the idea of 'priestcraft' had long defined the rights that priests allegedly denied. Price famously listed the 'rights' which, he contended, had been vindicated by the Revolution of 1688,[204] but even then wrote nothing new about the nature of rights as such or about any new rights (for example, for slaves and women) not discussed in 1688–9 but that might now be achieved.

He did not need to. For Price as for others, a theological doctrine, Arianism, meant that rights now became an engine of revolution. If the social institutions underwritten by a Trinitarian God had no divine authority, only the people could be sovereign and only their individual entitlements could be the principles validating their actions. Political clichés about delegated authority, trust, and contract, long familiar to Whigs, became sensational in this revived intellectual context. Price not only sought to redefine the love of one's country; he sought to internationalize patriotism by linking it to what, he argued, may 'be called the Religion of Benevolence. Nothing can be more friendly to the general rights of mankind.' He did not define either. Although best known for his peroration, memorably claiming, 'I have lived to see the rights of men better understood than ever', he did not explain how, or why they were better understood; and even Price could write in the familiar plural of men's 'common rights and liberties'.[205] The most powerful term, for Price, was 'religion', not 'rights'.

Paine is sometimes treated as a harbinger of a secular (and therefore potentially universal) theory of natural rights on the strength of his argument in 1777 that 'A *natural* right is an animal right; and the power to act it, is supposed, either fully or

---

[204] Price, *A Discourse on the Love of our Country*, 6, 12–14, 34.
[205] Price, *A Discourse on the Love of our Country*, 5, 8, 12, 49.

in part, to be mechanically contained within ourselves as individuals.' But this sentence appears in an anonymous article in the *Pennsylvania Journal* that has been wrongly attributed to Paine.[206] These were never his views. Paine's view of rights was premised on the assumptions generated by his Deism, with a residual influence from Trinitarian Anglicanism; because of his generalizing Deist creed, he seems never to have used the phrase 'the rights of Englishmen' in his published writings. Instead, as is argued here, Paine deployed two accounts of rights, slightly different but neither dependent on English institutions or underwritten by the Church: one, that they were given anew to every individual at the moment of that individual's creation, and so were personal to that individual rather than to a collective 'humanity'; two, that rights derived from divine grant at the creation of mankind, and then descended by indefeasible hereditary succession. In both accounts the key actor was God: Paine, like his English ancestors of the seventeenth century, began as a divine right theorist.

The phrase 'rights of man' proliferated at the end of the eighteenth century, and was accompanied by a growing if infrequent use of 'human rights'. Both have been seen as marking a step change in understandings of rights, but it is difficult to establish such a divide from Paine's writings. A word count within texts does not settle this question, but can help reveal meanings. *Rights of Man* included 'human rights' just once, and then only in the borrowed English translation of the text of the *Déclaration des droits de l'homme et du citoyen*; again, just once Paine used the singular 'human right', but evidently was not inspired by the French usage to employ it except rarely.[207] In *Rights of Man. Part the Second* the phrase also occurred just once: 'The hereditary system, therefore, is as repugnant to human wisdom, as to human rights', a locution that may have been driven by style.[208] In *The Age of Reason* Paine used many seemingly cognate phrases—'human inventions', 'human sight', 'human language', 'human reason', 'human speech', 'human opinions', 'human life', 'the human mind', 'human comprehension'—but 'human rights' not at all.[209] That the citizens of the new American republic considered Paine as 'the friend of human rights' was not Paine's phrase but James Monroe's, in a letter that Paine reprinted in 1796.[210] Paine, then, knew the phrase 'human rights' by 1791; despite knowing it, he made nothing of it.

His chosen titles for his most famous works were *Common Sense*, not *Rights of Americans*; *Rights of Man*, not *Human Rights*. Although Paine wrote in the second of rights being possessed by a universalist collective 'man' in the abstract, he wrote equally of rights being possessed by 'men', by all particular individuals, with no sense of an inconsistency.[211] He was also limited in his outreach to the whole of

---

[206] 'Candid and Critical Remarks on a Letter signed Ludlow': *CW*, ii. 274. For the de-attribution, see Appendix: Paine De-attributions.

[207] 'Immortal power is not a human right': Paine, *Rights of Man* (1791): *CW*, i. 254, 313.

[208] Paine, *Rights of Man. Part the Second* (1792): *CW*, i. 367.

[209] Paine, *The Age of Reason* (1794): *CW*, i. 464, 473, 477, 482, 483, 487, 492, 506.

[210] Paine, *Letter to George Washington* (1796): *CW*, ii. 701.

[211] 'That men, should take up arms, and spend their lives and fortunes, *not* to maintain their rights'; 'men are all of *one degree*, and consequently that all men are born equal, and with equal natural rights'; 'The rights of men in society are neither devisable, nor transferable, nor annihilable, but are descendible

humanity, since in this work Paine's conception of rights as the gift of a God understood still in derivative Christian terms inevitably limited the applicability of his theory to people of other religions. This global dimension was one that Paine nowhere explored. By appropriating the phrase for his title, Paine was bidding to identify a familiar and local natural rights doctrine solely with the idea of 'a Regeneration of man' that went beyond sudden and swiftly completed political change in any particular country.[212] This 'regeneration' could only be an echo of a spiritual rebirth.

One famous opponent of the French Revolution had already begun to back away from natural rights doctrine, but not because the Whig tradition had rejected rights. Burke had qualified his position, writing of the English supporters of the French Revolution: 'In denying their false claims of right, I do not mean to injure those which are real, and are such as their pretended rights would totally destroy.' But Burke's negations of 'natural rights', in rhetorical phrases, were more memorable.[213] Just as the American Revolution seemingly made a new arena for universalist rights language, in which Paine's often particularist *Common Sense* could be misread, so in turn did the French Revolution and *les droits de l'homme* do the same for Paine's *Rights of Man*. As in 1776, so in 1791, the circulation of Paine's works did not prove that he fully shared the political discourses of America or France.[214]

Paine's contribution to the later development of natural rights theory was negative as well as positive, the first an unintended consequence of the full working out of his Deism. Both of Paine's accounts of the acquisition of rights depended on divine grant, which arguably could only be known through historic record of revelation. But in *The Age of Reason* he wrote that 'Revelation is necessarily limited to the first communication—after this it is only an account of something which that person says was a revelation made to him', like the Ten Commandments. This called in question the hereditary descent of rights given to mankind at the Creation. Paine poured scorn on the biblical account of that event:

> As to the account of the creation, with which the book of Genesis opens, it has all the appearance of being a tradition which the Israelites had among them before they came into Egypt; and after their departure from that country they put it at the head of their history, without telling (as it is most probable) that they did not know how they came by it. The manner in which the account opens shows it to be traditionary...Why it has been called the Mosaic account of the creation, I am at a loss to conceive. Moses... neither told it nor believed it.

only'; 'Every man is proprietor in society, and draws on the capital as a matter of right'; 'Does Mr. Burke mean to deny that *man* has any rights?'; 'the divine origin of the rights of man at the creation'; 'the equality of man, so far from being a modern doctrine, is the oldest upon record'; 'Natural rights are those which appertain to man in right of his existence': Paine, *Rights of Man* (1791): *CW*, i. 250, 273–6, 325.

[212] Paine, *Rights of Man* (1791): *CW*, i. 317 (text corrected).

[213] Burke, *Reflections*, ed. Clark: for his qualifications, 217, 380; for his negations, 151, 162, 173, 232, 235, 244, 250, 272–3, 279, 281–2, 311, 347–8, 364, 390, 409.

[214] 'Rather than the result of gradual conceptual shifts in English discourse, or even the publication of Paine's influential book, the sudden explosion of this term is more likely explained by events across the Channel': Edelstein, 'Intellectual History and Digital Humanities'.

A rationale that was merely 'traditionary' had no other authority. Indeed, it was radically secular, and far short of Burke's theistic vision. According to Paine, 'the word of God cannot exist in any written or human language'. Instead, 'The creation speaks a universal language, independently of human speech or human language...it publishes itself from one end of the earth to the other.' But in celebrating this language Paine did not argue that it contained a specification of rights. It is not clear that Paine appreciated that his argument in *The Age of Reason* undermined his case for the authority of natural rights, although his own brief 'profession of faith' in that work did not mention them.

Indeed, were rights necessary in a Deist republic? 'What more does man want to know than that the hand or power that made these things [the heavens] is divine, is omnipotent? Let him believe this with the force it is impossible to repel, if he permits his reason to act, and his rule of moral life will follow of course.' 'The Almighty Lecturer' taught man that 'He can now provide for his own comfort, AND LEARN FROM MY MUNIFICENCE TO ALL, TO BE KIND TO EACH OTHER.' Paine's Almighty Lecturer included no teaching on rights in his lectures. 'Rights' was a term wholly missing from *The Age of Reason* apart from its title page, which ironically described Paine as the author of *Rights of Man*.[215] That Paine returned to a conception of something like ancient, divine rights in *Agrarian Justice*, his proposed reforms the consequence of a secularized echo of the Fall, did not reverse the trend: *The Age of Reason* had far more impact, and a far wider circulation, than *Agrarian Justice*.

Natural rights doctrine can only have been weakened by the contrast between its universalism and unfolding events in France; but this did not abolish the need of reformers to dignify their goals. 'Rights' could hardly be objected to, and reformers did not renounce them; but after the publication of *The Age of Reason* the misleading image of Paine as an infidel contributed to the debate in ways that he probably did not anticipate. Many English reformers in *c*.1800–30, among whom religious unbelief was increasingly common, tended to fall back on 'the Rights of Englishmen' to secure their political ends rather than to develop Paine's previous theistic accounts of rights into abstract but similarly metaphysical theories of universally valid 'human rights'.[216]

The English controversies of the 1790s over the French Revolution also helped to cast the debate on rights in more practical terms. In that debate defenders of the established order tended to divide. Some emphasized divinity: they held that rights had practical meaning only in relation to an omnipotent God's benign intentions for man. Others emphasized utility: they held that an individual's most general right was the pursuit of happiness, and that the best course of social action was always and only identified by an aggregate of individual human choices. Both schools distanced themselves from 'metaphysical' natural rights as the basis for appeals against actual outcomes, notably against a commercial society supported

---

[215] Paine, *The Age of Reason* (1794): *CW*, i. 464, 466, 473–4, 477, 485.
[216] See Ch. 7, section Britain.

by the state.[217] Reformers could follow the same path of disengagement from the-istic rights language, and this disengagement affected Paine as much as Burke. In 1792 Sir Brooke Boothby, a friend of the French Revolution but a critic of Paine, looked back on *Common Sense*, just republished: Paine's 'scripture politics are obso-lete and superannuated in these countries by an hundred years'; the work contained 'such monstrous nonsense as might, for what I know, be suited to the fanatics of Boston, where witchcraft was in great vogue the beginning of this century'.[218] Debate in England had already moved on.

For most defenders of the established order, but also for some reformers, the idea of natural rights as entitlements applying in a state of nature that had preceded the formation of civil society increasingly came to seem as at best a metaphysical con-struct with worryingly unlimited implications, at worst a historical claim that was inconveniently unproven. Both groups came to doubt, or openly to challenge, Paine's seeming revival of the idea of a state of nature as a historical reality.[219] Both came increasingly to emphasize instead the rights that were guaranteed to men within civil society by its laws:

> All *rights*, therefore, which a man is capable of exercising and enjoying (except those of breathing, and willing, and eating, and sleeping, which are rather necessary func-tions than natural rights, and which, without the protection of society, would be of short duration), are properly *civil*; to be enjoyed by all the members and subjects of a polity, according to the laws and government of that polity, for the good of the whole: which the *good of the whole* requires that they should be as *different* and *unequal* in many respects, as are the necessary stations and relations, the capacities and qualifica-tions, of the persons in the society and government to which they belong.[220]

By *The Age of Reason* (1794), the idea of a state of nature had implicitly become a casualty even in Paine's thought.

After *Rights of Man*, and during the ensuing controversies over equality and commercial wealth, this polarization of opinion rapidly progressed. The relation of natural rights to civil society had long been a question, one never capable of defini-tive resolution but often concealed beneath the hegemonic rationale for the Whig ascendancy that followed 1688: did men outside of the state, or in a state of nature, possess rights? If they did, were all, or some, or none of those rights carried over into civil society when men entered it? These questions had for some decades been evaded by Whigs; reformers could easily argue that their newly extended interpret-ation of the social role of rights was rooted in the work of some founding thinker like John Locke, or some foundational event like 1688. In general, reformers in the

---

[217] Thomas Philip Schofield, 'Conservative Political Thought in Britain in Response to the French Revolution', *HJ* 29 (1986), 601–22.

[218] Brooke Boothby, *Observations on the Appeal from the New to the Old Whigs, and on Mr Paine's Rights of Man* (London: John Stockdale, 1792), 99.

[219] 'Paine situait donc ses descriptions à mi-chemin entre l'hypothétique et le factuel': Lounissi, *Paine*, 73. This questioning had been present in critiques of Paine published during the American Revolution.

[220] Edward Tatham, *Letters to the Right Honourable Edmund Burke on Politics* (Oxford: J. Fletcher, 1791), 39–40.

early 1790s made a more assertive use of the familiar concepts of natural rights and the sovereignty of the people.[221]

This provoked a major reaction: universalizing rights were, once more, demonized. By 1794, William Pitt, warning the House of Commons against 'a plot... to form a Convention', argued:

> This whole system of insurrection... would appear... to be laid in the Rights of Man, that monstrous doctrine, under colour of which the weak and ignorant, who are most susceptible of impression from such barren and abstract speculations, were expected and attempted to be seduced to overturn Government, law, property, security, religion, order, and every thing valuable in this country, as they had already overturned and destroyed every thing in France, and endangered every nation in Europe.[222]

So natural right was stigmatized as 'abstract'; but this hardly corresponded with Paine's particularist use of the concept in his negations of hereditary institutions. By 1799, the lawyer and reformer James Mackintosh had to attempt to defend 'the law of nature and nations' by rescuing it from 'Shallow systems of metaphysics'.[223] Paine was not a systematic or a metaphysical thinker. But in the impassioned polemics of the early 1790s, men often found in his pages what they expected to find, not what he had written.

This uncertainty about what reformers intended only grew as some (but not all) reformers in the early 1790s made more use of 'the rights of man' rather than of 'the rights of Englishmen'; these activists tended to echo French naturalistic usage rather than Paine's theistic derivation of rights directly from God. It may be that this different source meant that many reformers in the 1790s went further than reformers of previous decades in looking for far more sweeping changes in society. The English law of seditious libel, harshly enforced by the ministry in the 1790s, partly checked the open expression of such demands.[224] Nevertheless, there is evidence for their existence and their potential into the 1840s.

Despite possible legal action, 'the rights of man' could be used to imply far more extensive outcomes than 'the rights of Englishmen'. In 1791, John Oswald professed in long-familiar moderate terms: 'all that we desire is a fair and equal representation.' But he added: 'Let us always remember, however, that liberty is only another name for equality, and that no nation deserves the appellation of free in which the conditions of men are greatly unequal.' Specifically, he recommended 'a just and enlightened policy respecting property in land', and that the people

---

[221] Notably [Mary Wollstonecraft], *A Vindication of the Rights of Men, in a Letter to the Right Honourable Edmund Burke; occasioned by his Reflections on the Revolution in France* (London: J. Johnson, 1790); Joseph Priestley, *Letters to the Right Honourable Edmund Burke, occasioned by his Reflections on the Revolution in France, &c.* (Birmingham: Thomas Pearson, 1791).

[222] *The Parliamentary Register; or History of the Proceedings and Debates of the House of Commons* (London: Debrett, 1794), xxxviii. 247 (16 May 1794).

[223] James Mackintosh, *A Discourse of the Study of the Law of Nature and Nations* (London: T. Cadell et al., 1799), 36.

[224] In the face of government action, British reformers now often took pains to disguise the full extent of their earlier revolutionary commitments: Jenny Graham, 'Revolutionary Philosopher: the Political Ideas of Joseph Priestley (1733–1804)', *Enlightenment and Dissent* 8 (1989), 43–68; 9 (1990), 14–45.

themselves should 'vindicate' the 'actual exercise of sovereignty', not delegating it to representatives in parliament. By the third edition of his tract, Oswald went far further:

> Let us not be deceived, for it is force alone that can vindicate the rights of the people. Force is the basis of right, or rather right and force are one. The will of God is right, for his power is almighty; and on the invincible power of the people the rights of man stand upright...let us therefore arm the whole to overturn the usurpation of the parts...let us rise up as one man, armed, to vindicate our rights...whoever shall dare to oppose the reformation of abuse, him let the *besom of destruction* sweep from the face of the earth.[225]

In 1792, Thomas Cooper, just back from Paris, repudiated the charge that he had 'no less a design than that of overturning the British Constitution' and professed to seek only 'peaceable but manly applications to Parliament, and associations among the People directed to this purpose', but matched these disavowals with extended negations of the House of Commons, the monarchy, the aristocracy, and the clergy, 'the PRIVILEGED ORDERS', as 'Incumbrances, absurd and useless, dangerous and unjust', invoked a French authority—'For a Nation to change the form of its Government, (says M. La Fayette), it is sufficient she wills it'—and reached his peroration:

> No reflecting Man can look back at the last half Century, or consider the probabilities of the next, without seeing clearly that the Revolution of Europe is at hand. In this Country, as in others, the day of Reformation must come. The true Friends of the People, aware of the Danger that must inevitably ensue from a long continuance of privileged Obstinacy, cry out for early and peaceable Reformation. For the sake of these orders, it is to be hoped they will not cry out in vain; lest tired with increasing Oppression, and bending under the burthen of public Servitude, an irritated People may *demand* a Restoration of their long lost Rights, and Kings, and Bishops, and Nobles, be irrevocably swept away in the dreadful torrent of public resentment.

It was an outcome that he had, perhaps only for form's sake, warned against. After all this, Cooper recorded that for his name to be 'connected' with that of Paine was 'an honour'.[226] Men like Oswald and Cooper helped create a context in Britain in which Paine's publications were read, their implications extended, and universalizing rights demonized.

If Paine in *Rights of Man* outlined ideas which could look back to the 1750s, some of those who celebrated him were already going in different directions.[227] For many members of the London Corresponding Society and its provincial allies,

---

[225] [John Oswald], *A Review of the Constitution of Great Britain* (London: J. Ridgway, 1791), 50–2, citing [William Ogilvie], *An Essay on the Right of Private Property in Land, with respect to its Foundation in the Law of Nature; Its present Establishment by the Municipal Laws of Europe; and The Regulations by which it might be rendered more beneficial to the lower Ranks of Mankind* (London: J. Walter, 1782); John Oswald, *Review of the Constitution of Great-Britain* (3rd edn, ?1792), 52–3.

[226] Thomas Cooper, *A Reply to Mr Burke's Invective against Mr Cooper, and Mr Watt, in the House of Commons, on the 30th of April, 1792* (London: J. Johnson, 1792), 14–16, 24, 53–4, 58.

[227] The extremist potential of many reformers, often concealed for prudential reasons, is revealed in Graham, *The Nation, the Law and the King*.

universal manhood suffrage, annual parliaments, the payment of MPs and the abolition of property qualifications for sitting in the Commons, annual elections, and equal electoral districts were no longer intended to re-pristinize existing society; they were intended as steps to a social revolution in which monarchy and aristocracy would be not merely restrained but expropriated and abolished. Paine was the most famous and widely read of the reformers, but he was already falling behind such developments. Even in his antipathy to wars and to the high taxes that they entailed, his case for the attainability of peaceful reform was weakened when in February 1793 the French republic declared war on the British monarchy, not vice versa.

Because of the seventeenth-century employment of the term 'rights', this growing use of 'the rights of man' did not necessarily make all reformers moderns overnight. The assumption that the American and French Revolutions were in some sense 'modern' episodes has led to the characterization of English reformers' commitments as similarly 'forward-looking'. But the revolutionaries could no more escape the past than their opponents. Just as English Nonconformists were largely detained in an ideological landscape created in the seventeenth century, so were many English political reformers. Indeed, they were often the same people. The Presbyterian Richard Price, who triggered the English debate on the French Revolution, championed his central principle 'that civil authority is a delegation from the people' by urging his followers to promote it though 'detesting the odious doctrines of passive obedience, non-resistance, and the divine right of kings'; he listed as a goal, even before remedying 'the INEQUALITY OF OUR REPRESENTATION', the repeal of 'the TEST LAWS' of 1673 and 1678.[228] Joseph Priestley denounced Burke's *Reflections*, 'the principles of it being, in fact, no other than those of *passive obedience and non-resistance*, peculiar to the Tories and the friends of arbitrary power, such as were echoed from the pulpits of all the high church party, in the reigns of the Stuarts, and of Queen Anne'.[229] James Mackintosh condemned 'the divine right of Kings to tyrannize and oppress mankind'.[230]

In 1795, John Thelwall explained why the tide of opinion flowed towards the cause of reform:

> The infallibility of the priesthood—the divine right of kings—the doctrine of non-resistance—the unqualified veneration for birth and title—the bulwarks of religious intolerance—all these once supposed impregnable fortresses have either yielded in their turn to the irresistable artillery of reason, or continue at present to make but feeble resistance.[231]

---

[228] Price, *A Discourse on the Love of our Country*, 34–9.
[229] Joseph Priestley, *Letters to the Right Honourable Edmund Burke* (1791), viii.
[230] Mackintosh, *Vindiciae Gallicae* (1791), 314.
[231] John Thelwall, *Political Lectures. Volume the First—Part the First* (London: Eaton and Smith, 1795), 70. 'Originally, Thelwall was a church and king man with pro-Tory prejudices imbibed from his father. He identified his radical epiphany not with the classic instance of reading *Rights of Man*, but in the attempts to close down the debating societies discussing the Regency controversy in 1789–90, followed by his experiences in the Westminster Election of 1790': Jon Mee, *Print, Publicity, and Popular Radicalism in the 1790s: The Laurel of Liberty* (Cambridge, 2016), 169–70.

If things had changed it was only because ministers found it 'more to their interest and advantage' to enforce a new doctrine, 'the infallibility of ministers, the divine right of 162 oligarchic proprietors of the rights and suffrage of the nation', the owners of 'the rotten boroughs'.[232] In 1806 the ardent reformer and Unitarian William Hazlitt, reviling the memory of the late Prime Minister, argued that Pitt had 'industriously diffused' a 'spirit of passive obedience and non-resistance'.[233] As in the American colonies in the 1770s, so in England in the 1790s, would-be revolutionaries could be found speaking a political language that was many decades old. Defenders of the established order came to write in rather different terms, commending a modern, commercial society whose wealth, they claimed, depended on the freedoms that necessarily brought inequality as well as prosperity.

Paine's response to this new commercial vision was limited, since he had already accepted free trade and freedom of contract. He focused his negative use of 'rights' on only a few targets, notably the hereditary principle. That clear focus was one reason for his polemical effectiveness. Indeed, an implication of the argument presented here is that the growing use of 'rights' and 'rights of man' in the decades after *c*.1776 was one result of the application of familiar ideas as negations during an era of major conflict, when there were many enemies to negate, more than as affirmations of any new meaning of rights defining a new vision of society and leading forward to the adoption of the Universal Declaration of Human Rights in 1948. Had such a new sense of 'rights' been born in the 'age of revolution', it would be inexplicable why it faded so quickly from view until 1948. Paine contributed greatly to the increasing use of rights language in the anglophone discourse of the 1790s, but it seems that he did not transform the widely prevalent meanings of that language from the particularist 'rights of Englishmen' to universal 'human rights'. One reason for that must be that Paine's Deism was still a minority commitment, and did not become the universal faith that he hoped it would; the formation and reception of Paine's political thought, as much as of Locke's, had theological premises.

Economic levelling: the image of Jacobinism

The growing salience of commercial society, together with Paine's appeal in *Common Sense* to original principles announced at the Creation, meant that the hostile outcry that greeted *Rights of Man* often focused on attributing to Paine a position that he did not hold: the levelling of all private property. Much British reaction against the French Revolution was concerned to defend the inequalities that were presented as consequences of Britain's successful commercial culture; but until *Rights of Man. Part the Second* the commercial nexus was not central to the works of either Burke or Paine.[234] This growing public preoccupation with levelling had a variety of sources, independent of either.

[232] *The Tribune, a Periodical Publication, consisting chiefly of the Political Lectures of J. Thelwall* (London: Eaton and Burks, 1795), i. 267; cf. 134, 178, 196, 265, 269.

[233] William Hazlitt, *Free Thoughts on Public Affairs* (1806), in *The Complete Works of William Hazlitt*, ed. Howe, i. 112–13.

[234] Gregory Claeys, 'The French Revolution Debate and British Political Thought', *History of Political Thought* 11 (1990), 59–80.

One was the visceral anti-monarchical (and by implication anti-aristocratic) political rhetoric that had never entirely disappeared in Britain; it had been resuscitated by the political conflicts of the 1760s and by the writings of Wilkes, Junius, and the authors of such periodicals as *The Crisis*. A second was the element of Protestant Dissenting hostility to ecclesiastical (and therefore to general social) hierarchy surviving from the seventeenth century and finding its greatest triumph in the American Revolution: there the physical violence offered to Loyalists, the expropriation of large amounts of their property, and their exile had been inescapable applications of the principle. Third was the wave of *émigrés* who were driven from France by sanguinary violence and the expropriation and destruction of property; related, and equally eloquent, was the disregard of these things by the French Revolution's British sympathizers.

Fourth was the evolving nature of the French Jacobins. Founded at Versailles as a single debating society for Breton deputies in early 1789, the society moved to Paris after the October Days; it opened its doors to all citizens, although its members were initially largely from the social elite. From there the idea spread, seeding a network of allied provincial Jacobin clubs. By July 1791 these numbered 921, including nearly a million members.[235] But the expulsion of Girondin deputies in June 1793 and their execution in October represented a Jacobin coup at the centre. It made possible social revolution, de-Christianization, and the Terror, implemented at local level by the provincial Jacobin clubs, and only ended after the executions of Robespierre and his circle on 28 July 1794; the membership of the clubs thereafter declined, but Jacobinism's image abroad was now indelible. In many English eyes, it came to symbolize the French Revolution as a whole; even after the end of the 'Jacobin republic' of 1792–4, the name stuck.

French Jacobinism was never a single position, but it became widely associated in England with the systematic use of violence. Punitive violence and economic levelling went together in the French Revolution from the outset, although economic redistribution also had its idealistic and bureaucratic side.[236] Violence too was not a single thing, differing greatly in its psychology and its manifestations; yet lurid reports reaching Britain tended to homogenize the complexities. Consequently, after France declared war in 1793, many English reformers turned away from the French example. Even John Thelwall wrote: 'nor shall I be backward in stigmatising with just epithets of abhorrence, the ferocious barbarity, the enormous, and almost unparalleled cruelty...with which the more energetic party abused their power!'[237] Such English reformers had recourse to a domestic tradition; necessarily, they looked backwards. Even in reforming circles, from 1793 'Paine's name dropped into the background, and his outspoken republican tone gave way to renewed emphasis

---

[235] Michael Kennedy, *The Jacobin Clubs in the French Revolution: The First Years* (Princeton, 1982), 3 and appendix B; Patrice Higonnet, *Goodness beyond Virtue: Jacobins during the French Revolution* (Cambridge, Mass., 1998), 14.

[236] Jean-Pierre Gross, *Fair Shares for All: Jacobin Egalitarianism in Practice* (Cambridge, 1997), 4–8. Gross emphasizes Jacobin idealism.

[237] John Thelwall, *Sober Reflections on the Seditious and Inflammatory Letter of the Rt. Hon. Edmund Burke to a Noble Lord* (London: Symonds, 1796), 63.

upon restoring the "purity" of the constitution.' Indeed 'public opinion' was 'saturated with constitutionalist rhetoric'.[238] Meanwhile, as one student of France has written, 'No historian of political discourse would deny the existence of a strong egalitarian commitment to revolutionary ideology, nor fail to recognise in the promise of civic equality the implicit prospect of greater economic equality.'[239] English observers were not necessarily wrong about French events.

Nevertheless, the use of the term 'Jacobin' by defenders of the established order was intended to disparage all domestic reformers in England and to obscure the wide variety of opinion among their ranks. It had just that effect. Paine appropriately ignored the label, though some English reformers, like John Thelwall, accepted it.[240] Even Thelwall protested, in reply to Burke's vilification: 'Some [Jacobins] wish for a greater change, and others for a less. There are, I fear, almost as many different opinions, among reformers, as to the extent of that change as there were among the allies about the objects of that ever to be renowned and glorious confederacy of kings.'[241] In Norwich, Richard Dinmore objected that 'the jacobins are not properly a party; each man thinks for himself, and is very little anxious about the opinions of others'. He added: 'I call them jacobins because their enemies chose so to call them, with a view to confound the public mind'; the 'jacobins' did not express 'French principles... but they are principles of pure English growth, Locke, Sydney, Marvel, Milton, &c were their authors.'[242]

Such authors had been diverse in their views, and had seldom anticipated the issues that came to prominence in the 1790s. There was no single, unified English Jacobin position that Paine might classically have expressed. Nor did the options remain constant. Just as French Jacobins evolved through internal conflict and schism away from constitutional monarchy and towards the use of violence to effect social change, so too did some of their English namesakes. Of this profoundly changing ideological scene in England Paine seems to have appreciated little: he had isolated himself while composing, and then left the country. But war, from 1793, polarized the options.

Growing extremism in France acted to place a different interpretation on earlier English domestic developments like the advocacy of universal manhood suffrage from the Westminster election of 1780 and the calls for land nationalization from 1775 by the otherwise untypical and isolated Thomas Spence. In *Rights of Man. Part the Second* especially, Paine set out an argument for commerce's role in promoting peace between individuals and between nations, and promising 'a revolution in the uncivilized state of governments'.[243] But Paine's eloquent case for the levelling of status was easily read in the 1790s as an implied demand for the levelling

---

[238] E. P. Thompson, *The Making of the English Working Class* (London, 1963), 122, 124.

[239] Gross, *Fair Shares for All*, 3.   [240] Higonnet, *Goodness beyond Virtue*, 325.

[241] John Thelwall, *Rights of Nature, against the Usurpation of Establishments. A Series of Letters to the People, in Reply to the False Principles of Burke* (London: Symonds, 1796), in *The Politics of English Jacobinism: writings of John Thelwall*, ed. Gregory Claeys (University Park, Pa, 1995), 409.

[242] Richard Dinmore, *An Exposition Of the Principles of the English Jacobins; with Strictures On the Political Conduct of Charles J. Fox, William Pitt and Edmund Burke* (Norwich: John March and London: J. S. Jordan, 1796), 6, 20, 25, 32. Paine appeared only once in Dinmore's discussion, 35.

[243] Paine, *Rights of Man. Part the Second* (1792): *CW*, i. 400.

of property. In this context his proposal for 'progressive taxation' conceded the principle of state redistribution: although it would be levied on income from estates, beginning at 1.25 per cent on estates producing an annual revenue of £50 to £500, the tax would reach 100 per cent on income over £23,000 p.a.[244] Although applied by Paine first to the redistribution of income, the same principle might be expected to extend logically to property also. Paine did nothing to deny that implication in later editions, but this should not be read as evasion or deceit; it suggests instead that his attention was elsewhere.

Paine's professed goal was the division of only the very largest estates, not the end of private property in land; but because his target was an older one, primogeniture and the aristocratic principle, not private wealth as such, it was possible for some of his contemporaries to conclude that the implications of Paine's doctrine as a whole were more extensive than the percentages expressed in his taxation proposals. In *Rights of Man*, Paine condemned the law of primogeniture: 'The nature and character of aristocracy shows itself to us in this law. It is a law against every law of nature, and nature herself calls for its destruction.' Aristocracy was 'a monster'.[245] If the abolition of primogeniture meant the break-up of aristocratic landed estates, the effect would have been far more extensive than that of the progressive taxation of incomes that Paine proposed in *Rights of Man. Part the Second*.

Once Paine had put this prospect onto the national agenda (*Rights of Man. Part the Second* was published on 16 February 1792), the publication in April and May that year of the early demands of the London Corresponding Society to 'a fair, equal and impartial Representation of the People in Parliament', rights withheld from people by 'Fraud or Force', looked more revolutionary in their implications than similar goals, universal suffrage and annual parliaments, had done in 1780. This was so even though the first LCS proposals made no explicit reference to events in France, and charged corrupt government with being 'a Diminution of our Property'. These proposals related to the English case; they rehearsed episodes in English history from 1429 to 1715 to show how the ancestral electoral rights of Englishmen had been abridged, and said nothing of economic levelling.[246] But this did not save them from being swept into a single category, 'Jacobinism'.

Reformers were therefore obliged repeatedly to insist that they sought an equality of rights, not of property.[247] In a publication dated 29 November 1792, Maurice Margarot and Thomas Hardy protested for the LCS: 'Whoever shall attribute to us (who wish only the Restoration of the lost Liberties of our Country) the expressions of NO KING! NO PARLIAMENT! or any design of invading the PROPERTY

---

[244] Paine, *Rights of Man. Part the Second* (1792): *CW*, i. 434–6.

[245] Paine, *Rights of Man* (1791): *CW*, i. 288.

[246] *First Address of the London Corresponding Society* (2 Apr. 1792) and *Address of the London Corresponding Society to the Nation at Large* (24 May 1792), in Thale (ed.), *LCS Papers*, 10–14.

[247] E.g. *The Perverse Definition Imposed on the Word Equality* (broadsheet, no printer, c.1792), in Gregory Claeys (ed.), *Political Writings of the 1790s* (8 vols, London, 1995), iii. 403–4; for its distribution in Manchester, see Thomas Walker, *A Review of Some of the Political Events which have occurred in Manchester, during the Last Five Years* (London: J. Johnson, 1794), 45–7. The 'equalization of property' was a 'wild and detestable...sentiment': 'Account of London Corresponding Society General Meeting, 12 November 1795', in Thale (ed.), *LCS Papers*, 327.

of other Men, is guilty of a wilful, an impudent, and a malicious Falsehood.' Rather, '*proportional Distinctions of Property*' were '*sacred and inviolable*'.[248] But as the events of the 1790s unfolded, some English reformers came to tread the same path as their French colleagues, exploring ways in which equality of rights could be interpreted as offering greater economic entitlements to the poor. William Godwin took this route, albeit in two expensive quarto volumes of 1793, there outlining 'the scheme of equal property'.[249] John Thelwall's thought developed in the same direction.[250] Paine's chapter in *Rights of Man. Part the Second* advocating a more extensive system of poor relief that overrode private property rights may have been an embarrassment to English reformers, and few discussed it in print; still more did they shy away from *Agrarian Justice* (1797). Yet these English reformers moved in that direction of their own volition.

Before *The Age of Reason* Paine seldom dwelt on his differences from French Jacobins, but these were significant. Until the flight to Varennes in June 1791, most French Jacobins favoured a reformed monarchy;[251] from 1776 Paine had repeatedly condemned monarchy as such. The French campaign of de-Christianization was undertaken in the name of atheism; Paine, according to his published work, was a believing theist. The Jacobin Goddess of Reason was a secular personification; Paine described reason as literally a divine gift. French Jacobinism had as an ideal the education of every child;[252] Paine sketched a plan for 'Education for one million and thirty thousand children' for 'every child under fourteen years of age',[253] but mentioned this plan only briefly, and only once; he was himself largely self-taught, and disparaged much of what then comprised a grammar school education.[254] The Jacobins moved away from their early free trade beliefs and from 4 May 1793 legislated for price and wage control, called the 'Maximum', consciously compromising the security of property; Paine favoured free trade, and on the basis of his American experience advised Danton against price fixing.[255] As some elements within Jacobinism moved closer towards ideals of economic redistribution, on 18 March 1793 the Convention made it a capital offence even to propose a *lex agraria* or 'any other law subversive of territorial, commercial and industrial

[248] *Address of the London Corresponding Society to the other Societies of Great Britain, united for obtaining a Reform in Parliament* (London: no printer, 1792), 7–8.

[249] William Godwin, *An Enquiry Concerning Political Justice, and Its Influence on General Virtue and Happiness* (2 vols, London: G. G. J. and J. Robinson, 1793), 842.

[250] 'Philosophy and Humanity forbid the propagation of this levelling doctrine.' Nevertheless, man is born only to find 'His inheritance is alienated, and his common right appropriated, even before his birth.' The contract between employer and labourer was an 'unjust agreement' and 'is, morally and politically, void'; hence 'the labourer has a right to a share of the produce, not merely equal to his support, but, proportionate to the profits of the employer... the landed proprietor is only the trustee for the community': Thelwall, *Rights of Nature, against the Usurpation of Establishments. A Series of Letters to the People, in Reply to the False Principles of Burke* (London: Symonds, 1796), in *Writings of John Thelwall*, ed. Claeys, 472, 476–8.

[251] Kennedy, *Jacobin Clubs*, i. 268, 273.

[252] Clarence Crane Brinton, *The Jacobins* (New York, 1930), 158; Higonnet, *Goodness beyond Virtue*, 57, 96–7, 206–8.

[253] Paine, *Rights of Man. Part the Second* (1792), in *CW*, i. 425–6, 431.

[254] Paine, *The Age of Reason* (1794): *CW*, i. 491–5.

[255] Paine to Danton, 6 May 1793: *CW*, ii. 1336–7.

properties';[256] Paine's goal of abolishing the law of primogeniture would have had just that effect.

The decrees of Ventôse (February 1794) would have seized the property of those convicted of counter-revolutionary acts and distributed it to the poor. The Jacobins instituted an effective progressive income tax to transfer wealth from the rich to the poor, with a top marginal rate of 50 per cent; here Paine went further, proposing a marginal top rate of 100 per cent.[257] The National Assembly abolished slavery in 1794; Paine showed little interest in the question. French Jacobins had extensive schemes of social reform; in *Rights of Man. Part the Second* Paine said nothing about them. French Jacobins sought symbolically to erase the old society, introducing a new calendar, a new numbering of years, new weights and measures: Paine ignored them all. But these differences were not often apparent to English critics of the French Revolution: they simplified a picture of great complexity by positing a single category, 'Jacobinism'. Paine's unresponsiveness to a wide swathe of French thought characterized reformers' discussions in London also: after the outbreak of war it became much harder to discover what was actually happening in France, and English partisans, for and against, both tended to debate the issues in terms of their antecedent English commitments. Where Paine, in Paris, might have briefed an English audience on the actual nature of Jacobinism, he did not do so.

The French political elite was itself overtaken by events after the storming of the Tuileries palace by the *sans-culottes* on 10 August 1792; the effective abolition of the monarchy that this entailed created a wholly new context for the contemporary reception of Paine's writings. Elite opinion in Britain now often swung away from him, and left behind his own preoccupations—the hereditary principle and the representative system—in favour of related but different preoccupations of the moment.

THE ESCALATING REVOLUTION, 1791–1792

Rights of Man was published in London on 13 March 1791; some time before 7 April Paine returned to Paris, where he remained until 13 July that year, staying as the guest of Lafayette (the hero of *Rights of Man*, perhaps returning Paine's favour in publishing his French friend's propaganda). Later, when Lafayette was in Austrian captivity, he either found it expedient to represent himself as a moderate, or disclosed what his views had always been. They had, he wrote, been importantly different from Paine's:

> I cast a longing eye upon the British constitution, and most devoutly wished to see it adopted, with some modifications necessary to the continental situation of France. This measure would have saved a vast deal of trouble, confusion, and tumult. I see no

---

[256] The '"red scare" was very real and the risk of such erosion [of property rights] taking place was clearly perceived': Gross, *Fair Shares for All*, 3–4, 93. R. B. Rose, 'The "Red Scare" of the 1790s: The French Revolution and the "Agrarian Law"', *P&P* 103 (1984), 113–30.

[257] Gross, *Fair Shares for All*, 128–36; Paine, *Rights of Man. Part the Second* (1792): *CW*, i. 435–6.

reason why a free people, should not adopt a constitution which had staunchly maintained a consistency with the liberty of the subject, in all the various ordeals of experience. I was, however, well satisfied with the constitution, as accepted by the king; it appeared to me a good foundation, upon which future experience might build an excellent fabric.

Now, however, his English friend had intervened. With the benefit of hindsight, Lafayette continued:

At this crisis, when the people were almost giddy with politics, Mr. Paine's Answer to Mr. Burke made its appearance, and was read with much avidity. When I perused this book, I considered its political errors, as we generally consider the literary errors of a friend, mere defects in the judgment, which could have no evil tendency, except in militating against the reputation and interest of the author. I did not imagine that the people of France could ever rush into such mad extravagancies, as to adopt so unstable, and undurable a form of government as that of a republic—a form of government which was so evidently inconsistent with the nature, extent, and situation of the country, and with the natural temper of the people.

In 1793 Lafayette claimed to idolize the British Constitution, and only blamed Lord North's ministry in the 1770s for 'strong intentions of totally overthrowing the constitution'. At some distance from 1776, he now wrote that a republic, in the abstract, was 'the most pleasing and plausible that can be presented to the uninformed or inexperienced bulk of mankind', but 'we find all to be a grievous delusion in the end'.[258] A republican outcome was unfolding in France, but even Lafayette did not claim that this happened because the French implemented Paine's theory.

Paine's return to France was in time for him to witness a darker turn in the Revolution. He was, for once, in France at the moment of the key event in the discrediting of monarchy, the royal family's 'flight to Varennes' on 20 June 1791, their attempt to escape to a royalist stronghold or to the Austrian Netherlands and their forcible return to Paris on the 25th. Even then, a clear majority in the National Constituent Assembly supported the fiction that the king had been kidnapped and forced to leave behind him a manifesto renouncing the Revolution. The constitution, providing for a constitutional monarchy, had almost been completed; there was little appetite in the Assembly for starting again. But fears of counter-revolutionary conspiracy at the heart of the state had received powerful confirmation, and the euphoria of 1789 was now far in the past.

Few of the leading revolutionary activists, until that point, had openly sought the toppling of the monarchy. Now, some did: the Cordeliers Club organized mass demonstrations in Paris, demanding the deposition of Louis. François Robert

---

[258] *The Marquis de la Fayette's Statement of his Own Conduct and Principles... Translated from the Original French, and most respectfully Inscribed to the Whig Club* (London: J. Deighton, 1793), 77–9. For Lafayette's praise of the British Constitution, and implicit rejection of Paine's critique of it, 35, 37–40, 54–60. They shared, however, a condemnation of aristocracy, the Church ('the unrelenting nightmare of theocracy'), the court ('the pompous raree-show of state'), wars ('Unnecessary wars' leading to 'loans, taxes, places, and pensions, which produce only poverty, and distress to the subject'), and corruption in the House of Commons, 26–7, 30–2, 38–40, 61, 64.

republished on 21 June his pamphlet of 1790 calling for a republic; Nicholas Bonneville's journal *La Bouche de fer* made the same demand on the 23rd. Some individuals in the circle of Mme. Roland met on the 20th and agreed to launch a journal, *Le Républicain*, four issues of which appeared on 3, 10, 16, and 23 July (Robespierre, who was present, disagreed).[259] As in America in 1775–6, Paine was not the first; indeed anti-monarchical opinion was already being organized.

The response of the philosopher Antoine-Nicolas de Condorcet to the flight to Varennes was to launch a new society, the Société des Républicains. Its leaders were hardly political heavyweights: the publisher Nicolas de Bonneville, author of the atheistical *De l'espirit des religions* (Paris: Cercle Social, 1792); the prominent politician and lawyer Jacques-Pierre Brissot de Warville;[260] the financial expert Étienne Clavière; the army officer Achille Duchâtelet; the businessman François Lanthenas, later the translator of *The Age of Reason*; and Paine. Significantly, these Frenchmen could speak English. In response to new circumstances, and especially to the widespread French disillusion with monarchy that followed the king's attempted escape, Paine adapted his message: he moved away from the group of Jefferson and Lafayette, self-styled moderates, and re-emphasized his long-standing anti-monarchical commitments. For Paine, the new United States now became a model not of stable, representative, anti-hereditarian government but of republican revolution, a vision Paine was to express in *Rights of Man. Part the Second*.[261]

It was Paine and Duchâtelet who wrote (Paine producing an English text) a republican proclamation announcing the end of the monarchy, not by deposition but by an alleged abdication. On 1 July 1791, eleven days after the king's flight was discovered, after anti-monarchical opinion in Paris had taken shape, and without wider consultation, copies were plastered on the walls of Paris and on the door of the National Assembly. It asserted that the king

> has abdicated the throne...the reciprocal obligation which subsisted between us is dissolved. He holds no longer any authority. We owe him no longer obedience. We see in him no more than an indifferent person; we can regard him only as Louis Capet. The history of France presents little else than a long series of public calamity, which takes its source from the vices of the Kings...The catalogue of their oppressions was complete, but to complete the sum of their crimes, treason was yet wanting. Now the only vacancy is filled up, the dreadful list is full; the system is exhausted; there are no remaining errors for them to commit, their reign is consequently at an end.[262]

The claim of abdication was that which many English Whigs had used against James II in 1688.

[259] Lounissi, *Paine*, 686–7.

[260] For Brissot's confidence in the American Revolution as 'the birth date of a world made anew' see Antonino De Francesco, 'The American Origins of the French Revolutionary War', in Pierre Serna, Antonino De Francesco, and Judith A. Miller (eds), *Republics at War, 1776–1840: Revolutions, Conflicts, and Geopolitics in Europe and the Atlantic World* (Basingstoke, 2013), 27–45, at 35. This perspective was not confined to Paine alone.

[261] Philipp Ziesche, *Cosmopolitan Patriots: Americans in Paris in the Age of Revolution* (Charlottesville, Va, 2010), 48.

[262] Conway, *Life*, 126.

On 2 July the text was published in Brissot's journal *Le Patriote français*. The Anglophile Étienne Dumont later described the circumstances of its composition. He, Dumont, had drafted a document exonerating the king, but then Achille Duchâtelet called.

> After a short preamble, he put into my hand an English manuscript, in the form of a proclamation to the French people. It was nothing less than a manifesto against royalty, and it called upon the nation to seize the opportunity, and become a republic. Paine was the author of it. Duchâtelet was determined to adopt it and put his name to it, to placard it on the walls of Paris and stand to the consequences. He came to request that I would translate it and add some necessary developments. I began by discussing with him this strange proposal; and pointed out the danger of raising the standard of republicanism without the concurrence of the national assembly. Nothing was yet known of the King's intentions or means; how he was supported, or what were his alliances, his army, and the assistance he would receive from the provinces. I asked Duchâtelet whether he had consulted with any of the most influential men, such as Sieyès, Lafayette, and others? He had not; he acted alone. Paine and he, the one an American, the other a thoughtless member of the French nobility, put themselves forward to change the whole system of government in France. I resisted all his entreaties, and peremptorily refused to translate his proclamation... Next day, the republican proclamation, signed Duchâtelet, appeared on the walls in every part of Paris, and was denounced to the assembly. The idea of a republic had presented itself to no one, and the first intimation of such a thing filled the *côté droit* and the moderates of the *côté gauche* with consternation. Mallouet, Cazalès, and several others proposed that the author should be prosecuted; but Chapelier, backed by a numerous party, fearful of adding fuel to the fire instead of extinguishing it, moved for the order of the day, on the plea that the proposal was an absurdity and the author a madman... But some of the seed thrown out by the audacious hand of Paine, began to bud forth in the minds of many leading individuals.[263]

Nevertheless, these leading individuals had been overtaken not by ideology but by events. The royal family's failed attempt to escape abroad was a public relations disaster for the king personally. According to Dumont, the flight to Varennes produced a dignified but widespread rejection of monarchy as such among the Parisian populace:

> A few hours after the King's flight, every sign of royalty disappeared, one after the other... in a few hours every one had found out that a King was not at all necessary... The famous Paine was at this time in Paris, and very intimate in Condorcet's family. He thought he had effected the revolution in America, and fancied himself called upon to bring about another in France.[264]

Even then, it was not clear that the principle of constitutional monarchy itself was doomed: one of Samuel Romilly's informants in Paris, James Trail, reported in June that 'Some very seditious resolutions have been adopted and published by

---

[263] Étienne Dumont, *Recollections of Mirabeau, and of the Two First Legislative Assemblies of France* (London: Edward Bull, 1832), 262–4.
[264] Dumont, *Recollections*, 260–1.

some of the inferior clubs, and some abominable libels have also been published against Lafayette and the municipality, but, it would seem, with very little effect.' George Wilson confirmed this, reporting in September of the royal family's continued popularity in many quarters. The same month, Trail added: 'The satisfaction with the King's unequivocal and decided mode of accepting the constitution is still manifest among all ranks of people. For the present, suspicion seems to be asleep; and I think it is not impossible, by a continuance of the same open and frank conduct, to prevent it from being waked.'[265] Paine evidently saw things differently. Gouverneur Morris, though no friend of Paine's, noted on 5 July 1791: 'Payne is here, inflated to the Eyes and big with a Litter of Revolutions.'[266] Even Robespierre disagreed, arguing before the Jacobins on 13 July that 'le mot république ne signifie aucune forme particulière de gouvernement, il appartient à tout gouvernement d'hommes libres qui ont une patrie', so that France was already both a monarchy and a republic.[267] Until 10 August 1792 the king remained, for some, a plausible head of a constitutional monarchy. Paine's placard of 1 July 1791 did not change that; and it evidently had little influence on the debates of the Assembly.[268]

Reacting to this anti-monarchical initiative, the abbé Sieyès, sometimes labelled the leading thinker of the Revolution, published in *Le Moniteur* of 6 July a defence of the proposed constitution, perhaps an implicit defence of himself against attacks by Robespierre and Danton. Sieyès evidently sought a way of redefining a constitutional monarchy as the representative of the nation, now that Louis XVI was unfit to fill the office.[269] In what seems to have been a staged and mutually complimentary exchange, Paine replied in a letter dated 8 July published in *Le Moniteur* and *Le Républicain* on 16 July; Sieyès replied. It was almost unique that Paine should engage in such an exchange of views with a named individual, and the reasons of both men for arranging it are unclear.[270] At issue was the planned constitution, and Paine again deployed his long-asserted theory of representation.

What, after all, was 'representation'? What was it to be 'represented'? Paine, perhaps implicitly echoing the English practice with which he was familiar, held to the assumption that voters were only represented by the individual for whom they had voted. This, indeed, was basic to his understanding of what a republic was.

---

[265] James Trail to Samuel Romilly, 27 June 1791; George Wilson to Romilly, 21 Sept. 1791; Trail to Romilly, 26 Sept. 1791: *Memoirs of the Life of Sir Samuel Romilly, Written by Himself, with a Selection from his Correspondence, edited by his Sons* (3 vols, London, 1840), i. 428, 436–7, 440.

[266] *A Diary of the French Revolution by Gouverneur Morris 1752–1816*, ed. Beatrix Cary Davenport (2 vols, London, 1939), ii. 213.

[267] Lounissi, *Paine*, 689.   [268] Lounissi, *Paine*, 686–7.

[269] 'He is, more than any other, the man who articulates the political theory of the French Revolution... Sieyes is *the* man of 1789': Murray Forsyth, *Reason and Revolution: The Political Thought of the Abbé Sieyes* (Leicester, 1987), 3, 176; Sonenscher, in Emmanuel Joseph Sieyès, *Political Writings Including the Debate between Sieyès and Tom Paine in 1791*, ed. Michael Sonenscher (Indianapolis, 2003), 163–4.

[270] For the claim of Joseph Lakanal in 1796 that Sieyès framed only a weak defence of monarchy in order to prepare French opinion for a republic see Aldridge, *Man of Reason*, 148–9. This is in doubt, if Sieyès's arguments are read as sophisticated and original. For an argument that Sieyès's points were 'compatible with his broader theory', see Sieyès, *Political Writings*, ed. Sonenscher, introduction, xxvi–xxxiii: 'Paine envisaged a single system of election that would always go upwards, while Sieyès envisaged a double system of election that would go both upwards and downwards at periodic intervals.'

I do not mean by Republicanism that which bears the name in Holland, or in some Italian States. I consider it simply as a Government by Representation; a Government founded upon the principles of the 'Declaration of Rights;' principles with which many parts of the French Constitution are at variance. The French and the American Declarations of Rights are but one and the same thing in principles, and almost in expressions; and this is the republicanism which I undertake to defend against what is called Monarchy and Aristocracy.

For Paine, the American and French cases had, by definition, to be the same. He seemed not to grasp the possibility of alternative theories of representation, and so did not anticipate the tradition of strong executives and weak elected legislatures that were to characterize French government under the Directory, under Bonaparte, and afterwards.

Sieyès indeed was the father of the division of France into *départements*, each the framework for a system of indirect election that echoed that which had been stand-ard in eighteenth-century France; Paine did not discuss this. Sieyès replied to Paine's letter at six times its length, focusing on the key point: for Sieyès, 'a representative system' and 'republicanism' were separate things, where for Paine they were the same. Arguing from first principles, Sieyès envisaged 'different sorts of representa-tions' and a constitution that ascribed substantial power to a monarch, 'the Elector', 'whose evident and palpable interest would be always inseparable from that of the majority': he would appoint ministers. Paine had demanded a government founded on the Declaration of Rights; Sieyès replied: 'I do not see why this government should not be a Monarchy.' Paine had argued that the American and French dec-larations of rights were the same; Sieyès replied 'So much the worse. I could wish that ours might be the best, and it would not be difficult to make it so.'

A more extended debate between Paine and Sieyès, the two leading theorists of their age, would have been invaluable to present-day scholars. In reality, their brief correspondence covered almost none of the matters then fought over in France. The text of Paine's letter reads like the preliminary to a full exchange in which he promised 'not to exceed the extent of fifty pages in my part of the controversy', but after Sieyès's second letter, Paine did not reply in the Parisian press.[271] Although Paine then left for London, the French republic did not declare war until February 1793; communication by post between London and Paris would have been easy. The absence of an exchange suggests that Paine's interests were elsewhere; he already knew the answer to French problems, which he repeatedly termed 'the representa-tive system'. Instead, Paine wrote and published *Rights of Man. Part the Second*, which was partly a response, but hardly an adequate theoretical reply, to Sieyès.[272] It was primarily addressed to an English-speaking audience.

In the turning tide of French opinion against monarchy it is likely that Paine did not act as the main gravitational force, but rather that Parisian democratic

[271] Paine to Sieyès, 8 July 1791, published in *Le Moniteur* (16 July 1791); Sieyès to Paine, n.d.: Sieyès, *Political Writings*, ed. Sonenscher, 165–73.
[272] For which, see Ch. 5, section France and America. For the exchange see Forsyth, *Reason and Revolution*, 176–9.

initiatives, driven by popular societies like the Cordeliers Club after the National Assembly replaced the old sixty districts with forty-eight sections on 21 May 1790, turned independently towards republicanism after the flight to Varennes.[273] Paine had no contact with these clubs, and did not anticipate that the Revolution would soon take such a violent turn away from his 'representative system' towards the direct democracy of the *sans-culottes*. The subsequent growing extremism of French politics was probably the result not of a single Paineite manifesto on the walls of certain buildings in Paris but of two large sets of causes, the priority of which historians still debate.

First were the consequences of revolutionary violence itself, one episode legitimizing and demanding the next; or, put a little differently, the dependence of revolutionary ideology on an ideal of direct democracy which led to direct action in the name of 'the people'. Second was the growing fear of even moderate reformers that royalists, everywhere numerous, were mounting a successful resistance and threatening to undo all that the Revolution had achieved. The comte d'Artois, the king's brother, had fled after the fall of the Bastille, had taken refuge in his father-in-law's court at Turin, and by mid-1791 had organized a small army in Trier and Mainz: he was a rallying point for the growing number of *émigrés*. Within France, armed resistance to the Revolution in several areas, notably Languedoc and the Rhone, posed a real threat to the revolutionary elites and masses in Paris. So did the resistance of most bishops and many clergy of the Catholic Church from early 1791 in the face of the new demand that they take an oath of loyalty to the revolutionary state. Each set of causes heightened the others.

PAINE IN LONDON: *RIGHTS OF MAN. PART THE SECOND*

Paine's chief focus had been on a comparatively restricted topic: the abolition of monarchy. Having written his anti-monarchist manifesto, he left for England on 8 July 1791 in company with two other republicans, Lord Daer and Étienne Dumont. Although Paine had his circle of admirers, not everyone close to him in France recorded a positive verdict. Dumont later wrote:

> I had met Paine five or six times before, and I could easily excuse, in an American, his prejudices against England. But his egregious conceit and presumptuous self-sufficiency quite disgusted me. He was drunk with vanity. If you believed him, it was he who had done every thing in America. He was an absolute caricature of the vainest of Frenchmen. He fancied that his book upon the Rights of Man ought to be substituted for every other book in the world; and he told us roundly that, if it were in his power to annihilate every library in existence, he would do so without hesitation in order to eradicate the errors they contained and commence with the Rights of Man, a new era of ideas and principles. He knew all his own writings by heart, but he knew nothing

[273] J. F. Bosher, *The French Revolution* (London, 1989), 171–3.

else...My curiosity concerning this celebrated writer was more than satisfied during this journey, and I saw him no more.[274]

It may be that Paine had already decided to add to his best-seller a sequel.

By returning to England, Paine just missed the massacre in the Champ de Mars on 17 July 1791 when a vast meeting of republicans, inspired by the political clubs, organized a petition for the king's abdication. The National Assembly, having just reinstated the king after the failed flight to Varennes, condemned the meeting in advance, and the city authorities ordered its dispersal. The National Guard broke it up by force, inflicting many civilian deaths, an atrocity never forgotten in Paris and one that made a peaceful outcome even more elusive. For the moment at least, it seemed that republican initiatives in France had failed. Opinion was now becoming more inflamed on both sides of the Channel: the second anniversary of the storming of the Bastille, 14 July 1791, saw sustained 'church and king' riots in Birmingham in which the reformer Joseph Priestley's house, other private houses, and four Dissenting chapels were gutted.

Paine responded by drawing closer to the Society for Constitutional Information. After its publication the SCI lent its backing to *Rights of Man*; the Society's resolution of 23 March 1791 commending the work as 'most masterly' and claiming Paine as 'a Member of that Society' was printed at the end of its fourth edition in April that year. The author of the resolution, Jeremiah Batley, privately acknowledged that 'There was certainly an apparent inconsistency in recommending a book which affirms we have no Constitution, by a Society instituted, as I conceive, for the preservation of one',[275] but it may be that the SCI, and its new activists like Horne Tooke, were carrying matters beyond what more moderate members had envisaged. The SCI went further, at a meeting on 28 May chaired by the unbelieving Anglican clergyman John Horne Tooke, to issue a veiled threat of resistance.

It may be that the exercise of such a long-familiar threat, not the nature of rights as such, was increasingly the point at issue; the first did not demand a deeper understanding of the universal nature of the second, but rather a particularist response to specific events or perceived injustices. The normally cautious John Horne Tooke illustrates the potential extension of rights claims. Even the reformer John Thelwall's second wife, who consistently excused the revolutionaries of the 1790s, described Tooke as 'one of the violent spirits of the age' and repeated a story she had heard, she thought, from John Frost: that Tooke, at one of his dinner parties, had been 'running on' about the need to execute Louis XVI, 'greatly to the annoyance of Tom Paine, who, whatever may have been his failings in other respects, was a man of humanity...after a long suspense of sullen forbearance, [Paine] broke silence with the indignant exclamation, "Ah, Tooke! You are a true royalist! You love

---

[274] Dumont, *Recollections of Mirabeau*, 270–1. Paine featured only briefly in Dumont's book, which focused on a much more important actor in the Revolution.

[275] Batley to Wyvill, 14 Apr. 1792, in *Political Papers, comprising the Correspondence of several Distinguished Persons in the Years 1792, 1793, &c. with the Editor, the Rev. Christopher Wyvill* (6 vols, York: L. Lund, [1794–1802]), v. 4.

blood!"'[276] Reformers could mean much more, even if they increasingly found it prudent, after the publication of *Rights of Man*, in public (or when on trial) to disavow the 'rights of man' and to base their claims instead on the apparently safer ground of the Saxon constitution, once it had been freed from the 'Norman Yoke'.[277]

Paine was present at the SCI's meeting on 22 July 1791; by 1792 he was a regular attender.[278] As events in France seemed to open up a republican future, Horne Tooke increasingly led the SCI in a revolutionary direction. It was Paine who wrote but Horne Tooke who signed and the SCI which subsidized Paine's first publication in England after his return, the *Address and Declaration*, agreed to at a meeting on 20 August 1791: in more heightened language than in *Rights of Man*, Paine denounced 'arbitrary power . . . passive obedience and court government' in Britain; 'We are oppressed with a heavy national debt, a burden of taxes, and an expensive administration of government, beyond those of any people in the world.' We 'profess and proclaim it as our principle that every nation has at all times an inherent indefeasible right to constitute and establish such government for itself as best accords with its disposition, interest, and happiness'. By implication, it recommended the establishment of a republic. On 4 November 1791 Paine was acclaimed at an inspirational meeting of the Revolution Society (which evidently now overlapped with the SCI) to honour a visiting French revolutionary, Jerome Pétion, where, after *ça ira* had been played three times by the orchestra, the chairman, Thomas Walker, proposed a toast to lasting friendship between England and France. Paine, asked for a toast, proposed 'the Revolution of the World': his extensive programme was already evident.[279] On the same day, in Manchester, its own Constitutional Society held a dinner at which one of the toasts was 'May the Stuart principles meet with the Stuart's fate': to such reformers the rising of 1745 was closer than the Terror.[280]

Yet in face of the pressures of the moment the Society began to fracture, moderates like the Revd Christopher Wyvill congratulating the SCI on adhering to 'the principles of our mixed form of Government' and warning against the adoption of 'Mr. Paine's ill-timed, and, in my opinion, pernicious counsels'. Wyvill warned also against 'the supporters of moderate measures' in the SCI being 'out-numbered' by 'new Members who are inclined to favour Mr. Paine's projects', not stopping short of anything but 'a Republic on the principles of the American States'. This was a real danger, Wyvill argued, since Paine's 'tempting offer of annuities to the poor out of the great estates of the rich, may raise him a formidable party among the lowest of the class, whose fury concurring with national distress on other accounts,

---

[276] [Henrietta Cecil Boyle Thelwall], *The Life of John Thelwall* (London: John Macrone, 1837), 242–3.

[277] Thompson, *The Making of the English Working Class*, 86–9.

[278] Graham, *The Nation, the Law and the King*, 283.

[279] Albert Goodwin, *The Friends of Liberty: The English Democratic Movement in the Age of the French Revolution* (London, 1979), 188.

[280] The toast was repeated in Manchester on 5 Nov. 1792: Graham, *The Nation, the Law and the King*, 248–54, 381; [Paine], *Address and Declaration, of the Friends of Universal Peace and Liberty, held at the Thatched House Tavern, St. James's Street, August 20th. 1791* (n.p. [London], n.d. [1791]): *CW*, ii. 534–7.

might be very destructive indeed'. All Wyvill wanted, he claimed, was 'a Repeal of the Test Act, and a moderate Reformation in Church and State'.[281]

For Wyvill, Paine set back the prospects of moderate reform 'more...than any other circumstance whatever'. 'It is unfortunate for the public cause, that Mr. Paine took such unconstitutional ground, and has formed a party for a Republic among the lower classes of the people, by holding out to them the prospect of plundering the rich.' By now, wrote Wyvill, the SCI had 'given their sanction to Paine's most pernicious projects'.[282] The newly formed and patrician Society of the Friends of the People now broke with the SCI, alarmed that that body was going too far; it was in the summer of 1792 that 'the Constitutional Society under Tooke seized the initiative in the reform movement', and set about distributing across the country large numbers of tracts, especially the writings of Paine.[283]

Paine was evidently unconcerned by reported threats of disorder; he was by now in a place of safety, staying with his friend Clio Rickman in his house in Marylebone Street. Rickman described (but sanitized) the agreeable life of a literary celebrity in a secure city:

> Mr. Paine's life in London was a quiet round of philosophical leisure and enjoyment. It was occupied in writing, in a small epistolary correspondence, in walking about with me to visit different friends, occasionally lounging at coffee-houses and public places, or being visited by a select few. Lord Edward Fitzgerald; the French and American ambassadors, Mr. Sharp the engraver, Romney the painter, Mrs. Wolstonecroft, Joel Barlow, Mr. Hull, Mr. Christie, Dr. Priestly, Dr. Towers, Col. Oswald, the walking Stewart, Captain Sampson Perry, Mr. Tuffin, Mr. William Choppin, Captain De Stark, Mr. Horne Tooke, &c. &c. were among the number of his friends and acquaintance; and of course, as he was my inmate, the most of my associates were frequently his. At this time he read but little[284]

yet he was busy in writing a second instalment to his most famous tract, to be published as *Rights of Man. Part the Second*. Its publication was even harder to arrange than its precursor's. The publishers Joseph Johnson and J. S. Jordan both refused to be involved, fearing legal action. Paine's relations with a replacement, Thomas Chapman, broke down; he returned to Jordan and Johnson, and on Paine's written undertaking that he was both the author and the publisher, the tract finally appeared on 16 February 1792.[285]

Like *Rights of Man*, this sequel was written largely or wholly in London. Gouverneur Morris, passing through the capital, met Paine on 16 February: 'I tell Payne that I am really afraid he will be punished. He seems to laugh at this and relies on the Force he has in the Nation. God knows what may happen but I should think the Example of France is not very inviting. He seems Cock Sure of bringing

---

[281] Wyvill to Jeremiah Batley, 4 Apr. 1792, in Wyvill, *Political Papers*, v. 1–2.

[282] Wyvill to Samuel Shore, 28 May 1792, in Wyvill, *Political Papers*, v. 51–2; R. R. Fennessy, *Burke, Paine and the Rights of Man: A Difference of Political Opinion* (The Hague, 1963), 246.

[283] Graham, *The Nation, the Law and the King*, 310–11, 323–5. The theme of Paine's relations with the LCS is resumed in Ch. 5, section The London Corresponding Society.

[284] Thomas Clio Rickman, *Life of Thomas Paine* (London, 1819), 100–1.

[285] Keane, *Paine*, 324–7.

about a Revolution in Great Britain, and I think it quite as likely that he will be promoted to the Pilory.' Morris added on 23 February:

> Payne comes in who seems to become every Hour more drunk with Self Conceit. It seems, however, that his Book excites but little Emotion and rather raises Indignation. I tell him that the disordered State of Things in France works against all Schemes of Reformation both here and elsewhere. He declares that the Riots and Outrages in France are Nothing at all. It is not worth while to contest such Declarations; I tell him therefore that as I am sure he does not believe what he says I shall not dispute it.[286]

But Paine did believe what he said.

PAINE'S ARGUMENT: *RIGHTS OF MAN. PART THE SECOND*

France and America

In *Rights of Man. Part the Second* Paine announced his sense of his mission, derived from 'the great Father of all':

> For my own part, I am fully satisfied that what I am now doing, with an endeavour to conciliate mankind, to render their condition happy, to unite nations that have hitherto been enemies, and to extirpate the horrid practice of war, and break the chains of slavery and oppression, is acceptable in his sight, and being the best service I can perform, I act it cheerfully.[287]

The Age of Reason was not far off. Judged by this Messianic standard, Paine accepted that his earlier work *Rights of Man*, had its limitations: 'it did not go far enough. It detected errors; it exposed absurdities; it shook the fabric of political superstition; it generated new ideas; but it did not produce a regular system of principles in the room of those which it displaced.' It may be inferred that in Paine's view natural rights was not such a 'regular system of principles'. The absence, he claimed, was remedied in what was now presented as the second part of that work (although in *Rights of Man* Paine had envisaged no such sequel).[288] Did *Rights of Man. Part the Second* achieve these ends?

In one respect Paine's text was puzzling. *Rights of Man. Part the Second*, its dedication to Lafayette dated not in Paris but in London on 9 February 1792, continued Paine's turn away from the French Revolution begun at the end of *Rights of Man* (1791); and it added little on France that was new. Given his republican initiative in Paris in June and July 1791, it might have been expected that Paine would at least seek to consider more closely the events of the Revolution in order to plan a peaceful and republican reconstruction of France's government; he did not do so. Instead, in *Part*

---

[286] *A Diary of the French Revolution by Gouverneur Morris 1752–1816*, ed. Beatrix Cary Davenport (2 vols, London, 1939) for 16, 23 Feb. 1792: ii. 368, 370. Morris told Lafayette on 26 Jan. 1790 'that Payne can do him no good for that although he has an excellent Pen to write he has but an indifferent Head to think': 389.

[287] Paine, *Rights of Man. Part the Second* (1792): *CW*, i. 452 (text corrected).

[288] Paine, *Letter Addressed to the Addressers* (1792): *CW*, ii. 471.

the Second, Paine shifted attention away from France (where events were already giving some Englishmen concern) and praised what he argued were the 'principles' of government of the new (but remote and therefore universalist) American republic.

> The Revolution of America presented in politics what was only theory in mechanics... no sooner did the American governments display themselves to the world, than despotism felt a shock, and man began to contemplate redress.
>
> The independence of America, considered merely as a separation from England, would have been a matter but of little importance, had it not been accompanied by a revolution in the principles and practice of governments...As America was the only spot in the political world, where the principles of universal reformation could begin, so also was it the best in the natural world. An assemblage of circumstances conspired, not only to give birth, but to add gigantic maturity to its principles... Government founded on a *moral theory, on a system of universal peace, on the indefeasible, hereditary Rights of Man*, is now revolving from west to east, by a stronger impulse than the government of the sword revolved from east to west.

But after these uplifting generalizations, Paine did not turn to specifics about the American Revolution, or the society of the new United States, or the constitution of 1787. It was sufficient that the American republic could be ascribed different premises from the old world for America to be held up as a 'moral' alternative to it.[289]

Instead, Paine's main point in chapter I of *Part the Second* was to argue not from the specifics of the French or American Revolutions but from 'a system of principles as a basis on which governments ought to be erected', and especially, as in *Common Sense*, for a pre-existing 'society' as a natural and peaceful formation against which the unnatural and warlike phenomenon of 'government' could be judged (the theological premises of this view were already evident in 1776): 'society performs for itself almost every thing which is ascribed to government'. To establish this point Paine used an American example, but an imaginary one: 'For upward of two years from the commencement of the American war, and to a longer period in several of the American States, there were no established forms of government...yet during this interval, order and harmony were preserved as inviolate as in any country in Europe.'[290] As a comment on the savage realities of civil war in North America this needed, itself, an explanation. It may also be that Paine was inconsistent: in the new American republic he favoured a stronger Federal government, but in the old monarchies of France and England he expressed hostility to government as such.

Paine did not attempt to demonstrate the innocence of 'society' from the much closer example of France, where such a claim would have been recognized as problematic. Indeed, he pronounced, in the United States 'by the simple operation of constructing government on the principles of society and the rights of man, every difficulty retires'. Such simple principles had their simple effects automatically:

> There the poor are not oppressed, the rich are not privileged. Industry is not mortified by the splendid extravagance of a court rioting at its expense. Their taxes are few, because

---

[289] Paine, *Rights of Man. Part the Second* (1792): *CW*, i. 353–6 (text corrected).
[290] Paine, *Rights of Man. Part the Second* (1792): *CW*, i. 351, 357–8 (text corrected).

their government is just; and as there is nothing to render them wretched, there is nothing
to engender riots and tumults.

Given this logical and simple operation, it followed that it was not necessary for
Paine, in his eyes, to trace the working out of those principles; but precisely this
problem of the implementation of principle was now inescapable in France. Paine
did not confront it, claiming that the correct course was obvious: 'One of the great
advantages of the American Revolution has been, that it led to a discovery of the
principles, and laid open the imposition, of governments.'[291] In the case of the
American Revolution, it is argued (in Chapter 4) that the realities had been different. Paine brought his principles with him to Pennsylvania in 1774, and found
there the perfect arena in which to think them instantiated. In France after 1792
Paine's adjustment to very different circumstances was agonized and limited.

After this praise of 'society', *Rights of Man. Part the Second* returned in a notably brief chapter II to familiar English terrain: denouncing the origin of existing
monarchies in 'plunder' by 'bands of robbers', each 'a banditti of ruffians', and
asserting the superiority of the representative over the hereditary system. Paine's
telling example was English: 'Though not a courtier will talk of the curfeu-bell,
not a village in England has forgotten it.'[292] He did not address the contradiction between this account of the origins of states and that in *Common Sense*, in
which men were pictured as entering freely into political association in order to
defend their natural rights.

Paine's chapter 3 was differently aimed. 'It is not to him [Burke], but to Abbé
Sieyes, that I address this chapter. I am already engaged to the latter gentleman, to
discuss the subject of monarchical government.' Uniquely, Paine continued the
controversy with his French counterpart that he had begun in the Paris press in
July 1791, but Sieyès had focused on the principle of representation, Paine on the
principle of monarchy.[293] Sieyès had supported the continuance of a redefined
constitutional monarchy in France: Paine sought monarchy's eradication, but did
not meet Sieyès's exact arguments about representation. Rather, Paine repeated
his familiar point that all monarchies had begun in 'tyranny and the sword'. Talent
did not descend in hereditary succession, Paine argued. 'All hereditary government is in its nature tyranny.' The 'hereditary system' caused war, he urged, citing
examples. He quoted Sieyès's acceptance, in his second letter, that the hereditary
principle 'can never accord with the laws of a true representation'. Paine replied:
'Though the comparison between hereditary and elective monarchy, which the
Abbé has made, is unnecessary to the case, because the representative system
rejects both; yet, were I to make the comparison, I should decide contrary to what
he has done.'

In *Part the Second* Paine held up the example of the American Revolution against
the French implicitly to counter Sieyès's claim in July 1791 that the new French
Constitution was 'the purest and the best which has hitherto appeared in the world'.

---

[291] Paine, *Rights of Man. Part the Second* (1792): *CW*, i. 360, 398.
[292] Paine, *Rights of Man. Part the Second* (1792): *CW*, i. 361–3.
[293] For this exchange with Sieyès, see Ch. 5, section The Escalating Revolution, 1791–1792.

Sieyès had sought to refine and reform an old government; Paine argued that government as such had few legitimate functions, and 'society' could do almost everything that was required. Significantly, Paine understood his French colleague's position in terms of his, Paine's, earlier preoccupations; he did not address Sieyès's abstract arguments. Instead, Paine responded with one of his most sweeping generalizations: 'The representative system takes society and civilization for its basis; nature, reason, and experience for its guide.' Where Sieyès had argued that the representative system and the republic were distinct, Paine asserted, baldly, that 'Republican government... most naturally associates with the representative form.' So it was, Paine claimed, in America. But on the different conceptions of representation that Sieyès had advanced, Paine was silent, writing only: 'All men can understand what representation is.'[294] He drew on his English experiences to the extent that he could imagine no other system. Even on this issue, then, Paine and Sieyès largely talked past each other; in his chapter 3, Paine soon reverted to a debate with Burke, Paine insisting on his distinction between 'representation' and 'simple democracy' in order to defend the former from Burke's critique.

Paine phrased precise negations of monarchy; by contrast, his affirmations were general. His most notable affirmation indeed echoed Robespierre: 'What is called a *republic*, is not any *particular form* of government'; it was merely government for 'the public good'. 'Republican government is no other than government established and conducted for the interest of the public, as well individually as collectively.'[295] How this public virtue was to be measured, Paine did not explain. Indeed the point of republicanism for Paine was its logically necessary antithesis to the hereditary principle (republicanism's performance did not, therefore, need to be assessed). Many states called themselves republics, 'But the government of America, which is wholly on the system of representation, is the only real republic in character and practice, that now exists.' France, then, did not qualify.

The single choice Paine offered was between 'everything hereditary' and 'the system of representation'. Although he had earlier argued that each generation was free to choose whatever form of government it wished, it became clear from Paine's text that it could not legitimately choose monarchy or aristocracy. Monarchy (repeating a key phrase in *Common Sense*) was 'the popery of government'. America's government was 'representation ingrafted upon democracy', the system that Paine had been urging all along. Its actual working in the United States, Paine did not here explain; the merit of republicanism, in his model, was that it was the opposite of monarchy. Paine therefore eulogized the representative system in general terms. It 'diffuses such a body of knowledge throughout a nation, on the subject of government, as to explode ignorance and preclude imposition', as in America must be the case.[296]

---

[294] Paine, *Rights of Man. Part the Second* (1792): *CW*, i. 353–4, 357–8, 363–70, 373 (text corrected).

[295] Paine, *Rights of Man. Part the Second* (1792): *CW*, i. 364, 366–7, 369–70.

[296] Paine, *Rights of Man. Part the Second* (1792): *CW*, i. 370–1, 375.

Constitutions, American and English

How did this paragon work in practice? In his lengthy chapter IV, 'On Constitutions', Paine now attempted an answer. Most republics had existed in the ancient world, but he rejected any search into 'the obscure field of antiquity' since the foundation of the United States meant that 'We are brought at once to the point of seeing government begin, as if we had lived in the beginning of time.' This ought to have implied that colonial Americans had lived in a state of nature until they formed the constitutions of their thirteen new states, but Paine sidestepped the problem of their prior government as colonies by arguing that Pennsylvania (and similarly the other states) had formed its constitution through the work of a 'convention', a representative assembly. It was an account with the politics removed: Paine recorded nothing of the political manoeuvres by which minorities had seized and exercised power, preferring to aim at generalized inspiration.[297] But perhaps, by adopting this approach, Paine was polemically more effective.

The same absence of politics characterized Paine's account of the gradual adoption of the Act of Confederation in 1781 and the federal constitution of 1787 by all the states. The problem of the chronological priority of the thirteen states to their constitutions was avoided by Paine's insistence on a definition: a constitution simply was 'a thing antecedent to government, and always distinct therefrom'. The formation of Pennsylvania's constitution in 1776 was a rare case in which Paine wrote from personal knowledge; when he turned to the convention that met at Philadelphia in May 1787 to frame a federal constitution, he did not disclose that he had already left for France that April. Indeed his account of American federal constitution-framing was not well informed.

Instead, he praised the Philadelphia Convention in English terms: 'they did not, like a cabal of courtiers, send for a Dutch stadtholder [as in 1688], or a German elector [as in 1714]; but they referred the whole matter to the sense and interest of the country.' Paine's opponent here was also English: 'From the want of understanding the difference between a constitution and a government, Dr. Johnson,[298] and all writers of his description, have always bewildered themselves.' Equally English were his examples of the transcendence of constitutions: William of Normandy, Magna Carta, 'the Edwards and the Henrys', James II and William III, the Bill of Rights, the Whigs' Septennial Act of 1716, 'the corruption introduced at the Hanover accession, by the agency of Walpole'. Finally, almost uniquely, a political observation intruded: 'As to what is called the Convention-parliament [of 1689], it was a thing that made itself, and then made the authority by which it acted.' Why this was not equally true of later conventions, Paine did not enquire.[299]

The English government 'appears, since its political connection with Germany [in 1714], to have been so completely engrossed and absorbed by foreign affairs, and the means of raising taxes, that it seems to exist for no other purposes'. The

---

[297] Paine, *Rights of Man. Part the Second* (1792): *CW*, i. 376–8.

[298] Paine evidently referred to [Samuel Johnson], *Taxation no Tyranny: an Answer to the Resolutions and Address of the American Congress* (London: T. Cadell, 1775).

[299] Paine, *Rights of Man. Part the Second* (1792): *CW*, i. 378–83, 390.

alternative ideal of cheap, simple government was similarly vouched for by a native example: "'*Government*," says Swift, "*is a plain thing, and fitted to the capacity of many heads.*"[300] Paine may have echoed one passage from that author:

> God... hath made the science of governing sufficiently obvious to common capacities; otherwise the world would be left in a desolate condition, if great affairs did always require a great genius, whereof the most fruitful age will hardly produce above three or four in a nation, among which, princes, who, of all other mortals, are the worst educated, have twenty millions to one against them that they shall not be of the number; and proportionable odds, for the same reasons, are against every one of noble birth, or great estates... I never yet knew a minister, who was not earnestly desirous to have it thought, that the art of government was a most profound science; whereas it requires no more, in reality, than diligence, honesty, and a moderate share of plain natural sense.[301]

But if governing was something of which men of common capacities were capable, it was not clear why princes of ordinary abilities were especially disqualified. Paine did not make clear the sources of his own negations. He did not often name the authors on whom he drew, but he did so here. His choice suggests that his repeated championing of the ideal of simplicity in politics derived not from a new world, from anticipations of a liberal-democratic future, but from an old world, from Tory critiques of Whig corruption and manoeuvre in the first half of the century. Only partly did Paine ever succeed in theorizing these antipathies.

Indeed there was a notable absence from Paine's writings, *Rights of Man* in particular: despite his condemnation of monarchy in general, and denunciation of George III, Paine wrote little specifically against Louis XVI and later even risked his own life by pleading for that of the French king in the National Convention. Paine's commitments were more specific and less abstract than they later appeared: a preoccupation with his defence of Louis XVI alone will seem to support a claim of his universalism, yet this needs to be balanced against his particularism, his denunciations of Hanoverian kings of England. Paine remained committed to his view that the French Revolution, like the American, was benign because it was a matter of general principle; but this was a default position, arrived at once specific objections to specific monarchs (notably George III) were registered.

Social security

From these familiar English points, Paine turned at the end of *Rights of Man. Part the Second*, in a lengthy chapter V, not to a deeper analysis of revolution as such, or of the events of the American or French Revolutions, but to what is often read as a prophetic sketch of a system of social security, paid for by the taxation of the rich.

---

[300] Paine, *Rights of Man. Part the Second* (1792): *CW*, i. 386, 392.

[301] *An Enquiry Into the Behaviour of the Queen's Last Ministry, With Relation to their Quarrels among themselves, and the Design charged upon them of altering the Succession of the Crown. June MDCCXV*, in *The Works of Dr Jonathan Swift, Dean of St. Patrick's Dublin*, ed. Deane Swift (London: W. Johnston, 1765), xv. 65–6.

In this outline he made no reference to American or French sources: no such social security system had achieved prominence in the revolutions of 1776 or 1789, and Paine's scheme has therefore conventionally been interpreted as anticipating revolutions still in the future. The data on which Paine's plans were based were drawn not from America or France, but from England: William Pitt's speeches in Parliament and Sir John Sinclair's study of taxation.[302]

Paine's pages outlining social reform[303] assumed increasing relevance in later decades, but even here his argument necessarily could not anticipate the class-based analysis, on economic premises, that was to characterize nineteenth-century reformist politics. Paine argued that his language was 'dictated by no passion but that of humanity';[304] he did not, indeed could not, defend class allegiance. Chapter V began instead with what Paine saw as the vast, unnecessary expense of corrupt governments. His scheme for redistributing wealth was preoccupied with alternative uses for some of the massive sums Paine thought could be freed by abolishing monarchy and aristocracy, and the wars, taxes, and national debts that Paine claimed they alone caused. The aristocracy, for Paine, was associated with the concept of luxury, and it was a moral condemnation of luxury more than an economic condemnation of inequality of property that influenced Paine's analysis. That, indeed, was why he was not inconsistent in arguing in *Rights of Man. Part the Second* for a degree of redistribution of income while arguing elsewhere (as has been seen)

> That property will ever be unequal is certain. Industry, superiority of talents, deterity of management, extreme frugality, fortunate opportunities, or the opposite, or the means of those things, will ever produce that effect, without having recourse to the harsh, ill-sounding names of avarice and oppression.[305]

Only after rehearsing in familiar fashion his negative critique of war, government expense, foreign dominion, chartered rights that excluded the rights of man, the inadequacy of parliamentary representation, the powers of the House of Lords, the inequity of the tax burden, and the emptiness of the idea of the crown did Paine turn to the theme for which chapter V is now best known.

Paine's pages on social reform began with statistical accounts not directly of people's daily experiences of poverty and their weekly budgets but of national tax revenues and excessive government expenditures. The most famous quantitative surveys or analyses of poverty and the life experiences of labourers still lay in the future; Paine hardly anticipated them.[306] Rather, he outlined a cheaper structure

---

[302] Paine, *Rights of Man. Part the Second* (1792): *CW*, i. 402, 404, 410, 416, 420, 423; John Sinclair, *The History of the Public Revenue of the British Empire* (London: W. and A. Strahan, for T. Cadell, 1785); Paine used the second edition of 1790.

[303] Paine, *Rights of Man. Part the Second* (1792): *CW*, i. 415–42.

[304] Paine, *Rights of Man. Part the Second* (1792): *CW*, i. 413.

[305] Paine, *Dissertation on First-Principles of Government* (1795): *CW*, ii. 580.

[306] Tho[mas] Ruggles, *The History of the Poor; their Rights, Duties, and the Laws respecting them* (2 vols, London: J. Deighton, 1793–4, 2nd edn, 1797); David Davis, *The Case of the Labourers in Husbandry Stated and Considered, in three parts. Part I. A View of their Distressed Condition. Part II. The Principal Causes of their Growing Distress and Number, and of the Consequent Increase of the Poor-Rate. Part III. Means of Relief Proposed. With an Appendix; containing A Collection of Accounts, shewing the*

of government, as a result of which 'there will remain a surplus of upwards of six millions out of the present current expenses. The question then will be, how to dispose of this surplus.' Paine's first plan was 'to abolish the poor-rates entirely, and, in lieu thereof, to make a remission of taxes to the poor to double the amount of the present poor-rates'. Since 'the poor are generally composed of large families of children, and old people unable to labour', Paine proposed transferring £4 million to them. The rest of the poor were 'incidental', and could be dealt with 'in great measure' by 'benefit clubs'. Paine showed no understanding of the many causes of adult underemployment and unemployment, whose victims would, in his plan, have been largely cut off from previously existing, if scanty, state support. An exception was his proposal for building workhouses 'capable of containing six thousand persons' to provide for 'the casual poor in the cities of London and Westminster'.[307] But for the adult unemployed in the rest of the nation there would have been no provision. Paine's understanding of 'the poor' was highly selective, as, it might be argued, was the case with other contemporaries who were not yet able to consult the subsequently published studies of David Davis and Frederick Morton Eden. Paine's own experience of economic adversity might have supplied at least some of this specific knowledge, but he did not record it in print.

Paine's plan therefore needs to be reconciled with his eloquent lament at the 'thousands… pining with want, and struggling with misery'. Or, again: 'there lies hidden from the eye of common observation, a mass of wretchedness that has scarcely any other chance than to expire in poverty or infamy'. It seems that his rhetorically memorable identification with the poor coexisted in Paine's mind with his plan, but with little practical engagement, since Paine assumed that the labour of poor individuals was fully capable of providing for their needs once the burden of unnecessary taxation (which took from the labourer 'a fourth part of his yearly earnings') was lifted.[308] Despite Paine's eloquent lament at a 'mass of wretchedness', he wrote nothing about its specific realities, its other causes, or its demoralizing impact on so many.

Paine's attention was elsewhere, on the goals of 'Restoring justice among families by distribution of property… Extirpating the overgrown influence arising from the unnatural law of primogeniture, and which is one of the principal sources of corruption at elections.' Paine's priority was a negative critique of injustice and

---

Earnings and Expences of Labouring Families, in Different Parts of the Kingdom (Bath: R. Cruttwell, for G. G. and J. Robinson, London, 1795); Frederick Morton Eden, *The State of the Poor: or, An History of the Labouring Classes in England, from the Conquest to the Present Period; In which are particularly considered, their Domestic Economy, with respect to Diet, Dress, Fuel, and Habitation; And the various Plans which, from time to time, have been proposed, and adopted, for the Relief of the Poor: together with Parochial Reports Relative to the Administration of Work-houses, and Houses of Industry; the State of Friendly Societies; and other Public Institutions; in several Agricultural, Commercial, and Manufacturing, Districts* (3 vols, London: B. and J. White, G. G. and J. Robinson, T. Payne et al., 1797); P[atrick] Colquhoun, *A Treatise on Indigence; exhibiting a General View of the National Resources for Productive Labour; with Propositions for Ameliorating the Condition of the Poor, and improving the moral Habits and increasing the Comforts of the Labouring People, particularly The Rising Generation, by Regulations of Political Economy* (London: J. Hatchard, 1806).

[307] Paine, *Rights of Man. Part the Second* (1792): *CW*, i. 415–24, 430–1.
[308] Paine, *Rights of Man. Part the Second* (1792): *CW*, i. 392, 405, 424.

'luxury', especially that luxury which arose from 'an overgrown estate'; his ideal was the small freeholder (as he himself now was, in America), whose interest was at odds with the interest of the great landowner. When one considered the incomes of landed families in higher and higher brackets, Paine contended, it became impossible to argue that such incomes were necessary; but he condemned this inequality with the term 'luxury'. Tracing ever higher wealth,

> we shall at last arrive at a sum that may not improperly be called a prohibitable luxury. It would be impolitic to set bounds to property acquired by industry, and therefore it is right to place the prohibition beyond the probable acquisition to which industry can extend; but there ought to be a limit to property, or the accumulation of it by bequest. It should pass in some other line. The richest in every nation have poor relations, and those very often near in consanguinity.

Instead, Paine offered a table of 'progressive taxation' that would 'supersede the aristocratical law of primogeniture'. What was the appropriate level of that tax? Paine proposed no answer, since he held that 'The object is not so much the produce of the tax as the justice of the measure.' Even his social security proposals, then, were driven more by his negations of the unjust 'aristocratical system' than by his affirmations, by any vision of the society which a just distribution of property would produce.[309]

Absent from Paine's plans for social security was the rising world of manufactures. In his discourse, 'industry' still meant what it had meant throughout the eighteenth century, namely personal industriousness; he could not anticipate the great inequalities of wealth in a society dominated by manufacturing (or, as it came later to be theorized, capitalism). Paine perceived humanity's enemy as the aristocrat in the old world, not the manufacturer in a new. His analysis was a moral rejection of the luxury drawn from landed rents, not an economic rejection of the wealth drawn from manufacturing profits. But by this rejection of luxury Paine gave a hostage to fortune. His moral language set no analytical limit to taxation and immediately led moderates to claim that his plan was to bribe the poor with annuities taken from the estates of the rich: not redistribution, but expropriation. Paine did not dispel their fears, and, it might be argued, his intentions were widely misunderstood.[310] Nor did he respond to one famous claim of eighteenth-century political economy: that the luxury of the rich meant the employment of the poor. Paine's incidental condemnation of great inequalities of property was soon overtaken by William Godwin's far more systematic and extensive critique in *An Enquiry Concerning Political Justice*, published in February 1793; Paine was retrospectively assimilated to a crusade of the nineteenth century, and the differences between Paine and the early socialists were lost to view.

Consequently, it is still often not made clear that Paine's schemes of state charity were extensions of (and sometimes reductions of) the provisions for poor relief

---

[309] Paine, *Rights of Man. Part the Second* (1792): *CW*, i. 413, 433–4, 436, 439.

[310] Paine 'makes no real attempt to justify these radical incursions on property rights': Philp, *Paine*, 87. This suggests that he did not see them as such, but rather as moral reforms.

already in place in England. Paine's schemes were therefore not necessarily inconsistent with his reliance on private enterprise, free trade, and their attendant inequalities of property.[311] His vision of a society governed through the representative
system implied a diversified society of different interests, not a homogeneous society for which one person, party, or class could claim to stand. As will be argued, his
tract *Agrarian Justice* (1797) had as its intellectual context his moral and theological
reflections in *The Age of Reason* (1794–5), not the reflections in *Rights of Man. Part
the Second* on social security payments.[312] And so, making no connection with his
scheme of social security, Paine turned at the end of *Rights of Man. Part the Second*
to an uplifting vision of cooperation between England, France, and America to
extinguish 'despotism and bad government'. Indeed, Paine's vocation was that of a
Deist, not of a political economist.[313]

Reactions to *Part the Second*

Despite these pacific professions, *Rights of Man. Part the Second* aroused a large
hostile reaction in England. The abolition of primogeniture and the break-up of
the great estates might have been seen there in the 1790s as revolution; however,
Paine did not present it in this way. He praised 'Reason and discussion...By such
a process no tumult is to be apprehended.' Paine is instead famous for what is often
taken to be a valid insight into the nature of modern revolution as such:

> What were formerly called revolutions, were little more than a change of persons, or
> an alteration of local circumstances. They rose and fell like things of course, and had
> nothing in their existence or their fate that could influence beyond the spot that pro-
> duced them. But what we now see in the world, from the revolutions of America and
> France, is a renovation of the natural order of things, a system of principles as universal
> as truth and the existence of man, and combining moral with political happiness and
> national prosperity.[314]

Here, then, seems to be Paine the universalist, celebrating a position often thought
to have been confirmed by events. But there are problems with crediting him with
such a valid prophecy.

First, he possessed no such insight, on the basis of his American experiences of
1774–83, before he arrived in France in 1787; and he might have been expected to
have drawn this lesson from America, had it been possible to draw it. Second, changes
in the recent interpretations of both revolutions now suggest that his benign and
cerebral characterization of them was, rather, a projection onto their cataclysmic
and sanguinary realities of Paine's prior commitments. Third, if Paine did not
anticipate the American and French Revolutions it was not because he was unwilling to try to look to the future, for he wrongly predicted many more. Revolutions
would break out across Europe: 'I do not believe that monarchy and aristocracy

---

[311] 'Paine's "social chapter" was not in fact extensively discussed, at least in print': Claeys, *Paine*, 121.
[312] See Ch. 6, section *The Age of Reason* as a Context for *Agrarian Justice*.
[313] Paine, *Rights of Man. Part the Second* (1792): *CW*, i. 449.
[314] Paine, *Rights of Man* (1791): *CW*, i. 341–2, 447.

will continue seven years longer in any of the enlightened countries in Europe...As revolutions have begun...it is natural to expect that other revolutions will follow.'[315] Fourth, revolution took a different course: it had to be exported across the European continent at the point of the bayonet, rather than being a spontaneous 'movement', the spontaneous instantiation of a series of universal principles. In Europe as well as North America, different societies reacted to the (universalist) discourse of the French Revolution in different (particularist) ways.

Paine predicted a revolution in the government of Britain that would follow a successful French invasion. He claimed that 'the plan for a descent upon England by gunboats was proposed by myself'. While in Paris in the late 1790s he sent the Council of Five Hundred a voluntary contribution of 500 livres towards this cause, with 'all the wishes of my heart for the success of the descent, and a voluntary offer of any service I can render to promote it'.[316] Paine's career in the French government was clearly at an end; it was rational for him to gamble on being the catalyst of revolution in his home country. In this scheme he made some progress. An English agent in Paris in 1798 reported Bonaparte's plan that, in the event of a successful invasion, an English Directory would be established consisting of '[Thomas] Paine, [John Horne] Tooke, [William] Sharpe, [John] Thelwall, and [the Marquis of] Lansdown'.[317] Even in America in September 1803 Paine expected to be tempted 'to make another passage cross the Atlantic to assist in forming a Constitution for England'.[318]

Paine, then, framed some arguments about the lessons that the British might learn from the new government established in the United States. But his own account of his published work was more abstract:

> In the first part of 'Rights of Man,' I have endeavored to show...that there does not exist a right to establish hereditary government...In the second part of 'Rights of Man,' I...have confined myself to show the defects of what is called hereditary government, or hereditary succession, that it must, from the nature of it, throw government into the hands of men totally unworthy of it...James II is recorded as an instance of the first of these cases.

Paine reserved a fuller comparison between a hereditary system of government and 'the representative system', the United States, for an open letter to Henry Dundas, Secretary of State.[319] Even here, Paine did not enter into a systematic comparison of the two countries' constitutions, but argued primarily that the American government was much cheaper, again using as his authority for English expenditure Sir John Sinclair's *History of the Revenue*.[320]

---

[315] Paine, *Rights of Man. Part the Second* (1792): *CW*, i. 352, 355.

[316] Paine to the Conseil des Cinq Cents (29 Jan. 1798): *CW*, ii. 1403; Alfred Owen Aldridge, 'Thomas Paine's Plan for a Descent on England', *WMQ* 14 (1957), 74–84.

[317] *Report on the Manuscripts of J. B. Fortescue, Esq. Preserved at Dropmore*, ed. Walter FitzPatrick (10 vols, London, 1905), iv. 69–70.

[318] Paine to Barras, 29 Dec. 1797; Paine to the Conseil des Cinq Cents, 28 Jan. 1798; Paine to Thomas Jefferson, 1 Oct. 1800, 9 June 1801, [Oct. 1801], 23 Sept. 1803, 30 Jan. 1806: *CW*, ii. 1402–3, 1415–16, 1420, 1424, 1449, 1474–5, 1478.

[319] Paine, *A Letter To Mr Secretary Dundas* (1792), the letter dated 6 June 1792: *CW*, ii. 447–9, 452.

[320] Paine, *Letter Addressed to the Addressers* (1792): *CW*, ii. 502.

America mattered more than that: as the English reformers steered away from the example of France in *c.*1791–3, embarrassed by the unfolding horrors of its revolution, they made increasing use of the more attractive example of the new American republic.[321] But English reformers typically knew little of the United States, and projected onto that society their wish-fulfilments. This was true even of a man who had briefly practised at the bar in Philadelphia. Joseph Gerrald, now an activist in the London Corresponding Society and soon to be transported to Australia, wrote:

> In America, that happy land of freedom and equality of rights, the blood of man is never shed to satiate the cruelty and ambition of crowned heads. America is without courts, and therefore she is without wars…In America, that country which God and man have concurred to render the blissful habitation of abundance and of peace, the poor are not broken down by taxes to support the expensive trappings of royalty, or pamper the luxury of an insolent nobility. No lordly peer tramples down the corn of the husbandman, no proud prelate wrings from him the tythe of his industry. They have neither chicanery in ermine [robes, i.e. peers], nor hypocrisy in lawn [sleeves, i.e. bishops]. The community is not there divided into an oppressed peasantry and an overgrown aristocracy, the one of whom lives by the plunder of the state, while the others are compelled to be the objects of it. Plenty is the lot of all, superfluity of none…The word subordination, a term unknown in the vocabulary of freemen, and which means only a reciprocation of slavery and tyranny, never wounds the ear of the high minded republican. Order, real order is preserved, because no man has an interest in disturbing it.[322]

This was an English Utopian vision, not a report on the situation on the ground in America. Such eulogies had to be true by definition, given Paine's identification of the negative features of English society. As a reformer who visited the republic admitted, 'Perhaps some part of my predilection for America, may be justly attributed to my political prejudices in favour of the kind of government established there.'[323]

Frenchmen could indulge in the same wishful thinking: J. P. Brissot's *Nouveau Voyage dans les États-Unis de l'Amerique Septentrionale* (1792) assured readers that 'A man in that country, works scarcely two hours in a day, for the support of himself and family.'[324] The ardent reformer and Unitarian Samuel Taylor Coleridge, lecturing in Bristol in the early 1790s and framing a project for a Utopian community called Pantisocracy to be established on the banks of the Susquehannah River, knew Brissot's book and echoed his prediction about the length of the American working day needed to produce necessities, as did Robert Lovell. Indeed

[321] Mark Philp, 'The Role of America in the "Debate on France" 1791–5: Thomas Paine's Insertion', *Utilitas* 5 (1993), 221–37; Wil Verhoeven, *Americomania and the French Revolution Debate in Britain, 1789–1802* (Cambridge, 2013).

[322] Joseph Gerrald, *A Convention the Only Means of Saving us from Ruin. In a Letter, addressed to the People of England* (London: D. I. Eaton, 1793), 71–3; partly quoted in Philp, 'The Role of America', 223. Philp finds that 'it is difficult to judge how deep lay the commitment, how far it extended beyond the most literate radical circles, and precisely when it developed', 225.

[323] Thomas Cooper, *Some Information respecting America* (London: J. Johnson, 1794), iv.

[324] J. P. Brissot de Warville, *New Travels in the United States of America. Performed in 1788* (London: J. S. Jordan, 1792), 260.

Coleridge later said that he had chosen the Susquehannah as a site because he liked the sound of the name.[325] Egalitarian self-rule was an appealing vision. Numbers of English activists emigrated to the new United States, including John Binns, Thomas Birch, John Daly Burk, James Thomson Callender, Matthew Carey, Thomas Cooper, Richard Dinmore, Denis Driscol, William Duane, Daniel Isaac Eaton, Thomas Emmet, Joseph Gales, Henry Jackson, William MacNeven, Robert Merry, Joseph Priestley, and others;[326] but *émigré* status did not establish the accuracy of their understanding of American society, and it did not remove from British minds the immediate and pressing case of France.

For inescapable reasons, France was to be at the centre of attention for British observers until 1815, and the limitations of Paine's account of the French Revolution outweighed, for his critics, his unspecific but golden image of the new American republic. After 1815, the ill-informed eulogies persisted, as in Jeremy Bentham's writings. Consequently, 'all political groupings managed to accommodate their images of America to their own traditions and framework of values', at least until the growing 'disenchantment with America's acquisitive and inegalitarian capitalism' that has been located in *c*.1820–50.[327] It has been suggested that the American example features little in the case put by the defenders of Church and state in England in the 1790s, 'as if there is a recognition among loyalist propagandists that the American example must be shut out, because it is not clear how it can be countered'. It may be that this infrequency is to be explained more by the implausibly Utopian nature of writing on America, and by an appreciation that its circumstances were unique, not exemplary: the arguments for America were distant, and generalized; the arguments for France were close, and specific.[328]

Nor does *Rights of Man. Part the Second* disclose a new debt to Rousseau and a consequent collective, communitarian attitude to government. Paine's remark in a private letter, probably about this time, even treated nations as an extrapolation of individuals: 'A nation is only a great individual, and that which is good or bad character for an individual is good or bad character for a Nation.'[329] Paine frequently wrote of 'the people'; he never explained what he meant by the term partly because he did not give 'the nation' a new and collective meaning. That remained a locution more French than English.

[325] J. R. MacGillivray, 'The Pantisocracy Scheme and its Immediate Background', in Malcolm W. Wallace (ed.), *Studies in English by Members of University College Toronto* (Toronto, 1931), 131–69, at 132, 143, 152; John Colmer, *Coleridge: Critic of Society* (Oxford, 1959), 7–8.

[326] Michael Durey, *Transatlantic Radicals and the Early American Republic* (Lawrence, Kan., 1997).

[327] Paul Crook, 'Whiggery and America: Accommodating the Radical Threat', in Michael T. Davis (ed.), *Radicalism and Revolution in Britain, 1775–1848: Essays in Honour of Malcolm I. Thomis* (London, 2000), 191–206, at 192–3; David Paul Crook, *American Democracy in English Politics 1815–1850* (Oxford, 1965); Gregory Claeys, 'The Example of America a Warning to England? The Transformation of America in British Radicalism and Socialism, 1790–1850', in Malcolm Chase and Ian Dyck (eds), *Living and Learning: Essays in Honour of J. F. C. Harrison* (Aldershot, 1996), 66–80, at 67.

[328] e.g. William Playfair, *Inevitable Consequences of Reform in Parliament* (London, 1792), pp. 16–17, in Philp, 'The Role of America', 231.

[329] Paine to anon., n.d. [?1792]: *CW*, ii. 1297 (there misdated 1789).

EXILE, THE TERROR, AND ITS
AFTERMATH, 1792–1794

The London Corresponding Society

Paine left Paris in July 1791, and was continuously in England until *Rights of Man.
Part the Second* was published in London on 16 February 1792.[330] By chance,
Paine was now on the spot to coincide with another notable development: the
foundation of the London Corresponding Society on about 25 January that year.
Perhaps covertly promoted by leading members of the more patrician Society for
Constitutional Information, the plebeian LCS was a quickly growing club of artisans sometimes influenced by Paine's ideas as no society in Philadelphia or Paris
had ever been: the Jacobins or the Cordeliers owed little to any reading of his
works. The LCS was soon joined by a small master, the shoemaker Thomas Hardy,
who by the spring was its secretary. Its central goal was, like the SCI (and presumably given to it by the SCI), universal suffrage and annual parliaments. This doctrine was already familiar ground in London from 1780, but the LCS supported it
with a plebeian identity. As Hardy wrote to a Scottish ally, the society had discussed
'the low and even miserable conditions the people of this Nation were reduced to',
the result of 'the avariciousness and extortions of that haughty voluptuous and lux-
urious class of beings who would have us to possess no more knowledge than to
believe all things were created for the use of that small group of worthless individuals'.[331] It seems from the perspective of recent historiography that the LCS was
Paine's natural home; yet he evidently did not see the populist significance of this
new phenomenon.

Little evidence survives for Paine's relations with the plebeian LCS or the provincial societies with which it developed contacts. It is not even clear how many of its
meetings he attended. Instead, Paine was closer to the patrician Society for
Constitutional Information, where he was the guest of honour at a meeting in April
1792. The SCI, founded in 1780 and associated with a talented group of theorists
including John Cartwright, Thomas Brand Hollis, John Jebb, and Capel Lofft, later
joined by John Horne Tooke, adopted from the beginning the goals of annual parliaments and universal manhood suffrage, and pursued them by the assiduous circulation of printed material;[332] Paine may now, in part, have caught up with what they
had been doing for a decade. But Paine's contacts were with a changed SCI, pushed
in a more extreme direction. Especially this may have been the achievement of the
evasive Tooke. In 1794 Tooke successfully played down his extremism in order to
defend himself at his trial; yet in 1792 Paine was frequently Tooke's guest at his house
at Wimbledon, and may have understood more than emerged in court.[333]

---

[330] For the popular reception of Paine, see especially Thompson, *The Making of the English Working
Class*; Claeys, *Paine*, chs 5 and 6; Nicholas Rogers, 'Burning Tom Paine: Loyalism and Counter-
Revolution in Britain, 1792–1793', *Histoire Sociale/Social History* 32 (1999), 139–71. Such perspectives
can now be supplemented by evidence for popular political consciousness and protest before the 1760s.
[331] Hardy to John Walker, 9 Apr. [1792]: Francis Place MSS, BL Add MSS 27,814, fo. 178.
[332] Graham, *The Nation, the Law and the King*, 42–7, 79.
[333] Graham, *The Nation, the Law and the King*, 81–9.

The publication of *Rights of Man. Part the Second* on 16 February 1792 meant that Paine had no time to incorporate in its pages anything learned from the LCS, launched with a handful of founder members late in the previous month. According to Thomas Hardy, Paine offered to help write an address for the LCS, setting out the principles of the new society, after it was unable to agree, on 26 March 1792, to John Horne Tooke's draft text (it is not clear that Paine was present at that meeting); but Paine (who wrote slowly) evidently did not produce a manifesto in time, for on 28 or 29 March the LCS adopted a text drafted instead by Maurice Margarot. On 11 May a division of the LCS heard a reading of Paine's letter of defiance to the Home Secretary, Henry Dundas, and began a subscription to help Paine's legal defence in the impending prosecution (it is unlikely that Paine was present); but the LCS finally raised only £10, hardly an overwhelming response, and even this was not used for its intended purpose.[334]

After the publication of *Rights of Man. Part the Second* Paine went into hiding in Bromley, Kent, to be out of the public eye while anti-Paine mobs burned his effigy across England in a 'ritual of loyalist celebration',[335] but he was working on a response to the controversy and on an address from the Manchester Constitutional Society. The latter was read in translation by James Watt, Jr and Thomas Cooper at the Jacobin Club in Paris on 27 May, announcing that their principles were not confined to their society but 's'étendent, avec une force toujours croissante, dans toutes les parties de la Grande Bretagne'.[336] It seems that Paine was undiscriminating in his French contacts, for he was also elected to the editorial circle of the Girondist journal *La Chronique du mois*, and wrote for it.[337] Just as Paine had not understood the realities of revolutionary violence in America and France, so he did not appreciate the possibility of revolutionary violence in Britain, and the reactions of even moderates against his own works in consequence.

If Paine's anticipations were limited, the opposite was also the case: his doctrines were simplified and partly misrepresented in their public reception. The rector of Wolsingham in the Durham coalfield reported in 1792:

> As the cheapness of Mr. Paine's books has put it in the power of the poorest man to purchase them, there are I believe many of them now in circulation amongst such people, who with great industry communicate those dangerous yet fascinating opinions of equality amongst their companions; They have not yet been at all riotous; but the conversation of many of them has a strong tendency to levelling and republicanism... They talk of equality and expect, that all property will be divided, in case of a Republic. They murmur against the heavy taxes, which they suppose to arise from the extravagance of the Prince of Wales and the rest of the royal family; and as they hear that his royal Highness has got into much debt at present they suppose that their bur-

[334] Thale (ed.), *LCS Papers*, xxi, 6, 9, 15, 108, 257, 259.
[335] Frank O'Gorman, 'The Paine Burnings of 1792–1793', *P&P* 193 (2006) 111–55, at 114.
[336] Keane, *Paine*, 340; Address to the Jacobin Club (27 May 1792), printed in Moncure Daniel Conway, *Thomas Paine (1737–1809) et la Révolution dans les deux mondes* (Paris, 1900), 210–12.
[337] Gary Kates, *The Cercle Social, the Girondins, and the French Revolution* (Princeton, 1985), 188, 202–9.

thens will be still increased in order to pay it off. As they hear that the king is the richest Monarch in Europe they speak disrespectfully of his Majesty, for not paying his son's debts, without squeezing money for that purpose out of the hands of poor labourers.[338]

There is no evidence that Paine appreciated how his arguments were received and amplified among a mass audience.

Paine returned to London on 14 May after the publisher of *Rights of Man. Part the Second*, J. S. Jordan, received a summons to appear before the Court of King's Bench; Paine himself was summonsed, on a charge of seditious libel, on 21 May. He appeared in court on 8 June only to learn that his trial was postponed until the winter. The period of Paine's possible interaction with the LCS was therefore between mid-May and early September 1792, for on 13 September he fled to France; yet of this period little is known. It seems that after his court appearance he again went into hiding in the house of a member of the SCI, Christopher Hull, while writing the pamphlet later published as *Letter Addressed to the Addressers*. It was in the summer of 1792 that the educated activists of the SCI came to dominate the deferential and inexperienced LCS.[339] Yet many other activists were involved in the LCS; Paine was one figure among many. Although his health was drunk at an LCS meeting on 20 January 1794, his was only one of seventeen toasts on that occasion.[340] The evidence does not establish that Paine was the presiding genius of that society. Nor was *Rights of Man* necessarily the perfect encapsulation of the views of that diverse body. As is argued in Chapter 7, the most influential of Paine's tracts with LCS members was probably *The Age of Reason*.

Yet *Rights of Man. Part the Second* was important, and Pitt's government now decided to act. On 21 May 1792 a royal proclamation was issued against seditious publications; in a debate in the Commons on 25 May on the royal proclamation against 'seditious writings', the ministry made clear that Paine was the prime target. William Pitt argued that he himself had opposed universal suffrage ten years before, but, since then, 'principles had been laid down by Mr. Paine, which went to a more dangerous and indefinite extent. Principles which struck at hereditary nobility, and which went to the destruction of monarchy and religion, and the total subversion of the established form of government.'[341] Pitt did not include universal manhood suffrage, which was not associated primarily with Paine; nor was it obviously the chief solvent of government and society: Paine's goals were wider. Yet it may be that the ministry thought a safer course than prosecution was to pressurize Paine into a voluntary exile. On 8 June the court postponed Paine's trial for seditious libel until December that year. On 4 July Paine offered the royalties of *Rights of Man*, now amounting to £1,000, to the Society for Constitutional Information (not the LCS), 'to apply it to such purposes as they shall see proper'.

---

[338] J. Wilson to John Reeves, 10 Dec. 1792: BL Add MSS 16,927 fos 47–8.
[339] Graham, *The Nation, the Law and the King*, 333–4, 338, 370.
[340] Thale (ed.), *LCS Papers*, 108.
[341] William Cobbett (ed.), *The Parliamentary History of England, from the Earliest Period to the Year 1803* (London: T. C. Hansard et al., 1817), xxix. col. 1513.

The SCI declined,[342] possibly seeing in Paine too dangerous a patron. Finally Paine's nerve broke; warned by William Blake of an imminent attempt to arrest him, Paine left London for France on the evening of 13 September.

Paine took with him a proof of his pamphlet *A Letter Addressed to the Addressers*, which was published in London on 18 October 1792. His starting point, just as in *Common Sense*, was a long quotation from the Bible, 1 Samuel 8, in order to negate kingship. He proceeded to ridicule gentlemen as being 'fed by the public, as a pauper is by the parish'. Consequently, the constitution was a good one only for 'courtiers, placemen, pensioners, borough-holders, and the leaders of parties', and was only sustained by 'perpetual corruption'. Rather, Paine insisted, he had 'shown, both in the first and second parts of "Rights of Man," that there is not such a thing as the English Constitution, and that the people have yet a constitution to form'.

Thus far, Paine re-trod familiar ground. But he may have considered that, if he were to be prosecuted or forced into exile, he would now set out his position much more emphatically. His pamphlet went further than many moderate English reformers had been willing to go, calling for 'a national convention, elected for the purpose [of parliamentary reform], by all the people'. Paine framed this demand in the context of a rejection of the utility of the monarch and the House of Lords, by which rejection 'every species of hereditary government might fall'. Instead, Paine invoked 'a mode of referring back' to 'the sovereign and original constituent power, the nation itself'. By a convention alone could 'the will of the nation' be known. 'Partial addresses, or separate associations, are not testimonies of the general will' (by implication, Paine did not recognize the London Corresponding Society as speaking for the nation). Since six parts in seven of the nation were unrepresented in Parliament, Paine looked forward to 'a general demur...as to the obligation of paying taxes', that is, a tax strike.[343]

This call for a convention had been made unemphatically and briefly in *Rights of Man* (1791).[344] Now it was made stridently and aggressively, as a complete rejection of monarchy and aristocracy. It was made, too, in the context of a demand for a new franchise for elections to parliament (rejecting 'the custom of attaching rights to *place*, or in other words, to inanimate matter, instead of to the *person*') and of an apparent call to action: 'When the rich plunder the poor of his [*sic*] rights, it becomes an example to the poor to plunder the rich of his property.' This sensational invocation gave a hostage to fortune. In temperate mood, Paine said something different: 'when the rich protect the rights of the poor, the poor will protect the property of the rich.'[345] But if this qualification were overlooked, or if emphasis were placed on the idea of 'plunder', Paine could be depicted as advocating a

---

[342] Paine to the Chairman of the SCI, 4 July 1792, quoted Keane, *Paine*, 342. Paine's donation to the SCI was known in the LCS in November 1792: Thale (ed.), *LCS Papers*, 29.

[343] Paine, *Letter Addressed to the Addressers* (1792): *CW*, ii. 475–7, 480, 482–5, 496, 498–9, 503–4.

[344] Paine, *Rights of Man* (1791): *CW*, i. 280.

[345] Paine, *Letter Addressed to the Addressers* (1792): *CW*, ii. 504, 506. For the difficulty of reading such remarks on rights by Paine as affirmations of universal suffrage, see Ch. 3, section Democracy, Rights, and 'the People'.

political revolution to bring about the expropriation of the rich and the levelling of property, a position he never soberly urged.

So Paine distanced himself from the reforming societies like the Society of the Friends of the People ('their incivility toward me is what I should expect from place-hunting reformers'), the SCI, and the LCS as well as from the unreformed Parliament: only a convention, for Paine, would declare the national will.[346] To his opponents, this new position was sensational: it threatened the immediate revolutionary overthrow of Parliament and monarchy together. But Paine dropped it coolly into his pamphlet, as a moral corrective: he did not announce it as the forerunner of social transformation. Even at his most outspoken, Paine did not here call for 'revolution'. He evidently had no understanding that such might be the consequence, and that he had undermined any defence at his forthcoming trial based on an argument that he was not far out of line with many other previous reformers, including aristocratic ones. He had burned his bridges, seemingly without realizing it. After 1783, Paine returned to Britain in no legal peril; after 1792, he could never return.

The British context continued to develop: if Paine had ignored the LCS, the LCS found no need to invoke Paine on the matter of a convention. In 1793 one of its leading members, Joseph Gerrald, reviewed with overt hostility the monarchies of William III and the Hanoverians, and set out a detailed plan for a convention elected by universal manhood suffrage as the 'only mode of national salvation'; his practical scheme followed the ringing exhortation 'THAT REBELLION TO TYRANTS IS OBEDIENCE TO GOD'. Gerrald did not mention Paine.[347] After a 'British Convention' reconvened in Edinburgh later in 1793 had been broken up in December by the authorities, one spokeman for that body appealed to the precedent of King Alfred ('that patriot king') and his constitution rather than to Paine or to natural rights as the ground for a convention (a Saxon convention being 'the annual meeting of all *freemen*'); the constitution as repaired by the Convention Parliament in 1689 'has long been mouldering in decay, and is now tottering to its fall'. To remedy that decay, 'THE ONLY OBJECTS OF OUR ASSOCIATION ARE THE RESTORATION OF ANNUAL PARLIAMENTS AND UNIVERSAL SUFFRAGE. WE GO NO FURTHER.'[348] But they had already gone much further than the French; and the Convention in 1689 had been integral to a revolution. Appropriately, the LCS resolved on 20 January 1794 (not mentioning Paine) to watch 'the proceedings of parliament' daily thereafter, and on any motion 'inimical to the liberties of the people' the General Committee would issue summonses

---

[346] Paine, *Letter Addressed to the Addressers* (1792): *CW*, ii. 498, 504. The Society of Friends of the People 'is made of men of various descriptions, but chiefly of those called Foxites... It is now amusing the people with a new phrase, namely, that of "a temperate and moderate reform," the interpretation of which is, *a continuance of the abuses as long as possible. If we cannot hold all let us hold some*': ii. 510.

[347] Joseph Gerrald, *A Convention the Only Means of Saving us from Ruin. In a Letter, addressed to the People of England* (London: D. I. Eaton, 1793), 59, 103, 113.

[348] *The Address of the British Convention, assembled at Edinburgh, November 19, 1793, to the People of Great Britain* (London: D. I. Eaton, [1793]), 5–6, 14.

'forthwith to call a GENERAL CONVENTION of the PEOPLE'.[349] In March, the LCS issued such invitations. It was a direct challenge: the ministry now arrested the leaders, and the famous trials of 1794 for treason now ensued. Revolutions did not depend on Paine alone, and could have other premises than natural rights theory.

The uncertain survival of the Revolution

Already, in 1791, an internal and external struggle for the Revolution's survival was compounded by desperate strife among its most ardent friends. After the king's flight to Varennes in June 1791, the Jacobins fell into bitter schism: most branches of the clubs were captured by their extremists when the moderates and constitutional-monarchists left in July to form their own society, meeting in a former Feuillant monastery. These 'Feuillants' provided many of the king's ministers and formed a majority in the National Constituent Assembly; their high-water mark was on 14 September 1791 when the king attended the Assembly and signed the new 'Constitution of 1791', the text of which, Sieyès later implied, 'had been largely "dictated" by himself to his colleagues in the Constitutional Committee'.[350] Over the course of two years, the National Constituent Assembly had completed its work, and now made way for its successor, the Legislative Assembly. The Revolution, the moderates hoped, was over; it had ended in a constitutional monarchy, not as Paine wished in a republic. But Paine had left France for England in July 1791 and would remain there until September 1792, a long absence.

This monarchical ending was not to be: distrust and disunity, fear and paranoia, conspiracy theories and denunciations formed the discursive context as the newly elected Legislative Assembly met on 1 October 1791, its deputies wholly replacing those of the preceding National Constituent Assembly but themselves soon gravitating towards the existing clubs of Feuillants or Jacobins and playing out those clubs' rivalries with greater ferocity. A faction now formed within the Jacobins around the charismatic figure of Jacques Brissot, most of them deputies from the Gironde and attracting the nicknames Brissotins or Girondins. This group generally advocated war with Austria and were opposed by the anti-war Robespierre; he attracted his own followers who became known as Montagnards from their favoured seating area in the Assembly and joined in the strident personal conflict between the two men.

The Legislative Assembly's fate was to be caught between the threats of counter-revolution and *sans-culotte* violence as distrust of the king escalated. His

---

[349] John Martin and Thomas Hardy, *At a General Meeting of the London Corresponding Society, held at the Globe Tavern Strand; on Monday the 20th Day of January, 1794 Citizen John Martin, in the Chair. The following Address to the People of Great Britain and Ireland, was read and agreed to* ([?London]: no printer, [1794]), 7; T. M. Parssinen, 'Association, Convention and Anti-parliament in British Radical Politics, 1771–1848', *EHR* 88 (1973), 504–33, at 513–15, argued that there is evidence of only two members of the LCS having intended such a convention as an anti-parliament, but added: 'The lack of precision on the part of the moderate leaders when writing about the convention's purpose was quite deliberate.' Open affirmations of revolutionary intent can hardly be expected.

[350] Forsyth, *Reason and Revolution*, 180.

brothers were raising Royalist armies just over the Rhine; the queen's brothers were Joseph II (1741–90) and Leopold II (1747–92), emperors of a now hostile Austria; Prussia too was interventionist. In the face of these threats, the Girondins encouraged a widespread enthusiasm for war. It was four Girondins who were brought into the king's ministry in March 1792, so greatly heightening the prevalent distrust and fear of conspiracy within and between the Feuillants, the Girondins, and the Montagnards. On 20 April 1792 Louis himself came to the Assembly to request war against Austria; after this popular gesture his position weakened as the early stages of the war went badly and conspiracy theories involving the royal family grew, especially when he dismissed his Girondin ministers on 12 June. The next day, Prussia declared war on France.

On 20 June 1792 the Paris *sans-culottes* took matters into their own hands, invading the Legislative Assembly and the Tuileries Palace, mobbing the king, and accusing him to his face that he was loyal to the *émigrés*, not to his kingdom. The military situation deteriorated when in July a Prussian army invaded France. More and more of the Paris sections now demanded the king's deposition; on 6 August a huge demonstration on the Champ de Mars signed a petition demanding that step, and, among other aims, universal male suffrage, a goal of the Cordeliers Club. On 9 August Danton and Robespierre seized control of Paris's municipal government. In the paranoid atmosphere created by the mobilization of local National Guard units to fight at the front, Paris's local government units, the sections, also began to petition for the deposition of the king. They were implicitly challenging the Assembly, which had inherited a constitution built around constitutional monarchy.

Paine was still in England. When the Assembly was still unable to agree to a deposition, on 10 August the *sans-culottes*, now backed by the reorganized and newly democratized National Guard, returned to the Tuileries, killing some 600 of the Swiss guards, capturing the royal family, who had taken refuge in the nearby Assembly, effectively terminating the constitutional monarchy, and initiating what has been described as the 'second revolution' or the 'first Terror' in the face of the Austro-Prussian advance. It was an episode marked by random killings of aristocrats, nonjuring priests, and suspected conspirators all over France. The events of 10 August constituted a decisive political moment and a key instance of revolutionary violence: power now lay with the Paris commune. Faced by mass violence, the Legislative Assembly was coerced into declaring the monarchy suspended and agreeing to its own replacement by a Convention whose task was to write a new, republican, constitution for France. In Paine's absence, France effectively, if not formally, had become a republic.

Paine's closest contact, Lafayette, suspected of complicity in the 'flight to Varennes' of the previous year, was dismissed from the command of the National Guard. Given a military command in the north-east but fearing that 'I should be assassinated at the head of the army'[351] since his soldiers now sided with the deposition of the king, Lafayette gave himself up to the Austrians on 19 August. His fears were

---

[351] *The Marquis de la Fayette's Statement of his Own Conduct and Principles* (1793), 87–9.

to be all too vividly justified. In this alarming situation, Paine's closest French ally was now depicted as a national enemy, but Lafayette had already been under suspicion. To some French observers, Paine's alliances were too apparent. When *Rights of Man. Part the Second* was published in Paris in April 1792, its translator Lanthenas omitted the English edition's dedication to Lafayette, apologizing in the translator's preface:

> Paine, that uncorrupted friend of freedom, believed too in the sincerity of Lafayette. So easy is it to deceive men of single-minded purpose! Bred at a distance from courts, that austere American does not seem any more on his guard against the artful ways and speech of courtiers than some Frenchmen who resemble him.[352]

This was written by a friend; but Paine also had to encounter the indifferent.

The French loss of Longwy (20 August 1792) and of Verdun (2 September), laying open the way to Paris for the Prussians, led immediately to panic, to fears of conspiracy by counter-revolutionary prisoners, and to the 'September Massacres' in which between 1,000 and 1,300 inmates in Paris gaols were summarily killed. The Girondins now dominated the Assemby; from fear, the moderate Feuillants largely ceased to attend. In their absence, the Girondins voted for the creation of a third legislature, the National Convention, in succession to the Legislative Assembly, to revise the constitution of 1791 by terminating the monarchy and adopting universal male suffrage. Chosen by hastily arranged elections that returned Brissot, Robespierre, and Paine, and initially once more including mutually antagonistic groups of Girondins and Montagnards, the Convention sat from 20 September 1792 to 26 October 1795. It was this body that tried and executed Louis and failed to control the widespread outbreaks of rural resistance to newly introduced conscription, most extensively, but not only, in the Vendée.

In the autumn of 1792 Paine acted the part of an international celebrity, wildly acclaimed as such in France, but unaware of his political mis-steps. In June 1792, while Paine was in England, Robespierre had attacked *Rights of Man* in his journal *Le Défenseur de la Constitution*, rejecting parts of Paine's account (in reality, as is suggested here, Lafayette's account) of Lafayette's role in the Revolution.[353] By accepting Lafayette's version, Paine had unknowingly taken sides in a complex political situation. The same happened on 26 August 1792, when a leading Girondin, Marguerite-Élie Guadet, carried in the National Convention a decree awarding French citizenship to a series of foreign fellow-travellers including Anacharsis Cloots and George Washington, together with six Britons: Thomas Clarkson, James Mackintosh, Thomas Paine, Joseph Priestley, William Wilberforce, and David Williams.[354]

Paine was now eligible to serve in the new and hurriedly arranged National Convention, and on 6 September was elected to that body. Achille Audibert, acting for the constituency of Pas-de-Calais, travelled to London to tell Paine the news and to upstage the three other constituencies that also elected him. This was

---

[352] Lanthenas, Translator's Preface: *CW*, i. 347.   [353] Aldridge, *Man of Reason*, 170.
[354] Aldridge, *Man of Reason*, 171.

evidence of Paine's widespread fame, but his election, like that of Anacharsis Cloots and Joseph Priestley, may also have been 'a partisan move to enhance the profile of the Girondins', with whom these three were connected, and to check the influence of the Jacobin Club:[355] perhaps unknowingly, Paine was being recruited to just one faction in a French battle.

Paine's alignment was not without cause. The Girondins were once depicted in anglophone historiography as moderates, yet in key respects the adjective is inappropriate for this loose but often fervent group of revolutionary ideologues. They were at one with Paine in urging the export of the French Revolution internationally and in championing a laissez-faire economy of deregulation and the career open to talent.[356] By contrast, many Jacobins were being influenced by their *sans-culotte* supporters towards the parochial goal of securing the revolution in one country, France, and sustaining a 'moral economy' of government price regulation.[357] Paine's choice of allies was partly determined by personal contacts, since his social origins and his openness to state social security systems, expressed in *Rights of Man. Part the Second* and later in *Agrarian Justice*, might in themselves have created some common ground with the Jacobins; but these potential affinities were not to prove decisive. Only by May 1793 had 'tumultous misconduct' in the political realm brought Paine to advise Danton: 'All that can now be hoped for is limited to France only, and I agree with your notion of not interfering in the government of any foreign country, nor permitting any foreign country to interfere in the government of France.'[358] By then, arguably, it was too late.

Paine had spent more than a year in England; now, having crossed the Channel and survived effusive welcomes along the way, he arrived in Paris on 19 September 1792 (he was to remain there until 1802). The Revolution had, in his absence, developed in ways that he could not have anticipated. Sanguinary conflicts had broken up the idealistic and fraternal spirit of 1789. The advance of the Prussian and Austrian armies in August and September 1792 had thrown the capital into panic. Yet Paine's republican initiative of June 1791 had not swept all before it. It was plebeian Paris opinion, with which Paine had no contact, that had changed this. It had done so only recently, beginning with the sensational invasion of the Tuileries by *sans-culottes* on 20 June 1792. The Jacobin Club followed by moving towards a demand for the overthrow of the monarchy, and on 29 July even Robespierre, hitherto cautious, declared himself in favour of that step. After the imprisonment of the king and the royal family, a majority of members of the previous Legislative Assembly fled or hid. Already, none were safe.

---

[355] Michael Rapport, *Nationality and Citizenship in Revolutionary France: The Treatment of Foreigners 1789–1799* (Oxford, 2000), 141.

[356] William Doyle, 'Thomas Paine and the Girondins', in Doyle, *Officers, Nobles and Revolutionaries: Essays on Eighteenth-Century France* (London, 1995), 209–19. It is not clear that Thomas Paine was the 'J. Payne' recorded as admitted to the Paris Jacobin Club on 23 September 1793: Lounissi, *Paine*, 735–45.

[357] Ian Dyck, 'Local Attachments, National Identities and World Citizenship in the Thought of Thomas Paine', *History Workshop Journal* 35 (1993), 117–35, at 128–9.

[358] Paine to Danton, 6 May 1793: *CW*, ii. 1335.

Euphoria was temporarily restored by the defeat of the Prussians at Valmy (20 September 1792) and of the Austrians at Jemappes (6 November). The new Convention opened on the day of Valmy: already, the Girondins and Jacobins had pulled apart, the Girondins supporting the war, the Jacobins condemning it. Each increasingly saw the other as the covert enemy of the Revolution. In this looming clash, Paine was pre-committed. Two days later the National Convention unanimously declared the monarchy abolished, Paine voting with the rest: France was henceforth formally a republic. When the next year a revolutionary calendar was adopted, it dated Year I of the Republic not from 1789 but from 22 September 1792. In this phase of wild optimism, the National Convention passed on 19 November 1792 its Girondin-inspired motion offering help to 'all people desirous of recovering their liberty', that is, a commitment to support its principles everywhere, by force of arms: Girondin strategy was to safeguard the Revolution by encircling France with revolutionary republics. The Revolution was now a militant and effective force, in arms.

The fragmentation of the Legislative Assembly into parties was no secret. But on 22 September 1792, soon after Paine's return to Paris, he crossed the new Minister of Justice, the Jacobin Georges-Jacques Danton. Danton proposed in the Convention that judges should be directly elected, to sweep away the remains of a royal elite; Paine, unaware of the history of the matter in France and echoing his English assumptions, urged that judges needed to be learned in the law, not elected by the people but appointed. Paine had not gauged the mood of the Convention, and Danton's proposal was overwhelmingly adopted. Paine was not deterred: the *Lettre de Thomas Paine au peuple François* was published on 25 September. His personal contacts were primarily with the Girondins, and he had neglected Jacobins like Barère, Danton, and Marat. More generally, Paine's internationalist address was arguably a less than optimal response to the growing divisions in the Convention, and to increasing French xenophobia and paranoia.

In his *Lettre de Thomas Paine au peuple François* he announced (echoing his rhetoric in America and the foreign policy of the Girondins) that 'the cause of France is the cause of all mankind'. It may be that Paine cared for France primarily as a weapon in his international crusade, and his remark had force in that context. 'It is to the peculiar honour of France, that she now raises the standard of Liberty for all nations; and in fighting her own battles, contends for the rights of all mankind.' It was 'no longer the paltry cause of kings, that calls France and her armies into action. It is the great cause of ALL', to institute 'the great Republic of Man'. France should now say to her enemies 'it is for you, it is for all Europe, it is for all mankind, and not for France alone, that she raises the standard of Liberty and Equality!'[359] There is no evidence that Paine understood that such plans distanced him from the Jacobin position. The existence of a consistent Girondin position on a host of policy questions has been doubted;[360] but the possibility now existed of Paine being aligned, however inappropriately, with a losing party.

[359] Paine, *Address to the People of France* (1792): *CW*, ii. 538–40.
[360] Lounissi, *Paine*, 723–7 questions whether there was a consistent Girondin position, including against state economic intervention, that marked them out as a group from the Jacobins.

On 11 October 1792, thanks to the support of the Girondins, the Convention elected Paine to serve on a committee of nine to draw up a new and republican constitution;[361] of the inner working of the committee nothing is now known. However, Paine did publish in *La Feuille villageoise* of 11 October a strident denunciation of monarchy, lest the French lose sight of what they had achieved by abolishing that institution.[362] Paine was then unsuccessful when he tried to check the outcry against the king when the Convention considered procedure for his trial in November. The drafting of the constitution was overtaken by events. What preoccupied the Convention was less the clauses in the proposed constitution than a series of conflicts on what to do with their prisoner.

On 11 December the king's trial began.[363] When Saint-Just demanded the immediate execution of Louis, Paine through his interpreter Jean Henri Bancal at once tried to stem the tide; Robespierre rose to reply. Paine had defined himself against the Jacobins. On 15 January 1793, Paine urged the Convention that Louis be sent into exile in the United States; it was an unrealistic outcome, with respect both to France and to the American republic, and on the 17th there was a clear majority for a verdict of guilty.

Paine nevertheless persisted in his attempts, at subsequent sessions, to avert a death sentence or to postpone it. The 'Mountain', the nickname for the area in the Convention where the Jacobins sat, was loud in its disapproval; Marat urged that Paine's vote not be counted, since he was a Quaker, and so unable to vote for the death penalty. Paine, through Bancal, who read a written translation of Paine's prepared speech, persisted:

> I may lay claim to the possession of a certain amount of experience; I have taken no inconsiderable part in the struggle for freedom during the Revolution of the United States of America; it is a cause to which I have devoted almost twenty years of my existence. Liberty and humanity have ever been the words that best expressed my thoughts, and it is my conviction that the union of these two principles, in all cases, tends more than anything also to insure the grandeur of a nation. I am aware of the excitement and anger aroused by the perils to which France, and especially Paris, have been subjected; and yet, if we could only catch a glimpse of the future, long after all this excitement and anger have passed away, it is not unlikely that the action which you have sanctioned today will assume the aspect of having been performed from a spirit of revenge rather than from a spirit of justice. (*Murmurs.*) My solicitude for the welfare of France has now been transformed into concern for her honour.

---

[361] Paine later wrote: 'I was one of the nine members that composed the first Committee of Constitution. Six of them have been destroyed. Sieyès and myself have survived—he by bending with the times, and I by not bending. The other survivor [Bertrand Barère] joined Robespierre; he was seized and imprisoned in his turn, and sentenced to transportation. He has since apologized to me for having signed the warrant, by saying he felt himself in danger and was obliged to do it': Paine, 'To the Citizens of the United States', III (29 Nov. 1802): *CW*, ii. 920.

[362] [Paine], 'An Essay for the Use of the New Republicans in their Opposition to Monarchy' (1792): *CW*, ii. 541–7, corrected by Lounissi, *Paine*, 699.

[363] For these events see William Doyle, *The Oxford History of the French Revolution* (Oxford, 1989), 183–96; Lounissi, *Paine*, 699–720. The Girondin motion offering support to all kindred movements was rescinded in the Convention, after Jacobin pressure, in April 1793.

Paine's justified boasting of his role in these two revolutions was not decisive. He now added an interpretation of the relations of the two countries in the American revolutionary war; again, this was not to tip the scale.

> Should I, after returning to America, spend my leisure in writing a history of the French Revolution, it would give me greater satisfaction to be able to set down a multitude of mistakes prompted by a feeling of compassion rather than to record a single deed prompted by even a just severity...France's sole ally is the United States of America. It is the only nation upon which France can depend for a supply of naval stores...Now, it is an unfortunate circumstance that the individual whose fate we are at present determining has always been regarded by the people of the United States as a friend to their own revolution. Should you come, then to the resolution of putting Louis to death, you will excite the heartfelt sorrow of your ally. If I were able to speak the French language, I would appear in person at your bar, and, in the name of the American people, ask that Louis be respited.

At this point Thuriot and Marat denounced the translation. Bancal continued:

> It is my fondest desire that when an ambassador has been sent by your executive committee to Philadelphia, he may carry with him the tidings from France of the respite granted by the National Convention to Louis, solely because of its friendship for America. In the name of the citizens of that Republic, I beg that you delay the execution. Do not, I beseech you, bestow upon the English tyrant [George III] the satisfaction of learning that the man who helped America, the land of my love, to burst her fetters, has died on the scaffold.[364]

Paine's experience of two revolutions did not compel his fellow deputies, since he had not engaged with the particular detail of French history and politics. His universalism, in invoking the brotherhood of Americans and French, children of related universalist revolutions, was unsuccessful. All this was rhetoric against the flood tide of particularist negation of monarchy.

Paine was arguably impractical in his belief that kingship could be terminated without consequences for the person of the monarch, although, unusually, six other members referred to him by name when casting their oral votes:[365] Paine was not without influence, although he did not carry the day. Louis's death had little effect in the United States. These two revolutionary regimes had never been the same: even their universalist rhetoric was significantly different. Indeed the new American republic now witnessed an anti-Jacobin reaction, but this was not an idealization of Louis XVI. The trial of the French king eclipsed Paine's own trial *in absentia* in London on 18 December; predictably, this resulted in Paine's conviction, but he was never to return to his native land.[366] The execution of Louis on 21 January 1793 raised the stakes in

---

[364] Paine, 'Shall Louis XVI be Respited?' (19 Jan. 1793): *CW*, ii. 556–8.

[365] Lounissi, *Paine*, 718.

[366] Paine was indicted on a charge of seditious libel (which did not carry the death penalty), not treason. Biographers have recorded different sentences passed on him, but none was pronounced on 18 December since Paine was tried *in absentia*: cf. T. B. Howell (ed.), *A Complete Collection of State Trials* (London: T. C. Hansard, 1817), xxii. cols. 357–471; Michael Lobban, 'Treason, Sedition, and

European politics, and on 1 February the National Convention declared war on Britain. It resolved also to appeal dirctly to the British people in an address to be drafted by Bertrand Barère, Philippe Fabre d'Eglantine, and Thomas Paine.[367]

Inopportunely, the committee on the constitution presented its final text to the Convention on 15 February. Its draft of 368 articles, most likely inspired by Condorcet, was hopelessly complex. Probably from this period dates the document entitled 'Plan of a Declaration of the Natural, Civil and Political Rights of Man'.[368] It too was an elaborate list of thirty-three constitutional points, high-minded, French in style but nevertheless lacking real engagement with the current state of French politics: it is not established that Paine was the primary author.

Paine evidently wanted a far simpler set of general principles, but not a constitution dominated by Jacobin direct democracy. As he rashly lectured Danton, Paine's ideal was still the representative system, not populist collective action: France 'must speak for other nations who cannot yet speak for themselves. She must put thoughts into their minds, arguments into their mouths, by showing the reason that has induced her to abolish the old system of monarchical government, and to establish the representative [system]'.[369] This was Paine's generalized language of international transformation: it did not respond to French aims and divisions, or to the growing challenge posed by Jacobin violence on the streets of Paris.

The king's trial seriously weakened the reluctant Girondins. When the Convention's committee, including Paine and many Girondins, submitted its proposed constitution it was defeated, that party's leading hostess, the clever but dangerously candid Mme. Roland, observing:

> I believed that, like most authors, Payne was worth less than his writings.
>
> The boldness of his thoughts, the originality of his style, his hard truths thrown audaciously in the middle of those they offended, had to cause a great sensation; but I thought him better at throwing out sparks, so to speak, than at discussing the foundations or preparing the formation of a government. Payne better illuminates a revolution than constructs a constitution. He grasps, he establishes grand principles which strike everyone, intoxicating a political club and rousing a tavern: but for cold discussion in a committee, for the work of the legislator that follows, I find *David Williams* infinitely better than him.

the Radical Movement in the Age of the French Revolution', *Liverpool Law Review* 22 (2000), 205–34; John Barrell and Jon Mee (eds), *Trials for Treason and Sedition, 1792–1794* (8 vols, London, 2006), i. xiii–xix, xliii–xlviii. Paine's counsel, Thomas Erskine, attempted to persuade the jury that Paine's pamphlet was merely 'a contribution to a long-term debate about rights, and … part of the more recent controversy initiated by Edmund Burke. The more the pamphlet could be regarded as part of a literary debate, the less could it be deemed an attempt to spread disaffection among the populace': xviii. Erskine's argument was unsuccessful. Paine's biographers have claimed that he was outlawed; but this would have required a subsequent legal procedure. Evidence is lacking that it was ever undertaken, perhaps because it was assumed that Paine would never return. I am grateful to Michael Lobban for advice on the procedure for outlawry.

[367] T. C. W. Blanning, *The Origins of the French Revolutionary Wars* (London, 1986), 157.

[368] 'Plan of a Declaration of the Natural, Civil and Political Rights of Man': *CW*, ii. 558–60, de-attributed in Appendix: Paine De-attributions.

[369] Paine to [Danton], n.d., Archives Nationales, AF II 49, Dossier 380, no. 5, quoted in Hawke, *Paine*, 264; Keane, *Paine*, 357.

Williams, equally made a French citizen, had not been nominated to the Convention where he would have been more useful; but the government invited him to visit Paris, where he passed several months and often conferred with working deputies. A wise thinker, a real friend of mankind, he seemed to me to concentrate on men's means of happiness, while Payne felt and described the abuses that created their misery. I saw him [Williams], from the first time he took part in the sessions of the Assembly, concerned by the disorder of the discussions, upset by the influence that the tribunes thought they had, doubting if it were possible for such men, in such a situation, ever to decree a reasonable Constitution. I think the knowledge he acquired of what we were, attached him still more to his own country, to which he eagerly returned. 'How can men debate', he asked me, 'who don't know how to listen? You other French, you no longer take the trouble to preserve a decent exterior, which has such influence in assemblies: carelessness, heedlessness and dirtiness don't recommend a legislator; nothing is unimportant that strikes people every day and is public knowledge.' What would he say, good God! if he saw the deputies since 31 May, dressed like harbour workers, in trousers, vest and bonnet, their shirts open to the stomach, swearing and gesticulating like drunken sans-culottes! He would think it very simple that the people should treat them like valets, and that the whole lot, dirtied with their excesses, end by falling under the rod of a despot who will know how to enslave them.

The face of Payne sometimes reminds me of the comparison which the Romans made of Sulla's face with a mulberry dusted with flour. Williams played his part with equal dignity in Parliament or in Senate, and carried throughout real dignity.[370]

With the balance of power swinging the other way, a new committee with a quite different and Jacobin composition was elected to draw up an alternative constitution.

The tide of war with Austria and Prussia turned with France's major defeat at Neerwinden (18 March 1793), which forced its withdrawal from the Austrian Netherlands; the republic's leading general, Charles François Dumouriez, now changed sides, and when his attempt to lead his army to Paris and restore the monarchy failed, he too fled to the Austrians on 4 April. A second revered champion of the Revolution, after Lafayette, was now identified as a traitor. In this moment of national peril, in the face of inflation and popular demands for price controls, urged by the Jacobins and resisted by the Girondins, the Convention voted on 6 April 1793 to establish a Committee of Public Safety with sweeping powers, later to be the chief instrument of political persecution.

With Girondins and Jacobins openly accusing each other of treason, cooperation became impossible, and the Girondins were denounced in mass demonstrations. In June 1793, coerced by the Parisian National Guard, the Convention expelled twenty-nine Girondin deputies, many of whom had voted against the king's execution; some twenty later fled to the provinces. The Jacobins were now identified as the organizers of a massive elimination of supposed traitors and conspirators, after its termination to be termed the Terror, a campaign of execution that unfolded in the coming months. Such a purge of traitors was just what the Girondins themselves had demanded. Now they were the losers; they largely stayed away from the Convention, and it was the Montagnards who drafted a new constitution, brief and without the academic elaborations of Condorcet's. Now Robespierre rose to

[370] *Mémoirs de Madame Roland*, ed. Paul de Roux (Paris, 1966), 169–70.

prominence, a consistent believer that the Girondins were at the heart of a grand conspiracy against the Revolution.[371]

Of these two broad sets of causes—the logic of *sans-culotte* violence and the mounting paranoia caused by the perceived threat of counter-revolution—Paine wrote nothing. Indeed there is no evidence that he understood either. Nor did he remark on the demands of the Jacobin clubs in Paris for social reforms,[372] or the activities of the Jacobin deputies during the Terror, imposing similar reforms in the provinces.[373] Given the important pages devoted to topics like social security and redistributive taxation in *Rights of Man. Part the Second* and in *Agrarian Justice*, Paine's silence on the practical reform programmes of the French Jacobins was significant. The Terror proper, conventionally dated from September 1793 to July 1794, was something that Paine cannot have anticipated in *Rights of Man* (1791) or *Rights of Man. Part the Second* (1792); he was, from prison, unable to write about it during its course; but it is notable that after his release he mentioned it so briefly, and so infrequently. For Paine, as for many in Paris, disillusionment largely meant silence; but on the interactions, in this key episode, of universalism and particularism Paine left few considered reflections.

Paine's imprisonment: nationality and cosmopolitanism

On 15 April 1793 the Jacobins denounced in the Convention a list of twenty-two alleged counter-revolutionaries; for the present, the attempt was defeated. Yet with the power of the Girondins crumbling and that of the Jacobins rising, Paine began to be pessimistic, writing to Jefferson on 20 April:

> Had this Revolution been conducted consistently with its principles, there was once a good prospect of extending liberty throughout the greatest part of Europe; but I now relinquish that hope...As the prospect of a general freedom is now much shortened, I begin to contemplate returning home. I shall await the event of the proposed Constitution, and then take my final leave of Europe.[374]

Although now pessimistic, Paine's universalist assumption was unchanged: politics for him was the application of general principles, and with this idealistic revolutionary consistency he associated the Girondins.

Perhaps because he expected his own early departure for America, Paine showed no political prudence in the face of Marat's denunciation. On 6 May 1793 Paine even wrote to Danton, lecturing him on the lessons to be learned from the American Revolution and warning him about the abuses of the French:

> As you read English, I write this letter to you without passing it through the hands of a translator. I am exceedingly disturbed at the distractions, jealousies, discontents and

---

[371] Tackett, *The Coming of the Terror in the French Revolution*, 277, 287, 292 and *passim*.

[372] Isser Woloch, *The New Regime: Transformations of the French Civic Order, 1789–1820s* (New York, 1994); Higonnet, *Goodness beyond Virtue*.

[373] Gross, *Fair Shares for All*; Michel Biard, *Missionaires de la République: les représentants du peuple en mission (1793–1795)* (Paris, 2002).

[374] Paine to Jefferson, 20 Apr. 1793: *CW*, ii. 1330–2.

uneasiness that reign among us, and which, if they continue, will bring ruin and disgrace on the Republic. When I left America in the year 1787, it was my intention to return the year following, but the French Revolution, and the prospect it afforded of extending the principles of liberty and fraternity through the greater part of Europe, have induced me to prolong my stay upwards of six years. I now despair of seeing the great object of European liberty accomplished, and my despair arises not from the combined foreign powers, not from the intrigues of aristocracy and priestcraft, but from the tumultuous misconduct with which the internal affairs of the present Revolution is conducted.

In constitutional matters, 'representation itself is publicly insulted, as it has lately been and is now by the people of Paris'. These were not the words of a believer in direct democracy, but of what Paine repeatedly called the representative system.

The tension between Paris and the departments was to be solved, as in the United States, urged Paine, by moving the Convention from Paris to its own local government jurisdiction. As in America, he continued, it was pointless to try to fix the price of provisions in Paris. French assignats were falling too much in value, as had happened to American paper money. Paine professed no 'personal interest...I attend only to general principles'.

> As soon as a constitution shall be established I shall return to America...In the mean time I am distressed to see matters so badly conducted, and so little attention paid to moral principles. It is these things that injure the character of the Revolution and discourage the progress of liberty all over the world...There ought to be some regulation with respect to the spirit of denunciation that now prevails. If every individual is to indulge his private malignancy or his private ambition, to denounce at random and without any kind of proof, all confidence will be undermined and all authority be destroyed...Calumny becomes harmless and defeats itself when it attempts to act upon too large a scale. Thus the denunciations of the Sections [of Paris] against the twenty-two deputies [Girondins] falls to the ground...Most of the acquaintances that I have in the Convention are among those who are in that list, and I know there are not better men nor better patriots than what they are.
>
> I have written a letter to Marat of the same date as this but not on the same subject. He may show it to you if he chuse.[375]

As a political intervention it was either bravely candid or tactically unwise, an appeal to a foreign case which had occurred in very different circumstances. What was blowing the principled French Revolution off course? Paine could offer no other account of the adverse forces than his phrases 'tumultuous misconduct' and 'private malignancy'. The records of the Convention 'suggest that he spoke only six times during this nine-month period, and only once on a topic other than the trial of the former king. He was presumably out of his depth in the complex republican politics that must otherwise have seemed so important to him.'[376]

---

[375] Paine to Danton, 6 May 1793: *CW*, ii. 1335–8.
[376] Thomas Munck, 'The Troubled Reception of Thomas Paine in France, Germany, the Netherlands, and Scandinavia', in Simon P. Newman and Peter S. Onuf (eds), *Paine and Jefferson in the Age of Revolutions* (Charlottesville, Va, 2013), 161–82, at 166–7.

Paine did not last long in this frenzied and complex political environment. When on 2 June 1793 an organized armed mob surrounded the Convention and compelled action against the leading Girondin deputies, Danton allegedly warned Paine not to try to enter the building and to be careful of being seen as an enemy of the Revolution;[377] Paine was in any case almost isolated in that body. Some Girondin deputies submitted to arrest; others fled, including Condorcet and Brissot, but almost all were later captured. On 7 June Robespierre moved for legislation against foreigners, and a law was soon passed for their imprisonment. For Paine, Paris became an even more violent and dangerous place. His national status was unclear; he withdrew from the Convention in June 1793, going into virtual hiding in the suburb of Saint-Denis where he had been living since March. It is not known whether Paine was present on 24 June when the Convention accepted what was later known as the 'constitution of 1793', providing for universal manhood suffrage, a unicameral legislature, and annual elections: London's SCI could have asked for no more, but the constitution was never put into effect. It was not Paine's achievement.

Later, Paine wrote of the weeks before he ceased to attend:

> I went but little to the Convention, and then only to make my appearance; because I found it impossible to join in their tremendous decrees, and useless and dangerous to oppose them. My having voted and spoke extensively, more so than any other member, against the execution of the King, had already fixed a mark upon me: neither dared any of my associates in the Convention to translate and speak in French for me, anything I might have dared to have written.
>
> Pen and ink were then of no use to me: no good could be done by writing, and no printer dared to print; and whatever I might have written for my private amusement, as anecdotes of the times, would have been continually exposed to be examined, and tortured into any meaning that the rage of party might fix upon it.[378]

Finally Paine had realized that he could do nothing, either personally or by his writings, to stem the torrent of events around him. He was probably not in the Convention when on 21 June a body of delegates from Arras arrived to announce that a number of deputies from the Pas de Calais region, Paine publicly named among them, had lost the delegates' confidence: Paine's status was now even more in doubt as the numbers executed in Paris, Lyon, Nantes, Toulon, and the dead in the massacres in the Vendée, rose steadily through the summer of 1793.

The murder of Marat by a Girondin sypathizer on 13 July 1793 created a Jacobin martyr; it launched an even more frenzied drive for retribution against the Girondins, whom the Jacobins held responsible. Even the Jacobin constitution, passed by the Convention in June, was now suspended. On 4 December the National Convention redefined itself: no longer a temporary assembly to draft a constitution, it now regarded itself as a ruling body, but was dominated by the Committee of Public Safety. Parisian politics did not speak with one voice: during this period Paine was

---

[377] Conway, *Life*, 177–9.
[378] Paine, 'Forgetfulness' [to Lady Smyth], n.d. [?1794]: *CW*, ii. 1124.

contacted by Bertrand Barère, former member of the centrist group nicknamed the Plain but now president of the Committee of Public Safety, for help in facilitating shipments of American grain to Paris, and (as Barère professed) in drafting a new constitution. This was not the only move that led the American minister in Paris, Gouverneur Morris, to suspect that Paine was conspiring to bring about his recall, which Paine may have been,[379] an opinion which, once formed in Morris's mind, confirmed his antipathy to Paine.[380]

Paine evidently intended to try to return to the United States on an American ship in October 1793,[381] but did not escape. Perhaps he judged that it would have been even more dangerous to draw attention to himself by preparations for departure. If so, this extreme caution was unavailing. Paine's name was included in a long list of deputies whom the deputy Jean-Pierre-André Amar denounced on 3 October for treasonable activity. On 16 October Marie Antoinette was executed. Despite attempts at restraint from Robespierre and Danton, the show trial of the Girondins took place on 30 October; one committed suicide, twenty were guillotined. Unknown to Paine, Robespierre had already written a reminder to himself to act in the matter of Paine also: 'Demander que Thomas Paine soit decreté d'accusation, pour l'interêt de l'Amérique autant que de la France.'[382] His wording may imply that someone, possibly the American minister to France, Gouverneur Morris, had suggested that the United States would also welcome it if Paine were out of the way.

On 25 December the Jacobin François Bourdon de l'Oise accused Paine in the Convention of absenteeism and conspiracy, and the Convention decreed the exclusion from their assembly of all foreigners. Bourdon may have sought to isolate Paine from his contacts with Edmond Genêt, a French emissary who was trying to stir up revolution in the Mississippi valley, and was damaging relations with France's only ally.[383] For whatever reason Paine was arrested on 28 December 1793 and imprisoned in the Luxembourg, where he was joined by more and more citizens arrested during the Terror and destined for swift execution.[384] Paine's account of how he escaped execution only by chance amid the general massacre of the Terror is unforgettable and has seemed self-evidently true for his biographers, but by his own account he was suffering from a fever which meant that he was unaware of what happened at the time; only a month later was he told of the accident that allegedly prevented his collection from his cell and dispatch to the guillotine. The story has not been verified from another source, and it is still a possibility that there was no death warrant; that the object of the Jacobins in imprisoning Paine was to prevent him from writing about the Terror, not to execute him—a step that might have alienated the United States at a time when France needed American aid. Indeed

---

[379] Paine to Barère, 5 Sept. 1793: *CW*, ii. 1332–3.   [380] Nelson, *Paine*, 255.

[381] Paine to Barère, 5 Sept. 1793, *CW*, ii. 1332–3.   [382] Keane, *Paine*, 599, n. 16.

[383] Rapport, *Nationality and Citizenship in Revolutionary France*, 191.

[384] There are records of 2,639 death sentences passed by revolutionary tribunals in Paris, and 16,594 in the country as a whole, including the capital. But many more (perhaps more than 400,000) were summarily murdered, committed suicide, or died in prison or in the related civil wars, notably in the Vendée. Donald Greer, *The Incidence of the Terror during the French Revolution* (Cambridge, Mass., 1935); Hugh Gough, *The Terror in the French Revolution* (2nd edn, Basingstoke, 2010), 2.

Paine anticipated such a possibility, writing to Gouverneur Morris from the Luxembourg: 'They have nothing against me—except that they do not choose I should be in a state of freedom to write my mind freely upon things I have seen.'[385]

On 20 January 1793 Joel Barlow attempted to secure Paine's release, leading a party of eighteen Americans to petition the Convention. Thomas Griffith, one of the party, wrote that 'not a few members hissed during the reading of parts of our memorial, in which Paine's attachment to republican principles was asserted'.[386] Republican principles were evidently not a universal language. The plea was rejected, as Marc Vadier, president of the Convention, explained:

> Thomas Paine is a native of England; this is undoubtedly enough to apply to him the measures of security prescribed by the revolutionary laws. It may be added, citizens, that if Thomas Paine has been the apostle of liberty, if he has powerfully co-operated with the American Revolution, his genius has not understood that which has regenerated France; he has regarded the system only in accordance with the illusions with which the false friends of our revolution have invested it. You must with us deplore an error little reconcilable with the principles admired in the justly esteemed works of this republican author.[387]

It was a penetrating analysis. To a French observer, Paine might always be an Englishman, expelled from the Convention for that reason; and his English generalizations about liberty did not align him with the Jacobin revolution. Individuals in revolutionary Paris might claim American citizenship in attempts to protect themselves, as did Lafayette;[388] but this tactic did not establish their claims.

The legal position was a complex one. From *Calvin's Case* in 1608 onwards, the English law of allegiance (what would now be called nationality law) described the individual's natural relation to the sovereign, not a contractual relation to a 'nation'. Not until 1871 did English law recognize the right of an individual born a subject of the English monarch to renounce that allegiance.[389] The American colonies began with this English law of nationality, and made only 'piecemeal changes and partial modifications' to it, emphasizing contract and the assimilation of new settlers, before that law finally developed into 'a new concept of citizenship' in the new republic, the idea that all allegiance rested on consent; but although 'general

---

[385] Paine to Gouvereur Morris, 24 Feb. 1794: *CW*, ii. 1338–9. John G. Alger, *Englishmen in the French Revolution* (London, 1889), 88, pointed out that 'Even at the height of the Terror men were not executed without trial, nor without an indictment having been drawn up by Fouquier Tinville, and served upon them at least overnight...Removal to the Conciergerie, which adjoined the tribunal, was likewise in almost all cases the first indication of an approaching trial. Not one of these preliminaries had been accomplished in Paine's case.'

[386] Griffith added: 'I considered that the partiality of my countrymen towards a republican form of government led them to mistake the character of the French Revolution': Griffith's journal, in Elizabeth Wormeley Latimer, *My Scrap-Book of the French Revolution* (Chicago, 1898), 51.

[387] Conway, *Life*, 200.

[388] Louis Gottschalk and Margaret Maddox, *Lafayette in the French Revolution: Through the October Days* (Chicago, 1969), 81.

[389] Clark, *Language of Liberty*, 46–62.

principles were clear, particular questions about the source, character, and effects of citizenship remained open well into the nineteenth century'.[390]

This evolution from natural to contractual ideals of citizenship was complex, but that evolution did not pass through the ideal that all Americans were citizens of the world, perhaps implying in some minds that all citizens of the world were Americans: the new republic still defined its citizens as distinct from aliens, although the basis for that definition evolved. The Westminster Parliament had greatly advanced that evolution of ideas with an Act in 1740 which provided a much easier procedure for naturalization in the American colonies, though still requiring a prior seven years' residence there and communion in 'some Protestant and Reformed Congregation'; but naturalization law remained a matter of controversy in Britain and its colonies, especially when the British government banned colonial naturalization acts in 1773.[391] Although this restriction featured as a grievance in the Declaration of Independence, Paine never wrote of the law of nationality or of these controversies. Public policy in the new republic sought more citizens, not the abolition or dilution of citizenship. If it is correct to argue that Paine never quite adopted the new doctrine of universal manhood suffrage, caution should be exercised before ascribing to him decisively modern positions about some necessary relation between democracy and nationhood.

So the Pennsylvania constitution, enacted on 28 September 1776, provided for all foreign settlers who took 'an oath or affirmation of allegiance' to acquire land, to be deemed a 'free denizen' after one year's residence, entitled to 'all the rights of a natural born subject of the state', except being a representative; this needed two years' residence.[392] Yet citizenship itself was 'ill-defined'; Article IV of the Articles of Confederation, imprecisely drafted, was unclear in seeming to create a common United States citizenship. Even the constitution of 1787 'left critical questions relating to citizenship unanswered', assuming but not stating that birth conferred citizenship. The position was unclear for many individuals: in 1794 even the Swiss-born Jeffersonian politician Albert Gallatin's election to the Senate was challenged on nationality grounds, despite his service in the War of Independence, and he was unseated. Gallatin had claimed that 'Every man who took an active part in the American Revolution, was a citizen according to the great laws of reason and nature', universalist arguments that Paine himself was compelled to use. But with the influx of refugees following the European wars, there were Naturalization Acts in 1790 and 1795; the Federalists' 'Alien and Sedition' Acts of 1798, including the Naturalization Act of that year, greatly tightened American definitions of who counted as a citizen, relaxed again by the Republicans' Act of 1802 but still exclusive rather than inclusive.[393]

[390] James H. Kettner, *The Development of American Citizenship, 1608–1870* (Chapel Hill, NC, 1978), 3, 9–10 and *passim*.

[391] Kettner, *American Citizenship*, 74–7, 105, 106–72.

[392] Francis Newton Thorpe (ed.), *The Federal and State Constitutions, Colonial Charters, and other Organic Laws of the States, Territories, and Colonies now or heretofore forming the United States of America* (7 vols, Washington, 1909), v. 3091.

[393] Kettner, *American Citizenship*, 219–22, 231–5, 240–7; Rogers M. Smith, 'Constructing American National Identity: Strategies of the Federalists', in Doron Ben-Atar and Barbara B. Oberg (eds), *Federalists Reconsidered* (Charlottesville, Va, 1998), 19–40, at 34 for a Supreme Court judge's

The French Revolution went through a similar trajectory, but more rapidly. In 1789 France welcomed foreigners in a euphoric spirit of cosmopolitanism; in August 1792 the Legislative Assembly extended French citizenship to eighteen foreign reformers, Paine among them. But in 1793 the National Convention returned to a latent xenophobia, purging foreigners like Paine and, in many cases, executing them in the Terror, like the German baron Anacharsis Cloots, going to his death with the unavailing universalist appeal 'Hurrah for the fraternity of nations! Long live the Revolution of the world!' Before then, revolutionaries might interpret patriotism, still synonymous with cosmopolitanism, as a peaceful preference for France. When this patriotism became paranoid, it turned against many foreigners: Paine was not alone.[394]

Irrespective of paranoia, however, 'in every constitution of the 1790s, a precondition for the exercise of the rights of citizenship was either birth on French soil, or, for foreigners, a period of residence followed by naturalization': the identity of the state with the nation was for successive republican regimes a leading ideal of the Revolution. As early as 20 October 1789, 'the Constituent Assembly stressed that, for a foreigner to acquire political rights, he would have first to assume French nationality... foreigners... were to lose their eligibility for communal and departmental administration, a disenfranchisement which sat uneasily with the universal implications of the rights of man'. Cosmopolitanism was steadily shut down as the Revolution proceeded.[395]

It is uncertain whether the law of the new French republic or the new American republic recognized dual citizenship in 1793; if not, Paine's acceptance of French citizenship would have cancelled his citizenship in the United States. Additionally, where English law did not recognize that a person born an English subject could voluntarily divest himself of that status, French law on that point was unclear.[396] The French insistence that Paine was an Englishman, and therefore a foreigner liable to be expelled from the Convention, contradicted Desforgues's claim that Paine, born an Englishman, had become 'successively an American and French citizen',[397] but the point was undecided. One American minister in Paris, Morris, thought Paine was not an American; his successor, Monroe, thought the opposite.

opinion in a case of 1795 that the universalist status of 'citizen of the world' was 'a creature of the imagination'. For the Federalist reaction of the 1790s against cosmopolitanism and the emergence of 'the figure of the proudly xenophobic American patriot', see also Seth Cotlar, *Tom Paine's America: The Rise and Fall of Transatlantic Radicalism in the Early Republic* (Charlottesville, Va, 2011), 82–114, at 83.

[394] The 'lobbying refugees in Paris failed to recognize the threat posed by universalism deployed in the service of a single nation': Janet Polasky, 'Revolutionaries between Nations, 1776–1789', *P&P* 232 (2016), 165–201, at 199.

[395] Rapport, *Nationality and Citizenship*, 1–4, 26, 85, 138, 190–2; Peter Sahlins, *Unnaturally French: Foreign Citizens in the Old Regime and After* (Ithaca, NY, 2004), 267–9, 283–4; Renée Waldinger, Philip Dawson, and Isser Woloch (eds,), *The French Revolution and the Meaning of Citizenship* (Westport, Conn., 1993). 'In the later 1790s, both governments [the United States and France] adopted more exclusive concepts of national citizenship, which were based as much on birth, heritage, natural allegiance, and political loyalty as on choice': Ziesche, *Cosmopolitan Patriots*, 5.

[396] The British government's refusal in the 1790s to accept the claims of British seamen captured on American ships and pressed into the Royal Navy to have transferred their nationality to the United States was a source of conflict; but in Jay's Treaty (1795) the American government dropped the point.

[397] Thomas D. Scoble, *Thomas Paine's Citizenship Record* (New Rochelle, NY, 1946), 27 and *passim*. Scoble, an American attorney, treated the question as self-evident, vindicating the American citizenship of a national hero. Scoble applied much later United States law to Paine's case, but largely or wholly omitted eighteenth-century American, French, and English law.

Paine had, of course, a personal interest in claiming to be an American, since the only state at all likely to intervene to secure his release from the Luxembourg and to save him from execution was the United States; but this did not make his wish a legal reality. Paine, then, fell into a legal grey area created by the unprecedented events of 1776–93: there was as yet no agreed answer to the problem. Lawyers confidently deliver a verdict on the clear meaning of the law; historians record that at any time the opinions of parties to the debate, including lawyers, differed.

Cosmopolitanism was therefore undergoing a subtle transformation, from meaning an ability to move easily and peacefully in elite society all over Europe to meaning an identification with universal rights and hence with the forcible export of the French Revolution beyond France.[398] From identity with all nations cosmopolitanism metamorphosed into identity with the French nation, the Revolution personified. The American Joel Barlow protested to the Convention on 7 November 1792: 'he appealed for citizenship to be detached from nationality, on the grounds that human rights are universal.' Condorcet agreed, but in the spring of 1793 the Convention rejected the idea that citizenship was a natural right. After the execution of the king, foreigners seeking naturalization would have to endorse the whole republican project.[399]

Paine himself had published almost nothing on the question of citizenship, but that little showed the evaporation of any attempt to devise a new cosmopolitanism. In *The American Crisis* no. XIII, dated from Philadelphia on 19 April 1783, he wrote in favour of closer federal union:

> I ever feel myself hurt when I hear the union, that great palladium of our liberty and safety, the least irreverently spoken of. It is the most sacred thing in the constitution of America, and that which every man should be most proud and tender of. Our citizenship in the United States is our national character. Our citizenship in any particular [American] state is only our local distinction. By the latter we are known at home, by the former to the world. Our great title is AMERICANS—our inferior one varies with the place.[400]

Paine, English by birth, had no particular attachment to Pennsylvania. He had every attachment to a strong, federal United States, to safeguard what he saw as his achievement in the Revolution.

Paine's early but hostile biographer James Cheetham argued that Paine was not given French citizenship as an honorary title alone; 'he went there in consequence of his adoption and election, and he *took the oath of allegiance to the French republick.* Every member of the convention took it as a matter of course, and so did Paine. If, therefore, in becoming a citizen of France by adoption, and taking the oath of allegiance, he could alienate his citizenship in the United States, he ceased to be a

---

[398] For a different argument, analysing cosmopolitanism as 'a part of our own idealistic vocabulary' and associating it with reformers and revolutionaries, see Margaret C. Jacob, *Strangers Nowhere in the World: The Rise of Cosmopolitanism in Early Modern Europe* (Philadelphia, 2006), 1. Yet Paine plays almost no role in Jacob's text or in Michael Scrivener, *The Cosmopolitan Ideal in the Age of Revolution and Reaction, 1776–1832* (London, 2007).

[399] Rapport, *Nationality and Citizenship*, 139–40.

[400] [Paine], *The American Crisis*, XIII (19 Apr. 1783): *CW*, i. 234.

citizen.'[401] Cheetham echoed the official French position. Paine's friend Achille Audibert petitioned the Committee of Public Safety on his behalf, but the result was the same.[402] Gouverneur Morris, the American minister in Paris, wrote on 14 February 1794 to Chemin Deforgues, the French Minister of Foreign Affairs:

> Thomas Paine has just applied to me to claim him as a Citizen of the United States. These (I believe) are the facts which relate to him. He was born in England. Becoming subsequently a citizen of the United States, he there acquired a great celebrity through his revolutionary writings. In consequence he was adopted as a French citizen, and then elected a Member of the Convention. His conduct since that period is out of my jurisdiction. I am ignorant of the reason for his present detention in the Luxembourg prison, but I beg you, (if there are reasons unknown to me which prevent his liberation) please be so good as to inform me of them, so that I may communicate them to the government of the United States.

On 19 February Desforgues wrote back:

> In your letter of the 26th of last month [26 Pluviôse or 14 February] you reclaim the liberty of Thomas Paine as an American citizen. Born in England, this ex-deputy has become successively American citizen and French citizen. In accepting the latter title and in occupying a seat in the Legislative Corps, he has submitted himself to the laws of the Republic and has in effect renounced the protection which the law of nations and the treaties concluded with the United States would have been able to assure him. I am not aware of the reasons for his detention, but I presume that they are well founded. I am nevertheless going to submit to the Council of Public Safety the request which you have addressed to me, and I shall promptly acquaint you with its decision.[403]

Paine demanded that Morris inform the American government, and Morris did so, writing to Jefferson on 21 January about Paine:

> I do not recollect whether I mentioned to you, that he would have been executed along with the rest of the Brissotines [i.e. Girondins] if the adverse party had not viewed him with contempt. I incline to think that, if he is quiet in prison, he may have the good luck to be forgotten. Whereas, should he be brought much into notice, the long suspended axe might fall on him. I believe he thinks, that I ought to claim him as an American citizen; but, considering his birth, his naturalization in this country [France], and the place he filled [in the National Assembly], I doubt much the right, and I am sure that the claim would be, for the present at least, inexpedient and ineffectual.

Morris wrote again to Jefferson on 6 March:

> Mr. Paine wrote me a note, desiring I would claim him as an American, which I accordingly did,[404] though contrary to my judgment, for reasons mentioned in my

[401] Cheetham, *Life*, 197.   [402] Keane, *Paine*, 406.

[403] Ministère des Affaires Etrangères, EU 40:91 and 50:102, quoted in Aldridge, *Man of Reason*, 211–12.

[404] Morris did not claim him as an American: Morris to Desforgues, 14 Feb. 1794 (translated) in Jared Sparks, *The Life of Gouverneur Morris* (3 vols, Boston, 1832), ii. 401–2. Morris had earlier written: 'I suspected, but I did not say so, that Paine was intriguing against me, although he put on a face of attachment': Morris to Robert Morris, 25 June 1793: iii. 46–7.

last. The Minister's letter to me of the first Ventose, of which I enclose a copy, contains the answer to my reclamation. I sent a copy to Mr Paine, who prepared a long answer, and sent it to me by an Englishman, whom I did not know.

I told him, as Mr Paine's friend, that my present opinion was similar to that of the Minister, but I might, perhaps, see occasion to change it, and in that case, if Mr Paine wished it, I would go on with the claim, but that it would be well for him to consider the result, that if the government meant to release him they had already a sufficient ground; but if not, I could only push them to bring on his trial for the crimes imputed to him; seeing that, whether he be considered as a Frenchman, or as an American, he must be amenable to the tribunals of France for his conduct while he was a Frenchman, and he may see in the fate of the Brissotins [Girondins] that to which he is exposed. I have heard no more of the affair since; but it is not impossible that he may force on a decision, which, as far as I can judge, would be fatal to him; for, in the best of times, he has a larger share of every other sense than of common sense, and lately the intemperate use of ardent spirits has, I am told, considerably impaired the small stock he originally possessed.[405]

These exchanges have generally been interpreted by recent American historians as evidence of Gouverneur Morris's covert attempt to secure Paine's execution, Paine being undoubtedly an American; but this is by no means obvious. Morris had even praised in his diary *Rights of Man*: 'There are good Things in the Answer as well as in the Book,' but noted also the opinion of Paine's countryman Hodges, then sharing a 'wretched' apartment with Paine: 'He speaks of Payne as being a little mad, which is not improbable.'[406] Both Morris and Desforgues agreed that Paine was now a French citizen; they had a strong legal case in a world in which the idea of multiple citizenships was not yet accepted, and it may be that Paine owed his life to Morris's prudent restraint.

French Jacobins, it seemed, lacked the present-day notion of a 'citizen of the world', a key absence which has often been concealed by the salience of a recent term of historical art, 'the cosmopolitan Enlightenment': in the eighteenth century no such reification promoted any such ideal. Indeed the American and French Revolutions displayed a common and important element: despite the widely shared euphoria, the sense of beginning the world over again, Paine and others did not embed in either revolution a transcendent notion of human brotherhood, of fraternity, of world citizenship. But Paine did not try very hard to convert these revolutions to that cause; for him, his claimed identity as a 'citizen of the world' was a position forced on him by his emigration from his native country, not any worked-out ideology that he had held before 1774. Paine did not make common cause on this point with Richard Price, whose sermon *A Discourse on the Love of our Country* (1789) had indeed proposed a fundamental transmutation of patriotism into cosmopolitanism, with implications for the revolutionary overthrow of 'most'

[405] Morris to Jefferson, 21 Jan. and 6 Mar. 1794, in Sparks, *Life of Morris*, ii. 392–400, at 393; 407–15, at 408–9.
[406] Morris, *Diary*, ed. Davenport, ii. 156 (8 Apr. 1791); ii. 163 (16 Apr. 1791).

existing governments.[407] Not only did the American and French republics not clearly formulate and embrace the international unity of mankind; both fell back on specific and exclusive definitions of national citizenship in the manner of antecedent European kingdoms. As is now obvious, the future in the nineteenth century was to be not world citizenship but its opposite, a new and virulent social, intellectual, and cultural formation: nationalism.

Nor did Paine's Deistic religion save him. On 24 March 1794 the chief architect of de-Christianization, the militant atheist Jacques-René Hébert and his followers, the *hébertistes*, were guillotined, Robespierre denouncing their atheism as contrary to the Revolution. 'Atheism', pronounced Robespierre, 'is aristocratic. The conception of a great Being who watches over oppressed innocence, and punishes successful crime, is democratic through and through.'[408] But Robespierre's Supreme Being was not the God of the English Deists, and Robespierre never made common cause with Paine on the territory of religion. Equally with citizenship, Deistical religion, present in some sense among both the American and French revolutionary elites, never became the common currency of a new spiritual benevolence. On the contrary, the future for the United States was to be one of conflict between conventionally identified Christian denominations; for the French republic, one of conflict between resurgent Roman Catholicism and secularism.

In September 1794 James Monroe arrived in Paris to replace Gouverneur Morris as American minister, but still with no instructions from Washington concerning Paine. Only on 18 September did Monroe write to Paine to express his personal opinion: 'By being with us through the revolution, you are of our country, as absolutely as if you had been born there; and you are no more of England, than every native of America is.'[409] But whether this counted as official recognition is debatable. The theoretical outcome of Paine's ordeal was, therefore, unclear. Nor did Paine clarify it. Paine never wrote the history of the French Revolution that he often spoke of, since—as with the American Revolution—he understood little of the French Revolution's particularist nature and causes. Neither in the autumn of 1793 nor following his release on 5 November 1794 did Paine reflect on the wider significance of recent political events. He had the time, the opportunity, the motives, the ability, and the intention to write; but he did not do so. Even on a smaller scale, he never published anything to analyse the September Massacres or the Terror.

Of the second, at least, he was well aware, complaining to George Washington of the peril he had been in, and from which Washington had done nothing to deliver him:

From about the middle of March (1794) to the fall of Robespierre July twenty-ninth (9th of Thermidor), the state of things in the prisons was a continued scene of horror. No man could count upon his life for twenty-four hours. To such a pitch of rage and suspicion were Robespierre and his committee arrived, that it seemed as if they feared

---

[407] Burke, *Reflections*, ed. Clark, 63–5.
[408] Ruth Scurr, *Fatal Purity: Robespierre and the French Revolution* (New York, 2006), 294–6, 306–7, 348.
[409] Aldridge, *Man of Reason*, 219.

to leave a man living. Scarcely a night passed in which ten, twenty, thirty, forty, fifty or more were not taken out of the prison, carried before a pretended tribunal in the morning and guillotined before night.

One hundred and sixty-nine were taken out of the Luxembourg one night, in the month of July, and one hundred and sixty of them guillotined. A list of two hundred more, according to the report in the prison, was preparing a few days before Robespierre fell. In this last list I have good reason to believe I was included.[410]

But Paine wrote nothing about any inherent relation between violence and revolution. After his release he was described by a perceptive French observer: 'Thomas Payne, whom I seldom saw, left the impression of a man of means, hazardous in doctrine, cautious in practice; likely to commit himself to revolutions, but incapable of accepting their dangerous consequences, good by nature and sophist by conviction. He is very imperfectly appreciated in the biographies.'[411]

---

[410] Paine, *Letter to George Washington* (1796): *CW*, ii. 689–723, at 698–9. This letter may contradict the usual account of Paine's escaping death by accident.

[411] Charles Nodier, *Souvenirs de la Révolution et de l'Empire* (3rd edn, 2 vols, Paris, 1864), i. 275.

6

Paine, Religion, and Politics
The Deist Legacy

THE AGE OF REASON

Paine retreated to a Paris suburb during the Terror, fearing arrest and execution. Yet instead of a work on the French Revolution, the subject of his intended intellectual legacy was not an affirmation, but a negation: not revolution, but revelation. *The Age of Reason* has seldom commanded the attention it deserves, since it is easy to assume that Paine's goal was an extension of what was assumed to be his prior purpose; that in *The Age of Reason* 'his mission [was] to democratize reason and religion'.[1] As is argued in Chapter 3, the image of Paine as a pioneer of political democracy now calls for more careful definition; a similar reconsideration is necessary of Paine's religion, for it is argued here that his Deism preceded his politics.

It also preceded any significant knowledge by Paine of French society. *The Age of Reason* did not greatly draw on his personal experience of French popular religiosity; on the contrary, he adopted too late the view that the driving force of the French Revolution was atheist, not Deist, in its nature. This atheist impulse had been sensed earlier by Paine's friend in 1787–90, Edmund Burke; without acknowledgement, Paine came by 1793 to agree with him. Even so, Paine's understanding was limited. Why it was that the French Revolution so suddenly took such a de-Christianizing turn, Paine never really understood. *The Age of Reason*, designed to recall France to theism, said almost nothing about the French Revolution itself, which was the major point at issue. Instead, *The Age of Reason* was expressed in Paine's most universalizing terms: 'A thing which every one is required to believe requires that the proof and evidence of it should be equal to all, and universal'.[2] For Paine, the religious doctrine to which all had equal access had to be Deism.

The Age of Reason was self-identified as a Deist work, not a democratic one. Deism was already old in England, as democracy was not. Paine's Deist views, like his Deist sources, could have dated from the 1750s, and were not obviously an innovation of the 1790s.[3] His writings nevertheless posed a problem of consistency,

---

[1] Edward Larkin, *Thomas Paine and the Literature of Revolution* (Cambridge, 2005), 8; cf. Nathan O. Hatch, *The Democratization of American Christianity* (New Haven, 1989). For an argument that Paine's Deism came first, see Nathalie Caron, *Thomas Paine contre l'imposture des prêtres* (Paris, 1998).

[2] Paine, *The Age of Reason* (1794): *CW*, i. 468.

[3] J. A. I. Champion, 'Deism', in Richard H. Popkin (ed.), *The Columbia History of Western Philosophy* (New York, 1999), 444–5, and Diego Lucci, *Scripture and Deism: The Biblical Criticism of*

for the denial in *The Age of Reason* of revelation as a source of prescription for government undermined the central argument in *Common Sense* that God had, in specific revelation, forbidden the adoption of monarchy. This denial also undermined the central argument in *Rights of Man* that each individual's natural rights were a divine grant at the moment of his or her creation, and that 'the equality of man' was based on 'The Mosaic account of the creation'. In addition, *The Age of Reason* made problematic the argument Paine was to use in *Agrarian Justice* that 'Land... is the free gift of the Creator in common to the human race',[4] an argument that might be held to depend on revelation. In places, Paine insisted that God did not intervene in Creation; elsewhere, Paine wrote as if his own survival and influence was providentially directed. Did his religious views change over time? Paine recorded no spiritual journey to Deism between the 1770s and the 1790s, and one possible inference is that none took place; that his use of Scripture and revelation in *Common Sense* had been for tactical reasons only. *The Age of Reason* used a language more extreme than anything in Paine's earlier publications, but recorded no authorial conversion where he might have done so.

The Age of Reason has previously been explained as an attempt to reverse the French campaign of de-Christianization; but however much this campaign contributed to provoke Paine to an opposite stance, there is evidence that he was engaged in writing even before the Revolution's assault on Christianity reached its height in the spring of 1793. Indeed, Paine had accepted the Revolution's early hostility to the Church and to Trinitarian Christianity (a hostility which was the main message of *The Age of Reason* itself), involving the confiscation of church property, the Civil Constitution of the Clergy, and the deportation of non-compliant priests. Only now was he surprised, and appalled, as these things led on to hostility to theism as such.[5] As its translator Lanthenas later wrote, *The Age of Reason* 'was written by the author in the beginning of the year '93 (old style). I undertook its translation before the revolution against the priests, and it was published in French about the same time.'[6]

There was a local memory in Diss, Norfolk, where Paine had worked as a staymaker in 1765–6: 'It is said that while employed at Diss by Mr. Gudgeon, he commenced "The Age of Reason," the greatest of his productions.'[7] This evidence is too tenuous to be reliable, but the possibility exists that, like *Common Sense*, Paine's *Age of Reason* embodied long-standing reflections. In 1786 John Adams had written, after an evening in Paine's company, that he had 'expressed a contempt of

---

the *Eighteenth-Century British Deists* (Bern, 2008), 212, both emphasize Paine's indebtedness to the English Deists of the early eighteenth century.

[4] [Paine], *Common Sense* (1776): *CW*, i. 10–12; *Rights of Man* (1791): *CW*, i. 273–4; *Agrarian Justice* ([1797]): *CW*, i. 606, 620. For an argument that Paine's Deism (understood as an assertion that a creator God established Creation on general principles but then stood aside from it) was inconsistent with his pantheism (understood as an assertion of God 'literally permeated the universe') see Jack Fruchtman, Jr, *Thomas Paine and the Religion of Nature* (Baltimore, 1993), 3 and *passim*.

[5] Caron, *Thomas Paine contre l'imposture des prêtres*, 167–8; *Letter from Thomas Paine, to Camille-Jordan* (1797): *CW*, ii. 756–63.

[6] Lathenas to Thionville, Archives Nationales, Paris, F7 4774 64, quoted in Keane, *Paine*, 389–90.

[7] *Historical Sketches and Tales of the Town of Diss* (Diss, 1931), quoted in Keane, *Paine*, 547 n. 55.

the Old Testament, and indeed of the Bible at large which surprised me'; Paine 'checked himself with these words: "I have some thoughts of publishing my thoughts on religion, but I believe it will be best to postpone it to the latter part of my life." '[8] It may be that Paine partly drafted his text at an earlier date; if so, he would still have had time to revise it to incorporate reflections on revolutionary France, but it contained no such reflections.[9]

The Age of Reason used the term 'Deism', but not often, and offered no systematic account of that position. Instead, it had two main components, partly contradicting each other: first a defence of theism, which might have been occasioned in Paine's mind specifically by the French revolutionary situation, and, second, an attack on Trinitarian Christianity, which is likely to have been Paine's much older commitment (as *The Age of Reason. Part the Second* also suggests). Yet in *The Age of Reason* the theist component was small compared with the anti-Trinitarian. Even this first component contained nothing specific about French culture or the French Revolution, an informed engagement with which would have been necessary in order to divert them from atheism. In this work Paine relied on the popular Newtonianism that he had imbibed in London in the 1750s or after, a Newtonianism that still normally led in England towards theism; he was evidently unaware of the different pathways of intellectual development in eighteenth-century France, where the intelligentsia's 'teachings, debates, tensions, and rivalries' had led many thinkers in the direction of an atheist materialism even before some of them later came to place that interpretation on imported Newtonian natural science.[10]

Paine seems also to have been unaware of the atheism that recent scholars have detected behind the carefully guarded statements of many early eighteenth-century English Deists,[11] and even in the case of France did not name the atheists against whom he may have written. It may be that the second component of *The Age of Reason*, the anti-Christian, frustrated the intention of the first: a generalized defence of theism would probably have been ineffective without a specific defence of the forms that theism might take, and especially of the form, Trinitarian Christianity, prevalent among European and American readers: not for nothing was Paine to become known as an 'infidel', although infidelity was, literally construed, the opposite of Paine's position.

In 1803, back in the United States and defending himself from charges of 'infidelity', Paine explained to Samuel Adams the circumstances in which this work was composed.

> I have said in the first page of the first part of that work that it had long been my intention to publish my thoughts upon religion, but that I had reserved it to a later time of life. I have now to inform you why I wrote it and published it at the time I did.

---

[8] Harry Hayden Clark, 'An Historical Interpretation of Thomas Paine's Religion', *University of California Chronicle* 35 (1933), 56–87, at 84.

[9] Paine, *The Age of Reason*, ed. Moncure Daniel Conway (New York, 1896), 4.

[10] Alan Charles Kors, *Atheism in France, 1650–1729* (Princeton, 1990), ix and *passim*.

[11] e.g. Wayne Hudson, *Enlightenment and Modernity: The English Deists and Reform* (London, 2009), 13–17.

In the first place, I saw my life in continual danger. My friends were falling as fast as the guillotine could cut their heads off, and as I every day expected the same fate, I resolved to begin my work. I appeared to myself to be on my death-bed, for death was on every side of me, and I had no time to lose. This accounts for my writing it at the time I did; and so nicely did the time and the intention meet that I had not finished the first part of that work more than six hours before I was arrested and taken to prison. Joel Barlow was with me and knows the fact.

In the second place, the people of France were running headlong into atheism, and I had the work translated and published in their own language to stop them in that career, and fix them to the first article (as I have before said) of every man's creed who has any creed at all, *I believe in God*.[12]

Awaiting arrest and execution, Paine claimed that there could now be no reason for continuing to conceal his religious opinions.

It may have been that something of Paine's indignation in *The Age of Reason* against the Old Testament's 'obscene stories...the cruel and torturous executions, the unrelenting vindictiveness...a history of wickedness that has served to corrupt and brutalize mankind'[13] was in part a projection onto Trinitarian Christianity of his fear and disgust at the Terror unfolding around him. The Revolution to which he had wholly committed himself had gone terribly wrong, but Paine could not admit it; he may have transposed his revulsion from revolution onto revelation. Equally, it may be that Paine's insistence in this text on the existence of a benign Creator was a way of defending the necessary truth of his principled optimism at a time when its earthly realizations were so difficult to demonstrate. But these hypotheses must be inconclusive, since evidence sufficient to assess them does not survive.

Paine was arrested on 28 December 1793. While in prison his mind was evidently still fixed on matters of religion rather than on the politics of the Jacobin ascendancy. An English surgeon surnamed Bond, imprisoned with him, spent many hours each day with Paine, who had with him the text of his latest work. Bond recorded: 'Mr. Paine, while hourly expecting to die, read to me parts of his "Age of Reason"; and every night when I left him to be separately locked up, and expected not to see him alive in the morning, he always expressed his firm belief in the principles of that book, and begged I would tell the world such were his dying opinions. He often said that if he lived he should prosecute further that work, and print it.'[14] After his release his main project was to write a sequel to *The Age of Reason*.

Paine's vilification for a work that was widely seen as a statement of infidelity began early. As he worked, Paine had passed the text to his translator, and the existence of the pamphlet became known in Paris. From the draft finished by March 1793 an imperfect or preliminary French version was published that spring as *Le*

---

[12] Paine to Samuel Adams, 1 Jan. 1803: *CW*, ii. 1436.
[13] Paine, *The Age of Reason* (1794): *CW*, i. 474.
[14] Thomas Clio Rickman, *The Life of Thomas Paine* (London: Rickman, 1819), 194. As so often, such evidence cannot be corroborated from other sources.

Siècle de la Raison, ou Le Sens Commun des Droits de l'Homme, with its translator, the Deputy and former Jacobin François-Xavier Lanthenas, rather than Paine listed as author on the title page. Its text was a positive affirmation of 'the choicest gift of God to man, the GIFT OF REASON' and of natural rights; the work was intended to persuade French readers to distance themselves from Catholicism. Two corrected editions in French followed in the autumn of 1793, these instead prioritizing the-ism and making explicit the author's negative response to the official campaign of de-Christianization.[15] Paine, then, had not anticipated the militant atheism that he now (perhaps belatedly) saw as undermining the French Revolution. Whether atheism or human rights were the essence of that episode is still debated by histor-ians (the present study contends that no such 'essence' can be diagnosed).

In the Thermidorian reaction that brought about the fall of Robespierre on 27 July 1794, Paine's views on Deism were less relevant still. On 12 February 1798 John Hurford Stone wrote from Paris to Joseph Priestley of 'Mr. Paine's Age of Reason; of which an immense edition in French was published, and not twenty copies were sold'.[16] Not anticipating this cold reception, Paine continued to revise his text, which was also published in Paris in English, with its author's name, as *The Age of Reason. Being an Investigation of True and Fabulous Theology* (Paris: Barrois, 1794), the Preface dated 27 January. On 21 January, Gouverneur Morris, the American minister in Paris, had written to Thomas Jefferson: 'lest I should forget it, I must mention that Thomas Paine is in prison, where he amuses himself with publishing a pamphlet against Jesus Christ'.[17] Although Jefferson was by now out of office, he did nothing to press his government to insist on Paine's American sta-tus. Paine's self-image as a citizen of the world received a setback when its theo-logical premises became public.

Paine has sometimes been explained as an ambassador within international Deism, but *The Age of Reason* does not bear this out. It contains no mention of the writings on theology of American or French freethinkers.[18] Indeed Paine's explan-ation of the occasion for *The Age of Reason* was profoundly anti-French:

> The circumstance that has now taken place in France of the total abolition of the whole national order of priesthood, and of everything appertaining to compulsive systems of religion, and compulsive articles of faith, has not only precipitated my intention, but rendered a work of this kind exceedingly necessary, lest in the general wreck of super-stition, of false systems of government and false theology, we lose sight of morality, of humanity and of the theology that is true.

---

[15] David C. Hoffman and Claudia Carlos, 'Thomas Paine's *Le Siècle de la Raison, ou Le Sens Commun Des Droits de L'Homme*: Notes on a Curious Edition of *The Age of Reason*', in Scott Cleary and Ivy Stabell (eds), *New Directions in Thomas Paine Studies* (New York, 2016), 133–54; Richard Gimbel, 'The First Appearance of Thomas Paine's *The Age of Reason*', *Yale University Library Gazette* 31 (1956), 87–9.

[16] *Copies of Original Letters recently written by Persons in Paris to Dr Priestley in America. Taken on board a Neutral Vessel* (London: J. Wright, 1798), 25.

[17] Morris to Jefferson, 21 Jan. and 6 Mar. 1794: Sparks, *The Life of Gouverneur Morris* (3 vols, Boston: Gray and Bowen, 1832), ii. 392–400, at 393.

[18] Paine did refer to Franklin, but only to the 'proverbs' in his *Poor Richard's Almanac*: Paine, *The Age of Reason* (1794): *CW*, i. 475.

Paine did, however, claim that politics came first: 'Soon after I had published the pamphlet "Common Sense," in America, I saw the exceeding probability that a revolution in the system of government would be followed by a revolution in the system of religion.'[19] This revolution, presumably, was to have been the acceptance of Deism.

This chronology is in doubt. Paine's religious opinions were probably formed as a child in England, not in America or France: as he wrote to Samuel Adams, it had 'long' been his intention to publish on the theme. Speculation has surrounded the possible tension between his Church of England mother and Quaker father, but there is little evidence apart from Paine's own autobiographical fragment:

> From the time I was capable of conceiving an idea, and acting upon it by reflection, I either doubted the truth of the christian system, or thought it to be a strange affair; I scarcely know which it was: but I well remember, when about seven or eight years of age, hearing a sermon read by a relation of mine, who was a great devotee of the church, upon the subject of what is called *Redemption by the Death of the Son of God*.[20] After the sermon was ended I went into the garden, and as I was going down the garden steps (for I perfectly recollect the spot) I revolted at the recollection of what I had heard, and thought to myself that it was making God Almighty act like a passionate man who killed his son when he could not revenge himself any other way; and as I was sure a man would be hanged that did such a thing, I could not see for what purpose they preached such sermons.

Paine concluded: 'How different is this to the pure and simple profession of Deism!'[21] The memory of revulsion at what is now called the doctrine of the atonement has the ring of truth, but this rejection of atonement was not necessarily synonymous with a full affirmation of Deism.

At some time in his life Paine also became aware of a famous literary passage. His Deistic vision he later described as a recapitulation of that outlined by Joseph Addison (1679–1719), whose verses of 1712 (adopted as a hymn) Paine quoted in 1794, beginning with the lines:

> The spacious firmament on high,
> With all the blue ethereal sky,
> And spangled heavens, a shining frame
> Their great original proclaim.[22]

---

[19] Paine, *The Age of Reason* (1794): *CW*, i. 464–5.

[20] The identity of this text has not yet been established, although sermons on the subject in the 1740s, the probable decade of Paine's experience, included [Caleb Fleming], *An Essay To State the Scripture-Account of Man's Redemption, by the Death of Christ* (London: M. Cooper, 1745) and Nicolaus Ludwig, Graf von Zinzendorf, *Sixteen Discourses on the Redemption of Man By the Death of Christ* (London: James Hutton, 1740), popularized by John Wesley as *Extract of Count Zinzendorf's Discourses on the Redemption of Man by the Death of Christ* (Newcastle: John Gooding, et al., 1744). Henry Felton had published, posthumously, *Sermons on the Creation, Fall, and Redemption of Man* (London: John Clarke, 1748), and George Whitefield had a sermon on 'Christ, the Believer's Wisdom, Righteousness, Sanctification, and Redemption' in his *Nine Sermons* (London: Sam. Mason and Gab. Harris, 1742). But the sermon could have been published earlier.

[21] Paine, *The Age of Reason* (1794): *CW*, i. 497–8 (text corrected).

[22] Paine, *The Age of Reason* (1794): *CW*, i. 481, 485 quoting Addison, 'Ode', in *The Spectator*, no. 465 (23 Aug. 1712).

Appropriately, Paine proceeded by 'referring to the ideas that occurred to me at an early part of life': his Quaker father, his education at Thetford grammar school, his attendance in London at 'the philosophical lectures of [Benjamin] Martin and [James] Ferguson', his acquaintance with Dr John Bevis of the Royal Society.[23] In this area too, Paine did not claim to have learned key lessons in America or France, although he may have learned from a tradition of English physico-theology dating from the 1660s.[24] There is evidence that he met the French Deist the Comte de Volney in 1801,[25] but nothing seems to have flowed from the meeting.

Paine's ideas had evidently been formed long before. In *The Age of Reason*, Paine argued that 'our ideas, not only of the almightiness of the Creator, but of His wisdom and His beneficence, become enlarged in proportion as we contemplate the extent and the structure of the universe'. Specifically, 'It is an idea I have never lost sight of that all our knowledge of science is derived from the revolutions (exhibited to our eye and from thence to our understanding) which those several planets or worlds of which our system is composed make in their circuit round the sun.'[26] This observation seems to have dated from 1757–8 or the 1760s, when, attending lectures on popular Newtonianism in London, he purchased (presumably at some expense) an orrery, a clockwork model of the orbits of the planets.[27] Paine recalled this decisive argument in the second part of *The Age of Reason*: 'could a model of the universe, such as is called an orrery, be presented before him [a man with "no knowledge of machinery"] and put in motion, his mind would arrive at the same idea', that is, of deriving 'some at least of the mechanical works we now have' from 'the structure and machinery of the universe' as well as 'impressing him with a knowledge of, and a belief in, the Creator'.[28] He mentioned no political inferences.

Englishmen had no need of Newtonianism to generate reforming politics: their culture was already full of critiques of existing political and religious forms. In 1778 Paine had complained of a central English example: 'The toleration act [of 1689] in England, which *granted* liberty of conscience to every man, in religion, was looked upon as the perfection of religious liberty. In America we consider the assumption of such power as a species of tyrannic arrogance, and do not *grant* liberty of conscience as a *favour* but *confirm* it as a *right*'.[29] He did not claim that he discovered that principle only after his migration to the American colonies.

The Age of Reason did what many English freethinkers of the early eighteenth century had done: it undermined the social authority of the clergy by ridiculing the Church's claims to interpret revelation, as recorded in its authoritative text. The nature of Jesus and the sacraments, and the doctrine of the atonement, those freethinkers had argued, were not defined in Scripture. Churches, they had

---

[23] Paine, *The Age of Reason* (1794): *CW*, i. 496.
[24] David C. Hoffman, '"The Creation We Behold": Thomas Paine's *The Age of Reason* and the Tradition of Physico-Theology', *Proceedings of the American Philosophical Society* 157 (2013), 281–303.
[25] Aldridge, *Man of Reason*, 266–7.   [26] Paine, *The Age of Reason* (1794): *CW*, i. 503.
[27] Vikki J. Vickers, '*My Pen and my Sword have ever gone together*': *Thomas Paine and the American Revolution* (London, 2006), ch. 4.
[28] Paine, *The Age of Reason. Part the Second* (1795): *CW*, i. 602–3.
[29] [Paine], 'A Serious Address to the People of Pennsylvania on the Present Situation of their Affairs' (Dec. 1778): *CW*, ii. 285.

concluded, lacked prescriptive authority. Similarly, Paine contended that 'My own mind is my own church'; it followed that 'I believe in the equality of man', that is, in each individual's unmediated access to the Deity.[30] This, rather than any demonstrably equal share of 'reason' given to all, established the equality of individuals (indeed it was of central importance that Paine did not need to explain what 'reason' signified other than that it allowed immediate access to God). This was, of course, not a secular argument for human equality, but a theistic argument (echoing Protestantism) for man's powerlessness in face of God's omnipotence. The French Trinity of *liberté, égalité, fraternité* embodied different assumptions, but Paine, in Paris, saw only an incomprehensible atheism. His response, again, was English: Trinitarian Christians in Paine's youth had routinely argued that Christianity was the necessary basis of sociability, and Paine now used the same argument on behalf of his Deism: for him, unmediated human benevolence created society, his alternative to the state.

Formally, Paine contended that each individual was equally able and therefore equally entitled to form religious opinions as every other individual. This position soon collapsed in *The Age of Reason* into disapproval of religious positions other than Paine's own, notably atheism and Catholicism. But if people were as gullible as Paine depicted them, misled into superstition by a self-interested priesthood, individuals' equal possession of reason was called in doubt. Nor was it clear in Paine's account why true revelation—the word of God writ large and visible in Creation—did not persuade all people everywhere in the world to be of one mind in religion.[31] Indeed investigation of the material universe had encouraged many French *philosophes* to adopt precisely the atheism that Paine deplored; but these thinkers did not feature in his analysis.

This gullibility and priestly self-interest, according to *The Age of Reason*, took one form in particular. Paine was eager to demolish 'All national institutions of churches', which were 'no other than human inventions, set up to terrify and enslave mankind, and monopolize power and profit'; he was unresponsive to Burke's argument that such a revolution would bring down theism also. On the contrary: for Paine, the end of the 'adulterous connection of church and state' would mean that 'man would return to the pure, unmixed and unadulterated belief of one God, and no more'.[32] But this return Paine did not demonstrate, and the atheism of the French Revolution therefore came to him as an unwelcome surprise.

For powerful reasons, Paine's chief theoretical target had to be 'revelation'. He therefore defined it in a way that turned it into a direct communication from God to all individuals (which Deists held to be possible), so disqualifying revelation as a restricted communication to just some, a communication on which authoritative institutions could be founded. This left Jesus as 'a virtuous and an amiable man', a 'virtuous reformer and revolutionist'.[33] But what was the content of Jesus's

---

[30] Paine, *The Age of Reason* (1794): *CW*, i. 464.
[31] Paine, *The Age of Reason* (1794): *CW*, i. 483–4.
[32] Paine, *The Age of Reason* (1794): *CW*, i. 464–5.
[33] Paine, *The Age of Reason* (1794): *CW*, i. 464–7, 469, 480.

revolutionary activity? This now became, as a result, unclear. Paine did not specifically invoke Jesus's teachings to promote revolution; in *Common Sense* he had cited the Old Testament but only to disprove the authority of monarchy, ignoring the New. Paine's unitary God did not intervene to prevent the Terror. Indeed, in Deism strictly conceived He did not intervene in the world at all. One weakness of Paine's Deism was that it did not recruit the Almighty, in any clear sense, in the revolutionary cause.

It might be argued that Paine's ridicule of the doctrine of the atonement was all too effective: he thereby sawed off the branch on which he sat.[34] If Paine could derive from a few un-Trinitarian parts of Scripture, like the Psalms, 'the power and benignity of the Almighty', then God's not acting in the face of human suffering became more incomprehensible, not less: suffering was more of a problem in a universe ruled by a Deist God. But Paine was pre-committed to a view of physical creation that ruled out divine interventions as 'miracles', and ruled out revelation. For if formal religion 'cannot have connection with mystery',[35] no more could politics.

Given this English frame of reference, it is understandable that the French version of *The Age of Reason* had no appreciable impact in slowing, let alone reversing, the current of atheism that flowed through the French Revolution. When theism eventually revived in France, it owed much to ultramontane Catholicism, little to Paine. In its main objective, to save the French Revolution from atheism, *The Age of Reason* was unsuccessful. Its second major characteristic was established by omission: it said nothing about the ways in which the American Revolution had been promoted covertly by religious heterodoxy, but openly by the varieties of Trinitarian Protestant Dissent, fundamentalist and even at times with a millenarian component. One consequence of the American Revolution was not widespread Deism, but, rather, a flood of evangelical Protestantism. Paine never wrote of these profound changes in the intellectual life of the early United States. For him, before his return there in 1802, that republic had to be a test case, immaculate, beyond reproach, even beyond historical analysis.

THE AGE OF REASON. PART THE SECOND

In *The Age of Reason. Part the Second*, published in Paris in October 1795 in French and English versions, Paine restated that he had been provoked to publish the first part by 'the circumstances' in France at the end of 1793: 'The just and humane principles of the Revolution, which philosophy had first diffused, had been departed from.' The passive voice disclosed his unwillingness to ascribe blame. Yet *Part the Second* was a more generally anti-French work: French Catholicism had 'prepared

---

[34] The 'internal evidence is that the theory or doctrine of redemption has for its basis an idea of pecuniary justice and not that of moral justice': Paine, *The Age of Reason* (1794): *CW*, i. 481. It seems that Paine knew of only one of the doctrines of the atonement. For others see L. W. Grensted, *A Short History of the Doctrine of the Atonement* (Manchester, 1920).

[35] Paine, *The Age of Reason* (1794): *CW*, i. 470–1, 474, 479–81, 506–10.

men for the commission of all crimes'. Paine, released from prison and now possessing 'a Bible and a [New] Testament', which he had lacked while writing *The Age of Reason*, returned to his favourite genre: in *Part the Second* he sought to prove his points by a relentlessly detailed exegesis of Scripture texts in the manner of early eighteenth-century English Deists.[36]

The Age of Reason. Part the Second was therefore nearly twice as long as *The Age of Reason*. In *Part the Second* Paine made no claims about the impact of his first pamphlet. He merely asserted that the French Church had been responsible for the Terror: 'The intolerant spirit of Church persecutions had transferred itself into politics; the tribunal styled revolutionary supplied the place of an inquisition; and the guillotine of the stake.' Paine cited no evidence from French society before the Revolution to support this assertion, but he did not seek to make an empirical point. His aim was to vindicate the 'just and humane principles of the Revolution' by associating its actual results with the old demonology of the English Deists, notably the Catholic Church.[37] This strategy was not helpful in explaining why the early stages of the French Revolution, with its seemingly Deistic worship of a 'Supreme Being', had turned to militant atheism.

To vindicate a benign Deism, Paine acknowledged that he had to counter the published criticisms of *The Age of Reason*, 'several' of which 'I have seen', and he claimed that he now refuted them: their 'cobweb' was 'brushed away', he wrote, by *Part the Second*. This work was however framed not as a study of religion in action, but as detailed textual criticism of the Bible for its internal inconsistencies. Thanks to these flaws, the Bible 'ceases to have authority, and cannot be admitted as proof of anything'. Without such authority, men taking the Bible to be the word of God merely 'ascribe the wickedness of man to the orders of the Almighty'. For this normative reason, as well as the inconsistencies of the text, Paine termed the Bible 'a book of lies and contradictions'.[38]

Paine's outspoken negations were unusual in the 1790s; but his textual criticism was very much of its age, in some ways echoing, for example, the work of the French sympathizer, political revolutionary, journalist, and biblical scholar Alexander Geddes (1737–1802). They had opportunities to meet in 1787–92 in the circle of their hospitable mutual publisher Joseph Johnson, to whose journal, the *Analytical Review*, Geddes was a frequent contributor, although direct evidence of meetings is lacking.[39] Geddes, a pupil at the heavily Jacobite Scots College in Paris in 1758–64, was a Scots Catholic priest in an age in which 'Catholic priests were Jacobites to a man';[40] as with some Englishmen of his generation, this orientation may have fed into a deep antipathy to the established (Hanoverian) order.[41]

---

[36] Paine, *The Age of Reason. Part the Second* (1795): *CW*, i. 514.
[37] Paine, *The Age of Reason. Part the Second* (1795): *CW*, i. 514.
[38] Paine, *The Age of Reason. Part the Second* (1795): *CW*, i. 517, 529–30.
[39] William Godwin's diary records Geddes circulating widely among famous London reforming intellectuals from 1789, but no social occasions at which both Paine and Geddes were present: <http://godwindiary.bodleian.ox.ac.uk/index2.html>.
[40] Thomas M. Devine, 'Alexander Geddes: the Scottish Context', in William Johnstone (ed.), *The Bible and the Enlightenment: A Case Study. Dr Alexander Geddes, 1737–1802: The Proceedings of the Bicentenary Geddes Conference held at the University of Aberdeen, 1–4 April 2002* (London, 2004), 35–43, at 40.
[41] See Ch. 2.

He also shared many of Paine's dispositions. Geddes's first biographer, John Mason Good, who knew him from 1793, claimed:

> He knew as well, and was ready to admit as largely, as any protestant whatever, the alternate systems of force and fraud by which the see of Rome has endeavoured to obtain an unjust temporal supremacy over the great body of the catholic church itself…He could ridicule the infallibility of the pope, and laugh at images and relics, at rosaries, scapulars, agnus Deis, blessed medals, indulgences, obiits and dirges, as much as the most inveterate protestant in his neighbourhood, and could as abundantly abhor the old-fashioned and iniquitous doctrine, that faith ought not to be held with heretics. Claiming the fullest liberty of conscience himself, he was ever ready to extend it in an equal degree to others, and could therefore with the utmost cordiality embrace the protestant as well as the catholic.

Geddes himself wrote in 1793 of the gospel: 'I would not make [it] my law, if Reason, pure Reason were not my prompter and preceptress.'[42] He was not a Deist, but such positions were ones that he held in common with Deists.

Paine did not explicitly acknowledge Geddes, but evidence does establish that Geddes was at least aware of Paine. In 1792 Geddes published a satirical attack on slavery, beginning, 'In this curious and inquisitive generation, when the most venerable and hoary prejudices seem to flee, with precipitancy, before that blazing meteor, called *The Rights of Man*' and arguing, by implication, that the abolition of slavery would logically entail the abolition of many other domestic abuses also.[43] For his part, Paine may have encountered Geddes's biblical work, which attracted a storm of controversy from the 1780s to the early 1790s by its scrutiny of the early books of the Old Testament, conceived as human compilations, in an attempt to establish a historically reliable (but not divinely inspired) text.[44] Geddes, too, treated the idea of the Fall as a fable, gave prominence to the injustice of the violent behaviour of the Jews to their neighbours, and denied the Mosaic authorship of the Pentateuch.[45] Paine is highly unlikely to have had access in Paris to Geddes's publications while composing *The Age of Reason* and *The Age of Reason. Part the Second*. But the parallels are such as to suggest that Paine may have acquired, in London, at least a general awareness of Geddes's methods and conclusions, and perhaps more. If so, Paine's methodology may be identified as a combination of biblical textual criticism in the manner of Geddes with the antipathies of early eighteenth-century

[42] John Mason Good, *Memoirs of the Life and Writings of the Reverend Alexander Geddes, LL.D.* (London: G. Kearsley, 1803), 36–7, 363.

[43] [Alexander Geddes], *An Apology for Slavery; or, Six Cogent Arguments against the Immediate Abolition of the Slave-Trade* (London: J. Johnson and R. Faulder, 1792), 7.

[44] *The Holy Bible, or the Books Accounted Sacred by Jews and Christians, otherwise called the Books of the Old and New Covenants*, ed. Alexander Geddes (London: J. Davis for R. Faulder and J. Johnson, 1792, 1797); only two folio volumes were published. Geddes had prepared the ground by preliminary publications in 1782 and 1786.

[45] Reginald Cuthbert Fuller, *Alexander Geddes, 1737–1802: A Pioneer of Biblical Criticism* (Sheffield, 1984), 43, 54–9. Edward H. Davidson and William J. Scheick, in *Paine, Scripture and Authority: The Age of Reason as Religious and Political Idea* (Bethlehem, Pa, 1994), 66–9, detect exact echoes of Geddes in *The Age of Reason*. In response to his political and scholarly activity, Bishop John Douglass suspended Geddes from holy orders on 27 June 1793: Gerard Carruthers, 'Alexander Geddes', *ODNB*.

English Deists. But this remains a hypothesis, not proven by evidence currently available.

Paine was, nevertheless, an independent thinker. He recorded that the 'glaring absurdities, contradictions and falshoods' in the Bible were 'more numerous and striking than I had any expectation of finding when I began this examination, and far more so than I had any idea of when I wrote the former part of "The Age of Reason"'. He undoubtedly worked out his position in more detail in *Part the Second*, but did not change that position. Of *The Age of Reason* he wrote:

> the opinions I have advanced in that work are the effect of the most clear and long-established conviction that the Bible and the [New] Testament are impositions upon the world, that the fall of man, the account of Jesus Christ being the son of God, and of his dying to appease the wrath of God, and of salvation by that strange means are all fabulous inventions, dishonourable to the wisdom and power of the Almighty; that the only true religion is Deism, by which I then meant, and mean now, the belief of one God, and an imitation of His moral character, or the practise of what are called moral virtues—and that it was upon this only (so far as religion is concerned) that I rested all my hopes of happiness hereafter.[46]

Although Paine now had his source in front of him after release from prison, it is likely that he would have been unable to compose *Part the Second* in the time available had he not drawn on his long-standing reflections on the Bible: Paine was evidently a lifelong Deist, not a recent convert, nor a man newly working out a religious position afresh in 1793–4 from first principles. True, he was reacting against Jacobinism: 'There are matters in that book [the Bible], said to be done by the *express command* of God, that are as shocking to humanity and to every idea we have of moral justice as anything done by Robespierre, by Carrier,[47] by Joseph le Bon.'[48] But Paine drew on more than that revulsion from the Terror, and his antecedents were, once again, chiefly English. There was as much of the word of God in Old Testament chronicles, he urged, 'as there is in any of the histories of France, or Rapin's "History of England," or the history of any other country'.[49] The *History of England* was the only history he specifically named.[50] Together with Paine's older English Deism went its present-day application: 'the French Revolution has excommunicated the Church from the power of working miracles'.[51]

---

[46] Paine, *The Age of Reason. Part the Second* (1795): *CW*, i. 582–3.

[47] Jean-Baptiste Carrier (1756–94), a member of the National Convention from September 1792, was *représentant-en-mission* responsible from October 1793 for atrocities in the suppression of the rising in the Vendée, including mass drownings; recalled to Paris, he was arrested on 3 September 1794, after the fall of Robespierre, and executed on 16 December.

[48] Joseph Le Bon (1765–95), a member of the Convention from 2 July 1793, was *représentant-en-mission* to the departments of the Somme and the Pas de Calais, where he presided over atrocities committed against anti-revolutionaries. For these crimes he was arrested on 10 July 1795, and executed.

[49] Paine, *The Age of Reason. Part the Second* (1795): *CW*, i. 518, 545–6.

[50] Paul Rapin de Thoyras, *The History of England: as well Ecclesiastical as Civil*, trans. Nicholas Tindal (15 vols, London: James and John Knapton, 1726–31) extended to 1688.

[51] Paine, *The Age of Reason. Part the Second* (1795): *CW*, i. 587.

There were hints in *Part the Second* at wider learning. On the authenticity of the Book of Job 'I have seen the opinion of two Hebrew commentators, Abenezra[52] and Spinoza'.[53] Only in the intended third part of *The Age of Reason* did Paine cite 'Spinoza on the Ceremonies of the Jews, p. 296, published in French at Amsterdam, 1678'.[54] In *Part the Second* Paine added translations of 'two extracts from Boulanger's "Life of Paul," written in French'.[55] This was his only quotation in *The Age of Reason* from a French source, yet even this was not quite French, for Paine drew on a loose translation into that language in 1761 by the baron d'Holbach of a work written by the English Deist Peter Annet (1693–1769); d'Holbach protected his own identity by falsely attributing authorship to the late Nicolas Antoine Boulanger (1722–59). Paine took from the French edition passages describing the views of Faustus of Milevis and other sects on the inauthenticity of the Gospels, passages which Annet had quoted from Augustine's *Contra Faustum Manichaeum* and Origen's *Contra Celsum*. If the translation was Paine's own, it makes it more notable that he cited no other French sources.[56] It is more likely that he relied on a translator, perhaps Lanthenas.

Paine, then, learned almost nothing in religious matters from America or from France. It was not from anything in his American or French experiences that Paine drew the argument: 'Of all the tyrannies that afflict mankind, tyranny in religion is the worst.'[57] Paine neither saw, nor reported on, religious tyranny in colonial America or in pre-Revolution France. He cooperated with the American Deist Elihu Palmer after his, Paine's, return to America in 1802,[58] but there is no evidence of similar cooperation there before his departure for Europe in 1787. On the contrary, it seems likely that the religious views that Paine brought to America in 1774 were already formed in his mind, from English models. Early eighteenth-century

---

[52] Rabbi Abraham ben Meir Ibn Ezra (1089–1164).

[53] Paine, *The Age of Reason. Part the Second* (1795): *CW*, i. 547. Baruch de Spinoza (1632–77). For an argument that Paine certainly knew Spinoza's work see Caron, *Thomas Paine contre l'imposture des prêtres*, 240 (a work which, however, does not mention Geddes, a comparable source).

[54] Paine, 'Extracts from a Reply to the Bishop of Llandaff', written *c.*1796–1800, printed in *The Theophilanthropist* (New York, 1810): *CW*, ii. 774. Paine referred to B. de Spinoza, *Traitté des Cérémonies superstitieuses des Juifs tant anciens que modernes*, trans. D. de Saint-Glain (Amsterdam: Jacob Smith, 1678), a translation of Spinoza's *Tractatus Theologico-Politicus*. For Paine's debt to Spinoza and Ezra see Davidson and Scheick, *Paine, Scripture and Authority*, 58–60.

[55] Paine, *The Age of Reason. Part the Second* (1795): *CW*, i. 586–7.

[56] [Nicolas Antoine Boulanger, attrib.], *Examen Critique de la Vie & des Ouvrages de Saint Paul. Avec une Dissertation sur Saint Pierre, par feu M. Boulanger* ('à Londres' [Amsterdam: M. M. Rey], 1770), 8–9, 19–20, 75–6. This work was a free translation by Paul Henri Thiry, baron d'Holbach (1723–89) of [Peter Annet], *The History and Character of Saint Paul, examined: In a Letter to Theophilus, a Christian Friend* (London: F. Page, [?1748]), 6. D'Holbach was evidently hiding behind the identity of a minor philosophe, Nicolas Antoine Boulanger, as d'Holbach had also done with his *Le Christianisme dévoilé* (1766).

[57] Paine, *A Letter to the Honourable Thomas Erskine* (1797): *CW*, ii. 727.

[58] Elihu Palmer admired Paine from at least 1794, but there is no evidence that Paine drew on Palmer. It was Palmer who sent Paine, in Paris, a copy of Palmer's *The Principles of Nature*, which Paine acknowledged in a letter of 21 February 1802 promising the publication of a third part of *The Age of Reason* and implying that it was already completed: G. Adolf Koch, *Republican Religion: The American Revolution and the Cult of Reason* (New York, 1933), 71–2, 86–7, 130–46.

American Deism was primarily an import from England.[59] Insofar as it had an open and public existence, it is not clear that Paine was in contact with any organized, self-aware American Deism before he left in 1787. In America, the contribution of the 'deist movement of the late 1790s' to 'the stock of artisan religious views' was 'only...minor'.[60] The American Society of Theophilanthropists, launched in New York by Palmer in 1795 but probably never exceeding a membership of a hundred, found its most active leaders in militant British *émigrés*. Even with their support, 'Deism as an organised religion had collapsed' by the time of Paine's return in 1802.[61]

Did Paine's Deism remain constant over time? In particular, the early eighteenth-century debate on Deism was concerned with the question whether a particular individual's Deism was a genuine attempt to formulate a more tenable conception of God, or a screen for atheism in an age in which open atheism would have been a perilous position to profess. After Paine's return to America in 1802, there is evidence from one witness, though a hostile one, James Cheetham.

> In deism, Paine was, in all probability, a hypocrite. Generally, he expressed detestation of atheism, and yet he has uttered opinions favourable to it. He believes, he asserts in his Age of Reason, in one God, but it is probable that he believed in nothing superiour to matter. In conversation with Mrs. Palmer, widow of the deistical haranguer, in the presence of Mr. Carver, of this city, from whom I have the fact, he let out his materialism. Stewart, "the traveler," an insane man, had published a pamphlet, which he called *Opus Maximum*, denying the existence of every thing but matter.[62] Referring to it, Mrs. Palmer remarked:—'Stewart's doctrine, Mr. Paine, may be correct.' 'It is well enough, replied Paine, to say nothing about it; the *time is not yet come!* Death then was with him, as well as with the French convention, *eternal sleep*.

Cheetham's hostile verdict was shaped by his own belief that 'The human mind is apt to run to extremes. From doubting the divinity of the Christian religion, it descends to deism, and it would be surprising if, in sinking, the deist stopped short of atheism.'[63]

This evidence for Paine's atheism is not reliable, set against his consistent and fervent statements of his theism; but it does illustrate if not establish the belief, widely shared even in the last decade of Paine's life, that his Deism was only a screen; that Paine's real aim, as Cheetham claimed, was not to state

---

[59] Herbert M. Morais, *Deism in Eighteenth Century America* (New York, 1934), 29–84; Kerry Walters, *Revolutionary Deists: Early America's Rational Infidels* (Amherst, NY, 2011), 15–50.

[60] Sean Wilenz, *Chants Democratic: New York City & the Rise of the American Working Class, 1788–1850* (New York, 1984), 78.

[61] Michael Durey, *Transatlantic Radicals and the Early American Republic* (Lawrence, Kan., 1997), 195–7.

[62] John Stewart, *Opus Maximum: or, the great essay to reduce the world from contingency to system, in the following new sciences: Psyconomy; or, the science of moral powers ... Mathemanomy; or, the laws of knowledge: Logonomy; or, the science of language: Anagognomy; or, the science of education: Ontonomy; or, the science of being* (London: J. Ginger, 1803).

[63] Cheetham, *Life*, 186–7.

a speculative point about which philosophers in their elaborate investigations of abstruse subjects may very harmlessly differ, but the propagation of licentious doctrines amongst the lower orders, with a view to weaken if not to destroy, in practice, that awful fear which restrains them from the commission of sins against God and crimes against man... I have associated with deists; I have listened to the dogmas of deism, and although priestly intolerance and persecution, the abuses of the Christian religion, are principally the alleged causes of their aversion from the one and their attachment to the other, yet I have found them in spirit more intolerant and persecuting, if possible, than any thing which distinguishes the sufferings of the Hugonots or the bloody reign of Mary.[64]

Such hostile rhetoric was, by 1802, commonplace in the United States.

If Paine had long-standing knowledge in this field, it was knowledge that he continued to develop. The Jewish account of the origins of the world was 'fabricated', argued Paine in 1804, 'from the cosmogony of Persia, rather than that of India';

All those ancient nations had their cosmogonies, that is, their accounts of how the creation was made, before there was such people as Jews or Israelites. An account of these cosmogonies of India and Persia is given by Henry Lord, Chaplain to the East India Company at Surat, and published in London in 1630. The writer of this has seen a copy of the edition of 1630, and made extracts from it.[65]

The great orientalist Sir William Jones, added Paine, had argued that Sanscrit might hold keys to human origin in proper names.[66] Paine did notice an American Rabbi's answer to *The Age of Reason*,[67] but it was his English audience that Paine had chiefly in mind.

Similarly, when Paine wrote of 'religion' he meant Christianity. 'Of all the systems of religion that ever were invented, there is none more derogatory to the Almighty, more unedifying to man, more repugnant to reason, and more contradictory in itself, than this thing called Christianity.' How much Paine knew of the other religions may be questioned. But of Christianity he knew, or thought he knew, that it meant that very English construct, 'church and state'. 'As an engine of power, it serves the purpose of despotism; and as a means of wealth, the avarice of priests.'[68]

---

[64] Cheetham, *Life*, 209–10.

[65] Paine, 'Hints Toward Forming a Society for Inquiring into the Truth or Falsehood of Ancient History, so far as History is Connected with Systems of Religion Ancient and Modern', *The Prospect* (21 July 1804): *CW*, ii. 808–9. Paine cited Henry Lord, *A Display of Two Forraigne Sects in the East Indies: vizt: the sect of the Banians the ancient natives of India and the sect of the Persees the ancient inhabitants of Persia* (London: T. and R. Cotes for Francis Constable, 1630).

[66] Paine, 'Hints Toward Forming a Society' (1804): *CW*, ii. 809, citing (without further reference) William Jones, *Asiatick Researches: or, Transactions of the Society Instituted at Bengal for inquiring into the history and antiquities, the arts, sciences, and literature, of Asia* (Calcutta, 1789–).

[67] Paine, *A Letter to the Honourable Thomas Erskine* (1797): *CW*, ii. 736, and *Examination of the Passages in the New Testament* ([1807]): *CW*, ii. 853; citing David Levi, *A Defence of the Old Testament, in a series of letters addressed to Thomas Paine, Author of a Book entitled 'The Age of Reason'* (New York: William A. Davis for Napthali Judah, 1797).

[68] Paine, *The Age of Reason. Part the Second* (1795): *CW*, i. 600–1.

Consequently, Paine produced, in *Part the Second*, a series of memorable remarks on the Bible: 'the grovelling tales and doctrines of the Bible and the [New] Testament are fit only to excite contempt'; 'the stupid Bible of the Church, that teacheth man nothing'.[69] It was such normative comments (generally absent from the guarded writings of early eighteenth-century Deists) that inspired one part of his contemporaries but alienated another, and brought down on him the charge of infidelity. Paine's unitary God, proved by Creation, could easily seem synonymous with Creation itself; that is, with a material Nature. Paine's claim that his political theory rested on an ethical basis was, therefore, a weak point in his position. A material Nature might be nature red in tooth and claw, not the wisely sufficient provision for mankind of an infinitely benevolent Creator.

Paine inherited the assumptions of an age for which Tennyson's image of nature still lay long in the future. As in the 1750s, so in the 1790s, the application of Deism for Paine was not to promote atheism but to attack a social form that was still widely understood as premised on Trinitarian Christianity. At national level, this hegemony was expressed in the often-repeated formula 'Church and state': the idea that the political order was not secular and voluntary, but had an integral relation to a divinely mandated ecclesiastical and moral order. At local and personal level, the same hegemony was captured in the terms 'subordination' or 'subjection': the idea that the social order, like the heavenly, was an undifferentiated hierarchy sustained by the mutual duties of individuals of equal value but unequal authority. Subjection, therefore, was 'mutual subjection', since 'in all the Relations between Man and Man, there is a mutual Dependence, whereby the one cannot subsist without the other'.[70] It was a theory which held that 'The state, like the church, is held together by love.'[71] Like all such theories, different groups in society accepted it to different degrees, and it evolved over time under the pressure of events; but it was prominent in British reactions to Paine in the 1790s.

As a theory, it was widely shared. Richard Price, in his sermon of 1789 that prompted Burke's *Reflections*, had argued that 'we ought to consider ourselves as citizens of the world' and called for a series of fundamental reforms; nevertheless, even Price had urged that 'Obedience...to the laws and to magistrates, are necessary expressions of our regard to the community; and without this obedience the ends of government cannot be obtained, or a community avoid falling into a state of anarchy that will destroy those rights and subvert that liberty, which government is instituted to protect.' Price feared that excessive adulation of men in power would produce its opposite; he therefore condemned 'spurning at all public authority, and throwing off

---

[69] Paine, *The Age of Reason. Part the Second* (1795): *CW*, i. 602–3.

[70] This was 'something more than the Compliment of Course, when our Betters are pleased to tell us they are our humble Servants, but understand us to be their Slaves': Jonathan Swift, *Three Sermons: I. On Mutual Subjection. II. On Conscience. III. On the Trinity* (London: R. Dodsley and M. Cooper, 1744) [5, 10]. A similar doctrine of reciprocity was in full repair in the 1790s, e.g. James Scott, *Equality Considered and Recommended, in a Sermon ... April the 6th, 1792* (London: John Nichols for J. Debrett, 1792), 9, 11.

[71] A. M. C. Waterman, 'Theology and Political Doctrine in Church and Dissent' and 'Intellectual Foundations of Tory Doctrine', in Waterman, *Political Economy and Christian Theology since the Enlightenment* (Basingstoke, 2004), 31–69, at 57; Clark, *English Society*, ch. 3.

that respectful demeanor to persons invested with it which the order of society requires'.[72] For Price, obedience and deference were merely prudential; they lacked the 'metaphysical or theological justification' which others still gave them.[73] Yet if even a reformer like Price spoke in these terms, the emphatic attachment of others to 'Church and state' becomes more comprehensible. Even before *The Age of Reason*, an old trope was being rehearsed with renewed confidence: in France, 'The infidel writings of their philosophers have undermined the king's throne, and struck a blow at all religion.'[74] Paine was about to fall into that category.

Paine's *Age of Reason* therefore met with an almost wholly hostile reaction from a wide spectrum of sources and a stream of adverse publications that did not soon fall away but lasted beyond 1802.[75] These publications came from churchmen and Dissenters; from metropolitan opinion, from provincial English writers, from Scots and Irish authors; from three leading journals of widely different politics, the *British Critic*, the *Critical Review* and the *Analytical Review*; and even from Unitarians, since they, although rejecting the alliance of Church and state, affirmed that religion in general was the foundation of civil society, and defended Unitarian Christianity on the basis of revelation. This hostile comment often stemmed from the argument that Deism was old news: according to a fictitious carpenter, his neighbour 'assures me, that after all the rout you have made about these things, you have not advanced a single syllable that has not been said forty times before, and which has not been confuted over and over again a hundred years ago'.[76]

Often, too, the criticism derived from the perception that *The Age of Reason* 'was geared towards the "uneducated masses" or the "lower orders"':[77] Deist theology was not new, but Paine's populist political orientation was. The Bishop of London identified the danger of Paine's tract:

It is not from the matter, which is most contemptible, and contains nothing new, but from the manner, from the plainness, the familiarity, and the air of authority and triumph with which it is written, that mischief may arise. It is *irreligion made easy* to the great bulk of mankind, and rendered intelligible to every capacity. It is a snare laid for

[72] Richard Price, *A Discourse on the Love of our Country, delivered on Nov. 4, 1789, at the Meeting-House in the Old Jewry, to the Society for Commemorating the Revolution in Great Britain* (London: George Stafford for T. Cadell, 1789), 10, 21, 27.

[73] Waterman, 'Intellectual Foundations of Tory Doctrine', 59.

[74] William Agutter, *Christian Politics; or, the Origin of Power, and the Grounds of Subordination. A Sermon ... September 2, 1792* (London: F. and C. Rivington, 1792), 11; [Ambrose Serle], *Equality no Liberty; or, Subordination the Order of God, and the Welfare of Man* (London: no printer, 1792), 19.

[75] Some 67 replies are listed in Michael L. Lasser, 'In Response to *The Age of Reason*, 1794–1799', *Bulletin of Bibliography and Magazine Notes* 25 (1967), 41–3; more are added in Gayle Trusdel Pendleton, 'Thirty Additional Titles Relating to the *Age of Reason*', *British Studies Monitor* 10 (1980), 36–45. See also Davidson and Scheick, *Paine, Scripture and Authority*, 108–16. Caron, *Thomas Paine contre l'imposture des prêtres*, 521–30, finds 110 replies. Patrick Wallace Hughes, 'Antidotes to Deism: A Reception History of Thomas Paine's *The Age of Reason*, 1794–1809', Ph.D. thesis, University of Pittsburgh, 2013, lists some 145 separate publications in the controversy, 309–31.

[76] *A Country Carpenter's Confession of Faith: With a Few Plain Remarks on The Age of Reason. In a Letter from Will Chip, Carpenter, in Somersetshire, to Thomas Pain, Stay-Maker, in Paris* (London: F. and C. Rivington, 1794), 11 (sometimes wrongly ascribed to Hannah More).

[77] Hughes, 'Antidotes to Deism', iv.

those numerous and valuable classes of men, who have hitherto, in a great measure, escaped the contagion of infidelity, and are perhaps scarce acquainted with its name, the mechanic, the manufacturer, the farmer, the servant, the labourer. On these (to whom the subject is quite new, and who have neither time nor talents for examining questions of this nature), the bold assertions, the intrepid blasphemies, and coarse buffoonery, which constitute the whole merit and character of this performance, are but too well calculated to impose and to supply the place of reasoning and of proof.[78]

One historian found only four English tracts in this controversy that sided with Paine, evidence of little support on this issue even within the reforming intelligentsia; she concluded that the evangelical phenomena of the 1790s 'testify either to an existing dissatisfaction [with the Church that] the *Age* only served occasionally to focus, not to create or lead, or to a spiritual hunger that Paine's cool rationalism was unable to address'. Very few authors 'sided with deism', so that 'The evidence thus mounts sharply against any widespread reception of the doctrines among the reading classes.' It was a reception in Britain very different from that which had greeted Paine's *Rights of Man*.[79]

Another historian concluded that criticism of Paine's tract was 'largely hyperbolic, used to frighten the public', rather than evidence that it had seriously undermined religion in Britain. Partly because of legal prosecutions, there were few British editions of *The Age of Reason* or *The Age of Reason. Part the Second* in 1794–6: a single edition of the first; two editions of the second; a combined edition of both from the bookseller Thomas Williams numbering 2,000 copies, for which he was prosecuted and imprisoned.[80] By contrast, there were seventeen editions in the United States between 1794 and 1796. In a letter from Pennsylvania of 16 October 1794, Joseph Priestley was alarmed that the work was 'much read' and had 'made [a] great impression here'.[81] Yet so too had Bishop Watson's *An Apology for the Bible*, which proved a runaway bestseller in Britain and sold widely in the United States.[82]

By contrast, there seems to have been no French controversy; evidently *The Age of Reason* and *The Age of Reason. Part the Second* made no significant impact there, and called for no reply. On his release from prison, Paine, ill and isolated, found that the Revolution had moved rapidly on. Ironically, he may have been associated in the public mind with the political and religious views of the executed and

---

[78] Beilby Porteus, *A Charge Delivered to the Clergy of the Diocese of London, at the Visitation of that Diocese in the Year MDCCXCIV* (London: F. and C. Rivington, 1794), 23.

[79] Pendleton, 'Thirty Additional Titles', 38; 'it is surprising how few voices were raised in Paine's defence outside of the radical press': Claeys, *Paine*, 191.

[80] Franklyn Prochaska, 'Thomas Paine's *The Age of Reason* Revisited', *Journal of the History of Ideas* 33 (1972), 561–76, at 569, 574.

[81] Jay Smith, 'Thomas Paine and *The Age of Reason*'s Attack on the Bible', *The Historian* 58 (1996), 745–61, at 757.

[82] R[ichard] Watson, *An Apology for the Bible, in a Series of Letters addressed to Thomas Paine, Author of a Book entitled, The Age of Reason, Part the Second, being an Investigation of True and Fabulous Theology* (London: T. Evans et al., 1796) reached its eighth London edition in 1797. In the British Isles, there were editions in Alnwick, Cork, Dublin, Dundee, and Glasgow; in the United States, in Albany, Boston, Lancaster, Pa, Lichfield, Conn., New Brunswick, NJ, New York, Philadelphia, and Shepherds-Town. Va.

vilified Robespierre. Nor did he speak effectively to a French audience. Close critical reading of the Scriptures in the vernacular had not played the same widespread part in Catholic French society that it had in Britain and the United States; unconsciously, Paine's assumptions were Protestant ones. As telling, the mockery of theism had already, for many decades, been undertaken in France by French authors of the ability of Diderot, Hélvetius, d'Holbach, Volney, and Voltaire, but they had typically not employed the detailed critiques of biblical texts favoured by the English Deists. In France, Deism had been upstaged by atheism: there, Paine was already out of date.[83]

After *The Age of Reason. Part the Second* Paine was now drawn to do what he had not done in the case of *Common Sense* and *Rights of Man*. He became fixated on a single issue: not the American Revolution; not the French; not the hoped-for revolution in his native England; not revolution in the abstract; but revelation. From 1794 to his death in 1809, theological controversy took centre stage in Paine's outlook.

As soon as Richard Watson's book appeared, Paine began a reply, intended as a third part of *The Age of Reason*; he could neither leave the issue alone nor complete his project, and worked at it intermittently. Extracts were printed only in 1810, after his death, in the New York magazine *The Theophilanthropist*.[84] In 1804 he contributed polemical articles on religion to the New York monthly journal *The Prospect, or View of the Moral World*, edited by the American Deist Elihu Palmer.[85] More of his work on similar themes appeared in 1807 in Paine's sixty-two-page pamphlet, announced as 'Printed for the Author': perhaps no publisher would give his name to it. Its closing sentence suggests why: 'HE THAT BELIEVES IN THE STORY OF CHRIST IS AN INFIDEL TO GOD.'[86] The subject was exhausted. *The Age of Reason* had been the last gasp of eighteenth-century British Deism rather than the beginning of a major new world of discourse. Only in the backward United States was the conflict with biblical fundamentalism still a live one.

THE AGE OF REASON AS A CONTEXT FOR *AGRARIAN JUSTICE*

In the early 1790s, his attention focused on political events, Paine could not always be up to date with recent theology. In particular, he did not mention a key work

---

[83] Yannick Bosc, 'Paine et Robespierre: propriété, vertu et révolution', in Jean-Pierre Jessenne, Gilles Deregnaucourt, Jean-Pierre Hirsch, and Hervé Leuwers (eds), *Robespierre: De la nation artésienne à la République et aux Nations* (Villeneuve d'Ascq, 1994), 245–51, at 249; Caron, *Thomas Paine contre l'imposture des prêtres*, 263–72. For the much older history of French Deism see C. J. Betts, *Early Deism in France: From the So-Called 'déistes' of Lyon (1564) to Voltaire's 'Lettres philosophiques' (1734)* (The Hague, 1984).

[84] Paine, 'Extracts from a Reply to the Bishop of Llandaff' (1810): *CW*, ii. 764–88.

[85] Paine, 'Prospect Papers': *CW*, ii. 788–830.

[86] *Examination of the Passages in the New Testament, quoted from the Old and called Prophecies concerning Jesus Christ. To which is prefixed, An Essay on Dream, Shewing by what operation of the mind a Dream is produced in sleep, and applying the same to the account of Dreams in the New Testament; With an Appendix containing my Private Thoughts of a Future State, And Remarks on the Contradictory Doctrine in the Books of Matthew and Mark. By Thomas Paine* (New York: printed for the author [1807]): *CW*, ii. 848–92.

published in London in 1779, by which time he was in America and preoccupied with its revolution. 'Paine's argument from design is...flawed, and shows a lamentable ignorance of Hume's *Dialogues on Natural Religion*, which is a more than adequate counter to his rather bald assertions.'[87] But Paine confessed that he had read replies to *The Age of Reason*;[88] it will be argued here that these replies created a more powerful context for the interpretation of *The Age of Reason. Part the Second* and *Agrarian Justice* than had been the case with *Common Sense* and *Rights of Man*, where Paine did not obviously follow closely the debates that he had launched.

Paine now drew on English sources of which he already had a considerable knowledge. In *Rights of Man. Part the Second*, he had paid a compliment to the reforming bishop Richard Watson: 'Among all the writers of the English church clergy, who have treated on the general subject of religion, the present Bishop of L[l]andaff has not been excelled.'[89] Yet, like Burke, the bishop turned against his former ally. Paine believed that the decision to prosecute the printers of the second part of *The Age of Reason* was taken because the Society for the Propagation of Christian Knowledge had learned that Paine intended to publish a third part of that work, replying to 'their champion' Richard Watson. Of Watson's *An Apology for the Bible*, Paine wrote: 'The Bishop's answer, like Mr. Burke's attack on the French Revolution, served me as a background to bring forward other subjects upon, with more advantage than if the background was not there. This is the motive that induced me to answer him, otherwise I should have gone on without taking any notice of him.'[90] It was this work that most exercised Paine among the replies to *The Age of Reason*, and to it he replied at length.

Paine's *Agrarian Justice* (1797) was once conventionally explained as an anticipation of socialism and an echo of the writings of Thomas Spence. It came to be seen in retrospect as a pioneering text of 'the modern land reform movement', as a secular revival of natural law, and as a secular argument about the structural economic causes of inequality.[91] *Agrarian Justice* certainly had an afterlife, and was later recruited in just that way. Yet neither Paine nor Spence succeeded in placing the redistribution or nationalization of land at the centre of most reformers' agendas in nineteenth- or twentieth-century Britain, France, or the United States: in Britain, reform came to address the redistribution of capital or income more than the redistribution of land. Spence also came to define his views in opposition to Paine's. Paine's afterlife, in this respect as in others, calls for careful reconsideration.

The neglect can be explained by a different context proposed for a reading of *Agrarian Justice*: on publication, this text was a practical application of the theoretical issues laid out in *The Age of Reason*, not in chapter V of *Rights of Man. Part the*

---

[87] Mark Philp, *Paine* (Oxford, 1989), 112; David Hume, *Dialogues Concerning Natural Religion* ([London; no printer], 1779).

[88] Paine, *The Age of Reason. Part the Second* (1795): *CW*, i. 518.

[89] Paine, *Rights of Man. Part the Second* (1792): *CW*, i. 453.

[90] Paine to Thomas Jefferson, 1 Oct. 1800: *CW*, ii. 1412.

[91] M. Beer (ed.), *The Pioneers of Land Reform: Thomas Spence, William Ogilvie, Thomas Paine* (London, 1920), v, who nevertheless judged Paine's proposals 'very moderate', ix. Beer cited Alfred Russel Wallace, *Land Nationalisation* (London, 1882) as a recent work in the tradition.

Second.[92] So *Agrarian Justice* began by rehearsing again the 'oppressions' of 'priestly imposture' as a cause of the agrarian wrongs Paine now sought to correct. 'France and all Europe' had been 'plunged' in a 'long and dense night' by 'their governments and their priests'. As soon as Paine turned to property, he drew a distinction between 'natural property', which 'comes to us from the Creator of the universe', and 'artificial or acquired property—the invention of men'. Paine's argument, then, was impelled by his familiar negations, and unsustainable without his Deistic premises.[93]

In artificial property, Paine conceded that 'equality is impossible'; but he made up for that with an argument on 'Equality of natural property', God's gift. It was this attribute of natural property that established also 'Equality of the right of suffrage'.[94] So Paine, urging a wide electorate, still grounded the franchise on property rights, where the new English advocates of universal suffrage based it on individual personality; and Paine did this as a consequence of his theory of literal divine grant. In *Agrarian Justice* he did not refer back to his plans for progressive taxation set out in *Rights of Man. Part the Second*; on the contrary, *Agrarian Justice* was not significantly dependent on that earlier text. Paine wrote *Agrarian Justice* not because he had become a follower of Babeuf, but because he remained a Deist.

Paine began the Inscription to *Agrarian Justice* with the universalist words: 'The plan contained in this work is not adapted for any particular country alone: the principle on which it is based is general.' He did not link his argument with any interpretation of the French Revolution, or claim that the French Revolution was his model. Yet although dedicated to the Directory, Paine's information was English, and his monetary calculations were expressed in pounds sterling, not in French francs.[95] His only data on the fiscal scope for social redistribution were English, drawn from Pitt's budget statement of December 1796.[96] Paine announced what had prompted him to write his tract: he did not mention the sufferings of the French people in 'the winter of 1795 and '96', but recorded only a theological affront to himself. This, too, had been English: in the preface to the English edition, Paine recorded that he was provoked to publish his tract by reading in the Bishop of Llandaff's *An Apology for the Bible* a list of Watson's publications, including a sermon entitled 'The Wisdom and Goodness of God, in having made both Rich and Poor; with an Appendix, containing Reflections on the Present State of England and France.'[97] A second trigger was Bishop Samuel Horsley's remark in

[92] For a contrasting argument that *Agrarian Justice* extended the social policies expressed in *Rights of Man. Part the Second* see Bernard Vincent, 'Paine's *Agrarian Justice* and the Birth of the Welfare State', in Vincent, *The Transatlantic Republican: Thomas Paine and the Age of Revolutions* (Amsterdam, 2005), 125–35.

[93] By contrast, William Blackstone, in his *Commentaries on the Laws of England*, had explained the inequalities of landed property as the result of human legislation alone, from which appeal could not be had to natural law or divine institution.

[94] Paine, *Agrarian Justice* ([1797]): *CW*, i. 606–7.

[95] Paine, *Agrarian Justice* ([1797]): *CW*, i. 606, 615–17.

[96] *The Parliamentary History of England, from the Earliest Period to the Year 1803* (London: T. C. Hansard et al., 1818), xxxii. cols 1256–64.

[97] Paine, *Agrarian Justice* ([1797]): *CW*, i. 609. The title Paine cited was from an advertisement; Richard Watson's sermon had been entitled *A Sermon preached before the Stewards of the Westminster*

the House of Lords in November 1795 that, in Paine's paraphrase, man '*has nothing to do with the laws but to obey them*'.[98]

Paine's objection to Watson was equally theological: 'It is wrong to say God made *rich* and *poor*; He made only *male* and *female*; and He gave them the earth for their inheritance.' It might be objected that this idea of a specific divine grant was at odds with the Deist idea of God as the author of general laws only; but Paine was here arguing against Trinitarians, whose stance on revelation meant that the Book of Genesis was to be interpreted historically, and it is not clear that God's provision of the land to mankind in common counted, for Paine, as anything other than a general provision. This equal right to natural property, argued Paine, continued to his present day. Indeed its continuance was the practical, economic counterpart to Paine's denial of the Fall of Man. So the original state of humanity had to be, for Paine, a mirror of the Christian account of humanity before the Fall: for Paine, 'The life of an Indian is a continual holiday, compared with the poor of Europe.' He did not explain further the idyllic state in which he supposed 'the Indians of North America' lived 'at the present day' other than to claim that 'Poverty...exists not in the natural state'; the point of his image was an abstract one, to create a definitional contrast.[99]

For Paine did not emancipate himself from the powerful inherited assumptions of the Fall by rejecting it. Rather, he silently translated it into material terms. Some original and disastrous event had occurred, he argued, which was irreversible: 'It is always possible to go from the natural to the civilized state, but it is never possible to go from the civilized to the natural state.' But for Paine that event was not man's first disobedience, but mankind's expulsion from the land, when 'cultivation' succeeded the grazing of 'flocks and herds', and 'the idea of landed property' was first devised to confine access to the land to the few. At least 'half the inhabitants of every nation' were now 'dispossessed' of 'their natural inheritance'.

He did not justify this choice of a fraction. Paine envisaged a national fund, created by a 10 per cent death duty on property; but why this tenth was equal to the value of the property of which mankind had been dispossessed, he did not explain. These omissions suggest that his attention was elsewhere. Paine's proposals for compensation (transfer payments of £15 to 'every person' at age 21, and a pension of £10 per annum to all those aged 50 or over) were also modest in size, arbitrarily set, and hardly transformative in practical terms; their point was, rather, an eschatological one, symbolically to counter a secular Fall. As Paine rightly appreciated, 'it is justice, and not charity, that is the principle of the plan'.[100] That is, he offered no rationale for the amount of wealth to be redistributed; what interested him was mankind's just right to redress.

Dispensary at their Anniversary Meeting, in Charlotte-Street Chapel, April 1785. With an Appendix. [followed by a text:] The Wisdom and Goodness of God, in having made both Rich and Poor (Loughborough: Adams, Jun. and London: T. Cadell and T. Evans, 1793).

[98] Paine, *Agrarian Justice* ([1797]): *CW*, i. 606, 609, 615, 621; for Horsley's speech, see *Parliamentary History*, xxxii. col. 258. Paine omitted Horsley's qualification: 'with the reserve of their undoubted right to petition against any particular law, as a grievance on a particular description of people'.

[99] Paine, *Agrarian Justice* ([1797]): *CW*, i. 609–11.

[100] Paine, *Agrarian Justice* ([1797]): *CW*, i. 610–13, 616, 618.

Only in theological terms could Paine plausibly claim that these modest payments would effect a 'revolution in the state of civilization'. It was the inherited perception of the Fall that created in Paine the view that everything in contemporary society was to be rejected: 'The present state of civilization is as odious as it is unjust. It is absolutely the opposite of what it should be, and it is necessary that a revolution should be made in it.' By contrast, Paine was no simple egalitarian in a material sense, writing: 'I am a friend to riches because they are capable of good. I care not how affluent some may be, provided that none be miserable in consequence of it.' His eloquent laments at this point at 'The contrast of affluence and wretchedness continually meeting and offending the eye... The sight of the misery, and the unpleasant sensations it suggests' warn against assuming that Paine was *not* aware of such things. That he wrote explicitly of them, but so briefly, rather highlights the general absence of such matters from his writings before and after *Agrarian Justice*. What Paine most objected to was not material poverty as such, although he did object to it, but the 'superstitious awe, the enslaving reverence, that formerly surrounded affluence'.[101] 'Superstitious' and 'reverence' were revealing terms. But his words did not attend to envy as a cause of misery in some people who resented affluence: if so, his words might be read as drawing no line beyond which the expropriation of wealth would be illegitimate.

It was this ideal of the natural equality of man by creation that led Paine in *Agrarian Justice* to a much more extensive position, expressed in an aside: even personal property accumulated by the industry of the individual was not beyond moral obligation. The individual 'owes on every principle of justice, of gratitude, and of civilization, a part of that accumulation back again to society from whence the whole came'.[102] For Paine, the exact size of that debt was not central; the point was the debt's moral status.

Paine, then, was a retro-Deist, not a proto-socialist. This is no disparagement of Paine, who was necessarily unable to adopt the second role, but *Agrarian Justice* was notable for his performance of the first. Even in his last published work, in 1807, an attack on the idea that prophecies in the Old Testament foretold the coming of Christ in the New, Paine reverted to early eighteenth-century English Deist controversies, citing William Whiston (1667–1752): 'Whiston was a man of great literary learning, and of deep scientific learning... He wrote so much in defence of the Old Testament, and of what he calls prophecies of Jesus Christ, that at last he began to suspect the truth of the Scriptures, and wrote against them.'[103] Paine added an attack on *Dissertations on the Prophecies* (1754–8) by Thomas Newton (1704–82), Bishop of Bristol 'but a superficial writer'.[104]

---

[101] Paine, *Agrarian Justice* ([1797]): *CW*, i. 617, 620–1.
[102] Paine, *Agrarian Justice* ([1797]): *CW*, i. 620.
[103] Paine, *Examination of the Passages in the New Testament* ([1807]): *CW*, ii. 869, citing William Whiston, *An Essay towards Restoring the True Text of the Old Testament; and for Vindicating the Citations made thence in the New Testament* (London: J. Senex and W. Taylor, 1722).
[104] Paine, *Examination of the Passages in the New Testament* ([1807]): *CW*, ii. 877, citing Thomas Newton, *Dissertations on the Prophecies which have been remarkably fulfilled, and at this time are fulfilling in the world* (3 vols, London: J. and R. Tonson and S. Draper, 1754–8; 10th edn, Edinburgh, 1793).

Paine denied any direct indebtedness in the early part of his life when he concluded his last pamphlet of 1807 and contrasted his previous self-reliance with his recent discovery of an English ally: 'When, in the first part of "The Age of Reason", I called the creation the true revelation of God to man, I did not know that any other person had expressed the same idea. But I lately met with the writings of Doctor Conyers Middleton, published the beginning of last century, in which he expresses himself in the same manner, with respect to the creation, as I have done in "The Age of Reason".' Paine now quoted lengthy passages from Middleton (1683–1750), including Middleton quoting Cicero. One of Middleton's critics had attacked him for calling creation, revelation. Paine quoted this Deist: '"Yet it is no other [term]", replied Middleton, "than what the wise in all ages have given to it, who consider it as the most authentic and indisputable revelation which God has ever given of Himself, from the beginning of the world to this day."' Middleton had quoted Cicero, and anticipated that 'Our Doctors perhaps will look on this as RANK DEISM; but let them call it what they will, I shall ever avow and defend it as the fundamental, essential, and vital part of all true religion.' These were, for Paine, 'sublime extracts'.[105] Paine probably had access to the works of William Whiston, Thomas Newton, and Conyers Middleton after his return to the United States in 1802; if he knew of them earlier, it is notable that he did not at least mention them in *The Age of Reason* or elsewhere.

Where Whiston and Middleton provided Paine with intellectual confirmation, it was not until 1802, from Paris, that he complimented an American Deist, Elihu Palmer, on Palmer's Deist work, *Principles of Nature: or, a Development of the Moral Causes of Happiness and Misery among the Human Species* (New York: no printer, 1801).[106] Paine's last published essay before his death on 8 June 1809 was an attack on the 'absurd and impious doctrine of predestination'. Here Paine finally turned to an American exemplar, Benjamin Franklin, for an affirmation of Deism. But what caught his eye in the recently published biography of Franklin was Franklin's response to English sources:

> He was in London at the time of which he speaks. 'Some volumes,' says he, 'against Deism, fell into my hands. They were said to be the substance of sermons preached at Boyle's lectures. It happened that they produced on me an effect precisely the reverse of what was intended by the writers; for the arguments of the Deists, which were cited in order to be refuted, appeared to me more forcible than the refutation itself. In a word I soon became a perfect Deist.'—New York edition of Franklin's Life, page 93.[107]

---

[105] Paine, *Examination of the Passages in the New Testament* ([1807]): *CW*, ii. 883–5, citing Conyers Middleton, *Vindication of the Free Inquiry into the Miraculous Powers, Which are supposed To have subsisted in the Christian Church, &c. From the Objections of Dr Dodwell and Dr Church* (London: R. Manby and H. S. Cox, 1751), 6–10. Paine's reference to Middleton's 'letters' from Rome suggests that Paine knew of Middleton's *A Letter from Rome, Shewing an Exact Conformity between Popery and Paganism: or, the Religion of the Present Romans to be derived entirely from that of their Heathen Ancestors* (London: W. Innys, 1729) or *Popery Unmask'd. Being the Substance of Dr Middleton's celebrated Letter from Rome* (London: R. Manby and H. Shute Cox, 1744). Davidson and Scheick, *Paine, Scripture and Authority*, 62–3, argue that Paine may have known Middleton's work earlier.

[106] Paine to Elihu Palmer, 21 Feb. 1802: *CW*, ii. 1426.

[107] Paine, 'Predestination': *CW*, ii. 897, citing *The Life of Dr Benjamin Franklin: written by himself* (New York: T. and J. Swords, 1794). The best-known abridgement was that later work, *A Defence of*

Even here Paine did not claim personal knowledge of Franklin's beliefs, and it seems likely that the cautious Franklin had not confided in the hot-headed Paine when Franklin met him in London in 1774.[108] Not until after 1794, the date of this edition's publication, did Paine become fully aware of his American ally's religious views; and Paine is unlikely to have read the New York edition before his return to the United States in 1802. Once back in America, Paine defended his Deist creed from the arguments of the English Baptist Robert Hall, *Modern Infidelity Considered with respect to its Influence on Society* (Cambridge, 1800): despite a hostile reaction to *The Age of Reason* in the new American republic that considerably exceeded that in England, Paine chose to reply to an English tract.[109]

By contrast, the reaction in Britain and America to *Agrarian Justice* was small, except insofar as it was quickly overtaken by Thomas Spence.[110] Paine was already categorized as the author of *Rights of Man* and *The Age of Reason* and as an 'infidel': there was little intellectual room for a new image of him as a land reformer to emerge to displace these, an image which could have responded aptly to his theism. But if *Agrarian Justice* is rightly located as sandwiched between *The Age of Reason* and Paine's later writings on religion, the religious context of his tract of 1797 comes into focus. There was, as yet, no such thing as 'secular liberalism' for Paine to adopt: for him, human equality and the equality of rights were always and only of divine institution.

Natural and Revealed Religion: being an abridgment of the sermons preached at the lecture founded by the Honble Robert Boyle, Esq. (4 vols, London: Arthur Bettesworth and Charles Hitch, 1737). Franklin wrote that he read the 'volumes ... against Deism' when 'scarce fifteen'; born in 1706, this would place the encounter in 1721. But he was in London in 1724–6, which is a more likely time-frame for his acquaintance with anti-Deist literature. Franklin may have confused an earlier source with the work of 1737. The best known of the Boyle lectures was Richard Bentley, *The Folly and Unreasonableness of Atheism ... In Eight Sermons preached at the Lecture Founded by the Honourable Robert Boyle, Esquire, in the first Year 1692* (London: J. H. for H. Mortlock, 1693); it reached its 5th edn in 1724.

[108] Franklin's 'Articles of Belief and Acts of Religion', dated 1728, describes a creed much like Paine's: Walters, *Revolutionary Deists*, 64–72. They came from the same source: English Deism.

[109] Paine, 'Prospect Papers', 'Remarks on R. Hall's Sermon' (1804): *CW*, ii. 789–91.

[110] For Spence see Ch. 7, section Land reform: Thomas Spence v. Thomas Paine. For reactions to *Agrarian Justice* see Claeys, *Paine*, 207.

PART III

DIVERGENCES AND LEGACIES

7

Receptions and Reinterpretations
Paine's Lasting Influence

FRANCE

The Directory, Paine's *Dissertation on First-Principles of Government* (1795), and Bonaparte

In France, Paine soon faced disillusionment. The thinning of the ranks of the Girondins and the Jacobins in turn during the Terror had left the National Convention swayed by men of property, eager to frame a constitution that would bring stability after years of chaos. The task was entrusted to a commission in November 1794; in January following Paine wrote a document on the constitution of 1793, probably translated into French by Lanthenas, never published but evidently used in an attempt to influence the debate, perhaps by being read in the Convention.[1] This reading evidently did not happen.

The draft constitution was presented to the Convention on 23 June 1795. This version was to be built on a franchise confined to those who paid direct taxes, or were soldiers; these voters would then choose a body of electors, a property qualification confining the numbers eligible for service at that level to about 30,000. These electors would in turn choose a bicameral legislature, the upper house of which would itself then choose the five members of the Directory, all of whom would have to be over the age of 40. The Directory would hold supreme executive power at national and local level.[2] Under the influence of the Thermidoreans, the tide was now running strongly against Jacobin populism, and the proposed constitution was clearly meant to prevent the Terror from ever returning.

This constitution would have been wholly contrary to Paine's long-standing orientation against oligarchy. He objected in a letter to a member dated 6 June,[3] but his considered reply was another tract, *Dissertation on First-Principles of Government*, perhaps dated 'Paris, July, 1795'.[4] It had been drafted, he later claimed, at the time

---

[1] Paine, *Observations sur la partie de la Constitution de 1793 (présentée par l'ancien Comité de salut public) qui concerne la formation et les pouvoirs du Conseil executive*, in Bernard Vincent (ed.), 'Cinq inédits de Thomas Paine', *Revue française d'études américaines* 40 (1989), 213–35, at 226–30. The English text does not survive. For Paine's attempts, after his release from prison, to influence the framing of a constitution see Lounissi, *Paine*, 382–98.

[2] Hawke, *Paine*, 310–11.   [3] Lounissi, *Paine*, 383.

[4] The date is given in *CW*, ii. 588; I have been unable to trace a dated edition. Lounissi, *Paine*, 387, gives the date 23 June.

of the attempted revolution in the United Provinces in 1787–8. If so, it does not seem that Paine significantly updated the text. Just as he had earlier lectured Danton on the lessons of the American Revolution, so Paine again held up the American example against the French. The 'science of government' had stood still until the American Revolution, he argued. 'No improvement has been made in the principle and scarcely any in the practice till the American Revolution began.' Against error, Paine held up 'principle'. Principle made politics an 'easy' question. The proposed constitution, by implication, was clearly in error.

But what were the alternatives? Paine's problem was that his analysis was unchanged. The 'primary divisions' of governments, he urged, 'are but two: First, government by election and representation. Secondly, government by hereditary succession.' Even now, Paine, ignoring the arguments of Sieyès, was still committed to his old argument that the great choice in politics was between 'the system of representation, and that of hereditary succession'.[5] However theoretically plausible, this analysis disclosed no understanding of the complex politics of the Revolution, or of how France had reached the point at which it now stood. Even the proposed Directory could claim to rest, in a sense, on a basis of representation. But Paine's tactics were less than optimal, since his revived tract began by rehearsing once more the old arguments against hereditary government, chiefly monarchy, and gave much space to familiar denunciations of aristocracy. Neither was still at immediate issue in the France of 1795.

Paine was deeply unhappy with the Directory. The trouble, indeed, began earlier. 'Had a constitution been established two years ago [in 1793] (as ought to have been done), the violences that have since desolated France and injured the character of the Revolution, would, in my opinion, have been prevented.'[6] This unhappiness provoked him to his most extensive advocacy to date of a wide electorate: 'The true and only true basis of representative government is equality of rights. Every man has a right to one vote, and no more in the choice of representatives.' Paine established this not by a disquisition on natural rights theory but by advancing a practical argument: 'Will the rich exclude themselves? No. Will the poor exclude themselves? No. By what right then can any be excluded?' It followed that 'In any view of the case it is dangerous and impolitic, sometimes ridiculous, and always unjust to make property the criterion of the right of voting.'[7]

This was a change from his position in *Rights of Man*. But the argument ignored the real reasons why different governments always had, and still had, contrasting machineries of representation, yet still commanded substantial legitimacy in the eyes of their citizens or subjects. Nowhere did Paine use the phrase, already current in England, 'annual parliaments and universal suffrage'. The closest he came was a moral critique of riches: 'this exclusion from the right of voting implies a stigma on the moral character of the persons excluded; and this is what no part of the community has a right to pronounce upon another part'. Whatever its effect as exhortation, this fell short of the new English doctrine of universal suffrage. The equal moral

---

[5] Paine, *Dissertation on First-Principles of Government* ([1795]): *CW*, ii. 571–2.
[6] Paine, *The Age of Reason. Part the Second* (1795): *CW*, i. 587.
[7] Paine, *Dissertation on First-Principles of Government* ([1795]): *CW*, ii. 577–9.

standing of individuals was also, arguably, compromised by Paine's concession: 'That property will ever be unequal is certain.' Instead, Paine launched his pamphlet with a backward-looking denunciation of the hereditary principle (which the Directory was not defending) and an assertion of 'the representative system' (whose existence in the Westminster Parliament Paine nowhere acknowledged).[8]

Paine was, here as elsewhere, still largely echoing English discourse of an earlier decade and still assumed the old rhetorical antithesis of liberty and slavery, most obviously in arguing:

> To take away this right [of voting] is to reduce a man to slavery, for slavery consists in being subject to the will of another, and he that has not a vote in the election of representatives is in this case... It is possible to exclude men from the right of voting, but it is impossible to exclude them from the right of rebelling against that exclusion; and when all other rights are taken away the right of rebellion is made perfect.[9]

Also oriented to the past was Paine's praise of 'the representative system' while saying little specifically about how that system was to be restructured and how it was to work: 'as in extensive societies, such as America and France, the right of the individual in matters of government cannot be exercised but by election and representation, it consequently follows that the only system of government consistent with principle, where simple democracy is impracticable, is the representative system.' Paine's praise of 'government by election and representation' was in order to frame the antithesis against 'government by hereditary succession', not to begin a deeper enquiry into the nature of the right to vote.

Indeed, he openly stated, in an older idiom, that 'Personal rights... are a species of property.' One new element was that Paine in the *Dissertation* now advocated a bicameral legislature (the members divided between the two houses by lot) rather than a unicameral one, but the single short paragraph he devoted to the subject revealed its unimportance in his wider scheme of things.[10] This may seem inconsistent with Paine's earlier support for unicameralism. Indeed one historian has identified in America a 'struggle between the unicameralists and the bicameralists in the 1770s and 1780s' for control over the constitution: 'The unicameralists, those who viewed the world anew, tabula rasa, and believed human nature plastic, moldable and remakeable, battled against historicists [the bicameralists] trying to remake the governing institutions they had known in the past in a new form.'[11] Paine's easy compromise on this issue is evidence that his political ideals had particularist as well as universalist elements. But Paine's deductive pattern of reasoning did not rule definitively on uni- or bicameralism. It was also unable to cope with ordinary political conflict:

> It will sometime happen that the minority are right, and the majority are wrong, but as soon as experience proves this to be the case, the minority will increase to a majority,

---

[8] Paine, *Dissertation on First-Principles of Government* ([1795]): *CW*, ii. 572, 579–80.

[9] Paine, *Dissertation on First-Principles of Government* ([1795]): *CW*, ii. 579–80.

[10] Paine, *Dissertation on First-Principles of Government* ([1795]): *CW*, ii. 571, 578, 584–5.

[11] Brendan McConville, *The King's Three Faces: The Rise & Fall of Royal America, 1688–1776* (Williamsburg, Va, 2006), 314.

and the error will reform itself by the tranquil operation of freedom of opinion and equality of rights. Nothing, therefore, can justify an insurrection, neither can it ever be necessary where rights are equal and opinions free.

But in order to 'overthrow despotism', 'insurrections' were 'justified by necessity'.[12]

Paine's *Dissertation* had no effect in revising France's proposed constitution. As a response to the world of the *sans-culottes* and the Terror, Paine's case lacked engagement with France as that nation had developed. Nor could Paine predict the next step, for the challenge faced by the Directory was not another populist revolution; it was military dictatorship. The *Dissertation* did not effectively recall the deputies to the founding principles of the French Revolution, for Paine did not understand how the origins of that episode were different from the event that he assumed had been triggered in 1776 by his own, English, principles. Indeed his *Dissertation* had little specific to say about France at all.

After his release from prison the Convention reinstated Paine as a Deputy on 8 December 1794, but he seems not to have returned as a regularly active member. After distributing copies of his *Dissertation* to the Deputies, he appeared in the Convention on 7 July 1795, once more standing silently on the tribune while a translation of his speech was read out. As political rhetoric the speech was less than optimal, for Paine began with an attempt to 'submit to the Convention the most unequivocal proofs of my integrity, and the rectitude of those principles which have uniformly influenced my conduct'. He soon turned to a blanket condemnation of the proposed constitution: 'certain it is that the plan of the Constitution which has been presented to you is not consistent with the grand object of the Revolution, nor congenial to the sentiments of the individuals who accomplished it'. He recalled the Deputies to 'principle'. The constitution's definition of citizenship would 'deprive half the people...of their rights as citizens'; it 'proposes as the object of society...the good only of a *few*'; the labourers would be 'consigned totally to the caprice and tyranny' of that few. A taxpayer franchise was subject in its application to 'caprice'. Adding soldiers to the list of those enfranchised was merely a 'trick and subterfuge' to disguise the restrictive franchise. It was politically ineffective language, although Paine evidently spoke from the heart.

Unflatteringly, Paine warned his fellow Delegates not to 'subvert the basis of the Revolution'; the proposed constitution would replace its principles with 'a cold indifference and self-interest'. What, then, were the principles of the Revolution? Paine could only point to a document, the Declaration of Rights that preceded the proposed constitution's text.[13] But it could equally be argued that the Declaration's generalizations were indeed embodied in the constitution's provisions. Paine wrote nothing more in specific detail about the leaders of the French Revolution, or the aims reflected in events. He may have identified accurately the self-interest that motivated his fellow Deputies of 1795, but he gave them no sufficient reason to

---

[12] Paine, *Dissertation on First-Principles of Government* ([1795]): *CW*, ii. 585, 587.
[13] Paine, 'The Constitution of 1795', speech in the French National Convention (7 July 1795): *CW*, ii. 589–91.

depart from their chosen course. He ended his speech by recommending that the constitution be referred back to its drafting committee in order to be brought into harmony with the Declaration of Rights, but this proposal won no support. His speech was not printed. Paine evidently had little influence on the outcome of the Convention's deliberations, just as he had had little influence on the framing of the United States' Constitution of 1787.[14]

Paine did not attend the Convention again. On 23 September 1795 it adopted the new constitution; in October elections were held to the new bicameral legislature, that is, the Committee of Five Hundred and the Council of Elders. Paine was not elected. He was henceforth no longer a legislator, and his ability to have even the slightest direct engagement with French politics was at an end. When the provision that two-thirds of the members of the new legislature be chosen from the existing Convention triggered an uprising in Paris on 5 October 1795, it was crushed, at the price of hundreds of dead, by the troops of a young general, Napoleon Bonaparte. Even then, Paine's response was to write not a history of the French Revolution but a pamphlet, *The Decline and Fall of the English System of Finance*, published in April 1796; it predicted that country's inexorable bankruptcy. Again, his sources were English, notably an English banker friend, Sir Robert Smyth, a sympathizer with the French Revolution.[15] Paine claimed to have been vindicated when in 1797 the British government suspended conversion of Bank of England notes into specie; but with a wholly paper currency the British economy found it easier to sustain the fiscal burden of war. In this pamphlet Paine predicted that, in twenty years, Britain's currency would fail; instead, in 1816 Britain returned to the gold standard.

By 1797, Paine was reported as pluming himself 'more on his theology than his politics'.[16] Increasingly his analysis of the public sphere turned on the question of religion. In an effort to promote Deism as an antidote to Christianity, he launched a group in Paris that he termed the Society of Theophilanthropists; but it did not flourish.[17] French politics continued to move away from the ideals of the Jacobins, as the election of a new third of the representatives made clear. In 1797, many in France began to fear a royalist revival, this time brought about by means of free elections. Paine shared this alarm, for the French as well as for the American republic. The Directory saw a threat to itself, and on 4 September 1797 (18 Fructidor) the Directory acted, bringing in the army to purge from the legislature 200 deputies it defined as anti-republicans. Of the five members of the Directory, François de Barthélemy was arrested; Lazare-Nicolas-Marguerite Carnot went into hiding; the remaining three henceforth ruled as a dictatorship, with army support. Paine

---

[14] For a defence of Paine's influence see Lounissi, *Paine*, 388–96.

[15] Hawke, *Paine*, 317.

[16] *The Writings of Theobald Wolfe Tone*, ed. T. W. Moody, R. B. McDowell, and C. J. Woods (3 vols, Oxford, 1997–2007), iii. 29–30.

[17] Hawke, *Paine*, 326. One of Paine's talks to the society appeared under the title *Atheism Refuted; in a Discourse to Prove the Existence of a God. By T. P.* (London: J. Johnson, 1798). Clio Rickman published his own edition as *A Discourse Delivered by Thomas Paine, at the Society of the Theophilanthropists at Paris, 1798* (London: Rickman, [1798]).

supported this military coup, urging that the republic itself was at stake, menaced by royalist conspiracy.

France was now, effectively, a military dictatorship; opposition was suppressed by force. Yet Paine now reversed his profound opposition to the constitution of 1795: 'A better *organized* Constitution has never yet been devised by human wisdom', he wrote in a pamphlet printed by his friend Bonneville in October 1797 (it is not clear that Paine intended a comparison with the American Constitution of 1787). It was, after all, a representative system. After ringing praise of its wisdom, Paine recorded a minor reservation: 'The only defect in the Constitution is that of having narrowed the right of suffrage', the point that he had made central to his complete repudiation of it in 1795. Now, he wrote that this constitution had worked miracles: 'Almost as suddenly as the morning light dissipates darkness, did the establishment of the Constitution change the face of affairs in France. Security succeeded to terror, prosperity to distress, plenty to famine, and confidence increased as the days multiplied.' Given these successes, the Directory was quite right to remove the 'hypocrites' and 'secret conspirators' aiming at 'counter-revolution' who had been returned in the elections for the new third of the legislature.[18]

Whatever Paine's analysis, the Directory had created a precedent: it was soon itself to be toppled by a military coup. Meanwhile, it staged a second coup on 11 May 1798 (22 Floréal), ejecting 106 newly elected members of the legislature, this time for the opposite reason: that they intended to revive the Terror.[19] Paine said nothing. The precedent had been strengthened, and Napoleon Bonaparte's military coup took place on 9 and 10 November (18 and 19 Brumaire) 1799. Soon Bonneville's newspaper *Le Bien informé* carried an article comparing Bonaparte with Oliver Cromwell;[20] its authorship is unknown. A week after the coup Paine left for Belgium, staying in Bruges with a former cellmate in the Luxembourg prison, and did not return to Paris until the spring of 1800.[21] On his return, he came again under the attention of the police, and was warned by a policeman that his writings in *Le Bien informé* were considered subversive; in the face of this threat, Paine fell silent for eighteen months, voicing only privately his hostile opinions of Bonaparte's government.[22] Finally, following the Peace of Amiens in March 1802, he was able to leave France for America that September. Safely back in Washington, Paine published his opinion that France's government had grown into a 'tyranny, as it did in England under Oliver Cromwell'.[23] Even then, his yardstick was an English one; it did not capture what was distinctively French about Napoleon.

Bonaparte had initially patronized Paine, seeming to draw on his advice for the project of the invasion of England, but Paine gave offence by arguing that the end could only be achieved by the destruction of English commerce. Later, after his return from Egypt, Bonaparte encountered Paine at a dinner given to honour French

[18] *Letter of Thomas Paine to the People of France, and the French Armies, on the Events of the 18th Fructidor, and its Consequences* (1797): *CW*, ii. 594–613, at 595, 598–601. A French edition was soon published.

[19] Hawke, *Paine*, 334.   [20] Lounissi, *Paine*, 772.   [21] Hawke, *Paine*, 338.

[22] Keane, *Paine*, 444–52.

[23] Paine, 'To the Citizens of the United States' (22 Nov. 1802): *CW*, ii. 914.

generals; facing him, Bonaparte said loudly to General Lasnes 'The English are all alike; in every country they are rascals.'[24] By 1802 former republicans had become 'an embarrassment' to the ambitious Bonaparte; Paine's works were removed from the *Bibliothèque nationale*.[25]

Paine's condemnation of tyranny was not his only commitment. By early 1804 the prospect of a French invasion of England, destroying 'the hereditary system', reawakened Paine's former hopes under the Directory and took precedence over his censure of dictatorship. Now, for Paine, a French invasion, led by 'Bonaparte', would have a wholly benign effect. He was 'too good a general to undiscipline and dissolute his army by plundering, and too good a politician, as well as too much accustomed to great achievements, to make plunder his object'. He would, on the contrary, establish a just republic. In 1794–5, Paine had had two main explanations for why the French Revolution had taken a wrong turn, but they were explanations internal to France.[26] In 1804, swept along by his aversion for his native country, Paine advanced a third explanation:

> With respect to the French Revolution, it was begun by good men and on good prin-
> ciples, and I have always believed it would have gone on so had not the provocative
> interference of foreign powers, of which Pitt was the principal and vindictive agent,
> distracted it into madness and sown jealousies among the leaders.[27]

Now the prospect of destroying the chief culprit among those intervening powers eclipsed, for Paine, any other consideration, while his brief and shifting explanations of the reasons for the French Revolution's having veered off course show the limitations of his appreciation of that complex episode.

Nor was his new admiration for Napoleon a temporary aberration on Paine's part. In a newspaper article of July 1805 he looked forward to England's defeat: 'France, at this time, has for its chief the most enterprising man in Europe, and the greatest general in the world; and besides these virtues or vices (call them what you please, for they may be either), he is a deep and consummate politician in every thing which relates to the success of his measures.'[28] The battle of Trafalgar on 21 October placed Paine's hopes beyond reach, but Paine chose not to admit this, assuring Jefferson: 'Nelson's victory, as the English papers call it, will have no influence on the campaign nor on the descent [the invasion of England]...it is probable he [Napoleon] will be in London in six months.'[29] In the summer of 1806 Paine insisted to a Scots visitor, John Melish, that England's political system 'was wrong, and it never would be set right without a revolution, which was as certain as fate, and at no great distance in time'.[30] Even in January 1807 he wrote of the

---

[24] Quoted in Aldridge, *Man of Reason*, 268.

[25] Marianne Elliott, *Partners in Revolution: The United Irishmen and France* (New Haven, 1982), 279.

[26] See Ch. 7, section Paine's retrospect on the Revolution.

[27] Paine, 'To the People of England on the Invasion of England' (6 Mar. 1804): *CW*, ii. 675, 680, 683.

[28] [Paine], 'Remarks on English Affairs' (8 July 1805): *CW*, ii. 684–7.

[29] Paine to Jefferson, 30 Jan. 1806: *CW*, ii. 1475, 1478.

[30] John Melish, *Travels in the United States of America, in the Years 1806 & 1807, and 1809, 1810, & 1811* (2 vols, Philadelphia: for the author, 1812), i. 65.

ruinous expense of England's navy; 'That the English Government does not depend upon the navy to prevent Bonaparte making a descent upon England, is demonstrated by the expensive preparations that Government puts itself to by land to repel it... If Bonaparte succeed in all his plans, I hope he will put an end to navies for the good of the world.'[31] In some respects Paine had learned nothing and forgotten nothing.

Paine's retrospect on the Revolution

Paine had a unique vantage point to observe the causes or nature of the French Revolution, but its faults, to him, were only instances of a familiar general principle: 'The right which any man, or any family, had to set itself up at first to govern a nation, and to establish itself hereditarily, was no other than the right which Robespierre had to do the same thing in France... The Capets, the Guelphs, the Robespierres, the Marats, are all on the same standing as to the question of right.' Paine now had a new reproach for English aristocrats with their 'great landed estates': they were acquired by 'robbery', and those who acquired them after 1066 were 'the Robespierres and the Jacobins of that day'.[32] The problem was that French events had not finally been guided by English norms, whether monarchical or (in Paine's writings) revolutionary.[33]

The French Revolution had obviously gone wrong, but Paine insisted that his initial (but English) commitments were right. How did he diagnose this mistaken course? First, the French revolutionaries had extended far beyond their initial campaign to reform the Church, ending with a crusade to institute atheism; in *The Age of Reason* (1794) Paine issued a recall to the principles of English Deism. It was unavailing. Second, as he argued in *Dissertation on First-Principles of Government* (1795), there was no right to set up 'hereditary government... as has been done in England', and 'in England... the great landed estates, now held in descent, were plundered from the quiet inhabitants at the conquest' in 1066. Hence 'All the disorders that have arisen in France, during the progress of the revolution, have had their origin, not in the *principle of equal rights*, but in the violation of that principle.' This was the case following the non-institution of the constitution proposed in 1793: 'instead of this, a revolutionary government [the Jacobins'], a thing without either principle or authority, was substituted in its place; virtue and crime depended on accident; and that which was patriotism one day, became treason the next.'[34] It was as close as Paine got to an analysis of the Terror; but it was problematic to claim that had the proposed constitution of 1793 been established, all would have been well.

---

[31] Paine, 'Of the English Navy' (1807): *CW*, ii. 687–8.

[32] Paine, *Dissertation on First-Principles of Government* (1795): *CW*, ii. 573, 582.

[33] For an argument that *Common Sense* had more influence in continental Europe than *Rights of Man*, see A. Owen Aldridge, 'The Influence of Thomas Paine in the United States, England, France, Germany and South America', in Werner P. Friederich (ed.), *Comparative Literature: Proceedings of the ICLA Congress* (Chapel Hill, NC, 1959), ii. 369–83, at 370, 372–3, 378.

[34] Paine, *Dissertation on First-Principles of Government* (1795): *CW*, ii. 574, 582, 585, 587.

Paine, evidently fearful and traumatized by the Terror, had compromised with reality, first with the Directory, then with its successor. Bonaparte, on his return from his campaign in Italy, met Paine, and according to Paine's friend Henry Yorke 'declared, that a statue of gold, ought to be erected to him [Paine] in *every city in the universe*; he also assured him [Paine], that he [Bonaparte] always slept with his book [*Rights of Man*] under his pillow, and conjured him [Paine] to honour him [Bonaparte] with his correspondence and advice'. According to Yorke, Paine was not taken in; he 'entertains the most despicable opinion of Bonaparte's conduct, military as well as civil, and thinks him the completest charlatan [that] ever existed'. Paine did not sound the alarm at the coup of 18–19 Brumaire (9–10 November 1799) when Bonaparte abolished the Directory and seized power as First Consul. Even when safely back in America, Paine did not protest when Bonaparte was crowned as the Emperor Napoleon on 2 December 1804.

Yet Paine, in Paris in 1802, had privately disclosed his deep unhappiness with France. 'It was not without considerable difficulty that I discovered his residence', wrote Yorke, 'for the name of Thomas Paine is now as odious in France as it is in England, perhaps more so.' Yorke recorded Paine's devastating judgement on the French:

They have shed blood enough for liberty, and now they have it in perfection. This is not a country for an honest man to live in; they do not understand any thing at all of the principles of free government, and the best way is, to leave them to themselves. You see they have conquered all Europe, only to make it more miserable than it was before...I know of no Republic in the world, except America, which is the only country for such men as you and I. It is my intention to get away from this place as soon as possible, and I hope to be off in autumn; you are a young man, and may see better times, but I have done with Europe, and its slavish politics...Ah! France, thou hast ruined the character of a Revolution virtuously begun, and destroyed those that produced it.[35]

Paine did not now claim to have played a leading role in the French Revolution. Indeed his role had been seldom more than marginal, and the great French historians of that very French episode seldom found it necessary to devote space to him.[36]

If he was well aware of the outcome of the Revolution as a political event, Paine necessarily could not anticipate the course taken by French religion in the nineteenth century, but here too it would be difficult to argue that *The Age of Reason* was a decisive text. Far from acting as a rallying point for a moderate, rational Deism, the work was largely ignored. Similarly, any influence by Paine on French political thought was almost wholly absent in the decades that followed.[37]

[35] Henry Redhead Yorke, *Letters from France, in 1802* (2 vols, London: H. D. Symonds, 1804), ii. 337, 341–2, 361, 367.

[36] A minor exception was François-Alphonse Aulard, *The French Revolution: A Political History 1789–1804*, trans. Bernard Miall (4 vols, New York, 1910), but even Aulard pointed out the un-French nature of Paine's arguments: 'It was as much in the name of the Bible as in the name of reason that Paine attacked the institution of royalty', i. 112.

[37] Paine does not appear in Henry Michel, *L'Idée de l'état: essai critique des théories sociales et politiques en France depuis la Révolution* (3rd edn, Paris, 1898); Albert Bayet and François Albert, *Les Écrivains politiques du XIXe siècle* (Paris, 1935); Jacques Droz, *Histoire des doctrines politiques en France*

A key element in Paine's later reputation was his role as an agent of revolutions, and therefore as a commentator with a special insight into the nature of revolution as such. Yet (as has been argued) Paine used the term 'revolution' in the common eighteenth-century sense, meaning a sudden and dramatic change. Appropriately, for him the French Revolution was over at an early date: as he wrote to Washington on 31 May 1790 (from London), 'the French Revolution is not only complete but triumphant'.[38] Even if a revolution embodied, for Paine, his principle of equal rights, he did not anticipate the later meaning of the term as a process, extending over time, with an inner dynamic.[39] It was in this new sense that France, after the Bourbon restoration, continually sought to re-enact its revolution,[40] and in a similar sense that political science in the twentieth century conceived of revolution as a reified phenomenon which could be expected to repeat itself in advanced nations as a shared rite of passage in their evolution towards what came in the late nineteenth century to be called 'modernity'.[41]

Paine undoubtedly had a rare experience of two transformative and violent episodes; but his status as a prophet requires qualification. It is no disparagement of him to record that he (like his contemporaries) could not exactly anticipate the American and French Revolutions, but even so he did not analyse them in American or French terms; the histories of both episodes that he envisaged, he never wrote; nor did he comment on the works of history on both revolutions that soon began to be published. He did not anticipate the revolution that broke out in Ireland in 1798, and which stood every chance of success at a moment of extreme British strategic weakness. By contrast, the revolutions that he did urge or expect—notably a revolution in Britain, both in the 1770s and the 1790s—did not take place.

AMERICA

The hereditary principle and Paine's *Letter to George Washington* (1797)

In the mid-1790s Paine's preoccupation with religion went with another growing theme: his resentment that the government of the United States had done nothing

(Paris, 1948); Roger Henry Soltau, *French Political Thought in the 19th Century* (New York, 1959); Jean Luc Chabot, *Histoire de la pensée politique: XIXe–XXe siècle* (Paris, 1988); Philip Loïc, *Histoire de la pensée politique en France: de 1789 à nos jours* (Paris, 1993); Dominique Bihoreau, *La Pensée politique et sociale en France au XIX siècle* (Paris, 1995). Jeremy Jennings, *Revolution and the Republic: A History of Political Thought in France since the Eighteenth Century* (Oxford, 2011) notes the rejection of Paine with France's increasing xenophobia, 203, but Paine makes no appearance in the book's account of subsequent French political thought.

[38] Paine to Washington, 31 May 1790: *CW*, ii. 1304–5.
[39] 'Breaking the Grip of the Social Sciences: The Case of Revolution', in J. C. D. Clark, *Our Shadowed Present: Modernism, Postmodernism and History* (London, 2003), 33–58, and work there reviewed.
[40] François Furet, *Revolutionary France 1770–1880* (1988; Oxford, 1992).
[41] Crane Brinton, *The Anatomy of Revolution* (1939; 3rd edn, New York, 1965); Lawrence Stone, 'Theories of Revolution', *World Politics* 18 (1965–6), 159–76.

for so long to rescue him from imprisonment in the Luxembourg, and from (as he saw it) almost certain execution. On his release Paine was taken into the house of the new American minister to France, James Monroe. While he was a guest, Monroe could restrain him from publishing his indignation; but as Paine recovered from the illnesses that he had contracted in prison, his indignation increasingly demanded an outlet. Monroe finally asked Paine to find another lodging, and on 30 July 1796 Paine dated, and sent off for publication in America, his *Letter to George Washington*, openly attacking the man whom he had supported during the revolutionary war. It has been interpreted as Paine's attempt to claim for himself the role of founding father of both the American and French Revolutions.[42] The resulting pamphlet was first advertised for sale in the United States by Benjamin Franklin Bache on 6 February 1797.[43]

Whether or not a psychological interpretation in terms of 'parricide' is valid, Paine's argument was a further application of an English preoccupation. Just as George III had assumed in Paine's mind the position of excessively powerful head of the executive, rhetorically described in the terms first made canonical by English Whigs in the Exclusion Crisis of 1679–81, so Paine now redirected a similar denunciation, with little modification, against Washington. Although Paine would have voted for the constitution of 1787, he wrote, it contained many defects, especially having a single person as head of the executive: this established 'the debasing idea of obeying an individual'. Even at the outset of the constitution, Paine claimed to detect 'the germ of corruption'. The results, 'injustice', were acted out in Washington's 'levee-room' (an allusion to monarchical ceremonial). The constitution of 1787 was, after all, 'a copy, though not quite so base as the original, of the form of the British Government'; hence 'an imitation of its vices was naturally to be expected'. Washington began his presidency 'by encouraging and swallowing the grossest adulation ... You have as many addresses in your chest as James II.' John Adams had said 'that as Mr. Washington had no child, the Presidency should be made hereditary in the family of Lund Washington' (George Washington's cousin). Paine even hinted that John Adams had an ambition for the Vice-Presidency to be hereditary in his own family; John Jay had called for a hereditary Senate.[44] That a hereditary presidency in the United States soon became inconceivable (until its recent semi-dynastic form) distracted attention from the continued salience in Paine's own mind of early eighteenth-century English anti-hereditarian principles. Paine was not alone in the new American republic in professing such fears, whether sincerely or not. But he wrote from Paris, and his critique of Washington was not primarily an American one.

---

[42] Paine misrepresented his role in the mission to France in 1781 of John Laurens, and in the financial, military, and naval assistance that Paine claimed resulted in the decisive Franco-American victory at Yorktown on 17 October 1781. He also passed over the evidence that Washington had arranged for Paine to be supported with a payment of $800 per annum from a secret fund to write for the American government (employment that lasted from 10 February 1782 to 18 April 1783) until other financial support could be found for him: Steven Blakemore, 'Revisionist Parricide: Thomas Paine's Letter to George Washington', in Blakemore, *Crisis in Representation: Thomas Paine, Mary Wollstonecraft, Helen Maria Williams, and the Rewriting of the French Revolution* (Madison, 1997), 57–73.

[43] Keane, *Paine*, 431.   [44] Paine, *Letter to George Washington* (1796): *CW*, ii. 692–3, 695–6.

Paine's disposition towards Washington had been confirmed when in November 1794 the American envoy in London, John Jay, signed a treaty with the British government; it averted maritime and military conflict but at a price that many in the United States thought too high, including giving up a claimed right of neutral ships to trade with belligerents and passing over the British practice of pressing American seamen to serve in the Royal Navy.

Paine reacted to this treaty as an affront to his position that he had become an American by fighting in the American Revolution. In his *Letter to George Washington* he wrote of Jay's treaty as a de facto Anglo-American alliance. So hostile was Paine to the new turn taken by the United States that on 26 Fructidor, an VI (12 September 1798) he allegedly published in *Le Bien informé*, the Parisian newspaper run by Nicolas de Bonneville, publisher of the French editions of *Rights of Man* and *The Age of Reason* and perhaps the joint author of this essay, a plan for a French invasion of the United States.[45] Just as France threatened to export revolution to her European neighbours, so she should do to the United States to rescue that republic from the Federalists and recall it to the principles of 1776. Paine offered France public advice drawn from Britain's failure to conquer the Thirteen Colonies on land in 1776–83: France's strategy should now be a naval campaign in association with 'the friends of liberty' within the American republic, who would rise and depose the government.[46] This, with a revolution in Britain, was one of the revolutions that Paine predicted but which did not materialize.

Paine thereby made his return to the United States deeply problematic: not only had he insulted Washington, widely revered as the father of the republic, but it was alleged in the American press that Paine had called for a second American Revolution with French armed intervention.[47] Only Washington's death (1799) and Jefferson's presidency (1801–9) made Paine's return possible. Indeed only Jefferson's presidency made it desirable. When John Adams was elected President in 1797, Paine interpreted this as the work of 'the mercantile wise-acres of America . . . for the purpose of supporting the British treaty'. It meant that 'I am mortified at the fall of the American character. It was once respectable even to eminence; now it is despised; and did I not feel my own character as an individual, I should blush to call myself a citizen of America.'[48]

---

[45] For the disputed attribution of this article see Aldridge, *Man of Reason*, 263; Lounissi, *Paine*, 757. The article promised the emancipation of American slaves, and Bonneville was a member of the Société des Amis des Noirs.

[46] David Freeman Hawke, *Paine* (New York, 1988), 335. The plan was published in America in *Porcupine's Gazette* (13 Feb. 1799), and reprinted in John Bristed, *Hints on the National Bankruptcy of Britain and on her Resources to Maintain the Present Contest with France* (New York: E. Sargeant, 1809), 267–71: Aldridge, *Man of Reason*, 338.

[47] The story reportedly originated in a London newspaper, *The Public Ledger*, of 8 July 1794 (it has not been possible to trace a copy of this issue). Since Paine had been in prison since December 1793, the report, if soundly based, can only have related to earlier in 1793. In the circumstances of 1793 Paine is unlikely to have submitted such a plan; it evidently dates from 1798. After his return to the United States in 1802, Paine was obliged repeatedly to ridicule the idea that the new American republic had ever been in danger of invasion from France: 'To the Citizens of the United States' (1802–5): *CW*, ii. 917, 919, 925, 951, 953; Keane, *Paine*, 484–5.

[48] Paine to James Madison, [27 Apr. 1797]: *CW*, ii. 1393–5.

Evangelicalism and Paine's reception

On 2 September 1802 Paine left France for the United States. He arrived in Baltimore only to find that one innkeeper after another refused him admittance: this was far from a hero's welcome.[49] His admirer Thomas Clio Rickman wrote that Paine was 'particularly unfortunate' in his retirement in the United States, since it was 'a country, abounding in fanatics'.[50] America had greatly changed.[51] *Rights of Man* enjoyed large sales in the United States in the 1790s, as two different interpretations of republicanism, that of Paine and that of John Adams, competed for ascendancy.[52] Neither secured a clear victory: the republic's myth of origins, its popular culture, and its political rhetoric were becoming (in present-day terms) democratic, egalitarian, and radical-individualist, but its social and political realities were becoming commercialized, increasingly unequal, economically plutocratic, and (perhaps partly in reaction) religiously fundamentalist-evangelical, even after Jefferson's election as President in 1800.[53]

In a political system now polarized between the parties of Federalists and Republicans, even some of Jefferson's allies now distanced themselves from Paine, whose *Age of Reason* and attack on George Washington had made him a political liability. For his part, Paine did not accept the sincerity of the outcry against him by his opponents in America: 'all this *war-whoop* of the pulpit has some concealed object. Religion is not the cause, but is the stalking-horse. They put it forward to conceal themselves behind it'; their real goal was 'to overturn the Federal Constitution established on the representative system, and place government in the New World on the corrupt system of the old'.[54] So heartfelt was his Deism that in his own eyes its critics had other purposes. 'Religion and War is the cry of the Federalists.'[55] This they concealed: 'the Feds do not declare what their principles are.' By contrast, 'The principles of the Republicans are to support the representative system of government... they know of no such thing as hereditary government.'[56]

This was the old binary alternative, but many citizens of the new republic thought differently. Britain's American colonies had been developing dynamically in the

[49] Seth Cotlar, *Tom Paine's America: The Rise and Fall of Transatlantic Radicalism in the Early Republic* (Charlottesville, Va, 2011), 1, 211; Alfred F. Young, 'The Celebration and Damnation of Thomas Paine', in Young, *Liberty Tree: Ordinary People in the American Revolution* (New York, 2006), 265–95; Lounissi, *Paine*, 663–80.

[50] Thomas Clio Rickman, *The Life of Thomas Paine* (London: Rickman, 1819), 5.

[51] 'Paine changed relatively little between 1776 and 1809, yet America changed a great deal': Simon P. Newman, 'Paine, Jefferson and Revolutionary Radicalism in Early National America', in Simon P. Newman and Peter S. Onuf (eds), *Paine and Jefferson in the Age of Revolutions* (Charlottesville, Va, 2013), 71–94, at 90.

[52] Young, 'The Celebration and Damnation of Thomas Paine', 265–95, at 272–3, 275–8.

[53] For the evolution away from early Jeffersonian agrarian and freethinking ideals see Joyce Appleby, *Capitalism and a New Social Order: The Republican Vision of the 1790s* (New York, 1984); Doron S. Ben-Atar, *The Origins of Jeffersonian Commercial Policy and Diplomacy* (Basingstoke, 1993); Joyce Appleby, *Inheriting the Revolution: The First Generation of Americans* (Cambridge, Mass., 2000).

[54] Paine to Samuel Adams, 1 Jan. 1803: *CW*, ii. 1436.

[55] Paine, 'To the Citizens of the United States' (letter VI, 12 Mar. 1803): *CW*, ii. 931.

[56] [Paine], 'A Challenge to the Federalists to Declare their Principles' (17 Oct. 1806): *CW*, ii. 1007–8.

century before 1776; after independence, the pace of change only accelerated as an increasingly redefined elite re-established political control in an ever more commercial setting. Under the impact partly of political and social revolution compelled by war and inflation, partly of economic development and migration, the new republic was significantly different from the place in which Paine had landed in 1774: in the 1790s Paineite politics and their increasingly redistributionist schemes were submerged by religiously inspired assertions of national destiny and evangelical repudiations of Paine's Deism.[57] From the mid-1820s Paine's memory was kept alive in working men's clubs, especially those touched by the freethinking of recent English Deist *émigrés*, and by some reforming or Deist newspapers on the eastern seaboard,[58] but there was no 'American working-class movement' in the nineteenth century to the degree that there was in the British Isles. The United States had diverged.

These profound and extensive developments Paine did not, perhaps could not, appreciate. For him, the United States still had to be the test case that proved the correctness of his initial principles, the more so since France had caused him such disillusionment. Paine's writings from the period 1802–9 give no evidence that he was willing seriously to explore the changes proceeding in American society. James Cheetham, an *émigré* from England, later wrote:

> After his return to the United States from France, I became acquainted with him on his arrival in New-York, in the year 1802 ... [on their first meeting] I soon perceived that he had a very retentive memory, and was full of anecdote. The Bishop of L[l]andaff was almost the first word he uttered, and it was followed by informing us, that he had in his trunk a manuscript reply to the Bishop's Apology. He then, calmly mumbling his stake, and ever and anon drinking his brandy and beer, repeated the introduction to his reply, which occupied him near half an hour. This was done with deliberation, the utmost clearness, and a perfect apprehension, intoxicated as he was, of all that he repeated. Scarcely a word would he allow us to speak. He always, I afterwards found, in

---

[57] For an argument of the wide extent of 'free enquiry' or 'lived deism' in the early Republic, countering the older historiographical orthodoxy of Deism's 'precipitous decline' after *c.*1800, see Eric R. Schlereth, *An Age of Infidels: The Politics of Religious Controversy in the Early United States* (Philadelphia, 2013): 'Though relatively few in number, these deists profoundly influenced how Americans viewed the relationship between religious belief and political actions', 8–9, 244. But for a 'reaction against skepticism' around 1800, after a decade in which the rejection of the British monarchy had 'stimulated criticism of the royalist authority of religion, challenging conceptions of God as a divine king and practices of humiliation and self-abnegation associated with belief in his absolute sovereignty', see Amanda Porterfield, *Conceived in Doubt: Religion and Politics in the New American Nation* (Chicago, 2012), 5, 12, 114–15 and *passim*.

[58] 'Since many of their [the freethinkers'] leaders had only recently arrived from Britain, their broadsides on religion, monarchy and moralism seemed oddly out of place in the post-Jeffersonian United States, as if the freethinkers were trying to transplant arguments pertinent enough in England without taking stock of American realities': Sean Wilenz, *Chants Democratic: New York City & the Rise of the American Working Class, 1788–1850* (New York, 1984), 153–7, at 156; Mark A. Lause, 'The "Unwashed Infidelity": Thomas Paine and Early New York Labor History', *Labor History* 27 (1986), 386–409 (I owe this reference to Jon Earle); Harvey J. Kaye, *Thomas Paine and the Promise of America* (New York, 2005), 91–257. Kaye's evidence may be read (contrary to his argument) as showing Paine's only small practical influence in the nineteenth- and twentieth-century United States, however occasionally he was invoked for rhetorical effect.

all companies, drunk or sober, would be listened to, but in this regard there were no *rights of men* with him, no equality, no reciprocal immunities and obligations, for he would listen to no one.[59]

Paine was not alone among British *émigrés* in not understanding how far the United States had changed. In general, they 'remained unaware of the growing distance between their image of America and its reality'.[60]

Party politics, Deism, and the Trinitarian interpretation of the new republic

Nor was Paine, in the United States after 1802, a wholly new man, despite his experiences in France. As late as 1777, he had affirmed an English view of American political identities as binary opposites: 'A person, to use a trite phrase, must be a Whig or a Tory in a lump. His feelings, as a man, may be wounded; his charity, as a Christian, may be moved; but his political principles must go through all the cases on one side or the other. He cannot be a Whig in *this* stage, and a Tory in *that*.'[61] In 1776, at the end of *Common Sense*, he had issued an invitation to a future that would be free from party political conflicts:

> Let each of us hold out to his neighbor the hearty hand of friendship, and unite in drawing a line, which, like an act of oblivion, shall bury in forgetfulness every former dissension. Let the names of Whig and Tory be extinct; and let none other be heard among us, than those of a *good citizen; an open and resolute friend;* and *a virtuous supporter of the* RIGHTS *of* MANKIND, *and of the* FREE AND INDEPENDENT STATES OF AMERICA.[62]

Yet after 1802 Paine was quickly drawn into American party-political conflicts which he still perceived in binary terms derived from those long-standing and divisive English conflicts. He may not have been alone in doing so, but his indebtedness was marked.

At the time of his return, he wrote, 'The people were divided into two classes, under the names of *republicans* and *federalists*'.[63] The Republicans were the Jeffersonians. The Federalists were 'in their principles anti-federal and despotic'. They 'show the cloven hoof of faction'. They were the 'hirelings' of the 'Government of England'.[64] 'The plan of the leaders of the faction was to overthrow the liberties of the New World, and place government on the corrupt system of the Old.'[65] The ministers of the recent administration of President John Adams, from that party,

---

[59] Cheetham, *Life*, xxi–xxii. Paine's early enemies spread reports of his excessive drinking in attempts to denigrate him. Other parts of their evidence may deserve consideration.
[60] Michael Durey, *Transatlantic Radicals and the Early American Republic* (Lawrence, Kan., 1997), 292.
[61] [Paine], *The American Crisis*, III (19 Apr. 1777): *CW*, i. 76.
[62] [Paine], *Common Sense* (1776): *CW*, i. 46.
[63] Paine, 'To the Citizens of the United States', VIII (7 June 1805): *CW*, ii. 951.
[64] Paine, 'To the Citizens of the United States', I (15 Nov. 1802): *CW*, ii. 911–12.
[65] Paine, 'To the Citizens of the United States', II (22 Nov. 1802): *CW*, ii. 917.

were 'apostates from the principles of the Revolution'.[66] It was as if Paine wrote of England's revolution of 1688. By 1806, the terms of Paine's abuse of Adams were still wholly English: standing army, taxes, debt, war, arbitrary power. The aim of the Federalists was 'to establish a Government of war and taxes on the corrupt principles of the English Government... the leaders of the Federal faction are an English faction'.[67] But this was not self-evidently the case, and other observers saw an opposite paradox in the politics of the new republic. A Scots visitor, John Melish, in New York in 1806, thought that 'the question between the parties not being well defined, it is difficult to understand it'. He consulted Washington's Farewell Address and Jefferson's Inaugural Speech, 'but the sentiments inculcated in these two papers appeared to me to be precisely the same'.[68] Paine, by contrast, had no doubts, and saw in American politics an antithesis that he immediately recognized.

How historians characterize America's social changes in the early republic controls the interpretation of Paine's reaction to them. The conventional interpretation was that the colonial American elite abandoned its older hierarchical attitudes during the Revolution, so permitting the emergence of 'a much more universal and socially progressive understanding [of liberty], reflected in the language of the Declaration of Independence... Hence, a Thomas Paine would appear not so much as an individual ahead of his time but as someone who simply complied with the essence of the Founders' new sense of liberty, while a John Adams with his Federalist views of social hierarchy would appear to be somewhat anomalous.'[69] If so, it would follow that Paine's profound unhappiness with the course of events in the United States from the 1790s is evidence for the republic's taking a direction antithetical to its 'founding principles': the Federalists, in other words, did indeed stand for those oligarchical, even aristocratic, principles that Paine claimed to detect in them.

This interpretation has been challenged. In an alternative explanation, the colonial elite, which had assiduously modelled itself on the English gentry, had absorbed English assumptions about liberties being privileges only possible within an unequal society, and made no sacrifice of them in the events or the classic documents of the Revolution. They intended no re-engineering of 'the English social order'; they merely sought to mobilize the colonial masses for the revolutionary war by developing a rhetoric of *inclusive* liberty' that was not intended as 'an objective description of social reality'. Returning a singular 'liberty' to plural 'liberties' understood as privileges allows an understanding of the Founders when—to present-day observers—they 'said one thing and did another' in respect of inequality,

[66] Paine, 'To the Citizens of the United States', VI (14 May 1803): *CW*, ii. 935.

[67] [Paine], 'A Challenge to the Federalists to Declare their Principles' (17 Oct. 1806): *CW*, ii. 1007, 1009.

[68] John Melish, *Travels in the United States of America, in the Years 1806 & 1807, and 1809, 1810, & 1811* (2 vols, Philadelphia: for the author, 1812), i. 62–3.

[69] Michal Jan Rozbicki, *Culture and Liberty in the Age of the American Revolution* (Charlottesville, Va, 2011), 78.

notably over slavery.[70] This reinterpretation entails a reinterpretation of Paine also: his critique of the new American republic was a projection of his antecedent English principles more than it was a well-informed response to changes in American politics and society.

For the new republic, the wartime rhetoric of 'liberty' posed problems after the war was over. The euphoria of 1783 soon gave way to growing internecine political conflict. When an American edition of *Rights of Man* was published, it carried a quotation from a private letter by Jefferson, now pressed into service by the publisher as a preface without Jefferson's knowledge:

> I am extremely pleased to find it will be reprinted, and that something is at length to be publicly said against the political heresies which have sprung up among us.
>
> I have no doubt our citizens will rally a second time round the standard of Common Sense.[71]

By 'political heresies' Jefferson meant the views of the Vice-President, John Adams, whose *Defence of the Constitutions* was interpreted by Jefferson's friends as a fundamental attack on the populist nature of the American polity. In 1791 Jefferson accused Adams of 'apostasy to hereditary monarchy and nobility'.[72] In 1796, Jefferson added:

> In place of that noble love of liberty and republican government which carried us triumphantly thro' the [revolutionary] war, an Anglican, monarchical and aristocratical party has sprung up, whose avowed object is to draw over us the substance as they already have the forms of the British government... It would give you a fever were I to name to you the apostates who have gone over to these heresies, men who were Samsons in the field and Solomons in the council, but who have had their head shorn by the harlot England.[73]

This was to become Paine's perspective also, for Paine's antipathy to England was undiminished.

Meanwhile, opinion in the American republic had been exercised on Paine's *Rights of Man* not least by a series of letters signed 'Publicola' that appeared in the *Columbian Centinel*, published in Boston, from 8 June to 27 July 1791. Their author was the rising star John Quincy Adams, son of the future second President John Adams and himself a holder of that office in 1825–9. Adams began by quoting Jefferson's remark about '*political heresies*': these words 'seem, like the Arabian prophet, to call upon all true believers in the *Islam* of democracy, to draw their swords, and, in the fervour of their devotion, to compel all their countrymen to cry out, "There is but one Goddess of Liberty, and Common Sense is her prophet."' His

---

[70] Rozbicki, *Culture and Liberty*, 78–80, citing Gordon S. Wood, *The Radicalism of the American Revolution* (New York, 1992).

[71] Jefferson to Jonathan B. Smith, 26 Apr. 1791: Jefferson, *Papers*, xx. 290. The publisher changed Jefferson's third person construction into first person speech.

[72] Jefferson to Washington, 8 May 1791: Jefferson, *Papers*, xx. 291.

[73] Jefferson to Philip Mazzei, 24 Apr. 1796: Jefferson, *Papers*, xxix. 81–5.

reply could only be a profound critique of *Rights of Man*, denying that work to have the coherence of a deduction from rights. Adams could not, of course, deny that

> The people of England have, in common with other nations, a natural and unalienable right to form a Constitution of Government, not because a whole nation has a right to do whatever it chooses to do, but because Government being instituted for the common security of the natural rights of every individual, it must be liable to alterations whenever it becomes incompetent for that purpose.

This did not negate 'The right of a people to legislate for succeeding generations... expressions of a similar nature may be found in all the Constitutions of the United States.' But the right to dissolve an existing government and form a wholly new one was only to be exercised in 'cases of extreme urgency' like that of 1776 when a people was 'compelled' to 'exercise this right'.

Was France in 1789 such a case? Adams was unwilling to say. Was Britain in such a situation in the 1790s? Adams, singing the praises of the English common law, which did not conform to Paine's model of a written constitution antecedent to government, denied it. The English were bound by 'a social compact now existing' unless it could be proved that it was 'clearly incompetent for the purposes for which it was instituted'. No 'mechanical horror against the name of a king, or of aristocracy' was enough to 'authorise a people to lay violent hands upon the Constitution'. The survival of the new United States, in Adams's eyes, now stood on the same ground as the survival of England; but England was in more peril because of the existence there of 'the *mob*', a 'tremendous power, which is competent only to the purposes of destruction... Should these people be taught that they have a right to do every thing, and that the titles of Kings and Nobles, and the wealth of Bishops, are all usurpations and robberies committed upon them, I believe it would not be difficult to arouse their passions, and to prepare them for every work of ruin and destruction.'[74] The American example is often cited by historians as having been an inspiration to early nineteenth-century British reformers, but via John Quincy Adams the opposite lesson from the new American republic was also communicated across the Atlantic.

Soon after his return, Paine published a series of long letters addressed 'To the Citizens of the United States' in a number of newspapers, chiefly *The National Intelligencer*; the first appeared on 15 November 1802, the eighth and last on 7 June 1805.[75] In 1783 he had complained that he found no home in America,[76] but in 1802 he reversed his position: now, the new republic was 'the country of my heart, and the place of my literary and political birth'.[77] He has often been taken at his word, especially by present-day citizens of that country who find in Paine's writings elements apparently flattering to their state's myth of origins. His role in the American Revolution sometimes led, much later, to his retrospective elevation

---

[74] Reprinted as John [Quincy] Adams, *An Answer to Pain's Rights of Man* (London: John Stockdale, 1793), 7, 10, 14–15, 18–19, 24, 30–1.

[75] Paine, 'To the Citizens of the United States' (1802–5): *CW*, ii. 908–57.

[76] See Ch. 4, section Paine: refugee.

[77] Paine, 'To the Citizens of the United States' (6 Dec. 1802): *CW*, ii. 926.

to the ranks of the Founding Fathers and propagated the assumption that he had a unique insight into American affairs. To Paine himself, the new American republic proved a disappointment: it was already importantly different from the society he had predicted would arise from revolution.

Paine had therefore to offer a new interpretation of what had gone wrong. In 1795 he had argued that the French Revolution had been derailed only through not adopting the constitution of 1793. Now he drew a comparison between the American and French Revolutions, and pointed to a similar problem in each: party politics.

> The French Revolution was beginning to germinate when I arrived in France. The principles of it were good, they were copied from America, and the men who conducted it were honest. But the fury of faction soon extinguished the one and sent the other to the scaffold...while I beheld with pleasure the dawn of liberty rising in Europe, I saw with regret the luster of it fading in America. In less than two years from the time of my departure some distant symptoms painfully suggested the idea that the principles of the Revolution were expiring on the soil that produced them...a faction, acting in disguise, was rising in America; they had lost sight of first principles. They were beginning to contemplate government as a profitable monopoly, and the people as hereditary property.

Paine was convinced of his own importance in this tactical conjuncture: 'In every part of the Union, this faction [the Federalists] is in the agonies of death, and in proportion as its fate approaches, gnashes its teeth and struggles. My arrival has struck it as with an hydrophobia, it is like the sight of water to canine madness.'[78] Paine's role, he thought, was to overturn the 'Reign of Terror that raged in America during the latter end of the Washington Administration, and the whole of that of Adams'. 'So far as respects myself, I have reason to believe and a right to say that the leaders of the Reign of Terror in America and the leaders of the Reign of Terror in France, during the time of Robespierre, were in character the same sort of men; or how is it to be accounted for, that I was persecuted by both at the same time?'[79]

This was self-absorbed, and a rhetorical overstatement about the Federalists.[80] Paine's remarks call in question the nature of his understanding of the Terror in France; but his conceptual apparatus was simple, and in 1802 as in 1776 he could only see politics in a binary system. This binary polarity trumped logic, for even if the American Federalists were the friends of the hereditary system that he claimed

---

[78] Paine, 'To the Citizens of the United States' (15 Nov. 1802): *CW*, ii. 908–12.

[79] Paine, 'To the Citizens of the United States' (29 Nov. 1802): *CW*, ii. 918–9. Paine cited as proof Robespierre's note that Paine should be accused 'pour les intérêts de l'Amérique autant que de la France'.

[80] For American Republicans allegedly approving Robespierre's defence of 'Terror', see Rachel Hope Cleves, *The Reign of Terror in America: Visions of Violence from Anti-Jacobinism to Antislavery* (New York, 2009), 78. 'Paine effectively linked the revolutionary founding of the American republic with other revolutions in a way that appeared to validate the ideology of the American revolution, thus providing a template for Republicans who sought to assess and critique what they interpreted as the counter-revolutionary tendencies of the Federalists...As the French Republic declined in popularity in the United States, Republicans disavowed the French and their supporters': Newman, 'Paine, Jefferson and Revolutionary Radicalism', 71–94, at 76.

them to be, that would have placed them at the opposite end of the political spectrum to the Jacobins. Paine's frame of reference was nevertheless still not French. In America in 1806, he claimed, 'The old names of *Whig* and *Tory* have given place to the later names of *Republicans* and *Federalists*',[81] but for Paine the principles were similar. The reality was that 'the principles of the [French] Revolution' were ones that Paine (believing the story evidently fed him by Lafayette) had only partly understood. In 1804, Paine let slip his opinion that 'the French Revolution has not exhibited to the world that grand display of principles and rights that would induce settlers from other countries to put themselves under a French jurisdiction in Louisiana',[82] but how and why that was the case he did not explain.

The closest he came to doing so was, once more, in an aside:

Inequality of rights has been the cause of all the disturbances, insurrections and civil wars that ever happened in any country, in any age of mankind. It was the cause of the American Revolution, when the English Parliament sat itself up to *bind America in all cases whatsoever*, and to reduce her to unconditional submission. It was the cause of the French Revolution; and also of the civil wars in England, in the time of Charles and Cromwell, when the House of Commons voted the House of Lords useless.[83]

This was Paine's familiar response, established in his writings by vivid statement rather than by an extended argument. His attempts to recall the new American republic to its origins were therefore not wholly persuasive. It might be argued that Paine had a decisive impact on American political rhetoric, with his claims about beginning the world over again and the moral purity of a polity without kings and bishops; yet Paine's unhappiness in the years from his return to the United States until his death points in another direction.

American party politics had come of age: its discourse was now as violently denigratory as Britain's had long been. Once his imminent return in 1802 was reported, many American newspapers assailed him, even before his arrival, as a 'drunken atheist', ringing the changes on similar terms of abuse.[84] The denunciations continued after his arrival. Paine was well aware of this: 'I arrived at Baltimore on the 30th of October, and you can have no idea of the agitation which my arrival occasioned. From New Hampshire to Georgia (an extent of 1500 miles), every newspaper was filled with applause or abuse.'[85] Paine replied to this invective with indignation and contempt, comparing it to the persecution he had suffered in France:

these men [the Federalists], these Terrorists of the New World, who were waiting in the devotion of their hearts for the joyful news of my destruction, are the same

[81] [Paine], 'A Challenge to the Federalists to Declare their Principles' (17 Oct. 1806): *CW*, ii. 1007.
[82] Paine, 'To the French Inhabitants of Louisiana' (1804): *CW*, ii. 966.
[83] *Thomas Paine to the Citizens of Pennsylvania, on the Proposal for Calling a Convention* (Aug. 1805): *CW*, ii. 1006.
[84] Keane, *Paine*, 456–7.
[85] Paine to Thomas Clio Rickman, 8 Mar. 1803: *CW*, ii. 1439–40. For a collection of responses to Paine in the American press after 1802 see Kenneth W. Burchell (ed.), *Thomas Paine and America, 1776–1809* (6 vols, London, 2009), vi.

banditti who are now bellowing in all the hackneyed language of hackneyed hypocrisy about humanity and piety, and often about something they call infidelity, and they finish with the chorus of *Crucify him, crucify him.* I am become so famous among them, they cannot eat or drink without me. I serve them as a standing dish, and they cannot make up a bill of fare if I am not in it.'[86]

In one instance this denigratory rhetoric touched Paine on a raw nerve. In an election in the spring of 1806 his vote was rejected, on the grounds that he was not an American citizen.

> Elisha Ward and three or four other Tories who lived within the British lines in the Revolutionary war, got in to be inspectors of the election last year at New Rochelle. Ward was supervisor. These men refused my vote at the election, saying to me: 'You are not an American; our minister at Paris, Gouverneur Morris, would not reclaim you when you were imprisoned in the Luxembourg prison at Paris, and George Washington refused to do it.' Upon my telling him that the two cases he stated were falsehoods, and that if he did me injustice I would prosecute him, he got up, and calling for a constable, said to me, 'I will commit you to prison.' He chose, however, to sit down and go no farther with it.[87]

Paine's vote was not counted; he sued, and was apparently unsuccessful in his action, although evidently on technical grounds. Paine's nationality in his last years was therefore undecided. Ironically, he was subject to taxation without representation in the very American republic that he had laboured to bring into being.[88]

Paine seems to have attracted little praise in America at this time for his role in the French Revolution. Rather, his reception in the new republic was mainly a response to his perceived position on religion. Colonial America beyond the social elite had been less exposed to Deism than eighteenth-century England; *The Age of Reason* came as more of a shock in the new republic than in Paine's homeland, where the Deist challenge had been long and loudly debated. In America, too, the currents were running strongly away from Deism, for the new republic was witnessing passionate evangelical revivals, fostering dispositions that could be exploited by the political opponents of the President, Thomas Jefferson, to disparage Jefferson's friend and ally. The feasibility of realizing Paine's Deist society was already being negated by the different varieties of English-inspired evangelical Trinitarian Christianity that conquered the new republic, especially Methodism and Baptism; Paine encountered both popular and elite hostility from Trinitarian Christians for writing *The Age of Reason.* This was not only 'the most widely circulated religious work of the eighteenth century' in America; it also met with the most widespread and sustained backlash.[89] Despite its many editions and wide circulation, the current of religious change flowed in the opposite direction.

---

[86] Paine, 'To the Citizens of the United States' (29 Nov. 1802): *CW*, ii. 920.

[87] Paine to George Clinton, 4 May 1807: *CW*, ii. 1487.

[88] America 'receives my portion of Taxes for my house in Bordentown and my farm at New Rochelle': Paine to James Monroe, 25 Aug. 1794: *CW*, ii. 1344. On the general issue, see Bernard Vincent, 'A National of Nowhere: The Problem of Thomas Paine's American Citizenship', in Vincent, *The Transatlantic Republican: Thomas Paine and the Age of Revolutions* (Amsterdam, 2005), 109–14.

[89] Marcus Daniel, *Scandal & Civility: Journalism and the Birth of American Democracy* (New York, 2009), 247–9. Similarly, the American Deist Elihu Palmer's 'keenest supporters were drawn from the

The pious Benjamin Rush,[90] a convert from Presbyterian Calvinism to the Arminianism of the Universalist Church, was outraged by Paine: 'His "Age of Reason" probably perverted more persons from the Christian faith than any book that ever was written for that purpose. Its extensive mischief was owing to the popular, perspicuous, and witty style in which it was written, and to its constant appeals to the feelings and tempers of his readers.' For Rush, *The Age of Reason* was 'absurd and impious'; its author was one of 'the infidel writers of the age' who 'seduce by the novelty of their manner and brilliancy of their style much more than by their arguments'. Rush's condemnation was the more marked, since his political views were closely parallel to Paine's. Yet in 1809 he wrote: 'I did not see Mr. Paine when he passed through Philadelphia a few years ago. His principles avowed in his *Age of Reason* were so offensive to me that I did not wish to renew my intercourse with him.'[91] By 1822 Isaac Candler, a traveller in America, noted that 'Instances of openly avowed deism are rare. Persons who hold deistical opinions generally either keep them to themselves, or veil them under the garb of flimsy hypocrisy. I recollect only two persons of all with whom I conversed on religion, who unhestitatingly proclaimed their disbelief in Christianity; though I met with several whom I suspected to be concealed deists. In many parts a man's reputation would have been seriously injured if he were to avow himself one.'[92]

Rush had been in line with a torrent of American pamphlet literature that condemned *The Age of Reason* from the year of its publication. The Revd James Jones Wilmer, an Episcopalian priest toying with Swedenborgianism, began with a critique of Paine's denial of revelation: 'if which is revealed to me ceases to be a revelation, in communication to another, then all truth is incommunicable.'[93] The Methodist Samuel Stilwell claimed a basic contradiction: 'Mr. Paine is indebted to the very book he endeavours to invalidate for the moral precepts he is labouring to make us believe are the productions of his fruitful reason.' It was unacceptable that Paine was 'endeavouring to make a revolution in the system of religion in America'; nor was it appropriate, 'because every person here may worship God agreeable to the dictates of his own conscience'.[94] George Keating urged that reason 'in its depraved state' could not be 'a *perfect* and unerring guide, to matters of Religion'.[95]

The Congregational minister William Patten refused to accept that Paine was well intentioned: 'in rejecting Christianity, as he rejected the only perfect system of

ranks of the British and Irish radical exiles who brought their deist beliefs with them to the United States', 366 n. 35. For the reception in the United States of Paine's religion see also Nathalie Caron, *Thomas Paine contre l'imposture des prêtres* (Paris, 1998), 299–336.

[90] He chose his wife on the basis of her praise for the sermons of Dr John Witherspoon: Rush, *Autobiography*, 115–16.

[91] Rush, *Autobiography*, 323; Rush to John Dickinson, 16 Feb. 1796: Rush, *Letters*, 770; Rush to James Cheetham, 17 July 1809, Rush, *Letters*, 1009.

[92] [Isaac Candler], *A Summary View of America* (London: T. Cadell, 1824), 163.

[93] James Jones Wilmer, *Consolation: being a Replication to Thomas Paine, and others, on Theologics* (Philadelphia: William W. Woodward, 1794), 11.

[94] Samuel Stilwell, *A Guide to Reason or an Examination of Thomas Paine's Age of Reason, And Investigation of True and Fabulous Theology* (New York: John Buel, 1794), 5–8.

[95] [George Keating], *The Folly of Reason. Being Our Perfect and Unerring Guide, to the Knowledge of True Religion* (New York: Tibbout and O'Brien, 1794), 8.

moral and religious truth, he cannot claim a pure motive for reflections dishonorary to GOD, and injurious to his fellow-men'. Patten therefore relentlessly listed Paine's contradictions.[96] From Alexandria the influential Presbyterian minister James Muir denied that Paine spoke for his epoch: 'Whatever revolutions have lately taken place, proceed not, I apprehend, merely from the principle of "reason" ... These events have arisen from the impulse of the moment. The first causes of these, had not in view what afterwards took place, and the issue may be vastly different from what the present agents in them propose.'[97] Another Presbyterian minister, Ebenezer Bradford, dedicated his rebuttal to George Washington as a man who had 'exhibited the most unequivocal demonstrations of a firm and constant faith in Revelation', even though surrounded by 'open and acknowledged Deists'.[98] This was not in reality true of Washington, but the new republic was already whitewashing those religious sceptics of an earlier age, now to be presented as Founding Fathers.

Such American critiques of Paine's theology continued through the 1790s. As early as 1803, Paine felt obliged to reply when his old friend Samuel Adams, aged 80 and living in retirement, wrote a short letter to praise Paine for his role in the American Revolution but to reproach him for his religious writings: 'when I heard that you had turned your mind to a defence of infidelity, I felt myself much astonished and more grieved that you had attempted a measure so injurious to the feelings and so repugnant to the true interest of so great a part of the citizens of the United States.' Jefferson, warned Adams, had been similarly suspected, and this did harm: 'Neither religion nor liberty can long subsist in the tumult of altercation, and amidst the noise and violence of faction.'[99] Paine appreciated that he needed to defend himself, and copied Adams's letter and his reply to the *National Intelligencer*, explaining: 'I give the letter the opportunity of reaching him by the newspapers.'[100]

Paine's reply was cautious and respectful, but insistent that he was a Deist, not an atheist. Paine rightly suspected that Adams had not read *The Age of Reason*, as perhaps many Americans had not who denounced Paine as an infidel. Paine replied that he was an infidel only with respect to superstition, as his ancestors, medieval Catholics, had been. But this would have made things worse in the eyes of Paine's readers.

The case, my friend, is that the world has been over-run with fable and creeds of human invention, with sectaries of whole nations against all other nations, and sectaries of those sectaries in each of them against each other. Every sectary, except the Quakers, has been a persecutor. Those who fled from persecution persecuted in their turn, and it is this confusion of creeds that has filled the world with persecution and deluged it with blood.

---

[96] William Patten, *Christianity the True Theology, and Only Perfect Moral System; in Answer to 'The Age of Reason'* (Warren, RI: Nathaniel Phillips, 1795), 9–10.
[97] James Muir, *An Examination of the Principles contained in the Age of Reason. In Ten discourses* (Baltimore: S. & J. Adams, 1795), 10–11, 23, 118.
[98] [Ebenezer Bradford], *Mr Thomas Paine's Trial; being an Examination of the Age of Reason* (Boston: Isaiah Thomas and Ebenezer T. Andrews, 1795), iii.
[99] Adams to Paine, 30 Nov. 1802: *CW*, ii. 1433.
[100] Paine to the editor of the *National Intelligencer*, 1 Jan. 1803: *CW*, ii. 1432–3.

It was as if Paine wrote of the Puritans. Even the books of the Bible held to be canonical were established only by 'the popish Councils of Nice and Laodicea': by implication, the Bible of the Puritans was as credulously received as that of the Papists. Worse still, Paine soon turned aside from these familiar points to pursue his hatred of the Federalists. 'Religion is not the cause, but is the stalking horse.' The Federalists, conspiring against the constitution, argued Paine, were merely using religion as a pretext to damage him. For Paine, the true worship of God was 'not by praying, but by endeavouring to make his creatures happy'. Paine himself had been

> exposed to, and preserved through, many dangers; but instead of buffeting the Deity with prayers as if I distrusted Him, or must dictate to Him, I reposed myself on His protection; and you, my friend, will find, even in your last moments, more consolation in the silence of resignation than in the murmuring wish of a prayer.[101]

To an English Deist this might have seemed a respectful restatement of a benign position, coupled with a late seventeenth-century English commonplace that religion was being used as a mask to conceal political purposes; to an American revivalist it would have seemed a provocation, as well as a second reproach to a Founding Father, Samuel Adams, following that to Washington. Paine now received widespread insults, ostracism, and even threats, as he travelled in the new republic.

Non-Trinitarians hardly made common cause there; on the contrary, these groups generally regarded each other as enemies. Their criticism, as well as the hostility of Trinitarians, damaged Paine's attempt to launch a widespread Deism. John Adams confided to his diary: 'The Christian Religion is, above all the Religions that ever prevailed or existed in ancient or modern Times, The Religion of Wisdom, Virtue, Equity and Humanity, let the Blackguard Paine say what he will.'[102] Yet however much Trinitarians feared that Paine had won many converts, his Deism, despite his efforts after 1802, largely fell on stony ground in America.[103]

In early 1804 Paine made contact in New York with the American Deist and ex-Presbyterian Elihu Palmer, whose views on the political role of Trinitarian Christianity were similar to Paine's own. Paine joined Palmer in founding the Deistical Society of New York, but evidence is lacking that it was dominated by Paine; its inspirer was, on the contrary, Palmer, and it did not long survive Palmer's death.[104] The manifesto of the Society set out a position similar to Paine's, but did not bear the hallmarks of his style. Palmer's last work did not record any debt to Paine, Palmer instead writing: 'Of all the men...whose philosophic researches have extended the farthest into the properties of the material world, John Stewart...a single individual who has dared to despise all compromise with prejudices, appears

---

[101] Paine to Samuel Adams, 1 Jan. 1803: *CW*, ii. 1434–8.

[102] Adams, *Diary*, 26 July 1796, in Adams, *Diary and Autobiography*, iii. 234.

[103] Caron, *Thomas Paine contre l'imposture des prêtres*, 337–57.

[104] Elihu Palmer's follower John Fellows wrote that 'It existed some years after the death of its founder; but at length was discontinued for want of zeal in its members': *Posthumous Pieces by Elihu Palmer, being three chapters of an unfinished work intended to have been entitled 'The Political World'* (London: R. Carlile, 1824), 9.

to be entitled to the highest estimation.' In his oration on the twenty-first anniversary of American independence, reviewing the American and French Revolutions, Palmer gave Paine only one passing mention in a list of other worthies.[105]

Paine did agree to write for Palmer's journal *Prospect; or, View of the Moral World*, contributing some seventeen essays in 1804.[106] These he wrote with pertinacious enthusiasm: the subject was still, for him, the heart of the matter, and his first essay was, again, a response to an English challenge: the Baptist minister Robert Hall's *Modern Infidelity Considered*, a work which quickly ran to six editions and enjoyed a wide circulation.[107] Once again, Paine revisited the themes of infidelity, human suffering, revelation, the incarnation, and the atonement, to show that 'The Christian system of religion is an outrage on common sense.'[108] Paine's understanding of his opponents did develop, however, since he now stigmatized 'the gloominess of the Calvinistic creed' for prohibiting the Calvinist of Connecticut from admiring the beauties of Creation on the Sabbath, a state whose laws commanded that people should on that day only go 'reverently to and from meeting'. Paine concluded: 'Everything in the creation reproaches the Calvinist with unjust ideas of God, and disowns the hardness and ingratitude of his principles.'[109] It was not language likely to win a mass following in the new republic.

Despite Paine's zealous writing, the circulation of *The Prospect* was probably modest. After Palmer's death in 1804 his journal ceased publication the next year. Paine was never an organizer, and in his last years he evidently lacked the energy or commitment to keep this society alive. Deism was a declining force in the new American republic: its great days had been in England in the first decades of the eighteenth century, and in religion as in politics Paine was more a survivor from an older era than the herald of a new one. Even Unitarianism was soon confined to be the religion of the New England intelligentsia, and was later swamped by waves of immigration of Roman Catholics from the European continent, especially Irish, Italians, and Poles: the rise of their denomination would have been anathema to Paine. It is sometimes said that Paine would have approved of the second Great Awakening, since it democratized American religion; but there is no evidence that he did so, and much evidence that he retained to the last a fervent Deism to which revivalist Evangelicalism was antithetical. A secularist tradition did develop in nineteenth-century America, and it honoured the memory of Paine; but it was small, and (like its British counterpart) reinterpreted Paine's Deism as an example of atheism.[110]

---

[105] Palmer, *Posthumous Pieces*, 11–12, 19, 49.

[106] Paine, 'Prospect Papers' (1804): *CW*, ii. 788–830.

[107] Robert Hall, *Modern Infidelity Considered With respect to its Influence on Society: In a Sermon, Preached at the Baptist Meeting, Cambridge* (Cambridge: M. Watson, 1800).

[108] Paine, 'Prospect Papers', 'Remarks on R. Hall's Sermon' (1804): *CW*, ii. 788–91.

[109] [Paine], 'Prospect Papers', 'Of the Sabbath-Day in Connecticut' (15 Sept. 1804): *CW*, ii. 804–5.

[110] It is striking how seldom Paine appears in the actions or writings of American secularist leaders after his death: James Turner, *Without God, Without Creed: The Origins of Unbelief in America* (Baltimore, 1985), 251; Susan Jacoby, *Freethinkers: A History of American Secularism* (New York, 2004), 65, 150, 264.

What Paine's perceived 'irreligion' did do was to strengthen the Federalists, making play with their Christianity, against Jefferson's Republicans, too easily tarred with the brush of Paine's alleged infidelity. The second American Revolution for which the American press reported that Paine had called, or any more peaceful equivalent of it, now rapidly receded from sight as 'French infidelity' was linked by Federalists with the rapid social changes that were undermining American social ties.[111] If Jacobin social policy was far away, Paine's *Age of Reason* brought the alleged consequences of Deism within reach: the effect was the opposite of what Paine had intended in condemning French atheism.

One of Paine's lasting premises conceived 'society' as a benign, self-generating form of social organization in which 'the people', freed from the heavy hand of aristocratic government, would cooperate together peacefully for the public good. As he wrote in 1805, 'The independence of America would have added but little to her own happiness, and been of no benefit to the world, if her government had been formed on the *corrupt models of the old world*. It was the opportunity of *beginning the world anew*, as it were; and of bringing forward a *new system* of government in which the rights of *all* men should be preserved that gave *value* to independence.'[112] Yet the new states' governments presided over an era of violent competition, slave-owning, genocide of Native Americans and acquisitive lawlessness that one historian has termed 'hustling', using the idea to characterize the new society.[113] To these characteristics Paine did not respond. In the 1790s Paine (thinking of England) had developed ideas of social justice revolving around a social security system involving transfer payments to the old, the sick, and children: where poor law costs steadily rose in Britain from the 1790s in a series of untheoretical local responses to circumstances, Paine's plan was ignored in the new United States; when social security became serious politics there in the twentieth century it was anathematized by Americans who identified with their 'usable' version of the Paine of 1776.

The new American Republic, at least on the still-dominant east coast, was evolving away from Paine's idealized image of the independent freeholder (an ancient English ideal) to become a plutocracy presided over by an elective monarch far more powerful than George III; it is difficult to square such institutions with Paine's values. The English Parliament's claim in 1689 to bind 'themselves, their heirs and posterities for ever' in subjection to William and Mary and their heirs, anathematized by Paine, now found its more effective and lasting expression in the American legal doctrine, today known as originalism, which contends that the United States is bound to the intentions of its Founders as expressed in documents like the constitution of 1787. Yet Paine had famously argued that no one generation had authority over the next: 'Every age and generation is, and must be (as a matter of right) as free to act for itself in all cases, as the age and generation that preceded it.

---

[111] Wood, *The Radicalism of the American Revolution*.
[112] Paine, 'To the Citizens of the United States' (7 June 1805): *CW*, ii. 956.
[113] Walter A. McDougall, *Freedom Just Around the Corner: A New American History 1585–1828* (New York, 2004).

The vanity and presumption of governing beyond the grave is the most ridiculous and insolent of all tyrannies.'[114] His position, instead, expressed in univeralist terms the particularist English legal doctrine that no Parliament could bind its successor. Most tragically of all, Paine had predicted that a republic could not fall into civil war.[115] Happily for his reputation, this prediction had been forgotten by the time that the war of 1861–5, with its immense casualties and destruction of property, indicated that republics and monarchies had many common problems.

Paine's pessimism extended to the international sphere:

> were America, instead of becoming an example to the Old World of good and moral government and civil manners, or, if they like it better, of gentlemanly conduct toward other nations, to set up the character of ruffian, that of *word and blow, and the blow first*, and thereby give the example of pulling down the little that civilization has gained upon barbarism, her independence, instead of being an honor and a blessing, would become a curse upon the world and upon herself.[116]

Nor was his condemnation of extreme inequalities of wealth easily assimilable in the new United States:

> The superstitious awe, the enslaving reverence, that formerly surrounded affluence, is passing away in all countries, and leaving the possessor of property to the convulsion of accidents. When wealth and splendor, instead of fascinating the multitude, excite emotions of disgust; when, instead of drawing forth admiration, it is beheld as an insult upon wretchedness; when the ostentatious appearance it makes serves to call the right of it in question, the case of property becomes critical, and it is only in a system of justice that the possessor can contemplate security.[117]

These words were written in France, not America. An Englishman who visited Paine in his last year noted that he was 'completely deserted by those who formerly had almost deify'd him'.[118]

Some present-day citizens of the United States have become ever more preoccupied with that state's 'founding principles'; here Paine still plays a part thanks to his linked arguments that society is an autonomous formation antecedent to government, and that governments are built on constitutions as a building is constructed from a previously existing blueprint. Both arguments still provide vocabularies for political action, even if limited by comparison with the vocabularies of the 1770s. Yet both arguments call for reconsideration. England's American colonies were

---

[114] Paine, *Dissertation on First-Principles of Government* (1795): *CW*, ii. 576; repeating *Rights of Man* (1791): *CW*, i. 251.

[115] [Paine], *Common Sense* (1776): *CW*, i. 26–7. Recent studies of US censuses have revised upwards the older estimated death toll of the civil war of the 1860s to 750,000–850,000.

[116] Paine, 'To the Citizens of the United States' (14 May 1803): *CW*, ii. 933.

[117] Paine, *Agrarian Justice* ([1797]): *CW*, i. 620–1.

[118] 'His appearance was that of a man of superior mind...His conversation was calm and gentleman-like, except when religion or party politics were mentioned. In this case he became irrascible, and the deformity of his face, rendered so by intemperance, was then disgusting. His intellect did not seem impaired. He died as he lived, a professed deist': T. Adams, *Democracy Unveiled; in a Letter to Sir Francis Burdett, Bart M.P.* (London: C. Chapple, 1813), 292–4.

founded long before 1776, some in the early seventeenth century; in each case governments were established first, civil society followed. Even in 1776, rebellion and a claim to the political independence of each colony came first; those states then sought to devise their own constitutions and to frame the Articles of Confederation to govern the cooperation of the states; the constitution of 1787 was later still. After the Revolution, American citizens began to appeal, for party-political advantage, to different understandings of the Founding; this mythmaking in the pursuit of partisan goals was inventive, impassioned, distorting, and powerfully persistent.[119] Paine in the debates of the 1800s was unable to obtain political leverage from a recall to the founding principles of the United States, since he could not give a persuasive account of what they had been, just as, in France in the 1790s, he could not effectively obstruct the Directory by issuing a recall to the principles of 1789. Paine, therefore, helped reveal the methodological difficulties that obstructed attempts to announce universalist 'founding principles' and to treat them as normative at some remove in time.

For a series of reasons Paine was not at ease in the new republic, and may have returned to his opinions of 1783. On his deathbed in New York in 1809, according to Mme Bonneville (not a hostile witness), he said to Albert Gallatin: '*I am very sorry that I ever returned to this country.*'[120] In the same setting he complained to his physician, Dr James Manley, of 'the want of respect which he conceived he merited';[121] this had indeed been a preoccupation since his return to the United States in 1802. Before the publication of *Rights of Man* (1791) he had, according to a recent historian, 'fallen into obscurity' in America. Subsequently he was a symbol, invoked to validate greater plebeian involvement in politics, the equalization of property, and the disrespect of independent plebeians towards members of the elite;[122] but this role was generalized, and it is not clear that it had specific consequences. Jefferson's Republicans combined with the Federalists to exclude Paine, so that he died in effective isolation.[123] The new republic soon developed a professional political class; it became a place of wide inequalities of property, both landed and financial, and of rampant speculation in both. Cultural populism was much older than Paine, and it neither democratized American politics nor levelled property.

---

[119] Rozbicki, *Culture and Liberty in the Age of the American Revolution*, 106–9.

[120] M. and Mme Bonneville, 'Thomas Paine: A Sketch of his Life and Character', in Conway, *Life*, 337.

[121] Cheetham, *Life*, 304.

[122] Seth Cotlar, *Tom Paine's America: The Rise and Fall of Transatlantic Radicalism in the Early Republic* (Charlottesville, Va, 2011), 37–44 at 38; 132–3; 159. For a contrary argument that 'Endowing American experience with democratic impulses and aspirations, Paine had turned Americans into radicals—and we have remained radicals at heart ever since...His contributions were too fundamental and his vision of America's meaning and possibilities too firmly imbued in the dynamic of political life and culture to be...easily shed or suppressed', see Kaye, *Thomas Paine and the Promise of America*, 4, 6 and *passim*.

[123] Cotlar, *Tom Paine's America*, 214. In 1803, Paine, rejected in Baltimore, was fêted at the Tontine City Hotel in New York; but the hotel was run by John Lovett, an English immigrant and former member of the London Corresponding Society.

The framing of a national myth of origins

Paine never wrote his history of the American Revolution, and did not, by that means, help to shape the self-understandings of the new republic. This task was undertaken by others, and the republic's early historiography concerning its nature and origins demoted Paine to a minor role. That historiography had clear purposes: 'The histories produced during the early national period represent the beginnings of a genre of writing new to America, one characterized by the subjugation of history to the service of nationalism...the effect, if not the intent, was a turn away from the Enlightenment ideal of the universality of human experience to a preoccupation with a distinctly national experience.' As such, these early and particularist histories 'reveal an almost obsessive preoccupation with the problem of union', as the new citizens sought to hold their state together in the face of centrifugal forces. Even the few Deists among these historians 'enlisted God in the service of nationalism'.[124] But these were ends that Paine did not easily serve: as a particularist Englishman he had worked to break up an empire, not to found one; his most memorable invocations had been universalist and not nationalist ones; and he did nothing to enlist a Deist God as the patron of a new republic.

Early American historians of the American Revolution had therefore subtly to misrepresent the nature of that conflict. They often disguised the localist imperatives that had animated most of the colonial participants and omitted the colonists' divided opinions on the way forward, instead framing general, principled theories of the Revolution's significance. But these theories differed. The anniversary of 1776 was celebrated each Fourth of July on party lines. The Republican tradition emphasized Thomas Jefferson (not often dwelling on his inconvenient friendship with Paine), the Declaration of Independence (which Paine had not claimed he had written), and the extensive future promise of social revolution (which Paine had not mapped out). The Federalist tradition of celebration focused on George Washington (again not dwelling on Paine's broken friendship with the national hero), minimized the revolutionary nature of what had happened (which Paine had talked up), and explained away the ideological motivations of elites (which Paine had sought to idealize).[125] In both these new historiographical scenarios, Paine did not quite fit.

These imperatives meant that Paine would be given a modest, and not a transformative, role in the early versions of the national myth. In 1789 the South Carolina physician, politician, and historian David Ramsay (1749–1815) argued that the decision to pursue independence was the result of 'Necessity not choice'. 'The revolution was not forced on the people by ambitious leaders grasping at supreme power, but every measure of it was forced on Congress, by the necessity

---

[124] Arthur H. Shaffer, *The Politics of History: Writing the History of the American Revolution 1783–1815* (Chicago, 1975), 1–3, 166–8; Peter C. Messer, *Stories of Independence: Identity, Ideology and History in Eighteenth-Century America* (Dekalb, Ill., 2005), 7, 13.

[125] Knouff, *The Soldiers' Revolution*, 233–71; Simon P. Newman, *Parades and the Politics of the Street: Festive Culture in the Early American Republic* (Philadelphia, 1997), in which Paine does not feature; Len Travers, *Celebrating the Fourth: Independence Day and the Rites of Nationalism in the Early Republic* (Amherst, Mass., 1997), recording, 90, only one newspaper republication of *Rights of Man*.

of the case, and the voice of the people.' It was the British Act of Parliament passed in December 1775 'for throwing them [the colonists] out of British protection' that meant that 'They considered themselves to be thereby discharged from their allegiance, and that to declare themselves independent, was no more than to announce to the world the real political state, in which Great-Britain had placed them.' Ramsay downplayed the significance of *Common Sense* by placing it in that highly conservative interpretative framework.

By devising a model of the colonists as having from the beginning been orderly, law-bound, liberty-loving moderates (a misleading, but appealing, model), Ramsay diminished the significance of the revolutionary transition and of the contributions of contingency and the negation of English institutions. To argue that 'Nothing could be better timed than this performance [*Common Sense*]' downplayed the significance of its intellectual content, even though Ramsay conceded that 'In union with the feelings and sentiments of the people, it produced surprising effects.'[126] Consequently, in 1789 Ramsay could present Paine as working within orthodox colonial religious discourse:

> With the view of operating on the sentiments of a religious people, scripture was pressed into his service, and the powers, and even the name of a king was rendered odious in the eyes of the numerous colonists who had read and studied the history of the Jews, as recorded in the Old Testament. The folly of that people in revolting from a government, instituted by heaven itself, and the oppressions to which they were subjected in consequence of their lusting after kings to rule over them, afforded an excellent handle for prepossessing the colonists in favour of republican institutions, and prejudicing them against kingly government.

Ramsay, writing in a phase of nation building, had to emphasize (what had not been the case) the unanimity of the colonists of 1776 in adopting the goal of independence. He relegated to an appendix the argument that since the revolution had been 'the people's war', it followed that 'the pen and the press had merit equal to that of the sword', and that the goal of independence had needed to be urged by fervent propaganda. Even then, in the appendix he merely listed Paine's name as one of twenty-two notable authors. Ramsay also began the emphasis on the importance of key official documents, notably the Declaration of Independence and the constitution of 1787; but in drafting these, Ramsay could not claim that Paine had played any part.[127]

Ramsay's work, published in 1789, had been written before two developments that further changed American perceptions of Paine: the French Revolution, and Paine's publications on religion. In 1805, three years after Paine's return to the United

---

[126] Ramsay here largely copied sentences from William Gordon's *The History of the Rise, Progress, and Establishment, of the Independence of the United States of America* (4 vols, London: for the author, 1788), ii. 275. The English Dissenting minister and *émigré* Gordon had gone much further: *Common Sense* was 'read by almost every American'; 'It has satisfied multitudes . . . has been greatly instrumental in producing a similarity of sentiment through the continent, upon the subject [independence] under the consideration of congress.' Even so, this was the only mention of Paine in Gordon's *History*.

[127] David Ramsay, *The History of the American Revolution* (2 vols, Philadelphia: R. Aitken, 1789); ed. Lester H. Cohen (2 vols, Indianapolis, 1990), i. xviii–xxii, 315–17; ii. 633–4.

States in a storm of controversy, the Massachusetts political activist Mercy Otis Warren (1728–1814) almost airbrushed him out of the picture in her own *History of the Rise, Progress and Termination of the American Revolution*, a work in which 'virtue' was a leading category. *Common Sense* was relegated to a footnote and an appendix in which Warren offered cool praise for Paine's political writings, only to distance herself from his other publications:

> His celebrity might have been longer maintained, and his name have been handed down with applause, had he not afterwards have left the line of politics, and presumed to touch on theological subjects of which he was grossly ignorant, as well as totally indifferent to every religious observance as an individual, and in some instances his morals were censured.
>
> Persecuted in England he repaired to France, some time before *monarchy* was subverted in that nation. There, after listening to the indigested rant of infidels of an antecedent date, and learning by rote the jargon of the modern French *literati*, who zealously laboured in the field of *scepticism*, he attempted to undermine the sublime doctrines of the gospel, and annihilate the Christian system. Here he betrayed his weakness and want of principle, in blasphemous scurrilities and impious raillery, that at once sunk his character, and disgusted every rational and sober mind.

That this was done during 'the confusions and despotism of the *Robespierrian reign*' was 'no apology'.[128]

Such squeamish averting of the public gaze was a feature of the historians of the early republic: Paine had to be given some praise as the author of *Common Sense*, but not too much. In any case, such historians correctly understood that Paine had been but one in a large cast of actors on the historical stage. Loyalist historians, who might have been expected to single Paine out for vilification or to use his writings to characterize the rebellion, generally ignored him altogether. Their interpretative framework prioritized Puritanism or its denominational successors and a covert, long-intended design of independence engineered by self-interested individuals, rather than the late contributions of Deism or natural rights theory.

Joseph Galloway, the well-informed former Speaker of the Pennsylvania Assembly, looked back to the long-term goals of the seventeenth-century Puritans, as inherited by the colonial Presbyterians, but ignored Paine.[129] From Massachusetts, Chief Justice Peter Oliver blamed the revolution on ambitious individuals, 'an *Otis*, an *Adams*, a *Franklin*, & a few others of the most abandoned Characters, aided by a set of Priests, who are a disgrace to Christianity', but did not list Paine among the former.[130] Justice Thomas Jones, from the perspective of New York, wrote of 'the Presbyterian faction and republican party' in that state as synonymous. The wishes

---

[128] Mercy Otis Warren, *History of the Rise, Progress and Termination of the American Revolution* (3 vols, Boston: Manning and Loring, 1805); ed. Lester H. Cohen (2 vols, Indianapolis, 1988), i. xix, 292, 378–80.

[129] The 'first settlers in New England had nothing less in view than an independent establishment, both in religion and government': [Joseph Galloway], *Historical and Political Reflections on the Rise and Progress of the American Rebellion* (London: G. Wilkie, 1780), 32.

[130] *Peter Oliver's Origin & Progress of the American Rebellion: A Tory view*, ed. Douglass Adair and John A. Schutz (San Marino, Calif., 1961), 149.

of the majority for a redress of grievances but 'a firm union' with Britain were frustrated by 'the artful cabals of the republicans in Congress'. Jones briefly mentioned *Common Sense*, but not as transforming opinion, and did not name its author.[131] Reflecting on his experience in Massachusetts, Thomas Hutchinson wrote primarily of organized mob violence and the exploitation of popular fears by opposition politicians: 'groundless fears, artfully raised by men, whose views were their own advancement by the ruin of the present easy, happy model of government, and the establishment of another form, but under their own real, if not nominal authority, in the place of it'; Paine did not feature in his *History*.[132] For such men, 1642 represented Presbyterian intolerance, not the republican 'virtue' of the 'Commonwealthmen'. In neither nexus of ideas did Paine fit.

But whatever the influence of these historiographical exercises in self-imaging, the politics of the new republic were already complex, large in scale, and self-referential: in the development of American democracy after 1802 Paine played only a modest role, occasionally invoked as a symbol but with little real traction on events.[133] Given the need of the United States periodically to engage in agonized redefinitions of its relation to its Revolution, it might be argued that it was significant how seldom Paine featured in such American reconsiderations, not how often. Even close to his lifetime, the issues raised in the seething political and social conflicts of the early decades of the new republic were seldom the issues addressed by Paine in 1776.[134] John Adams, who became almost obsessive about Paine, summed him up in 1809: 'Mr. Cheetham's project [a biography of Paine] is of uncertain utility. The sooner Paine is forgotten, perhaps, the better. I fear he has done more harm than good.' Paine's

> political writings, I am singular enough to believe, have done more harm than his irreligious ones. He understood neither government nor religion. From a malignant heart he wrote virulent declamations, which the enthusiastic fury of the times intimidated all men, even Mr. Burke, from answering as he ought. His deism, as it appears to me, has promoted rather than retarded the cause of revelation, at least in America and indeed in Europe. His billingsgate, stolen from Blount's *Oracles of Reason*,[135] from Bolingbroke, Voltaire, Bérenger, &c., will never discredit Christianity, which will hold

[131] Thomas Jones, *History of New York during the Revolutionary War, and of the Leading Events in the Other Colonies at that Period*, ed. Edward Floyd De Lancey (2 vols, New York, 1879), i. 35, 46, 63; cf. 3–4, 6, 15, 23, 46, 59.

[132] Thomas Hutchinson, *The History of the Colony and Province of Massachusetts-Bay*, ed. Lawrence Shaw Mayo (3 vols, Cambridge, Mass., 1936), iii. 253; cf. 67, 69, 162, 183–4, 186, 193–5, 203–4, 212, 214, 276, 326, 329.

[133] Paine is largely irrelevant to the story told in Gordon S. Wood, *Empire of Liberty: A History of the Early Republic, 1789–1815* (New York, 2009) and Daniel Walker Howe, *What Hath God Wrought: The Transformation of America, 1815–1848* (New York, 2007).

[134] 'Today, democracy in America means enfranchisement, at a minimum, of the entire adult citizenry. By that standard, the American democracy of the mid nineteenth century was hardly a democracy at all: women of all classes and colors lacked political and civil rights; most blacks were enslaved; free black men found political rights they had once enjoyed either reduced or eliminated; the remnant of a ravaged Indian population in the eastern states had been forced to move west, without citizenship': Sean Wilentz, *The Rise of American Democracy: Jefferson to Lincoln* (New York, 2005), xviii and *passim*.

[135] Charles Blount, *The Oracles of Reason* (London: no printer, 1693).

its ground in some degree as long as human nature shall have anything moral or intellectual left in it.[136]

Even as Adams reviled Paine's impact on American religion, he conceded that his view that Paine had had a greater harmful effect on American politics was 'singular'. Adams, though a hostile witness, had made a significant admission.

BRITAIN

Paine as exiled prophet: English 'Jacobinism'

Paine's influence in Britain and Ireland was considerable. It was greater than his influence in America, and far greater than that in France; but it was limited especially by the keen attention of many sectors of British society to the French Revolution, and by reactions to the wars that followed from 1793. British preoccupations with France also created for Paine a unique role. In France and America, Paine was engaged with daily politics; he was therefore a dangerous if a defamed presence. In Britain he became for some after 1792 the heroic exile: a generation could grow up looking to Paine as a prophet, inspirational but unaccountable. The young Robert Southey, lecturing in Bristol in 1795, claimed he hailed Paine as the 'hireless Priest of Liberty! Unbought teacher of the poor! Chearing to me is the reflection that my heart hath ever acknowledged—that my tongue hath proudly proclaimed—the Truth and Divinity of thy Doctrines!'[137] But the debate on the French Revolution developed in new ways, far from its origins in 1789–90, and after 1795 'The great names of the early years, like Paine, Burke, Tooke, Priestley and Price were now rarely invoked.'[138]

In the English provinces Paine's lasting role could be less prominent than it had been in London, and the cohesion of reformers was often threatened by government action. After the execution of the conspirator Colonel Edward Despard in 1803, surviving 'groups of Painites in manufacturing communities will have lost any national links. They drew back into their own communities, and their influence will have been shaped by local problems and experiences... The Jacobins or Painites disappeared.'[139] In the 1810s the most widespread network of political debating societies since the 1790s was composed of bodies called, evidently without controversy, Hampden Clubs rather than Paine Clubs. When extra-parliamentary agitation after 1819 displayed 'the growing weakness of the English *ancien régime*', Paine did not figure prominently.[140] Paine's exact contribution to British

[136] John Adams to Benjamin Rush, 31 Aug., 25 Oct. 1809, in John A. Schutz and Douglass Adair (eds), *The Spur of Fame: Dialogues of John Adams and Benjamin Rush, 1805–1813* (San Marino, Calif., 1966), 152–3, 160.

[137] Robert Southey to Tom Southey, 9 May 1795: Geoffrey Carnall, *Robert Southey and his Age* (Oxford, 1960), 45.

[138] *Political Writings of the 1790s*, ed. Gregory Claeys (8 vols, London, 1995), introduction, i. xlvii.

[139] E. P. Thompson, *The Making of the English Working Class* (London, 1963), 499.

[140] Thompson, *The Making of the English Working Class*, 671. By 1812, there is evidence that Luddites in Lancashire and Yorkshire could think of themselves, as one supporter wrote, in various

politics from the 1790s into the early nineteenth century therefore demands careful qualification. British parliamentary politics, both among the ministry and the opposition, was a wide and complex field; its participants were well able to formulate their positions without reference to Paine. Much the same was true of extra-parliamentary politics also.[141]

Paine's works had a very extensive circulation in Britain and Ireland. *Common Sense* was reprinted in London during the American war and long after, and these reprintings prepared the ground for the much wider circulation of *Rights of Man* and other of Paine's writings in the 1790s. In exile in France, Paine became for his English admirers an iconic figure, known primarily through his texts. This status has distracted attention from the way in which what became known as English 'Jacobinism' in and from the 1790s was not always primarily indebted to Paine. John Thelwall, recently identified as 'the chief orator, strategist and theoretician of the London Corresponding Society',[142] after attending medical lectures in London, published in 1793 an account of the nature of life itself which embraced 'the simple principles of materialism' and implicitly rejected the separate existence of a soul; he recalled in 1796 that 'it was not *Tom Paine* but *Edmund Burke* that made me so zealous a reformer, and convinced me of the necessity of annual Parliaments and universal suffrage'. In 1790 John Horne Tooke had even offered to send Thelwall to Cambridge in place of Tooke's own son, whom Tooke had 'disowned', so that Thelwall could 'rise to eminence' in the Church;[143] it would hardly have been with the intention that Thelwall should return to orthodoxy. By the mid-1790s Thelwall has been described as 'much the most prominent of Godwin's admirers'.[144] Paine became less and less central to an evolving political debate; the turn to questions of economic equality in a commercial society from the mid-1790s has been held to owe more to Thelwall.[145] This may be because economic themes were less central to Paine's thought in the 1790s than they have conventionally been depicted.

---

ways—'They may be called Hampdenites, Sidneyites, or Paineites'—but with no specific consequences from the choice of name: 597. Cobbett satirically listed seventeen different sorts of clubs in 1817, but did not find it necessary to mention Paine clubs among them: 617. In 1819 Cobbett returned from America to Britain, bringing Paine's exhumed bones: 'Then (it turned out) it was not Paine's republicanism but his notions of currency reform which Cobbett wished to honour': 699. If Paine 'anticipates the tone' of Cobbett, it was Cobbett who talked in that tone to English audiences 'for thirty years', and had an immense 'democratic influence': 749.

[141] It is remarkable that Paine features only in occasional asides in scholarly studies like Emma Vincent Macleod, *A War of Ideas: British Attitudes to the Wars against Revolutionary France 1792–1802* (Aldershot, 1998) and William Thomas, *The Philosophic Radicals: Nine Studies in Theory and Practice 1817–1841* (Oxford, 1979).

[142] *The Politics of English Jacobinism: Writings of John Thelwall*, ed. Gregory Claeys (University Park, Pa, 1995), xiii.

[143] [Henrietta Cecil Boyle Thelwall], *The Life of John Thelwall* (London: John Macrone, 1837), 78. I owe this reference to Gregory Claeys.

[144] John Thelwall, *An Essay, Towards a Definition of Animal Vitality* (London: G. G. J. and J. Robinson, 1793), 7–9, 13 and *The Tribune*, 3 (1796), 95, quoted in *Writings of Thelwall*, ed. Claeys, xvi–xvii, xxix; 221, 309.

[145] *Writings of Thelwall*, ed. Claeys, xxxvi–lv; Gregory Claeys, 'The Origins of the Rights of Labor: Republicanism, Commerce, and the Construction of Modern Social Theory in Britain, 1796–1805', *Journal of Modern History* 66 (1994), 249–90, at 263–74.

Reforming discourse extended beyond economics, even if Paine's natural rights language of the 1790s was not to be the dominant discourse of the early nineteenth century. 'Plebeian democrats might have revered the memory of Tom Paine, but as often as not they ignored his strictures against invoking the legitimating force of the past. They turned more often to a radicalized British constitutionalism than to the language of the French Revolution in order to draw legitimacy for their own democratic claims and actions and to censure the claims and actions of their social betters.'[146] Unexpectedly, the 'rights of Englishmen' enjoyed a new vogue.

Land reform: Thomas Spence v. Thomas Paine

British reformers in the 1790s sometimes went beyond Paine's positions, as had a few writers in England from at least the 1770s, but not in order to praise Paine as their precursor or to salute Paine as a figure to whom they needed to respond. The clearest example of a reformer countering Paine in a hostile spirit was Thomas Spence (1750–1814).[147] His choice of Paine as a thinker to define himself against is further evidence of Paine's fame; but Spence was not intimidated. Raised in Newcastle in the Glassite sect but now in London, he published in 1795 his own pamphlet that referred back to his earlier tract of 1793, also entitled *Rights of Man*, and to his lecture of 1775 urging the collective ownership of land. Writing in the third person of himself, Spence pointed out: 'there is another RIGHTS OF MAN by *Spence*, that goes farther than *Paine's*…it suffers *no* private Property in Land, but gives it all to the Parishes.' It is not clear whether Spence knew that Paine was a landowner, but Spence's critique caught him: 'Y[oung]. M[echanic]. It is amazing that Paine and the other Democrats should level all their Artillery at Kings, without striking like Spence at this root of every abuse and grievance. O[ld]. M[echanic]. The reason is evident: They have no chance of being Kings; but many of them are already, and the rest foolishly and wickedly hope to be sometime or other Landlords, lesser or greater.' Paine was, by now, a lesser landlord in the United States, where the common ownership of land was not demanded; he had already argued against the early communism of Gracchus Babeuf in France, where, again, the abolition of private property did not figure in 1789.

Spence now took what seemed to him to be a logical step: 'a Convention or Parliament of the People would be at eternal War with the Aristocracy.' Despite the landlords' power, 'a true and universal knowledge of Spence's plain and simple System' would 'overturn them, and sweep all their Greatness and Lordliness away in one Day'. This could be done by 'a provisionary Government…at once'; but 'if the Aristocracy arose to contend the matter, let the People be firm and desperate, destroying them Root and Branch, and strengthening their Hands by the rich Confiscations, Thus the War would be carried on at the expence of the wealthy

---

[146] James A. Epstein, *Radical Expression: Political Language, Ritual and Symbol in England, 1790–1850* (New York, 1994), 9 and *passim*.

[147] For Spence as 'a chiliast, prophesying the Millennium' see T. M. Parssinen, 'Thomas Spence and the Origins of English Land Nationalization', *Journal of the History of Ideas* 34 (1973), 135–41, at 140.

enemy.' This would not be, Spence urged, 'a barren Revolution of mere unproduct-ive Rights, such as many contend for';[148] in his mind, Paine would have been among the many.

Paine was indeed a theorist, authorized in his own perception by his universal benevolence to urge sweeping, beneficent reform, and not greatly attending to its consequences. His *Rights of Man* therefore criticized French institutions, but did not denounce by name the king, aristocrats, or churchmen; it did not demand their execution, or the expropriation of private property. Paine's writings acted as catalysts in a fevered environment in which hatred and resentment were not abstract, but deeply rooted and practical: a British world, from the 1790s to the 1830s, in which assassination, expropriation, and revolution were feared by well-informed individuals as real possibilities.

Spence's *Rights of Man*, in a Preface dated 19 November 1792, had condemned 'Partial Reforms, or . . . Piece-meal Reformation'. He anticipated in 1793 the objec-tion of 'a Gentleman': 'But who, pray, among all the Revolutionists in either America, France, or England, or any where else, ever disputed or attempted to invalidate the rights of the landed interest? Or, does Paine, whose publications seem to satisfy the wishes of the most sanguine Reformers, glance in the least on their rights?' Spence replied: 'Mr. Paine acts more cautiously, and does not hurt the feelings of any gentleman that is unconnected with government, and so, of course, may retain their good will, notwithstanding all the lengths he goes; and may, even with a good grace, consistent with his reform, enjoy a very handsome estate, and with all his boasted liberty and equality, may roll in his chariot on the labours of his tenants.'[149] It was exaggerated, but not untrue: Paine, on his American estate, had a tenant farmer.

Nor was this an isolated instance. In *The Rights of Infants* (1797), Spence offered an extended critique of Paine's *Agrarian Justice*. This work strengthened Spence's conviction that 'deism and republicanism in themselves would not suffice to secure real justice'.[150] Spence envisaged a wholesale return to the land; Paine had not. Spence wanted something much more extensive than Paine had offered. Indeed he responded to Paine by taunting him with Burke's phrase: Paine had at last accepted that God had given the earth to mankind in common, 'But, O dire disappoint-ment! Behold! Mr. Paine, instead of erecting on this rock of ages an everlasting Temple of Justice, has erected an execrable fabric of compromissory expediency, as if in good earnest intended for a Swinish Multitude.' For Spence, 'All dominion is rooted and grounded in land, and thence spring every kind of lordship'; Spence was determined to root out this iniquity, not to compromise with it.

---

[148] [Thomas Spence], *The End of Oppression; Being a Dialogue between an Old Mechanic and a Young One. Concerning the Establishment of the Rights of Man* (2nd edn, London: T[homas] Spence, [1795]), 3, 5–9.

[149] T[homas] Spence, *The Rights of Man, as Exhibited in a Lecture, Read at the Philosophical Society, in Newcastle, To which is now added, an Interesting Conversation, Between a Gentleman and the Author, on the Subject of his Scheme. With The Queries sent by the Rev. Mr J. Murray, to the Society in Defence of the Same* (London: T. Spence, 1793), iii–iv, 19, 32.

[150] Malcolm Chase, 'Paine, Spence and the "Real Rights of Man"', *Bulletin of the Society for the Study of Labour History* 52 (1987), 32–40, at 34.

In two columns, Spence contrasted Paine's system with his own. Under Paine's, 'The people will, as it were, sell their birth-right for a mess of porridge, by accepting of a paltry consideration in lieu of their rights.' Under Spence's, 'The people will receive, without deduction, the whole produce of their common inheritance.' Under Paine's, 'The people cannot derive right of suffrage in national affairs, from their compromissory stipends.' Under Spence's, 'Universal suffrage will be inseparably attached to the people both in parochial and national affairs.' Under Paine's, 'After admitting that the earth belongs to the people, the people must nevertheless compromise the matter with their conquerors and oppressors, and still suffer them to remain as a distinct and separate body among them, in full possession of their country.' Under Spence's, 'After insisting that the land is public property, the people's oppressors must either submit to become undistinguishable in the general mass of citizens or fly the country.'[151] Spence's list extended over five pages: his differences from Paine could hardly have been more clearly set out. In London revolutionary circles, no open schism developed between Paineite and Spencean wings:[152] Paine was in exile, and was therefore swept forward, in the perceptions of many Britons, in initiatives that owed steadily less to him. Yet *Agrarian Justice* arguably 'reveals an estrangement between its author and English popular radicalism, the consequences perhaps of Paine's years of exile'.[153]

Paine was, as has been shown, part of an older world. For powerful reasons, he was not in the vanguard of those in Britain who sought to base a new politics on economic analysis. Paine was an obsessive critic of absolute power but his mid-eighteenth-century mindset led him to identify that power primarily with hereditary power, that is, monarchy and aristocracy. By the last decade of his life, a new target was beginning to cohere against which old suspicions could redirect themselves: manufacturing industry and its owners. Yet this evolution only created contrasts between those few who began to perceive a newly emerging social formation and that much larger number of people, including Paine, who did not.

Manufacturing, capitalism, and poverty

In 1805 the English physician Charles Hall, moved by the human suffering he witnessed among his patients, made his sense of an emerging economic contrast explicit in his book *The Effects of Civilisation*.[154] Hall began with the same 'two orders' as Paine, 'the rich and the poor'. The power of the rich

---

[151] T[homas] Spence, *The Rights of Infants; or, the Imprescriptable Right of Mothers to such a Share of the Elements as is sufficient to enable them to suckle and bring up their Young. In a Dialogue between the Aristocracy and a Mother of Children. To which are added, by Way of Preface and Appendix, Strictures on Paine's Agrarian Justice* (London: T. Spence, 1797), 3–4, 11, 13.

[152] No such schism is recorded in Malcolm Chase, *'The People's Farm': English Radical Agrarianism 1775–1840* (Oxford, 1988).

[153] Chase, 'Paine, Spence', 36.

[154] John Dinwiddy, 'Charles Hall: Early English Socialist', *International Review of Social History* 21 (1976), 256–65, reprinted in Dinwiddy, *Radicalism and Reform in Britain, 1780–1850* (London, 1992), 87–107. Although Hall did not acknowledge Paine, Dinwiddy argued, 103, that Hall at one point echoed him.

is as strong and effective as that of the most absolute monarch that ever lived, as far as relates to the labour of the poor; indeed probably more so, since it is doubtful whether any power ever existed, in any kind of government whatever, that could impose on the people what is imposed on them by the power of wealth. To condemn so many to the mines; to confine such numbers to such nauseous, irksome, unwholesome, destructive employments; is more than equal to any kingly power on earth. To enforce the execution of such punishments, would require an army almost equal in number to the people so punished. The punishments of tyrants are generally confined to those that are near them; but the power of wealth pervades the whole country, and subjects every poor man to its dominion... Adam Smith thinks Mr. Hume has great merit in having been the first that observed that manufactures had abolished the servile dependence of the people on the great feudal barons; but Dr. Smith was not aware of this new species of dependence of the lower orders on the rich, which is established in its stead, in most civilized states.[155]

But of this social formation, the world of manufactures, Paine never wrote. Even Hall wrote of it to reject it, and to advocate a return of the population to the land.

Although Paine often witnessed poverty, he did not discuss the specifics of that phenomenon; generally, he mentioned it only to blame it on government. When Paine had written of 'the rich' he had primarily envisioned the nobleman, the great landowner in the old order. Gradually, in the early nineteenth century, the image of 'the rich' came to be associated more with the employer, finally meaning the industrialist. Hall wrote at an early stage in this association. He began, like Paine, with an account of the inequality of landed property, but to Hall poverty was caused by 'too many' of the rural labourers, the people who produced necessary things, being 'thrown into the manufactures', where they produced mainly luxuries for the rich. Paine's solution to the ills of the old order was republican government; but to Hall, a republic in itself would make little difference to the disparity between rich and poor. This disparity now took place in a new setting: 'The manufactures soon became the employment of a great proportion of the people, and made a very great alteration in the situation of them: and as this forms a very striking feature in the face of civilized countries, and is of great consequence, we think it deserves particular notice and discussion.'

For both Hall and Paine, the riches of the rich caused the poverty of the poor, but for Hall this happened through the newly burgeoning means of production and exchange; for Paine, through men's ancient dispossession from God's original gift, their landed inheritance. Even Hall had not reached socialism: by 'the manufacturers' he still meant the workers in manufactures, as opposed to what he termed 'their masters'. He did not yet write of 'capitalism',[156] but analysis soon moved in

---

[155] Charles Hall, *The Effects of Civilization on the People in European States* (London: for the author, 1805), 43, 46, 49–50.

[156] The term 'capitalism' was absent from Hall's text. It included only two perfunctory uses of 'capitalist' and one of 'capitalists' (72, 268, 316), evidently untheorized synonyms for the term 'the rich' (268). Capitalists were composed of 'the tradesmen or manufacturers', but these were not yet clearly distinct from an older economy: 'A very great proportion of such people are the owners of land, and the occupiers of it' (71). The term 'capitalist' could occasionally be found in anglophone discourse in

that direction with the economic writings of David Ricardo. Nor were the new phenomena of manufacturing confined to Europe. Hall also noticed 'how earnest and impatient the people in America are to arrive at a similar situation to that of the nations of Europe; and, in consequence, what endeavours are making to obtain it' by 'the introduction of manufactures'. Already, 'an aristocracy has...considerable footing and weight there', whether or not they bore formal titles. 'There is the same division of the people observable in America, that there is in Europe; the inhabitants are divided into rich and poor there also.'[157] This was not Paine's vision of an American Arcadia.

The new social constituency of mass industry most clearly generated a new political discourse in early nineteenth-century Britain, since there (unlike in France and the United States) these phenomena were not overlaid by the consequences of a founding revolution. For some scholars it was tempting in retrospect to create genealogies linking Paine with later reforming initiatives, notably socialism; but this is seldom a valid exercise. Charles Hall did not find it necessary to cite Paine;[158] nor, in his *Autobiography*, did Robert Owen.[159] After 1830, 'The social vision of a Paine or a Cobbett could no longer have an immediate relevance to a population of factory workers.'[160] Although the culture of the factory did not at once replace the culture of the artisan workshop, the trend eventually became evident. Through the nineteenth century, reforming groups in Britain could sometimes appeal to Paine; but these appeals were both infrequent, and specific appropriations for later purposes, not the acknowledgement of a lasting because universalist political discourse. It might be objected that this is always the case, and that appropriations were always related to the needs of a later moment; but that objection would be

the 1790s, sometimes in unexpected places, but was uncommon before the 1800s: Edmund Burke, *Reflections on the Revolution in France, and on the Proceedings in Certain Societies in London relative to that Event* (London: J. Dodsley, 1790), 236; James Mackintosh, *Vindiciae Gallicae. Defence of the French Revolution and its English Admirers against the Accusations of the Right Hon. Edmund Burke: including some Strictures on the late Production of Mons. De Calonne* (London: G. G. J. and J. Robinson, 1791), 160; *Reflections on the Formation and Distribution of Wealth. By M. [Anne-Robert-Jacques] Turgot* (London: J. Good et al., 1793), 111–12, 114, 116–17; [Sir George Onesiphorous Paul], *Observations on a Bill before Parliament* (London: no printer, [1796]), 14; John Thelwall, *Rights of Nature, against the Usurpation of Establishments. A Series of Letters to the People, in Reply to the False Principles of Burke. Part the Second* (London: H. D. Symonds, 1796), 88–9, 91–2; Helen Maria Williams, *A Tour in Switzerland; or, A View of the Present State of the Governments and Manners of those Cantons: with Comparative Sketches of The Present State of Paris* (2 vols, London: G. G. and J. Robinson, 1798), i. 21, 23; Earl of Lauderdale, *A Letter on the Present Measures of Finance; in which the Bill now Depending in Parliament is Particularly Considered* (London: J. Debrett, G. G. and J. Robinson, 1798), 29, 33. As with other words, what is notable is how long it took for an old term to be given a new and reified meaning.

[157] Hall, *Effects of Civilization*, 75–6, 78, 94, 112, 250, 252–3.

[158] Charles Hall, *Observations on the Principal Conclusion in Mr Malthus's Essay on Population* (London: for the author, 1805) equally did not refer to Paine.

[159] Paine was not mentioned in Robert Owen, *A New View of Society* (2nd edn, London: Longman et al., 1816) or in *The Life of Robert Owen. Written by Himself* (London, 1857–8): *Selected Works of Robert Owen*, ed. Gregory Claeys (4 vols, London, 1993), iv.

[160] Gareth Stedman Jones, *Languages of Class: Studies in English Working Class History 1832–1982* (Cambridge, 1983), 56; 'the aim was no longer simply a Jacobin republic of free and independent producers, but a co-operative commonwealth of associated producers', 60.

exactly the contention of this book. Founders are often less determinative than their later appropriations make them appear. Paine's greatest impact was less on factory reform, trades unions, or emergent socialism, than on a surviving element from his own age: Trinitarian Christianity.

Atheism and Christianity in English reform: the reception of Paine's *The Age of Reason*

Natural rights language was not necessarily dominant, even among reformers. Francis Place, the London-based artisan leader, wrote: 'My landlord was a member of the London Corrersponding Society, and at his request I also became a member. That was in the month of June 1794.' Place's imagination had been captured on 28 April that year by a chance reading of Paine's *The Age of Reason* in his landlord's room (the one book by Paine, recorded Place, that until then he 'had not seen'), waiting for his wife to give birth; 'I read it with delight... It was the first deeistical book I ever saw, excepting the writings of David Hume.' Place sought the acquaintance of the book's owner, a member of the London Corresponding Society, who persuaded Place to join that body.[161] Place, then, had never met Paine, and was mobilized by only one of Paine's writings, although Place recorded that, with the exception of *The Age of Reason*, he had already read them all: even as intelligent and committed a reformer as Place had not been turned into a disciple of Paine's by this earlier scrutiny. For Place (and perhaps for others like him) Paine was famous, and even emancipatory, without being necessarily determinative of their future thinking. Place's work for the Society in the 1790s was also different in kind from Paine's. Place's efforts were mainly organizational, and the organization of mass action, a thing of the future, was an area into which Paine had never ventured. For residents in the British Isles, the problem of communication also tended to detain Paine in the intellectual landscape of 1792 and earlier. Cut off in France by the war, Paine never, for example, wrote for the Society's ill-starred magazine, published from July 1796 to May 1797, *The Moral and Political Magazine of the London Corresponding Society*.

Paine made only occasional appearances in the papers of the LCS, and although some of its divisions organized the distribution of his works, they were usually of titles like *Agrarian Justice* and *Letter to the People of France*: the Society was not primarily dedicated to distributing *Rights of Man*.[162] The Society's *Correspondence*, collected and published in book form in 1795, did not mention Paine; instead, it gave often-repeated prominence to '*universal suffrage and annual parliaments*' as 'the political creed of the London Corresponding Society', goals in which the published correspondence acknowledged no indebtedness to him.[163] This was appro-

---

[161] Dudley Miles, *Francis Place 1771–1854: The Life of a Remarkable Radical* (Brighton, 1988), 23–4, citing the first draft of Place's autobiography, BL Add MSS 27,808, fo. 3; *The Autobiography of Francis Place (1771–1854)*, ed. Mary Thale (Cambridge, 1972), 126–7, 129. Place arranged for the printing of 'a cheap edition' of *The Age of Reason* in 1796: 159.

[162] Thale (ed.), *LCS Papers*, 25, 327, 380, 438.

[163] *The Correspondence of the London Corresponding Society revised and corrected, With Explanatory Notes and a Prefatory Letter, by the Committee of Arrangement, deputed for that purpose: Published for the*

priate, since Paine had not embraced that already well-known formula. Indeed these goals had reached the national political agenda in England in the 1780s, while Paine was in America, and had been worked out by others. The phrase now became a mantra, as the leaders of the LCS tried to create a common front with other societies, for example in Sheffield, and to disguise the extent of their own republican intentions.

The LCS volume however presented a sanitized, moderate, constitutionalist image of the Society.[164] It showed Maurice Margarot writing from Sydney, Australia, where he had been transported, appealing to 'the British constitution, as it was established by the revolution of 1688; which placed the present family on the throne, for the immediate purpose of more effectually protecting British freedom'; Paine was an open critic of the Revolution of 1688 and of the Hanoverians. The volume contained a letter dated 15 February 1795 from the President and Secretary of the LCS to the Duke of Portland, Secretary of State for the Home Department, presenting 'a Constitutional Renovation of the Commons House of Parliament' as a means to 'secure this country from those evils which menace it, and which have already filled with desolation and calamity the surrounding nations'; Paine was a friend to the extension of revolution across Europe. The LCS, then, at least professed to be politically far more moderate than Paine.

But there were other elements in the Society that hardly appeared in its correspondence. The LCS volume showed the Secretary and Assistant Secretary writing to their sister society in Birmingham on 23 October 1795: 'We earnestly recommend to all our associated friends to avoid themes of religious opinion. The object we have in view is temporal.'[165] The letter did not reveal the occasion of the remark, a motion brought to the General Committee in London on 17 September 1795 from Division 27 that

> there are in the Society Atheists, Deists & other blasphemous Persons who go about propagating the most horrible Doctrines, contrary to every Principle of Liberty, & which frighten all good Christians from the Society. They likewise make use of the most diabolical expressions such as calling the Deity 'Mr Humbug.' 'Damning the Bible' Blasting all Christians & declaring the Society will never do any good untill they are without them. This division do recommend that the President of the General [Committee] do severely reprimand them for the 1st offence & that they be expelld from the Society for the second.

Use of Members, pursuant to the 17th Article of the Society's Regulations (London: Printed by Order of the London Corresponding Society, [1795]), 5, 6, 19, 27–9, 37, 40, 42, 48–9, 54, 56–7, 66, 68, 70, 72–3, 79.

[164] For the excision of many pages from the Journal of the LCS from 3 May 1792 to 2 January 1794 in order to conceal its more extreme activities at the time of the trials of 1794, and Thomas Hardy's later rewriting of history to dissociate the SCI from the LCS, see Jenny Graham, *The Nation, the Law and the King, Reform Politics in England, 1789–1799* (2 vols, Lanham, Md, 2000), 293–5.

[165] *Correspondence of the London Corresponding Society*, 12, 16. Occasionally, a reference slipped out to 'Superstitious delusion', 79. The 'Conclusory Address' from the Committee of Arrangement also repudiated 'the Agrarian position of equalizing property' and assured the supporters of the LCS that 'the charge of your being inimical to Monarchical government takes its rise from your having dared to resist the Treasonable and Jacobitical Doctrine of the DIVINE RIGHT OF KINGS', 82.

The charge was too well aimed, and the General Committee, disagreeing, recorded that the Committee '*passed to the order of the day with contempt*'.[166] The supporters of the motion therefore seceded to form another body with a Christian test for admission, 'The Friends of Religious and Civil Liberty'.[167]

Francis Place confirmed this situation in text he later deleted from his autobiography:

> Nearly all the leading members [of the LCS] were either Deists or Atheists—I was an Atheist... This was also the opinion of many others—There were however a number of very religious persons in the society. If ever toleration in its best sense ever prevailed in any society it was in this. Religious topics never were discussed scarcely ever mentioned. It was a standing rule in all the divisions and in the committees also That no discussions or disputes on any subject connected with religion should be permitted and none were permitted. In private, religion was frequently the subject of conversation, and it was well known [that the] most conspicuous members were free thinkers but no exception was ever taken, to those opinions nor were they ever brought into discussion.[168]

As with the LCS's involvement in attempted insurrection, Place laboured to play down the degree and significance of freethought. Significantly, though, he identified the 'Deists' with the 'Atheists'. The LCS, then, was split between the theists like Thomas Hardy, who had an apocalyptic sense that the 'reign of the Beast of Civil and Ecclesiastical Power is almost at an end—Thanks to the Supreme Ruler of the Universe—for his great goodness hitherto—and the bright prospect before us',[169] and the atheists.

Despite this necessary reticence of the LCS, Place promoted the cause of freethought in its ranks. In 1796 he sought to launch his career as a publisher with an edition of Paine's *The Age of Reason*, sold via the LCS; the distribution system was evidently effective, for in 1797 Place was cheated out of his share of the profits in the venture by his partner, the printer Thomas Williams.[170] By contrast, it is not clear that the LCS circulated Paine's *Rights of Man*. At a debating society on 12 December 1794, John Gale Jones, a prominent member, argued that 'the C[orresponding] S[ociety] did not officially circulate that pamphlet; the C.S. always leaves it to the choice of it's Members to read what political pamphlets they think proper'.[171] *Rights of Man* was undoubtedly influential, but was not the foundation text of the LCS and its associated societies. Members of the LCS were driven by their own pre-commitments.

---

[166] Thale (ed.), *LCS Papers*, 306; *The Autobiography of Francis Place*, ed. Thale, 159.

[167] Miles, *Place*, 32–4.

[168] BL Add MSS 27,808 fos 115–16, in Thale (ed.), *LCS Papers*, 307.

[169] National Archives, Treasury Solicitor's Papers, TS 11/953/3497, in Thale (ed.), *LCS Papers*, 307. For Hardy's millenarianism, which he carefully concealed from most of his contemporaries in the LCS, see Jon Mee, *Print, Publicity, and Popular Radicalism in the 1790s: The Laurel of Liberty* (Cambridge, 2016), 69–72.

[170] Miles, *Place*, 32–4; Thale (ed.), *Autobiography of Francis Place*, 159–72.

[171] National Archives, Home Office Papers, HO 42/37, in Thale (ed.), *LCS Papers*, 307.

These often concerned religion. William Hamilton Reid, a member of the LCS from, at the latest, May 1793[172] but who later left that body, writing in 1800 of *The Age of Reason*, pointed out the 'early predilection of the London Corresponding Society for this performance'. It was 'the sole medium which, for the first time, made infidelity as familiar as possible with the lower orders'; 'till the Age of Reason was adopted by the political societies in the metropolis, Deism, to say nothing of Atheism, was rather the affair of a few isolated individuals, than, as it has been since that period, the concern of a considerable part of the community'. Reid gave as 'the most prominent reason' for 'the late inclination to infidelity' the work of 'a certain society, assisted by the politics of the moment'. There were other reasons, including the predisposition among Protestants to see the French as 'the select *agents* of Providence' in destroying Roman Catholicism, which would lead on to the destruction of all other denominations; but the LCS was, for Reid, the major cause of 'infidelity'.

> If the facts I am about to adduce were not well warranted, posterity would not believe, that in consequence of the publication of a rhapsody against the doctrines of Christianity, hazarded by a theoretical politician in 1794, and under favour of the French revolution, a very considerable number of our countrymen adopted his notions; and became equally as violent for the extermination of the Christian religion, as for the remedy of those *civil abuses*, for which alone their society was at first established!
>
> Without experience of the fact, who would believe that while the infatuated disciples of the new philosophy were declaiming against their clergy, for mingling politics with religion, they themselves, employed missionaries to add deism to the democracy of their converts![173]

Reid conceded:

> It is still fair to admit, that the adoption of Paine's Age of Reason was not agreed to in the London Corresponding Society, without considerable opposition, especially in the general committee; but as zeal superseded judgment, in their discussions upon the subject, the epithets of d-m-d fool, and d-m-d Christian, ultimately prevailed...In the hour of its admiration, this rhapsody was ridiculously termed the *New Holy Bible*; a circumstance which fully evinced the intentions of Mr. Paine's partisans: in fine, the attachment of the party was carried so far, that the bare circumstance of having the Age of Reason in a house, was deemed a collateral proof of the *civism* of the possessor.
>
> It may be urged, that this conduct of the society was never justified by any act of the body at large: this is granted; but when it is considered, that their inclination for deism was sufficiently powerful to occasion a schism, which produced a *new society*, under the denomination of the *Civil and Religious*; it follows, that the preponderance of a party, in the original body, was equal to a decision of the whole, and fixes the charge of a partiality to infidelity, beyond the possibility of doubt...Still, nothing like a miracu-

---

[172] Thale (ed.), *LCS Papers*, 67.
[173] William Hamilton Reid, *The Rise and Dissolution of the Infidel Societies in the Metropolis: including, the origin of modern Deism and Atheism; the genius and conduct of those associations; their lecture-rooms, field-meetings, and deputations; From the Publication of Paine's Age of Reason till the present Period* (London: J. Hatchard, 1800), 1–4, 34.

lous conversion of the London Corresponding Society is to be imputed to Mr. Paine's Anti-theological Work. On the contrary, their minds were prepared for this more popular performance, by the more learned and elaborate productions of Mirabaud's System of Nature, and Volney's Ruins of Empires: the latter, in point of style, is looked upon as the Hervey of the Deists; the former, as the Newton of the Atheists.

From whatever source, 'such a torrent of abuse and declamation appeared to burst from all quarters at once, that as the idea of a *Deist* and a good *Democrat* seemed to have been universally compounded, very few had the courage to oppose the general current... in the recommendation of any person to an office among them, it was common to distinguish him as "*A good Democrat and a Deist.*" Or, to fix the character more strongly, to add, "*That he is no Christian.*" '[174]

Reid argued that 'between such Deism as this, and stark Atheism, there may be a nominal *distinction*, but no *difference*'. He misquoted the *Charge* of Beilby Porteus, Bishop of London, in 1794: the French were

> pretended Deists, but real Atheists. And although the name of a Supreme Being was sometimes mentioned, yet it was seldom mentioned but with ridicule and contempt. They acknowledged nothing beyond the grave; and they stigmatized all opinions different from these, with the names of superstition, bigotry, priestcraft, fanaticism, and imposture.[175]

It was this schism within the LCS, argued Reid, that fatally weakened it: 'After these notions of infidelity were in a manner established in the divisions, it is natural to suppose, that in choosing their delegates, those persons were preferred who were doubly recommended by *their religion*, and their politics. However, from this period, when the leaders began to force their anti-religious opinions upon their co-associates, it is undeniable that their intestine divisions hastened their dissolutions more than any external obstacles.'[176]

Nineteenth-century secularism and the revial of Paineite Deism: Richard Carlile

Economics, more than theology, came to predominate in early nineteenth-century British political discourse. In effecting this shift there was a key intermediary, a

---

[174] Reid, *Rise and Dissolution*, 5–6, 8–9. Reid referred to *Système de la Nature. Des Loix du Monde Physique & du Monde Moral. Par M. Mirabaud* [i.e. Paul Henri Thiry, baron d'Holbach] (2 vols., 'Londres' [i.e. Amsterdam], 1770), first published in English as *The System of Nature: or, the Laws of the Moral and Physical World... translated from the French of M. Mirabaud... by William Hodgson* (London: for the translator, 1795); Constantin François Chasseboeuf, comte de Volnay, *Les Ruines: ou Méditation sur les révolutions des empires* (Paris, 1791), first translated as *The Ruins: or a survey of the revolutions of empires by M. Volney... Translated from the French* (London: J. Johnson, 1792). Reid recorded that *The System of Nature* was 'published in weekly numbers', and may have been influential before its publication in book form.

[175] Reid, *Rise and Dissolution*, 80; for the accurate text, see Beilby Porteus, *A Charge delivered to the Clergy of the Diocese of London, at the Visitation of that Diocese, in the Year MDCCXCIV* (London: F. and C. Rivington, 1794), 13.

[176] Reid, *Rise and Dissolution*, 9. 'Bone and Lee, two seceding members, and booksellers by profession, were proscribed for refusing to sell Volney's *Ruins*, and Paine's *Age of Reason*': 6. The secessionists were often Methodists, subsequently harassed by the LCS: 17–18; Albert Goodwin, *The Friends of Liberty: The English Democratic Movement in the Age of the French Revolution* (London, 1979), 484–5.

former Dissenting minister, the son and grandson of Dissenting ministers. The most important theorist of the 1790s for Francis Place was not Thomas Paine but William Godwin. In 1825, William Hazlitt (1778–1830) similarly looked back to 1793: 'No work in our time gave such a blow to the philosophical mind of the country as the celebrated *Enquiry concerning Political Justice*. Tom Paine was considered for the time as a Tom Fool to him.'[177] It was Godwin's book that Place consistently recommended. It formed his utilitarianism and his preference for political gradualism; it led him into the circle of Jeremy Bentham and James Mill from the 1810s; it led him away from the LCS's fixation on parliamentary reform as the sole cure for all of society's ills. After the 1790s Paine disappeared from Place's preoccupations, reappearing only briefly in 1819 when Place offered to help the reformer Richard Carlile, prosecuted and convicted for selling Paine's *The Age of Reason*. Indeed Place's biographer argues that Place 'was a principal influence behind Carlile's move from deism to atheism'.[178]

Carlile's temporary revival of Paineite Deism was not unique. The Society for the Suppression of Vice had prosecuted the bookseller Daniel Isaac Eaton in 1812 for selling *The Age of Reason*, but this conflict between Evangelicalism and atheism was now about to become a defining framework of a new ideology, conceptualized in the early 1820s, newly termed 'radicalism'. The press campaign mounted by Richard Carlile and his associate William Sherwin (both biographers of Paine) from about 1817 onward carried the message that, as Carlile put it, Britain was a 'continued mass of Corruption, Falsehood, Hypocrisy, and Slander', sustained by excessively high taxes.[179] This was common ground with Paine, whose political writings Carlile edited.[180] But what Carlile responded to most were Paine's writings on religion, which he republished, and which stood behind Carlile's strident tone. He was indeed zealous in this cause, reprinting Paine and the American Deist Elihu Palmer, and launching a magazine, *The Deist: or, Moral Philosopher*, that carried long extracts from d'Holbach, Palmer, Voltaire, and others. Carlile was convicted of blasphemy in October 1819, and this sense of persecution informed his own *Life of Thomas Paine*, which appeared in November 1820.[181]

Paine's *Age of Reason* had its first impact in the 1790s; from 1819 it was circulated to an additional audience. Legal persecution brought Carlile welcome publicity and large sales. Paine was therefore back on the agenda in the new politics of the 1820s, but as an 'infidel' and a 'radical' (neither of which he had been) rather than as a Deist and an enemy of the hereditary principle (which he had). In Carlile's case, persecution had the opposite effect from that which the Vice Society intended:

---

[177] [William Hazlitt], *The Spirit of the Age: or Contemporary Portraits* (2 vols, London: Henry Colburn, 1825), i. 33.

[178] Miles, *Place*, 41, 103.

[179] Joel H. Wiener, *Radicalism and Freethought in Nineteenth-Century Britain: The Life of Richard Carlile* (Westport, Conn., 1983), 19.

[180] *The Political and Miscellaneous Works of Thomas Paine* (2 vols, London: R. Carlile, 1819).

[181] Thomas Paine, *The Age of Reason, part the first* (London: R. Carlile, 1818); Thomas Paine, *The Age of Reason, part the second* (London: R. Carlile, 1818); Thomas Paine, *The Age of Reason. Part the third* (London: R. Carlile, 1818); also as *The Theological Works of Thomas Paine* (London: R. Carlile, 1818); Wiener, *Radicalism and Freethought*, 27–8, 33–54.

the formation of 'a cohesive "republican and infidel" movement, the first of its kind in nineteenth-century Britain'. But it was not to be a dominant phenomenon: 'Carlile's radicalism, as it developed from the pressure of events in the early 1820s, was essentially preindustrial... Carlile hated social injustice. But he blamed the "traditional" enemies of the poor for it: kings, lords, taxgatherers, fundholders, magistrates, and, above all, clergymen. They were the appropriators of the soil and of common property, and those who profited from privileged institutions.'

Like Paine, Carlile had been born in a small and declining rural town (in his case, Ashburton, Devon); both rejected their early Anglican upbringing; neither prospered as workers in a declining handicraft industry (in Carlile's case, tinplate manufacture); both moved to the old economy of London, not to an area of new manufacturing industry in the north. Like Paine, Carlile was a supporter of free trade, condemning the Speenhamland system of outdoor relief for the poor and arguing that 'The great radical failure is in the people themselves, who waste, by their bad habits, by drunkenness and religion, the means of consuming those more necessary comforts in diet, dress, and dwelling, which would give a high degree of activity to trade, and create a greater demand for labour.' But unlike Paine, Carlile would countenance, as he wrote in 1820, the 'shedding of blood' when 'indispensable' to 'annihilate the existing order of things and to begin de novo'. When Carlile receded from this physical-force position in the 1830s, he was found declaring in 1836, 'I am not an atheist, not a blasphemer, not an infidel' and in 1837 asserted that he was 'wholly, and in every respect a Christian'. Moving away from socialism and Chartism, a relocation that increasingly marginalized him, he adopted a Christian rationalism of his own devising.[182] Even Paine's most fervent follower of the 1820s found Paine's politics less and less appealing after 1832.

The conceptualization of radicalism and the retrospective appropriation of Paine

Carlile's views alienated him from a large part of the emerging radicalism of the 1820s. Writing from Dorchester gaol in 1821, he nailed his colours to a single, and already outdated, mast:

> The Writings of Thomas Paine, alone, form a standard for any thing worthy of being called Radical Reform. They are not Radical Reformers who do not come up to the whole of the political principles of Thomas Paine... There can be no Radical Reform short of what is commonly called a Republican form of Government... The advocates of universal suffrage, who talk about their affection and esteem for royal families, and titled legislators, and certain priests and religions, are deeply tinged either with timidity or hypocrisy and corruption... Below the principles of Thomas Paine there can be nothing but sham-fighting with the enemies of the liberties of mankind.

Carlile threatened: 'I will divide the country, or all who call themselves Reformers, upon these principles.' He insisted on an endorsement of Paine, 'the Reformer of

---

[182] Wiener, *Radicalism and Freethought*, 4, 101–2, 155, 217, 222.

Priestcraft, as well as Kingcraft'.[183] 'Those unwilling to conform to Paineite reasoning were, in effect, excommunicated' from Carlile's following.[184]

For Carlile, atheism and republicanism were the linked legacy of Paine. But by the late 1820s, 'the Paine–Carlile tradition had acquired a certain stridency and air of unreality'.[185] For Henry Hunt, founder in 1821 of a mass phenomenon, the Great Northern Union, dedicated to universal manhood suffrage, annual parliaments, and the secret ballot, this insistence on the salience of anti-religious ideology was a mistake for a grouping that included among its members many reforming Christians. Hunt denounced Carlile's position that 'no Reform can be of service till "*all religion* is destroyed"'; Hunt insisted: 'I believe the great mass of the Reformers are religious.' The result was that Carlile and Hunt 'were never reconciled', so that Carlile 'stood widely divorced from popular radicalism, culture and experience'.[186] But neither Hunt nor Carlile echoed exactly what Paine had demanded. Universal suffrage and annual parliaments, the mantra of the London Corresponding Society in the 1790s, had some way yet to run: Henry Hunt stood on that platform in the election for the Westminster constituency in 1818, but was soundly beaten. Soon, parliamentary reform expressed in terms other than republican ones was to develop into a central commitment for the cohort of 1832 in a way that it had never been for Paine. If English republicanism fell away after the Reform Act, it was not because monarchy and aristocracy were abolished but because republicanism's late eighteenth-century Deist and Paineite premises were overtaken by other reforming commitments.

Meanwhile, English freethinking survived. Reid had written in 1800 of 'the rancour of Infidel fanatics'.[187] Such remarks are often discounted as reflections of the author's vehemence; but such dismissal misses the centrality of anti-Christian discourse in both France and Britain from the 1790s into the nineteenth century. So Paine, the ardent and universalist Deist, was caught up in an assertive and particularist English secularism that he never sanctioned; Paine's affirmations in religion were often swamped by the atheists' negations. But he was not in England to see this happen, and there is no evidence that he appreciated the secularist ends to which his Deist teachings were put in his home country.

It would otherwise be a paradox that Paine's influence was most significant in England, the country least touched by the revolution for which he had called. There Paine indirectly fed a stream that merged in the 1820s into a new river, 'radicalism', a combination of universal suffrage, Ricardian economics, and militant

---

[183] John Belchem, *'Orator' Hunt: Henry Hunt and English Working-Class Radicalism* (Oxford, 1985), 149, 154.

[184] Epstein, *Radical Expression*, 119.

[185] Thompson, *Making of the English Working Class*, 763.

[186] Belchem, *Hunt*, 155, 157, 198. For the instinctive alliance with Carlile of John Gast, a radical and a Deist, see I. J. Prothero, *Artisans and Politics in Early Nineteenth-Century London: John Gast and his Times* (Folkestone, 1979). Gast supported a republic, a taxpayer franchise, and a single tax on income: 84–5, 88, 332.

[187] Reid, *Rise and Dissolution*, v.

atheism.[188] None of these three components were Paine's own. His advocacy of a wide (although never clearly defined) franchise came closest to the first, but had different origins, while he neither anticipated the economics of Ricardo nor subscribed to atheism. On the contrary, the Deist Paine became a small landowner.

Yet in the nineteenth century, British freethinkers typically abandoned Deism and adopted atheist principles. Secularists were often influenced by the negations of *The Age of Reason*, and kept it in print as a work of current relevance, but after Richard Carlile they drew from it conclusions very different from Paine's theism.[189] Carlile, however, was 'distinctly non-committal' about Paine's welfare schemes, not mentioning those in *Rights of Man*, and treating the proposal for death duties in *Agrarian Justice* as, in Carlile's words, merely 'the offspring of humanity and benevolence'. Consequently, Paine's 'social insurance proposals attracted little attention and no sustained commitment'. His long-term influence in the late nineteenth century was in such circles as the Secularism of Charles Bradlaugh, but 'on questions of social welfare, Bradlaugh was a dedicated follower of Malthus... The welfare legislation of the Liberal governments of 1906–14 owed nothing to the ideas of Paine or Condorcet.'[190]

To a considerable degree, Paine's memory was kept alive less by his followers, intellectually indebted to him, than by those who most denounced him. Yet these posthumous opponents misread Paine, importing him into their own day. In 1819 John Harford reacted against the effects of Carlile's reprinting of *The Age of Reason*, newspaper reports of it, and Carlile's trial: these

> have given, of late, an unusual currency to the name and to the opinions of Paine. The Radical Reformers are also grown bold enough to acknowledge him as their Apostle and their Idol. It therefore becomes a duty to expose the wickedness of this man's principles, and the corresponding enormity of his life.

The key term 'radicalism' did not feature in Harford's book of 1819, appearing only in its third edition of 1820. In 1819, however, he correctly appreciated that 'radical reformers' were committed to a clear programme: 'As to the scheme of universal Suffrage and annual Parliaments, a notion borrowed from Paine, which is the watchword of this party, it is so triumphantly absurd as hardly to justify a serious refutation.' But this programme was not borrowed from Paine: Harford projected it back onto him. Harford continued: 'It is impossible to overlook the striking resemblance which exists between the Revolutionists of 1793, and the Radicals of 1819.—They all belong to the same family, and are wedded to the same principles... The whole system of 1793, and that of 1819, are equally founded on

---

[188] J. C. D. Clark, 'How Ideologies are Born: The Case of Radicalism', in Clark, *Our Shadowed Present: Modernism, Postmodernism, and History* (London, 2004), 110–45.

[189] Edward Royle, *Victorian Infidels: The Origins of the British Secularist Movement 1791–1866* (Manchester, 1974); Susan Budd, *Varieties of Unbelief: Atheists and Agnostics in English Society 1850–1960* (London, 1977); Edward Royle, *Radicals, Secularists and Republicans: Popular Freethought in Britain, 1866–1915* (Manchester, 1980); David Berman, *A History of Atheism in Britain: From Hobbes to Russell* (London, 1988).

[190] Gareth Stedman Jones, *An End to Poverty? A Historical Debate* (London, 2004), 194, 210–11, citing R. Carlile, *The Life of Thomas Paine written purposely to bind with his writings* (2nd edn, London, 1821), 23.

Thomas Paine's doctrines of the Rights of Man.'[191] This analysis did not address how the world had changed: as has been shown, those changes seldom resulted from direct applications of Paine's ideas.

An Anglican clergyman, Francis Thackeray, argued similarly in 1831. He was moved by the 'frantic violence' of 'the labouring classes' at the time of the French Revolution of 1830: 'Who shall say that the late revolution, which commenced like that of 1789, with a professed horror of shedding human blood, may not proceed, like the latter, with fury and carnage, and terminate at length in despotism?' Thackeray, like Harford, launched a ferocious attack on Paine's character, but linked it with two strands of argument. First, he responded as had Edmund Burke to the three rights claimed by Richard Price in his sermon of 1789, Burke denying that 'nature' had engraved natural rights in the heart of man. Second, Thackeray criticized the proposals for social security payments in Paine's *Rights of Man. Part the Second*, arguing that the work of Robert Malthus had shown how such proposals would lead only to larger families. Nor was there a solution to poverty: 'there probably will be Poor unto the end of time.'

Yet Paine had never engaged in explicit controversy with Malthus, and Paine's social analysis had not anticipated Malthus's positions, first published in 1798. In his first edition Malthus had engaged with Godwin and Condorcet, not with Paine, despite sharing a publisher with him.[192] In Thackeray's vision of 1831, 'Every member of the political body is interested in preserving *Order against Anarchy*.'[193] Paine had never entered into such an argument, and had had no conception of the social dynamics of 'anarchy' in either the American or French Revolutions that might have identified order as being at risk during the revolutions he recommended.

Positive affirmations of Paine could still be heard. In 1837 the East London Democratic Association was founded, its manifesto declaring that its goal would be to advance the condition of the working class 'by disseminating the principles propagated by that great philosopher and redeemer of mankind, the Immortal Thomas Paine'.[194] Yet despite the extent of and the momentum behind the phenomenon soon known as Chartism, it is notable how seldom, and how perfunctorily,

---

[191] John S. Harford, *Some Account of the Life, Death, and Principles of Thomas Paine, together with Remarks on his Writings, and on their Intimate Connection with the Avowed Objects of the Revolutionists of 1793, and of the Radicals in 1819* (Bristol: J. M. Gutch, 1819), vi, 17–19. In 1819, the term 'radicalism' was also absent from Harford's appendix of writings of 'The Radicals', 85–93. Significantly, in the extended 3rd edition (Bristol, 1820), to which an anonymous reader alerted me, Harford wrote of 'Radicalism' that it had not dared go so far as to make men 'savage and barbarous', 90; of 'the tenets of Radicalism', 91, and of 'the spirit of Radicalism', 93. Such evidence supports my argument that 'radicalism' was conceptualized quite suddenly around the year 1820: it was not a logical extension of the older use of the substantive noun 'radical'.

[192] [Thomas Robert Malthus], *An Essay on the Principle of Population, as it affects the Future Improvement of Society, with Remarks on the Speculations of Mr Godwin, M. Condorcet, and other Writers* (London: J. Johnson, 1798). Paine featured only in the second edition of 1803.

[193] Francis Thackeray, *Order against Anarchy. Being a Reply to Thomas Paine's Attack upon the British Constitution, entitled 'The Rights of Man;'—with Observations addressed to all Classes of the Community, and Particularly Applicable to the Present Period* (London: C. J. G. and F. Rivington, 1831), v, 4, 9–12, 22, 29–30, 34–6.

[194] *Prospectus of the East London Democratic Association* (London, 1837), quoted in A. R. Schoyen, *The Chartist Challenge: A Portrait of George Julian Harney* (London, 1958), 14. Paine does not thereafter feature in Schoyen's book.

the name of Paine appears in the pages of its historians.[195] One recent historian has emphasized, instead, the role in Chartism of Thomas Spence and his ideas of land reform.[196] Paine was even repudiated in Bronterre O'Brien's *Poor Man's Guardian* for adhering to the French constitution of 1791, defending the middle classes against Robespierre's more extensive social reforms: 'There was nothing radical in Paine, he never saw to the bottom.'[197] Elsewhere Paine was remembered, honoured, toasted; but practical politics had moved on.

The French Revolution naturally cast a shadow over the British reformers and conservatives of the early nineteenth century, but Paine's name initially appeared seldom in arguments about the nature and significance of that French example; Paine's writings did not create a dominant image of the French Revolution for English-speaking readers until the growth of the new discipline of political science in the early twentieth century.[198] Similarly the example of America, an example that Paine came to urge by 1792, was influential in early nineteenth-century Britain, but not mainly because Paine had urged it: British Whigs could independently use the American republic to advance their tactical goals in Britain.[199]

Paine's influence on the mainstream of British political thought in the nineteenth century, conceived as a secular subject, was marginal: the revolution that Paine had sought never arrived in Britain, and Paine did not achieve canonical status in a tradition that he is thought to have inspired.[200] His works continued to be revered by freethinkers and reprinted by radical publishers,[201] but the debate had developed away from Paine's preoccupations of the 1750s. Perhaps this explains why British republicanism remained so weak, even after the rise of a powerful

---

[195] R. G. Gammage, *History of the Chartist Movement 1837–1854* (1854; 2nd edn, New York, 1969), 38; J. L. and Barbara Hammond, *The Age of the Chartists 1832–1854* (London, 1930), 18; David Goodway, *London Chartism 1838–1848* (Cambridge, 1982), 12–13, 23; Dorothy Thompson, *The Chartists* (London, 1984), 166, 243; 'so far as a more consistently humanist and universalist tone was present in the claim for democratic rights made by large numbers of Chartists than had been present among the advocates of manhood suffrage in the 1790s or the 1810s, it was the Owenite movement rather than Paine that had accomplished this transformation': Stedman Jones, *Languages of Class*, 126.

[196] Chase, 'Paine, Spence', 39. This revision 'challenges any view of labour history which sees Chartism as part of an unproblematic apostolic succession stretching back to Thomas Paine, mainly via Carlile'.

[197] Hedva Ben-Israel, *English Historians on the French Revolution* (Cambridge, 1968), 160–1; Stedman Jones, *Languages of Class*, 158.

[198] J. R. Dinwiddy, 'English Radicals and the French Revolution, 1800–1850', in F. Furet and M. Ozouf (eds), *The French Revolution and the Creation of Modern Political Culture*, iii, *The Transformation of Political Culture 1789–1848* (Oxford, 1989), 447–66, reprinted in Dinwiddy, *Radicalism and Reform*, 207–28.

[199] Gregory Claeys, 'The Example of America a Warning to England? The Transformation of America in British Radicalism and Socialism, 1790–1850', in Malcolm Chase and Ian Dyck (eds), *Living and Learning: Essays in Honour of J. F. C. Harrison* (Aldershot, 1996), 66–80; David Paul Crook, *American Democracy in English Politics 1815–1850* (Oxford, 1965); Paul Crook, 'Whiggery and America: Accommodating the Radical Threat', in Michael T. Davis (ed.), *Radicalism and Revolution in Britain, 1775–1848* (Basingstoke, 2000), 191–206.

[200] Many works of scholarship on British political thought in the nineteenth and early twentieth centuries find no need to discuss Paine. The absence of evidence is not necessarily evidence of absence; but sometimes it can be.

[201] David Vincent (ed.), *Testaments of Radicalism: Memoirs of Working Class Politicians 1790–1885* (London, 1977), 105, 113.

socialism. British society in the nineteenth century was not the world Paine had envisaged; his career is the most eloquent example in the recent history of political thought not of the realization and instantiation of universalist ideals but of the law of unintended consequences. That, ultimately, is why Paine's life and thought has a tragic quality.

The writings of Paine nevertheless retain a specialized currency, even into the present, and notably in two areas. One is the project of secularists, primarily British, to call on his support to promote a present-day crusade against 'religion', by which they normally mean Christianity.[202] The effectiveness of this retrospective recruitment is limited by evidence that Paine consistently repudiated atheism, which he termed 'a *nominal nothing* without principles',[203] and fervently advocated Deism. Second, some citizens of the United States seek to invoke Paine in order to place a more extensive interpretation on the present-day significance of the American Revolution.[204] This in turn has its problems, for Paine's politics in the new republic were substantially a continuation of his negative reaction against what he perceived as a threat of hereditary government, and he did little to extend his positive plans for the future development of American society beyond that English starting point. Paine, to his last days, was more a cultural Englishman than an assured cosmopolitan, but more a cosmopolitan than an American. He was not at all a Frenchman.

---

[202] A. J. Ayer, *Thomas Paine* (London, 1988); Christopher Hitchens, *Thomas Paine's Rights of Man: A Biography* (New York, 2006); Christopher Hitchens, *God Is Not Great: The Case Against Religion* (London, 2007).

[203] Paine, 'To the Citizens of the United States' (7 June 1805): *CW*, ii. 949.

[204] 'Paine remains a minor player in contemporary political, historical, and literary interpretations of the Revolution in large part because he continues to pose as much of a threat to elite intellectual and political power today as he did in 1776': Edward Larkin, *Thomas Paine and the Literature of Revolution* (Cambridge, 2005), 11.

Conclusion
The Age of Revolution, the Enlightenment, and the Dynamics of Reforming Traditions

Political theories are instinctively judged, whether appropriately or not, against widespread understandings of the results attributed to them: how did it all turn out? In recent decades, in which popular sovereignty acting through representative democracy and resting on natural rights premises could seem the new and cosmopolitan international norm, indeed to symbolize not just 'modern politics' but 'modernity' and the 'end of history', it was understandable that Paine should have been acclaimed as a pioneer, or even *the* pioneer. Yet these outcomes are in doubt; 'democracy' can now be a term conventionally applied to a variety of techniques by which the few govern the many, and the most bloody tyrannies designate themselves 'people's republics'. As some commentators on current politics are anxiously observing, 'history' is not turning out as expected. From the perspective of the present, it has been argued that these older assumptions have been significantly eroded around the world.[1] This loss of confidence justifies new questions: was that linked set of ideas really Paine's? Was it present at the heart of the 'age of revolution'? And was it ever accurately diagnosed?

Political historians have for some time disputed the assumption that the arrival of democracy was a matter of appealing in the 1790s, through newly populist language, to a wide audience hitherto excluded from political involvement and discourse. In Britain such popular involvement dated from the Reformation, and was continually reaffirmed in the crises of 1660–1760 by such figures as the Duke of Monmouth, Henry Sacheverell, and Charles Edward Stuart before it found new forms with activists like John Wilkes, John Cartwright, Lord George Gordon, Thomas Hardy, John Gale Jones, John Lovett, John Thelwall, William Cobbett, and Henry Hunt. Paine had some later devoted followers, like Richard Carlile and W. T. Sherwin, but they were increasingly unusual. From the 1640s to the 1840s the English, Welsh, Scots, and Irish needed no permission to judge for themselves, and did not explicitly or implicitly learn such a right from any pamphleteer, even from the most widely circulated of them all, Thomas Paine. He worked brilliantly within a tradition, but

[1] For cautions against 'our current sense of historical felicity' about 'liberal democracy' see John Dunn, *Breaking Democracy's Spell* (New Haven, 2014); 'there are stronger grounds today for us to view it far more sceptically: less as a serene, deeply adhesive, and self-subsistent totality, and more as a complex and largely opaque historical accident, the internal relations of which remain unstable, vulnerable, and replete with continuing danger', 2–4 and *passim*.

like all traditions it changed after his time. Political history, then, still has much to contribute to political science.

It is argued above that the age of revolution was not solely or even primarily a series of affirmations, or instantiations of general principles; it must be understood also as a series of particularist responses to circumstance, and of particularist negations. This, in turn, links with a re-evaluation of the most famous political writer of that age. To understand Paine's thought it has been necessary to contextualize him within an older chronological framework, within the diverse discourses available to him, and within wider geographical settings. It is inappropriate to censure him for not saying what he was in no intellectual position to say; it is necessary, to judge his achievement, to know what he was able to achieve.

Attending to the intellectual options of Paine's age shows how ideologies coined only after his death cannot provide such knowledge. Widening the conventional chronological framework makes it possible to dispense with the proleptic assumption that the 'age of revolution' was an intellectually self-sufficient era. Finally, comparisons between England, the American colonies, and France highlight the differences between those societies and warn against assuming that universalist generalizations (which were certainly made at the time) took precedence over particularist local circumstances. In the present day, when the specific and the pragmatic is so often reasserting itself against generalizing discourses alleged to date only from the 1970s,[2] this conclusion may be more widely, if reluctantly, received. If so, the study of Paine should remind readers that humanity does not have it in its power to begin the world over again.

The recent ascendancy of rights-based democracy has succeeded formerly hegemonic socialist models in the interpretation of Paine. Both schools are aspects of the intellectual history of the last century, and to understand them demands an understanding of the age of revolution. A renewed study of Paine is valuable since the assumption, though weakening, still survives that a great divide can be located somewhere in the late eighteenth century, a fundamental transition between a 'pre-modern' world and a 'modern' one. This master assumption is supported by an unremarked division within academe. Scholarship on the political thought of the eighteenth century and scholarship on that of the nineteenth often have few professional points of contact. A silent separation within the ranks of historians means that two adjacent but incompatible orthodoxies have grown up. Recent historiography on the political thought of the eighteenth century is dominated by the two discourses of 'the Enlightenment' and of natural rights theory, each supposedly finding its triumphant instantiation in the age of revolution; the historiography devoted to nineteenth-century political thought is written very differently as a series of intellectual responses to the advance of industrial society, the responses most obviously of utilitarianism and socialism. So constructed, these two intellectual worlds are quite different. Each is assumed to have been intellectually independent and self-referential.[3] Each nexus seems plausible in its own terms. But how the

---

[2] Samuel Moyn, 'The End of Human Rights History', *P&P* 233 (2016), 307–22.

[3] For an argument that 'nineteenth-century English political thought was distinct from that of the eighteenth... The political debates of the 1790s mark the conclusion of early modern political thinking

transitions from the first world to the second came about is a question seldom, if ever, asked.

The incompatibility between these two orthodoxies is, however, a problem. In neither utilitarianism nor socialism did natural rights play a central role. Jeremy Bentham, who dismissed natural rights as 'nonsense upon stilts', did not anticipate the notion of an Enlightenment, any more than did the early British socialists; even that learned historian of philosophy Karl Marx hardly used the German term *die Aufklärung*. In anglophone political thought, then, a large question emerges: how did eighteenth-century discourse, so depicted, turn into the political discourse of the nineteenth? One conventional argument is that the characteristic eighteenth-century Whig discourse of natural rights appropriately lost a battle in the 1790s against the advance of working-class radicalism; but this scenario becomes problematic when it is accepted that the 1790s did not witness 'the making of the English working class', and that 'radicalism' was a new ideology of *c.*1820 that had nothing to do with class formation.

This book suggests that the transitions to utilitarianism and socialism were not brought about by any cataclysmic confrontation between two rival systems of ideas during the age of revolution; there was no confrontation in the 1770s or the 1790s between natural rights and utilitarianism in which Paine might have played a key part as a champion of one discourse or an opponent of another. Instead, late eighteenth-century atheism developed to feed into British utilitarianism; Christianity survived Deism to help inspire British socialism. Neither development was significantly forwarded by human rights discourse or any defined Enlightenment discourse.[4] The heroic theory of the evolution of political thought does not fit this period.

Paine's insistence on the individual, as against the calls of revealed religion or of hierarchy, certainly mattered. But the anglophone political world also changed for other reasons than mass conversion to Paine's teaching. His wide currency derived from his speaking the older discourses of his societies more than from framing new discourses, adopted in the years that followed.[5] Paine died in America in 1809. An important phase of conceptual formation in Britain in the decades after 1815 did see the definition of the new ideologies of liberalism, radicalism, socialism, and conservatism; but this new cast list was more the filling of a vacuum than a contested displacement of incompatible but still vital older ideas, and these ideologies

---

in Britain because then one can discern the swan-song of seventeenth- and eighteenth-century discourses on contractarian conceptions of government and natural rights', see Mark Francis and John Morrow, *A History of English Political Thought in the Nineteenth Century* (London, 1994), 4, 7 and *passim*. Paine does not feature in this book.

[4] Natural rights discourse did not disappear entirely. By the mid-nineteenth century 'its shards and remnants could be adduced to support a bewildering variety of contradictory positions': Jeremy Waldron, 'The Decline of Natural Right', in Allen W. Wood and Songsuk Susan Hahn (eds), *The Cambridge History of Philosophy in the Nineteenth Century (1790–1870)* (Cambridge, 2012), 623–50, at 625. But its old ubiquity was over.

[5] For an argument that major changes in British political attitudes are to be dated to the 1850s rather than to the period from the 1780s to the 1840s see Boyd Hilton, *A Mad, Bad, and Dangerous People? England 1783–1846* (Oxford, 2006), 628ff.

arrived on one side of the Atlantic only.[6] One cause of this vacuum was the fading of universalist natural rights discourse, a decline that Paine did not prevent but that he might paradoxically have forwarded by his wide circulation and by the hostile reactions that this inspired. Paine was also innocent of the idea of 'the Enlightenment': this was a term of historiographical art widely adopted in anglophone discourse only from the mid-twentieth century, and was not available even to theorists in the eighteenth. Utilitarianism was not new: it was little more than an emphasis on, and finally a secular translation of, a principle widely entertained in a weak sense throughout eighteenth-century anglophone Christianity. In the history of political thought, evolution often offers a better model than revolution. So does the law of unintended consequences.

The leading practical problems of the early and mid-nineteenth century in Western Europe were ones that developed after the exhaustion of earlier discourses. But 'exhaustion' is only a metaphor, and further enquiry is needed. Two themes in particular, seemingly central to Paine's thought, display such a pattern of decline: natural rights, and republicanism.

It is still widely assumed that natural rights discourse was on an upward trend in the long eighteenth century; that it was a leading cause of the outbreak of the American and French Revolutions; and that it was centrally embodied in what later became known as the 'founding principles' of the new American and French republics. These episodes, examined outside of those republics' myths of origin, make that model problematic. A longer chronological perspective than just 'the age of revolution' shows that natural rights language reached its peak of effectiveness in the seventeenth century, not the eighteenth.[7] An examination of the 1770s and 1790s casts doubt on any fundamental transition in those years from particularist legal rights, 'the rights of Englishmen', to universalist human rights. In these respects, as in others, the American Revolution represented a throwback to older patterns of conflict and involved a re-run of older discourses, ignited not least by religious conflicts.[8] Even the French Revolution had its long antecedents in specifically French theological conflicts, and in the lasting local divisions caused by the wars of religion of the late sixteenth and early seventeenth centuries.[9]

Britain formed an arena whose political discourses were not overlaid by revolution in 1776 or 1789. Natural rights language proliferated but weakened in Britain during the eighteenth century as rights broadened into ubiquitous truisms. The very over-extension of rights in the 1790s diluted them to the point where they

---

[6] Historians still debate the question 'why was there no socialism in America?' But the same question can be asked of other European ideologies also.

[7] Richard Tuck, *Natural Rights Theories: Their Origin and Development* (Cambridge, 1979). For the antiquity of the discourse see Brian Tierney, *The Idea of Natural Rights: Studies on Natural Rights, Natural Law and Church Law 1150–1625* (Atlanta, 1997). In the eighteenth century, natural rights theory survived in an intellectually powerful form primarily in the German-speaking world: 174–7 and T. J. Hochstrasser, *Natural Law Theories in the Early Enlightenment* (Cambridge, 2000).

[8] Clark, *Language of Liberty, passim.*

[9] e.g. Mack P. Holt, *The French Wars of Religion, 1562–1629* (1995; 2nd edn, Cambridge, 2005); Dale K. Van Kley, *The Religious Origins of the French Revolution: From Calvin to the Civil Constitution, 1560–1791* (New Haven, 1996).

became shared rhetoric, uplifting but with less and less specific leverage. Paine, despite his frequent but usually undeveloped use of rights language, did not win any titanic struggle; he was a man of his age in appealing to premises that so many English-speaking people on both sides of the Atlantic already held.[10] But he could not rescue natural rights from the more revolutionary implications of the phrase 'the rights of man', implications widely resisted. From Thomas Paine, present-day readers can learn of the declining effectiveness of even widely accepted values.

Paine was evidently unaware that the natural rights tradition was dividing in the 1790s into theistic and atheistic branches, with major consequences for its long-term future. Because Paine's Deism was often (if wrongly) read by his contemporaries as atheism, he unintentionally helped undermine natural rights conceived in his own earlier terms as divine gifts. The French Revolution propagated a different conception of natural rights unindebted to divine intervention; but the course of that revolution acted widely to damage the idea. Even English reformers in the 1790s often moved away from the generalized 'rights of man' and fell back on the historic 'rights of Englishmen': yet this last was an older language of historic constitutionalism and was to have little future after the unanticipated consequences of the Reform Act of 1832.[11]

In the new American republic the development of political discourse was different from Britain's, for heightened talk of 'the rights of man' soon faded in the realities of war and national formation. The diverse and negotiable 'liberties' of the English common law were reified into a non-negotiable 'Liberty' and so created a 'civil religion' that treated the United States as unquestionably the realization of natural rights doctrine. This merely shut down attention to the debatable nature of rights. Over time, 'Liberty' became a rhetorical ratification of actually existing social forms and practices in the new republic rather than a series of calls for freedom from them. As 'Liberty' became a synonym for the totality of the pattern of life actually in place, claims came to be expressed in terms of 'civil liberties', practices allegedly already guaranteed by a homogeneous set of national values. Paine anticipated no such development. This reification was beyond the understanding of those who had employed mid-eighteenth-century natural rights doctrine; it was effected mainly by the impact of revolution and its associated demands for social solidarity, not by any inner logic of intellectual development.

If the account given in this book is justified, it is no longer possible to characterize the American or French Revolutions, in the broadest outlines, as rational, consensual reactions to natural rights denied by governments. In America the controversies of 1765–75 saw growing appeals to a religiously grounded right of resistance against a threat partly perceived in religious terms, partly in terms of constitutional disputes over the relation between centre and periphery; but these problems were not solved in the Articles of Confederation, in the Constitution of 1787, or in the test cases in the Supreme Court that followed. The result was a second and yet

---

[10] Paine made no significant lasting contribution to the intellectual development of the tradition. Appropriately, he does not feature in John Finnis, *Natural Law and Natural Rights* (Oxford, 1980).

[11] For which see Clark, *English Society*, 547–64.

more destructive civil war in 1861–5, nowhere anticipated in the writings of Paine or of the Founding Fathers. France, in turn, witnessed the affirmation of natural rights as a consequence, not a cause, of its Revolution, but there too rights quickly became claims and lost their glamour as those claims were expressed in the setting of civil and European war.

Paine's proposed solutions to the issues of conflict between denominations and between centre and periphery were to favour the widespread adoption of Deism and the establishment of a powerful central government in America and France. In the first, he was unsuccessful, since as a Deist he was not sensitive to the grounds of conflict between hitherto-traditional religious denominations and what these conflicts revealed about a still current, and shared, Trinitarianism. The second, the emergence of a powerful central government and an elective monarchy in the person of the American President (in France, the First Consul),[12] was a consequence of the debates of the Constitutional Convention of 1787 in which Paine was not present and in which debates he seems not to have been cited. Although an Englishman, he had not learned lessons from the problems of England's constitutional relations with Scotland and Ireland, and had not recognized both those problems in the forms they took in their transatlantic dimension. In 1775 the Thirteen Colonies still stood some chance of securing peaceful redress of grievances via the route of negotiation, urged by John Dickinson;[13] but Paine contributed to diverting events from negotiation into the pathway of civil war.

The American Revolution, then, was very Anglo-American, dominated by emphatic negations of the British monarchy and by Protestant Nonconformist religious discourse; as Paine's writings suggest, it did not in any strong sense of ideological inspiration or innovation lead into the early stages of the French Revolution, which generally looked to re-pristinize the monarchy and the national Church. If the key narrative in *Rights of Man* is de-attributed, the French Revolution can hardly now be conceived as, in the broadest terms, the ideological offspring of the American. It should be a truism, since the decline of Marxist and rights-based historiographies in the late twentieth century, that the French Revolution emerges as very French both in its particularist causes and in its particularist consequences. For deep-rooted historical reasons the French nation hardly followed Paine's tactical lead, and the Revolution hardly exemplified the adoption and instantiation of American ideas of natural rights: a secularized natural rights language was already at home in francophone culture before 1776. Revolution did, however, obviously occur. France became, if intermittently, a republic, and republicanism obviously spread in nineteenth-century Europe. What, then, of republicanism?

In the English-speaking world republicanism had been in decline since the 1650s, and had only a limited currency after 1688. After their Declaration of Independence Britain's American colonists were obliged to revitalize a now largely academic political

---

[12] F. H. Buckley, *The Once and Future King: The Rise of Crown Government in America* (New York, 2014).

[13] Jane E. Calvert, *Quaker Constitutionalism and the Political Thought of John Dickinson* (Cambridge, 2009).

tradition in a hurry; poorly prepared for that task, they launched a new republic embodying major constitutional flaws, with consequences evident in 1861–5. France in 1789–95 was similarly unsuccessful in establishing a workable republican polity, and its troubled history in the nineteenth century followed no steady path to a republican constitution.

In neither case did Paine contribute decisively to framing the structure of effective, stable republican systems; but nor did his contemporaries. Knowing little of the classics, he could make scant use of the histories of Greek or Roman republics. For him the dominant idea of republicanism derived from one recent and deliberately limited usage: in this usage, it signified only government for the public good, a widely adaptable but disastrously unspecific ideal. A theory of government built around a non-monarchical head of state was therefore only a default position, inevitable once monarchy and the hereditary principle were negated but not clear in its consequences. Paine's role was to help discredit both monarchy and the hereditary principle, but the later alternatives emerged more by chance than by design.

His religious commitments contributed. Paine carried forward and revitalized early eighteenth-century English Deism, but (perhaps in part by linking it with emergent late eighteenth-century biblical criticism) he revived Deism in a way that for many readers pointed to atheism rather than to his own passionate and philanthropic theism. Paine evidently did not appreciate that this was happening. The Deism that he re-launched therefore proved to be negative more than positive, particularist more than universalist: it was a powerful weapon in assaults, in England, on 'Church and state' and on the expressions of Trinitarian Christianity, but was limited in any positive contribution to British socialism (itself initially, in large part, a Christian response to atheist radicalism). Similarly, his Deism issued in a set of attitudes, now labelled individualism, that coexisted easily with free trade and therefore proved less useful to the collective moral sense of labourers who were increasingly being made aware of themselves as an interest group. Paine had an afterlife within that new creation, early nineteenth-century radicalism, but he played that posthumous role not least because his actual teaching had been misunderstood or misrepresented for later use.

In part because of the American and French Revolutions, republics are today commonplace around the world; but presidential systems have a high correlation with military dictatorships. A peaceful, benign Deism did not emerge as the denominational foundation for present-day republicanism, and Paine, despite his efforts, was not able to make it so.

This sequence of events draws attention to a more general truth. In the twentieth century, the new academic discipline of the history of political thought assembled a canon of major figures whose writings were conventionally read in terms of their affirmations; those affirmations were interpreted as cumulatively building 'modernity'. It is now necessary to recognize that in many cases those authors' negations were both prior in time, and to different degrees influential in shaping the content of their theories. Consequently, the discipline of the history of political thought now needs to extend balanced attention to both affirmations and negations. Readers may see in this book an argument for the deletion of Paine from that canon, but this would be a misconception. First, if the concept of a canon has validity, it should help identify many canons. Paine stood in no canon debating the implications of Aristotle's *Politics*, as some of his contemporaries into the 1790s still did; but he was certainly in a canon of those who debated the meaning of the revolutions of 1688, 1776, and 1789. Secondly, it is argued in this book that the canonical works do not explain the revolutions; rather, the wider political and ideological contexts of the societies have to be brought to bear in order to explain the 'canonical' texts themselves.

Paine's negations caught the imaginations of many people in North America, Britain, and Ireland (although fewer in France). He fought a series of campaigns against what he condemned as the hereditary principle in politics and in religion; the two were profoundly linked in ways that later became unfamiliar or forgotten. Conventional accounts of 'the Enlightenment' in terms of its affirmations presumed a natural affinity between reforming causes, and expected the champions of one cause in the eighteenth century to have identified with others also. These accounts embodied a projection backwards in time of a simplifying universalism. Paine saw no such affinity; he was necessarily unaware that the revolutionary changes for which he called were exemplifications of any unified position, much later summed up in the reified category 'the Enlightenment'. Indeed, Paine's thought shows how the absence of any such sense of common cause was one limitation on the effectiveness of a notion of 'the Enlightenment', when it was finally conceptualized.

Yet the expectation that Paine was committed to any linked set of causes only declares present-day assumptions, not Paine's. He was a man of extraordinary talents who played significant (though not dominating) roles in a series of extraordinary episodes. Like many other reformers, he took for granted most of his society's values and structures, dissenting only in a few, but important and clearly defined, respects. What were those respects? Paine inherited a dynastic political discourse of the early eighteenth century that he (like a few others, notably Jeremy Bentham) extended to a rejection of monarchy itself. He was not an atheist, as Bentham was. He was a Deist of the mid-eighteenth century who inferred from his Deism the illegitimacy of the hereditary principle; having identified that principle, he saw it everywhere, and fought against it in diverse campaigns the religious premises of which were nevertheless largely consistent.

The consistency of Paine's thought is therefore to be understood as much in its negations as in its affirmations. Fear and hatred drove the American and French Revolutions, as well as polite discussions of abstract principle; however unappealing, fear and hatred must be subjects for the historian, and must be related to the trajectories of such arguably epiphenomenal discourses as natural rights theory and republicanism. Nevertheless, negations were not timeless, however much reformers or their opponents wished to use them to construct traditions of thought and action and to draw support from the resulting myths.

What does the reforming tradition look like, when reconstructed in these terms? Paine's critique of monarchy, aristocracy, and Trinitarian Christianity came, after a few decades, to be marginal to the rapidly evolving internal social conflicts of the United States, Britain, and France. Their reformist politics derived from fast-changing practice and from continual ideological innovation rather than from the overriding force of revolutionary traditions; from the contributions of thousands of activists and authors, not from the few famous writers once credited with having set the terms of debate. Nevertheless, in Paine's lifetime his critique of the existing order was explosive. Paine was England's greatest revolutionary in the scope of his engagement with world-historical events and in the extensive implications of his political ideas. But not even such revolutionaries achieve negations as ambitious as Paine's.

APPENDIX

Paine De-attributions

The canon of writings attributed to Paine was significantly inflated in the late nineteenth century at a time when scholarship in this area was at an early stage.[1] Moncure Daniel Conway, an able historian and a pioneer in the field, was however also responsible for a series of unsupported attributions to Paine of anonymous items, attributions that misled subsequent generations. The short list of de-attributions below begins to redress the balance. It is, however, only a provisional list. Further attributions and de-attributions may emerge from a computer analysis of the prose styles of Paine and his leading contemporaries currently being undertaken by a team at Iona College; I shared drafts of this appendix with the team, and was assured that I and they were in agreement. What follows does not report the conclusions of that project's quantitative research, but my own; my conclusions are based on traditional methods of contextual analysis, and are open to correction as more is learned in this field.

Weight should be given to the essays printed in an early edition, *The Works of Thomas Paine* (2 vols, Philadelphia: James Carey, 1797), for which Carey asked the publisher Robert Aitken to identify Paine's anonymous essays in the *Pennsylvania Magazine* for 1775. Of major pieces Carey reprinted only 'To the Public', 'To the Publisher of the Pennsylvania Magazine', 'Useful and Entertaining Hints', 'New Anecdotes of Alexander the Great', 'The Snow Drop and the Critic', 'An Account of the Burning of Bachelor's Hall', and 'Farmer Short's Dog Porter'. The essays de-attributed below were not included in Carey's edition.

Several scholars have previously expressed cautions about the canon hitherto attributed to Paine.[2] In this book I have found it appropriate to go beyond their reservations to a more extensive reinterpretation.

'Humanus' letters
Published in the *Sussex Weekly Advertiser* (June 1772, 9 October 1773), signed 'Humanus'. Attributed to Paine in Colin Brent, 'Thirty Something: Thomas Paine at Bull House in Lewes 1768–74—Six Formative Years', *Sussex Archaeological Collections* 147 (2009), 153–67. No evidence links these letters with Paine; their prose style is unlike his; he nowhere else used a Latinate pen name.

'A Forester' articles
Published in the *Sussex Weekly Advertiser* (1772–3) signed 'A Forester' (this was the pen name Paine used for his own essays in the *Pennsylvania Journal* of 3 April–8 May 1776: *CW*, ii. 60–87). Attributed to Paine in G. Hindmarch, 'Thomas Paine: The Methodist Influence', *Bulletin of the Thomas Paine Society* 6 (1979), 59–78, but de-attributed in George Spater, 'The Author of the "A Forester" Articles', *Bulletin of the Thomas Paine Society* 7 (1982), 53–5.

---

[1] For a similar deflation of the Defoe canon, see P. N. Furbank and W. R. Owens, *Defoe De-Attributions: A Critique of J. R. Moore's Checklist* (London, 1994).
[2] Notably Aldridge, *American Ideology*, 286–91.

'A Dialogue between General Wolfe and General Gage in a Wood near Boston'

First published in the *Pennsylvania Journal* (4 Jan. 1775); attributed in Conway (ed.), *Writings*, i. 10–13 and *CW*, ii. 47–9. Paine disembarked in Philadelphia from the *London Packet* on 30 November 1774 suffering from an acute fever, probably typhus. He is unlikely to have been physically able to make contacts with the press and to write such an essay in time for its publication. The article praised three army officers: William, Baron Blakeney (1671/2–1761) was most famous for his defence of Minorca in 1756; William Augustus, Duke of Cumberland (1721–65), remembered partly as the victor of Culloden in 1746, partly as the British commander in Germany during the Seven Years War; and John Manners, Marquess of Granby (1721–70), who fought in Germany during the Seven Years War, notably at the battle of Minden. Paine did not display such knowledge, and elsewhere vilified Cumberland. The essay shows an interest in the transatlantic dispute that Paine recorded was awakened in himself only later, by the battles of Lexington and Concord on 19 April. No evidence connects Paine with this essay.

'African Slavery in America'

Published in the *Pennsylvania Journal* (8 Mar. 1775), attributed in Conway (ed.), *Writings*, i. 4–9 and *CW*, ii. 15–19. De-attributed in Hazel Burgess, *Thomas Paine: A Collection of Unknown Writings* (Houndmills, 2010), 6. Foner's edition omitted the salutation (printed by Conway) with which the anonymous author had addressed the article to the editors of the *Journal*: 'Messrs. BRADFORD, *Please to insert the following, and oblige yours* A. B.' This suggests the Pennsylvania Quaker, anti-slavery activist and author Anthony Benezet. The pamphlet's first footnote appealed to an array of learned sources largely beyond Paine's repertoire in 1774: 'Dr. [William] Ames, [Richard] Baxter, [James] Durham, [John] Locke, [Gershom] Carmichael, [Francis] Hutcheson, [baron] Montesquieu, and [William] Blackstone, [Robert] Wallace, etc. etc. [William Warburton] Bishop of Gloucester.' The author wrote of 'our religion' as Christianity, and claimed that the slave trade had been carried on 'in opposition to the Redeemer's cause': the Deist Paine never wrote in such terms. Nor did Paine echo the author's objection: 'With what consistency, or decency they [the colonists] complain so loudly of attempts to enslave them, while they hold so many hundred thousands in slavery.' The syntax, in addition, is not Paine's.

'Reflections on the Life and Death of Lord Clive'

Published in the *Pennsylvania Magazine* (Mar. 1775), signed 'ATLANTICUS'. Attributed in Conway (ed.), *Writings*, i. 29–35 and *CW*, ii. 22–7. J. M. Opal, '*Common Sense* and Imperial Atrocity: How Tom Paine Saw South Asia in North America', *Common-place* 8 (July 2009), <http://www.common-place.org/vol-09/no-4/forum/opal.shtml>, argues that Paine was converted to hostility to the British empire by the publicity given in 1772–4 to Robert Clive's maladministration in India. But this rests chiefly on Opal's attribution to Paine of 'Reflections on the Life and Death of Lord Clive', and of a second anonymous paragraph, 'A Serious Thought' (de-attributed below). Although Paine may have read these articles, his authorship has not been established. Some of their phrases were echoed in Paine's 'Forester's Letter' III (1776), citing the same incidents proving 'the cruelties practised by the British army in the East Indies' and similarly referring as his authority to 'the Proceedings of the Select Committee on Indian Affairs' (*CW*, ii. 76–7), but this may only indicate Paine's having read the paragraphs of 'ATLANTICUS' and 'HUMANUS', not Paine's authorship of either. 'Reflections on the Life and Death of Lord Clive' seems unlike Paine's syntax and vocabulary. A. O. Aldridge recorded of this piece that 'there are circumstances which place the attribution in doubt': *American Ideology*, 287.

'A Serious Thought'

Published in the *Pennsylvania Journal* (18 Oct. 1775), signed 'HUMANUS'. Attributed in Conway (ed.), *Writings*, i. 65–6 and *CW*, ii. 19–20. Paine never elsewhere wrote to the press with indignation equal to that of HUMANUS against the slave trade; nor did Paine echo the religious language of HUMANUS about 'the great cause of the King of kings', or demand the setting of 'Christian examples to the Indians' of the Orient. HUMANUS demanded that the first act of an independent America be 'an act of continental legislation, which shall put a stop to the importation of Negroes for sale, soften the hard fate of those already here, and in time procure their freedom': Paine had time until he left for France in 1787 to call for such legislation, but did not do so. The prose of 'A Serious Thought' makes use of repeated dashes, a stylistic convention that Paine did not use.

'Cupid and Hymen'

First published in the *Pennsylvania Magazine* (Mar. 1775); attributed in Conway (ed.), *Writings*, i. 36–9 and *CW*, ii. 1115–18. It seems to have been attributed to Paine because of its proximity in the magazine to two other anonymous essays, 'An Occasional Letter on the Female Sex' and 'Reflections on Unhappy Marriages'. The de-attribution of those two pieces leaves 'Cupid and Hymen' without any obvious relation to Paine's output. The twee style is wholly unlike Paine's. The vocabulary and syntax are not his. No evidence connects Paine with this essay.

'Duelling'

First published in the *Pennsylvania Magazine* (May 1775); attributed in Conway (ed.), *Writings*, i. 40–5 and *CW*, ii. 28–32. The syntax is not Paine's; nor is the vocabulary ('postulata', 'irrefragable'). No evidence connects Paine with this essay.

'Reflections on Titles'

First published in the *Pennsylvania Magazine* (May 1775). Attributed in Conway (ed.), *Writings*, i. 46–7 and *CW*, ii. 33–4. Paine in *Common Sense* was shortly to repudiate the hereditary principle, but there made no use of criticism of titles as such when he might easily have done so. The epigram from Whitehead that precedes this piece suggests an author with more knowledge of recent literature than Paine possessed. The syntax is not his. No evidence connects Paine with this essay.

'The Dream Interpreted'

Published in the *Pennsylvania Magazine* (May 1775); attributed in Conway (ed.), *Writings*, i. 48–50 and *CW*, ii. 50–2. The fanciful imagery resembles nothing else in Paine's writings; the syntax is not Paine's; it was signed 'Bucks County', a place with which Paine had no association. No evidence connects Paine with this essay.

'Reflections on Unhappy Marriages'

First published in the *Pennsylvania Magazine* (June 1775); attributed in Conway (ed.), *Writings*, i. 51–4 and *CW*, ii. 1118–20. It was de-attributed by Edward R. Pitcher, *The Pennsylvania Magazine, or American Monthly Museum, 1775–1776: An Annotated Index of Sources, Signatures, and First Lines of Literary Sources* (Lewiston, NY, 2001), 97, who showed 'Unhappy Marriages' to have been an essay copied from the London *Gentleman's Magazine* 9 (May 1739).

'Thoughts on Defensive War'

First published in the *Pennsylvania Magazine* (July 1775). Attributed in Conway (ed.), *Writings*, i. 55–8 (as 'Probably by Paine') and *CW*, ii. 52–5. It 'cannot conclusively be attributed to Paine, but the probabilities of his authorship are high': Aldridge, *American Ideology*, 31. The argument that 'political as well as spiritual freedom is the gift of God through Christ' is hardly consistent with Paine's Deism; nor is the defence of 'the church militant' and 'the visible church'. The syntax is not strongly reminiscent of Paine's. No evidence connects Paine with this essay.

'An Occasional Letter on the Female Sex'

First published in the *Pennsylvania Magazine* (Aug. 1775); attributed in Conway, *Writings*, i. 59–64 and *CW*, ii. 34–8. This is de-attributed in Frank Smith, 'The Authorship of "An Occasional Letter on the Female Sex"', *American Literature* 2 (November 1930), 277–80 and Mary Catherine Moran, *'L'Essai sur les femmes/Essay on Women*: An Eighteenth-Century Transatlantic Journey', *History Workshop Journal* 59 (2005), 17–32. They demonstrate that the text was taken from William Russell's 'Preface' to *Essay on the Character, Manners, and Genius of Women in Different Ages, Enlarged from the French of M. Thomas* (2 vols, Philadelphia: R. Aitken, 1774), itself taken from Antoine-Léonard Thomas, *Essai sur le caractère, les moeurs, et l'esprit des femmes dans les différens siècles* (Paris, 1772). Foner knew of Smith's work but nevertheless included the essay on the insufficient ground that 'it indicates his [Paine's] interest as editor of the magazine in the subject, and because some of the language of the essay is his'. No evidence survives on Paine's exact role in determining the contents of the *Pennsylvania Magazine* and only one much later report that he was ever its editor; throughout his career he showed little interest in the rights of women. It remains to be proved whether any phrases were Paine's. The *Pennsylvania Magazine* version was prefixed by an epigraph from Otway, not in Russell's edition; since Paine nowhere else referred to Otway, this may suggest another hand in the choice of this article for reprinting, presumably that of the actual editor—who was probably Aitken.

'A Dialogue between the Ghost of General Montgomery Just arrived from the Elysian Fields; and an American Delegate, in a Wood near Philadelphia'

Attributed in Conway (ed.), *Writings*, i. 161–7 and *CW*, ii. 88–93. This essay first appeared, anonymously, in *The Pennsylvania Packet, or, the General Advertiser* on 19 February 1776. It was republished as a pamphlet by Robert Bell the same year, and was also reprinted by him as an appendix to his second edition of *Common Sense*: this seemed to later readers conclusive proof of Paine's authorship. Yet Paine had by the time the second edition appeared broken from Bell, the first publisher of *Common Sense*, after a dispute over royalties; Bell was unlikely to have had private knowledge of Paine's authorship; and Bell was seeking to pad out his own edition to compete with the genuinely extended editions of *Common Sense* produced by Paine's new publishers, W. and T. Bradford. Although 'A Dialogue' urged independence, as did Paine, its range of reference was not Paine's. It hailed 'the immortal Montesquieu'; Paine used no such praise of him (the passage in *Rights of Man* that did so was not, it is suggested below, by Paine). It cited the stance on America of a succession of British politicians—Lord Chatham, Lord North, the Marquis of Rockingham, John Wilkes, the Duke of Grafton, and Lord Lyttelton—in ways that Paine did not elsewhere do. Paine never invoked 'Aristides, Epaminodas, Pericles, Scipio, Camillus and a thousand other illustrious Grecian and Roman heroes'. Nor did he elsewhere argue that American independence would be 'a jubilee to Hampden—Sidney—Russell—Warren—Gardiner—Macpherson—Cheeseman', that is: John Hampden (1595–1643), MP, opponent of Charles I in the Ship Money and other controversies; Algernon Sidney (1623–83) and William, Lord Russell (1639–83), Whig politicians executed under Charles II and hailed as martyrs by the Whigs. Warren may be John Warren (1621–96), a clergyman who became a Congregationalist after the Restoration; James Gardiner (1686–1745) was an army officer, killed resisting the Jacobite rising at the battle of Prestonpans when his troops deserted him but made famous by Philip Doddridge's *Some Remarkable Passages in the Life of . . . Colonel James Gardiner* (1747). Captain John McPherson and Captain Cheeseman were aides-de-camp to the American General Richard Montgomery; they all died in the failed American attempt to conquer Canada in December 1775. None of them were figures on whom Paine greatly relied in writings known to be his. The author praised 'The revolution' of 1688; Paine elsewhere condemned it. The author wrote of George III as 'a ROYAL CRIMINAL', which is reminiscent of Paine in *Common Sense*, but this may only show the currency of such language, or suggest that Paine may have read the article.

The People the Best Governors: or a Plan of Government Founded on the Just Principles of Natural Freedom (no place, ?Boston, 1776)

This pamphlet has formerly been attributed to Paine in the Library of Congress catalogue: Claeys, *Paine*, 61. Like *Common Sense*, it argued that the Jews '*might have continued in that state of liberty, had they not desired a King*', [3]. But it displayed knowledge of the classical world beyond Paine's, 4, 10. It proposed that no person hold public office who did not believe in God, 'and that the bible is his revealed word', 11: Paine disagreed. Its syntax is not Paine's.

'Retreat Across the Delaware'

First published in the *Pennsylvania Journal* (29 Jan. 1777); attributed in Conway (ed.), *Writings*, i. 381–3 and *CW*, ii. 93–6. Paine did not elsewhere publish detailed accounts of troop movements; the syntax is not his. No evidence connects this essay with Paine.

'Candid and Critical Remarks on a Letter signed Ludlow'

Published in the *Pennsylvania Journal* (4 June 1777), signed 'Common Sense'. Attributed in *CW*, ii. 272–7. This essay debated the forthcoming Pennsylvania constitution. But it argued that 'were all the *great natural* rights, or principles . . . to be admitted [i.e. carried over from a state of nature to "civil government"], it would be impossible that any government could be formed thereon', 274. Paine argued that many natural rights did carry over to civil society. No evidence connects this essay with Paine.

Preamble to the Act Passed by the Pennsylvania Assembly, March 1, 1780

Attributed in Conway, *Writings*, ii. 29–30 and *CW*, ii. 21–2, where it is entitled 'Emancipation of Slaves'; de-attributed, with reasons, by Keane, *Paine*, 572–3 and James V. Lynch, 'The Limits of Revolutionary Radicalism: Tom Paine and Slavery', *PMHB* 123 (1999), 177–99, at 183.

'For The-Times'

Published in *The Times*, 13 February 1789. Attributed in Burgess, *Thomas Paine*, 65–6. De-attributed by Mark Philp, *EHR* 126 (2011), 185–7. The essay was signed 'Common Sense'; but this was a pen name often used at the time, and Paine had no monopoly of it. The author wrote of George III as 'our gracious king'; lavished effusive praise on the Prime Minister, William Pitt; and condemned the 'morals' of the Foxite Whigs. Paine did none of these. No evidence links Paine with this essay, and he is not known to have published in *The Times*. The syntax is not Paine's.

Rights of Man (1791), a passage

Rights of Man was undoubtedly by Paine, and previous editors have therefore not noticed that it contains a key passage which appears to be not solely his own work ('The despotism of Louis XIV . . . and to act in unison with its object': *CW*, i. 298–313). The 6,000-word passage contains a detailed high-political narrative of the approach to the French Revolution; but Paine was consistently uninterested in politics, calling it 'Jockeyship'.[3] The section briefly mentions earlier French monarchs, 'philosophers' like Montesquieu[4] and Voltaire[5] and economists like Quesnay and Turgot, but picks up the story in detail from 1778: 'The French officers and soldiers who after this went to America, were eventually placed in the school of Freedom, and learned the practice as well as the principles of it by heart', *CW*, i. 299–300.

---

[3] Paine, *The Age of Reason* (1794): *CW*, i. 496.

[4] Paine cited Montesquieu once, in 1782, but only quoted from 'a former declaration of Congress' rather than from the original: *CW*, ii. 344. There were no other explicit citations in Paine's published works.

[5] Paine cited Voltaire once, in 1776: *CW*, i. 53. There were no other explicit citations in Paine's published works.

This was, in brief, the interpretation of Lafayette, who served in the French army in America and is the hero of this section. He was Paine's probable source for its account of court intrigues surrounding figures like Necker, Calonne, the comte d'Artois, the Archbishop of Toulouse, the ducs de la Rochefoucauld and de Luxembourg, and the vicomte de Noailles, up to the taking of the Bastille and the choice of Lafayette himself 'to preside in the National Assembly' in July 1789. Paine cannot have had personal knowledge of these intrigues. He cited, 308, a French book, *L'Intrigue du Cabinet*, that he is unlikely to have found, or translated, without help: this was evidently Louis-Pierre Anquetil, *L'Intrigue du cabinet sous Henri IV et Louis XIII terminée par la Fronde* (4 vols, Paris: Moutard, 1780). Paine admitted: 'N.B. Since the taking of the Bastille, the occurrences have been published; but the matters recorded in this narrative are prior to that period; and some of them, as may easily be seen, can be but very little known', *CW*, i. 317; this suggests that Paine drew on a source. The syntax of the passage, *CW*, i. 298–313, is not Paine's, although if he transcribed another document he presumably put some of it into his own words.

Rights of Man (1791), a translation

Paine included an English translation of the *Déclaration des droits de l'homme et du citoyen*: Paine, *Rights of Man* (1791): *CW*, i. 314. But this was almost identical with the English translation in Richard Price's *A Discourse on the Love of our Country* (1789), appendix, 6. Price's own fluency in French is in doubt, and he was probably supplied with the translation by another. Price and Paine may independently have copied from an English source. However, there was no separate publication of an English translation of the *Déclaration* in 1789–91, which makes it likely that Paine copied the text from Price's widely known *Discourse*.

Reflections on the Present State of the British Nation by British Common Sense (London: James Ridgway, 1791); also published as *British Common Sense; or, Reflections on the Present State of the British Nation* (London: W. Miller, 1791)

Attributed in Burgess, *Thomas Paine*, 71–132. De-attributed by Mark Philp, *EHR* 126 (2011), 185–7. The author wrote of himself as 'an individual but little known, stiling himself *Common Sense*', 5; by that date Paine saw himself as an international celebrity. The title page carried a Latin tag from Horace, and the author showed a knowledge of Latin phrases and figures elsewhere unmatched by Paine, 14, 33, 52, 76, 92, 103, 117, 124. He showed a detailed knowledge of forms of crime and poverty that Paine did not elsewhere echo, e.g. 28. The author wrote scathingly of 'the idle, noxious poor' and recommended the entire abolition of the poor relief system in favour of a scheme of state-organized labour for 'breaking in barren lands' to fit them for agriculture, a reform which would produce an end to 'weak minded charity'. After its institution, 'giving charity to a vagrant beggar' would become a crime, 47, 59, 61; this was not Paine's plan. 'Common Sense' was an often-used pen name. No evidence connects this essay with Paine. Its leaden syntax was far from Paine's.

A Letter from Common Sense, addressed to the King and People (London: Printed for the Author, and sold by J. Bew . . . and J. Debrett, [1791])

Attributed in Burgess, *Thomas Paine*, 133–46. De-attributed by Mark Philp, *EHR* 126 (2011), 185–7. The author hailed Britain's as 'a form of government the most perfect under heaven', 5; 'the constitution of this country is formed of three parts, each part possessing distinct rights'; George III was 'immaculate as virtue, and without a fault', 11, 30. Problems had been found 'not in the constitution . . . not in sovereignty , , , not in defective laws' but in the 'popular insanity' inspired by Wilkes and Fox, 6. Fox was guilty of 'an endeavour to establish a democratical power', 31. Paine took opposite views. The author provided a commentary on high-political events from the end of Lord North's administration, 16–28, of which Paine can have known little. He offered an offhand comment opposite to Paine's deepest commitments: 'The deist in religion, and the sophist in politics . . . bewilder reason in the chaos of uncertainty' 31. 'Common Sense' was an often-used pen name. No evidence connects this essay with Paine. Its syntax was not Paine's.

Old Truths and Established Facts, being an Answer to a Very new Pamphlet indeed! (?London, ?1792)

Signed 'Vindex'. Attributed in Claeys, *Paine*, 27, 37. The pamphlet is wholly a discussion of the African slave trade, and a defence of 'The Society for Abolition', that is, the Society for Effecting the Abolition of the Slave Trade, founded in London on 22 May 1787. There is no evidence for Paine's membership of the Society; he nowhere displayed the detailed knowledge of its affairs revealed in this pamphlet. It praised anti-slavery MPs as 'Gentlemen of the most distinguished abilities in the House of Commons', and denied that abolition 'involves any thing hostile to the present Constitution of Great Britain', 4, not known to be sentiments of Paine. Its syntax is significantly different from Paine's.

'Plan of a Declaration of the Natural, Civil and Political Rights of Man'

Attributed in Conway (ed.), *Writings*, iii. 128–31 under the title 'Declaration of Rights' and *CW*, ii. 558–60. This document reads like that of one of Paine's French associates, at the time when the new Convention was drawing up an impractically elaborate constitution in late 1792. Paine may have had some input into it, but it does not bear the marks of a composition by him. Foner omitted Conway's note: 'The present translation is from "Oeuvres Complètes de Condorcet," tome xviii'; Condorcet may have been the author. No evidence connects Paine with this essay. Indeed some of its clauses—'26. The national sovereignty is one, indivisible, imprescriptible and inalienable. 27. It resides essentially in the entire people, and each citizen has an equal right to concur in its exercise'—contradicted Paine's idealized internationalism of a similar period: Paine, *Address to the People of France* (1792), in *CW*, ii. 537–40.

Ten Minutes Advice to the People of England, On the Two Slavery-Bills Intended to be Brought into Parliament in the Present Sessions ([London, 1795])

Attributed in Burgess, *Thomas Paine*, 149–54. De-attributed by Mark Philp, *EHR* 126 (2011), 185–7. A protest against what were passed as the Treasonable and Seditious Practices Act and the Seditious Meetings Act. The text is signed 'COMMON SENSE 12th November, 1795'. 'Common Sense' was a frequently used pen name, which Paine could not monopolize. After his departure for France and his conviction for publishing *Rights of Man. Part the Second* Paine had no reason for concealing his identity, and good reason for publishing with his own name. Paine did not elsewhere protest against these acts. No evidence connects Paine to this pamphlet. The syntax is not Paine's.

Bibliography

CITED WORKS BY PAINE

Listed in date order. The author's name in square brackets signifies that the work was initially published anonymously. Paine's works are often given inaccurate titles in recent scholarship (e.g. *The Rights of Man: Part One*); the published titles are given here.

[Paine], *The Case of the Officers of Excise; With Remarks on the Qualifications of Officers; and on the Numerous Evils arising to the Revenue, From the Insufficiency of the Present Salary. Humbly addressed to the Hon. and Right Hon. Members of Both Houses of Parliament* (no place, no printer, [Lewes: William Lee, 1772]; 2nd edn, London: J. S. Jordan, 1793; 3rd edn, London: W. T. Sherwin, 1817). *CW*, ii. 3–15 (where a signature, 'Thomas Paine', is added at the end of the text which was absent in the original).

[Paine], 'The Magazine in America', *Pennsylvania Magazine* (24 Jan. 1775), attributed to Paine in *CW*, i. 1109–13

[Paine], *Common Sense; Addressed to the Inhabitants of America, On the following interesting Subjects. I. Of the Origin and Design of Government in general, with concise Remarks on the English Constitution. II. Of Monarchy and Hereditary Succession. III. Thoughts on the present State of American Affairs. IV. Of the present Ability of America, with some miscellaneous Reflections* (Philadelphia: R. Bell, 1776). Published on 9 or 10 Jan. *CW*, i. 3–46

[Paine], 'To the Representatives of the Religious Society of the People called Quakers' (1776), part of the Appendix to the third edition of *Common Sense* (Philadelphia: W. and T. Bradford, 1776). *CW*, ii. 55–60

[Paine], *Four Letters on Interesting Subjects* (Philadelphia: Steiner and Cist, 1776). Not in *CW*

[Paine], 'The Forester's Letters' [attributed collective title], four essays printed in the *Pennsylvania Journal* for 3, 10, 24 Apr. and 8 May 1776, each signed 'The Forester'. *CW*, ii. 60–87

'To the People', *Pennsylvania Gazette* (26 June 1776): attributed to Paine in Keane, *Paine*, 137. Not in *CW*

[Paine], 'To the People' [attributed title], *Pennsylvania Packet* (18 Mar. 1777), signed 'Common Sense'. *CW*, ii. 269–72

[Paine], *The American Crisis*, the title used for the first five of a numbered series of pamphlets, plus one entitled *The Crisis Extraordinary* and two entitled *A Supernumerary Crisis*, between Dec. 1776 and Apr. 1783. The main series was titled *The American Crisis. Number I [et seq.]. By the Author of Common Sense*. The last was titled *The Last Crisis, Number XIII*. Some carried a subtitle; from no. II they often appeared with a printer's name: Philadelphia, Styner & Cist. Each is signed at the end 'Common Sense', and dated. For the publishing history see Paine, *Collected Writings*, ed. Eric Foner (New York, 1955), 854–8; Aldridge, *American Ideology*, 240–53. *CW*, i. 48–239

[Paine], 'A Serious Address to the People of Pennsylvania on the Present Situation of their Affairs' [attributed collective title], four essays printed in the *Pennsylvania Packet*, 1, 5, 10, 12 Dec. 1778, unsigned. *CW*, ii. 277–302

[Paine], *Public Good, Being An Examination Into the Claim of Virginia to the Vacant Western Territory, and Of the Right of The United States to the Same. To which is Added, Proposals for laying off a new State, to be Applied as a Fund for Carrying on the War, or Redeeming the*

National Debt. By the Author of Common Sense (Philadelphia: John Dunlap, 1780). *CW*, ii. 303–33

Letter Addressed to the Abbe Raynal on the Affairs of North-America: In which the Mistakes in the Abbe's Account of the Revolution of America are Corrected and Cleared Up. By Thomas Paine, M.A. of the University of Pennsylvania, and author of the pamphlet and other publications, entitled, 'Common Sense' (Philadelphia: Printed by Melchior Steiner... and sold by Robert Aitken, 1782; reprinted London: C. Dilly, 1782). [In both editions, 'Abbe' was printed without an acute accent.] *CW*, ii. 211–63

[Paine], 'Six Letters to Rhode Island' [attributed collective title], six essays published in the *Providence Gazette*, 21 Dec. 1782–1 Feb. 1783, each with its separate title and each signed 'A Friend to Rhode-Island and the Union'. *CW*, ii. 333–66

Thoughts on the Peace, and the Probable Advantages thereof to the United States of America (Philadelphia; reprinted London: J. Stockdale, 1783). A reprint of *The American Crisis*, XIII

'To a Committee of the Continental Congress' [attributed title] [Oct 1783]. *CW*, ii. 1226–42

Dissertations on Government, the Affairs of the Bank, and Paper-Money. By the Author of Common Sense (Philadelphia: Charles Cist, 1786). *CW*, ii. 367–414

Prospects on the Rubicon. Or, An Investigation into the Causes and Consequences of the Politics to be Agitated at the Meeting of Parliament (London: J. Debrett, 1787). Signed 'Thomas Paine'. *CW*, ii. 621–50

Rights of Man: Being an Answer to Mr Burke's Attack on the French Revolution. By Thomas Paine, Secretary for Foreign Affairs to Congress in the American War, and Author of the Work Intitled Common Sense (London: J. Johnson, 1791; reprinted London: J. S. Jordan, 16 Mar. 1791). *CW*, i. 243–344

Address and Declaration, of the Friends of Universal Peace and Liberty, held at the Thatched House Tavern, St. James's Street, August 20th. 1791. By Thomas Paine, Author of the Works intitled Common Sense, and the Rights of Man (no place, no printer [London, 1791]). *CW*, ii. 534–7

Opinion de Thomas Paine sur l'affaire de Louis Capet, adressée au Président de la Convention Nationale. Imprimée par ordre de la Convention Nationale (Paris, Jan. 1792)

Rights of Man. Part the Second. Combining Principles and Practice. By Thomas Paine, Secretary for Foreign Affairs to Congress in the American War, and Author of the Work entitled Common Sense; and the First Part of the Rights of Man (London: J. S. Jordan, 16 Feb. 1792). *CW*, i. 345–458

A Letter To Mr Secretary Dundas. In Answer to His Speech on the Late Proclamation. By Thomas Paine (London: J. Parsons, 1792). *CW*, ii. 446–57

A Letter to Mr Henry Dundas, one of His Majesty's Principal Secretaries of State and Treasurer of the Navy, in Answer to his Speech on the late excellent Proclamation. First Published in a Patriotic Paper entitled The Argus. By Thomas Paine, Author of Common Sense, A Letter to the Abbe Raynal, A Letter to the Marquis of Lansdown, and Rights of Man (London: James Ridgway, 1792)

Two Letters to Lord Onslow, Lord Lieutenant of the County of Surry: and one to Mr Henry Dundas, Secretary of State, on the Subject of the Late Excellent Proclamation (London: James Ridgway, 1792)

Letter Addressed to the Addressers, on the late Proclamation. By Thomas Paine, Secretary for Foreign Affairs to Congress in the American War, and Author of the Works Intitled 'Common Sense,' 'Rights of Man, Two Parts,' &c (London: H. D. Symonds and Thomas Clio Rickman, 1792). Signed 'Thomas Paine'. *CW*, ii. 469–511

'Answer to Four Questions on the Legislative and Executive Powers' [attributed title], trans. Condorcet, published in *Chronique du Mois*, June–July 1792, the fourth signed 'Thomas Paine'. *CW*, ii. 521–34

'On the Propriety of Bringing Louis XVI to Trial' [attributed title], 20 Nov. 1792. Signed 'Thomas Paine'. *CW*, ii. 547–51

Lettre de Thomas Paine au peuple françois: Paris, le 25 Septembre (Paris: Imprimerie du Cercle social, [1792]), translated as *Letter of Thomas Paine, to the People of France. Published and Distributed Gratis by the London Corresponding Society* (London: no printer, 1792). Reprinted as *Address to the People of France* (attributed title), signed 'Thomas Paine'. *CW*, ii. 537–40

Reasons for Wishing to Preserve the Life of Louis Capet. As Delivered to the National Convention. By Thomas Paine, Member of the National Convention, and Author of Common Sense, A Letter to the Rayntl [sic], &c. &c. &c. (London: James Ridgway, [1793]). Printed (without the anonymous editorial preface) as 'Reasons for Preserving the Life of Louis Capet'. *CW*, ii. 551–5

'Shall Louis XVI be Respited?' [attributed title] (Speech read in the National Convention, 19 Jan. 1793). *CW*, ii. 555–8

Observations sur la partie de la Constitution de 1793 (présentée par l'ancien Comité de salut public) qui concerne la formation et les pouvoirs du Conseil executive, in Bernard Vincent (ed.), 'Cinq inédits de Thomas Paine', *Revue française d'études américaines* 40 (1989), 213–35

The Age of Reason. Being an Investigation of True and of Fabulous Theology. By Thomas Paine, Citizen and Cultivator of the United States of America;—Secretary for Foreign Affairs to Congress in the American War;—and Author of the Works entitled, 'Common Sense, and Rights of Man.' (Paris: Barrois senior, [Feb. 1794]); English edn, London: D. I. Eaton, 1794. *CW*, i. 460–514

The Age of Reason. Part the Second. Being an Investigation of True and Fabulous Theology ([Paris]: for the author, 1795). A pirated edition was published, with errors: (London: H. D. Symonds, 25 Oct. 1795). An authorized edition followed: (London: Daniel Isaac Eaton, 1 Jan. 1796). *CW*, i. 514–604

Dissertation on First-Principles of Government; by Thomas Paine, Author of Common Sense; Rights of Man; Age of Reason, &c (Paris, 'Printed at the English Press', [1795]; English edn, London: Daniel Isaac Eaton, 1795). *CW*, ii. 570–88

'The Constitution of 1795' [attributed title] (speech in the National Convention, 7 July 1795). *CW*, ii. 588–94

The Decline and Fall of the English System of Finance. By Thomas Paine, Author of Common Sense, American Crisis, Rights of Man, Age of Reason, &c. (Paris: Adlard & Son; London: T. Williams, 1796). *CW*, ii. 651–74

Letter to George Washington, President of the United States of America. On Affairs Public and Private. By Thomas Paine, Author of the Works entitled, Common Sense, Rights of Man, Age of Reason, &c (Philadelphia: Benj. Franklin Bache, 1796), the text dated 30 July 1796. *CW*, ii. 691–723

Letter, from Thomas Paine to Camille Jordan, of the Council of Five Hundred: Occasioned by the report on the priests, public worship, and the bells (London: 'Printed and sold by all booksellers', 1797). *CW*, ii. 756–63

A Letter to the Honourable Thomas Erskine, on the Prosecution of Thomas Williams, for publishing The Age of Reason. By Thomas Paine, Author of Common Sense, Rights of Man, Agrarian Justice, &c. &c. (Paris: for the Author, 1797). *CW*, ii. 727–48

Agrarian Justice, opposed to Agrarian Law, and to Agrarian Monopoly. Being a Plan for Meliorating the Condition of Man, By Creating in every Nation a National Fund, To Pay to every Person, when arrived at the Age of Twenty-one Years, the Sum of Fifteen Pounds Sterling, to enable him or her to begin the World; and also, Ten Pounds Sterling per Annum during life to every Person now living of the Age of Fifty Years, and to all others when they shall arrive at that Age, to enable them to live in Old Age without Wretchedness, and go decently out of the World. By Thomas Paine, Author of Common Sense, Rights of Man, Age of Reason, &c. &c. (Paris: W. Adlard, [1797]; reprinted with some omissions, London: J. Adlard and J. Parsons, [1797]). *CW*, i. 605–23

Letter of Thomas Paine to the People of France, and the French Armies, on the Events of the 18th Fructidor, and its Consequences (Paris: At the printing-office of the Social-Circle, 1797). *CW*, ii. 594–612

'A Discourse at the Society of Theophilanthropists' [attributed title], (1797), published in *The Temple of Reason*, 3 Jan. 1801. *CW*, ii. 748–56

A Discourse delivered by Thomas Paine, at the Society of the Theophilanthropists, at Paris, 1798 (London: Thomas Clio Rickman, 1798)

The Works of Thomas Paine (2 vols, Philadelphia: James Carey, 1797)

Atheism Refuted; in a Discourse to Prove the Existence of a God. By T[homas] P[aine] (London: J. Johnson, 1798)

Paine to the Conseil des Cinq Cents, printed in *Le Bien informé*, 29 Jan. 1798. *CW*, ii. 1403

'To the Citizens of the United States, and Particularly to the Leaders of the Federal Faction' [attributed title], a series of seven letters published from 15 Nov. 1802 to 7 June 1805, in the *National Intelligencer* (I–V), the Philadelphia *Aurora* (VI) and the Trenton *True-American* (VII). Signed Thomas Paine. *CW*, ii. 908–57

'Prospect Papers' [attributed collective title], a series of seventeen articles published in *The Prospect, or a View of the Moral World* (New York) from 18 Feb. to 8 Sept. 1804, signed 'Thomas Paine', 'T.P.' or with pen names like 'A True Deist'. *CW*, ii. 788–830

'To the People of England on the Invasion of England' [attributed title], first published in the *Philadelphia Aurora*, 6 Mar. 1804. Signed Thomas Paine. *CW*, ii. 675–83

'To the French Inhabitants of Louisiana' [attributed title] (1804). Signed 'Common Sense'; dated 22 Sept. 1804. First publication not traced. *CW*, ii. 963–8

[Paine], 'Origin of Freemasonry' [attributed title] [1805]. *CW*, ii. 830–41, claiming a subsequent publication as a pamphlet in 1818 (not identified)

[Paine], 'Remarks on English Affairs' [attributed title], *Baltimore Evening Post* (8 July 1805). Signed 'C.S.' *CW*, ii. 684–7

Thomas Paine to the Citizens of Pennsylvania, on the Proposal for Calling a Convention (Philadelphia: Wm. Duane, 1805, dated Aug. 1805). *CW*, ii. 992–1007

[Paine], 'A Challenge to the Federalists to Declare their Principles' (17 Oct. 1806) [attributed title]. In *The Political and Miscellaneous Works of Thomas Paine* (2 vols, London: R. Carlile, 1819), ii. 188–90. Signed 'Common Sense.' *CW*, ii. 1107–10

[Paine], 'Of the English Navy' [attributed title], published in New York and Philadelphia newspapers (7 Jan. 1807). Signed 'Common Sense'. *CW*, ii. 687–8

Examination of the Passages in the New Testament, quoted from the Old and called Prophecies concerning Jesus Christ. To which is prefixed, An Essay on Dream, Shewing by what operation of the mind a Dream is produced in sleep, and applying the same to the account of Dreams in the New Testament; With an Appendix containing my Private Thoughts of a Future State, And Remarks on the Contradictory Doctrine in the Books of Matthew and Mark. By Thomas Paine (New York: printed for the author [1807]). *CW*, ii. 848–92

'Predestination' [attributed title]. First published in London, 1820. Signed 'Thomas Paine'. *CW*, ii. 894–7

'The Will of Thomas Paine' [18 Jan. 1809]. *CW*, ii. 1498–503

[Paine], 'Extracts from a Reply to the Bishop of Llandaff' [attributed title], written *c.*1796–1800, printed in *The Theophilanthropist* (New York, 1810). *CW,* ii. 764–88

The Political and Miscellaneous Works of Thomas Paine (2 vols., London: R. Carlile, 1819)

The Age of Reason, part the first (London: R. Carlile, 1818)

The Age of Reason, part the second (London: R. Carlile, 1818)

The Age of Reason. Part the third (London: R. Carlile, 1818)

The Theological Works of Thomas Paine (London: R. Carlile, 1818)

PRIMARY

[Adams, John], *Thoughts on Government: Applicable to the Present State of the American Colonies. In a Letter from a Gentleman To his Friend* (Philadelphia: John Dunlap, 1776)

Adams, John, *Statesman and Friend: Correspondence of John Adams with Benjamin Waterhouse 1784–1822,* ed. Worthington Chauncey Ford (Boston: Little, Brown, 1927)

Adams, John, *The Diary and Autobiography of John Adams,* ed. L. H. Butterfield (4 vols, Cambridge, Mass.: Belknap Press, 1961)

Adams, John, *The Spur of Fame: Dialogues of John Adams and Benjamin Rush, 1805–1813,* ed. John A. Schutz and Douglass Adair (San Marino, Calif.: The Huntington Library, 1966)

[Adams, John], *A Dissertation on the Canon and Feudal Law,* printed in the *Boston Gazette* (Aug. 1765), in *Papers of John Adams,* ed. Robert J. Taylor (Cambridge, Mass.: Belknap Press, 1977–), i. 103–28

Adams, John, *The Adams–Jefferson Letters: The Complete Correspondence between Thomas Jefferson and Abigail and John Adams,* ed. Lester J. Cappon (Chapel Hill, NC: University of North Carolina Press, 1988)

Adams, John, *The Works of John Adams, Second President of the United States: With a Life of the Author,* ed. Charles F. Adams (10 vols, Boston, 1850–6)

Adams, John [Quincy], *An Answer to Pain's Rights of Man* (London: John Stockdale, 1793)

Adams, Samuel, *The Writings of Samuel Adams,* ed. Harry Alonzo Cushing (4 vols, New York: G. P. Putnam's Sons, 1904–8)

Adams, T., *Democracy Unveiled; in a Letter to Sir Francis Burdett, Bart M.P.* (London: C. Chapple, 1813)

Address of the London Corresponding Society to the other Societies of Great Britain, united for obtaining a Reform in Parliament (London: no printer, 1792)

The Address of the British Convention, assembled at Edinburgh, November 19, 1793, to the People of Great Britain (London: D. I. Eaton, [1793])

'Africanus', *Remarks on the Slave Trade, and the Slavery of Negroes* (London: J. Phillips and T. Payne, and Norwich: Chase, 1788)

Agutter, William, *Christian Politics; or, the Origin of Power, and the Grounds of Subordination. A Sermon...September 2, 1792* (London: F. and C. Rivington, 1792)

[Annet, Peter], *Deism Fairly Stated, and Fully Vindicated from the Gross Imputations and Groundless Calumnies of Modern Believers...By a Moral Philosopher* (London: W. Webb, 1746)

[Annet, Peter], *The History and Character of Saint Paul, examined: In a Letter to Theophilus, a Christian Friend* (London: F. Page, [?1748])

Bacon, Francis, *The Essays or Counsels, Civill and Morall, of Francis Lo. Verulam, Viscount St. Albans. Newly enlarged* (London: Iohn Haviland, 1629)

Bain, Alexander, *James Mill. A Biography* (London: Longmans, Green, 1882)

Barber, Daniel, *The History of my Own Times* (3 vols, Washington: S. C. Ustick, 1827–32)

Barclay, Robert, *An Apology For the True Christian Divinity, As the same is held forth, and preached by the People, Called, in Scorn, Quakers* (London: no printer, 1678)

Barrel, John and Jon Mee (eds), *Trials for Treason and Sedition, 1792–1794* (8 vols, London: Pickering and Chatto, 2006), i

Barruel, Augustin, *Mémoires pour servir à l'histoire du Jacobinisme* (4 vols, London: de l'Imprimerie Françoise, 1797–8)

Belsham, W[illiam], *Examination of an Appeal from the New to the Old Whigs; to which is prefixed, An Introduction, containing Remarks on Mr Burke's Letter to a Member of the National Assembly* (London: C. Dilly, 1792)

[Benezet, Anthony], *Observations On the Inslaving, importing and purchasing of Negroes* (Germantown, Pa: Christopher Sower, 1759; 2nd edn, 1760)

Benezet, Ant[hony], *A Caution and Warning to Great Britain and Her Colonies, in a Short Representation of the Calamitous State of the Enslaved Negroes in the British Dominions* (Philadelphia: Henry Miller, 1766)

[Benezet, Anthony], *Some Historical Account of Guinea . . . With an inquiry into the rise and progress of the slave trade* (Philadelphia: Joseph Cruckshank, 1771)

Bentham, Jeremy, *A Fragment on Government: Being an Examination of what is delivered, On the Subject of Government in General, In the Introduction to Sir William Blackstone's Commentaries; with a Preface in which is given a Critique of the Work at Large* (London: T. Payne, P. Elmsly and E. Brooke, 1776)

Bentham, Jeremy, *An Introduction to the Principles of Morals and Legislation* (London: T. Payne, 1789)

Bentham, Jeremy, *The Works of Jeremy Bentham*, ed. John Bowring (11 vols, London: Simpkin, Marshall, 1843)

Bentham, Jeremy, *An Examination of the Declaration of the Rights of Man and the Citizen Decreed by the Constituent Assembly in France*, in Bentham, *Works*, ed. Bowring, ii

Bentley, Richard, *The Folly and Unreasonableness of Atheism . . . In Eight Sermons preached at the Lecture Founded by the Honourable Robert Boyle, Esquire, in the first Year 1692* (London: J. H. for H. Mortlock, 1693)

Biddle, Charles, *Autobiography of Charles Biddle, Vice-President of the Supreme Executive Council of Pennsylvania 1745–1821* (Philadelphia: E. Claxton, 1883)

Bisset, Robert, *Sketch of Democracy* (London: J. Smeeton, 1796)

Bisset, Robert, *The Life of Edmund Burke* (2nd edn, 2 vols, London: George Cawthorn, 1800)

[Blackburne, Francis], *The Confessional* (London: S. Bladon, 1766)

[Blackburne, Francis], *Reflections on the Fate of a Petition For Relief in the Matter of Subscription, Offered to the Honourable House of Commons, February 6th, 1772* (London: no printer, 1772)

Blackstone, William, *Commentaries on the Laws of England* (4 vols, Oxford: Clarendon Press, 1765–9)

Blount, Charles, *The Oracles of Reason* (London: no printer, 1693)

Blount, Thomas, *Glossographia: or a Dictionary, Interpreting all such Hard Words . . . as are now used in our refined English Tongue* (London: Tho. Newcomb, 1656)

Bolingbroke, Lord, *Contributions to The Craftsman*, ed. Simon Varey (Oxford: Clarendon Press, 1982)

Bolingbroke, Lord, *Bolingbroke's Political Writings: The Conservative Enlightenment*, ed. Bernard Cottret (Basingstoke: Macmillan, 1997)

Bolingbroke, Lord, *The Unpublished Letters of Henry St John, First Viscount Bolingbroke*, ed. Adrian Lashmore-Davies (5 vols, London: Pickering and Chatto, 2013)

[Boothby, Sir Brooke], *A Letter to the Right Honourable Edmund Burke* (London: J. Debrett, 1791)

Boothby, Brooke, *Observations on the Appeal from the New to the Old Whigs, and on Mr Paine's Rights of Man* (London: John Stockdale, 1792)

Boswell, James, *The Life of Samuel Johnson, LL.D.* (2 vols, London: Henry Baldwin for Charles Dilly, 1791)

[Boulanger, Nicolas Antoine, attrib.], *Examen Critique de la Vie & des Ouvrages de Saint Paul. Avec une Dissertation sur Saint Pierre, par feu M. Boulanger* ('à Londres' [Amsterdam: M. M. Rey], 1770)

[Bradford, Ebenezer], *Mr Thomas Paine's Trial; being an Examination of the Age of Reason* (Boston: Isaiah Thomas and Ebenezer T. Andrews, 1795)

Brissot de Warville, J. P., *New Travels in the United States of America. Performed in 1788* (London: J. S. Jordan, 1792)

Bristed, John, *Hints on the National Bankruptcy of Britain and on her Resources to Maintain the Present Contest with France* (New York: E. Sargeant, 1809)

Burchell, Kenneth W. (ed.), *Thomas Paine and America, 1776–1809* (6 vols, London: Pickering and Chatto, 2009)

Burgess, Hazel, *Thomas Paine: A Collection of Unknown Writings* (Houndmills: Palgrave, 2010)

[Burgh, James], *Political Disquisitions: or, An Enquiry into public Errors, Defects, and Abuses* (3 vols, London: E. and C. Dilly, 1774–5)

[Burke, Edmund], *Thoughts on the Cause of the Present Discontents* (London: J. Dodsley, 1770)

Burke, Edmund, *Reflections on the Revolution in France, and on the Proceedings in Certain Societies in London relative to that Event* (London: J. Dodsley, 1790)

[Burke, Edmund], *An Appeal from the New to the Old Whigs, in consequence of some late Discussions in Parliament, relative to the Reflections on the French Revolution* (London: J. Dodsley, 1791)

Burke, Edmund, *A Letter from the Right Honourable Edmund Burke to a Noble Lord* (London: J. Owen, 1796)

Burke, Edmund, *The Correspondence of Edmund Burke*, ed. Thomas W. Copeland et al. (10 vols, Cambridge: Cambridge University Press, 1958–78)

Burke, Edmund, *Reflections on the Revolution in France*, ed. J. C. D. Clark (1790; Stanford, Calif.: Stanford University Press, 2001)

Burney, Frances, *The Early Journals and Letters of Frances Burney*, ed. Lars E. Troide (5 vols, Kingston: McGill-Queens University Press, 1988)

[Candler, Isaac], *A Summary View of America* (London: T. Cadell, 1824)

Carlile, R., *The Life of Thomas Paine written purposely to bind with his writings* (2nd edn, London, 1821)

Cartwright, John, *American Independence the Interest and Glory of Great-Britain* (London: [H. S. Woodfall], 1774; new edn, 1775)

[Cartwright, John], *A Declaration of the Rights of Englishmen* (no place, no printer, [?1784])

Cartwright, John: F. D. Cartwright, *The Life and Correspondence of Major Cartwright* (2 vols, London: Henry Colburn, 1826)

A Catalogue of the Genuine Library and Philosophical Instruments of the late ingenious James Horsfall, Esq. Sub-Treasurer of the Middle Temple, and Fellow of the Royal Society, Deceased: Including the Library, Manuscripts, and Instruments of the late learned John Bevis, M.D. F.R.S. deceased…which…Will be Sold at Auction, By Mr Paterson…On Saturday the 17th of December, 1785 (?London, no printer, ?1785)

[Chalmers, George], *The Life of Thomas Pain, The Author of Rights of Men. With a Defence of his Writings. By Francis Oldys, A.M. of the University of Pennsylvania* (London: Stockdale, 1791; 2nd edn, 1793)

[Chalmers, James], *Plain Truth; addressed to the Inhabitants of America, Containing, Remarks on a late Pamphlet, entitled Common Sense. Wherein are shewn, that the Scheme of Independence is Ruinous, Delusive, and Impracticable: That were the Author's Asseverations, Respecting the Power of America, as Real as Nugatory; Reconciliation on liberal Principles with Great Britain, would be exalted Policy: And that circumstanced as we are, Permanent Liberty, and True Happiness, can only be obtained by Reconciliation with that Kingdom. Written by Candidus* (Philadelphia: R. Bell, 1776)

Cheetham, James, *The Life of Thomas Paine, author of Common Sense, The Crisis, Rights of Man, &c. &c. &c.* (New York: Southwick and Pelsue, 1809)

Christie, Thomas, *Letters on the Revolution in France, and on the New Constitution established by the National Assembly: occasioned by the Publications of the Right Hon. Edmund Burke, M.P. and Alexander de Calonne, late Minister of State* (Part I, London: J. Johnson, 1791)

Claeys, Gregory (ed.), *Political Writings of the 1790s* (8 vols, London: William Pickering, 1995)

Clark, Jonas, *The Fate of Blood-Thirsty Oppressors, and GOD's Tender Care of His Distressed People. A Sermon, Preached at Lexington, April 19, 1776* (Boston: Powars and Willis, 1776), in Jonas Clark, *The Battle of Lexington: A Sermon & Eyewitness Narrative* (Ventura, Calif.: Nordskog, 2007)

Clarkson, T[homas], *An Essay on the Comparative Efficiency of Regulation or Abolition, as applied to the Slave Trade* (London: James Phillips, 1789)

Clarkson, Thomas, *The History of the Rise, Progress and Accomplishment of the Abolition of the African Slave-Trade by the British Parliament* (2 vols, London: Longman et al., 1808)

Colquhoun, P[atrick], *A Treatise on Indigence; exhibiting a General View of the National Resources for Productive Labour; with Propositions for Ameliorating the Condition of the Poor, and improving the moral Habits and increasing the Comforts of the Labouring People, particularly The Rising Generation, by Regulations of Political Economy* (London: J. Hatchard, 1806)

Common Sense: or, the Englishman's Journal (2 vols, London: J. Purser and G. Hawkins, 1738–9)

Cooper, Thomas, *Letters on the Slave Trade, first published in Wheeler's Manchester Chronicle* (Manchester: C. Wheeler, 1787)

Cooper, Thomas, *A Reply to Mr Burke's Invective against Mr Cooper, and Mr Watt, in the House of Commons, on the 30th of April, 1792* (London: J. Johnson, 1792)

Cooper, Thomas, *Some Information respecting America* (London: J. Johnson, 1794)

Copies of Original Letters recently written by Persons in Paris to Dr Priestley in America. Taken on board a Neutral Vessel (London: J. Wright, 1798)

The Correspondence of the London Corresponding Society revised and corrected, With Explanatory Notes and a Prefatory Letter, by the Committee of Arrangement, deputed for that purpose: Published for the Use of Members, pursuant to the 17th Article of the Society's Regulations (London: Printed by Order of the London Corresponding Society, [1795])

A Country Carpenter's Confession of Faith: With a Few Plain Remarks on The Age of Reason. In a Letter from Will Chip, Carpenter, in Somersetshire, to Thomas Pain, Stay-Maker, in Paris (London: F. and C. Rivington, 1794)

Crèquy, Comte de Courchamps, *Souvenirs de la Marquise de Créquy, de 1710 à 1803* (10 vols, Paris: Garnier, 1903)

Crèvecoeur, J. Hector St. John de, *Letters from an American Farmer and Sketches of Eighteenth-Century America*, ed. Albert E. Stone (Harmondsworth: Penguin, 1986)

Curwen, Samuel. *The Journal of Samuel Curwen Loyalist*, ed. Andrew Oliver (2 vols, Cambridge, Mass.: Harvard University Press, 1972)

[Dalrymple, Sir John], *The Address of the People of Great-Britain to the Inhabitants of America* (London: T. Cadell, 1775)

Davis, David, *The Case of the Labourers in Husbandry Stated and Considered, in three parts. Part I. A View of their Distressed Condition. Part II. The Principal Causes of their Growing Distress and Number, and of the Consequent Increase of the Poor-Rate. Part III. Means of Relief Proposed. With an Appendix; containing A Collection of Accounts, shewing the Earnings and Expences of Labouring Families, in Different Parts of the Kingdom* (Bath: R. Cruttwell, for G. G. and J. Robinson, London, 1795)

[Dawson, Benjamin], *A Free and Candid Disquisition on Religious Establishments in General, and the Church of England in Particular* (London: B. White, 1771)

A Defence of Natural and Revealed Religion: being an abridgment of the sermons preached at the lecture founded by the Honble Robert Boyle, Esq. (4 vols, London: Arthur Bettesworth and Charles Hitch, 1737)

DeLolme, J. L., *The Constitution of England, or An Account of the English Government; In which it is compared with the Republican Form of Government, and occasionally with the other Monarchies in Europe* (London: T. Spilsbury for G. Kearsley, 1775)

Derham, W[illiam], *Physico-Theology: or, a Demonstration of the Being and Attributes of God, from his Works of Creation. Being the Substance of XVI Sermons Preached in St. Mary le Bow-Church, London, at the Honble Mr Boyle's Lectures, in the Years 1711 and 1712* (London: W. Innys, 1713; 12th edn, 1754)

[Dickinson, John], *Letters from a Farmer in Pennsylvania, to the Inhabitants of the British Colonies* (Philadelphia: David Hall and William Sellers, 1768)

Dinmore, Richard, *An Exposition Of the Principles of the English Jacobins; with Strictures On the Political Conduct of Charles J. Fox, William Pitt and Edmund Burke* (Norwich: John March and London: J. S. Jordan, 1796)

[Disney, John], *A Short View of the Controversies occasioned by the Confessional, and the Petition to Parliament for Relief in the Matter of Subscription to the Liturgy and Articles of the Church of England* (London: J. Johnson, 1773)

Dodd, William, *An Oration: delivered at the Dedication of Free-Masons' Hall, Great Queen-Street, Lincoln's-Inn-Fields, on Thursday, May 23, 1776* (London: G. Robinson et al., 1776)

Dragonetti, Giacinto, marchese, *A Treatise on Virtues and Rewards* (London: Johnson and Payne, and J. Almon, 1769)

Dumont, Étienne, *Recollections of Mirabeau, and of the Two First Legislative Assemblies of France* (London: Edward Bull, 1832)

D'Urfey, Thomas, *The Famous History of the Rise and Fall of Massaniello* (London, 1700)

Early Proceedings of the American Philosophical Society for the Promotion of Useful Knowledge compiled by one of the Secretaries, from the Manuscript Minutes of its Meetings from 1744 to 1838 (Philadelphia: McCalla and Stavely, 1884)

Eden, Frederick Morton, *The State of the Poor: or, An History of the Labouring Classes in England, from the Conquest to the Present Period; In which are particularly considered, their Domestic Economy, with respect to Diet, Dress, Fuel, and Habitation; And the various Plans which, from time to time, have been proposed, and adopted, for the Relief of the Poor: together with Parochial Reports Relative to the Administration of Work-houses, and Houses of Industry; the State of Friendly Societies; and other Public Institutions; in several Agricultural, Commercial, and Manufacturing, Districts* (3 vols, London: B and J. White, G. G. and J. Robinson, T. Payne et al., 1797)

Emerson, William, *Diaries and Letters of William Emerson 1743–1776*, ed. Amelia Forbes Emerson (privately printed, Concord, Mass., 1972)

English Historical Documents: American Colonial Documents to 1776, ed. Merrill Jensen (London: Eyre and Spottiswood, 1955)

English Liberty Established: or, The most material Circumstances relative to John Wilkes Esq (London: no printer, 1768)

Entick, John, *A New Naval History: or, Compleat View of the British Marine* (London: R. Manby et al., 1757)

Extracts From the Votes and Proceedings Of the American Continental Congress, Held at Philadelphia on the 5th of September 1774 (Philadelphia: William and Thomas Bradford, October 27th, 1774)

Farington, Joseph, *The Farington Diary*, ed. James Greig (8 vols., London: Hutchinson, 1922–8)

Farrand, Max (ed.), *Records of the Federal Convention of 1787* (rev. edn, 4 vols, New Haven: Yale University Press, 1966)

Felton, Henry, *Sermons on the Creation, Fall, and Redemption of Man* (London: John Clarke, 1748)

Ferguson, James, *An Idea of the Material Universe, Deduced from a Survey of the Solar System* (London: for the Author, 1756)

Ferguson, James, *Astronomy Explained upon Sir Isaac Newton's Principles, and made easy to those who have not studied Mathematics* (London: for the Author, 1756)

[Fleming, Caleb], *An Essay To State the Scripture-Account of Man's Redemption, by the Death of Christ* (London: M. Cooper, 1745)

Force, Peter (ed.), *American Archives: Fourth Series. Containing a Documentary History of the English Colonies in North America, from the King's Message to Parliament, of March 7, 1774, to the Declaration of Independence of the United States* (Washington: M. St Clair Clarke and Peter Force, 1833)

Ford, Worthington Chauncey (ed.), *Journals of the Continental Congress, 1774–1789* (34 vols, Washington: US Govt. Printing Office, 1904–37)

Fortescue, *Report on the Manuscripts of J. B. Fortescue, Esq. Preserved at Dropmore*, ed. Walter FitzPatrick (10 vols, London: HMSO, 1905), iv

Foster, James, *Discourses on all the Principal Branches of Natural Religion and Social Virtue* (2 vols, London: for the author, 1749–52)

Franklin, Benjamin, *The Life of Dr Benjamin Franklin: written by himself* (New York: T. and J. Swords, 1794)

Franklin, Benjamin, *Benjamin Franklin's Autobiographical Writings*, ed. Carl Van Doren (London: Cresset Press, 1946)

Franklin, Benjamin, *The Papers of Benjamin Franklin*, ed. Leonard W. Labaree et al. (New Haven: Yale University Press, 1959–)

Franklin, Benjamin, *Benjamin Franklin: Writings*, ed. J. A. Leo Lemay (New York: Library of America, 1987)

Furneaux, Philip, *An Essay on Toleration* (London: T. Cadell, 1773)

Gage, Thomas. *By His Excellency The Hon. Thomas Gage, Esq....A Proclamation* (broadsheet, no place [Boston]: no printer, 12 June 1775)

[Galloway, Joseph], *Historical and Political Reflections on the Rise and Progress of the American Rebellion* (London: G. Wilkie, 1780)

[Geddes, Alexander], *An Apology for Slavery; or, Six Cogent Arguments against the Immediate Abolition of the Slave-Trade* (London: J. Johnson and R. Faulder, 1792)

Geddes, Alexander (ed.), *The Holy Bible, or the Books Accounted Sacred by Jews and Christians, otherwise called the Books of the Old and New Covenants* (London: J. Davis for R. Faulder and J. Johnson, 1792, 1797)

[George III], *By the King. A Proclamation for suppressing Rebellion and Sedition* [23 Aug. 1775] (London: Charles Eyre and William Strahan, 1775)

[George III], *His Majesty's most Gracious Speech to both Houses of Parliament, on Thursday the 26th of October, 1775* (no place, no printer, [1775])

George III, *Letters from George III to Lord Bute 1756–1766*, ed. Romney Sedgwick (London: Macmillan, 1939)

Gerrald, Joseph, *A Convention the Only Means of Saving us from Ruin. In a Letter, addressed to the People of England* (London: D. I. Eaton, 1793)

Gibbon, Edward, *The Autobiographies of Edward Gibbon*, ed. John Murray (London: John Murray, 1896)

Godwin, William, *An Enquiry Concerning Political Justice, and Its Influence on General Virtue and Happiness* (2 vols, London: G. G. J. and J. Robinson, 1793)

Godwin, William, *Memoirs of Mary Wollstonecraft*, ed. W. Clark Durant (London: Constable, 1927)

Godwin, William, *The Letters of William Godwin, Volume I 1778–1797*, ed. Pamela Clemit (Oxford: Oxford University Press, 2011)

Good, John Mason, *Memoirs of the Life and Writings of the Reverend Alexander Geddes, LL.D.* (London: G. Kearsley, 1803)

Gordon, William, *The History of the Rise, Progress, and Establishment, of the Independence of the United States of America* (4 vols, London: for the author, 1788)

Grant, Alfred, *Our American Brethren: A History of Letters in the British Press During the American Revolution, 1775–1781* (Jefferson, NC: McFarland, 1995)

Graydon, Alexander, *Alexander Graydon's Memoirs of his Own Time*, ed. John Stockton Littell (Philadelphia: Lindsay and Blakiston, 1846)

Green, Ashbel, *The Life of Ashbel Green, V.D.M.*, ed. Joseph H. Jones (New York: Robert Carter, 1849)

Gregory, G[eorge], *Essays Historical and Moral* (London: J. Johnson, 1785)

Grellet, Stephen, *Memoirs of the Life and Gospel Labours of Stephen Grellet*, ed. Benjamin Seebohm (2 vols, Philadelphia: Henry Longstreth, 1860)

A Guide to the Knowledge of the Rights and Privileges of Englishmen (London: J. Scott, 1757)

Hall, Charles, *The Effects of Civilization on the People in European States* (London: for the author, 1805)

Hall, Charles, *Observations on the Principal Conclusion in Mr Malthus's Essay on Population* (London: for the author, 1805)

H[all], J[ohn], *The Grounds and Reasons of Monarchy Considered and exemplified out of the Scottish History* (Edinburgh: Evan Tyler, 1651)

[Hall, John], *The History of the Civil War in America. Vol. I. Comprehending the Campaigns of 1775, 1776, and 1777. By an Officer of the Army* (London: T. Payne and J. Sewell, 1780)

Hall, Robert, *Modern Infidelity Considered With respect to its Influence on Society: In a Sermon, Preached at the Baptist Meeting, Cambridge* (Cambridge: M. Watson, 1800)

Hamilton, Adrian, *The Infamous Essay on Woman* (London: André Deutsch, 1972)

[Hamilton, Alexander], *The Farmer Refuted: or, A more impartial and comprehensive View of the Dispute between Great-Britain and the Colonies, intended as a Further Vindication of the Congress* (New York: James Rivington, 1775)

[Hanway, Jonas], *Common Sense: in nine conferences, between a British Merchant and a Candid Merchant of America, in their private capacities as friends; tracing the several causes of the present contests between the mother country and her American subjects...* (London: J. Dodsley, 1775)

Hardy, Thomas, *Memoir of Thomas Hardy, Founder of, and Secretary to, the London Corresponding Society... written by himself* (London: James Ridgway, 1832)

Harford, John S., *Some Account of the Life, Death, and Principles of Thomas Paine, together with Remarks on his Writings, and on their Intimate Connection with the Avowed Objects of the Revolutionists of 1793, and of the Radicals in 1819* (Bristol: J. M. Gutch, 1819)

Harris, J[oseph], *The Description and Use of the Globes, and the Orrery. To which is prefixed, By way of Introduction, a Brief Account of the Solar System* (London: Thomas Wright et al., 1731; 12th edn, 1783)

Hartley, David, *Substance of a Speech in Parliament. Upon the State of the Nation and the Present Civil War with America* (London: J. Almon, 1776)

[Hazlitt, William], *The Spirit of the Age: or Contemporary Portraits* (2 vols, London: Henry Colburn, 1825)

Hazlitt, William, *The Complete Works of William Hazlitt*, ed. P. P. Howe (21 vols, London: Dent, 1930–4)

Henderson, Ebenezer, *Life of James Ferguson, F.R.S.* (Edinburgh: A. Fullarton, 1867)

Henry, John Joseph, Journal (1812), reprinted in *Pennsylvania Archives*, 2nd series, ed. William H. Egle (Harrisburgh: E. K. Meyers, 1890)

Herbert, Edward, *The Life of Edward Lord Herbert of Cherbury* (London: J. Dodsley, 1770)

[Heywood, Samuel], *The Right of Protestant Dissenters to a Compleat Toleration Asserted* (London: J. Johnson, 1789)

[Heywood, Samuel], *High Church Politics: being a Seasonable Appeal to the Friends of the British Constitution, against the Practices and Principles of High Churchmen; as exemplified in the late opposition to the repeal of the Test Laws, and in the riots at Birmingham* (London: J. Johnson, 1792)

Hoadly, Benjamin, *The Measures of Submission to the Civil Magistrate Consider'd. In a Defence of the Doctrine Deliver'd in A Sermon Preach'd before the Rt. Hon. The Lord Mayor, Aldermen, and Citizens of London, Sept. 29. 1705* (London: Tim[othy] Childe, 1706)

[d'Holbach, Paul Henri Thiry, baron], *Système de la Nature. Des Loix du Monde Physique & du Monde Moral. Par M. Mirabaud* (2 vols, 'Londres' [i.e. Amsterdam], 1770)

[d'Holbach, Paul Henri Thiry, baron], *The System of Nature: or, the Laws of the Moral and Physical World... translated from the French of M. Mirabaud... by William Hodgson* (London: for the translator, 1795)

Howell, T. B. (ed.), *A Complete Collection of State Trials*, xxii (London: T. C. Hansard, 1817)

[Hulme, Obadiah, attrib.], *A Historical Essay on the English Constitution: or, An impartial Inquiry into the Elective Power of the People, from the first Establishment of the Saxons in this Kingdom* (London: Edward and Charles Dilly, 1771)

Hulton, Anne, *Letters of a Loyalist Lady, Being the letters of Anne Hulton, sister of Henry Hulton, Commissioner of Customs at Boston, 1767–1776* (Cambridge, Mass.: Harvard University Press, 1927)

Hulton, Henry, 'An Englishman Views the American Revolution: The Letters of Henry Hulton, 1769–1776', ed. Wallace Brown, *Huntington Library Quarterly* 36 (1972–3), 1–26, 138–51

[Hume, David], *Essays, Moral and Political* (2 vols, Edinburgh: A. Kincaid, R. Fleming and A. Alison, 1741–2)

Hutcheson, Francis, *A Short Introduction to Moral Philosophy* (Glasgow: Robert Foulis, 1747)

Hutchinson, Thomas, *The History of the Colony and Province of Massachusetts-Bay*, ed. Lawrence Shaw Mayo (3 vols, Cambridge, Mass.: Harvard University Press, 1936)

An Impartial Sketch of the Life of Thomas Paine, author of 'Common Sense,' 'Rights of Man,' &c. &c. (London: T. Browne, 1792)

[Inglis, Charles], *The True interest of America Impartially Stated, in certain Strictures On a Pamphlet Intitled Common Sense. By an American* (Philadelphia: James Humphreys, jun., 1776)

Jackson, John, *The Grounds of Civil and Ecclesiastical Government Briefly Consider'd, To which is added, A Defence of the Bishop of Bangor, Against the Objections of Mr Law* (2nd edn, London: James Knapton, 1718)

[Jebb, John], *An Address to the Freeholders of Middlesex, assembled at Free Masons Tavern, in Great Queen Street, Upon Monday the 20th of December 1779, Being the Day appointed for a Meeting of the Freeholders, for the Purpose of Establishing Meetings to Maintain and Support the Freedom of Election* (London: J. Dixwell, T. Cadell and J. Bew, [1779])

[Jefferson, Thomas], *A Summary View of the Rights of British America. Set forth in some Resolutions Intended for the Inspection Of the present Delegates Of the People of Virginia, Now in Convention* (Williamsburg, Va: Clementina Rind, 1774)

Jefferson, Thomas, *The Writings of Thomas Jefferson*, ed. Andrew A. Lipscomb and Albert Ellery Bergh (Washington, DC: Thomas Jefferson Memorial Association, 1905)

Jefferson, Thomas, *The Papers of Thomas Jefferson*, ed. Julian P. Boyd et al. (Princeton, 1950–)

[Johnson, Samuel], *Taxation no Tyranny: an Answer to the Resolutions and Address of the American Congress* (London: T. Cadell, 1775)

Jones, Thomas, *History of New York during the Revolutionary War, and of the Leading Events in the Other Colonies at that Period*, ed. Edward Floyd De Lancey (2 vols, New York: New York Historical Society, 1879)

The Judgment of Whole Kingdoms and Nations…Shewing…An Account of the British Government, and the Rights and Priviledges of the People in the time of the Saxons, and since the Conquest (London: T. Harrison, 1710)

Junius, *The Letters of Junius*, ed. John Cannon (Oxford: Clarendon Press, 1978)

[Keating, George], *The Folly of Reason. Being Our Perfect and Unerring Guide, to the Knowledge of True Religion* (New York: Tibbout and O'Brien, 1794)

Kippis, Andrew, *A Sermon preached at the Old Jewry On the Fourth of November, 1788, before the Society for Commemorating the Glorious Revolution* (London: G. G. J. and J. Robinson, 1788)

Knight, Charles, *Passages of a Working Life during Half a Century*, ed. James Thorne (3 vols, 2nd edn, London: Knight & Co., 1873)

[Knox, William], *The Controversy between Great Britain and her Colonies Reviewed* (London: J. Almon, 1769)

[Knox, William], *The Interest of the Merchants and Manufacturers of Great-Britain, in the Present Context with the Colonies, stated and considered* (London: T. Cadell, 1774)

Lafayette, *The Marquis de la Fayette's Statement of His Own Conduct and Principles…Translated from the Original French, and most respectfully Inscribed to the Whig Club* (London: J. Deighton, 1793)

Langdon, Samuel, *A Rational Explication of St. John's Vision of the two Beasts, In the XIIIth Chapter of the Revelation. Shewing That the Beginning, Power, and Duration of Popery are plainly predicted in that Vision, and that these Predictions have hitherto been punctually verified* (Portsmouth, NH: Daniel Fowle, 1774)

Langdon, Samuel, *Government corrupted by Vice, and recovered by Righteousness. A Sermon Preached Before the Honourable Congress Of the Colony of the Massachusetts-Bay Assembled at Watertown, On Wednesday the 31st Day of May, 1775* (Watertown, Mass.: Benjamin Edes, 1775)

Larson, Jon Erik Larson (ed.), *Richard Price and the Ethical Foundations of the American Revolution* (Durham, NC: Duke University Press, 1979)

Lauderdale, Earl of, *A Letter on the Present Measures of Finance; in which the Bill now Depending in Parliament is Particularly Considered* (London: J. Debrett, G. G. and J. Robinson, 1798)

[Law, Edmund], *Considerations on the Propriety of Requiring a Subscription to Articles of Faith* (Cambridge: J. Archdeacon for T. & J. Merrill et al., 1774)

Lee, Charles, *General [Charles] Lee's Letter to General Burgoyne, upon his Arrival in Boston* (New York: J. Anderson, 1775)

Lee, Charles, *The Lee Papers* (4 vols, New York: New York Historical Society, 1871–4)

Leland, John, *An Account Of the Principal Deistical Writers that have Appeared in England in the last and present Century* (3 vols, London: B. Dod, 1754–6)

Leland, Thomas, *The History of Ireland from the Invasion of Henry II* (3 vols, London: J. Nourse et al., 1773)

[Leonard, Daniel], *Massachusettensis* ([Boston: no printer, 1775])

A Letter to a Member of the National Assembly [London, no printer, ?1791]

Levi, David, *A Defence of the Old Testament, in a series of letters addressed to Thomas Paine, Author of a Book entitled 'The Age of Reason'* (New York: William A. Davis for Napthali Judah, 1797)

List of the Society, Instituted in 1787, For the Purpose of effecting the Abolition of the Slave Trade (London: no printer, 1788)

Lister, Jeremy, *Concord Fight: Being so much of the narrative of Ensign Jeremy Lister of the 10th Regiment of Foot as pertains to his services on the 19th of April, 1775, and to his experiences in Boston during the early months of the siege* (Cambridge, Mass.: Harvard University Press, 1931)

Locke, John, *An Essay Concerning Humane Understanding* (London: Thomas Basset, 1690)

[Locke, John], *Two Treatises of Government*, ed. Peter Laslett (Cambridge: Cambridge University Press, 1988)

Lofft, Capel, *Remarks on the Letter of the Rt. Hon. Edmund Burke, Concerning the Revolution in France, and on the Proceedings in Certain Societies in London, Relative to that Event* (London: J. Johnson, 1790)

Lord, Henry, *A Display of Two Forraigne Sects in the East Indies: vizt: the sect of the Banians the ancient natives of India and the sect of the Persees the ancient inhabitants of Persia* (London: T. and R. Cotes for Francis Constable, 1630)

Mackintosh, James, *Vindiciae Gallicae. Defence of the French Revolution and its English Admirers against the Accusations of the Right Hon. Edmund Burke: including some Strictures on the late Production of Mons. De Calonne* (London: G. G. J. and J. Robinson, 1791)

Mackintosh, James, *A Discourse of the Study of the Law of Nature and Nations* (London: T. Cadell et al., 1799)

[Malthus, Thomas Robert], *An Essay on the Principle of Population, as it affects the Future Improvement of Society, with Remarks on the Speculations of Mr Godwin, M. Condorcet, and other Writers* (London: J. Johnson, 1798)

Marshall, Christopher, *Extracts from the Diary of Christopher Marshall, 1774–1781*, ed. William Duane (New York: New York Times, 1969)

Martin, Benjamin, *Bibliotheca Technologica: or a Philological Library of Literary Arts and Sciences* (London: S. Idle for John Noon, 1737)

Martin, Benjamin, *A Plain and Familiar Introduction to the Newtonian Philosophy, In Six Sections* (London: W. Owen, 1751)

Martin, Benjamin, *A New and Comprehensive System of Philology; or, a Treatise of the Literary Arts and Sciences, According to their present State* (2 vols, London: W. Owen, 1759–64)

Martin, John and Thomas Hardy, *At a General Meeting of the London Corresponding Society, held at the Globe Tavern Strand; on Monday the 20th Day of January, 1794 Citizen John Martin, in the Chair. The following Address to the People of Great Britain and Ireland, was read and agreed to* ([?London]: no printer, [1794])

Mayhew, Jonathan, *A Discourse Concerning Unlimited Submission and Non-Resistance to the Higher Powers* (Boston: D. Fowle, 1750)

[Mayhew, Jonathan], *A Mysterious Doctrine Unriddled, or Unlimited Submission and Non-Resistance to the Higher Powers Considered* (Boston and Newry: Daniel Carpenter and J. Gordon, 1775)

Melish, John, *Travels in the United States of America, in the Years 1806 & 1807, and 1809, 1810, & 1811* (2 vols, Philadelphia: for the author, 1812)

[Meredith, Sir William], *Letter to Dr Blackstone, By the Author of the Question Stated* (London: G. Woodfall, 1770)

Michell, Richard, *Fugitive Pieces on Various Subjects* (2 vols, Lewes: for the Author, by W. and A. Lee, 1787)

Middleton, Conyers, *A Letter from Rome, Shewing an Exact Conformity between Popery and Paganism: or, the Religion of the Present Romans to be derived entirely from that of their Heathen Ancestors* (London: W. Innys, 1729)

Middleton, Conyers, *Popery Unmask'd. Being the Substance of Dr Middleton's celebrated Letter from Rome* (London: R. Manby and H. Shute Cox, 1744)

Middleton, Conyers, *Vindication of the Free Inquiry into the Miraculous Powers, Which are supposed To have subsisted in the Christian Church, &c. From the Objections of Dr Dodwell and Dr Church* (London: R. Manby and H. S. Cox, 1751)

[?Middleton, Henry], *The True Merits of a Late Treatise, printed in America, Intitled, Common Sense, Clearly pointed out. Addressed to the Inhabitants of America. By a late Member of the Continental Congress, a Native of a Republican State* (London: W. Nicoll, 1776)

[Midon, Francis], *Remarkable History of the Rise and Fall of Masaniello, the Fisherman of Naples* (London: H. Fenwick, [?1770])

Milton, John, *A Defence of the People of England. In Answer to Salmasius's Defence of the King* (no place: no printer, 1695)

Moore, William, *The Address for Blood and Devastation: and the addressers exposed; together with the idolatrous worship of kings and tyrants, and the Americans justified by several precedents from Scripture, in their Resistance to the Depredations and Lawless Violence of an English King, and his bribed servile Parliament. Which may serve as an answer to Tax[a]tion no tyranny, Wesley's Calm address, &c. &c* (London [1776])

[Morgan, Thomas], *The Moral Philosopher. In a Dialogue between Philalethes a Christian Deist, and Theophanes a Christian Jew* (3 vols, London: for the Author, 1737–40)

Morris, Gouverneur, Jared Sparks, *The Life of Gouverneur Morris* (3 vols, Boston: Gray and Bowen, 1832)

Morris, Gouverneur, *A Diary of the French Revolution by Gouverneur Morris 1752–1816*, ed. Beatrix Cary Davenport (2 vols, London: Harrap 1939)

Muir, James, *An Examination of the Principles contained in the Age of Reason. In Ten discourses* (Baltimore: S. & J. Adams, 1795)

Newton, Thomas, *Dissertations on the Prophecies which have been remarkably fulfilled, and at this time are fulfilling in the world* (3 vols, London: J. and R. Tonson and S. Draper, 1754–8; 10th edn, Edinburgh, 1793)

Nodier, Charles, *Souvenirs de la Révolution et de l'Empire* (3rd edn, 2 vols, Paris: Charpentier, 1864)

[Ogilvie, William], *An Essay on the Right of Private Property in Land, with respect to its Foundation in the Law of Nature; Its present Establishment by the Municipal Laws of Europe; and The Regulations by which it might be rendered more beneficial to the lower Ranks of Mankind* (London: J. Walter, 1782)

Old Truths and Established Facts, being an Answer to a Very new Pamphlet indeed! (?London, ?1792), 15 pp. signed 'Vindex'

[Oldmixon, John], *The British Empire in America, Containing The History of the Discovery, Settlement, Progress and present State of all the British Colonies, on the Continent and Islands of America* (2 vols, London: John Nicholson et al., 1708)

Oliver, Peter, *Peter Oliver's Origin & Progress of the American Rebellion: A Tory view*, ed. Douglass Adair and John A. Schutz (San Marino, Calif.: The Huntington Library, 1961)

Opinion de Thomas Paine sur l'affaire de Louis Capet, adressée au Président de la Convention Nationale. Imprimée par ordre de la Convention Nationale (Paris: Jan. 1792)

[Oswald, John], *A Review of the Constitution of Great Britain* (London: J. Ridgway, 1791)

Otis, James, *The Rights of the British Colonies Asserted and Proved* (Boston: Edes and Gill, 1774)

Owen, Robert, *A New View of Society* (2nd edn, London: Longman et al., 1816)

Owen, Robert, *The Life of Robert Owen. Written by Himself* (London: Effingham Wilson, 1857–8), in *Selected Works of Robert Owen*, ed. Gregory Claeys (4 vols, London: William Pickering, 1993)

Paley, William, *The Principles of Moral and Political Philosophy* (London: R. Faulder, 1785)

Palmer, Elihu, *Posthumous Pieces by Elihu Palmer, being three chapters of an unfinished work intended to have been entitled 'The Political World'* (London: R. Carlile, 1824)

The Parliamentary Register; or History of the Proceedings and Debates of the House of Lords . . . During the Third Session of the Fifteenth Parliament of Great Britain, xi (London: J. Almon, 1783)

The Parliamentary History of England, from the Earliest Period to the Year 1803, ed. William Cobbett (36 vols, London: T. C. Hansard et al., 1806–20)

Patten, William, *Christianity the True Theology, and Only Perfect Moral System; in Answer to 'The Age of Reason'* (Warren, RI: Nathaniel Phillips, 1795)

Peckard, Peter, *Justice and Mercy recommended, particularly with reference to the Slave Trade. A Sermon preached before the University of Cambridge* (Cambridge: J. Archdeacon et al., 1788)

[Peckard, Peter], *Am I Not a Man? And a Brother? With all Humility addressed to the British Legislature* (Cambridge: J. Archdeacon, 1788)

The Perverse Definition Imposed on the Word Equality (broadsheet, no printer, c.1792)

Pigott, Charles, *A Political Dictionary: Explaining the True Meaning of Words* (London: D. I. Eaton, 1795)

Place, Francis, *The Autobiography of Francis Place (1771–1854)*, ed. Mary Thale (Cambridge: Cambridge University Press, 1972)

Playfair, William, *The Commercial and Political Atlas: representing, by means of stained copper-plate charts, the exports, imports, and general trade of England: the national debt, and other public accounts, with observations and remarks* (London: J. Debrett et al., 1786)

Playfair, William, *Inevitable Consequences of Reform in Parliament* (London, 1792)

'Political Observations, without Order: addressed to the People of America', *Pennsylvania Packet*, 14 Nov. 1774, reprinted in *English Historical Documents: American Colonial Documents to 1776*, ed. Merrill Jensen (London: Eyre and Spottiswood, 1955), 816–18

Porteus, Beilby, *A Charge delivered to the Clergy of the Diocese of London, at the Visitation of that Diocese, in the Year MDCCXCIV* (London: F. and C. Rivington, 1794)

Price, Richard, *Britain's Happiness, and The Proper Improvement of it, Represented in a Sermon, Preach'd at Newington-Green, Middlesex, On Nov. 29. 1759. Being the Day appointed for a General Thanksgiving* (London: A. Millar and R. Griffiths, 1759)

Price, Richard, *Four Dissertations. I. On Providence. II. On Prayer. III. On the Reasons for expecting that virtuous Men shall meet after Death in a State of Happiness. IV. On the Importance of Christianity, the Nature of Historical Evidence, and Miracles* (London: T. Cadell, 1772)

Price, Richard, *Observations on the Nature of Civil Liberty, the Principles of Government, and the Justice and Policy of the War with America* (2nd edn, London: T. Cadell, 1776)

Price, Richard, *Observations on the Importance of the American Revolution, and The Means of making it a Benefit to the World* (London: no printer, 1784)

Price, Richard, *The Evidence for a Future Period of Improvement in the State of Mankind, with the Means and Duty of Promoting it, represented in a Discourse, delivered on Wednesday the 25th of April, 1787, at the Meeting-House in the Old Jewry, London, to the Supporters of a New Academical Institution among Protestant Dissenters* (London: H. Goldney for T. Cadell and J. Johnson, 1787)

Price, Richard, *Sermons on the Christian Doctrine as received by Different Denominations of Christians* (London: T. Cadell, 1787)

Price, Richard, *A Discourse on the Love of our Country, delivered on Nov. 4, 1789, at the Meeting-House in the Old Jewry, to the Society for Commemorating the Revolution in Great Britain* (London: George Stafford for T. Cadell, 1789)

Prichard, Samuel, *Masonry Detected: being a universal and genuine description of all its branches from the original to the present time* (London: J. Wilford, 1730; 21st edn, ?1790)

Priestley, Joseph, *An Essay on the First Principles of Government; and on the Nature of Political, Civil, and Religious Liberty* (London: J. Dodsley, T. Cadell and J. Johnson, 1768)

Priestley, Joseph, *A Letter to the Right Honourable William Pitt, First Lord of the Treasury, and Chancellor of the Exchequer; on the Subjects of Toleration and Church Establishments; Occasioned by his Speech against the Repeal of the Test and Corporation Acts, on Wednesday the 28th of March 1787* (London: J. Johnson and J. Debrett, 1787)

Priestley, Joseph, *Defences of Unitarianism for the Year 1786, containing Letters to Dr Horne, Dean of Canterbury . . . On the Subject of the Person of Christ* (Birmingham: Pearson and Rollason, 1788)

Priestley, Joseph, *The Conduct to be observed by Dissenters in order to procure the Repeal of the Coropration and Test Acts, recommended in a Sermon, preached before the Congregations of the Old and New Meetings at Birmingham, November 5, 1789* (Birmingham: J. Thompson, [1789])

Priestley, Joseph, *Defences of Unitarianism for the Years 1788 & 1789. Containing Letters to Dr Horsley, Lord Bishop of St. Davids* (Birmingham: J. Thompson, [1790])

Priestley, Joseph, *A Discourse on Occasion of the Death of Dr Price; delivered at Hackney, on Sunday, May 1, 1791* (London: J. Johnson, 1791)

Priestley, Joseph, *Letters to the Right Honourable Edmund Burke, occasioned by his Reflections on the Revolution in France, &c.* (Birmingham: Thomas Pearson, and London: J. Johnson, 1791)

Priestley, Joseph, *Discourses relating to the Evidences of Revealed Religion. Vol. I. Delivered at Hackney in 1793, 1794* (London: J. Johnson, 1794)

Priestley, Joseph, *Letters addressed to the Philosophers and Politicians of France, on the Subject of Religion. To which are prefixed, Observations relating to the General Prevalence of Infidelity* (Philadelphia: Thomas Dobson, 1794)

Proceedings and Debates of the British Parliaments Respecting North America 1754–1783, ed. Richard C. Simmons and P. D. G. Thomas (6 vols, White Plains, NY: Kraus, 1982–6)

Prospectus of the East London Democratic Association (London, 1837)

Quincy, Josiah, 'Journal of Josiah Quincy, Jun., during his Voyage and Residence in England from September 28th, 1774, to March 3d, 1775', *Proceedings of the Massachusetts Historical Society* 3rd ser. 50 (1916–17), 433–96

[Ramsay, Allan], *Thoughts on the Origin and Nature of Government. Occasioned by The late Disputes between Great Britain and her American Colonies. Written in the Year 1766* (London: T. Becket and P. A. De Hondt, 1769)

[Ramsay, Allan], *A Plan of Reconciliation between Great Britain and her Colonies... By which the Rights of Englishmen, in Matters of Taxation, are preserved to the Inhabitants of America, and the Islands beyond Atlantic* (London: J. Johnson, 1776)

Ramsay, David, *The History of the American Revolution* (2 vols, Philadelphia: R. Aitken, 1789); ed. Lester H. Cohen (2 vols, Indianapolis: Liberty Classics, 1990)

Rapin de Thoyras, Paul, *The History of England: as well Ecclesiastical as Civil*, trans. Nicholas Tindal (15 vols, London: James and John Knapton, 1726–31)

Raynal, Guillaume-Thomas, Abbé, *The Revolution of America* (London: Lockyer Davis, 1781)

Reid, William Hamilton, *The Rise and Dissolution of the Infidel Societies in the Metropolis: including, the origin of modern Deism and Atheism; the genius and conduct of those associations; their lecture-rooms, field-meetings, and deputations; From the Publication of Paine's Age of Reason till the present Period* (London: J. Hatchard, 1800)

Reid, Thomas, *An Inquiry into the Human Mind, On the Principles of Common Sense* (Edinburgh: A. Kincaid and J. Bell, and London: A. Millar, 1764)

Revolution Society, *An Abstract of the History and Proceedings of the Revolution Society, in London. To which is annexed a copy of the Bill of Rights* ('Printed by Order of the Committee', 1789)

Rickman, Thomas Clio, *The Life of Thomas Paine* (London: Rickman, 1819)

The Rights and Liberties of the People of England Vindicated (London: W. Nicoll, [?1770])

Ritson, Joseph, *The Letters of Joseph Ritson, Esq.* (2 vols, London: William Pickering, 1833)

Rivers, David, *Observations on the Political Conduct of the Protestant Dissenters* (London: T. Burton, [?1799])

[Roebuck, John], *An Enquiry, whether the Guilt of the Present Civil War in America, Ought to be Imputed to Great Britain or America* (London: John Donaldson, 1776)

Roland, Mme, *Mémoirs de Madame Roland*, ed. Paul de Roux (Paris: Mercure de France, 1966)

Romilly, *Memoirs of the Life of Sir Samuel Romilly, Written by Himself, with a Selection from his Correspondence, edited by his Sons* (3 vols, London: John Murray, 1840)

[Rous, George], *Thoughts on Government: occasioned by Mr Burke's Reflections, &c. In a Letter to a Friend* (London: J. Debrett, 1790)

Rousseau, Jean-Jacques, *On the Social Contract, or Principles of Political Right* (1762), in *The Collected Writings of Rousseau*, ed. Roger D. Masters and Christopher Kelly (Hanover, NH: University Press of New England, 1994), iv

Ruggles, Tho[mas], *The History of the Poor; their Rights, Duties, and the Laws respecting them* (2 vols, London: J. Deighton, 1793–4)

[Rush, Benjamin], *An Address to the Inhabitants of the British Settlements in America, upon Slave-Keeping* (Philadelphia: John Dunlap, 1773; 2nd edn, 1773)

Rush, Benjamin, *The Autobiography of Benjamin Rush*, ed. George W. Corner (Princeton: Princeton University Press for the American Philosophical Society, 1948)

Rush, Benjamin, *The Letters of Benjamin Rush*, ed. L. H. Butterfield (2 vols, Princeton: Princeton University Press for the American Philosophical Society, 1951)

Russell, William, 'Preface' to *Essay on the Character, Manners, and Genius of Women in Different Ages, Enlarged from the French of M. Thomas* (2 vols, Philadelphia: R. Aitken, 1774)

Schutz, John A. and Douglass Adair (eds), *The Spur of Fame: dialogues of John Adams and Benjamin Rush, 1805–1813* (San Marino, Calif.: Huntington Library, 1966)

Scott, James, *Equality Considered and Recommended, in a Sermon…April the 6th, 1792* (London: John Nichols for J. Debrett, 1792)

[Scott, John], *A Letter to the Right Hon. Edmund Burke, In Reply to his 'Reflections on the Revolution in France, &c.' By a Member of the Revolution Society* (Dublin: J. Sheppard et al., 1791)

[Serle, Ambrose], *Equality no Liberty; or, Subordination the Order of God, and the Welfare of Man* (London: no printer, 1792)

Sharp, Granville, *A Representation of the Injustice and Dangerous Tendency of Tolerating Slavery; or of Admitting the Least Claim of Private Property in the Persons of Men, in England* (London: Benjamin White and Robert Horsfield, 1769)

Sharp, Granville, *A Declaration of the People's Natural Right to a Share in the Legislature; Which is the Fundamental Principle of the British Constitution of State* (London: B. White, 1774)

[Shipley, Jonathan], *A Speech, Intended to have been Spoken on the Bill for Altering the Charters of the Colony of Massachusett's Bay* (London: T. Cadell, 1774)

Sieyès, Emmanuel Joseph, *An Essay on Privileges, and particularly on Hereditary Nobility. Written by the Abbe Sieyes, a Member of the National Assembly; and Translated into English, with Notes, by a Foreign Nobleman, now in England* (London: J. Ridgway, 1791)

Sieyès, Emmanuel Joseph, *Political Writings Including the Debate between Sieyès and Tom Paine in 1791*, ed. Michael Sonenscher (Indianapolis: Hackett, 2003)

Smith, Adam, *An Inquiry into the Nature and Causes of the Wealth of Nations*, ed. R. H. Campbell and A. S. Skinner (2 vols, Oxford: Clarendon Press, 1976)

Smith, Captain George, *The Use and Abuse of Free-Masonry: a work of the greatest utility to the brethren of the society, to mankind in general, and to the ladies in particular* (London: G. Kearsley, 1783; 2nd edn, 1785)

Smith, Paul H. (ed.), *Letters of Delegates to Congress 1774–1789* (Washington: Library of Congress, 1976–)

Smollett, T[obias], *A Complete History of England, from the Descent of Julius Caesar, to the Treaty of Aix la Chapelle, 1748* (3rd edn, 11 vols, London: Richard Baldwin, 1760)

Somers, John, 1st Baron, *The Judgment of Whole Kingdoms and Nations concerning the Rights, Power, and Prerogative of Kings* (London: T. Harrison, 1710)

Southey, Robert, *Essays, Moral and Political* (2 vols, London: John Murray, 1832)

[Spence, Thomas], *The End of Oppression; Being a Dialogue between an Old Mechanic and a Young One. Concerning the Establishment of the Rights of Man* (2nd edn, London: T[homas] Spence, [1795])

Spence, T[homas], *The Rights of Man, as Exhibited in a Lecture, Read at the Philosophical Society, in Newcastle, To which is now added, an Interesting Conversation, Between a Gentleman and the Author, on the Subject of his Scheme. With The Queries sent by the Rev. Mr J. Murray, to the Society in Defence of the Same* (London: T. Spence, 1793)

Spence, T[homas], *The Rights of Infants; or, the Imprescriptable Right of Mothers to such a Share of the Elements as is sufficient to enable them to suckle and bring up their Young. In a Dialogue between the Aristocracy and a Mother of Children. To which are added, by Way of Preface and Appendix, Strictures on Paine's Agrarian Justice* (London: T. Spence, 1797)

Spinoza, B. de, *Traitté des Cérémonies superstitieuses des Juifs tant anciens que modernes*, trans. D. de Saint-Glain (Amsterdam: Jacob Smith, 1678)

[Stevens, John], *Examen du gouvernement d'Angleterre, compare aux constitutions des États-Unis... Par un cultivateur de New-Jersey. Ouvrage traduit de l'anglois, & accompagné de notes*, [trans. J. L. Faure?] (Londres [i.e. Paris?]: et se trouve à Paris, chez Froullé, 1789)

Stewart, John, *Opus Maximum: or, the great essay to reduce the world from contingency to system, in the following new sciences: Psyconomy; or, the science of moral powers... Mathemanomy; or, the laws of knowledge: Logonomy; or, the science of language: Anagognomy; or, the science of education: Ontonomy; or, the science of being* (London: J. Ginger, 1803)

Stiles, Ezra, *The Literary Diary of Ezra Stiles, D.D., LL.D.*, ed. Franklin Bowditch Dexter (4 vols, New York: Charles Scribner's Sons, 1901)

Stillwell, Samuel, *A Guide to Reason or an Examination of Thomas Paine's Age of Reason, And Investigation of True and Fabulous Theology* (New York: John Buel, 1794)

Stokes, Anthony, *A View of the Constitution of the British Colonies, in North-America and the West Indies, at the Time the Civil War broke out in the Continent of America* (London: for the author, 1783)

Swift, Jonathan, *Three Sermons: I. On Mutual Subjection. II. On Conscience. III. On the Trinity* (London: R. Dodsley and M. Cooper, 1744)

Tatham, Edward, *Letters to the Right Honourable Edmund Burke on Politics* (Oxford: J. Fletcher, 1791)

Thackeray, Francis, *Order against Anarchy. Being a Reply to Thomas Paine's Attack upon the British Constitution, entitled 'The Rights of Man;'—with Observations addressed to all Classes of the Community, and Particularly Applicable to the Present Period* (London: C. J. G. and F. Rivington, 1831)

Thale, Mary (ed.), *Selections from the Papers of the London Corresponding Society 1792–1799* (Cambridge: Cambridge University Press, 1983)

Thelwall, John, *An Essay, Towards a Definition of Animal Vitality* (London: G. G. J. and J. Robinson, 1793)

Thelwall, John, *Political Lectures. Volume the First—Part the First* (London: Eaton and Smith, 1795)

Thelwall, John, *The Tribune, a Periodical Publication, consisting chiefly of the Political Lectures of J. Thelwall* (London: Eaton and Burks, 1795)

Thelwall, John, *Rights of Nature, against the Usurpation of Establishments. A Series of Letters to the People, in Reply to the False Principles of Burke* (London: H. D. Symonds, 1796)

Thelwall, John, *Rights of Nature, against the Usurpation of Establishments. A Series of Letters to the People, in Reply to the False Principles of Burke. Part the Second* (London: H. D. Symonds, 1796)

Thelwall, John, *Sober Reflections on the Seditious and Inflammatory Letter of the Rt. Hon. Edmund Burke to a Noble Lord* (London: Symonds, 1796)

Thelwall, John, *The Life of John Thelwall* [by Henrietta Cecil Boyle Thelwall] (London: John Macrone, 1837)

Thelwall, John, *The Politics of English Jacobinism: Writings of John Thelwall*, ed. Gregory Claeys (University Park, Pa: Pennsylvania State University Press, 1995)

Thomas, Antoine Léonard, *Essai sur le caractère, les moeurs et l'esprit des femmes dans les différens siècles* (2 vols, Paris, 1772)

Thomson, James, *Antient and Modern Italy Compared: Being the First Part of Liberty, a Poem* (London: A. Millar, 1735); *Greece: Being the Second Part of Liberty, a Poem* (London: A. Millar, 1735); *Rome: Being the Third Part of Liberty, a Poem* (London: A. Millar, 1735); *Britain: Being the Fourth Part of Liberty, a Poem* (London: A. Millar, 1736)

Thomson, James, *The Seasons* (London: no printer, 1736)

Thorpe, Francis Newton (ed.), *The Federal and State Constitutions, Colonial Charters, and other Organic Laws of the States, Territories, and Colonies now or heretofore forming the United States of America* (7 vols, Washington: Government Printing Office, 1909)

[Tindal, Matthew], *An Essay Concerning the Power of the Magistrate, and the Rights of Mankind, in Matters of Religion* (London: Andrew Bell, 1697)

Tocqueville, Alexis de, *The Old Regime and the Revolution*, ed. François Furet and Françoise Mélonio (2 vols, Chicago: University of Chicago Press, 1998–2001)

Tone, Theobald, *The Life of Theobald Wolfe Tone edited by his Son*, William T. W. Tone (2 vols, Washington: Gales and Seaton, 1826)

Tone, Theobald, *The Writings of Theobald Wolfe Tone 1763–98*, ed. T. W. Moody, R. B. McDowell, and C. J. Woods (3 vols, Oxford: Clarendon Press, 1998–2007)

Toulmin, Joshua, *Two Letters on the late Applications to Parliament by the Protestant Dissenting Ministers* (London: J. Johnson, 1774)

Towers, Joseph, *An Oration delivered at the London Tavern, on the Fourth of November, 1788, on Occasion of the Commemoration of the Revolution, And the Completion of a Century from that great Event* (London: Charles Dilly, 1788)

Towers, Joseph, *Thoughts on the Commencement of a New Parliament. With an Appendix, containing Remarks on the Letter of the Right Hon. Edmund Burke, on the Revolution in France* (London: Charles Dilly, 1790)

[Trenchard, John], *Cato's Letters* (4 vols, London: W. Wilkins et al., 1723–4)

Turgot, [Anne-Robert-Jacques], *Reflections on the Formation and Distribution of Wealth* (London: J. Good et al., 1793)

An Unconnected Whig's Address to the Public; upon the Present Civil War, the State of Public Affairs, and the Real Cause of all the National Calamities (London: G. Kearsley, 1777)

Vincent, David (ed.), *Testaments of Radicalism: Memoirs of Working Class Politicians 1790–1885* (London: Europa Publications, 1977)

Volnay, Constantin François Chasseboeuf, comte de, *Les Ruines: ou Méditation sur les révolutions des empires* (Paris, 1791)

Volnay, Constantin François Chasseboeuf, comte de, *The Ruins: or a survey of the revolutions of empires by M. Volney... Translated from the French* (London: J. Johnson, 1792)

Voltaire, J. B. Arouet de, *Letters Concerning the English Nation* (London: C. Davis and A. Lyon, 1733)

Voltaire, J. B. Arouet de, *The White Bull, an Oriental History. From an Ancient Syrian Manuscript, communicated by Mr Voltaire* [trans. Jeremy Bentham] (London: J. Bew, 1774)

[Wagstaffe, Thomas], *The Rights and Liberties of Englishmen* (London: A. Baldwin, 1701)

Waldegrave, Lord, *The Memoirs and Speeches of James, 2nd Earl Waldegrave, 1742–1763*, ed. J. C. D. Clark (Cambridge: Cambridge University Press, 1988)

Walker, John. John Epps, *Life of John Walker, M.D.* (London: Whittaker, Treacher, 1831)

Walker, Thomas, *A Review of Some of the Political Events which have occurred in Manchester, during the Last Five Years* (London: J. Johnson, 1794)

Walpole, Horace, *Memoirs of King George II*, ed. John Brooke (3 vols, New Haven: Yale University Press, 1985)

Warburton, William, *A Sermon Preached before the Incorporated Society for the Propagation of the Gospel in Foreign Parts; at their Anniversary Meeting in the Parish Church of St. Mary-le-Bow, On Friday February 21, 1766* (London: E. Owen and T. Harrison, 1766)

Warren, Mercy Otis, *History of the Rise, Progress and Termination of the American Revolution* (3 vols, Boston: Manning and Loring, 1805); ed. Lester H. Cohen (2 vols, Indianapolis: Liberty Classics, 1988)

Washington, George, *The Writings of Washington from the Original Manuscript Sources, 1754–1799*, ed. John C. Fitzpatrick (39 vols, Washington, 1931–44)

Washington, George, *The Diaries of George Washington*, ed. Donald Jackson and Dorothy Twohig (6 vols, Charlottesville, Va, 1976–9)

Washington, George, *The Papers of George Washington*, ed. W. W. Abbott and Dorothy Twohig (Charlottesville, Va, 1981–): *The Colonial Series*; *The Revolutionary War Series*

Washington, George, *The Papers of George Washington. Presidential Series*, ed. W. W. Abbot and Dorothy Twohig (Charlottesville, Va: University Press of Virginia, 1987–)

Watson, Elkanah, *Men and Times of the Revolution; or, Memoirs of Elkanah Watson*, ed. Winslow C. Watson (New York: D. Appleton, 1861)

[Watson, Richard], *A Letter to the Members of the Honourable House of Commons; respecting the Petition for Relief in the Matter of Subscription. By a Christian Whig* (London: W. Bowyer and J. Nichols, 1772)

Watson, Richard, *A Sermon preached before the Stewards of the Westminster Dispensary at their Anniversary Meeting, in Charlotte-Street Chapel, April 1785. With an Appendix. The Wisdom and Goodness of God, in having made both Rich and Poor* (Loughborough: Adams, Jun. and London: T. Cadell and T. Evans, 1793)

Watson, R[ichard], *An Apology for the Bible, in a Series of Letters addressed to Thomas Paine, Author of a Book entitled, The Age of Reason, Part the Second, being an Investigation of True and Fabulous Theology* (London: T. Evans et al., 1796)

Wesley, John, *Extract of Count Zinzendorf's Discourses on the Redemption of Man by the Death of Christ* (Newcastle: John Gooding, et al., 1744)

Wesley, John, *The Journal of the Rev. John Wesley, A.M.*, ed. Nehemiah Curnock (London, 1916)

Wesley, John, *The Letters of the Rev. John Wesley, AM*, ed. John Telford (8 vols, London: Epworth Press, 1931)

Whitefield, George, 'Christ, the Believer's Wisdom, Righteousness, Sanctification, and Redemption', in his *Nine Sermons* (London: Sam. Mason and Gab. Harris, 1742)

Willard, Margaret Wheeler (ed.), *Letters on the American Revolution 1774–1776* (Boston: Houghton Mifflin, 1925)

Williams, Helen Maria, *A Tour in Switzerland; or, A View of the Present State of the Governments and Manners of those Cantons: with Comparative Sketches of The Present State of Paris* (2 vols, London: G. G. and J. Robinson, 1798)

Williams, Samuel, *The Natural and Civil History of Vermont* (Walpole, NH: Isaiah Thomas and David Carlisle, 1794)

Wilmer, James Jones, *Consolation: being a Replication to Thomas Paine, and others, on Theologics* (Philadelphia: William W. Woodward, 1794)

[Wollstonecraft, Mary], *A Vindication of the Rights of Men, in a Letter to the Right Honourable Edmund Burke; occasioned by his Reflections on the Revolution in France* (London: J. Johnson, 1790)

Wollstonecraft, Mary, *An Historical and Moral View of the Origin and Progress of the French Revolution; and the Effect it has Produced in Europe* (London: J. Johnson, 1794)

Wollstonecraft, Mary, *Collected Letters of Mary Wollstonecraft*, ed. Ralph M. Wardle (Ithaca, NY: Cornell University Press, 1979)

Wollstonecraft, Mary, *The Works of Mary Wollstonecraft*, ed. Janet Todd and Marilyn Butler (7 vols, London: William Pickering, 1989)

Woolsey, Robert, *Reflections upon Reflections, including some Observations on the Constitution and Laws of England; particularly On Pressing, on the Excise, on Libels, &c. In Two Letters, to the Right Hon. Edmund Burke, In answer to his Pamphlet* (London: for the author, and sold by W. Stewart, 1790)

Wyvill, Christopher, *Political Papers, comprising the Correspondence of several Distinguished Persons in the Years 1792, 1793, &c. with the Editor, the Rev. Christopher Wyvill* (6 vols, York: L. Lund, [1794–1802])

Yorke, Henry Redhead, *Letters from France, in 1802* (2 vols, London: H. D. Symonds, 1804)

Zinzendorf, Nicolaus Ludwig, Graf von, *Sixteen Discourses on the Redemption of Man By the Death of Christ* (London: James Hutton, 1740)

SECONDARY

Abel, Darrell, 'The Significance of the Letter to the Abbé Raynal in the Progress of Thomas Paine's Thought', *PMHB* 66 (1942), 176–90

Adams, Thomas R., *American Independence: The Growth of an Idea: A Bibliographical Study of the American Political Pamphlets Printed between 1764 and 1776 Dealing with the Dispute between Great Britain and her Colonies* (Providence, RI, 1965)

Adams, Thomas R., *The American Controversy: A Bibliographical Study of the British Pamphlets about the American Disputes, 1764–1783* (2 vols, Providence, RI, 1980)

Adams, W. Paul 'Republicanism in Political Rhetoric before 1776', *Political Science Quarterly* 85 (1970), 397–421

Albertone, Manuela and Antonino De Francesco (eds), *Rethinking the Atlantic World: Europe and America in the Age of Democratic Revolutions* (Basingstoke, 2009)

Alden, John Richard, *General Charles Lee: Traitor or Patriot?* (Baton Rouge, La, 1951)

Aldridge, Alfred Owen, 'Thomas Paine's Plan for a Descent on England', *WMQ* 14 (Jan. 1957), 74–84

Aldridge, Alfred Owen, 'Condorcet et Paine', *Revue de la literature compare* 32 (1958), 47–65

Aldridge, A. Owen., 'The Influence of Thomas Paine in the United States, England, France, Germany and South America', in Werner P. Friederich (ed.), *Comparative Literature: Proceedings of the ICLA Congress* (Chapel Hill, NC, 1959), ii. 369–83

Aldridge, Alfred Owen, *Man of Reason: The Life of Thomas Paine* (London, 1960)

Aldridge, A. Owen, 'Thomas Paine and the Classics', *Eighteenth-Ccentury Studies* 1 (1968), 370–80

Aldridge, A. Owen, 'Paine and Dickinson', *Early American Literature* 11 (1976), 125–38

Aldridge, A. Owen, 'The Problem of Thomas Paine', *Studies in Burke and his Time* 19 (1976), 127–43

Aldridge, Alfred Owen, *Thomas Paine's American Ideology* (Newark, Del., 1984)

Aldridge, Alfred Owen, 'Condorcet, Paine and Historical Method', in Leonora Cohen Rosenfield (ed.), *Condorcet Studies I* (Atlantic Highlands, NJ, 1984), 49–60

Aldridge, A. Owen, 'Natural Religion and Deism in America before Ethan Allen and Thomas Paine', *WMQ* 54 (1997), 835–48

Alexander, John K., *Render Them Submissive: Responses to Poverty in Philadelphia, 1760–1800* (Amherst, Mass., 1980)

Alger, John G., *Englishmen in the French Revolution* (London, 1889)

Andrews, Dee E., *The Methodists and Revolutionary America, 1760–1800: The Shaping of an Evangelical Culture* (Princeton, 2000)

Anon., 'Catholics and the American Revolution', *The American Catholic Historical Researches* new ser. 2 no. 1 (Jan. 1906), 1–40

Appleby, Joyce, *Capitalism and a New Social Order: The Republican Vision of the 1790s* (New York, 1984)

Appleby, Joyce, *Inheriting the Revolution: The First Generation of Americans* (Cambridge, Mass., 2000)

Arendt, Hannah, *On Revolution* (New York, 1963)

Armitage, David, *The Declaration of Independence: A Global History* (Cambridge, Mass., 2007)

Aulard, François-Alphonse, *The French Revolution: A Political History 1789–1804*, trans. Bernard Miall (4 vols, New York, 1910)

Ayer, A. J., *Thomas Paine* (London, 1988)

Bailyn, Bernard, *The Ideological Origins of the American Revolution* (Cambridge, 1967)

Bailyn, Bernard, 'Common Sense', in *Fundamental Testaments of the American Revolution* (Washington, 1973), 7–22

Baker, Keith Michael, *Inventing the French Revolution: Essays on French Political Culture in the Eighteenth Century* (Cambridge, 1990)

Baker, Keith Michael, 'Revolutionizing Revolution', in Keith Michael Baker and Dan Edelstein (eds), *Scripting Revolution: A Historical Approach to the Comparative Study of Revolutions* (Stanford, Calif., 2015), 71–102

Barlow, Richard Burgess, *Citizenship and Conscience: A Study in the Theory and Practice of Religious Toleration in England during the Eighteenth Century* (Philadelphia, 1962)

Bayet, Albert and François Albert, *Les Écrivains politiques du XIXe siècle* (Paris, 1935)

Beeman, Richard R., *The Varieties of Political Experience in Eighteenth-Century America* (Philadelphia, 2004)

Beer, M. (ed.), *The Pioneers of Land Reform: Thomas Spence, William Ogilvie, Thomas Paine* (London, 1920)

Belchem, John, *'Orator' Hunt: Henry Hunt and English Working-Class Radicalism* (Oxford, 1985)

Belchem, John, *Popular Radicalism in Nineteenth-Century Britain* (London, 1996)

Belissa, Marc, 'La Légende grise des dernières années de Thomas Paine en Amérique, 1802–1809', *Annales historiques de la Révolution Française* no. 360 (Apr. –June 2010), 133–72

Bell, David A., *The Cult of the Nation in France: Inventing Nationalism, 1680–1800* (Cambridge, Mass., 2001)

Bell, David A., *The First Total War: Napoleon's Europe and the Birth of Warfare as We Know It* (Boston, 2007)

Bell, James B., *The Imperial Origins of the King's Church in Early America, 1607–1783* (Basingstoke, 2004)

Bell, James B., *A War of Religion: Dissenters, Anglicans, and the American Revolution* (Basingstoke, 2008)

Ben-Atar, Doron S., *The Origins of Jeffersonian Commercial Policy and Diplomacy* (Basingstoke, 1993)

Ben-Israel, Hedva, *English Historians on the French Revolution* (Cambridge, 1968)

Berman, David, *A History of Atheism in Britain: From Hobbes to Russell* (London, 1988)

Betts, C. J., *Early Deism in France: From the So-Called 'Déistes' of Lyon (1564) to Voltaire's 'Lettres philosophiques' (1734)* (The Hague, 1984)

Bewley, Christina and David, *Gentleman Radical: A Life of John Horne Tooke 1736–1812* (London, 1998)

Bickham, Troy, *Making Headlines: The American Revolution as Seen through the British Press* (De Kalb, Ill., 2009)

Biard, Michel, *Missionaires de la République: les représentants du peuple en mission (1793–1795)* (Paris, 2002)

Bihoreau, Dominique, *La Pensée politique et sociale en France au XIX siècle* (Paris, 1995)

Black, Jeremy, *War for America: The Fight for Independence 1775–1783* (Stroud, 1991)

Blackburn, Robin, 'Slavery, Emancipation and Human Rights', in Kate E. Tunstall (ed.), *Self-Evident Truths? Human Rights and the Enlightenment* (London, 2012), 137–55

Blakemore, Steven, *Crisis in Representation: Thomas Paine, Mary Wollstonecraft, Helen Maria Williams, and the Rewriting of the French Revolution* (London, 1997)

Blakemore, Steven, *Intertextual War: Edmund Burke and the French Revolution in the Writings of Mary Wollstonecraft, Thomas Paine, and James Mackintosh* (London, 1997)

Blanning, T. C. W., *The Origins of the French Revolutionary Wars* (London, 1986)

Bloch, Ruth H., *Visionary Republic: Millennial Themes in American Thought, 1756–1800* (Cambridge, 1985)

Bonwick, Colin, *English Radicals and the American Revolution* (Chapel Hill, NC, 1977)

Bosher, J. F., *The French Revolution* (London, 1989)

Bosworth, Timothy W., 'Anti-Catholicism as a Political Tool in Mid-Eighteenth-Century Maryland', *Catholic Historical Review* 61 (1975), 539–63

Bouton, Terry, 'A Road Closed: Rural Insurgency in Post-Independence Pennsylvania', *Journal of American History* 87 (2000), 855–87

Bouton, Terry, *Taming Democracy: 'The People', the Founders, and the Troubled Ending of the American Revolution* (New York, 2007)

Breen, T. H., 'Retrieving Common Sense: Rights, Liberties and the Religious Public Sphere in Late Eighteenth Century America', in Josephine F. Pacheco (ed.), *To Secure the Blessings of Liberty: Rights in American History* (Fairfax, Va, 1993), 55–65

Breen, T. H., 'An Appeal to Heaven: The Language of Rights on the Eve of American Independence', in Robert Fatton Jr and R. K. Ramazani (ed.), *The Future of Liberal Democracy: Thomas Jefferson and the Contemporary World* (Basingstoke, 2004), 65–83

Breen, T. H., *American Insurgents, American Patriots: The Revolution of the People* (New York, 2010)

Brent, Colin, 'Thirty Something: Thomas Paine at Bull House in Lewes 1768–74—Six Formative Years', *Sussex Archaeological Collections* 147 (2009), 153–67

Brewer, John, *Party Ideology and Popular Politics at the Accession of George III* (Cambridge, 1976)

Brinton, Clarence Crane, *The Jacobins* (New York, 1930)

Brinton, Crane, *The Anatomy of Revolution* (1939; 3rd edn, New York, 1965)

Bronson, Bertrand H., *Joseph Ritson: Scholar-at-Arms* (2 vols., Berkeley, 1938)

Brown, Richard D., *Knowledge is Power: The Diffusion of Information in Early America, 1700–1865* (New York, 1989)

Brown, Thomas More, 'The Image of the Beast: Anti-Papal Rhetoric in Colonial America', in Richard O. Curry and Thomas M. Brown (eds), *Conspiracy: The Fear of Subversion in American History* (New York, 1972), 1–20

Buckley, F. H., *The Once and Future King: The Rise of Crown Government in America* (New York, 2014)

Budd, Susan, *Varieties of Unbelief: Atheists and Agnostics in English Society 1850–1960* (London, 1977)

Buel, Richard, *In Irons: Britain's Naval Supremacy and the American Revolutionary Economy* (New Haven, 1998)

Bushell, T. L., *The Sage of Salisbury: Thomas Chubb 1679–1747* (London, 1968)

Calvert, Jane E., *Quaker Constitutionalism and the Political Thought of John Dickinson* (Cambridge, 2009)

Calvert, Jane E., 'Thomas Paine, Quakerism and the Limits of Religious Liberty during the American Revolution', in *Selected Writings of Thomas Paine*, ed. Ian Shapiro and Jane E. Calvert (New Haven, 2014), 602–29

Cannon, John, *Parliamentary Reform 1640–1832* (Cambridge, 1973)

Carnall, Geoffrey, *Robert Southey and his Age* (Oxford, 1960)

Caron, Nathalie, *Thomas Paine contre l'imposture des prêtres* (Paris, 1998)

Carp, Benjamin L., *Rebels Rising: Cities and the American Revolution* (Oxford, 2007)

Carruthers, Gerard, 'Alexander Geddes', *ODNB*

Casino, Joseph J., 'Anti-Popery in Colonial Pennsylvania', *PMHB* 105 (1981), 279–309

Chabot, Jean Luc, *Histoire de la pensée politique: XIXe–XXe siècle* (Paris, 1988)

Champion, J. A. I., 'Deism', in Richard H. Popkin (ed.), *The Columbia History of Western Philosophy* (New York, 1999), 437–45

Chase, Malcolm, 'Paine, Spence and the "Real Rights of Man"', *Bulletin of the Society for the Study of Labour History* 52 (1987), 32–40

Chase, Malcolm, *'The People's Farm': English Radical Agrarianism 1775–1840* (Oxford, 1988)

Cheng, Eileen Ka-May, *The Plain and Noble Garb of Truth: Nationalism & Impartiality in American Historical Writing, 1784–1860* (Athens, Ga, 2008)

Christian, William, 'The Moral Economics of Tom Paine', *Journal of the History of Ideas* 34 (1973), 367–80

Claeys, Gregory, *Thomas Paine: Social and Political Thought* (London, 1989)

Claeys, Gregory, 'The French Revolution Debate and British Political Thought', *History of Political Thought* 11 (1990), 59–80

Claeys, Gregory 'The Origins of the Rights of Labor: Republicanism, Commerce, and the Construction of Modern Social Theory in Britain, 1796–1805', *Journal of Modern History* 66 (1994), 249–90

Claeys, Gregory, 'The Example of America a Warning to England? The Transformation of America in British Radicalism and Socialism, 1790–1850', in Malcolm Chase and Ian Dyck (eds), *Living and Learning: Essays in Honour of J. F. C. Harrison* (Aldershot, 1996), 66–80

Claeys, Gregory, *The French Revolution Debate in Britain* (Basingstoke, 2007)

Claeys, Gregory, 'Paine's *Rights of Man* and the Religiosity of Rights Doctrines', in Rachel Hammersley (ed.), *Revolutionary Moments: Reading Revolutionary Texts* (London, 2015), 85–92

Clark, Harry Hayden, 'An Historical Interpretation of Thomas Paine's Religion', *University of California Chronicle* 35 (Jan. 1933), 56–87

Clark, J. C. D., *The Language of Liberty 1660–1832: Political Discourse and Social Dynamics in the Anglo-American World* (Cambridge, 1994)

Clark, J. C. D., *Samuel Johnson: Literature, Religion and English Cultural Politics from the Restoration to Romanticism* (Cambridge, 1994)

Clark, J. C. D., *English Society 1660–1832: Religion, Ideology and Politics during the Ancien Regime* (Cambridge, 2000)

Clark, J. C. D., 'Protestantism, Nationalism and National Identity 1660–1832', *HJ* 43 (2000), 249–76

Clark, J. C. D., 'Edmund Burke's *Reflections on the Revolution in America* (1777); or, How Did the American Revolution Relate to the French?', in Ian Crowe (ed.), *An Imaginative Whig: Reassessing the Life and Thought of Edmund Burke* (Columbia, SC, 2005), 73–92

Clark, J. C. D., 'Religion and the Origin of Radicalism in Nineteenth-Century Britain', in Glenn Burgess and Matthew Festenstein (eds), *English Radicalism, 1550–1850* (Cambridge, 2007), 241–84

Clark, J. C. D., 'The Eighteenth-Century Context', in William J. Abraham and James E. Kirby (eds), *The Oxford Handbook of Methodist Studies* (Oxford, 2009), 3–29

Clark, J. C. D., 'The Enlightenment: catégories, traductions et objets sociaux', in Gérard Laudin and Didier Masseau (eds), *Lumières*, special issue 17–18 (2011), 19–39

Clark, Jonathan and Howard Erskine-Hill, (eds), *Samuel Johnson in Historical Context* (Basingstoke, 2002)

Clark, Jonathan and Howard Erskine-Hill (eds), *The Politics of Samuel Johnson* (Basingstoke, 2012)

Clark, Jonathan and Howard Erskine-Hill (eds), *The Interpretation of Samuel Johnson* (Basingstoke, 2012)

Clark, J. C. D., 'Secularization and Modernization: The Failure of a "Grand Narrative"', *HJ* 55 (2012), 161–94

Clark, J. C. D., 'Thomas Paine: The English Dimension', in *Selected Writings of Thomas Paine*, ed. Ian Shapiro and Jane E. Calvert (New Haven, 2014), 579–601

Clark, J. C. D., *From Restoration to Reform: The British Isles 1660–1832* (London, 2014)

Clark, J. C. D., 'Monuments to Liberty', *Times Literary Supplement*, 18 Sept. 2015, 14–15

Clark, Thomas, 'A Note on Tom Paine's "Vulgar" Style', *Communications Quarterly* 26:2 (1978), 31–4

Cleary, Scott and Ivy Stabell (eds), *New Directions in Thomas Paine Studies* (New York, 2016)

Cleves, Rachel Hope, *The Reign of Terror in America: Visions of Violence from Anti-Jacobinism to Antislavery* (New York, 2009)

Cogliano, Francis D., *No King, No Popery: Anti-Catholicism in Revolutionary New England* (Westport, Conn., 1995)

Colmer, John, *Coleridge: Critic of Society* (Oxford, 1959)

Conway, Moncure Daniel, *Thomas Paine (1737–1809) et la Révolution dans les deux mondes* (Paris, 1900)

Conway, Moncure Daniel, *The Life of Thomas Paine* (2 vols, New York, 1902; ed. Hypatia Bradlaugh Bonner, London, 1909)

Conway, Stephen, *The American War of Independence 1775–1783* (London, 1995)

Copeland, Thomas W., 'Burke, Paine and Jefferson', in Copeland, *Our Eminent Friend Edmund Burke: Six Essays* (New Haven, 1949), 146–89

Cotlar, Seth, *Tom Paine's America: The Rise and Fall of Transatlantic Radicalism in the Early Republic* (Charlottesville, Va, 2011)

Cotlar, Seth, 'Languages of Democracy in America from the Revolution to the Election of 1800', in Joanna Innes and Mark Philp (eds), *Re-imagining Democracy in the Age of Revolutions: America, France, Britain, Ireland 1750–1850* (Oxford, 2013), 14–27

Cotter, William R., 'The Somerset Case and the Abolition of Slavery in England', *History* 79 (1994), 31–56

Crary, Catherine S., *The Price of Loyalty: Tory Writings from the Revolutionary Era* (New York: McGraw-Hill, 1973)

Crook, David Paul, *American Democracy in English Politics 1815–1850* (Oxford, 1965)

Crook, Paul, 'Whiggery and America: Accommodating the Radical Threat', in Michael T. Davis (ed.), *Radicalism and Revolution in Britain, 1775–1848: Essays in Honour of Malcolm I. Thomis* (Basingstoke, 2000), 191–206

Cruickshanks, Eveline, *Political Untouchables: The Tories and the '45* (London, 1979)

Daniel, Marcus, *Scandal & Civility: Journalism and the Birth of American Democracy* (New York, 2009)

Davidson, Edward H. and William J. Scheick, *Paine, Scripture and Authority: The Age of Reason as Religious and Political Idea* (Bethlehem, Pa, 1994)

Davidson, Philip Grant, *Propaganda and the American Revolution 1763–1783* (Chapel Hill, NC, 1941)

Davis, David Brion, *The Problem of Slavery in the Age of Revolution 1770–1823* (Ithaca, NY, 1975)

De Bolla, Peter, *The Architecture of Concepts: The Historical Formation of Human Rights* (New York, 2013)

De Francesco, Antonino, 'The American Origins of the French Revolutionary War', in Pierre Serna, Antonino De Francesco, and Judith A. Miller (eds), *Republics at War, 1776–1840: Revolutions, Conflicts, and Geopolitics in Europe and the Atlantic World* (Basingstoke, 2013), 27–45

Derry, John W., *The Radical Tradition: Tom Paine to Lloyd George* (London, 1967)

Dickson, David, 'Paine and Ireland', in Dickson, Dáire Keogh and Kevin Whelan (eds), *The United Irishmen: Republicanism, Radicalism and Rebellion* (Dublin, 1993), 135–50

Dickinson, H. T., 'Thomas Paine and his British Critics', *Enlightenment and Dissent* 27 (2011), 19–82

Dinwiddy, J. R., 'Charles Hall: Early English Socialist', *International Review of Social History* 21 (1976), 256–65, reprinted in Dinwiddy, *Radicalism and Reform in Britain, 1780–1850* (London, 1992)

Dinwiddy, J. R., 'Conceptions of Revolution in the English Radicalism of the 1790s', in Eckhart Hellmuth (ed.), *The Transformation of Political Culture: England and Germany in the Late Eighteenth Century* (Oxford, 1990), 535–60, reprinted in Dinwiddy, *Radicalism and Reform in Britain, 1780–1850* (London, 1992)

Dinwiddy, J. R, 'English Radicals and the French Revolution, 1800–1850', in F. Furet and M. Ozouf (eds.), *The French Revolution and the Creation of Modern Political Culture*, iii, *The Transformation of Political Culture 1789–1848* (Oxford, 1989), 447–66, reprinted in Dinwiddy, *Radicalism and Reform in Britain, 1780–1850* (London, 1992)

Dixon, Thomas, *From Passions to Emotions: The Creation of a Secular Psychological Category* (Cambridge, 2003)

Dorigny, Marcel and Bernard Gainot, *La Société des Amis des Noirs 1788–1799: Contribution à l'histoire de l'abolition de l'esclavage* (Paris, 1998)

Doyle, William, *The Oxford History of the French Revolution* (Oxford, 1989)

Doyle, William, *Officers, Nobles and Revolutionaries: Essays on Eighteenth-Century France* (London, 1995)

Doyle, William, *Aristocracy and its Enemies in the Age of Revolution* (Oxford, 2009)

Doyle, William, 'Thomas Paine and the Girondins', in Doyle, *Officers, Nobles and Revolutionaries*, 209–19

Doyle, William, 'The Principles of the French Revolution', in Doyle, *Officers, Nobles and Revolutionaries*, 163–72

Droz, Jacques, *Histoire des doctrines politiques en France* (Paris, 1948)

Duncan, Jason K., *Citizens or Papists? The Politics of Anti-Catholicism in New York, 1685–1821* (New York, 2005)

Dunn, John, 'The Politics of Locke in England and America in the Eighteenth Century', in John W. Yolton (ed.), *John Locke: Problems and Perspectives* (Cambridge, 1969), 45–80

Dunn, John, *Democracy: A History* (London, 2005)

Dunn, John, *Breaking Democracy's Spell* (New Haven, 2014)

Durey, Michael, *Transatlantic Radicals and the Early American Republic* (Lawrence, Kan., 1997)

Dworetz, Steven M., *The Unvarnished Doctrine: Locke, Liberalism and the American Revolution* (Durham, NC, 1990)

Dyck, Ian (ed.), *Citizen of the World: Essays on Thomas Paine* (New York, 1988)

Dyck, Ian, 'Local Attachments, National Identities and World Citizenship in the Thought of Thomas Paine', *History Workshop Journal* 35 (1993), 117–35

Echeverria, Durand, *Mirage in the West: A History of the French Image of American Society to 1815* (Princeton, 1957)

Edelstein, Dan, 'A Reply to Jonathan Israel', in Kate E. Tunstall (ed.), *Self-Evident Truths? Human Rights and the Enlightenment* (London, 2012), 127–35

Edelstein, Dan, 'Enlightenment Rights Talk', *Journal of Modern History* 86 (2014), 530–65

Edelstein, Dan, 'From Constitutional to Permanent Revolution: 1649 and 1793', in Keith Michael Baker and Dan Edelstein (eds), *Scripting Revolution: A Historical Approach to the Comparative Study of Revolutions* (Stanford, Calif., 2015), 118–30

Edelstein, Dan, 'Intellectual History and Digital Humanities' *Modern Intellectual History*, 31 (2016), 237–46

Egnal, Marc, *A Mighty Empire: The Origins of the American Revolution* (Ithaca, NY, 1988)

Elliott, Marianne, *Partners in Revolution: The United Irishmen and France* (New Haven, 1982)

Elliott, Marianne, *Wolfe Tone* (New Haven, 1988)

Elton, G. R., 'Human Rights and the Liberties of Englishmen', *University of Illinois Law Review* (1990), 329–46

Epstein, James A., *Radical Expression: Political Language, Ritual and Symbol in England, 1790–1850* (New York, 1994)

Erdman, David V., *Commerce des Lumières: John Oswald and the British in Paris, 1790–1793* (Columbia, SC, 1986)

Erskine-Hill, Howard, 'Alexander Pope: The Political Poet in his Time', *Eighteenth Century Studies* 15 (1981–2), 123–48

Eustace, Nicole, *Passion is the Gale: Emotion, Power, and the Coming of the American Revolution* (Williamsburg, Va, 2008)

Fara, Patricia, *Newton: The Making of Genius* (London, 2002)

Fennessy, R. R., *Burke, Paine and the Rights of Man: A Difference of Political Opinion* (The Hague, 1963)

Ferguson, Robert A., 'The Commonalities of *Common Sense*', *WMQ* 57 (2000), 465–504

Ferling, John, *Setting the World Ablaze: Washington, Adams, and the American Revolution* (New York, 2000)

Finnis, John, *Natural Law and Natural Rights* (Oxford, 1980)

Fischer, David Hackett, *Albion's Seed: Four British Folkways in America* (New York, 1989)

Fischer, David Hackett, *Paul Revere's Ride* (New York, 1994)

Flavell, Julie, 'British Perceptions of New England and the Decision for a Coercive Colonial Policy, 1774–1775', in Julie Flavell and Stephen Conway (eds), *Britain and America go to War: The Impact of War and Warfare in Anglo-America, 1754–1815* (Gainesville, Fla, 2004), 95–115

Foner, Eric, *Tom Paine and Revolutionary America* (London, 1976)

Foner, Eric, 'Tom Paine's Republic: Radical Ideology and Social Change', in Alfred F. Young (ed.), *The American Revolution: Explorations in the History of American Radicalism,* (DeKalb, Ill., 1976), 189–232

Ford, Paul Leicester, 'The Crisis', *The Bibliographer* 1 (1902), 139–52

Forsyth, Murray, *Reason and Revolution: The Political Thought of the Abbé Sieyes* (Leicester, 1987)

Francis, Mark and John Morrow, *A History of English Political Thought in the Nineteenth Century* (London, 1994)

French, Allen, *The Day of Lexington and Concord: The Nineteenth of April, 1775* (Boston, 1925)

Fruchtman, Jack, Jr, *Thomas Paine and the Religion of Nature* (Baltimore, 1993)

Fruchtman, Jack, Jr, *Thomas Paine: Apostle of Freedom* (New York, 1994)

Fruchtman, Jack, Jr, 'Two Doubting Thomases: The British Progressive Enlightenment and the French Revolution', in Michael T. Davis (ed.), *Radicalism and Revolution in Britain, 1775–1848* (New York, 2000), 30–40

Fruchtman, Jack, Jr, *The Political Philosophy of Thomas Paine* (Baltimore, 2009)

Fuller, Reginald Cuthbert, *Alexander Geddes, 1737–1802: A Pioneer of Biblical Criticism* (Sheffield, 1984)

Furet, François and Denis Richet, *The French Revolution* (1965; London, 1970)

Furet, François, *Revolutionary France 1770–1880*, trans. Antonia Nevill (1988; Oxford, 1992)

Gammage, R. G., *History of the Chartist Movement 1837–1854* (1854; 2nd edn, New York, 1969)

Gaustad, Edwin S., *Neither King nor Prelate: Religion and the New Nation 1776–1826* (Grand Rapids, Mich., 1993)

Gaxotte, Pierre, *The French Revolution*, trans. Walter Alison Phillips (London, 1932)

Gegenheimer, Albert Frank, *William Smith Educator and Churchman 1727–1803* (Philadelphia, 1943)

Gerrard, Christine, *The Patriot Opposition to Walpole: Politics, Poetry, and National Myth, 1725–1742* (Oxford, 1994)

Gilbert, Felix, 'The English Background of American Isolationism in the Eighteenth Century', *WMQ* 3rd ser. 1 (1944), 138–60

Gilje, Paul A., *The Road to Mobocracy: Popular Disorder in New York City, 1763–1834* (Chapel Hill, NC, 1987)

Gilje, Paul A., *Rioting in America* (Bloomington, Ind., 1996)

Gimbel, Richard, *Thomas Paine: A Bibliographical Check List of Common Sense with an Account of its Publication* (New Haven, 1956)

Gimbel, Richard, 'The First Appearance of Thomas Paine's *The Age of Reason*', *Yale University Library Gazette* 31 (1956), 87–9

Glickman, Gabriel, 'Cultures and Coteries in Mid-Century Toryism: Johnson in Oxford and London', in Jonathan Clark and Howard Erskine-Hill (eds), *The Politics of Samuel Johnson* (Basingstoke, 2012), 57–89

Godechot, Jacques, *The Counter-Revolution: Doctrine and Action 1789–1804*, trans. Salvator Attanasio (New York, 1971)

Goetzmann, William H., *Beyond the Revolution: A History of American Thought from Paine to Pragmatism* (New York, 2009)

Goodrich, Amanda, *Debating England's Aristocracy in the 1790s: Pamphlets, Polemics and Political Ideas* (Woodbridge, 2005)

Goodrich, Amanda, 'Surveying the Ebb and Flow of Pamphlet Warfare: 500 Rival Tracts from Radicals and Loyalists in Britain, 1790–1796', *British Journal for Eighteenth-Century Studies* 30 (2007), 1–12

Goodway, David, *London Chartism 1838–1848* (Cambridge, 1982)

Goodwin, Albert, *The Friends of Liberty: The English Democratic Movement in the Age of the French Revolution* (London, 1979)

Gordon, Lyndall, *Mary Wollstonecraft: A New Genus* (London, 2005)

Gottschalk, Louis and Margaret Maddox, *Lafayette in the French Revolution: Through the October Days* (Chicago, 1969)

Gough, Hugh, *The Terror in the French Revolution* (2nd edn, Basingstoke, 2010)

Graham, Jenny, 'Revolutionary Philosopher: The Political Ideas of Joseph Priestley (1733–1804)', *Enlightenment and Dissent* 8 (1989), 43–68; 9 (1990), 14–45

Graham, Jenny, *The Nation, the Law and the King: Reform Politics in England, 1789–1799* (2 vols, Lanham, Md, 2000)

Grant, Alfred, *Our American Brethren: A History of Letters in the British Press During the American Revolution, 1775–1781* (Jefferson, NC, 1995)

Green, Dominic, 'From Jacobite to Jacobin: Robert Watson's Life in Opposition', in Allan I. Macinnes, Kieran German and Lesley Graham (eds), *Living with Jacobitism, 1690–1788: The Three Kingdoms and Beyond* (London, 2014), 185–96

Greene, Jack P., 'Bridge to Revolution: The Wilkes Fund Controversy in South Carolina, 1769–1775', *Journal of Southern History* 29 (1963), 19–52

Greene, Jack P., 'Paine, America, and the "Modernization" of Political Consciousness', *Political Science Quarterly* 93 (1978), 73–92

Greene, Jack P., *The Constitutional Origins of the American Revolution* (Cambridge, 2011)

Greenwood, David, *William King, Tory and Jacobite* (Oxford, 1969)

Greer, Donald, *The Incidence of the Terror during the French Revolution* (Cambridge, Mass., 1935)

Grensted, L. W., *A Short History of the Doctrine of the Atonement* (Manchester, 1920)

Griffin, Patrick, Robert G. Ingram, Peter Onuf, and Brian Schoen (eds), *Between Sovereignty and Anarchy: The Politics of Violence in the American Revolutionary Era* (Charlottesville, Va, 2015)

Gross, Jean-Pierre, *Fair Shares for All: Jacobin Egalitarianism in Practice* (Cambridge, 1997)

Gross, Robert A., *The Minutemen and their World* (New York, 1976)

Hammersley, Rachel, *French Revolutionaries and English Republicans: The Cordeliers Club, 1790–1794* (Woodbridge, 2005)

Hammersley, Rachel, *The English Republican Tradition and Eighteenth-Century France: Between the Ancients and the Moderns* (Manchester, 2010)

Hammond, J. L. and Barbara, *The Age of the Chartists 1832–1854* (London, 1930)

Handlin, Oscar, 'Learned Books and Revolutionary Action, 1776', *Harvard Library Bulletin* 34 (1986), 362–79

Hatch, Nathan O., *The Democratization of American Christianity* (New Haven, 1989)

Hawke, David Freeman, *Paine* (New York, 1974)

Herrick, James A., *The Radical Rhetoric of the English Deists: The Discourse of Skepticism, 1680–1750* (Columbia, SC, 1997)

Higonnet, Patrice, *Sister Republics: The Origins of French and American Republicanism* (Cambridge, Mass., 1988)

Higonnet, Patrice, *Goodness beyond Virtue: Jacobins during the French Revolution* (Cambridge, Mass., 1998)

Hill, Christopher, 'The Norman Yoke', in Hill, *Puritanism and Revolution: Studies in Interpretation of the English Revolution of the 17th Century* (London, 1958; Panther edn, 1969)

Hilton, Boyd, *A Mad, Bad, and Dangerous People? England 1783–1846* (Oxford, 2006)

Hindle, Steve, *On the Parish: The Micro-Politics of Poor Relief in Rural England c.1550–1750* (Oxford, 2004)

Hindmarch, G., 'Thomas Paine: The Methodist Influence', *Bulletin of the Thomas Paine Society* 6 (1979), 59–78

Hindmarch, George, *Thomas Paine: The Case of the King of England and his Officers of Excise* (printed for the author, 1998)

Hinkhouse, Fred Junkin, *The Preliminaries of the American Revolution as Seen in the English Press, 1763–1775* (New York, 1926)

Hirst, Désirée, *Hidden Riches: Traditional Symbolism from the Renaissance to Blake* (London, 1964)

Hitchens, Christopher, *Thomas Paine's Rights of Man: A Biography* (London, 2006)

Hitchens, Christopher, *God Is Not Great: The Case Against Religion* (London, 2007)

Hochstrasser, T. J., *Natural Law Theories in the Early Enlightenment* (Cambridge, 2000)

Hodson, Jane, *Language and Politics in Burke, Wollstonecraft, Paine, and Godwin* (Aldershot, 2007)

Hoffman, David C., 'Cross-Examining Scripture: Testimonial Strategies in Thomas Paine's *The Age of Reason*' *Rhetorica* 31 (2013), 261–96

Hoffman, David C., ' "The Creation We Behold": Thomas Paine's *The Age of Reason* and the Tradition of Physico-Theology', *Proceedings of the American Philosophical Society* 157 (2013), 281–303

Hoffman, David C. and Claudia Carlos, 'Thomas Paine's *Le Siècle de la Raison, ou Le Sens commun des droits del'homme*: Notes on a Curious Edition of *The Age of Reason*', in Cleary and Stabell (eds), *New Directions in Thomas Paine Studies*, 133–54

Hoffmann, Stefan-Ludwig, 'Human Rights and History', *P&P* 232 (2016), 279–310

Hone, J. A., *For the Cause of Truth: Radicalism in London 1796–1821* (Oxford, 1982)

Hoock, Holger, 'Mangled Bodies: Atrocity in the American Revolutionary War', *P&P* 230 (2016), 123–59

Howe, Daniel Walker, *What Hath God Wrought: The Transformation of America, 1815–1848* (New York, 2007)

Hudson, Wayne, *Enlightenment and Modernity: The English Deists and Reform* (London, 2009)

Hughes, Patrick Wallace, 'Antidotes to Deism: A Reception History of Thomas Paine's *The Age of Reason*, 1794–1809', Ph.D. thesis, University of Pittsburgh, 2013

Hunt, Lynn (ed.), *The French Revolution and Human Rights: A Brief Documentary History* (Boston, 1996)

Hunt, Lynn, *Inventing Human Rights: A History* (New York, 2007)

Hunt, Lynn, 'The Declaration of the Rights of Man and of the Citizen, August 1789: A Revolutionary Document', in Rachel Hammersley (ed.), *Revolutionary Moments: Reading Revolutionary Texts* (London, 2015), 77–84

Hunt, Lynn, 'The Long and the Short of the History of Human Rights', *P&P* 233 (2016), 323–31

Huyler, Jerome, *Locke in America: The Moral Philosophy of the Founding Era* (Lawrence, Kan., 1995)

Innes, Joanna and Mark Philp (eds), *Re-imagining Democracy in the Age of Revolutions: America, France, Britain, Ireland 1750–1850* (Oxford, 2013)

Ireland, Owen S., 'The Ethnic-Religious Dimension of Pennsylvania Politics, 1778–1779', *WMQ* 30 (1973), 423–48

Ireland, Owen S., 'The Crux of Politics: Religion and Party in Pennsylvania, 1778–1789', *WMQ* 42 (1985), 453–75

Israel, Jonathan, *A Revolution of the Mind: Radical Enlightenment and the Intellectual Origins of Modern Democracy* (Princeton, 2010)

Israel, Jonathan, *Democratic Enlightenment: Philosophy, Revolution, and Human Rights 1750–1790* (Oxford, 2011)

Jacob, Margaret, *The Radical Enlightenment: Pantheists, Freemasons and Republicans* (London, 1981)

Jacob, Margaret C., *Strangers Nowhere in the World: The Rise of Cosmopolitanism in Early Modern Europe* (Philadelphia, 2006)

Jacoby, Susan, *Freethinkers: A History of American Secularism* (New York, 2004)

Jasanoff, Maya, *Liberty's Exiles: American Loyalists in the Revolutionary World* (New York, 2011)

Jennings, Francis, *The Creation of America: Through Revolution to Empire* (Cambridge, 2000)

Jennings, Jeremy, *Revolution and the Republic: A History of Political Thought in France since the Eighteenth Century* (Oxford, 2011)

Jensen, Merrill, *The American Revolution within America* (New York, 1974)

Johnstone, William (ed.), *The Bible and the Enlightenment: A Case Study. Dr Alexander Geddes, 1737–1802: The Proceedings of the Bicentenary Geddes Conference held at the University of Aberdeen, 1–4 April 2002* (London, 2004)

Jones, Emily, 'Conservatism, Edmund Burke and the Invention of a Political Tradition, c.1885–1914', *HJ* 58 (2015), 1115–39

Jones, Emily, *Edmund Burke and the Invention of Modern Conservatism, 1830–1914* (Oxford, 2017)

Jones, G. H., 'The Jacobites, Charles Molloy, and *Common Sense*', *Review of English Studies* new series 4:13 (1953), 144–7

Jordan, Winthrop D., 'Familial Politics: Thomas Paine and the Killing of the King, 1776', *Journal of American History* 60 (Sept. 1973), 294–308

Juster, Susan, *Disorderly Women: Sexual Politics and Evangelicalism in Revolutionary New England* (Ithaca, NY, 1996)

Kaminski, Thomas, 'The Nature of Johnson's Toryism', in Jonathan Clark and Howard Erskine-Hill (eds), *The Politics of Samuel Johnson* (Basingstoke, 2012), 9–56

Kates, Gary, *The Cercle Social, the Girondins, and the French Revolution* (Princeton, 1985)

Kaye, Harvey J., *Thomas Paine and the Promise of America* (New York, 2005)

Keane, John, *Tom Paine: A Political Life* (London, 1995)

Kennedy, Michael L., *The Jacobin Clubs in the French Revolution: The First Years* (Princeton, 1982)

Kenyon, John P., 'Rights: Where Did the Concept of Rights Come From?', in Josephine F. Pacheco (ed.), *To Secure the Blessings of Liberty: Rights in American History* (Fairfax, Va, 1993), 21–36

Kettner, James H., *The Development of American Citizenship, 1608–1870* (Chapel Hill, NC, 1978)

Keyssar, Alexander, *The Right to Vote: The Contested History of Democracy in the United States* (2nd edn, New York, 2009)

Kidd, Thomas S., ' "Let Hell and Rome Do Their Worst": World News, Anti-Catholicism and International Protestantism in Early-Eighteenth-Century Boston', *New England Quarterly* 76 (2003), 265–90

Klooster, Wim, *Revolutions in the Atlantic World: A Comparative History* (New York, 2009)

Knouff, Gregory T., *The Soldiers' Revolution: Pennsylvanians in Arms and the Forging of Early American Identity* (University Park, Pa, 2004)

Koch, G. Adolf, *Republican Religion: The American Revolution and the Cult of Reason* (New York, 1933)

Kors, Alan Charles, *Atheism in France, 1650–1729* (Princeton, 1990)

Kramnick, Isaac, 'Tommy Paine and the Idea of America', in Paul J. Korshin (ed.), *The American Revolution and Eighteenth-Century Culture* (New York, 1986), 75–91

Labaree, Benjamin W., 'The Idea of American Independence: The British View, 1774–1776', *Proceedings of the Massachusetts Historical Society* 3rd ser. 82 (1970), 3–20

Lamb, Robert, *Thomas Paine and the Idea of Human Rights* (Cambridge, 2015)

Lambert, Frank, *'Pedlar in Divinity': George Whitefield and the Transatlantic Revivals, 1737–1770* (Princeton, 1994)

Langford, Paul, 'British Correspondence in the Colonial Press, 1763–1775: A Study in Anglo-American Misunderstanding before the American Revolution', in Bernard Bailyn and John B. Hench (eds), *The Press & the American Revolution* (Worcester, Mass., 1980), 273–313

Larkin, Edward, *Thomas Paine and the Literature of Revolution* (Cambridge, 2005)

Lasser, Michael L., 'In Response to *The Age of Reason*, 1794–1799', *Bulletin of Bibliography and Magazine Notes* 25 (1967), 41–3

Lause, Mark A., 'The "Unwashed Infidelity": Thomas Paine and Early New York Labor History', *Labor History* 27 (1986), 386–409

Le Bon, Gustave, *La Psychologie des foules* (Paris, 1895)

Le Bon, Gustave, *La Révolution française et la psychologie des révolutions* (Paris, 1912)

Lees, Lynn Hollen, *The Solidarities of Strangers: The English Poor Laws and the People, 1700–1948* (Cambridge, 1998)

Lefebvre, Georges, *The French Revolution* (2 vols, London, 1962–4)

Lessay, Jean, *L'Américain de la convention, Thomas Paine: professeur de révolutions, député du Pas-de-Calais* (Paris, 1987)

Levin, Yuval, *The Great Debate: Edmund Burke, Thomas Paine, and the Birth of Right and Left* (New York, 2014)

Liddle, William D., ' "A Patriot King, or None": Lord Bolingbroke and the American Renunciation of George III', *Journal of American History* 65 (1979), 951–70

Lobban, Michael, 'Treason, Sedition, and the Radical Movement in the Age of the French Revolution', *Liverpool Law Review* 22 (2000), 205–34

Loïc, Philip, *Histoire de la pensée politique en France: de 1789 à nos jours* (Paris, 1993)

Lottes, Günther, *Politische Aufklärung und plebejisches Publikum: Zur Theorie und Praxis des englischen Radikalismus im späten 18. Jahrhundert* (Munich, 1979)

Lottes, Günther, 'Radicalism, Revolution and Political Culture: An Anglo-French Comparison', in Mark Philp (ed.), *The French Revolution and British Popular Politics* (Cambridge, 1991), 78–98

Loughran, Trish, 'Disseminating *Common Sense*: Thomas Paine and the Problem of the Early National Bestseller', *American Literature* 78 (2006), 1–28

Loughran, Trish, *The Republic in Print: Print Culture in the Age of U.S. Nation Building, 1770–1870* (New York, 2007)

Lounissi, Carine, 'Lexique de la révolution, révolution du lexique: subversions politiques et sémantiques chez Thomas Paine', *Cercles* 7 (2003), 91–105

Lounissi, Carine, 'Penser la Revolution américaine en France (1778–1788): enjeux philosophiques et historiographiques', *Cercles* 16 (2006), 97–113

Lounissi, Carine, *La Pensée politique de Thomas Paine en contexte: théorie et pratique* (Paris, 2012)

Lounissi, Carine, 'De l'utilité des contextes en histoire des idées: l'exemple de *Rights of Man* de Thomas Paine', *Alphée* 1 (2012), 24–36

Lounissi, Carine, 'Thomas Paine's Reflections on the Social Contract: a Consistent Theory?', in Cleary and Stabell (eds), *New Directions in Thomas Paine Studies*, 175–93

Lovejoy, David S., *The Glorious Revolution in America* (1972; 2nd edn, Middletown, Conn., 1987)

Lucas, Stephen E., *Portents of Rebellion: Rhetoric and Revolution in Philadelphia, 1765–76* (Philadelphia, 1976)

Lucci, Diego, *Scripture and Deism: The Biblical Criticism of the Eighteenth-Century British Deists* (Bern, 2008)

Lutnick, Solomon, *The American Revolution and the British Press 1775–1783* (Columbia, SC, 1967)

Lutz, Donald S., 'The Relative Influence of European Writers on Late Eighteenth-Century American Political Thought', *American Political Science Review* 78 (1984), 189–97

Lynch, James V., 'The Limits of Revolutionary Radicalism: Tom Paine and Slavery', *PMHB* 123 (1999), 177–99

McBride, I. R., *Scripture Politics: Ulster Presbyterians and Irish Radicalism in the Late Eighteenth Century* (Oxford, 1998)

McConville, Brendan, *These Daring Disturbers of the Public Peace: The Struggle for Property and Power in Early New Jersey* (Ithaca, NY, 1999)

McConville, Brendan, *The King's Three Faces: The Rise and Fall of Royal America, 1688–1776* (Williamsburg, Va, 2006)

McDonnell, Michael A., *The Politics of War: Race, Class, and Conflict in Revolutionary Virginia* (Chapel Hill, NC, 2007)

McDougall, Walter A., *Freedom Just Around the Corner: A New American History 1585–1828* (New York, 2004)

MacGillivray, J. R., 'The Pantisocracy Scheme and its Immediate Background', in Malcolm W. Wallace (ed.), *Studies in English by Members of University College Toronto* (Toronto, 1931), 131–69

Mackesy, Piers, *The War for America 1775–1783* (London, 1964)

Mackesy, Piers, *Could the British have Won the War of Independence?* (Worcester, Mass., 1976)

Macleod, Emma Vincent, *A War of Ideas: British Attitudes to the Wars against Revolutionary France 1792–1802* (Aldershot, 1998)

McPhee, Peter, *Living the French Revolution, 1789–99* (Basingstoke, 2006)

McPhee, Peter, *Liberty or Death: The French Revolution* (New Haven, 2016)

Madelin, Louis, *The French Revolution* (New York, 1916)

Mahaffey, Jerome Dean, *Preaching Politics: The Religious Rhetoric of George Whitefield and the Founding of a New Nation* (Waco, Tex., 2007)

Mahaffey, Jerome Dean, *The Accidental Revolutionary: George Whitefield and the Creation of America* (Waco, Tex., 2011)

Maier, Pauline, 'John Wilkes and American Disillusionment with Britain', *WMQ* 3rd ser. 20 (1963), 373–95

Maier, Pauline, 'Popular Uprisings and Civil Authority in Eighteenth-Century America', *WMQ* 3rd ser. 27 (1970), 3–35

Maier, Pauline, *From Resistance to Revolution: Colonial Radicals and the Development of American Opposition to Britain, 1765–1776* (London, 1973)

Maier, Pauline, *American Scripture: Making the Declaration of Independence* (New York, 1997)

Marshall, Peter H., *William Godwin* (New Haven, 1984)

Mathiez, Albert, *After Robespierre: The Thermidorian Reaction*, trans. Alison Phillips (New York, 1931)

Mathiez, Albert, *The French Revolution*, trans. Alison Phillips (New York, 1962)

Mayer, Arno, *The Furies: Violence and Terror in the French and Russian Revolutions* (Princeton, 2000)

Mee, Jon, *Print, Publicity, and Popular Radicalism in the 1790s: The Laurel of Liberty* (Cambridge, 2016)

Messer, Peter C., *Stories of Independence: Identity, Ideology and History in Eighteenth-Century America* (Dekalb, Ill., 2005)

Metzger, Charles H., *Catholics and the American Revolution* (Chicago, 1962)

Meyer, Jean and Jean-Pierre Poussou, *La Révolution Française* (2 vols, Paris, 1991)

Michel, Henry, *L'Idée de l'état: essai critique des théories sociales et politiques en France depuis la Révolution* (3rd edn, Paris, 1898)

Michelet, J[ules], *Historical View of the French Revolution*, trans. C. Cocks (London, 1890)

Miles, Dudley, *Francis Place 1771–1854: The Life of a Remarkable Radical* (Brighton, 1988)

Millburn, John R., *Benjamin Martin: Author, Instrument-Maker, and 'Country Showman'* (Leiden, 1976)

Millburn, John R., *Wheelwright of the Heavens: The Life and Work of James Ferguson, FRS* (London, 1988)

Miller, John C., *Origins of the American Revolution* (Stanford, Calif., 1959)

Miquel, Pierre, *La Grande Révolution* (Paris, 1988)

Monod, Paul Kléber, *Jacobitism and the English People, 1688–1788* (Cambridge, 1989)

Morais, Herbert M., *Deism in Eighteenth Century America* (New York, 1934)

Moran, Mary Catherine, '*L'Essai sur les femmes/Essay on Women*: An Eighteenth-Century Transatlantic Journey', *History Workshop Journal* 59 (2005), 17–32

Mori, Jennifer, *Britain in the Age of the French Revolution 1785–1820* (London, 2000)

Morris, Marilyn, *The British Monarchy and the French Revolution* (New Haven, 1998)

Morton, Alan Q. (ed.), *Science Lecturing in the Eighteenth Century*, special issue of *British Journal for the History of Science* 28 (Mar. 1995)

Moyn, Samuel, *The Last Utopia: Human Rights in History* (Cambridge, Mass., 2010)

Moyn, Samuel, 'The End of Human Rights History', *P&P* 233 (2016), 307–22

Nash, Gary, 'Philadelphia's Radical Caucus that Propelled Pennsylvania to Independence and Democracy', in Alfred F. Young, Gary B. Nash and Ray Raphael (eds), *Revolutionary Founders: Rebels, Radicals, and Reformers in the Making of the Nation* (New York, 2011), 67–85

Nash, Gary and Jean R. Soderlund, *Freedom by Degrees: Emancipation in Pennsylvania and its Aftermath* (New York, 1991)

Nelson, Craig, *Thomas Paine: Enlightenment, Revolution, and the Birth of Modern Nations* (New York, 2006)

Nelson, Eric, *The Royalist Revolution: Monarchy and the American Founding* (Cambridge, Mass., 2014)

Newman, A. N., 'Leicester House Politics, 1748–1751', *EHR* 76 (1961), 577–89

Newman, Gerald, *The Rise of English Nationalism: A Cultural History 1740–1830* (New York, 1987)

Newman, Simon P., *Parades and the Politics of the Street: Festive Culture in the Early American Republic* (Philadelphia, 1997)

Newman, Simon P. and Peter S. Onuf (eds), *Paine and Jefferson in the Age of Revolutions* (Charlottesville, Va, 2013)

Newman, Stephen, 'A Note on *Common Sense* and Christian Eschatology', *Political Theory* 6 (Feb. 1978), 101–8

O'Gorman, Frank, 'The Paine Burnings of 1792–1793', *P&P* 193 (2006), 111–55

Opal, J. M., '*Common Sense* and Imperial Atrocity: How Tom Paine Saw South Asia in North America', *Common-place* 8 (July 2009), <http://www.common-place.org/vol-09/no-4/forum/opal.shtml>

Ousterhout, Anne M., 'Controlling the Opposition in Pennsylvania during the American Revolution', *PMHB* 105 (1981), 3–34

Owen, Kenneth, 'Violence and the Limits of the Political Community in Revolutionary Pennsylvania', in Patrick Griffin, Robert G. Ingram, Peter Onuf and Brian Schoen (eds), *Between Sovereignty and Anarchy: The Politics of Violence in the American Revolutionary Era* (Charlottesville, Va, 2015), 165–86

Oxley, Geoffrey W., *Poor Relief in England and Wales 1601–1834* (Newton Abbot, 1974)

Page, Anthony, *John Jebb and the Enlightenment Origins of British Radicalism* (Westport, Conn., 2003)

Palmer, R. R., *The Age of the Democratic Revolution: A Political History of Europe and America, 1760–1800* (2 vols, Princeton, 1959–64)

Parssinen, T. M., 'Thomas Spence and the Origins of English Land Nationalization', *Journal of the History of Ideas* 34 (1973), 135–41

Parssinen, T. M., 'Association, Convention and Anti-parliament in British Radical Politics, 1771–1848', *EHR* 88 (1973), 504–33

Pasley, Jeffrey L., '*The Tyranny of Printers': Newspaper Politics in the Early American Republic* (Charlottesville, Va, 2001)

Pendleton, Gayle Trusdel, 'The English Pamphlet Literature of the Age of the French Revolution Anatomized', *Eighteenth-Century Life* 5 (1978), 29–37

Pendleton, Gayle Trusdel, 'Thirty Additional Titles Relating to the *Age of Reason*', *British Studies Monitor* 10 (1980), 36–45

Pendleton, Gayle Trusdel, 'Towards a Bibliography of the *Reflections* and *Rights of Man* Controversy', *Bulletin of Research in the Humanities* 85 (1982), 65–103

Philp, Mark, *Godwin's Political Justice* (London, 1986)

Philp, Mark, *Paine* (Oxford, 1989)

Philp, Mark, 'Burke and Paine: Texts in Context', *Enlightenment and Dissent* 9 (1990), 93–105

Philp, Mark (ed.), *The French Revolution and British Popular Politics* (Cambridge, 1991)

Philp, Mark, 'The Role of America in the "Debate on France" 1791–5: Thomas Paine's Insertion', *Utilitas* 5 (1993), 221–37

Philp, Mark, 'English Republicanism in the 1790s', *Journal of Political Philosophy* 6 (1998), 235–62

Philp, Mark, 'Talking about Democracy: Britain in the 1790s', in Joanna Innes and Mark Philp (eds), *Re-imagining Democracy in the Age of Revolutions: America, France, Britain, Ireland 1750–1850* (Oxford, 2013), 101–13

Philp, Mark, 'Revolutionaries in Paris: Paine and Jefferson', in Philp, *Reforming Ideas in Britain: Politics and Language in the Shadow of the French Revolution, 1789–1815* (Cambridge, 2014), 187–209

Philp, Mark, *Reforming Ideas in Britain: Politics and Language in the Shadow of the French Revolution, 1789–1815* (Cambridge, 2014)

Piquet, Jean-Daniel, *L'Émancipation des Noirs dans la Révolution française* (Paris, 2002)

Pitcher, Edward R., *The Pennsylvania Magazine, or American Monthly Museum, 1775–1776: An Annotated Index of Sources, Signatures, and First Lines of Literary Sources* (Lewiston, NY, 2001)

Pocock, J. G. A., *The Machiavellian Moment: Florentine Political Thought and the Atlantic Republican Tradition* (Princeton, 1975)

Pocock, J. G. A., 'The Myth of John Locke and the Obsession with Liberalism', in J. G. A. Pocock and Richard Ashcraft (eds), *John Locke: Papers Read at a Clark Library Seminar 10 December 1977* (Los Angeles, 1980), 3–24

Pocock, J. G. A., 'The Varieties of Whiggism from Exclusion to Reform: A History of Ideology and Discourse', in Pocock, *Virtue, Commerce, and History: Essays on Political Thought and History, Chiefly in the Eighteenth Century* (Cambridge, 1985), 215–310

Pocock, J. G. A., 'Between Gog and Magog: The Republican Thesis and the *Ideologia Americana*', *Journal of the History of Ideas* 48 (1987), 325–46

Pocock, J. G. A., 'Negative and Positive Aspects of Locke's Place in Eighteenth-Century Discourse', in Martyn P. Thompson (ed.), *John Locke und/and Immanuel Kant* (Berlin, 1991), 45–61

Pocock, J. G. A., *Barbarism and Religion. Volume One: The Enlightenments of Edward Gibbon, 1737–1764* (Cambridge, 1999)

Polasky, Janet, *Revolutions without Borders: The Call to Liberty in the Atlantic World* (New Haven, 2015)

Polasky, Janet, 'Revolutionaries between Nations, 1776–1789', *P&P* 232 (2016), 165–201

Pole, J. R., *Political Representation in England and the Origins of the American Republic* (London, 1966)

Popkin, Richard H., 'The Deist Challenge', in Ole Peter Grell, Jonathan I. Israel, and Nicholas Tyacke (eds), *From Persecution to Toleration: The Glorious Revolution and Religion in England* (Oxford, 1991), 195–215

Porter, Roy (ed.), *The Cambridge History of Science*, iv, *Eighteenth-Century Science* (Cambridge, 2003)

Porterfield, Amanda, *Conceived in Doubt: Religion and Politics in the New American Nation* (Chicago, 2012)

Potofsky, Allan, 'The One and the Many: The Two Revolutions Question and the "Consumer-Commercial" Atlantic, 1789 to the Present', in Albertone and De Francesco (eds), *Rethinking the Atlantic World*, 17–45

Powell, David, *Tom Paine: The Greatest Exile* (London, 1985)

Poynter, J. R., *Society and Pauperism: English Ideas on Poor Relief, 1795–1834* (London, 1969)

Price, Benjamin Lewis, *Nursing Fathers: American Colonists' Conception of English Protestant Kingship, 1688–1776* (Lanham, Md, 1999)

Prochaska, Franklyn, 'Thomas Paine's *The Age of Reason* Revisited', *Journal of the History of Ideas* 33 (1972), 561–76

Prothero, I. J., *Artisans and Politics in Early Nineteenth-Century London: John Gast and his Times* (Folkestone, 1979)

Rakove, Jack, 'Constitutionalism: The Happiest Revolutionary Script', in Keith Michael Baker and Dan Edelstein (eds), *Scripting Revolution: A Historical Approach to the Comparative Study of Revolutions* (Stanford, Calif., 2015), 103–17

Rakove, Jack N. 'The Decision for American Independence: A Reconstruction', *Perspectives in American History* 10 (1976), 217–75

Rakove, Jack N., *The Beginnings of National Politics: An Interpretive History of the Continental Congress* (New York, 1979)

Rapport, Michael, *Nationality and Citizenship in Revolutionary France: The Treatment of Foreigners 1789–1799* (Oxford, 2000)

Ray, Sister Mary Augustina, *American Opinion of Roman Catholicism in the Eighteenth Century* (New York, 1936)

Redwood, John, *Reason, Ridicule and Religion: The Age of Enlightenment in England 1660– 1750* (London, 1976; 2nd edn, 1996)

Reid, John Philip, *Constitutional History of the American Revolution: The Authority of Rights* (Madison, 1986)

Rials, Stéphane, *La Déclaration des droits de l'homme et du citoyen* (Paris, 1988)

Richard, Carl J., *The Founders and the Classics: Greece, Rome, and the American Enlightenment* (Cambridge, Mass., 1994)

Robbins, Caroline, *The Eighteenth Century Commonwealthman* (Cambridge, Mass., 1959)

Robbins, Caroline, 'The Lifelong Education of Thomas Paine (1737–1809): Some Reflections upon his Acquaintance among Books', *Proceedings of the American Philosophical Society* 127 (June 1983), 135–42

Rogers, Nicholas, 'Burning Tom Paine: Loyalism and Counter-Revolution in Britain, 1792– 1793', *Histoire Sociale/Social History* 32 (1999), 139–71

Rose, R. B., *Gracchus Babeuf: The First Revolutionary Communist* (Stanford, Calif., 1978)

Rosenfeld, Sophia, 'Tom Paine's Common Sense and Ours', *WMQ* 65 (2008), 633–68

Rosenfeld, Sophia, *Common Sense: A Political History* (Cambridge, Mass., 2011)

Royle, Edward, *Victorian Infidels: The Origins of the British Secularist Movement 1791–1866* (Manchester, 1974)

Royle, Edward, *Radicals, Secularists and Republicans: Popular Freethought in Britain, 1866– 1915* (Manchester, 1980)

Royle, Edward, 'The Reception of Paine', *Bulletin of the Society for the Study of Labour History* 52 (1987), 14–20

Rozbicki, Michal Jan, *Culture and Liberty in the Age of the American Revolution* (Charlottesville, Va, 2011)

Ryerson, Richard Alan, *The Revolution is Now Begun: The Radical Committees of Philadelphia, 1765–1776* (Philadelphia, 1978)

Sack, J. J., 'The Memory of Pitt and the Memory of Burke: English Conservatism Confronts its Past, 1806–29', *HJ* 30 (1987), 623–40

Sack, James J., *From Jacobite to Conservative: Reaction and Orthodoxy in Britain c.1760– 1832* (Cambridge, 1993)

Sahlins, Peter, *Unnaturally French: Foreign Citizens in the Old Regime and After* (Ithaca, NY, 2004)

Sainsbury, John, *Disaffected Patriots: London Supporters of Revolutionary America 1769– 1782* (Kingston, Canada, 1987)

St Clair, William, *The Reading Nation in the Romantic Period* (Cambridge, 2004)

Schama, Simon, *Citizens: A Chronicle of the French Revolution* (New York, 1989)

Schlenther, Boyd Stanley, *Queen of the Methodists: The Countess of Huntingdon and the Eighteenth-Century Crisis of Faith and Society* (South Church, 1997)

Schlereth, Eric R., *An Age of Infidels: The Politics of Religious Controversy in the Early United States* (Philadelphia, 2013)

Schlesinger, Arthur M., 'Political Mobs and the American Revolution, 1765–1776', *Proceedings of the American Philosophical Society* 99 (1955), 244–50

Schlesinger, Arthur M., *Prelude to Independence: The Newspaper War on Britain 1764–1776* (1957; Boston, 1980)

Schnorrenberg, Barbara Brandon, 'Who Was George Lewis Scott?', *New Perspectives on the Eighteenth Century* 2 (2005), 39–53

Schofield, Robert E., *The Enlightenment of Joseph Priestley: A Study of his Life and Work from 1733 to 1773* (University Park, Pa, 1997)

Schofield, Robert E., *The Enlightened Joseph Priestley: A Study of his Life and Work from 1773 to 1803* (University Park, Pa, 2004)

Schoyen, A. R., *The Chartist Challenge: A Portrait of George Julian Harney* (London, 1958)

Scoble, Thomas D., *Thomas Paine's Citizenship Record* (New Rochelle, NY, 1946)

Schofield, Thomas Philip, 'Conservative Political Thought in Britain in Response to the French Revolution', *HJ* 29 (1986), 601–22

Scrivener, Michael, *The Cosmopolitan Ideal in the Age of Revolution and Reaction, 1776–1832* (London, 2007)

Scurr, Ruth, *Fatal Purity: Robespierre and the French Revolution* (New York, 2006)

Sedgwick, Romney (ed.), *The History of Parliament: The House of Commons 1715–1754* (2 vols, London, 1970)

Seeber, Edward Derbyshire, *Anti-Slavery Opinion in France during the Second Half of the Eighteenth Century* (Baltimore, 1937)

Sellers, M. N. S., *American Republicanism: Roman Ideology in the United States Constitution* (Basingstoke, 1994)

Selsam, J. Paul, *The Pennsylvania Constitution of 1776: A Study in Revolutionary Democracy* (Philadelphia, 1936)

Serna, Pierre, 'In Search of the Atlantic Republic: 1660–1776–1799 in the Mirror', in Albertone and De Francesco (eds), *Rethinking the Atlantic World*, 257–75

Shaffer, Arthur H., *The Politics of History: Writing the History of the American Revolution 1783–1815* (Chicago, 1975)

Shaffer, Arthur H., *To be an American: David Ramsay and the Making of the American Consciousness* (Columbia, SC, 1991)

Shain, Barry Alan (ed.), *The Nature of Rights at the American Founding and Beyond* (Charlottesville, Va, 2007)

Sheps, Arthur, 'The American Revolution and the Transformation of English Republicanism', *Historical Reflections* 2 (1975), 3–28

Skinner, Quentin, *The Foundations of Modern Political Thought* (2 vols, Cambridge, 1978)

Skinner, Quentin, 'Language and Political Change', in Terence Ball, James Farr, and Russell L. Hanson (eds), *Political Innovation and Conceptual Change* (Cambridge, 1989), 6–23

Skinner, Quentin, *Liberty before Liberalism* (Cambridge, 1998)

Skinner, Quentin, *Visions of Politics* (3 vols, Cambridge, 2002)

Slack, Paul, *The English Poor Law 1531–1782* (Basingstoke, 1990)

Slauter, Eric, 'Reading and Radicalization: Print, Politics, and the American Revolution', *Early American Studies* 8 (2010), 5–40

Smith, Frank, 'The Authorship of "An Occasional Letter on the Female Sex"', *American Literature* 2 (Nov. 1930), 277–80

Smith, Jay, 'Thomas Paine and The Age of Reason's Attack on the Bible', *The Historian* 58 (1996), 745–61

Smith, Olivia, *The Politics of Language 1791–1819* (Oxford, 1984)

Smith, Rogers M., 'Constructing American National Identity: Strategies of the Federalists', in Doron Ben-Atar and Barbara B. Oberg (eds), *Federalists Reconsidered* (Charlottesville, Va, 1998)

Smith, William Raymond, *History as Argument: Three Patriot Historians of the American Revolution* (The Hague, 1966)

Soboul, Albert, *The French Revolution, 1787–1799: From the Storming of the Bastille to Napoleon*, trans. Alan Forrest and Colin Jones (New York, 1975)

Soltau, Roger Henry, *French Political Thought in the 19th Century* (New York, 1959)

Sonenscher, Michael, *Before the Deluge: Public Debt, Inequality, and the Intellectual Origins of the French Revolution* (Princeton, 2007)

Sonenscher, Michael, *Sans-Culottes: An Eighteenth-Century Emblem in the French Revolution* (Princeton, 2008)

Sorel, Albert, *L'Europe et la Révolution française* (8 vols, Paris, 1885)

Spater, George, 'The Author of the "A Forester" Articles', *Bulletin of the Thomas Paine Society* 7 (1982), 53–5

Speck, W. A., *A Political Biography of Thomas Paine* (London, 2013)

Stanwood, Owen, *The Empire Reformed: English America in the Age of the Glorious Revolution* (Philadelphia, 2011)

Stedman Jones, Gareth, *Languages of Class: Studies in English Working Class History 1832–1982* (Cambridge, 1983)

Stedman Jones, Gareth, *An End to Poverty? A Historical Debate* (London, 2004)

Stewart, Larry, *The Rise of Public Science: Rhetoric, Technology and Natural Philosophy in Newtonian Britain, 1660–1750* (Cambridge, 1992)

Stewart, Larry, 'Seeing through the Scholium: Religion and Reading Newton in the Eighteenth Century', *History of Science* 34 (1996), 123–65

Stone, Lawrence, 'Theories of Revolution', *World Politics* 18 (1965–6), 159–76

Tackett, Timothy, *The Coming of the Terror in the French Revolution* (Cambridge, Mass., 2015)

Taine, Hippolyte, *Origines de la France contemporaine* (6 vols, Paris, 1876–94), partly translated as *The French Revolution*, trans. John Durand, ed. Mona Ozouf (3 vols, Indianapolis, 2002)

Taussig, Harold E., 'Deism in Philadelphia during the Age of Franklin', *Pennsylvania History* 37 (July 1970), 217–36

Taylor, Alan, *American Revolutions: A Continental History, 1750–1804* (New York, 2016)

Thale, Mary, 'London Debating Societies in the 1790s', *HJ* 32 (1989), 57–86

Thayer, Theodore, *Pennsylvania Politics and the Growth of Democracy 1740–1776* (Harrisburg, Pa, 1953)

Thomas, Chantal, *The Wicked Queen: The Origins of the Myth of Marie-Antoinette*, trans. Julie Rose (New York, 1999)

Thomas, William, *The Philosophic Radicals: Nine Studies in Theory and Practice 1817–1841* (Oxford, 1979)

Thompson, Dorothy, *The Chartists* (London, 1984)

Thompson, E. P., *The Making of the English Working Class* (London, 1963)

Thompson, Ira M., *The Religious Beliefs of Thomas Paine* (New York, 1965)

Tierney, Brian, *The Idea of Natural Rights: Studies on Natural Rights, Natural Law and Church Law 1150–1625* (Atlanta, 1997)

Todd, Janet, *Mary Wollstonecraft: A Revolutionary Life* (London, 2000)

Travers, Len, *Celebrating the Fourth: Independence Day and the Rites of Nationalism in the Early Republic* (Amherst, Mass., 1997)

Tuck, Richard, *Natural Rights Theories: Their Origin and Development* (Cambridge, 1979)

Tunstall, Kate E. (ed.), *Self-Evident Truths? Human Rights and the Enlightenment* (London, 2012)

Turner, James, *Without God, Without Creed: The Origins of Unbelief in America* (Baltimore, 1985)

Verhoeven, Wil, *Americomania and the French Revolution Debate in Britain, 1789–1802* (Cambridge, 2013)

Vickers, Vikki J., *'My Pen and my Sword have ever gone together': Thomas Paine and the American Revolution* (London, 2006)

Villers, David H., '"King Mob" and the Rule of Law: Revolutionary Justice and the Suppression of Loyalists in Connecticut 1774–1783', in Robert M. Calhoon et al. (eds, *Loyalism and Community in North America* (Westport, Conn., 1994), 17–30

Vincent, Bernard, *Thomas Paine, ou la religion de la liberté* (Paris, 1987)

Vincent, Bernard (ed.), *Thomas Paine, ou la république sans frontières* (Nancy, 1993)

Vincent, Bernard, *The Transatlantic Republican: Thomas Paine and the Age of Revolutions* (Amsterdam, 2005)

Wagner, Corinna, 'Loyalist Propaganda and the Scandalous Life of Tom Paine: "Hypocritical Monster!"', *British Journal for Eighteenth-Century Studies* 28 (2005), 97–115

Wahnich, Sophie, *In Defence of Terror: Liberty or Death in the French Revolution*, trans. David Fernbach (2003; London, 2012)

Waldinger, Renée, Philip Dawson, and Isser Woloch (eds), *The French Revolution and the Meaning of Citizenship* (Westport, Conn., 1993)

Waldron, Jeremy, 'The Decline of Natural Right', in Allen W. Wood and Songsuk Susan Hahn (eds), *The Cambridge History of Philosophy in the Nineteenth Century (1790–1870)* (Cambridge, 2012), 623–50

Waldstreicher, David, *In the Midst of Perpetual Fetes: The Making of American Nationalism, 1776–1820* (Chapel Hill, NC, 1997)

Wallace, Alfred Russel, *Land Nationalisation* (London, 1882)

Wallis, Ruth, 'John Bevis, M.D., F.R.S. (1695–1771), Astronomer Loyal', *Notes and Records of the Royal Society* 36 (1981–2), 211–25

Walters, Kerry, *Revolutionary Deists: Early America's Rational Infidels* (Amherst, NY, 2011)

Ward, Lee, *The Politics of Liberty in England and Revolutionary America* (Cambridge, 2004)

Waterman, A. M. C., 'Theology and Political Doctrine in Church and Dissent', in Waterman, *Political Economy and Christian Theology since the Enlightenment* (Basingstoke, 2004), 31–54

Whatmore, Richard, '"A gigantic manliness": Paine's Republicanism in the 1790s', in Stefan Collini, Richard Whatmore, and Brian Young (eds), *Economy, Polity and Society: British Intellectual History 1750–1950* (Cambridge, 2000), 135–57

Whatmore, Richard, 'The French and North American Revolutions in Comparative Perspective', in Albertone and De Francesco (eds), *Rethinking the Atlantic World*, 219–56

Wiener, Joel H., *Radicalism and Freethought in Nineteenth-Century Britain: The Life of Richard Carlile* (Westport, Conn., 1983)

Wigelsworth, Jeffrey R., *Deism in Enlightenment England: Theology, Politics, and Newtonian Public Science* (Manchester, 2009)

Wilenz, Sean, *Chants Democratic: New York City & the Rise of the American Working Class, 1788–1850* (New York, 1984)

Wilentz, Sean, *The Rise of American Democracy: Jefferson to Lincoln* (New York, 2005)

Williams, Gwyn, *Artisans and Sans-Culottes: Popular Movements in France and Britain during the French Revolution* (2nd edn, London, 1989)

Williamson, Audrey, *Thomas Paine: His Life, Work and Times* (London, 1973)

Williamson, Chilton, *American Suffrage from Property to Democracy 1760–1860* (Princeton, 1960)

Wills, Garry, *Inventing America: Jefferson's Declaration of Independence* (Garden City, NY, 1978)

Winch, Donald, *Riches and Poverty: An Intellectual History of Political Economy in Britain, 1750–1834* (Cambridge, 1996)

Woloch, Isser, *The New Regime: Transformations of the French Civic Order, 1789–1820s* (New York, 1994)

Wood, Gordon S., 'A Note on Mobs in the American Revolution', *WMQ* 3rd ser. 23 (1966), 635–42

Wood, Gordon, *The Creation of the American Republic 1776–1787* (Chapel Hill, NC, 1969)

Wood, Gordon, *The Radicalism of the American Revolution* (New York, 1992)

Wood, Gordon S., *The Americanization of Benjamin Franklin* (New York, 2004)

Wood, Gordon S., 'Thomas Paine, America's First Public Intellectual', in Wood, *Revolutionary Characters: What Made the Founders Different* (New York, 2006), 203–22

Wood, Gordon S., *Empire of Liberty: A History of the Early Republic, 1789–1815* (New York, 2009)

Wood, Gordon S., 'The Radicalism of Thomas Jefferson and Thomas Paine Considered', in Wood, *The Idea of America: Reflections on the Birth of the United States* (New York, 2011), 213–28

Wootton, David, 'The Republican Tradition: From Commonwealth to Common Sense', in Wootton (ed.), *Republicanism, Liberty and Commercial Society, 1649–1776* (Stanford, Calif., 1994), 1–41

Worden, Blair, 'Liberty for Export: "Republicanism" in England, 1500–1800', in Gaby Mahlberg and Dirk Wiemann (eds), *European Contexts for English Republicanism* (Farnham, 2013), 13–32

York, Neil, 'George III, Tyrant: *The Crisis* as Critic of Empire, 1775–1776', *History* 94 (2009), 434–60

Young, Alfred F., 'The Celebration and Damnation of Thomas Paine', in Young, *Liberty Tree: Ordinary People in the American Revolution* (New York, 2006), 265–95

Young, Brian, 'Newtonianism and the Enthusiasm of Enlightenment', *Studies in the History and Philosophy of Science* 35 (2004), 645–63

Young, Henry J., 'Treason and its Punishment in Revolutionary Pennsylvania', *PMHB* 90 (1966), 287–313

Ziesche, Philipp, *Cosmopolitan Patriots: Americans in Paris in the Age of Revolution* (Charlottesville, Va, 2010)

Zimmerman, Doron, *The Jacobite Movement in Scotland and in Exile, 1746–1759* (Basingstoke, 2003)

Zuckert, Michael, 'Natural Rights in the American Revolution: The American Amalgam', in Jeffrey N. Wasserstrom, Greg Grandin, Lynn Hunt, and Marilyn B. Young (eds), *Human Rights and Revolutions* (2nd edn, Lanham, Md, 2007)

Index